T0360743

Quantitative Enterprise Risk Management

This well-balanced introduction to enterprise risk management (ERM) integrates quantitative and qualitative approaches and motivates key mathematical and statistical methods with abundant real-world cases – both successes and failures. Worked examples and end-of-chapter exercises support readers in consolidating what they learn. The mathematical level, which is suitable for graduate and senior undergraduate students in quantitative programs, is pitched to give readers a solid understanding of the concepts and principles involved without diving too deeply into more complex theory. To reveal the connections between different topics, and their relevance to the real world, the presentation has a coherent narrative flow, from risk governance, through risk identification, risk modelling, and risk mitigation, capped off with holistic topics – regulation, behavioural biases, and crisis management – that influence the whole structure of ERM. The result is a text and reference that is ideal for graduate and senior undergraduate students, risk managers in industry, and anyone preparing for ERM actuarial exams.

MARY R. HARDY is Professor in the Department of Statistics and Actuarial Science at the University of Waterloo. She is a past vice president of the Society of Actuaries and was initiated as a Chartered Enterprise Risk Analyst through the Thought Leadership program. She has a Ph.D. in actuarial science from Heriot-Watt University, and she is a fellow of the Society of Actuaries, and of the Institute and Faculty of Actuaries, which awarded her the prestigious Finlaison Medal for service to the profession in 2012. Her past books include *Actuarial Mathematics for Life Contingent Risks* and *Investment Guarantees: Modelling and Risk Management*.

DAVID SAUNDERS is Associate Professor in the Department of Statistics and Actuarial Science at the University of Waterloo. He is a financial mathematician whose research focusses on the application of stochastic optimization and probability to problems in finance and insurance. Professor Saunders has served as a risk management consultant for over two decades, having worked for several firms in the banking and financial software industries. He has a Ph.D. in mathematics from the University of Toronto.

INTERNATIONAL SERIES ON ACTUARIAL SCIENCE

Editorial Board
Christopher Daykin (Independent Consultant and Actuary)
Angus Macdonald (Heriot-Watt University)

The *International Series on Actuarial Science*, published by Cambridge University Press in conjunction with the Institute and Faculty of Actuaries, contains textbooks for students taking courses in or related to actuarial science, as well as more advanced works designed for continuing professional development or for describing and synthesizing research. The series is a vehicle for publishing books that reflect changes and developments in the curriculum, that encourage the introduction of courses on actuarial science in universities, and that show how actuarial science can be used in all areas where there is long-term financial risk.

A complete list of books in the series can be found at www.cambridge.org/isas. Recent titles include the following:

Solutions Manual for Actuarial Mathematics for Life Contingent Risks (3rd Edition)
David C. M. Dickson, Mary R. Hardy & Howard R. Waters

Actuarial Mathematics for Life Contingent Risks (3rd Edition)
David C. M. Dickson, Mary R. Hardy & Howard R. Waters

Modelling Mortality with Actuarial Applications
Angus S. Macdonald, Stephen J. Richards & Iain D. Currie

Claims Reserving in General Insurance
David Hindley

Financial Enterprise Risk Management (2nd Edition)
Paul Sweeting

Insurance Risk and Ruin (2nd Edition)
David C.M. Dickson

Predictive Modeling Applications in Actuarial Science, Volume 2: Case Studies in Insurance
Edited by Edward W. Frees, Richard A. Derrig & Glenn Meyers

QUANTITATIVE ENTERPRISE RISK MANAGEMENT

MARY R. HARDY
University of Waterloo

DAVID SAUNDERS
University of Waterloo

CAMBRIDGE
UNIVERSITY PRESS

University Printing House, Cambridge CB2 8BS, United Kingdom

One Liberty Plaza, 20th Floor, New York, NY 10006, USA

477 Williamstown Road, Port Melbourne, VIC 3207, Australia

314–321, 3rd Floor, Plot 3, Splendor Forum, Jasola District Centre,
New Delhi – 110025, India

103 Penang Road, #05–06/07, Visioncrest Commercial, Singapore 238467

Cambridge University Press is part of the University of Cambridge.

It furthers the University's mission by disseminating knowledge in the pursuit of
education, learning, and research at the highest international levels of excellence.

www.cambridge.org
Information on this title: www.cambridge.org/9781009098465
DOI: 10.1017/9781009089470

© Mary R. Hardy and David Saunders 2022

This publication is in copyright. Subject to statutory exception
and to the provisions of relevant collective licensing agreements,
no reproduction of any part may take place without the written
permission of Cambridge University Press.

First published 2022

A catalogue record for this publication is available from the British Library.

ISBN 978-1-009-09846-5 Hardback

Cambridge University Press has no responsibility for the persistence or accuracy
of URLs for external or third-party internet websites referred to in this publication
and does not guarantee that any content on such websites is, or will remain,
accurate or appropriate.

To Phelim and Ruth

Contents

Preface

Enterprise risk management (ERM) is an increasingly popular university course within actuarial science, finance, risk management, and business programmes. The evolution of ERM over the past couple of decades has proceeded along two lines: the qualitative approach, which covers, for example, governance frameworks, risk identification procedures, and ERM processes; and the quantitative approach, which takes a more technical, mathematical perspective on risk modelling and risk measurement.

The aim of this book is to bring the qualitative and quantitative approaches together in a coherent and integrated text, at a level suitable for graduate and upper-level undergraduate students in mathematical and engineering sciences. It is also designed to be a useful self-study aid for students working towards professional actuarial exams, such as those offered by the Society of Actuaries towards the Chartered Enterprise Risk Analyst (CERA) certification.

This book has been a work in progress for many years. The rapidly changing ERM environment led to significant updates before publication to deal with changes in regulations and in risk management practice. As we write this preface, the global COVID-19 pandemic is ongoing, and it is difficult to predict how this will change risk management, even in the short term. The regulation of financial institutions is constantly evolving, and while we have strived to keep our presentation of the material current, one is always best advised to consult the regulatory documents themselves for the most detailed and up-to-date requirements.

There are several decisions that we made in writing the text, which may not meet with universal agreement. There are no exact start and end dates for the crisis that shook the global financial system in the first decade of this century. We have referred to it as the global financial crisis of 2007–8 throughout, in full recognition that this period omits the failures of many subprime lenders in 2006 and concerns about the potential for sovereign defaults that extended into

2009 and beyond. We have generally used LIBOR (London Interbank Offered Rate) as the underlying floating rate in our examples of interest rate derivative securities, acknowledging its impending obsolescence.

There are also things that we would have done differently if we had the time to start over. Re-reading the final draft, we felt that more attention should have been given to climate change, which presents not only a serious risk to all businesses but an existential threat to humanity.

This book contains over 175 exercises. The exercises are of several different types, including qualitative discussions, mathematical calculations and derivations, and computational exercises on real data sets. We encourage readers to attempt as many of these exercises as possible, as this is the only path to true mastery of the material. We are particularly grateful to the Society of Actuaries for allowing us to reproduce some problems from their past professional examinations. Whenever we have done so, it is indicated explicitly in the text. We have, on occasion, made minor modifications in the wording of these problems so that they fit more closely with the presentation in the text.

The material in this book is suitable for a sequence of two one-semester courses. Chapters 1–6 provide a solid foundation in qualitative and quantitative ERM; Chapters 7–10 could round off the first course, adding context with a slight focus on market risk and banking. In the second course, Chapters 11–20 provide a more in-depth look at some specific risks, and in the final chapters, the material returns to the top-down perspective, considering institutional issues that can promote or undermine the organization's risk management.

Chapter Summary

We begin, in Chapter 1, with an introduction to ERM. We present a historical view of the evolution of the subject and show how modern ERM has its origins in the individual areas of risk management that preceded it. We discuss ERM as an ongoing process and an integral part of the firm. We introduce the stages of the ERM cycle, including risk identification and analysis, risk evaluation, and risk treatment, each of which is to receive more detailed treatment later on in the book.

Chapter 2 presents a classification and description of the major types of risk that may be faced by an organization. We cover both external risks (those that arise from outside the organization) and internal risks (risks that are generated from within the organization). External risks are divided into economic, political, and environmental risks, and internal risks into operational and strategic risks. We also look at reputational risk, which may be either internally or externally generated. We consider several examples of how risks have arisen in high profile cases, illustrating as well how different types of risks can be driven by the same event.

Chapter 3 presents an introduction to risk measures, with a focus on Value at Risk (VaR), and Expected Shortfall, the two most commonly employed measures in quantitative risk management in practice. We study several important issues, including key properties that risk measures may possess (or fail to possess), that is, the axioms for a coherent risk measure, and computational issues, including estimating risk measures and how to calculate standard errors for risk measures estimated using Monte Carlo simulation.

Chapter 4 discusses frequency-severity analysis, a key workhorse in many real-world applications of quantitative risk management. In these models, the losses incurred are modelled as a compound random variable: the sum of a random number of independently and identically distributed losses. We discuss several common distributions used for both the frequency variable (the number of losses) and the severity distribution (the amount of each loss). Basic analytical results that can be used to calculate moments for frequency and severity models are presented, as are numerical methods needed to compute more complicated functions of loss distributions, such as risk measures.

Chapter 5 presents the basics of the application of extreme value theory to risk management. Extreme value theory provides us with a collection of tools that can be used to supplement traditional statistical analysis with asymptotic and statistical methods that focus on the extreme tails of loss distributions. We study both the block maxima and points-over-thresholds approaches, including the fundamental limiting results and corresponding statistical techniques. Approximation formulas for VaR and Expected Shortfall derived from the asymptotic limit theorems are presented.

Chapter 6 introduces copulas, the fundamental tool for modelling the dependence between loss random variables. We discuss copula basics, including Sklar's theorem, bounds for dependent risks, and basic implicit and explicit copulas. We also discuss measures of dependence and, in particular, how rank dependence can provide more information than the ubiquitous Pearson correlation coefficient. In keeping with our interest in the tails of loss distributions, we present measures of tail dependence. The chapter concludes with a discussion of the construction and estimation of copulas.

Chapter 7 discusses stress testing and scenario analysis, in which the behaviour of a portfolio under a collection of possible future scenarios is analysed. We consider important properties that stress scenarios should have, and the use and limitations of stress tests in practice. Different approaches for generating stress scenarios, including top-down and bottom-up approaches, and reverse stress testing are discussed. Finally, we discuss regulatory stress tests and consider some examples of past failures and successes of real-world stress tests.

Chapter 8 considers mathematical models commonly employed in the analysis of market risk. We begin by presenting an analysis of the behaviour of some series of equity returns, as an example of how to identify important empirical properties that should be reproduced by the mathematical models. We then describe three models that are commonly used to model asset returns in practice: the independent lognormal model, the GARCH (generalized autoregressive conditionally heteroscedastic) model, and the regime-switching lognormal model. We discuss the properties of the different models and the extent to which they reproduce our empirical observations about stock returns. We also study methods for estimating the model parameters and how to choose between the different models in practice.

Chapter 9 looks at techniques employed in the calculation of short-term portfolio risk. We review analytical approximations such as the delta-normal and delta-gamma-normal approaches, and then we discuss historical simulation. We conclude with a discussion of backtesting risk measure estimates.

Economic scenario generators (ESGs) for the modelling of risk over long time horizons are the subject of Chapter 10. We look both at models with a cascade structure, such as the Wilkie model, and vector autoregressive models. Important properties of ESGs are discussed, and we consider some of the challenges of model and parameter selection for long-term forecasting, such as structural breaks in the historical data. The application of ESGs to problems in risk management is illustrated through an example of an employer-sponsored pension plan.

Chapter 11 presents an overview of interest rate risk and the techniques for its management. We begin with a brief review of the term structure of interest rates and the mathematics of interest. We then proceed to a discussion of interest rate derivative securities. This is followed by a study of measures of interest rate sensitivity, including duration, convexity, and key rate duration, and their application to the mitigation of interest rate risk. The chapter concludes with an empirical discussion of the dynamics of the interest rate curve using principal component analysis.

Chapter 12 studies mathematical models for credit risk. We begin with an overview of credit sensitive instruments and the types of credit risk faced by financial market participants. We then discuss the three key components of mathematical credit risk models: probability of default, loss given default, and exposure at default. Models for the default of individual borrowers, including structural and reduced form models, are then presented and the role of credit ratings is also discussed. Finally, we discuss portfolio credit risk models, which dramatically illustrate the importance of the dependence modelling techniques discussed in Chapter 6.

Chapter 13 looks at liquidity risk. Access to highly liquid assets is a critically important consideration for firms that need to meet their short-term cash needs, either in normal operations or in crises. We distinguish between funding and market liquidity, as well as between systemic and idiosyncratic liquidity risk, and illustrate how cash flow scenario tests can be used to identify and mitigate liquidity risks. Liquidity adjusted risk measures and their application in banking are discussed. The chapter concludes with a discussion of emergency plans for managing extreme and unexpected liquidity shocks.

Chapter 14 presents a detailed discussion of model risk and governance. We discuss different sources of model risk, including defective models, inappropriate applications, and inadequate or inappropriate interpretation of the results. We review the model life cycle and quantitative approaches to measuring model and parameter uncertainty. Finally, we discuss model governance and methods for mitigating model risk.

Chapter 15 covers the use of options and other derivative securities for risk mitigation. We consider several types of risk including equity prices, interest rates, credit, exchange rates, and commodity prices and discuss the use of derivatives for managing the risk of each.

Chapter 16 studies risk transfer. We first consider general principles of risk transfer and then present several relatively recent innovations in the transfer of insurance risk. In particular, we study the use of captive insurance companies and the securitization of insurance risk, including Catastrophe (Cat) Bonds, pandemic bonds, and longevity derivatives.

Chapter 17 discusses regulation of financial institutions and, in particular, the Basel Accords in the banking industry and the Solvency II regime for regulating insurers in the European Union (EU). We do not attempt a comprehensive summary of all the different capital charges in each regime, but summarize the main aspects of each regime and focus on the underlying principles for the regulation of financial institutions.

Chapter 18 discusses capital allocation and performance measurement. Once the risk of a portfolio has been calculated, an important next step is to understand how that risk comes about; in particular, is it possible to assign to different portfolio constituents a quantitative measure of how much they contribute to overall portfolio risk? This has several applications in ERM, including assigning capital to different business units, hedging, and performance measurement. We present many different methods that have been proposed in the literature for the allocation of capital based on a quantitative risk measure. We also discuss characteristics that a capital allocation methodology should have and several real-world considerations in the application of capital allocation.

Over the past few decades, behavioural finance has grown in importance, highlighting several of the shortcomings of neoclassical economic and financial theory and studying how humans make financial decisions in the real world. In Chapter 19, we discuss the implications of behavioural finance for ERM. In particular, we study behavioural biases and how they can lead to risk management failures. We also present an introduction to Cumulative Prospect Theory, which provides a quantitative model of decision-making that reflects some universal cognitive biases.

Chapter 20 presents a discussion of crisis management, focussing on how to prepare for, and respond to, crises. We present several examples of good and bad responses to crises and discuss the impact of corporate structure and ethics on crisis response.

The appendix collects some material on probability and statistics that should be familiar to readers of the book. It is there for convenience and should not be mistaken for a comprehensive introduction to the subject matter.

Acknowledgements

Drafts of chapters of this book have been used in courses on risk management that have been taught at the University of Waterloo over the past few years, and we have received many helpful comments and suggestions from students and colleagues. Particular thanks go to Carole Bernard, Phelim Boyle, Jessica Dang, Ben Feng, Charlie Ford, Marius Hofert, Joseph Hyun Tae Kim, Johnny Siu-Hang Li, Ken Seng Tan, Ruodu Wang, Saisai Zhang, and Xiaobai Zhu. John Hardy, David Hardy, and Peter Hardy all provided insight into real-world project management. Special thanks go to Felice Liang, whose research assistance was invaluable during the final months of writing. All remaining errors in the book are, of course, our responsibility.

The Department of Statistics and Actuarial Science at the University of Waterloo has provided us with a wonderful environment in which to teach, collaborate, and study. One of the most painful aspects of the recent pandemic has been our inability to interact in person with our colleagues and students.

As always, our most profound debt of gratitude goes to our families. Completing a project of this size can be an imposition on life at home in the best of times, and is especially challenging during a pandemic. Mary thanks Phelim for his unstinting support, generosity, and forbearance. David thanks Ruth for her love and support, and Andrew, Sean, and Sofia for bringing joy and excitement to every day.

1

Introduction to Enterprise Risk Management

1.1 Summary

In this chapter, we present an overview of enterprise risk management (ERM). We begin by discussing the concepts of risk and uncertainty. We then review some of the more important historical developments in different areas of risk management, propose a definition for ERM, and show how ERM has its origins in all of the individual areas of risk management that came before.

We discuss how ERM can be implemented as an ongoing process, which is optimally built into the operations of an organization from the top down through a risk governance framework. Stages of the ERM cycle include risk identification and analysis, risk evaluation, and risk treatment. Each of these stages is introduced in this chapter and then developed in more detail in subsequent chapters.

1.2 Risk and Uncertainty

Suppose you are planning an outdoor party. You check the weather forecast and see that there is a 10% probability that it will rain during the event. That means there is a risk that your party will not be successful, unless you provide some shelter for your guests. It is uncertain whether or not the shelter will be needed, but you have very good information about the uncertainty – there is a 90% chance that the shelter will not be needed and a 10% chance that it will save your party from being washed out. More problematic in planning your party are the things about which you have no information. Perhaps, without your knowledge, two of the guests hate each other; if they meet at your party, a big fight will ensue, ruining the event. That is a risk out of the blue – you did not know that there was any risk of a fight, and, even if you had, it would have

1

been hard to assign probabilities to the events that unfolded. Both the rain and the fight represent risks to the success of your party, but the risks are different in nature. The risk of rain is much easier to handle – you can decide whether the risk justifies the cost of renting a temporary shelter for the day. The risk of a fight is a more difficult problem – you cannot prepare for it, or avoid it, if you are unaware that the risk exists.

Some writers use the term **risk** specifically for events which are identifiable and quantifiable, like the risk of rain at the party, and **uncertainty**, or **Knightian uncertainty**[1] for events which are not foreseeable, or are impossible to quantify, like the fight risk. In this text, we will use the term 'risk' in the broadest sense to encompass all uncertainty, but we will also refer to Knightian uncertainty when it is useful to make the distinction.

Risk is an essential feature of all business. A manufacturer must invest substantial amounts in research and development, equipment, and raw materials to establish a new product line, in the expectation that their product will prove profitable but allowing for the possibility that it does not. A bank that wishes to avoid all risk would never lend money to its customers. An insurer pursues risk because the purpose of insurance is to profit from managing the risks transferred to it by its customers.

In the business context, taking a risk can have a positive or negative outcome. In common usage, 'risk' is often used to refer only to the possibility of an unwelcome outcome; we refer to this type of risk as **downside risk**.

For many years, business education sought ways to incentivize higher risk-taking by managers in order to benefit from the extra returns attainable. The reasoning was based on the theory that, although managers tended to be risk-averse, businesses should be risk-neutral – meaning (loosely) that any risk that was expected to generate profit was worth pursuing, even if the potential downside could be catastrophic to the firm.[2]

More recently, it has become better recognized that, while some risk-taking is necessary for all business, it is also appropriate to manage those risks, avoiding some and perhaps mitigating others. Modern organizations aim to operate in a risk corridor: not too little, or the business cannot thrive, but not too much, in case the business is destroyed by foreseeable adverse events. The **risk tolerance** of the business sets the upper and lower limits of the risk corridor, and the **risk appetite** describes the target level of risk within the corridor under normal circumstances (although it should be noted that the precise definitions

---

[1] After Frank Knight, who distinguished risk and uncertainty in his 1921 book *Risk, Uncertainty and Profit*.

[2] For more in-depth explanation of these arguments, see, e.g., Grossman and Hart (1982) and Mayers and Smith (1982).

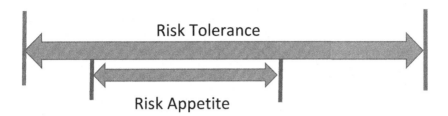

Figure 1.1 Risk appetite and risk tolerance

of risk appetite and risk tolerance vary across the literature) (see Figure 1.1). Risk appetite and risk tolerance are discussed in more detail in Section 1.12.1.

The objective of risk management is closely tied to the management of the **capital** of a firm. Broadly, capital refers to the funds available to absorb unexpected losses. Typically, a firm's capital includes all of its equity (excess of assets over liabilities) and some, or all, of its long-term debt. Following common usage, we will use the term 'capital' in this very loose sense. Where more precision is required, the calculation depends on the context. In some cases, long-term debt will be excluded, as it is less flexible than equity. In other cases, long-term debt is included, as it can be applied to absorb losses in the short term.

The term '**risk management**' is used by accountants, actuaries, project managers, quants (quantitative finance specialists), business leaders, engineers, and professional risk managers, and each of these groups has adopted a slightly different interpretation of the term. In the following sections, we describe the meaning and origins of a range of types of risk management, and we then discuss how the various strands of risk management converge in enterprise risk management.

1.3 Insurance Risk Management

The field of **risk management and insurance** (RMI) emerged in the 1960s as the study of the impact of insurable risk, or **pure risk**, on firms. Pure risks are all downside, such as the loss from windstorms or cyberattacks. Many pure risks are insurable, which means that firms may transfer the risk to an insurer, but at a cost. The RMI discipline was essentially a subfield of corporate finance, as it developed methods for determining the optimal financial approach to pure risk in reference to its impact on share values. That means that the firm might seek opportunities to reduce risks, but only if the analysis showed the cost of risk reduction to be less than the benefit. For example, a firm's risk of losses from fire damage may be reduced through insurance or through better-quality building materials or fire prevention strategies; the calculation the firm should make is to weigh up the costs and risks to decide on the best approach.

The choices available for managing pure risk are:

- Transfer – typically by purchasing insurance.
- Retain – self-insure.
- Avoid – by not engaging in the risky activity.
- Reduce – take actions to reduce the frequency and/or severity of loss.

These are not exclusive, as we shall see in later chapters. The firm might insure against severe losses but self-insure minor losses.

The analysis of pure risk, including the analysis of risk reduction or elimination (through insurance or otherwise), is now a major element of ERM. The options for managing risk in an ERM framework include the choices for pure risk, but ERM addresses both risk and risk management more comprehensively. In Section 1.12.4, we describe an expanded list of management strategies that recognizes potential rewards as well as losses.

1.4 Financial Risk Management

Two strands of modern finance deal, in different ways, with risk analysis and risk management. The first, is the quantitative assessment of the risk-return trade-off through modern portfolio theory. The second is pricing and hedging financial options.

1.4.1 Portfolio Risk

Portfolio analysis traditionally measures the risk associated with a portfolio of assets using the standard deviation of the portfolio return. The risk-reward trade-off is captured in the calculation of the efficient frontier, where the expected return on a portfolio of risky assets is plotted against the risk, as represented by the standard deviation. An example is given in Figure 1.2.

The efficient frontier represents the set of optimal portfolios, where optimal means that no other combination offers a higher expected return for any given standard deviation. When a risk-free asset is included in the portfolio mix, the efficient frontier is a straight line with y-intercept equal to the risk-free rate of return, denoted here by r_f. This is illustrated by the grey line in Figure 1.2.

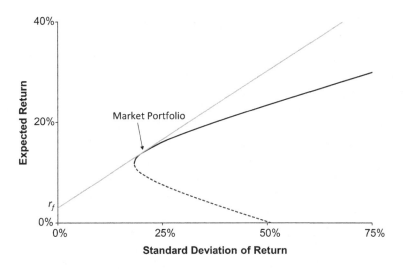

Figure 1.2 Illustration of a portfolio frontier – dark line is the efficient frontier for the risky asset portfolios; the straight line includes the risk-free asset.

There is a unique point on the efficient frontier that is achieved with zero investment in the risk-free asset. This is illustrated in Figure 1.2 by the point where the straight line is tangent to the original frontier. This point represents the mean and standard deviation of the return on the market portfolio, denoted by R_M; the market portfolio is a portfolio of all the investments represented in the market, each held in proportion to their total market capitalization. Any point on the efficient frontier can be achieved with a combination of an investment in the risk-free asset (possibly a negative, or short position), and an investment in the market portfolio. This implies that, under the model assumptions, there can be no reason to invest in anything other than the market portfolio, in respect of the risky asset allocation.

Now consider a single asset, for example, an investment in shares of XYZ company. The capital asset pricing model (CAPM) shows that the random return on shares of XYZ, denoted by R_X, must be related to the return on the market portfolio, denoted by R_M, as:

$$E[R_X] = r_f + \beta_X \left(E[R_M] - r_f \right). \tag{1.1}$$

The beta term is defined as follows: let $\rho_{X,M}$ denote the correlation between the return on the market portfolio and the return on the XYZ shares, and let σ_X and σ_M represent the standard deviation of returns on shares of XYZ and on the market portfolio, respectively. Then

$$\beta_X = \frac{\rho_{X,M}\,\sigma_X}{\sigma_M}. \tag{1.2}$$

Hence, the beta of the asset is a measure of the dependence of the returns of the XYZ shares on the market overall return; it is sometimes referred to as the **systematic risk**.

Non-systematic risk is the variation in the asset value that is independent of the market as a whole. In theory, this risk can be eliminated for investors through diversification, so the systematic risk of a portfolio, or of any investment, is considered the key risk.

There are some important considerations missing from this analysis. The first is that standard deviation, in general, is not a very good measure of risk. One reason is that it counts both upside and downside deviations equivalently; in addition, it may not capture rare events that could have significant impact. Furthermore, the efficient frontier analysis and equation (1.1) assume that the expected returns, standard deviations, and correlations of the individual investments are known by all and are (reasonably) static over time. In reality, each of these parameters can only be estimated, with a lot of associated uncertainty, and the parameters change significantly over time.

1.4.2 Options and Derivatives

The second major development in financial risk grew out of the seminal work of Black, Scholes, and Merton (BSM) in the field of options and other derivatives.

A derivative is an asset with a payoff that is dependent on another (underlying) security. A European call option with strike price K and term T years, written on an underlying security with price S_t at t, pays out the greater of $S_T - K$ and 0 at time T. A European put option with strike price K, term T years, and underlying asset price process S_t, pays out the greater of $K - S_T$ and 0 at T. Options are described and explored in depth in Chapter 9. The BSM work combined a scientific approach to pricing options with a consistent method for hedging the resulting cash flows. That is, as well as measuring risk, the approach offers important insight into the management of risk.

The BSM analysis of option pricing was significant in risk management for several reasons. The first is that options and other derivatives can be used to hedge risk, and so the development of scientific pricing methods expanded the options market and, therefore, the availability of pseudo-insurance within capital markets. For example, an investor might hold 10 shares in Gaggle.com with a current value $100 per share. Suppose she wishes to ensure that, in six months her portfolio does not fall in value below $850. She could purchase six-month put options with a strike price of $85 per share at a cost of around $1.50 per share or $15 in total. In the (unlikely) event that Gaggle.com shares fall below $85 at the maturity date, the put option would pay the shortfall, maintaining the portfolio value. If the share price is higher than $85 per share at the end of the six-month period, then the options expire without value.

More exotic derivatives can be used to hedge more exotic risks. Derivatives can be used to offset currency risk for businesses working in different markets or to offset default risk using credit derivatives. More simple forward and futures contracts, which set a fixed price for a commodity some time in advance of a transaction, can be used by businesses to lock in prices – for example, a farmer might lock-in the price of corn or pork bellies that they plan to sell, or an airline might lock-in the price of fuel that it plans to buy. Unlike options, under futures contracts the agreed price is paid at maturity even if the market price is more favourable. It is important to note that derivatives can be used for speculation as well as for hedging, unlike traditional insurance.

The second major contribution of the BSM analysis was to provide a systematic framework for hedging derivatives that is integrated with the pricing methodology. For example, consider the Black–Scholes formula for the price of a T-year put option, on a non-dividend paying stock with price S_t at time t, and with strike price K. The price at time 0 is

$$p_0 = Ke^{-rT}\Phi(-d_2(0,T)) - S_0\Phi(-d_1(0,T)),$$

where r is the continuously compounded risk-free rate of interest, Φ is the distribution function of the standard normal ($N(0,1)$) distribution, and, for any t_1, t_2 where $0 \le t_1 < t_2$

$$d_1(t_1, t_2) = \frac{\log(S_{t_1}/K) + (r + \sigma^2/2)(t_2 - t_1)}{\sigma\sqrt{t_2 - t_1}}, \tag{1.3}$$

$$d_2(t_1, t_2) = d_1(t_1, t_2) - \sigma\sqrt{t_2 - t_1}. \tag{1.4}$$

Here, $\sigma > 0$ is a measure of the volatility of the returns on the underlying stock. This formula[3] is also used to find the price at intermediate dates $0 < t < T$,

$$p_t = Ke^{-r(T-t)}\Phi(-d_2(t,T)) - S_t\Phi(-d_1(t,T)). \tag{1.5}$$

Now, although the formula is written in terms of the $N(0,1)$ distribution function, the development is based on the cost of replicating the option payoff,

---

[3] Note that the t_1 and t_2 arguments are usually omitted from the d_1, d_2 notation and that in finance texts N is generally used in place of Φ.

not on evaluating the expected costs under real-world probabilities. That is, under the BSM assumptions, the option seller can eliminate their risk by holding the replicating portfolio at time t, which is then costlessly rebalanced throughout the rest of the term. At time t, the replicating portfolio comprises $\Phi(-d_2(t, T))$ units of a $(T - t)$ year risk-free zero-coupon bond, with total face value K, together with $-\Phi(-d_1(t, T))$ units (the minus sign indicating that this is a short position) of the underlying stock at t, where each unit of stock has price S_t. The total value of this replicating portfolio is then exactly p_t at t, as given in equation (1.5). The $-\Phi(-d_1(t, T))$ term represents the derivative of the option price with respect to the stock price at time t; this is the option **delta**.

This is the real beauty of the Black–Scholes formula, that it simultaneously offers a valuation framework and a risk management strategy. The fundamental principle underlying the formula, which applies far more widely than vanilla European options, is the no-arbitrage principle, which requires that two portfolios with identical payoffs must have identical prices. There are some strong assumptions involved in the BSM framework, but years of research and experience have shown that the approach can be useful in practice, even where the underlying assumptions are breached.

1.5 Actuarial Risk Management

Actuaries typically work on quantitative analysis for insurance companies and pension plans. The traditional actuarial role in insurance includes determining premiums, setting reserves, and contributing to investment and risk management strategies.

Actuarial risks involve a combination of financial and non-financial uncertainty. For example, a term life insurance policy involves financial uncertainty with respect to the return earned by investing the premiums, and non-financial uncertainty in the benefit payout, which is contingent on the death of the insured life. Similarly, an auto insurance policy involves financial uncertainty in the value of accumulated premiums, non-financial uncertainty in the claim frequency (that is, the probability of a claim), and some financial and non-financial uncertainty in the claim severity because, when a claim arises, the amount will depend not only on the nature of the accident but also, potentially, on the inflation rates applying in the time between the loss event and the claim settlement. Most non-life insurance is quite short-term and involves little financial risk, but some life insurance liabilities are much more sensitive to financial risk than demographic risk and the risk management techniques for those are very similar to the techniques used by investment banks.

Actuarial risk management integrates RMI and financial risk management, but from a different perspective. The objective of RMI is to use insurance as a tool in risk management with the ultimate goal of maximizing share value of the firm. Financial risk management generally takes the perspective of pure investment enterprises, such as banks or hedge funds, where the objective is to create investment return with mitigation of downside risk. Actuarial risk management takes the perspective of the insurer but adds a broader public responsibility beyond maximizing profitability. For example, the actuary is responsible for the security of the policyholders' contingent benefits, and for ensuring that there is broad equity of treatment of different groups of policyholders. Some actuaries work for pension plans, where profit is not an objective. In this case, actuarial risk management consists of understanding the risks involved and advising plan managers as to the best strategy for balancing cost and benefit security without excessive risk-taking.

In the 1990s, actuaries developed **dynamic financial analysis** (DFA) techniques as an extension of their traditional risk management toolkit. DFA used integrated projections of assets and liabilities to assess the net effect of different investment and risk scenarios on the liabilities. The key insight in DFA was that the uncertainty in asset values should not be analysed separately from the uncertainty in liability values. Furthermore, different liability classes could be aggregated, allowing simultaneous modelling of risk from all sources with respect to a portfolio of liabilities and supporting assets. The scenarios analysed comprised paths for all key factors influencing cash flows (such as interest rates, claim frequency, and inflation rates), allowing the insurer to stress test their financial strength through a range of adverse scenarios. Additionally, the cash flows could be projected through a large number of stochastically simulated scenarios, thereby offering a probabilistic analysis of the portfolio solvency over a specified time horizon.

A major contribution to ERM was the recognition that jointly modelling assets and liabilities is essential where they are connected, for example, through common dependencies on capital market factors or on other factors influencing claim frequency and severity. The idea of projecting cash flows with dynamic control mechanisms, which means that the projection in each future year depends to some extent on the experience up to that year, is still a widely used tool in ERM.

1.6 Asset-Liability Management

Traditionally, financial risk management has focussed on asset values, and insurance risk management on liabilities. Asset liability management (ALM) considers risks arising from mismatching of assets and liabilities. It is an integral part of dynamic financial analysis and, hence, of actuarial risk management.

The main focus of ALM is interest rate risk. Often, the assets supporting an uncertain liability have different sensitivity to interest rate movements than the liability itself. This can create a situation where the assets appear to be sufficient to meet liabilities, but after a shift in interest rates the asset values fall below the liability values. We illustrate this with the following example.

Example 1.1 A company has a debt of 1,000 due in 10 years ('the liability'). It makes provision for the debt by purchasing a zero-coupon bond with term 8 years and face value 920 ('the asset').

The company demonstrates that the asset is sufficient to meet the liability based on market values. Market values are determined by discounting the cash flows at the risk-free rate of interest. Assume that the risk-free rate of interest (annually compounded) is 3.25% for an 8-year term and 3.5% for a 10-year term.

(a) Calculate the market value of the surplus of assets over liabilities.
(b) Assume that one year later interest rates have fallen, such that the 9-year risk-free rate of interest (annually compounded) is 3.0% and the 7-year risk-free rate is 2.8%.

   Calculate the change in value from time 0 to time 1 in: (i) the asset and (ii) the liability.
(c) Discuss the impact of the interest rate movement on the sufficiency of the assets with respect to meeting the liabilities.

Solution 1.1

(a) At time 0, the market value of the liability is

$$V_L(0) = 1{,}000(1.035)^{-10} = 708.92.$$

The market value of the asset is $V_A(0) = 920(1.0325)^{-8} = 712.31$.
The surplus is, therefore, $V_A(0) - V_L(0) = 3.39$.
(b) (i) At time 1, the market value of the asset is $V_A(1) = 920(1.028)^{-7} = 758.29$. The asset value has increased by 6.455% over the year.
   (ii) The market value of the liability is
   $V_L(1) = 1{,}000(1.030)^{-9} = 766.42$. The liability value has increased by 8.11% over the year.

(c) The asset manager is very happy to have made a return on investment of 6.5% over the year. Unfortunately, the liability value has increased by 8.1%. The surplus of 3.39 at time 0 has turned into a deficit of 8.13 at time 1 because of the asset-liability mismatch. □

In this example, the company could eliminate all risk by hedging the liability with an investment in a zero-coupon bond with face value 1,000, maturing at the same time as the liability; this is the replicating portfolio for the liability. The surplus will be zero regardless of the interest rate movements. However, it is not always possible or desirable to construct an exact match for the asset and liability cash flows, and ALM investigates methods of managing risk in more complex situations.

One of the earliest developments in ALM came when Frank Redington, a British actuary, published his work on immunization. He showed that by matching the value and duration of assets and liabilities, and selecting assets with greater convexity than the liabilities, the surplus ratio, Assets/Liabilities, would not decrease (and would slightly increase) on a level shift in interest rates, in either direction.[4] Redington's method involves some strong assumptions and simplifications, but, nevertheless, has been a critical tool in managing assets and liabilities in the financial sector.

ALM has been broadened to include other potential sources of asset-liability mismatch. It is also the precursor to **liability driven investment** (LDI). In both ALM and LDI, the principle is that the assets supporting uncertain future liabilities should be invested with reference to the nature of the liabilities, rather than simply to maximize return.

1.7 Quantitative Risk Management

Quantitative risk management (QRM) refers to the mathematical methods and paradigms used in risk management, predominantly in financial risk management. Models and theory from the fields of probability, statistics, econometrics, and financial mathematics are commonly applied.

The main focus of QRM is on the following topics.

(1) Modelling Extreme Events
Extreme value theory (EVT), which is the subject of Chapter 5, is a tool used to model rare events, where data is scarce, frequency of events is very low, but

---

[4] See Chapter 11 for further discussion of immunization.

the severity is high. Examples include losses arising from severe natural disasters. The first applications of extreme value theory were in environmental risk assessment, but it has been adapted to problems in financial and insurance risk.

There are two approaches to developing probability distributions for extreme values. The first considers the distribution of a sample maximum for different underlying distributions. As the sample size increases, the maximum value can be considered an extreme value. The second approach considers a threshold for a distribution, beyond which values are possible, but rare. The extreme value distribution is derived by considering the distribution of values given that they lie beyond the threshold. This leads to the 'points (or peaks) over threshold' approach.

(2) Aggregating Risks

Financial risks are highly dependent, and the nature of the dependency is not well captured, in general, with simple measures of correlation. Managing risks that are dependent requires models which apply even in the tails of the individual distributions. When we are interested in combining risks across an enterprise, we often need to pay special attention to the dependencies between different risks and different business units.

One important tool for modelling dependency is the **copula**, which is used to describe the full joint distribution of random variables, given their individual marginal distributions. This is the subject of Chapter 6.

(3) Risk Measures

The quantitative analysis of risks often involves modelling a probability distribution for future losses. We use risk measures to determine how much capital an enterprise would need to have available to absorb potential losses, with high probability, given the loss probability distribution.

The risk measure may be set by regulation, or by internal assessment of the firm's risk appetite. The well-known **Value at Risk** (VaR) metric is a risk measure that is based on a quantile of the loss distribution; that is, the α-VaR of a loss distribution represents the amount that, with probability at least α, will not be exceeded. The **Expected Shortfall** risk measure is the average loss, conditional on the loss lying in the tail of the distribution. That is, the α-Expected Shortfall represents the average loss given that the loss falls in the worst $1 - \alpha$ part of the distribution. The Expected Shortfall measure has many different names, as it was developed more or less simultaneously by a number of different groups. In banking, it may be called **Tail Value at Risk** (TailVaR) (although Expected Shortfall is becoming the more popular nomenclature); in insurance it is often called **Conditional Tail Expectation** (CTE); it is also referred to as **Conditional Value at Risk** (CVaR).

The VaR risk measure was in use by actuaries long before it was reinvented for investment banking. In actuarial contexts it is known as the quantile risk measure or quantile premium principle. VaR and Expected Shortfall are always specified with a given confidence level α, typically 95% or 99%. In Chapter 3, we discuss these and other risk measures in more detail and consider their uses in different contexts.

1.8 Project Risk Management

Project risk management (PRM) is the analysis and management of risks inherent in implementing business projects.

A project is an operation established to accomplish a specified goal in a specified period of time. For example, a firm may initiate a project to develop a new product, or to implement new software. Engineering and IT firms are particularly project-based, as the major objective of these firms is developing solutions to specific problems. Projects are temporary – they have a defined beginning and end. They often involve complex scheduling of interrelated tasks and goals.

Project management is used to execute projects efficiently, achieving the required results within the required budget and time frame. PRM is a subset of project management, applying classic risk management techniques to the project selection, planning, and implementation phases.

The techniques used in PRM are, broadly, a subset of those used for general ERM. PRM is discussed further in Chapter 2.

1.9 Operational Risk Management

While PRM deals with the risks specific to projects, **operational risk management** (ORM) is concerned with ensuring, as far as possible, that the day-to-day operations of a firm run smoothly.

ORM would include, for example, developing processes to limit losses from fraud; ensuring compliance in employment practices; developing processes to create safe work environments; and ensuring key employees have the right skills to fulfil their responsibilities. It would also cover risks arising from technology, such as software or hardware failures, data entry errors, or cyberattacks. Legal risks ranging from product defect liability, through improper accounting, to bribery, would all fall under the ORM remit.

ORM is predominantly concerned with processes and controls, with the objective of avoiding preventable losses.

1.10 Crisis Management

Crisis management is concerned with preparing for, working through, and recovering from crisis events. However strong a firm's risk strategy, from time to time a crisis will arise. It may be environmental, for example, an extreme weather event, or a global pandemic. Or it may be internal, for example, as a result of failure of quality control procedures. The first stage of crisis management, which involves trying to avoid crises that are avoidable and preparing for crises that are unavoidable, overlaps significantly with ORM. Crisis management is discussed further in Chapter 20.

1.11 Enterprise Risk Management (ERM)

We have stated that risk is an integral part of a successful operation; every firm must assume some level of risk and uncertainty to achieve meaningful goals. The challenge is to ensure that the risks are identified and understood, and that overall the treatment of risk is commensurate with the firm's strategic objectives.

The best way to meet this challenge is to integrate the analysis and management of all types of risk throughout the organization. This is the basis of ERM.

The Committee of Sponsoring Organizations of the Treadway Commission (COSO), a US-based coalition of accountants and financial managers, uses the following definition of ERM:

> Enterprise risk management is a process, effected by an entity's board of directors, management and other personnel, applied in strategy setting and across the enterprise, designed to identify potential events that may affect the entity, and manage risk to be within its risk appetite, to provide reasonable assurance regarding the achievement of entity objectives.

In the following comments, we expand on this brief definition, to give some guidance into the practical implementation of ERM.

- ERM is holistic. This means that individual business units do not manage their risks independently of each other. Instead, the risks across the organization are considered in aggregate. Individual units cannot opt-out of the organization's risk management policies.
- ERM is integrated across organizational units and across different types of risk. Risks can be categorized, broadly, into financial and non-financial risks and may be exogenous or endogenous to the organization. The ERM

process considers all risks together, recognizing the connectivity of different risks, and the differing impacts of different risk events on different areas of the business.

- ERM is applied 'top-down'. It is a primary responsibility of the Board of Directors of a firm, and corporate governance is a key component of ERM. The broad risk appetite of the institution will be set by the Board of Directors and is then translated into more detailed risk tolerance limits that are applied in the operations of the organization.

- The Board and senior officers of a firm are also responsible (explicitly or implicitly) for establishing and communicating the **risk culture** of the firm. The risk culture refers to the attitudes and practices accepted and applied by the employees of the organization, at all levels. A poor risk culture arises, for example, when employees are unaware of the risks to the firm, or where risk management is viewed as an annoying constraint on profitability, or where risk management procedures are treated as a mere compliance exercise. A strong risk culture arises when employees are encouraged to see risk management as integral to their own work and to the successful operations of the firm. A strong risk culture is demonstrated when risk management is not solely the responsibility of a separate risk unit. It is a key function of line management.

- Although the risk appetite and risk culture are communicated from the top down, the identification of key organizational risks will usually involve a combination of top-down and bottom-up analysis; for some risk categories, front-line employees have more insight into the day-to-day risks than senior management.

- ERM is not merely a defensive strategy; it is also used to add value to a firm, by understanding and exploiting risks that can offer an acceptable risk-return trade-off and by treating the allocation of the firm's risk budget, implemented through risk limits for example, as carefully as the allocation of the financial budget.

- ERM is a continuous process, not a discrete or one-off exercise. The identification of risks needs to be ongoing, to allow for timely identification of emerging risks and opportunities. Strategies for managing risks will change, for example, as the economic environment changes, or as technology evolves, or as new methods of risk transfer are developed.

As ERM is concerned with all risks and all institutions are likely to be subject to a combination of financial risk, insurable risk, operational risk, and project risk, all of the different strands of risk management described above are combined in ERM.

Many risk managers, consultants, and writers of ERM books focus on the qualitative aspects of ERM, such as the processes for identifying risks and the mechanisms for preventing fraud or improper accounting. But using ERM to add value requires quantitative analysis alongside the qualitative. ERM is only truly an integrated process when the qualitative and quantitative are conflated to produce strategic and ORM processes that are understood, absorbed, and implemented throughout the institution, vertically from the Board of Directors down to the front-line workers and horizontally across all functional areas.

1.12 The ERM Process

In Figure 1.3, we show a generic ERM cycle. At the centre is the risk appetite, which defines the level of risk/reward trade-off targeted by the organization. This is translated into detailed statements of risk limits for each unit of the organization.

To assess whether the organization is meeting its risk targets, it will establish processes for identifying and evaluating risks. It will then decide how the risks should be treated, based on the overall risk appetite. Each of these stages is described in more detail below.

1.12.1 ERM Stage 1: Risk Appetite and Risk Tolerance

The **risk appetite** of an organization is the amount of risk the organization expects to take on in order to achieve its mission. Setting the risk appetite is a

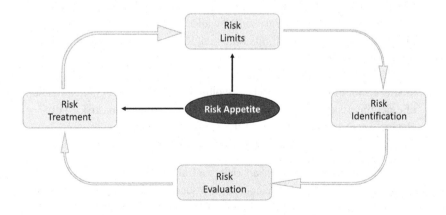

Figure 1.3 ERM cycle

responsibility of the Board of Directors, as it is highly interconnected with the other Board functions, including the determination of the strategic plan for the firm, setting compensation packages, and oversight of financial and operational management.

The full risk appetite statement may include a mix of quantitative and qualitative measures of risk. The statement should be forward-looking, and should be incorporated in, and influenced by, the strategic and financial plans of the firm. Qualitative measures might include a statement of significant risk exposures that the firm is willing to pursue and significant risks that the firm is aiming to avoid. Quantitative measures might include probabilistic statements, such as the acceptable probability of a specified loss of firm value, or earnings, or of a downgrade in the firm's credit rating classification.

The **risk tolerance** of a firm[5] adds specificity, and sets a corridor, around the risk appetite. Typically, risk tolerance statements are quantitative, defining bounds that can be embedded in the operations of the different business units, and for which compliance can be verified; breaching the risk tolerance limits would trigger immediate action to return to a risk profile that is consistent with the organization's risk appetite.

Sometimes, a firm will express its risk appetite qualitatively and support that statement with more detailed quantitative and qualitative risk tolerance thresholds.

A firm may also identify its **risk capacity**, which may be a wider range than defined by the risk thresholds, and signals the maximum amount of risk that a firm can support. Exceeding the risk capacity might breach regulatory requirements or jeopardize the organization's ability to meet its contractual obligations. The risk tolerance represents the maximum amount of risk that a firm is comfortable supporting and the risk appetite represents the amount of risk that the firm is targeting.

The firm's **risk profile** is a snapshot of the actual risk exposure at some point in time. Compliance with risk appetite and tolerance limits are assessed through regular monitoring and reconciliation of the firm's risk profile.

For example, suppose a bank issues loans to small businesses. Their risk appetite, in terms of defaults may be quite low – perhaps a 0.5% default rate. Their risk tolerance might be a 0.8% default rate; at that level, the loan portfolio is within tolerable bounds, though not within the target or optimal range. Their risk capacity might be a 2% default rate, meaning that their operations would

---

[5] Risk tolerance has a range of interpretations; here we use the most common, which is a tolerable range for the firm's risk.

be jeopardized, to some extent, if the default rate turns out to be more than 2%. A reasonable question might be 'why would the bank have any appetite for default risk?'. The answer is that, by taking on risk, the bank can charge higher interest on the loans and, therefore, potentially, make more profit than if their appetite was for 0% defaults. For some pure downside risks, such as cyberattacks, or workplace injuries, the appetite for risk may be set at zero, but zero risk-tolerance is generally unrealistic.

While precise definitions vary, there are many points of agreement about the risk appetite and tolerance framework:

- Setting and monitoring the organization's risk appetite is the responsibility of the Board and senior management.
- The risk appetite and tolerance framework should take into consideration the **external** context of the firm's operations.

  - The organization should consider the exposure to current and potential external factors impacting the firm's ability to achieve its strategic objectives.
  - The organization should review all its key external relationships and their contribution to risk. For example, when considering business interruption or reputational risk, the organization would need to consider the quality of diversification of its supply chain. When considering liquidity funding risk, which is the risk that cash is not available when needed, the organization would consider its relationship with its banking partners to assess the potential availability of overdrafts or lines of credit.
  - The organization should take into consideration the views and objectives of key external stakeholders, including, for example, customers, creditors, and regulators. Risks that appear to have only a minor potential financial impact could be more severe than they appear if the organization's reputation is damaged.

- The risk appetite and tolerance framework should take into consideration the **internal** context of the operations of the firm.

  - The Board should consider and respect the interests of internal stakeholders.
  - The risk appetite should be realistic in the context of the firm's governance, culture, and competency.
  - The risk appetite should take into consideration the firm's resources for managing risk in terms of finance and expertise.
  - The risk appetite statement may specify areas of zero risk appetite (e.g., for serious injuries in the workplace).

- The risk appetite should address strategic, financial, reputational, regulatory, and operational risks.
- Quantitative metrics should be well defined, and specify the relevant time horizon (e.g., 'limit the probability of a 20% drop in earnings over the next two years to no more than 5%').
- Qualitative risk appetite statements are often relative or categorize risk appetite into broad buckets (e.g., 'high', 'medium', or 'low').
- Once the risk appetite and tolerance parameters have been established, it is critical to monitor compliance.
- The risk appetite will change over time. The risk policy should include procedures for review and adjustment of the risk tolerance and appetite, but this must be overseen at the Board level.

Typical metrics that are covered in risk appetite or risk tolerance statements include share price, earnings volatility, excess capital over regulatory minimum requirements, credit rating, credit risk, customer satisfaction, and reputation. In a review of insurance companies' risk statements, Ingram (2017) mentions the following common themes for risk appetite statements: (1) linkage between risk appetite, risk management, and business strategy; (2) qualitative statements of overall security objective; (3) diversification of investments; (4) risk trajectory – that is, is the plan to grow risk or grow surplus? and (5) different strategies for different risk categories. For risk tolerance statements, Ingram (2017) noted several common metrics, including: (1) overall surplus to risk; (2) credit rating; (3) regulatory compliance; and (4) maximum tolerable loss.

We end our discussion with extracts from the public risk appetite statements of two institutions.

A. Excerpt from the Reserve Bank of Australia (RBA) Risk Appetite Statement.

> The Bank holds domestic and foreign currency-denominated financial instruments to support its operations in financial markets in pursuit of its policy objectives. These instruments account for the majority of the Bank's assets and expose the balance sheet to a number of financial risks, of which the largest is exchange rate risk. The Bank does not aim to eliminate this risk as this would significantly impair its ability to achieve its policy objectives. Instead, the risks are managed to an acceptable level through a framework of controls. The Bank acknowledges that there will be circumstances where the risks carried on its balance sheet will have a material impact on its financial accounts. The Bank regards it as desirable to hold sufficient reserves to absorb potential losses.
> The Bank has a very low appetite for credit risk. The Bank manages this risk carefully by applying a strict set of criteria to investments, confining its dealings to institutions of high creditworthiness and ensuring exposures to counterparties are appropriately secured.

Risk tolerances for the Bank's activities in financial markets are outlined in policies which are approved by the Governor and the Assistant Governor (Financial Markets) under delegation from the Governor. Performance against these measures is monitored daily and reported to the Assistant Governor (Financial Markets), the Head of Risk and Compliance and other senior staff.

This example shows a qualitative risk appetite statement, with an explanation that the quantitative metrics are included in a separate document of risk tolerance.

B. Excerpts from the University of Edinburgh statement of risk policy and risk appetite.

Reputation: It is regarded as critical that the University preserves its high reputation. The University therefore has low appetite for risk in the conduct of any of its activities that puts its reputation in jeopardy, could lead to undue adverse publicity, or could lead to loss of confidence by the Scottish and UK political establishment, and funders of its activities.

. . .

Financial: The University aims to maintain its long term financial viability and its overall financial strength. Whilst targets for financial achievement will be higher, the University will aim to manage its financial risk by not breaching the following minimum criteria: It will

- achieve a surplus of a minimum of 2% of gross income over any 3 year period;
- operate with a Staff Cost/Total Expenses ratio of less than 60%;
- achieve a rate of return of at least 2% above inflation on its endowment investments over a 3 year period;
- ensure long term borrowings never exceed 20% of net assets;
- ensure its surplus before interest always exceeds 2 times net interest charge;
- ensure that at least three months equivalent spend is held in cash or cash equivalents or in negotiated bank facilities.

In this example, we see that the risk appetite statement includes both qualitative constraints (for reputational risk) and quantitative constraints (for financial risk).

1.12.2 ERM Stage 2: Risk Identification

Identifying the risks that the organization must manage is the second step in the ERM process, after the risk appetite has been established. For some categories of risk, such as fraud or poor customer retention, the people working at the front end of an organization may have better information than those at more senior levels. Other types of risk are better assessed at more senior levels of an organization. For example, cyber risks may be best assessed by the

Chief Information Officer, perhaps with input from their team. The director of human resources would be asked to assess risks arising from failure to recruit adequate numbers of new hires or failure to recruit candidates with the necessary competency.

There are many suggestions in the literature on how to design the risk identification programme. The following steps are common to most of the suggested methodologies:

(1) Select key personnel from different units and from all levels of the organization. It would be natural to include all senior management, and a selection from the rest of the employees, ensuring different business units and functions are represented.

(2) Initiate training to ensure that the participants are engaged in, and understand, the process.

(3) Ask each participant to list a number of key risks (e.g., between two and five), and assess for each risk: (1) the likelihood or frequency of the associated risk event; and (2) the likely financial loss arising if the risk event does occur.

Participants may be asked to use a **risk map**. The risk map is a qualitative assessment in diagram form of the likelihood of a risk event occurring and the potential severity of loss if the event does occur. An example of the template is given in Figure 1.4. This type of template is also referred to as either a risk quadrant or a heat map. Participants in the risk identification exercise would be asked to mark the point on the diagram that describes their best estimate of the combination of likelihood and severity associated with each risk event. Risks which are located in the darker shaded areas are assessed as higher likelihood and/or higher severity.

Note that there are limitations of this approach. First, it is inherently subjective. It is well documented that individuals tend to discount the impact of events which have very high severity but very low probability. Second, if dependent risks are considered separately, two 'low likelihood, medium severity' risks may really be a single 'low likelihood, high severity' risk. A fundamental principle of ERM is that risks should be considered holistically, and the risk identification process should incorporate a stage where the relationship between individual risks is assessed, and risks which are likely to be highly interconnected are properly identified.

(4) The team managing the risk assessment process would consolidate the input from all participants in the identification exercise to prioritize risks for further analysis and evaluation.

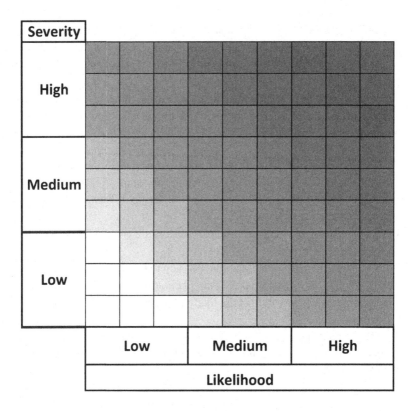

Figure 1.4 Example of a risk map template

1.12.3 ERM Stage 3: Risk Analysis and Evaluation

PESTLE and SWOT Analysis

In the **risk analysis** step the key risks identified in the second step are measured, as far as possible. There are many ways to do this, and most of this book will be concerned with the technical models and tools that may be used, so the discussion here will be brief.

Firms will update their strategic goals fairly regularly, and identifying and updating risks and opportunities will be an important step in setting strategic goals. **PESTLE** and **SWOT** analyses are commonly used tools in setting strategic objectives which encompass risk identification and analysis, at least in a qualitative sense.

PESTLE is an acronym for political, economic, social, technical, legal, and environmental. A PESTLE analysis identifies external forces that impact the organization, both positively, in the sense of potential opportunities for investment, and negatively, in the sense of emerging risks to the organization.

We see here that risk and opportunity are closely related; risk assessment and management should be core to every organization as they seek new opportunities, not an afterthought:

- **Political** factors relate to how political policies and trends may influence the organization's activities. Key issues could include government policy, public sentiment, civil unrest, tax policies, and trade restrictions. The risks to suppliers and other business partners should be considered in addition to potential direct impacts on the organization.
- **Economic** factors relate to capital markets, availability and cost of capital, volatility of local and global markets, and macroeconomic factors, such as gross domestic product (GDP), recession/growth cycles, unemployment rates, inflation rates, and exchange rates.
- **Social** factors include culture, lifestyle, demographic trends (e.g., aging population), use of technology, education levels, and provision of health services. Relevant factors are selected for their impact on customers, markets, and workforce.
- **Technical** factors include technology innovation, research and development, exposure to cyber threats, changes in consumer behaviour and expectations arising from technology trends.
- **Legal** factors include all legislation and regulation that pertain to the business environment. Relevant areas might include consumer protection, intellectual property rights, antitrust, laws relating to corporate liability, and employment law.
- **Environmental** factors include pandemics, extreme weather events and other natural hazards, and climate change.

SWOT is an acronym for strengths, weaknesses, opportunities, and threats. The SWOT analysis normally follows the PESTLE analysis and incorporates the external forces identified in the PESTLE framework with internal forces specific to the organization. The external forces identified through the PESTLE analysis will be used as inputs, particularly in the 'threat' and 'opportunity' categories of the SWOT analysis; risks that are more internally generated would largely fall under the 'weaknesses' category.

Quantitative vs Qualitative Analysis

A popular sentiment in financial risk management is 'you cannot manage what you cannot measure'[6] – and it is a helpful maxim, up to a point, but some

---

[6] This is sometimes attributed to Peter Drucker, but there is no evidence that he said it, or believed it.

risks are unmeasurable, and yet must be managed. Quantitative modelling techniques are appropriate when there is sufficient relevant data available to find statistical models and theory that can be applied with confidence. Where sophisticated risk modelling is not appropriate (because the risk is too nebulous or lack of relevant data would make modelling spurious), simple estimates of likelihood and severity may be used to quantify impact, but the possibility of spurious or nonsense metrics must be considered.

There are two major methods of quantifying future uncertain losses:

The **deterministic** approach assumes specific values for the various factors which determine the outcome of a risk event. For example, an insurer might be very interested in potential losses from earthquakes in a region. A deterministic risk model might be constructed to capture the potential impact over a specified area, broken down into different categories of loss (e.g., commercial property, homes, ships at sea, business interruption costs) given specified inputs of the exact location and severity of the earthquake. The insurer could then determine its liability under a number of different deterministic scenarios.

Financial risk is also sometimes modelled with deterministic scenarios (although, in general, stochastic modelling is more appropriate). For example, a company with a defined benefit pension plan might be concerned about the future costs of benefits, relative to asset values. A deterministic projection would utilize individual scenarios of relevant economic indicators (e.g., inflation, salary growth, interest rates, longevity, returns on equity investments) to produce individual paths of possible pension benefit costs. We call this approach **scenario testing**. Often, the individual scenarios are very complex, involving a large number of interacting processes.

The **stochastic** approach treats the future loss as a random variable or a stochastic process. We use the term *random variable* (broadly) if the loss event is defined at a specified time point or a one-off event, such as a single earthquake, and we use the term *stochastic process* for a loss which is developed over time, such as the annual costs from earthquake damage or the annual cost of pension benefits.

The tools and methods for the stochastic approach come from probability and statistics. We aim to identify suitable distributions for the random losses. Using these distributions, we can project estimates for the future losses and, also, determine measures of uncertainty associated with those estimates. Where the loss distribution is relatively straightforward, the results may be determined analytically, but in most cases the models and interactions are sufficiently complex that analytic results are not possible. In these cases, we commonly use **Monte Carlo methods**, also called **stochastic simulation**, to determine the full loss distribution over time.

The Monte Carlo approach is closely related to deterministic scenario methods. In the deterministic scenario approach the risk is evaluated using a small number of individual scenarios, each selected by the risk analyst. Using stochastic simulation, we create a model to generate a large number (from 1,000 to 1,000,000, typically) of separate, random scenarios. Each is equally likely; the basis of scenario creation is a random number generator and the subjectivity of the deterministic scenario approach is significantly reduced (although there can also be considerable subjectivity in the model and parameter selection process within a Monte Carlo approach). The full range of outcomes is an approximation to the distribution of the loss being modelled, so the mean, standard deviation, and associated probabilities of future loss can all be estimated using the output of the Monte Carlo simulation as if it were a data sample for the loss.

In Appendix A, we provide a review of some foundational concepts of probability and statistics. In the following chapters, we develop more specialized results that are particularly important for enterprise risk modelling.

Risk evaluation involves comparing the measured risks against the risk criteria established through the appetite and tolerance statements. If the risks are too great, relative to the tolerance limits, or to the returns generated, then the firm may choose to modify them using one or more of the risk treatment options described in Section 1.12.4.

1.12.4 ERM Stage 4: Risk Treatment

Through previous steps in the process, the firm should have identified key risks and, possibly, quantified the potential losses. In this step, the firm will assess whether there are strategies for managing the key risks that will add value or will eliminate risks that are outside the risk tolerance metrics of the firm.

The list of ways to manage risks set out below has its origins in the much shorter list in Section 1.3, which dealt only with pure, downside risk. For those risks, the list was 'Transfer; Retain; Avoid; Reduce'. Here, we consider the possibility that the firm may want to pursue (i.e. seek out more of) a certain risk, if that would add value, and we add some specificity to the 'Reduce' category:

• **Avoid the risk** – perhaps because it is a pure risk (no upside) or because it lies outside the risk appetite constraints.

   For example, a firm might avoid or withdraw from conducting business in a country that is financially or socially unstable if the associated risks are incompatible with its risk appetite.

- **Pursue the risk** – if the risk is essential to the core business of the firm, and can be exploited to increase firm value, then it may be pursued. Not all risk is bad risk. Insurance companies take on risk with every policy sold; banks take on risk with every loan arranged. In both cases, the aim of the business is to manage risk to create value. But other businesses must also pursue risks. For example, an airline company might open a new route, risking capital to establish the necessary infrastructure, etc. anticipating a good return on its investment.
- **Mitigate the likelihood** that the risk occurs or the frequency of the occurrence. For example, a firm might improve the quality of its workplace health and safety training, to reduce the frequency of worker injury. A car manufacturer might introduce more stringent quality control to reduce the likelihood of legal liability from selling defective vehicles.
- **Mitigate the severity** of the loss if the risk does occur. Some examples: (1) a hotel installs sprinklers so that if a fire occurs, it will be quickly extinguished and the losses will be small; (2) a manufacturer might choose to purchase its raw materials from several suppliers to reduce the severity of loss on the failure of any individual supplier; (3) a firm might hedge an exchange rate risk by entering into a swap contract with a bank. If the adverse currency movement occurs, the hedge will limit the loss.
- **Transfer the risk** to a third party. The firm may transfer all of a specific risk or may retain a share if that is more cost-effective. Often, the third party is an insurance company – property and casualty insurance is an important resource for risk transfer for business. Insurance companies also transfer risk by ceding business to reinsurers.

  More recently developments in **alternative risk transfer** (ART) have been devised to offer alternatives to insurance or reinsurance for transfer of pure risk. Examples of ART include catastrophe bonds, under which principal may be forfeited if a specified loss event occurs.
- **Retain by informed decision**. Also called '**running the risk**' or '**self-insuring**', this refers to risks which are not pursued for profit, but which cannot be avoided (at reasonable cost) and for which further mitigation options (remove source, change frequency, change severity) are not possible or cost-effective. Often, even where a firm purchases insurance, there is a co-pay or deductible retained by the firm. The reason for retention would be cost efficiency, compared with full insurance coverage. For example, a firm that operates supermarkets in a hurricane zone might retain the risk of loss from hurricanes up to, say, $1 million per year, but transfer all risk above that to an insurer.

1.13 Risk Governance

Risk governance refers to the way that the Board and management of an organization work together to manage risk.

The Board has the initial key responsibility for establishing and communicating the risk culture of the organization. It is also responsible for determining the organization's risk appetite and for creating formal structures and processes for implementing and monitoring risk management practices throughout the organization.

The management of the firm are then responsible for implementing the structures and processes determined by the board and setting internal control mechanisms for monitoring the implementation.

For many organizations, some of the work of monitoring and managing risk will be delegated through the committee structure. The precise roles and responsibilities will depend on the context of the organization. Figure 1.5 illustrates a possible committee structure. In this illustration, the Board creates a Risk Management Committee, which is a subcommittee of the Board. A Chief Risk Officer (CRO) supervises the Risk Management Unit. The CRO reports to the CEO but also has direct access to the Board through the Risk Management Committee. The Chief Financial Officer is primarily responsible for financial management and reporting, but also has responsibility for auditing the risk management processes, and so would also have access to the Risk Management Committee to report on compliance and effectiveness of the work of the Risk Management Unit.

1.13.1 Three Lines of Defence

The three lines of defence model was developed originally by the Committtee of Sponsoring Organizations of the Treadway Commission (COSO) and has been widely adopted. The following is a summary of the description provided by the Institute of Internal Auditors (IIA (2013)):

- **Risk Owner** – The first line of risk management is delegated to the employees who 'own' the risk – that is, who have a direct connection to the risks being managed. Managers at the front-line of the organization are the key players here, responsible for the design and implementation of risk management policies and procedures within their teams.
- **Oversight** – The second line of defence refers to the risk management specialists who are responsible for implementation and oversight of risk management across the organization. In the risk committee diagram in

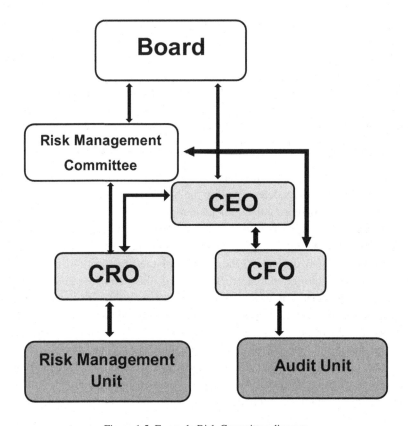

Figure 1.5 Example Risk Committee diagram

Figure 1.5, the risk management unit would comprise the second line of defence. Their main communication is with the risk owners and their main responsibilities are:

– Working with the risk owners to design and implement risk control procedures.
– Monitoring adequacy and effectiveness of first line controls.
– Monitoring compliance with organizational policies and procedures.
– Developing risk management frameworks, processes, and controls for the organization.
– Monitoring emerging risks and regulations.
– Providing guidance and training on risk management.
– Monitoring compliance with laws and regulations.

- **Audit** – The third line of defence is an internal audit of the first two lines. This is typically delegated to the audit committee, who are assumed to be independent of the risk committee and can, therefore, provide an objective review. To maintain independence, the third line should report directly to the Board (possibly through the Board's Risk Management Committee) with an assessment of the following issues:

    – Whether the risk management processes are compliant with relevant laws and regulations.
    – Whether processes are compliant with the internal policies and controls set by the organization.
    – Whether reporting and documentation processes are adequate and reliable.
    – Whether all required phases of risk management (e.g., as laid out in Figure 1.3) are adequately documented.
    – Whether the processes are efficient and effective.

Although the framework of the Three Lines Model has proved popular, there has been some debate about the optimal separation and delegation of responsibilities (not surprisingly, auditors and risk managers disagree about the priority of their respective roles) and some criticism of the effectiveness of the model.

The first problem with the model is that it contradicts the fundamental top-down principle of ERM. The Board should have a primary role in risk governance, but it is barely mentioned in the Three Lines framework. There is no mechanism for the Board decisions on risk appetite and risk culture to be communicated and implemented down through the organization. The model proposes that the first and second lines should work together and that the third line and the Board should communicate. There is no path for the Board to work with the specialist risk managers from the second line of defence, who are best qualified to support the Board in establishing risk management principles and strategies. Indeed, the original Three Lines Model documentation states that risk owners should develop their own risk controls, which implies a bottom-up risk management approach. A better implementation of the Three Lines Model would have the second line act as the intermediary between the decisions of the Board and the day-to-day operations of the organization, and, indeed, this is how the model has evolved in many organizations.

Another problem that has emerged in implementation of the model is that the third line of defence may be entirely focussed on record keeping and compliance. An auditor who only looks at whether the documentation is complete and the processes are complied with, but not at the adequacy or appropriateness of the processes and documentation, is not adding much defence to the system. But with risk management developing into some very technical areas, it is not clear that the internal audit committee will have the expertise to provide a robust review.

These, and other problems, were recognized in 2013 by the UK Parliamentary Commission on Banking Standards (PCBS) (Parliamentary Commission on Banking Standards (2013)), which was responsible for investigating unlawful and unethical banking practices. In their summary, the PCBS wrote that:

> The 'three lines of defence' system for controlling risk has been adopted by many banks with the active encouragement of the regulators. It appears to have promoted a wholly misplaced sense of security. Fashionable management school theory appears to have lent undeserved credibility to some chaotic systems. Responsibilities have been blurred, accountability diluted, and officers in risk, compliance and internal audit have lacked the status to challenge front-line staff effectively. Much of the system became a box-ticking exercise whereby processes were followed, but judgement was absent. In the end, everyone loses, particularly customers.

The PCBS specifically noted that the second and third lines of defence were considered secondary to the revenue generating functions of the front-line employees. Putting the first line of defence onus on the front-line employees ignored the fact they they are not employed to be risk managers – in fact, they are often rewarded for chasing risk. The remuneration policies, where big gains led to big bonuses for the employees, meant that the front-line workers were likely to earn more if they bypassed the risk controls than if they complied and, as long as the employees were creating profits, flags raised by the second or third lines of defence were not acknowledged.

1.14 Risk Budgeting

The risk budget of an organization is the allocation to individual units of the total risk that the firm takes on. This is often measured in terms of the firm's **economic capital** which refers to the excess of the value of its assets over the value of its liabilities. The firm's economic capital represents a cushion that can absorb adverse experience.

There are several ways to measure asset and liability values; in risk management we are interested in the most realistic and objective assessment, which is achieved by using market values rather than accounting values. So, we define:

Economic Capital = Market Value of Assets

− Market Value of Liabilities

The economic capital may be quite different from the figure for Assets − Liabilities in the company accounts, particularly where historical cost accounting is used. Also, note that the economic capital is changing more or less continuously, as asset and liability values are dependent on changeable market conditions.

If market values are not readily available, the evaluation of economic capital is done by modelling on a market-consistent basis, meaning that items are valued using a mathematical model that is calibrated to current market conditions.

The risk budget may also reference the **regulatory capital** of a firm, which is the amount of capital that the firm is required to hold to comply with regulation. This is particularly relevant for financial services companies such as banks and insurance companies, which are more strongly regulated than other sectors due to (1) the uncertain nature of their liabilities, (2) the complexity of their operations, making it difficult for individual policyholders or depositors to assess the quality of the organization, and (3) the importance of the continued solvency of the institutions to the smooth running of the economy. Investment banking regulation is broadly determined by the **Basel Committee on Banking Supervision**, an international organization widely known as the **Basel Committee**, whose standards, summarized in the Basel Accords and associated amendments, are adopted with some local variation by banking supervisors worldwide. Insurance company regulations are less centralized, though the European Union's Solvency II framework has become a benchmark for many other jurisdictions. Both the Basel rules and the Solvency II framework are described in Chapter 17.

1.15 Notes and Further Reading

1.15.1 Types of Risk Management Failure

Stulz (2008) proposes five types of risk management failures:

(1) Failure to use appropriate risk metrics.
(2) Mismeasurement of known risks.
(3) Failure to take known risks into account.
(4) Failure in communicating risks to top management.
(5) Failure in monitoring and managing risks.

In later chapters, we will discuss these topics in detail. In Chapter 2, we present a categorization of risks that is intended to assist in risk identification. In Chapter 3, we will define some key risk metrics and analyse their appropriateness. In Chapters 4 to 10, we present methods, models, and other tools for measuring quantifiable risks. In Chapters 11 to 14, we consider the characteristics, measurement, and management of several key risks in more detail. In Chapters 15 and 16, we discuss other methods of managing risks through offsetting, using hedging, or offloading, using insurance. Chapter 18 is concerned with taking risks into account, specifically in measuring profitability and allocating capital. In Chapters 19 and 20, we discuss monitoring, management, and communications with respect to some non-quantitative risks.

The PCBS report (quoted in Section 1.13) was commissioned in response to a scandal involving the London Interbank Offered Rate (LIBOR). This rate has been used as a benchmark rate for billions of dollars in transactions. It was set, essentially, by polling the major UK banks, but this laid the rate open to manipulation, as bankers misstated their rates to try to shift the LIBOR in a direction favourable to their transactions.

1.15.2 The Global Financial Crisis of 2007–8

The global financial crisis of 2007–8 began in the US, sparking a severe worldwide recession, with the aftereffects lasting well over a decade. The origins of the crisis lay in the period of deregulation in the US and several other countries in the years prior to 2007. This led to some creative and extremely high risk strategies developed by investment and retail banks, particularly relating to portfolios of mortgage debt. Retail banks issued mortgages to low-income home buyers, without much consideration of the ability of the borrowers to repay the loans. The mortgages were termed **subprime**, reflecting that they were issued with a high probability of default. Borrowers were lured into excessive loans through ultra-low initial repayments and aggressive marketing. After an initial period, the repayments would increase substantially, leading to a very large number of defaults and foreclosures. The loan portfolios were sold wholesale to investment banks who pooled the loans together in packages designed to be attractive to capital market investors. The principle was that, by pooling, the risk of loss from defaulting borrowers would be reduced. As the mortgage backed securities became more prevalent, banks created new securities that only paid out if the level of default on the **mortgage-backed securities** (MBS) exceeded some threshold. These products were called **credit default swaps** (CDS). The CDS contracts were significantly underpriced, due to a lack of understanding of the nature of the risks involved. A downturn in the economy sent the value of the loan portfolios plummeting, as borrowers defaulted en masse and the collateral for the loans – that is, the borrowers' homes – proved inadequate due to falling house values. The issuers of the CDS contracts were now in danger of being required to compensate the holders of the mortgage backed securities for payment shortfalls in such large numbers that the CDS issuers would be unable to meet their obligations. In September 2008, Lehman Brothers, which was then the fourth-largest investment bank in the US, filed for bankruptcy. Because of the interconnectedness of the major banks, the failure of Lehmann Brothers threatened the solvency of several other major institutions, in the US and internationally, through **default contagion**, which refers to the fact that one default can trigger many others. Markets plummeted around the world. Governments were required to provide billions of dollars in loans and guarantees to keep the financial markets afloat. This was not intended to protect the bankers and bank shareholders, but rather to ensure that manufacturers could access funds to pay their workers and that bank customers would not face the loss of their investments.

The crisis has had a significant and ongoing impact on ERM, particularly in the financial sector. The deregulation trend was reversed, at least for a time. A new risk category, systemic risk, representing the risk of a system-wide failure of financial markets became a concern of risk managers everywhere. Global regulations attempted to limit the influence of the largest banks, those that are 'too big to fail' in common language, or 'Systemically Important Financial Institutions' in the language of regulators. The Basel Committee embarked on a widespread revision of its capital and liquidity standards. In the US, the Dodd–Frank Act of 2010 consolidated the supervision of financial institutions and restricted the ability of banks to make more extreme speculative investments. Similar laws were passed in other countries that had followed the deregulation trend. The Dodd–Frank Act was credited with creating a stable market environment and restoring public trust in financial institutions. However, after heavy lobbying from the banks, it was partially repealed in 2017.

1.15.3 Further Reading

See Doherty (2000) for a presentation of the traditional RMI treatment of risk in corporate finance.

Modern portfolio theory was pioneered by Markowitz (1952) and Sharpe (1964). The seminal works on BSM theory are Black and Scholes (1973) and Merton (1973). See Boyle and Boyle (2001) for the story of derivatives, and their uses for good or ill.

The COSO definition of ERM is from 'Enterprise Risk Management –
Integrated Framework' (COSO, 2004).

For a deeper dive into risk governance, and the evolution of the 'three lines
of defence' framework, see Lam (2017).

The economics of insurance company regulation is discussed in 'When
Insurers Go Bust' by Plantin and Rochet (2016), who propose inversion of
the production cycle, and the absence of a tough, sophisticated claim holder as
key motivating factors for the prudential regulation of insurance companies.

For more information on the global financial crisis, see, for example, Lewis
(2011) and Stiglitz (2010).

1.16 Exercises

Exercise 1.1 Explain briefly the meaning of each of the following terms. Give
examples where possible.

(a) Risk appetite.
(b) Risk map.
(c) Regulatory capital.
(d) Risk governance.

Exercise 1.2 Explain why maximizing return may not be an optimal short-
term asset strategy.

Exercise 1.3 Describe three key differences between PRM and ORM.

Exercise 1.4 The Board of Directors of a firm is asked to consider the
following questions:

(a) How much risk is the firm currently taking?
(b) How much risk should the firm be taking?
(c) What is the maximum amount of risk that the Board wants the firm to
    take?
(d) What is the maximum risk that the firm can take without jeopardizing its
    operations?

Identify how these questions relate to the Board's risk appetite statement.

Exercise 1.5 WatAir is an airline company, targeting low-cost holiday travel
between Canada and the Caribbean:

(a) Give examples of risks that WatAir might pursue.
(b) Give examples of risks that WatAir might avoid.

(c) Give examples of risks that WatAir might transfer and explain where the risk could be transferred to.

(d) Give examples of risks that might be frequency-mitigated.

(e) Give examples of risks that might be retained by informed decision.

Exercise 1.6 A car manufacturer uses the following strategies/decisions relating to risk. Identify which of the risk treatment methods is being used in each case:

(a) Uses multiple suppliers from multiple countries for key raw materials.

(b) Enters into an exchange rate swap with a bank.

(c) Improves workplace safety training and resources in its factories.

(d) Invests in research and development of a self-driving car.

(e) Buys product liability insurance, which will partially reimburse the manufacturer in the event of legal liability from a defective product.

(f) Closes its factory in a country which is experiencing civil unrest.

Exercise 1.7 An insurer is considering entering the US individual health insurance market with a policy that would offer the following benefits only. The insurance is designed to supplement health insurance cover offered through the policyholder's employment ('the primary plan'):

• Hospital inpatient expenses (that is, the expenses of a hospital stay) exceeding coverage in the primary plan.

• Hospital outpatient expenses (clinic visits that do not require overnight stay) exceeding coverage in the primary plan.

• Specialist physician consultation exceeding coverage in the primary plan.

• Prescription drug costs exceeding coverage in the primary plan.

Identify at least one external factor from each of the PESTLE categories that would be significant for the risk management of this insurance product.

Exercise 1.8 An insurer is designing a policy that would cover any excess loan outstanding when a car is written off as a total loss (through accident or theft). The claim amount would be the difference (if positive) between the outstanding loan and the amount recovered from the policyholder's auto insurance policy. The term of the insurance would be the term of the loan, typically three to five years.

Using the PESTLE framework, describe briefly four key external factors that might impact the success of this product.

Exercise 1.9 A firm has the risk management and reporting structure illustrated below. Units 1 and 2 are involved in front end customer service and Unit 3 is the finance office.

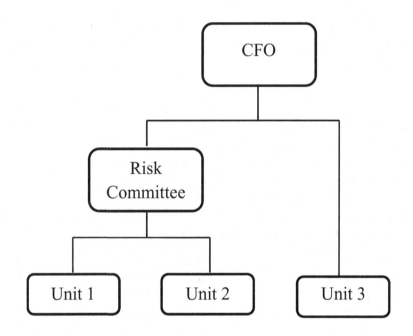

(a) Describe how the structure should be changed to comply with the three lines of defence framework.
(b) Explain the shortcomings of the three lines of defence framework and explain how the committee structure could be further adapted to overcome these.

Exercise 1.10 A car manufacturer decides to revise its risk appetite to be more conservative with respect to variability in annual earnings.
Explain how this might impact the following stakeholders:

(a) The marketing department.
(b) Shareholders.
(c) The agency assessing the firm's credit rating.
(d) Customers.

Exercise 1.11 Dearbourne Corporation is an innovative electronics corporation, bringing customers the latest in today's best computerized gadgets. Dearbourne has suffered losses recently due to both operational failures and emerging competition.

Dearbourne has only two divisions:

Division A: Manufacturing and quality control of product

Division B: Research and development of new electronic technologies

(a) Currently, Dearbourne uses the following practices to identify its top risks:

    I. Survey managers

    II. Use expert/industry surveys

    III. Use internal data

    Identify the potential shortcomings with each of these practices.

(b) Dearbourne is in the process of completing its next manager risk survey. These surveys are completed by individually interviewing selected managers.

    Outline the methodology that could be used and state the objectives.

(c) The following managers are among those selected to be surveyed.

    I. Building Security Manager

    II. Chief Information Officer

    III. Chief Officer of Quality Control

    Propose key survey questions specific to each manager.

Copyright 2013. The Society of Actuaries, Schaumburg, Illinois. Reproduced with permission.

Exercise 1.12 Poutine Inc.'s business is removing impurities in silver. The refining process is very energy-intensive, so energy costs are a large proportion of its total costs.

Customers provide raw silver to Poutine, which Poutine then refines for a fixed fee. Poutine uses coal as its only source of energy. Its fixed costs are extremely stable. The cost of coal is the only variable cost Poutine incurs.

Poutine's coal costs currently exceed the refining fee it charges. This situation has occurred several times in recent history.

The CEO asks you to apply the PESTLE framework to identify the general environmental risks Poutine faces.

(a) Identify each of the risks considered in the PESTLE framework.
(b) Provide an example for two of the risks identified above which are specific to Poutine.

Copyright 2014. The Society of Actuaries, Schaumburg, Illinois. Reproduced with permission.

2
Risk Taxonomy

2.1 Summary

A taxonomy is a classification system. In this chapter, we present a risk taxonomy, by which we mean that we shall categorize and describe all the major risks that may be faced by a firm or institution. We will describe risks that arise from outside the organization – 'external risks' – and those that come from within the organization – 'internal risks'. External risks are further categorized into economic, political, and environmental subcategories, while internal risks include operational and strategic risks. Reputational risk may be internally or externally generated. We describe some examples of how risks have arisen in several high profile cases, showing the intersectionality of the different risk categories – that is, how the different risk types can all be driven by a single risk event.

2.2 Introduction

In our taxonomy, as far as possible we define and classify risks based on events. That is, we identify events with potentially adverse consequences to an enterprise and categorize them into risk classes. The list is designed to be fairly generic and comprehensive so that it can be utilized across a wide range of industry sectors and types of institutions. The most important point is not the classification itself, but how the classification can help to develop an understanding of the various types of risk and how they are connected. For example, extreme weather may create environmental risk for a firm, the political response may create political risk, and regulations created as a result of the political response create potential regulatory risk. The overall classifications are convenient but should not be thought of as creating separate, distinguishable pigeon holes for the different risks.

External risks are classified into four categories:

- Financial market risk.
- Political and regulatory risk.
- Macroeconomic risk.
- Environmental risk.

Internal risks are classified into two categories:

- Operational risk – that is, relating to the day-to-day operations of the firm.
- Strategic risk relating to the strategic decisions and directions of the organization.

Reputational risk may be internally or externally triggered. This is the potential loss from damage to a firm's reputation or standing.

Within each of these categories there are several subcategories which we describe in more detail in the rest of this chapter. As with all risk taxonomies, this classification is not very rigorous. Many risks can be classified in different or multiple categories. Many different risks are closely related, with one risk event in one category generating other events in the same or other categories. Even the broad headings 'external' and 'internal' are not entirely satisfactory. For example, some of the risks listed under 'exchange rate risk' below are internal, but it is usual to include exchange rate risk with other financial market risk.

The risk types described in this chapter are not specific to a single sector of business or type of company, but the nature of the firm which is managing its risk will determine which of the risks are more or less critical. For example, all firms are subject to some financial market risk, but, clearly, it comprises a more important and more complex area for firms operating in financial services.

There are methods for measuring and managing most of the risks described. The purpose of this chapter is to define and classify the major risk categories. In later chapters, we will consider measurement and management of the risks.

2.3 External Risks: Financial Markets

2.3.1 Stock Market Risk

This is risk arising from general movements in financial markets. This is a key business risk for financial sector organizations, such as banks and hedge funds, where the firm's results are directly linked to the performance of their capital market investments. It is also an issue for other industry sectors because market movements impact shareholder value and availability of capital.

The major risk could arise from price movements or from changes in volatility. Firms may hedge their market risk to some extent.

Firms may also speculate – that is, take market positions that will generate profits if their predictions of market performance are correct, and losses if not. There is both upside potential and downside risk associated with stock market changes.

2.3.2 Interest Rate Risk

As interest rates rise, the value of bonds and bond-like investments will fall. Movements in interest rates may create major problems for financial firms, especially those with bond-like liabilities that are matched on the asset side of the balance sheet with fixed interest investments. Without careful management, the value of the liabilities may move less or more than the value of the supporting assets as interest rates change, potentially creating losses. Insurance companies and pension plans are particularly vulnerable because annuities and premium payment streams for long-term insurance contracts are highly interest-sensitive.

Interest rate movements also affect investor behaviour. Increasing rates may create a demand for fixed interest instruments, which could create downward pressure on prices of stocks and other assets as demand moves away. Higher interest rates limit consumer spending, as a larger proportion of income is applied to paying loans and mortgages. This tends to dampen economic growth, and puts downward pressure on house prices. On the other side, low interest rates discourage savings and other investments.

Losses may arise from movements in the whole yield curve or because of a change in the shape of the yield curve. The changing shape may create spread risks, which are described in Section 2.3.5.

2.3.3 Exchange Rate Risk

There are several ways that institutions might be exposed to unanticipated changes in exchange rates.

Transaction risk is the risk arising when a firm has current contractual obligations which are specified in different currencies. The firm is exposed to losses from exchange rate movements in the time period between entering a contract and settling it. If a contract calls for a series of payments which are specified in non-domestic currency, then the transaction risk continues as long as the contract is in force.

Economic risk refers to a firm's general economic exposure to exchange rate fluctuations. Examples include:

- Firms that import or export goods or raw materials.
- Firms that invest in foreign markets.
- Firms whose goods experience demand slumps when exchange rate movements make imported competitive goods relatively cheaper.
- Firms whose suppliers and customers are exposed to exchange rate risk.

Translation risk arises from the requirements of financial reporting for a firm with assets and liabilities designated in different currencies. For example, a foreign subsidiary of a firm might show significant volatility in net assets (assets – liabilities) from exchange rate movements between reporting periods, even if the value has been quite stable in the subsidiary's home currency.

2.3.4 Credit Risk

Credit risk covers a range of situations, all relating to exposure to loss as a result of a change in the credit status of a debtor or counterparty. We divide the risk into two categories. The first is **market risk**, which is the risk that assets held by a firm lose value because of changes in the credit standing of the issuer. The second is **default risk**, which refers to losses caused by the failure of other businesses or individuals with whom the firm has a financial relationship.

Market Risk

Market risk refers to the potential for losses driven by the decline in the market value of a contract owing to a deterioration in the creditworthiness of a debtor or counterparty. The losses are on a mark-to-market basis, and no default or bankruptcy needs to occur for the contract to lose value. For example, if an insurance company owns a bond issued by Bank A (or an option written by Bank A) and Bank A's creditworthiness declines, then that security is worth less to the insurer. If the insurer were interested in selling the security to a third party, buyers would not be willing to pay as much for it, owing to the increased probability that Bank A will fail to meet its obligations. In this sense not only default, but the perceived likelihood of future default, can cause credit risk losses. Market risk losses can be very significant. The Basel Committee on Banking Supervision (Basel Committee on Banking Supervision, 2009b) estimated that roughly two-thirds of counterparty credit risk losses during the global financial crisis were due to market risk.

Market risk is frequently measured and monitored using the spreads on credit default swaps. A **credit default swap** (CDS) is derivative security that behaves like an insurance contract on the default of an organization, referred to as the reference entity. In a CDS, one side (the protection buyer) will make periodic premium payments to the other side (the protection seller). In return, the protection seller will make a payment to the protection buyer if and when the reference entity defaults on its debts. The level of the premium payments is determined by the CDS spread and will be higher if the reference entity is perceived to be a worse credit risk. Hence, the CDS spread provides a market assessment of the creditworthiness of the reference entity; when the spread increases, companies owning securities issued by the reference entity will tend to suffer mark-to-market credit risk losses.

In addition to CDS spreads, credit ratings are also used to assess the creditworthiness of many securities. Credit ratings are assessments of the creditworthiness of debt issued by companies, governments, and other institutions assigned by specialist agencies. The 'big three' credit rating agencies are Standard and Poor's (S&P), Moody's, and Fitch.

When credit risk is associated with debt issued by a country, it is called **sovereign risk**. Sovereign risk also covers situations where a country changes rules specifically for foreign investors, for example, by imposing regulations preventing foreign investors from collecting the full proceeds of their investments, leading to lower bond valuation.

Credit ratings, credit default swaps, and mark-to-market credit losses are discussed further in Chapter 12.

Default Risk

Default risk is the risk that a borrower or contract counterparty of a firm fails to meet its obligations to the firm, whether through corporate failure or for other reasons – for example, it may be late with supplies or services. **Counterparty risk** is used when the default risk is associated with a counterparty in an over-the-counter financial contract such as an interest rate swap or a forward contract on a stock.

Concentration risk is a form of credit risk, arising when a firm is heavily dependent on a single counterparty or a small set of mutually dependent counterparties. Concentration risk amplifies default risk.

2.3.5 Spread Risk

The spread between two assets refers to the difference between the returns on those assets. The difference between corporate bond yields and government bond yields reflects their different levels of credit and liquidity risk.

The long-short bond spread is the difference between yields on long bonds and yields on short bonds, which reflects different levels of risk, as long-term bonds are more exposed to interest rate and credit risk, different levels of liquidity, and market segmentation.

Spread risk is the risk arising from changes in spreads. It is a problem, for example, if a firm holds short-term bonds, but has liabilities tied to long-term yields.

2.3.6 Systemic Risk

The International Monetary Fund Financial Stability Board (2009) defines systemic risk as 'risk of disruption to financial services that is caused by an impairment of all or parts of the financial system and that has the potential to cause serious negative consequences for the real economy.'

This is a very broad definition; it would cover disruption from all causes and does not capture some elements that are often considered critical features of systemic risk. Schwarcz (2008) defines systemic risk as the risk that a trigger event, such as an economic shock or an institutional failure, causes a cascading reaction of institutional losses or failures, ultimately destabilizing the financial system itself.

Systemic risk became a much more urgent area of research after the 2007–8 financial crisis, when the entire US banking system came perilously close to meltdown following the failure of Lehman Brothers and the near collapse of several other major investment banks, all triggered by unpredicted correlated defaults of subprime mortgages. The subprime mortgage crisis impacted all sectors of the US economy through the cascade of defaults and liquidity failures. Firms were unable to access capital, stock prices fell, and investors withdrew billions of dollars from the falling markets, creating an even deeper market decline and exacerbating the liquidity crisis. The cascade also impacted markets across the world, showing the interconnectedness of global markets and, in particular, the influence of the US market on all others.

2.3.7 Liquidity Risk

An institution may have sufficient assets to meet liabilities, in principle, but may still be unable to make payments as they fall due if the assets are not sufficiently liquid. Liquid assets include cash as well as other investments that can be easily and quickly converted to predictable amounts of cash.

Examples include government bonds and stocks that are publicly traded on major exchanges. Illiquid assets are those which take time to sell or which are highly unpredictable in terms of their value at sale. Illiquid asset categories include, for example, property, works of art, and private debt.

Organizations all have some inherent liquidity risk. The nature and significance differs according to the type of organization. Companies with fast turnover of inventory tend to have fewer liquidity problems because it is easy to match income and outgo. For example, supermarket chains have a very fast turnover of stock, so the period between paying suppliers and selling the products is very short; typically, there will be a continuous and predictable flow of cash in and cash out. Firms with longer periods between outgo and income are more exposed to liquidity gaps. For example, consider a boutique, high-end fashion retailer, who may have taken out a loan to purchase their stock at the start of the season and must then meet loan payments and other expenses before the inventory is sold over the following weeks and months. Similarly, construction firms typically receive payment in tranches, with final payment received shortly after completion of the project, but their outgo may be more or less continuous, with cash payments to workers and subcontractors and retailers of the building materials. Construction projects are very long term and involve a lot of uncertainty in timing, leading to a major risk of liquidity gaps. Another example of income-outgo mismatch is in insurance, where premiums at the start of the contract are invested to meet claims some considerable time later. If the premiums are invested in illiquid assets, the insurer may be faced with a liquidity gap when a claim arises.

Market liquidity risk is the risk that access to liquidity is restricted through general market conditions – typically, in a volatile, falling market (which is the systemic risk described in Section 2.3.6 above). Firms that are short of liquidity need to borrow cash or sell assets. When markets are in turmoil, for example, in a systemic market crisis, lending institutions are less likely to provide loans, or will only do so at excessive cost, and assets put up for sale may achieve far less than their intrinsic value as there are so few buyers in the market.

Funding liquidity risk arises when a firm has sufficient assets to meet liabilities, but insufficient cash. This may arise from market liquidity risk, reducing availability of loans or liquid assets, or it may be an idiosyncratic risk, arising from the specific circumstances of the firm. Firms generally hold a mix of liquid and illiquid assets. A firm that needs to make a cash payment, but only has access to illiquid assets, has a liquidity gap. Generally, the firm would seek to borrow sufficient cash to meet their liabilities, but the loan may only be available at significant cost.

2.4   External Risks: Macroeconomic

2.4.1   Business Cycles

The term **business cycles** refers to economy-wide fluctuations in the economic environment: as supply and demand curves shift, unemployment rises or falls, and countries move between low and high growth phases. These changes will usually be associated with financial market risk as exchange rates, stock prices, and interest rates may all be affected.

Although termed 'cycles', the incidence, severity, and length of fluctuations in the economy are not regular or predictable. Some industries or organizations are more impacted by the fluctuating economic conditions than others and, in fact, some firms may prosper through economic downturns. For example, in the recession following the 2007-8 global financial crisis, Walmart and McDonalds were reported to have increased market share because more consumers were seeking less expensive shopping and dining options.

2.4.2 Inflation

Inflation risk refers to the reduction in real returns arising because of falling purchasing power of cash. Long-term fixed amount cash flows are most vulnerable to inflation.

In the most developed countries, managing inflation has been a critical element of government management of the economy. The high inflation rates experienced in the 1980s in Europe and North America, with inflation at times exceeding 10%, appear to be a thing of the past – although, it is possible that governments may change their priorities with respect to management of the economy at some future date.

Inflation is a much more immediate issue in the developing world, impacting organizations operating within the affected countries and also those external firms who do business with the affected countries. Inflation risk is closely connected to exchange rate risk, through the principle of 'purchasing power parity'. This principle states that if there is price inflation in country A, say, but not in country B, the value of country A's currency will fall relative to country B, such that the purchasing power of a unit of currency in country B remains the same.

Anticipated inflation is not really a risk – it can be allowed for and managed. Even unanticipated inflation need not be a major source of risk, if cash flows move in parallel, maintaining the real returns. The problem arises when net incoming cash flows are fixed in monetary terms, so that the impact of inflation reduces their value and, therefore, the real return.

2.5 External Risks: Political and Regulatory

2.5.1 Political Risk

Political risk arises from adverse political changes in an organization's home country or in a foreign country where there is some exposure.

There may be political instability resulting in difficulty managing contracts or meeting obligations, or a supplier may not be able to move goods according to the original requirements. In extreme cases, there may be a virtual shut down of commerce in a country while the political situation is unstable. In less extreme cases, there may be problems with liquidity and capital markets.

Other examples of political risk include cases where the political climate of a country directly opposes the institution. For example, an international mining firm may find increased challenges to their operations in a country where the political climate shifts as a result of the negative impact of mining on the environment: in several countries mining operations have been nationalized, due to the local unpopularity of some multinational corporations.

One way that political risk is manifested is through changes in legislation, creating new regulatory hurdles and constraints. Political risk is, therefore, closely related to regulatory risk.

An illustration of how political risk can create a vicious cycle of losses, with surprisingly wide impact, was the decision made in 2018 by the US to impose new tariffs on imported steel and aluminium as part of a political campaign blaming foreign trade for domestic problems. The negative impact was felt not only by exporters, but also by US manufacturers who relied on the imported raw materials. Subsequent retaliatory tariffs on US exports then damaged the firms within the US that were accustomed to being able to sell their products across borders, who may have had no connection to the original issue with steel and aluminium.

The exit of the United Kingdom (UK) from the European Union (EU) in 2021 is another (long and drawn out) example of a political risk event, for industry, financial companies, as well as universities and other not-for-profit organizations, with ramifications being felt through the curtailing of, for example, free trade agreements, free movement agreements, and grants and subsidies provided to support infrastructure and educational projects.

2.5.2 Regulatory Risk

Regulatory risk arises from changes in laws or regulations which adversely impact an organization's operations or cash flow. There are many examples – changes in labour laws may increase salary expenses; changes in laws on transferring funds out of the country may create problems for firms operating in different markets; and changes in licensing rules may create barriers for firms trying to acquire the necessary permissions to conduct their business.

Regulatory changes may originate in political risk – for example, introducing penalties or exclusions for international companies – or may simply reflect modernizing trends. For example, many countries have developed more comprehensive laws on employee health and safety. A firm which ignored this trend may find its business adversely impacted by the need to improve workplace safety standards. That does not mean the regulatory development is targeting that firm or sector. Regulatory changes often reflect societal changes.

Firms that operate in more socially controversial areas of business are more vulnerable to regulatory risk. Cigarette companies have been subject to increasing constraints on marketing and sales in many countries, for obvious reasons. Companies that are accustomed to using secretive financial incentives to lubricate business arrangements may find themselves regulated out of business through anti-bribery legislation. Companies that exploit monopolistic positions may find regulations introduced to curtail their power.

In the financial sector, for around 20 years up to 2008, there was a general trend to deregulate under the controversial economic theory that regulation had only negative effects on a healthy market economy. Since this position was quite forcefully undermined by the global financial crisis of 2007–8, the positions of most commentators have become more balanced.

2.6 External Risks: Environmental

Environmental risk arises from changes in the environment and in the way organizations and society in general interact with the environment. Examples include natural environmental disasters, such as hurricanes, drought, or earthquakes; pandemic risks; and climate change.

Climate change is a long-term, and potentially existential, risk to businesses and communities. The nature of the risks and uncertainty around climate change make this a very complex challenge. It has been seen as a problem of Knightian uncertainty, unknowable and unmeasurable, although the scientific projections are increasingly specific. Public corporations have relatively short-term goals and the costs of climate change have, until recently, been perceived not only as unquantifiable, but also as falling beyond current planning horizons. Often, environmental risks that are not well suited to corporate planning, but which are significant to the economy as a whole, are handled through government intervention and, to some extent, that is taking place with climate change. But it has also become a political football, with many governments unwilling to collaborate on taking the substantive steps required to mitigate the problem, preferring instead to defer the problem or to argue speciously over the science.

Climate change will significantly impact all areas of society, including the economic environment. Global wealth will be diverted to managing the environmental changes; political instability is likely; much essential infrastructure, including major highways, railways, and airports is highly vulnerable to increasing sea levels. Natural resources will be depleted and energy, food, and water security are likely to be diminished in most developed countries. Some effects, such as the increasing frequency of hurricanes and wildfires, and increasing drought and desertification are already impacting global business.

Pandemic risk is another form of environmental risk. The COVID-19 pandemic illustrated the wide range of potential areas of impact created by a severe pandemic, including economic slump, workforce disruption, supply chain management problems, and political turmoil. Virtually all areas of the economy felt the impact of the pandemic and associated restrictions, but some sectors were far more affected than others, including leisure and hospitality, as well as some manufacturing and construction, which were impacted by stay-at-home orders.

Pandemics are unavoidable risks; risk management, therefore, focuses on preparedness, which falls under the crisis management sub-area of risk management. The key tasks of pandemic crisis management include: preparing an action plan, with alternative strategies for different levels of severity; maintaining and updating the action plan, running role-playing simulations to ensure the action plan works and is well understood by key players; monitoring the environment for early warning of developing pandemics; implementing the action plan; and dynamically adjusting the response through the crisis.

Natural disaster risk is similar to pandemic risk. It is unavoidable, in the sense that hurricanes, floods, and wildfires will happen and are largely out of the control of individual organizations. The frequency can be mitigated by positioning key structures away from the more common sites, with respect to hurricanes, floods, and earthquakes, for example. The severity can be mitigated by ensuring construction is robust to the likely natural hazards. Crisis management plans can ensure that when a natural disaster occurs, the response is planned and effective at minimizing impact. Insurance can be used to transfer some financial risk.

2.7 Internal Risks: Operational

The Basel Committee defines operational risk as 'the risk of loss resulting from inadequate or failed internal processes, people and systems, or from external events'.

The Basel Committee is concerned with banks, but the definition can be applied to any organization as it is extremely broad in scope. We will reference the Basel definition for our discussion of internal operational risk, particularly since many institutions have adopted the definition or a slightly rewritten version of it. However, we exclude external events from this section as they are covered in the previous sections.

The Basel Committee specifically excluded reputational risk from the list of operational risks, and we follow that distinction here. However, we do not use the Basel Committee's list of subcategories of operational risk. Instead, we have developed a list in which each subcategory is more specific, and more event-driven. It is also less focused on banking operations and, therefore, more widely applicable.

So, we are concerned with risks that are associated with the specific day-to-day operations of the company or organization. The risks are classified as internal, even though some, such as theft or fraud, may involve external agents. We claim that even these risks are essentially internal as they involve failure of internal processes which should prevent theft or fraud. As with all the risk classifications, the categories are neither exclusive nor exhaustive.

2.7.1 People and People Process Risk

The Basel Committee definition of operational risk specifies (in an awkward grammatical structure) 'inadequate or failed internal processes, people'.

People risk is the risk that individuals working for the organization, directly or through outsourcing, fail to follow the organization's rules, processes, or procedures. The failure may be deliberate, in which case the risk is theft, fraud, or sabotage perpetrated by an employee. If the failure is not deliberate, it may be caused by error, carelessness, lack of training, or lack of adequate competency. Human error emerges as a common component in catastrophic failures in many areas, including engineering, manufacturing, and medicine. Even where the original risk event was unavoidable, we often find that human error exacerbated the situation.

Behavioural risk refers to poor behaviour or poor decision-making caused by the corporate culture, combined with psychological biases. For example, a trader in a bank may be rewarded for making large gains through potentially enormous bonuses. Large losses may be punished with a job loss, but this is not too significant if the individual can quickly move to a new position, or if a few years of large bonuses precedes the job loss. So the incentives are aligned for the trader to take large risks for the potential of a large reward. If the trader's supervisor then asks the trader to take less risk, there is a conflict between the supervisor's instruction and the incentive structure. The trader may choose to hide the risks taken and the supervisor (who will also be rewarded if the trader's gambling pays off) may choose not to look too hard to see whether the risk limits are being complied with. Both are subject to behavioural risk caused by the incentive structure.

People process risk is the risk that the human resource process fails. For example, an organization may face losses on the resignation of one or two key people, if a succession plan has not been implemented, or if the work required has not been sufficiently documented for another person to take over. New recruits might not meet required standards of competency to maintain the quality of output for the organization. This will lead to instances of the non-deliberate type of people risk.

A subset of people risk is **dominance risk**. This risk arises where an individual – typically the CEO – is given too much power, without sufficient oversight, and uses that power to the detriment of the firm. Typically, the dominant CEO surrounds themself with a willing and unquestioning team, often over-promoted, and thus lacking the experience or expertise to question the CEO's decisions. The CEO is supposed to be subject to the oversight of the Board, but a dominant CEO can often manipulate the Board as well as the senior management of the firm. Often, the CEO takes the role of Board Chair, although that is contrary to ethical corporate governance. Even if they are not Chair, they may dominate the choice of directors, ensuring that the directors feel obligated to the CEO and will, therefore, be unquestioning of the CEO's actions.

2.7.2 Cyber Risk

Cyber risk may refer to the potential for losses arising from the failure of a firm's IT systems, but it is most commonly associated with criminal attempts to breach a firm's security system. The objective of cybercrime may be to: steal data (e.g., customer credit card information), blackmail firms using stolen intellectual property, collect ransom from firms that have been locked out of their systems, or possibly simply to embarrass the firm or organization.

State sponsored cybercrime is used to embarrass governments, steal state secrets, or to foment unrest in enemy countries.

Cyber risk has become one of the most critical challenges for modern organizations, particularly in financial services or for other organizations with significant online activities, but even small firms, with relatively low level online activity, are vulnerable.

Although cyber risk usually originates from outside the organization, it is included as an internal risk because in most cases, the breach represents a failure of the firm to secure its data, update its software, or implement good IT practices.

Data Breach

A data breach is an event in which information is accessed by hackers from outside the firm. The main objective of the hackers is often personal data, such as credit card numbers and social security numbers, that can be sold on to criminal organizations. Some of the more infamous data breach examples include the theft of credit/debit card information of up to 110 million customers of Target Stores in 2013 and the Equifax data breach of 2017. Equifax is a consumer credit reporting agency; the nature of its work requires it to collect detailed information on the financial records and transactions of vast numbers of individuals and businesses around the world. Equifax reported that around 50% of the US population were affected by the breach. The breach was not made public for several weeks after the company became aware of the losses. The result for Equifax was a sharp drop in share price and the resignation of several senior officers, including the CEO and CIO. The firm had been provided with a patch that would have blocked the data theft several months earlier, but the patch was not applied. The tools that Equifax had put in place to identify possible data theft attempts had not been renewed, allowing the hackers to continue accessing the data for several months before Equifax belatedly renewed its certificate, revealing the data theft. The loss was announced to the public one month later, in September 2017. Despite a very high potential black market value, there is no evidence that the stolen data was sold, leading security experts to conjecture that the Equifax breach was state sponsored.

Ransomware

Ransomware refers to malware (malicious software) that blocks the victim's access to their data until a ransom is paid to the perpetrators. The malware encrypts the victim's files and the decryption key is only provided once the victim has paid the required ransom, usually in cryptocurrency such as bitcoin. The malware is often introduced to the victim's computer through an attachment to an email or through a network service vulnerability. A variant on ransomware is where, instead of encrypting the data, the perpetrators threaten to publish the stolen data. In most cases, the victims of ransomware are individuals or small businesses; larger firms are more likely to maintain adequate cybersecurity to avoid the risk. Vulnerability to ransomware can be mitigated, for example, by having a rigorous backup system, by implementing good email practices (e.g., blocking the downloading of suspicious emails or attachments), by timely and diligent software updating, and by limiting access to computer systems.

Denial of Service (DoS) Attack

A denial of service attack is designed to render the victim's network unusable by either flooding the network with traffic or creating a network crash. A **distributed denial of service attack** (DDoS) is a denial of service that is generated from multiple systems. A DDoS can be difficult to manage as it is harder to identify the legitimate traffic from the malicious traffic. Denial of service attacks may be used for extortion, similarly to ransomware. Some firms suspect their competitors of launching DDoS attacks in order to direct more business to the perpetrator and to damage the reputation of the victim. Some activist groups use DDoS attacks for political purposes in an attempt to embarrass agencies that they oppose.

2.7.3 Other Information Technology Risk

IT risks that are not related to the deliberate criminal activity behind cyber risk arise from the reliance of the organization on its IT.

Key IT risks include:

(a) Accidental loss or corruption of data. .
(b) Unidentified bugs/errors in programs.
(c) System failure from inadequate capacity.
(d) Outages and interruptions to service.
(e) Failure of internet service providers (ISPs).
(f) Loss of data through destruction of physical storage through, for example, a natural disaster.

2.7.4 Project Risks

A project is a task with both a specific objective and a defined end point. All organizations use projects and project management at times; for example, in introducing new computer systems or implementing a new product line. For some firms, the main business objective is project management. This would be true, for example, of many engineering firms or management consultants.

Projects often involve a substantial investment of money and resources and major project failure can be devastating to the organization's finances, as well as, potentially, its reputation.

The key risks associated with project development and implementation are scope risk, defect risk, schedule risk, and resource risk.

Scope risk is the risk that the project goals are changed during the implementation phase, leading to potential overruns in time or budget and also, potentially, failing to meet the original project objectives. Scope risk can arise from **scope creep**, where the scope of the project is redefined gradually over time, perhaps as the project team identifies potential improvements or new ideas.

Another source of scope risk is called **gap risk**, where the original project planning was not sufficiently thorough and gaps appear (for example, in the resources allocated to the project or in the necessary steps for completion of the project) that require adjustments to the original scope. Gap risk can also lead to improvisation in the project implementation, which, in turn, can lead to multiple problems with ensuring the different parts of a project are consistent and coherent.

The project scope may also be altered as a result of external dependencies, for example, changes in regulation or failure of infrastructure.

Defect risk is the risk that hardware or software acquired or developed in order to implement a project does not meet the project needs. For example, the firm might purchase software for a project that cannot be tailored for the tasks required, or the firm might order engineering equipment that cannot manage the required loads.

Schedule risk is the risk of loss due to schedule failure. Project scheduling is a key component of project management. It is used to ensure that resources (human, engineering, financial) are available when required, but are not sitting idle while different parts of the project are being completed. If the scheduling is too aggressive, there will be bottlenecks and wasted resources from over runs in different sub-parts of the project. Overly conservative scheduling may also be wasteful if resources are allocated for longer than they are really required.

Resource risk is the risk of loss due to resources not being available when required. Projects often depend on a team of individuals collaborating, bringing different competencies to the task. One source of resource risk is losing key persons before the project is completed. The replacement may have different skills and may not have the same level of knowledge and engagement in the project as their predecessor. Resource risk also includes the possibility of running out of money to complete the work, especially if the cost exceeds the budgeted amounts.

2.7.5 Legal Risk

All organizations may find themselves subject to costly legal proceedings from time to time. Legal risk, broadly defined, is the risk of loss arising from lawsuits against the firm or from losses arising from pursuing unsuccessful lawsuits.

More specifically, McCormick (2010) suggests two different types of legal risk:

- **Risk of lawsuit** or similar claim or proceeding arising from infringement of laws or regulations, or from negligence leading to civil liability.
- **Defective contracts**, where, for example, a contract is not legally enforceable because of errors or omissions in the contract terms or process.

The first category was emphasized in the Basel Committee's definition of legal risk, which specifically mentions supervisory actions. This is particularly important in financial services, where supervision is complex and compliance with regulations may be viewed as inhibiting the firm's operations and, hence, not given sufficient priority in resource allocation. The first category also includes lawsuits arising from a range of possible sources of civil liability, including product liability arising from sale of unsafe products, liability to employees under workplace health and safety rules, or liability to third parties from patent infringement.

The second category covers losses arising from transactions that failed due to legal defects in the contracts. A classic example is the Hammersmith and Fulham derivatives case. In 1988 the London Borough of Hammersmith and Fulham, through its Chief Executive, entered into major financial transactions with a number of banks, speculating on interest rates falling. Interest rates rose, leading to massive liability from the borough to the banks. However, it emerged that Hammersmith and Fulham did not have the authority to enter into the transactions in the first place, and the banks therefore had no claim, and had to absorb the resulting losses, along with substantial legal costs arising from several stages of decision and appeal.

The International Bar Association (IBA) adds a category:

- **Failure to protect assets.** Assets include intellectual property, so this category would include the cost of recovering physical assets which have been misappropriated, as well as the costs of enforcing patents or copyright.

The IBA also adds a category for changes in law, but we include this risk in the political/regulatory category above.

2.7.6 Pricing Risk

Pricing risk arises if a product is priced too low or too high. If the price is too low, the firm will not recover the costs of production. If the price is too high, the firm may not capture a large enough share of the market to recoup its initial outlay. This can be a particular problem for businesses where there are delays between the price being agreed and the product or service being delivered. There are several possible explanations for mispricing. Some examples follow:

- There may be a change in exchange rates in the period between payment and delivery for cross-currency transactions. In this case, pricing risk is a special case of exchange rate risk.
- The pricing assumptions could be wrong. For example, pricing might be based on models that do not sufficiently capture the range and variability of the factors which affect the costs. Another common situation is changing the pricing assumptions to give a lower bid, to gain the business, without recognizing that the assumptions are overly optimistic. This may be an example of **model risk** – that is, risk from making decisions based on models which do not adequately capture the critical features of the problem being analysed, or **parameter risk**, which arises when the underlying model is adequate, but the parameters used are not.
- The enterprise might just be unlucky; for example, an insurer might set a premium sufficient to cover a potential loss with 95% probability. Even if all the assumptions are correct, there remains a 5% chance of underpricing through adverse experience.
- Insurers (and, to a lesser extent, other service providers) are at risk of underpricing due to **adverse selection**. Adverse selection is a consequence of information asymmetry. A purchaser of insurance has full knowledge of their own individual risk profile; the insurer will have less information on

each individual risk. Adverse selection, in the insurance context, relates to the fact that the buyers of insurance may transfer a higher expected loss than the insurer has allowed for. This is a very important source of risk in all areas of insurance.

2.7.7 Process Risk

Every enterprise depends on processes – to manufacture goods, to deliver services, to meet whatever the mission of the enterprise requires. In Section 2.7.1, we mentioned failure of 'people processes' – that is, the processes involved in recruiting, training, retaining, and terminating personnel. This section covers all risks affecting businesses or institutions that are not covered elsewhere. In each case, there is a failure at some stage of a business process or there is a failure to establish adequate processes. Different types of enterprise involve different processes and it is not possible to capture the full range here. Instead, we describe some higher level categories, and illustrate with a few examples:

- **Health and Safety**

  - Risk of **defective equipment** or resources – e.g., emergency exits which are inaccessible.
  - Risk of **flawed processes** – e.g., failure to establish a maintenance protocol for safety equipment or failure to provide enough lifeboats on a cruise ship.
  - Risk of **human error** – e.g., failure to recognise a health risk and follow the appropriate protocol.

- **Manufacturing and Engineering**

  - Risk of **defective components**, construction, or machinery.
  - Risk of **defective technical specification** arising, perhaps, from model risk or human error (or both).
  - **Flawed maintenance processes**.
  - **Human error** in implementation, maintenance, or monitoring of processes.

- **Model Risk**

  - **Model risk** arises when the technical, quantitative models used by a firm do not adequately capture the critical features of the issues which the model is designed to manage.

For example, it might be assumed that the failure of individual components will be independent. That means, if there are two components, each with a failure probability of 1:100, then, assuming independence, the probability of both failing would be 0.0001 or 0.01%. However, suppose the model is flawed, and that, rather than being independent, the components depend on some common factor; in that case, the probability of both components failing could be much higher.

This happens surprisingly frequently; the assumption of independence, implicit or explicit, appears to be very compelling, even when it is untrue. Hubbard (2020) gives an example of an airline crash, in which all three hydraulic systems failed, thereby rendering an aircraft uncontrollable. Since each system was supposed to have a failure probability of $1/1,000$, the failure of all three was cited as a one in one-billion (that is, $(1/1,000)^3$) event. But, in fact, all three systems were cut by shrapnel from the engine turbine blades. The mutual failure was almost inevitable given the breakup of the blades, so the *ex ante* probability of all three components failing was in fact much greater than the model predicted. In engineering, this is called **common mode failure** – that is, multiple failures with a common cause. In statistics, we would identify the component dependency, and consider the aggregate risk rather than the individual component risks.

– **Parameter risk** refers to the use of model inputs that are incorrect or inappropriate for the particular model use, even if the model itself is fine. The problem usually arises when there is insufficient data to estimate parameters accurately. Another common source is where parameters come from a data set or are developed for a problem which differs in some fundamental way from the current problem. For example, if we use whole population data to model the mortality of individual members of a pension plan, we are ignoring the fact that pension plan members tend to have significantly better health than the general population, and may be expected to live rather longer. This is an example of **basis risk**, because the basis of the model (population mortality) is different from the basis of the problem (pension plan member mortality).

2.8 Internal Risks: Strategic

Strategic risk refers to losses arising from adverse effects of strategic decisions made at the senior organizational level. The risk event is the decision to take some action which, subsequently, adversely impacts the organization.

Now, it is important to remember that it is the function of the executive to make strategic decisions and that every decision will involve risk. Sometimes, the absence of a decision involves even more risk than a definitive decision. In all decision-making at the enterprise level, it is inevitable that some choices will turn out well and some badly. Further, even knowing a decision turned out badly, after the event, does not mean that the decision was faulty, based on the information and opportunities available at the time the decision was made.

In Chapter 1 we noted that, in some cases, the appropriate strategies for particular risks might be 'pursue' or 'retain by informed consent'. So we might adopt risky strategies – such as expanding the business, changing manufacturing processes, launching a new product, developing a new IT system, or reducing insurance cover – because without risk there is no reward, or because the cost of transferring or eliminating the risk is disproportionate to the potential loss.

Strategic risk is not really an event-driven risk, and is not really a separate risk category. It is used more as a catch-all term for the potential adverse outcome of a strategic plan or decision. So, for example, a firm might decide to expand into a new country. The strategic risk refers to the possibility that the expansion does not prove to be profitable or successful. The reasons why the expansion could fail might fall under different categories, such as political or regulatory risk, exchange rate risk, or people risk, etc.

However, there are strategic decisions that have been so egregiously poor that it would be inappropriate to assume that all risks from strategic decisions are justifiable and appropriate. A risk management process should incorporate continuous assessment of the quality of the decisions made at the executive level, the quality of the analysis available to support the decisions, and the expertise and commitment to process of the directors and senior managers.

An example of a strategic risk taken that may not have involved the highest quality decision-making arises in the management of guarantees in life insurance policies with benefits linked to equity investment returns. These policies are known as Variable Annuities in North America. In the early 2000s, some insurers made the strategic decision not to hedge their exposure to stock market movements arising from their portfolios of variable annuity policies. The strategy paid off for several years but, in 2008, the economic crisis left those firms with a risk management crisis as the guarantees began to bite and the income stream (which is based on the underlying asset value) diminished.

This strategic decision would have paid off if markets had not experienced a crash, followed by a prolonged period of very low returns. Hedging is like buying insurance, if a firm does not hedge and there is no adverse market movement, it will make more profit than a competitor firm that did hedge.

Ex ante, the decision not to hedge could have been a sound decision, made in the clear understanding of the risks involved and, in particular, the exposure to and likelihood of extreme stock price movements, and an assessment of whether the risks were consistent with the firm's risk appetite and within its risk tolerances. Or, it could have been made without that understanding, based on a more subjective view of the risks involved. If the decision not to hedge was based on a full understanding of the risks, with a plan of action to follow if the adverse events occurred, then the risk process could be viewed as appropriate. If there was a failure of understanding, together with a failure to plan for the adverse event, that would be an example of poor strategic risk management.

2.9 Reputational Risk

Reputational risk refers to any risk that could damage the enterprise by damaging its reputation with customers or other stakeholders. Often, damage to reputation follows some other risk event. For example, in 2012 a trader at JP Morgan, named Bruno Iksil, created huge losses by speculating on credit spreads. This could be an example of people risk (if Iksil acted as a rogue trader by exceeding his trading limits) or people process risk (e.g., if Iksil's manager did not set appropriate limits or if Iksil did not have the competency required for his position). However, the resulting publicity, which was very critical of JP Morgan, was a fairly severe reputational loss. In this case, and many like it, reputational risk is really just a consequence of other risk events.

The purpose of separately identifying reputational risk is that the management of risk needs to take into consideration the potential reputational impact of any risk event.

Consider a hypothetical example. A subsidiary of a large global conglomerate is involved in mining. The local regulations require the firm to have insurance cover for at least $20 million of liability to cover losses in the event that the mining operations accidentally contaminate the local ecology. The firm has to consider how much insurance to purchase. If it chooses to purchase the minimum required cover, it will minimize the cost. There is a small chance that the actual losses are much greater than the insurance limit. In this case, the local subsidiary could wind up. The firm may decide to accept the small probability of failure, in return for the larger probability that the operation succeeds without mishap. However, when reputational risk to the global enterprise is taken into consideration, the ramifications of an ecological disaster might be much greater than the loss of the local subsidiary. This might lead to a decision to purchase insurance cover well beyond the minimum, to cover more extreme cases, and protect the worldwide reputation of the conglomerate.

2.10 Risk Management Examples

2.10.1 BP Deepwater Horizon

The *Deepwater Horizon* was a drilling rig in the Macondo prospect oilfield in the Gulf of Mexico. In April 2010, while drilling an exploratory well, there was an explosion and fire aboard the rig, during which 11 crew members were killed and a further 16 injured. The subsequent massive oil spill was an environmental disaster, the largest in US history up to that time.

Several commissions and teams of investigators reviewed the causes of the explosion and subsequent oil spill. The Bureau of Ocean Energy Management, Regulation and Enforcement and the United States Coast Guard prepared a joint report. The National Academy of Engineering conducted an independent investigation, focussing on the technical failures, and the 'Bipartisan National Commission on the BP Deepwater Horizon Oil Spill and Offshore Drilling' was asked to 'consider the root causes of the disaster and offer options on safety and environmental precautions.' In addition, BP published its own findings through the summer of 2010. Although each group had a different focus, the conclusions of each were substantially overlapping. The failure was initiated when a portion of drill pipe became trapped and the mechanism designed to seal the drill pipe did not work.

The following issues were identified in some or all of the reports. The risk categorization is ours.

- The initial triggering event arose because the cement used in construction was defective (**project or engineering risk** – defective components).
- There was insufficient training of personnel on when and how to shut down engines (**people process risk** – insufficient training).
- Poor maintenance of electrical equipment (**engineering process risk** – flawed maintenance).
- Bypassing of alarms and automatic shutdown systems by operators (**engineering process risk** – human error).
- Lack of a safety management system (**health and safety** – flawed process).
- Lack of a culture that emphasizes safety; selection of cheaper, more high risk materials and methods (**strategic risk** – strategic decision to reduce costs and quality).

- BP rejected the findings of its own modelling software that indicated more centralizers were required. Centralizers are used to keep the liner in the centre of a wellbore (**people risk – human error; model risk**).

The bipartisan National Commission concluded: 'Better management of decision-making processes within BP and other companies, … and effective training of key engineering and rig personnel would have prevented the Macondo incident.'

Poor decision-making at management level is a signal of mismanaged strategic risk. Lack of effective training of personnel is a signal of mismanaged people (process) risk.

Although three companies – BP, Halliburton, and Transocean – were directly involved in the management of the rig and the construction of the exploratory well, the **reputational risk** was mainly assumed by BP. The share value plunged and boycotts were organized that began to impact BP's retail gas stations throughout the US. In addition to the billions of dollars of fines and compensation, BP invested in a major advertising campaign to attempt to recover its reputation in the US.

2.10.2 Northern Rock

Northern Rock was originally a building society (that is, a mutual company offering savings accounts and mortgage loans) – and, subsequently, a bank – headquartered in the north of England.

Around 2006, Northern Rock developed a strategy that involved substantial borrowing in international money markets, to expand its capacity to offer mortgages. The mortgages were then bundled into new securities and sold off in the capital markets. The proceeds of the sales were used to service the money market loans. The strategy allowed the firm to grow its business dramatically, but the high leverage involved was risky.

In August 2007, the market for securitized mortgages fell as the subprime crisis became apparent – even though Northern Rock was not involved in subprime lending. Even more critically, the short-term loans which Northern Rock relied upon dried up, as the institutional lenders retrenched as the financial crisis developed. Northern Rock applied to the UK government for liquidity relief. Retail customers of the bank became concerned about the security of their savings, leading to scenes of queues of customers anxiously waiting for branches to open in order to withdraw their deposits. It appeared to be a classic 'run on the bank'. In 2008, Northern Rock was nationalized to stem the developing crisis. In 2011, it was sold back into the private sector, when it was subsumed by another British bank, Virgin Money.

The key risks demonstrated in the Northern Rock example include:

- **Systemic risk:** The start of the liquidity crisis for the bank was the non-renewal of short-term wholesale loans from institutional investors, probably as the lenders were facing their own issues managing liquidity and risk through the early days of the crisis.
- **Liquidity risk:** The run on the bank did not necessarily indicate that the bank was insolvent. The immediate problem was that the depositors wanted to take cash, but the assets were tied up in mortgages.
- **Interest rate risk, spread risk:** Contributing to the bank's problems was a mismatch between assets (the long duration mortgages) and the liabilities, comprising mainly short-term loans through the international money market and the deposits of the retail banking customers.
- **Strategic risk:** Northern Rock adopted a strategy with associated risks. The fact that it turned out so very badly is an example of strategic risk – but, as we have said, just because a strategy does not work out does not imply that the risk was unacceptable. Lack of strategic risk management would be indicated if the risk associated with the strategy of growth through leverage was not adequately understood or assessed.

2.10.3 Edinburgh Trams

In March 2006, the Scottish Parliament approved the building of two tram routes in Edinburgh. Construction began in June 2008, with an initial cost estimate of $498 million and a target completion date in 2011.

The project suffered multiple challenges and setbacks, with the result that the final tram routes are considerably smaller, and, with a final cost of around $1 billion, considerably more expensive than the initial plans. It also took around six years to complete, compared with the initial estimate of three years.

The project was subject to the project management risks described in Section 2.7.4 and several others:

- Disagreement amongst the political parties as to the scope of the project resulted in changes to the scope being introduced well after the project was underway (**scope risk, political risk**).
- Late delays were caused by the discovery that part of the concrete bed for the tracks did not meet specifications and a large section of track and road had to be dug out and replaced (**defect risk**).

- The defects and political disagreements created schedule overruns, which were exacerbated by extreme weather conditions (**schedule risk, environmental risk**).
- As the initial budget proved inadequate, there were problems acquiring the necessary funding as the project progressed, creating funding shortfalls (**resource risk**).
- Contractual disputes arose between the project management company and one of the construction companies, relating partly to whether the original contracts were fixed-price or not – that is, did the construction firm or the project management group bear the cost of the project risk? (**legal risk**).
- The original project management firm was established as a company wholly owned by the City of Edinburgh Council. In 2011, the company was disbanded and the project management transferred to an international consultancy. This points to possible **people risk** – that is, that the original company may have lacked the necessary competencies to manage such a major project.

2.10.4 COVID-19 and the US Government

The COVID-19 virus was first identified in December 2019. Over the following two years it caused over 5.5 million recorded deaths worldwide.[1] The rate of long-term health impairment is not yet known. A significant factor in the persistence and severity of the pandemic was the fact that it could be spread by asymptomatic carriers, making it very difficult to isolate infectious individuals.

In many ways, the US government had prepared well for a pandemic. Over several years, from the mid 2000s, the National Security Council put together the 'Playbook for Early Response to High-Consequence Emerging Infectious Disease Threats and Biological Incidents' – a crisis management plan specifying responsibilities and laying out key strategies and thresholds. The playbook was based on expert opinion, together with the results from large and small scale role-playing simulations. The plans were regularly reviewed and updated. In 2016, the US government was preparing for a severe global pandemic, which was considered a likely event in the short to medium term. The change of administration in 2017 resulted in a change of attitude. The pandemic response team was disbanded and the playbook was discarded. Nevertheless, the new administration ran its own widespread simulation in 2019, called 'Crimson Contagion'. The simulation identified several weaknesses and limitations of pandemic preparedness, including insufficient funding, unclear allocation of roles and responsibilities, limited ability to maintain

---

[1] The true numbers are likely to be very much higher due to limitations of testing and recording.

operational capacity, and problems with the process for states to request resources (ventilators, PPE, vaccines) from federal government emergency stockpiles. Despite all this preparation and activity, the US response to the COVID-19 pandemic was disastrous. The recommendations emerging from the Crimson Contagion simulation were not implemented. The 'playbook' was ignored. President Trump claimed – repeatedly, and falsely – that the pandemic was completely unpredictable and out of the blue. The US failure to manage the COVID-19 crisis arose from politicization of health measures (mask wearing, social distancing, lockdowns, quarantine recommendations and vaccinations), lack of supplies, failure to distribute supplies to the key regions, and failure to adequately restrict travel and other social gatherings. The crisis was exacerbated by mixed messaging about the severity, persistence, and treatment of the disease. By the end of April 2021, the recorded death rate from COVID-19 in the US was more than 2.5 times the rate in Canada, more than 12.5 times the rate in Norway, and more than 300 times the rate in New Zealand.

The key risks involved in the COVID-19 pandemic, and in the US government response, are,

- The pandemic crisis is an **environmental risk**.
- The widespread economic impact of COVID represents a **systemic risk**.
- The decisions that led to minimal implementation of recommended closures of schools and businesses represent **strategic risk**. The administration chose a strategy, against the advice of its scientists, that turned out to be very costly in terms of lives impacted by the virus.
- The decision to politicize distribution of the emergency stockpile; to limit the influence of infectious disease scientists; to promote false messaging about the severity, persistence, and infectiousness of the disease; and to ignore the advice of specialists in public health represents, potentially, a **dominance risk**.

2.10.5 COVID-19 and H-E-B Grocery Company

H-E-B Grocery Company is a supermarket chain, operating in Texas. It maintains an emergency preparedness unit, which is mainly tasked with managing the natural disasters, such as wind storms and floods, that regularly affect different parts of Texas. Pandemics were added to the list of emergencies covered in their crisis management plan – many years before COVID-19 – in response to outbreaks of avian and swine flu. Like the US government, H-E-B ran pandemic simulations, identifying where the pressures and shortages were likely to be most critical. Unlike the US government, H-E-B turned identification of risks and vulnerabilities into actions. And, unlike the US government, H-E-B implemented their crisis management plan early, before a single case had been recorded in Texas, based on what they saw happening in other states and other countries. Whilst still managing the COVID crisis, much of Texas was struck by an unprecedented winter storm, leaving millions without power or water, in freezing conditions. H-E-B was able to implement further emergency plans to manage the double contingency.

The result was that customers embraced the store, journalists praised it for its ability to manage the crisis and for its humanity in dealing with the needs of its customers and employees.

The external risks for H-E-B were the same as for the US government – the environmental risk of pandemic and the economic risks arising from the public health measures to contain the spread. H-E-B took a strategic risk in investing in pandemic preparedness – if there had been no pandemic, that investment might have seemed wasteful. In this case though, the risk paid off. The reputational reward from its much admired management of the crisis and the enhanced customer loyalty from its humane response to the two crises indicate the potential for social and economic benefit from strong risk management.

2.11 Notes and Further Reading

In this chapter, we have categorized a long list of risks and demonstrated how the risks have adversely impacted some firms or projects with specific examples. What we have seen is that risks do not, in fact, separate neatly into different buckets; very few real-world problems have arisen from a single identifiable event. In fact, we see from the examples that, the most obvious common problem is not a risk event or series of events – it is the failure of the organization involved to understand and plan for the risk events in order to mitigate their impact. The real risk to an organization is the failure to manage risk.

The risks outlined in this chapter are useful as a starting point in managing risk. First, we must identify what we seek to manage. In subsequent chapters, we will discuss how firms can model and manage these risks to avoid catastrophe and to add value.

See Shin (2009) for an excellent account of the Northern Rock crisis.

2.12 Exercises

Exercise 2.1 Explain briefly the meaning of each of the following terms (give examples, where possible):

(a) Dominance risk.
(b) Political risk.
(c) Scope risk.
(d) Cyber risk.

Exercise 2.2 The risks listed below have been proposed as relevant to a major Canadian university.

(a) For each risk, identify the type or types of risk involved.
(b) Sketch a risk map and mark on it where you think each of the risks above should be placed.

- Failure of campus construction projects to be completed on time or on budget.
- Government regulations restrict the number of international students permitted to study in Canada.
- A pandemic causes a prolonged campus shutdown.
- A university sports team is exposed in a hazing or drugs scandal.
- Job placement of graduates declines in a new economic downturn.
- The university pension plan falls into deficit as a result of a decline in the value of assets.

Exercise 2.3

(a) Describe four major risks which are suitable for quantitative analysis.
(b) Describe four major risks which are not generally suitable for quantitative analysis.

Exercise 2.4

(a) Explain why long-term government bonds are less liquid than short-term government bonds.
(b) Explain why a corporate bond is generally less liquid than a government bond with the same term to maturity.
(c) Explain why a work of art is an illiquid asset. Why would an individual invest in a work of art, given its lack of liquidity?

Exercise 2.5

(a) (i) Describe liquidity risk.
  (ii) Describe regulatory risk.
  (iii) Describe pricing risk.
(b) Describe how the following companies might be exposed to the risks defined in (a):

  (i) A general insurance company that specializes in pet insurance.
  (ii) A global airline company.
  (iii) A real estate hedge fund.

Exercise 2.6 You are given the following information on the General Motors Ignition Switch scandal:

Between April and September of 2014, General Motors (GM) issued a global recall of about 30 million of its small cars. The cars had faulty ignition switches, which could shut down the engine during driving, resulting in a loss of power steering and braking, and preventing the airbags from activating. The fault was said to be responsible for over 100 deaths and a large number of serious injuries. Many of the casualties were under 30 years old.

The unintended ignition shut-down happened because a component of the ignition system was not strong enough to provide the necessary mechanical resistance to prevent accidental rotation of the key. General Motors became aware of the problem as early as 2005, but decided to continue using the inadequate component to save costs.

In November 2014 emails surfaced that showed GM ordered a half-million replacement ignition switches nearly 2 months before ordering a recall.

A large number of lawsuits have been filed in response to the recall. On July 29, 2014, a lawsuit was filed in US District Court in Manhattan on behalf of 658 people who were injured or killed, allegedly because of the faulty ignition switches. The Orange County District Attorney has also filed a lawsuit against GM on behalf of the People of the State of California, alleging the company engaged in unfair competition and false advertising in violation of California law when it failed to disclose defects.

GMs share price fell by around 20% as a result of the recall.

For each of the following types of risk, explain the relevance, if any, to the events at GM. For each one, briefly explain how GM might have managed the risk more successfully:

(a) Legal risk.
(b) Behavioural risk.
(c) Project management risk.

(d) Process risk.

(e) Reputational risk.

Exercise 2.7 Yonge Life is a US-based life insurance company with the following characteristics:

- Yonge currently offers short-term life insurance products with face amounts up to $50 million.
- It has the second largest share of annual sales volume for the 10- and 20-year US term life insurance market.
- Recent mortality experience has been higher than expected.
- Yonge reinsures all policies that have a face amount in excess of $5 million with a US-based reinsurer.
- Yonge mostly invests in high-yield US corporate bonds.
- Over the past several years, management and staff turnover has been low.
- Yonge has followed a consistent corporate strategy for several years.
- External auditors and regulators have not found any major issues with the company's management or processes.
- Yonge's systems use state-of-the-art technology.

The enterprise risk management (ERM) department created the following list of ten risk categories for classifying company risks:

(1) Market and economic risk.

(2) Interest rate risk.

(3) Foreign exchange risk.

(4) Credit risk.

(5) Liquidity risk.

(6) Systemic risk.

(7) Demographic risk.

(8) Pricing risk.

(9) Operational risk.

(10) Strategic risk.

(a) Classify each of the ten risks as high, medium, or low importance for Yonge Life. Justify your choices.

(b) Yonge Life is considering expanding its presence by acquiring a Chinese company that sells 5, 10, and 20 year term policies with face amounts up to the equivalent of US $1 million. There is currently no reinsurance on this book of business and the company's investments are in Chinese investment grade corporate bonds.

Identify which risk categories would be of high importance if Yonge Life makes the acquisition. Justify your choices.

Copyright 2014. The Society of Actuaries, Schaumburg, Illinois. Reproduced with permission.

3
Risk Measures

3.1 Summary

Risk measures are used to give a numerical value, measuring risk, to a random variable representing losses. In this chapter, we introduce several risk measures, including the two most commonly used in risk management: **Value at Risk** (VaR), and **Expected Shortfall** (ES). The risk measures are tested for 'coherence' based on a list of properties that have been proposed as desirable for risk measures used in internal and regulatory risk assessment. We consider computational issues including estimating risk measures and standard errors from Monte Carlo simulation.

3.2 Introduction

Where we have sufficient data, we can model potential losses, measure risk, and analyse risk management strategies quantitatively using statistical models and methods. In these cases, risk measures are important for measuring potential adverse outcomes and assessing the adequacy of the firm's capital.

The first step is to identify a suitable distribution for losses. Often, we will use Monte Carlo simulation to generate a sample from the underlying loss distribution, though we may also work with empirical distributions (that is, a sample from the history of the loss process) or parametric distributions.

The next stage is to use the loss distribution to make decisions about how serious a threat, or opportunity, the risk represents. We will do this by looking at a range of summary statistics of the distribution, including, of course, the mean and the standard deviation. However, neither of these measures is designed to capture the overall riskiness of the distribution. To answer the question 'How much is the firm likely to lose if things go wrong?' we use **tail**

risk measures, that is, statistics that focus on the tail of the loss distribution. Tail loss events are rare but, if they do occur, they can have significant adverse impact.

Definition 3.1 Given a random loss L, measured over a specified time horizon, a **risk measure** is a real-valued function of L, denoted $\varrho(L)$, which quantifies the potential losses arising from the risk.

In modern usage, risk measures are commonly used to determine regulatory or economic capital. That is, the risk measure is used to quantify the appropriate level of capital needed to ensure that the uncertain future costs associated with the risk can be met with high probability. Where the risk measure is imposed by a regulator, the resulting capital requirement is **regulatory capital**. Where it is imposed internally, to comply with the firm's risk appetite, it is termed **economic capital**.

Risk measures are widely used in banking and insurance risk management. The convention in banking is to use profit random variables, say, W where a loss outcome would be $W < 0$; the risk measure is a measure of loss not profit, so it is usually expressed as $-\varrho(W)$ for some function ϱ representing the risk measure and the part of the distribution of W that is of most interest is $W < 0$. The convention in actuarial risk management is to use loss random variables, $X = -W$, which means that we do not need the sign change to give a measure of loss. In this book, we use the actuarial convention of working with loss random variables. All the definitions that we present need to be suitably adapted for risk measures of profit random variables.

It is sometimes appropriate to assume that the loss X is non-negative, for example, when we are dealing with pure loss with no upside or profit potential. It is not an essential assumption, however, and the risk measures that we describe can be applied to random variables with support spanning any part of the real line.

Risk measures have their origins in the **premium principles** of actuarial science. These were applied to a loss distribution to determine an appropriate premium to charge for the loss. Traditional premium principle examples include:

- The expected value premium principle – The risk measure is

$$\varrho(X) = (1 + \alpha)\mathrm{E}[X], \qquad \text{for some } \alpha \geq 0.$$

- The standard deviation premium principle – Let $\mathrm{Var}[X]$ denote the variance of the loss random variable, then the standard deviation principle risk measure is:

$$\varrho(X) = E[X] + \alpha\sqrt{\text{Var}[X]}, \qquad \text{for some } \alpha \geq 0.$$

• The variance premium principle

$$\varrho(X) = E[X] + \alpha\,\text{Var}[X], \qquad \text{for some } \alpha \geq 0.$$

Clearly, these measures have some things in common: for pure loss distributions (that is, where $X \geq 0$), each generates a premium which is greater than or equal to the expected loss. The difference between the premium and the expected loss is the **premium loading**, which acts as a cushion against adverse experience. In the standard deviation and variance principles the loading is related to the variability of the loss, which seems reasonable. However, none of these premium principles has its focus on the tail of the loss distribution, which is often the critical area for economic capital calculations.

3.3 Risk Measures for Capital Requirements

3.3.1 Example Loss Distributions

In this section, we describe the two most important risk measures in current use. We illustrate the calculation of the risk measures using the following two examples:

• A loss which is normally distributed with mean 33.0 and standard deviation 109.0.
• A loss from a put option, of $1{,}000\max(1 - S_{10}, 0)$, where S_{10} is the price at time 10 of an underlying equity investment, with initial value $S_0 = 1$. We assume that $S_{10} \sim \text{lognormal}(\mu = 0.8, \sigma = 0.69570)$.
  This loss distribution has mean value 33.0 and standard deviation 109.0.[1]

Although these loss distributions have the same mean and variance, the risks are actually very different. In Figure 3.1, we show the probability density functions of the two loss distributions in the same diagram. The put option loss has a probability mass at 0 and is continuous for $L > 0$.

3.3.2 Value at Risk – The Quantile Risk Measure

The **Value at Risk** (VaR) risk measure is always specified with a given confidence level α; values commonly used in practice are $\alpha = 90\%$, 95%, 99%, 99.5%, or 99.9%.

---

[1] We are not assuming any hedging of the risk. This is the 'naked' loss.

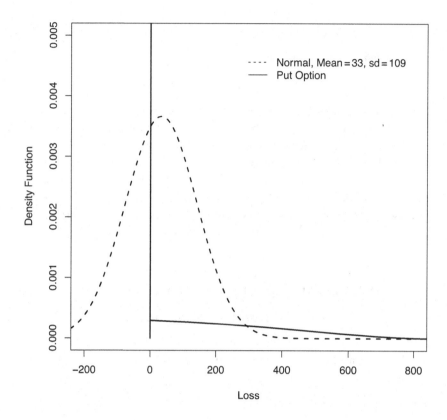

Figure 3.1 Probability density functions for the example loss distributions.

In broad terms, the α-VaR represents the loss that with probability α will not be exceeded. This value falls at the α-quantile of the loss distribution, so the VaR risk measure is also referred to as the quantile risk measure. For continuous random variables, the VaR function is exactly the quantile. For discrete random variables, the quantile may not be uniquely defined for any given α. In these cases the convention is to set the quantile, and the VaR, at the minimum of the range. We will generally use Q_α to denote the VaR at confidence level α, but, in line with common practice, we will also use VaR_α when it is more convenient.

Definition 3.2 The α**-Value at Risk** for a random loss L, for $0 \leq \alpha \leq 1$, is

$$Q_\alpha = \min\{Q : \Pr[L \leq Q] \geq \alpha\}. \tag{3.1}$$

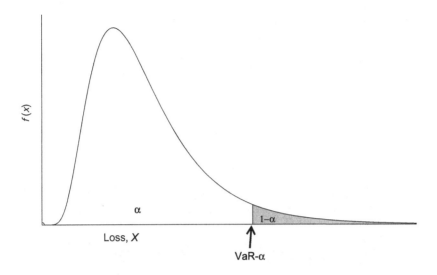

Figure 3.2 Probability density function with Value at Risk (VaR)

For a continuous random variable with strictly increasing cumulative distribution function $F_L(x)$, this simplifies to Q_α such that

$$\Pr[L \leq Q_\alpha] = \alpha, \text{ or, equivalently, } Q_\alpha = F_L^{-1}(\alpha). \qquad (3.2)$$

This result will also hold for a mixed (discrete and continuous) distribution, provided that the quantile of interest falls in the continuous part of the distribution.

In Figure 3.2, we show a loss density function, with the VaR identified, as the loss at which a portion, α, of the distribution lies below, and $1 - \alpha$ lies above.

The reason for the 'min' term in equation (3.1) is that for loss random variables that are discrete or mixed, there may be no value that exactly matches equation (3.2). For example, suppose we have the following discrete loss random variable:

$$L = \begin{cases} 100 & \text{with probability } 0.005 \\ 50 & \text{with probability } 0.045 \\ 10 & \text{with probability } 0.10 \\ 0 & \text{with probability } 0.85. \end{cases}$$

From this we can construct the following table:

x	$\Pr[L \leq x]$
100	1.000
50	0.995
10	0.950
0	0.850

Consider the 99% VaR:

- There is no value Q for which $\Pr[L \leq Q] = 0.99$, so we choose the smallest value for the loss that gives *at least* a 99% probability that the loss is smaller.
- For $Q < 50$, $\Pr[L \leq Q]$ is either 0.85 (at $0 \leq Q < 10$) or 0.95 (at $10 \leq Q < 50$), so the criterion is not satisfied for any $Q < 50$.
- The criterion $\Pr[L \leq Q] \geq 0.99$ is satisfied for all $Q \geq 50$;
- The smallest value that satisfies the criterion is 50, which is the 99% VaR.

Example 3.1 What are the 95%, 90%, and 80% VaR risk measures for the discrete loss distribution above?

Solution 3.1 $\Pr[L \leq Q] \geq 0.95]$ is true for all $Q \geq 10$. So the 95% VaR is 10.0.

$\Pr[L \leq Q] \geq 0.90]$ is also true for all $Q \geq 10$. So the 90% VaR is also 10.0.
$\Pr[L \leq Q] \geq 0.80]$ is true for all $Q \geq 0$. So the 80% VaR is 0.0.   □

We now calculate the VaR for the two example loss distributions from Section 3.3.1.

Example 3.2 Calculate the 95% VaR for the Normal($\mu = 33, \sigma^2 = 109^2$) loss random variable.

Solution 3.2 Since the loss random variable is continuous, we simply determine its 95% quantile. This is $Q_{0.95}$, where

$$\Pr[L \leq Q_{0.95}] = 0.95$$

$$\Longrightarrow \Phi\left(\frac{Q_{0.95} - 33}{109}\right) = 0.95$$

$$\Longrightarrow \left(\frac{Q_{0.95} - 33}{109}\right) = 1.6449$$

$$\Longrightarrow Q_{0.95} = 33 + 1.6449 \times 109 = 212.29 = \text{VaR}_{0.95}. \qquad □$$

In general, for a loss $L \sim N(\mu, \sigma^2)$, the α-VaR is

$$\text{VaR}_\alpha(L) = Q_\alpha = \mu + z_\alpha \sigma, \tag{3.3}$$

where z_α is the α-quantile of the $N(0, 1)$ distribution; that is

$$\Phi(z_\alpha) = \alpha \iff z_\alpha = \Phi^{-1}(\alpha).$$

Example 3.3 Calculate the 95% VaR for the 10-year put option.

Solution 3.3 Recall from Section 3.3.1 that the underlying stock price at maturity has a lognormal distribution, with $\mu = 0.8$ and $\sigma = 0.6957$.

We first find out whether the quantile falls in the area of probability mass at zero. The probability that the loss is zero is

$$\Pr[L = 0] = \Pr[S_{10} > 1] = 1 - \Phi\left(\frac{\log(1) - \mu}{\sigma}\right) = 0.8749. \tag{3.4}$$

As this is less than 0.95, the 95% quantile lies in the continuous part of the loss distribution.

The 95% VaR is $Q_{0.95}$ such that:

$$\Pr[L \leq Q_{0.95}] = 0.95$$

$$\Rightarrow \Pr[1,000(1 - S_{10}) \leq Q_{0.95}] = 0.95$$

$$\Rightarrow \Pr\left[S_{10} > \left(1 - \frac{Q_{0.95}}{1,000}\right)\right] = 0.95$$

$$\Rightarrow \Phi\left(\frac{\log\left(1 - \frac{Q_{0.95}}{1,000}\right) - \mu}{\sigma}\right) = 0.05$$

$$\Rightarrow \frac{\log\left(1 - \frac{Q_{0.95}}{1,000}\right) - \mu}{\sigma} = -1.645$$

$$\Rightarrow Q_{0.95} = 291.30. \qquad \square$$

We note that the 95% VaR of the loss distribution is found by assuming the underlying stock price falls at the 5% quantile of the stock price distribution, because the put option liability is a decreasing function of the stock price process.

In Section 3.5, we demonstrate how to estimate the VaR when the loss distribution is simulated using Monte Carlo.

3.3.3 Expected Shortfall

The VaR risk measure is the 'worst case' loss, where worst case is defined as the event with probability $1 - \alpha$. One problem with VaR is that it does not take into consideration the implications of that $1 - \alpha$ worst case event actually occurring. The loss distribution above the quantile does not affect the risk measure. The Expected Shortfall addresses this by taking the average loss, given that the loss lies in the right tail of the distribution.

Like the quantile risk measure, the Expected Shortfall is defined using some confidence level α, $0 \leq \alpha \leq 1$. Common values for α include 90%, 95%, 97.5%, or 99%.[2]

Definition 3.3 The α-**Expected Shortfall** is the expected loss given that the loss falls in the worst $(1 - \alpha)$ part of the loss distribution.

Let Q_v denote the v-VaR for the loss L. Then the α-Expected Shortfall for L is ES_α, where

$$\text{ES}_\alpha = \frac{1}{1 - \alpha} \int_\alpha^1 Q_v \, dv. \tag{3.5}$$

□

If Q_α falls in a continuous part of the loss distribution (that is, not in a probability mass) then we have a more intuitive expression. In this case $\Pr[L > Q_\alpha] = 1 - \alpha$, which means that the worst $1 - \alpha$ part of the loss distribution is exactly the losses greater than the α-quantile, which is equal to the α-VaR, so the Expected Shortfall is

$$\text{ES}_\alpha = \text{E}\,[L|L > Q_\alpha]\,. \tag{3.6}$$

We illustrate the Expected Shortfall in Figure 3.3. The distribution beyond the α-VaR is normalized to a conditional distribution by dividing the density function by $1 - \alpha$. The mean of the resulting conditional distribution is the Expected Shortfall at confidence level α.

If Q_α *does* fall within (and not on the upper boundary of) a probability mass, then there is some $\epsilon > 0$ such that $Q_{\alpha+\epsilon} = Q_\alpha$. Define $\beta' = \max\{\beta : Q_\alpha = Q_\beta\}$, so $\beta' \geq \alpha$ is the probability on the right end of the probability mass containing Q_α. Then $\Pr[L > Q_\alpha] = 1 - \beta'$ which is less than $1 - \alpha$, which means that $\text{E}\,[L|L > Q_\alpha]$ does not capture the expectation in the top $1 - \alpha$ part of the distribution. That is, if we consider only losses strictly greater than Q_α, we are using less than the worst $(1 - \alpha)$ of the distribution.

To ensure that, in these cases, we are using all of the top $1 - \alpha$ portion of the distribution, we adapt the formula of Equation (3.6) to be consistent with equation (3.5), as follows.

---

[2] Sometimes the Expected Shortfall is described in terms of $1-\alpha$ rather than α. Usually, the context makes it clear which is meant.

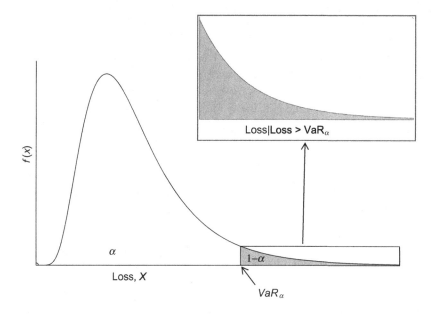

Figure 3.3 Probability density function illustrating the Expected Shortfall

Define $\beta' = \max\{\beta : Q_\alpha = Q_\beta\}$ as above. Then the expected loss given that the loss is in the upper $1 - \alpha$ part of the loss distribution is

$$\text{ES}_\alpha = \frac{(\beta' - \alpha)Q_\alpha + (1 - \beta')\,\text{E}[L|L > Q_\alpha]}{1 - \alpha}. \tag{3.7}$$

The intuition here is that the upper $1 - \alpha$ of the tail is made up of $L|L > Q_\alpha$, which accounts for $1 - \beta'$ of probability, plus a mass at Q_α accounting for $(1-\alpha)-(1-\beta') = \beta'-\alpha$ of probability. Taking the expected value conditional on being in the tail gives the Expected Shortfall.

We illustrate with a short example.

Example 3.4 A loss L has the following distribution.

$$L = \begin{cases} 0 & \text{with probability } 0.5 \\ 10 & \text{with probability } 0.47 \\ U & \text{with probability } 0.03, \end{cases}$$

where U is a random variable uniformly distributed on the interval $(10,110)$.
Calculate the 90% Expected Shortfall.

Solution 3.4 The 90% Expected Shortfall is the expected value of the loss, conditional on being in the worst 10% of the distribution. The 90% quantile falls in the probability mass at $L = 10$, so $Q_\alpha = 10$. The probability at the right end of this mass is $\beta' = 0.97$. We have that $E[L|L > Q_\alpha] = E[L|L > 10] = E[U] = 60$. This is the expected loss, given that the loss lies in the top 3% of the distribution, (the 97% Expected Shortfall), which is not what we are looking for here. To capture the top 10% of the distribution, we must include some of the loss within the probability mass, using equation (3.7):

$$ES_{0.90} = \frac{(0.97 - 0.90)(10) + 0.03(60)}{0.10} = 25.0.$$

The Expected Shortfall risk measure has become very widely used in practice. It is very intuitive and easy to apply, particularly with Monte Carlo simulation output. It is used extensively for regulatory and economic capital in North American insurance (where it is commonly called the **conditional tail expectation** (CTE)) as well as for short-term risk limits and regulatory capital measures in banking, under the Basel III regulations.

Notes on the Expected Shortfall Risk Measure

(1) The Expected Shortfall risk measure was proposed more or less simultaneously by several research groups, so it has a number of identities, including CTE, **tail value at risk** (Tail-VaR), **tail conditional expectation** (TCE), and **worst conditional expectation** (WCE). We have adopted the **ES** terminology as it has emerged as the most used in financial risk management. However, the term 'shortfall' is misleading, as it suggests some relative calculation (shortfall compared to what?) which is not relevant to the actual risk measure.

(2) In practice, equations (3.6) and (3.7) are more easily applied than (3.5).

(3) If the loss distribution is fully discrete, then we use equation (3.7). In this case, the cumulative distribution function $F(x)$ is a step function.

(4) The outcome of equation (3.7) will be the same as equation (3.6) when the quantile falls in the continuous part of a mixed distribution, or if the quantile lies at the upper bound of a probability mass in a mixed distribution. In both cases, we have $\beta' = \alpha$.

(5) If the loss distribution is continuous, then we can use equation (3.6) in the following form, where $f(y)$ is the density function of the loss:

$$ES_\alpha = \frac{1}{1 - \alpha} \int_{Q_\alpha}^{\infty} y \, f(y) dy. \tag{3.8}$$

Example 3.5 Expected Shortfall for a Discrete Loss Distribution

Suppose X is a loss random variable with probability function:

$$X = \begin{cases} 0 & \text{with probability } 0.9 \\ 100 & \text{with probability } 0.06 \\ 1,000 & \text{with probability } 0.04. \end{cases}$$

Calculate the 90% and 95% Expected Shortfall.

Solution 3.5 As the loss is discrete, we use Equation (3.7).
Consider first the 90% Expected Shortfall. This is the average loss, given that the loss lies in the worst 10% of the distribution. Now, if we look at the probability function for the loss, the values $X = 1,000$ and $X = 100$ account for exactly the worst 10% of the distribution, so the Expected Shortfall is

$$\text{ES}_{0.90} = \text{E}[X|X > 0] = \frac{(0.06)(100) + (0.04)(1,000)}{0.10} = 460.$$

That is, 460 is the mean loss given that the loss lies in the upper 10% of the distribution. In this case, the Expected Shortfall reduces to the form in equation (3.6), because the α quantile corresponds exactly to a stepping point in the distribution function, which means that $\beta' = \alpha$, in the notation of equation (3.7).

Now consider the 95% Expected Shortfall. The stepping points in the distribution function are at $F(x) = 0.9$, 0.96, and 1.0. So we do not have $\beta' = \alpha$ here. Instead we go to the next stepping point above α, which is $\beta' = 0.96$, giving

$$\text{ES}_{0.95} = \frac{(0.01)(100) + (0.04)(1,000)}{0.05} = 820.$$

Note that the Expected Shortfall uses all of the loss distribution at $X = 1,000$, which accounts for the worst 4% of the distribution, and then uses enough of the distribution at $X = 100$ to make up the 5% required for the 95% Expected Shortfall. $\square$

Example 3.6 Expected Shortfall for the Normal Distribution
Calculate the 95% Expected Shortfall for the Normal ($\mu = 33, \sigma = 109$) loss distribution.

Solution 3.6 The loss is continuous, so the 95% Expected Shortfall is $E[L|L > Q_{0.95}]$. Let $\phi(z)$ denote the p.d.f. of the standard normal distribution – that is,

$$\phi(z) = \frac{1}{\sqrt{2\pi}} e^{-\frac{1}{2}z^2}.$$

Then

$$ES_\alpha = E[L|L > Q_\alpha] = \frac{1}{1-\alpha} \int_{Q_\alpha}^{\infty} y\, f(y)\,dy$$

$$= \frac{1}{1-\alpha} \int_{Q_\alpha}^{\infty} \frac{y}{\sqrt{2\pi}\,\sigma} e^{-\frac{1}{2}\left(\frac{y-\mu}{\sigma}\right)^2} dy.$$

Let $z = \dfrac{y - \mu}{\sigma}$, then changing the integration variable gives

$$ES_\alpha = \frac{1}{1-\alpha} \int_{\frac{Q_\alpha-\mu}{\sigma}}^{\infty} \frac{\sigma z + \mu}{\sqrt{2\pi}} e^{-\frac{1}{2}z^2} dz \qquad (3.9)$$

$$= \frac{1}{1-\alpha} \left\{ \int_{\frac{Q_\alpha-\mu}{\sigma}}^{\infty} \frac{\sigma z}{\sqrt{2\pi}} e^{-\frac{1}{2}z^2} dz + \mu \int_{\frac{Q_\alpha-\mu}{\sigma}}^{\infty} \phi(z)\,dz \right\}. \qquad (3.10)$$

Substituting $u = z^2/2$ in the first integral gives

$$\int_{\frac{Q_\alpha-\mu}{\sigma}}^{\infty} \frac{\sigma z}{\sqrt{2\pi}} e^{-\frac{1}{2}z^2} dz = \sigma \int_{\left(\frac{Q_\alpha-\mu}{\sigma}\right)^2/2}^{\infty} \frac{1}{\sqrt{2\pi}} e^{-u}\,du$$

$$= \sigma\, \frac{e^{-\left(\frac{Q_\alpha-\mu}{\sigma}\right)^2/2}}{\sqrt{2\pi}}$$

$$= \sigma\, \phi\left(\frac{Q_\alpha - \mu}{\sigma}\right)$$

$$= \sigma\, \phi(z_\alpha)$$

where z_α is the α-quantile of the standard Normal distribution.

Also, note that the second integral in equation (3.10) is

$$\mu\left(1 - \Phi\left(\frac{Q_\alpha - \mu}{\sigma}\right)\right) = \mu(1 - \alpha).$$

Putting this together gives the Expected Shortfall formula for the Normal distribution as

$$ES_\alpha = \mu + \frac{\sigma}{1-\alpha} \phi \left(\frac{Q_\alpha - \mu}{\sigma} \right) \tag{3.11}$$

$$= \mu + \frac{\sigma}{1-\alpha} \phi(z_\alpha). \tag{3.12}$$

Hence, the 95% Expected Shortfall for the Normal distribution with $\mu = 33$ and $\sigma = 109$, is 257.83. □

Example 3.7 Expected Shortfall for the Put Option
Calculate (a) the 95% Expected Shortfall and (b) the 80% Expected Shortfall for the put option loss distribution.

Solution 3.7 (a) We know from Example 3.3 that the probability mass at zero accounts for 87.5% of the loss distribution, so the 95% quantile is in the continuous part of the loss distribution. We also know that for any $\alpha > 0.875$, the α-VaR for the put option loss happens when the underlying stock price at maturity (S_{10}) is at the lower α-quantile of its distribution (which is lognormal). To find the Expected Shortfall, it is simpler to work with the lognormal distribution of the underlying stock than to transform this into the distribution of the loss.

Let $Q_{1-\alpha}^S$ denote the $(1-\alpha)$-quantile of the S_{10} distribution, and let $f_S(y)$ denote the density function of the S_{10} distribution. Then for $\alpha > 0.875$ the α-Expected Shortfall of the loss is

$$ES_\alpha = \frac{1}{1-\alpha} \int_0^{Q_{1-\alpha}^S} 1{,}000(1-y) f_S(y) dy$$

$$= \frac{1}{1-\alpha} \int_0^{Q_{1-\alpha}^S} 1{,}000(1-y) \frac{1}{\sqrt{2\pi}\sigma y} \exp\left\{ -\frac{1}{2} \left(\frac{\log(y)-\mu}{\sigma} \right)^2 \right\} dy$$

$$= \frac{1{,}000}{1-\alpha} \left\{ \int_0^{Q_{1-\alpha}^S} \frac{1}{\sqrt{2\pi}\sigma y} \exp\left(-\frac{1}{2} \left(\frac{\log(y)-\mu}{\sigma} \right)^2 \right) dy \right.$$

$$\left. - \int_0^{Q_{1-\alpha}^S} \frac{y}{\sqrt{2\pi}\sigma y} \exp\left(-\frac{1}{2} \left(\frac{\log(y)-\mu}{\sigma} \right)^2 \right) dy \right\}.$$

Now, the first term in the { } is

$$\int_0^{Q_{1-\alpha}^S} f_S(y)\,dy = 1 - \alpha.$$

The second term can be simplified by substituting

$$u = \frac{\log(y) - \mu - \sigma^2}{\sigma}$$

so that the integral simplifies to

$$e^{\mu+\sigma^2/2} \int_{-\infty}^{\left(\log\left(Q_{1-\alpha}^S\right) - \mu - \sigma^2\right)/\sigma} \frac{1}{\sqrt{2\pi}} e^{-\frac{1}{2}u^2}\,du$$

$$= e^{\mu+\sigma^2/2}\, \Phi\left(\frac{\log\left(Q_{1-\alpha}^S\right) - \mu - \sigma^2}{\sigma}\right).$$

Then, for $\alpha > 0.875$,

$$\mathrm{ES}_\alpha = \frac{1{,}000}{1-\alpha}\left\{(1-\alpha) - e^{\mu+\sigma^2/2}\, \Phi\left(\frac{\log\left(Q_{1-\alpha}^S\right) - \mu - \sigma^2}{\sigma}\right)\right\} \qquad (3.13)$$

$$= 1{,}000\left\{1 - \frac{e^{\mu+\sigma^2/2}}{1-\alpha}\, \Phi\left(\frac{\log\left(Q_{1-\alpha}^S\right) - \mu - \sigma^2}{\sigma}\right)\right\}. \qquad (3.14)$$

Note that, by construction,

$$\frac{\log\left(Q_{1-\alpha}^S\right) - \mu}{\sigma} = z_{1-\alpha}$$

where $z_q = \Phi^{-1}(q)$ is the q-quantile of the standard normal distribution, so equation (3.14) can be written as

$$\mathrm{ES}_\alpha = 1{,}000\left\{1 - \frac{e^{\mu+\sigma^2/2}}{1-\alpha}\, \Phi\left(z_{1-\alpha} - \sigma\right)\right\}. \qquad (3.15)$$

Using this formula gives a 95% Expected Shortfall for the put option loss of 454.14.

(b) For the 80% Expected Shortfall we adjust the result above, as the 80%-quantile of the loss lies in a probability mass. Recall that, in this case, we define $\beta' = \max\{\beta : Q_\alpha = Q_\beta\}$ and use the formula (from equation (3.7))

$$\mathrm{ES}_\alpha = \frac{(\beta' - \alpha)Q_\alpha + (1 - \beta')\,\mathrm{E}[L|L > Q_\alpha]}{1-\alpha}.$$

All the quantile values $Q_\nu(L) = 0$ for $0 < \nu < 0.875$, so $\beta' = 0.875$, $\alpha = 0.80$, and $Q_\alpha(L) = Q_{\beta'}(L) = 0$. Using equation (3.15), we have $E[L|L > Q_\beta] = ES_{0.875}[L] = 262.24$, so the 80% Expected Shortfall is

$$\frac{(0.875 - 0.8) \times 0 + (1 - 0.875)(262.24)}{1 - 0.8} = 165.2. \qquad \square$$

3.3.4 Some Comments on VaR and Expected Shortfall

(1) Clearly $ES_\alpha \geq Q_\alpha$ with equality only if Q_α is the maximum value of the loss random variable.
(2) $ES_{0\%}$ is the mean loss.
(3) We define $Q_{0\%}$ to be the minimum loss.
(4) $Q_{50\%}$ is a median of the loss distribution.
(5) In Figure 3.4, we show the quantile and Expected Shortfall risk measures for both example loss distributions, for all values of α between zero and one. In the top diagram, the quantile risk measures at $\alpha = 0$ are zero for the put option example, because that is the minimum loss. The normal loss example allows profits, so the lower quantile risk measures are negative. The put option quantile risk measure remains at zero for all $\alpha < 0.875$, which is the probability that the put option matures in the money.

In the lower diagram the Expected Shortfall values meet at the left side, as the examples have the same mean loss. At the far right side, the maximum value of α shown in the plot is 0.999; at this level the normal loss example Expected Shortfall is \$400 and the put option example is \$783.

(6) In some cases, negative values may be excluded from the calculation, in which case the normal loss example quantile risk measure would be zero for $\alpha < 0.38$ and would follow the same path as shown in the upper diagram after that.

For the Expected Shortfall, the early values for the normal loss example would increase, as the Expected Shortfall would be defined for the loss random variable L as

$$E[\max(L, 0)|L > Q_\alpha].$$

(7) The Expected Shortfall is related to the **limited expected value** function, $E[L \wedge k] = E[\min(L, k)]$. For a continuous loss $L \geq 0$, with probability density $f(y)$, and for confidence level $\alpha > 0$, we have:

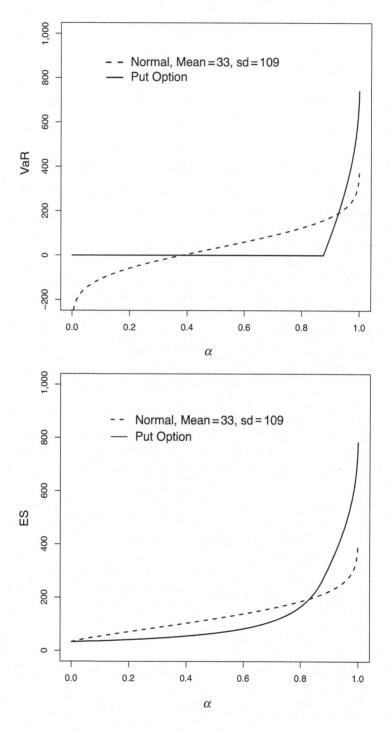

Figure 3.4 Risk measures for the example distributions.

$$\text{ES}_\alpha = \frac{1}{1-\alpha} \int_{Q_\alpha}^{\infty} y \, f(y) dy$$

$$= \frac{1}{1-\alpha} \left(\int_0^{\infty} y \, f(y) dy - \int_0^{Q_\alpha} y \, f(y) dy \right)$$

$$= \frac{1}{1-\alpha} \left(\text{E}[L] - \int_0^{Q_\alpha} y \, f(y) dy \right).$$

Now $\text{E}[L \wedge Q_\alpha] = \int_0^{Q_\alpha} y f(y) dy + Q_\alpha (1 - F(Q_\alpha))$

$$= \int_0^{Q_\alpha} y f(y) dy + Q_\alpha (1 - \alpha)$$

$$\implies \int_0^{Q_\alpha} y f(y) dy = \text{E}[L \wedge Q_\alpha] - Q_\alpha (1 - \alpha)$$

$$\implies ES_\alpha = \frac{1}{1-\alpha} \left(\text{E}[L] - \big(\text{E}[L \wedge Q_\alpha] - Q_\alpha (1 - \alpha) \big) \right)$$

$$\implies ES_\alpha = Q_\alpha + \frac{1}{1-\alpha} \big(\text{E}[L] - \text{E}[L \wedge Q_\alpha] \big).$$

3.4 Coherent Risk Measures

With all these risk measures to choose from it is useful to have some way of determining whether each is equally useful. In Artzner et al. (1999), some desirable characteristics for a risk measure were proposed, in the form of four criteria. A risk measure that satisfies the criteria is said to be **coherent**.

3.4.1 Criteria for Coherence of a Risk Measure $\varrho(X)$

Translation Invariance (TI): For any non-random c

$$\varrho(X + c) = \varrho(X) + c. \tag{3.16}$$

This means that adding a constant amount (positive or negative) to a risk adds the same amount to the risk measure.

Positive Homogeneity (PH): For any non-random $\lambda > 0$,

$$\varrho(\lambda X) = \lambda \varrho(X). \tag{3.17}$$

This criterion implies that changing the units of loss, for example, to express the loss in a different currency, or in millions instead of thousands, changes the risk measure in proportion. It also implies that $\varrho(0) = 0$. Combined with translation invariance, this implies that $\varrho(c) = c$ for any constant c.

Subadditivity (S): For any two random losses X and Y,

$$\varrho(X + Y) \leq \varrho(X) + \varrho(Y). \tag{3.18}$$

The subadditivity criterion has probably been the most examined of the axioms of coherence. The essential idea is that it should not be possible to reduce the total economic capital required for a risk by splitting it into smaller parts. Or, in other words, consolidating risks cannot make the risk greater, but it might make the risk smaller, if there is any diversification benefit.

Monotonicity (M): If $\Pr[X \leq Y] = 1$ then $\varrho(X) \leq \varrho(Y)$.

This is an intuitively appealing axiom, that if one risk is always bigger then another, the risk measures should be similarly ordered. This axiom, together with the TI axiom also requires that the risk measure must be no less than the minimum loss, and no greater than the maximum loss. This is easily shown by replacing X by $\min Y$ for the lower bound, then $\Pr[\min Y \leq Y] = 1$, so $\varrho(\min Y) \leq \varrho(Y)$ and using axiom TI, noting that $\min Y$ is not random, $\varrho(\min Y) = \min Y$ giving the lower bound.

Note that $\Pr[X \leq Y] = 1$ is often written $X \leq Y$.

3.4.2 Is VaR Coherent?

We can determine whether VaR satisfies the coherence criteria, in the general case. We assume a continuous loss distribution (except in the subadditivity section) to make the proofs and explanations easier to follow, but the general results apply to continuous, discrete, and mixed distributions.

For a continuous random loss X, the VaR_α risk measure is characterized by

$$\varrho(X) : \Pr[X \leq \varrho(X)] = \alpha. \tag{3.19}$$

Translation Invariance requires that

$$\varrho(X + c) = \varrho(X) + c \text{ for any constant } c.$$

Consider $Y = X + c$, where c is a constant. Then

$$
\begin{aligned}
\Pr[Y \le \varrho(Y)] = \alpha \implies & \Pr[X + c \le \varrho(Y)] = \alpha \\
\implies & \Pr[X \le \varrho(Y) - c] = \alpha \\
\implies & \varrho(X) = \varrho(Y) - c \\
\implies & \varrho(X) + c = \varrho(X + c),
\end{aligned}
$$

which demonstrates that VaR satisfies the translation invariance requirement.

Positive homogeneity requires that $\varrho(\lambda X) = \lambda \varrho(X)$ for any $\lambda > 0$.
Consider $Y = \lambda X, \lambda > 0$.

$$
\begin{aligned}
\Pr[Y \le \varrho(Y)] = \alpha \implies & \Pr[\lambda X \le \varrho(Y)] = \alpha \\
\implies & \Pr\left[X \le \frac{\varrho(Y)}{\lambda} \right] = \alpha \\
\implies & \varrho(X) = \varrho(Y)/\lambda \\
\implies & \lambda\varrho(X) = \varrho(\lambda X),
\end{aligned}
$$

which demonstrates that VaR satisfies the positive homogeneity requirement.

Subadditivity requires that for any $X, Y, \varrho(X + Y) \le \varrho(X) + \varrho(Y)$.

VaR is not subadditive, in general, and we prove this here with a counterexample.

Suppose we have losses X and Y, both dependent on the same underlying Uniform random variable $U \sim U(0, 1)$ as follows:

$$
X = \begin{cases} 1{,}000 & \text{if } U \le 0.04 \quad \text{with prob } 0.04 \\ 0 & \text{if } U > 0.04 \quad \text{with prob } 0.96, \end{cases}
$$

$$
Y = \begin{cases} 0 & \text{if } U \le 0.96 \quad \text{with prob } 0.96 \\ 1{,}000 & \text{if } U > 0.96 \quad \text{with prob } 0.04 \end{cases}
$$

so that

$$
X + Y = \begin{cases} 0 & \text{with prob } 0.92 \\ 1{,}000 & \text{with prob } 0.08. \end{cases}
$$

Let $\varrho(X)$ represent the 95% VaR risk measure for random loss X. Then $\varrho(X) = \varrho(Y) = 0$ since, in both cases, the probability of a non-zero loss is less than 5%. On the other hand, the sum, $X + Y$ has an 8% chance of being equal to 1,000, and the 95% quantile risk measure of the sum is, therefore,

$$\varrho(X + Y) = 1,000.$$

The VaR of the sum is greater than the sum of the two VaR's, so VaR is not subadditive.

Monotonicity requires that if $X \leq Y$ then $\varrho(X) \leq \varrho(Y)$.

Recall that $X \leq Y$ is shorthand for

$$\Pr[X \leq Y] = 1.$$

As ϱ is the α-quantile, and X, Y are continuous, we have

$$\Pr[X \leq \varrho(X)] = \alpha, \quad \text{and } \Pr[Y \leq \varrho(Y)] = \alpha.$$

Now,

$$X \leq Y \implies \Pr[X \leq k] \geq \Pr[Y \leq k] \text{ for any } k.$$

Set $k = \varrho(X)$ to give

$$\Pr[X \leq \varrho(X)] \geq \Pr[Y \leq \varrho(X)] \implies \alpha \geq \Pr[Y \leq \varrho(X)].$$

Then, since $\Pr[Y \leq \varrho(Y)] = \alpha$, we have

$$\alpha = \Pr[Y \leq \varrho(Y)] \geq \Pr[Y \leq \varrho(X)] \implies \varrho(Y) \geq \varrho(X),$$

which proves monotonicity for VaR.

3.4.3 Is Expected Shortfall Coherent?

Again, we assume a continuous loss random variable for convenience, but the results are also valid for discrete or mixed random variables.[3]

For a continuous random loss X, with α-quantile $Q_\alpha(X)$, the α-Expected Shortfall risk measure is

$$\varrho(X) = E[X|X > Q_\alpha(X)]. \tag{3.20}$$

Translation Invariance requires that $\varrho(X+c) = \varrho(X)+c$ for any constant c.

$$\varrho(X + c) = E[X + c|X + c > Q_\alpha(X + c)]$$

and since VaR is translation invariant we have $Q_\alpha(X + c) = Q_\alpha(X) + c$, so

---

[3] Provided the Expected Shortfall is defined correctly, as in equation (3.5), not equation (3.6).

$$\varrho(X + c) = \mathrm{E}[X + c | X + c > Q_\alpha(X) + c]$$
$$= \mathrm{E}[X + c | X > Q_\alpha(X)]$$
$$= \mathrm{E}[X | X > Q_\alpha(X)] + c$$
$$= \varrho(X) + c,$$

which demonstrates that the Expected Shortfall is translation invariant. **Positive homogeneity** requires that $\varrho(\lambda X) = \lambda \varrho(X)$ for any $\lambda > 0$.

$$\varrho(\lambda X) = \mathrm{E}[\lambda X | \lambda X > Q_\alpha(\lambda X)]$$

and since VaR is positive homogeneous we have $Q_\alpha(\lambda X) = \lambda Q_\alpha(X)$, so

$$\varrho(\lambda X) = \mathrm{E}[\lambda X | \lambda X > \lambda Q_\alpha(X)]$$
$$= \mathrm{E}[\lambda X | X > Q_\alpha(X)]$$
$$= \lambda \varrho(X),$$

which demonstrates that the Expected Shortfall is positive homogeneous. **Subadditivity** requires that $\varrho(X + Y) \leq \varrho(X) + \varrho(Y)$.

To demonstrate that the Expected Shortfall is subadditive, we use the following result.

Consider a random loss X with distribution function F_X. Let X_1, $X_2, \ldots, X_n$ denote a random sample from F_X, and let $X_{(j)}$ be the jth smallest value from the sample (this is the jth order statistic of the sample). Then the Expected Shortfall of X at confidence level α can be written as

$$\mathrm{ES}_\alpha(X) = \lim_{n \to \infty} \frac{1}{n(1 - \alpha)} \sum_{j = \lfloor n\alpha \rfloor + 1}^{n} X_{(j)}, \qquad (3.21)$$

where $\lfloor \ \rfloor$ indicates the floor function. This result can be explained intuitively as follows. Suppose we have a random sample of, say, $n = 1{,}000$ values from the loss distribution. The 95% Expected Shortfall is the expected value of the worst 5% of the loss distribution, which we estimate with the largest 5% of the sample. As the sample size $n \to \infty$, this estimate will converge to the Expected Shortfall.

Now we review subadditivity of the Expected Shortfall by assuming that we have two losses, X and Y, not necessarily independent. The joint distribution function is $F_{X,Y}$. Consider a random sample of n values of (X, Y),

$$(X_1, Y_1), (X_2, Y_2), \ldots, (X_n, Y_n).$$

From this we construct three different samples, one with the X_j values, one with the Y_j values, and one with $Z_j = X_j + Y_j$. We order each sample, and use the (j) subscript to indicate the ordered sample, $X_{(1)} \leq X_{(2)} \leq X_{(3)} \cdots$.

$$X_1, X_2, \ldots, X_n \rightarrow X_{(1)}, X_{(2)}, \ldots, X_{(n)},$$

$$Y_1, Y_2, \ldots, Y_n \rightarrow Y_{(1)}, Y_{(2)}, \ldots, Y_{(n)},$$

$$Z_1 = (X_1 + Y_1), \quad Z_2 = (X_2 + Y_2), \ldots,$$

$$Z_n = (X_n + Y_n) \rightarrow Z_{(1)}, Z_{(2)}, \ldots, Z_{(n)}.$$

Consider first $Z_{(n)} = X_k + Y_k$ for some k. We know that $X_k \leq X_{(n)}$ and, similarly, $Y_k \leq Y_{(n)}$, so we must have

$$Z_{(n)} \leq X_{(n)} + Y_{(n)}.$$

Now consider $Z_{(n-1)} = X_l + Y_l$ for some $l \neq k$. Then

$$Z_{(n-1)} + Z_{(n)} = X_l + Y_l + X_k + Y_k.$$

We know that $X_l + X_k \leq X_{(n-1)} + X_{(n)}$, and similarly $Y_l + Y_k \leq Y_{(n-1)} + Y_{(n)}$, so

$$Z_{(n-1)} + Z_{(n)} = X_j + Y_j + X_k + Y_k \leq X_{(n)} + Y_{(n)} + X_{(n-1)} + Y_{(n-1)}.$$

Note that when $Z_{(n-1)} = X_l + Y_l$, it is **not** true in general that $X_l \leq X_{(n-1)}$. What *is* true is that the sum of any two distinct values of X_j must be no greater than the sum of the two largest values of X_j.

Continuing this argument for $Z_{(n\alpha+1)} + Z_{(n\alpha+2)} + \cdots Z_{(n)}$, we have

$$\sum_{j=n\alpha+1}^{n} Z_{(j)} \leq \sum_{j=n\alpha+1}^{n} X_{(j)} + \sum_{j=n\alpha+1}^{n} Y_{(j)}$$

$$\Rightarrow \lim_{n \to \infty} \frac{1}{(1-\alpha)n} \sum_{j=n\alpha+1}^{n} Z_{(j)} \leq \lim_{n \to \infty} \frac{1}{(1-\alpha)n} \sum_{j=n\alpha+1}^{n} X_{(j)}$$

$$+ \lim_{n \to \infty} \frac{1}{(1-\alpha)n} \sum_{j=n\alpha+1}^{n} Y_{(j)}$$

$$\Rightarrow \mathrm{ES}_\alpha(Z) \leq \mathrm{ES}_\alpha(X) + \mathrm{ES}_\alpha(Y),$$

which proves the subadditivity of the Expected Shortfall.

Monotonicity requires that $X \leq Y \implies \varrho(X) \leq \varrho(Y)$.

We have, from equation (3.5),

$$\mathrm{ES}_\alpha(X) = \frac{1}{1-\alpha} \int_\alpha^1 Q_v(X) \, dv$$

and we also know that the quantiles are monotonic (since VaR is monotonic). So

$$X \leq Y \Rightarrow Q_\nu(X) \leq Q_\nu(Y) \quad \text{for any } \nu, 0 < \nu \leq 1$$

$$\Rightarrow \frac{1}{1-\alpha} \int_\alpha^1 Q_\nu(X)\, d\nu \leq \frac{1}{1-\alpha} \int_\alpha^1 Q_\nu(Y)\, d\nu$$

$$\Rightarrow \text{ES}_\alpha(X) \leq \text{ES}_\alpha(Y),$$

which proves that the Expected Shortfall is monotonic.

So, the Expected Shortfall satisfies all four criteria and is, therefore, a coherent risk measure.

3.5 Estimating Risk Measures Using Monte Carlo Simulation

3.5.1 Using Monte Carlo Simulation

In risk management applications we often use Monte Carlo simulation to estimate loss distributions, particularly when the underlying processes are too complex for analytic manipulation.

Using standard Monte Carlo simulation we generate a large number of independent simulations of the loss random variable L. Suppose we generate N such values, and order them from smallest to largest, such that $L_{(j)}$ is the jth smallest simulated value of L. We assume the distribution of L_j is an estimate of the true underlying distribution of L, and we treat the simulated values exactly as if they were a sample of observed values. In the context of this chapter, we are interested in using the sample to estimate the α-quantile risk measure and the α-Expected Shortfall for the underlying loss. We have two important questions (1) how do we use the output to estimate the risk measures and (2) how much uncertainty is there in the estimates?

3.5.2 Estimating VaR

Suppose we want to estimate the 95%-quantile risk measure of L. An obvious estimator is $L_{(950)}$, because it is the 95% quantile of the empirical distribution defined by the Monte Carlo sample $\{L_{(j)}\}$. That is, 95% of the simulated values of L are less than or equal to $L_{(950)}$. This is the **order statistic approach**, as it uses the αN order statistic from the sample to estimate the α-VaR.

On the other hand, 5% of the sample is greater than or equal to $L_{(951)}$, so that is another possible estimator.

The **smoothed empirical estimate** uses $L_{(j)}$ as an estimate of the $j/(N+1)$ quantile of the distribution, so that $L_{(950)}$ is assumed to be an estimate of the $950/1{,}001 = 94.905\%$ quantile. To estimate the 95% quantile, we use $L_{(0.95(1{,}001))} = L_{(950.95)}$, which we calculate by interpolating between the values for $L_{(950)}$ and $L_{(951)}$, to give

$$Q_{95\%} \approx (0.05)\, L_{(950)} + (0.95)\, L_{(951)}.$$

In summary, we have three possible estimators for Q_α, from a sample of N simulated values of a loss random variable L, where $N\alpha$ is assumed to be an integer (non-integer values of $N\alpha$ are not common in practice, as N is usually large, and α is usually a round number, in percentage terms):

(1) $L_{(\alpha N)}$;
(2) $L_{(\alpha N+1)}$;
(3) $L_{(\alpha(N+1))}$.

None of these estimators is guaranteed to be better than the others. Each is likely to be biased, though the bias is generally small for large samples as all three estimators are asymptotically unbiased. In practice, most people will use $L_{(\alpha N)}$, which we call the **raw empirical estimate**, although for loss distributions in common use, we usually get lower bias from using the smoothed empirical estimate, $L_{(\alpha(N+1))}$.

Example 3.8 Monte Carlo VaR Estimation Table 3.1 shows an excerpt from one sample of 1,000 values simulated from a loss distribution. The table shows the 100 largest values simulated.

(a) Estimate the 95% and 99% VaR for this sample using the three estimators above.
(b) What is the relative 'error' given the underlying distribution?[4]

Solution 3.8 The true values are

$$Q_{95\%} = \mu + 1.645\sigma = 212.3, \qquad Q_{99\%} = \mu + 2.326\sigma = 286.6.$$

Using the first estimator, $L_{(\alpha N)}$, we have

$$Q_{95\%} \approx L_{(950)} = 209.2 \qquad Q_{99\%} \approx L_{(990)} = 287.8$$

giving relative errors of -1.46% and 0.42% respectively.

---

[4] The relative error is the difference between the estimated value and the true value, expressed as a percentage of the true value.

Table 3.1. *Largest 100 values from a Monte Carlo sample of 1,000 values from a loss distribution – the underlying distribution is* $N(33.0, 109.0^2)$

$L_{(901)}$ to $L_{(910)}$									
169.1	170.4	171.3	171.9	172.3	173.3	173.8	174.3	174.9	175.9
$L_{(911)}$ to $L_{(920)}$									
176.4	177.2	179.1	179.7	180.2	180.5	181.9	182.6	183.0	183.1
$L_{(921)}$ to $L_{(930)}$									
183.3	184.4	186.9	187.7	188.2	188.5	191.8	191.9	193.1	193.8
$L_{(931)}$ to $L_{(940)}$									
194.2	196.3	197.6	197.8	199.1	200.5	200.5	200.5	202.8	202.9
$L_{(941)}$ to $L_{(950)}$									
203.0	203.7	204.4	204.8	205.1	205.8	206.7	207.5	207.9	209.2
$L_{(951)}$ to $L_{(960)}$									
209.5	210.6	214.7	217.0	218.2	226.2	226.3	226.9	227.5	227.7
$L_{(961)}$ to $L_{(970)}$									
229.0	231.4	231.6	233.2	237.5	237.9	238.1	240.3	241.0	241.3
$L_{(971)}$ to $L_{(980)}$									
241.6	243.8	244.0	247.2	247.8	248.8	254.1	255.6	255.9	257.4
$L_{(981)}$ to $L_{(990)}$									
265.0	265.0	268.9	271.2	271.6	276.5	279.2	284.1	284.3	287.8
$L_{(991)}$ to $L_{(1,000)}$									
287.9	298.7	301.6	305.0	313.0	323.8	334.5	343.5	350.3	359.4

Using the second estimator, $L_{(\alpha N+1)}$, we have

$$Q_{95\%} \approx L_{(951)} = 209.5 \qquad Q_{99\%} \approx L_{(991)} = 287.9$$

giving relative errors of -1.32% and 0.45% respectively.

Using the third estimator, $L_{(\alpha(N+1))}$, we have

$$Q_{95\%} \approx L_{(950.95)} = 209.5 \qquad Q_{99\%} \approx L_{(990.99)} = 287.9$$

giving relative errors of -1.32% and 0.45% respectively.   □

3.5.3 Estimating the Expected Shortfall

The Expected Shortfall is the mean of the worst $100(1 - \alpha)\%$ of the loss distribution, so we estimate the Expected Shortfall using the mean of the worst $100(1 - \alpha)\%$ simulations. That is, assuming $N(1 - \alpha)$ is an integer,

$$\widehat{\text{ES}}_\alpha = \frac{1}{N(1-\alpha)} \sum_{j=N\alpha+1}^{N} L_{(j)}. \qquad (3.22)$$

For example, given the information in Table 3.1 (showing the worst 100 simulations from a sample of $N = 1,000$), we estimate the 95% Expected Shortfall using the average of the worst 50 values, giving an estimate of 260.68. This compares with the true value of 257.83, which was calculated in Section 3.3.3.

3.6 Quantifying Uncertainty in VaR and Expected Shortfall Estimates

3.6.1 Standard Errors for Monte Carlo Estimates

In this section, we assume the sample of losses is generated by Monte Carlo simulation, but the principles apply equally to any sample that we assume to be independently drawn from an underlying distribution.

Method 1: Order Statistics

We can derive an approximate standard error for the estimated α-VaR without any further distributional assumptions, using properties of order statistics. Suppose we use the raw empirical estimator, $L_{(\alpha N)}$ as an estimate of the α-quantile from a sample of N values. This estimate will be subject to sampling variability. We use the simulations around the estimate to construct a non-parametric confidence interval for the the expected $N\alpha$ order statistic, which is a close approximation (for sufficiently large N) to a confidence interval for the true α-quantile, Q_α.

Consider an ordered random sample of N values from a loss distribution, denoted $L_{(1)}, L_{(2)}, \ldots, L_{(N)}$. Let M denote the random number of observations which are less than or equal to the unknown quantile, Q_α. If we knew M, we would know that $Q_\alpha \in \left[L_{(M)}, L_{(M+1)} \right)$.

Each simulated value of L either does fall below Q_α, with probability α, or does not, with probability $(1-\alpha)$. So M has a binomial distribution, $M \sim \text{Bin}(N, \alpha)$, which means that

$$\text{E}[M] = N\alpha \quad \text{and} \quad \text{Var}[M] = N\alpha(1-\alpha).$$

We construct a q-confidence interval for M, say, (m_L, m_U), such that

$$\Pr[m_L < M \le m_U] = q$$

where $m_L = E[M] - k = N\alpha - k$ and $m_U = E[M] + k = N\alpha + k$, and where, using the Normal approximation to the binomial distribution, we have

$$k = \Phi^{-1}\left(\frac{1+q}{2}\right)\sqrt{N\alpha(1-\alpha)}. \tag{3.23}$$

Let $z_v = \Phi^{-1}(v)$ for $0 < v < 1$, then $k = z_{1+q/2}\sqrt{N\alpha(1-\alpha)}$.

Now, the probability that $M \in (m_L, m_U)$ is equal to the probability that $L_{(M)} \in (L_{(m_L)}, L_{(m_U)})$, so that

$$\Pr[m_L < M \le m_U] = q \implies \Pr[L_{(m_L)} < L_{(M)} \le L_{(m_U)}] = q$$
$$\implies \Pr[L_{(N\alpha-k)} < Q_\alpha \le L_{(N\alpha+k)}] = q$$

and so $(L_{(N\alpha-k)}, L_{(N\alpha+k)})$ is a q-confidence interval for Q_α.

If $(N\alpha - k)$ is not an integer, we can interpolate between the nearest integers, or round k up to the next integer for a confidence interval that will be slightly more conservative.

For the normal approximation to be valid, we need $N(1 - \alpha)$ (or $N\alpha$ if smaller) to be at least around 30.

Example 3.9 Calculate 95% confidence intervals for the empirical 95% VaR and 99% VaR estimates in Example 3.8.

Solution 3.9 The confidence interval is bounded by $L_{(N\alpha-k)}$ and $L_{(N\alpha+k)}$ where, for the 95% VaR,

$$k = \Phi^{-1}(0.975)\sqrt{1,000\alpha(1-\alpha)}.$$

So for $\alpha = 0.95$ we have $k = 1.96\sqrt{(1,000(0.95)(0.05))} = 13.5$, giving a 95% confidence interval for the 95% VaR of

$$\left(L_{(950-13.5)}, L_{(950+13.5)}\right) = \left(L_{(936.5)}, L_{(963.5)}\right) = (200.5, 232.4)$$

using linear interpolation.

Similarly, for $\alpha = 0.99$ we have $k = 1.96\sqrt{(1,000(0.99)(0.01))} = 6.2$, giving a 95% confidence interval for the 99% VaR of

$$\left(L_{(990-6.2)}, L_{(990+6.2)}\right) = \left(L_{(983.8)}, L_{(996.2)}\right) = (270.7, 325.9).$$

□

Method 2: Repeat Simulations

Another way to explore the uncertainty in a Monte Carlo setting would be to use the technique described in Appendix A.8.4 – that is, repeat the simulations many times. Suppose we run 100 sets of 1,000 simulations. Each simulation set is used to estimate the VaR, giving a sample of 100 different estimates of the VaR, independent and identically distributed. The final VaR estimator would be the mean of the sample and the standard error is estimated by the standard deviation of the sample.

We can illustrate this with the normal loss example. With 100 replications, each with a sample size of 1,000, we find the mean values and standard deviations of the Monte Carlo estimators are:

$$\bar{L}_{(950.95)} = 212.94, \qquad s_{L_{(950.95)}} = 7.66.$$

Assuming that the estimators are approximately normally distributed, we have a 95% confidence interval for the true quantile value of

$$(212.94 \pm 1.96 \times 7.66) = (197.93, 227.95)$$

which compares with the true 95% quantile of 212.3.

Similarly, for the 99% estimators

$$\bar{L}_{(990.99)} = 291.09, \qquad s_{L_{(990)}} = 14.25,$$

which gives an estimated 95% confidence interval of

$$(291.09 \pm 1.96 \times 14.25) = (263.2, 319.0),$$

which compares with the true 99% quantile value of 286.6. We note that nearer the tail the standard deviation and the relative errors increase.

The repeat simulation method is reliable, but it requires substantially more computational resources. If the sample is not generated by simulation, it may not be possible to use the repeat method. The order statistics method is non-parametric; it usually generates a wider confidence interval, but it does not require any additional simulations nor any additional assumptions or approximations.

3.6.2 Standard Errors for Monte Carlo Estimates of Expected Shortfall

The most obvious candidate for estimating the standard deviation of the Expected Shortfall estimate is $s_u / \sqrt{N(1-\alpha)}$ where s_u is the standard deviation of the upper $100(1-\alpha)\%$ of simulated losses:

$$s_u = \sqrt{\frac{1}{N(1-\alpha)-1} \sum_{i=N\alpha+1}^{N} \left(L_{(j)} - \widehat{\mathrm{ES}}_\alpha\right)^2}.$$

We might use this because, in general, we know that the variance of the mean of a sample is equal to the sample variance divided by the sample size. However, this will underestimate the uncertainty, on average. The quantity that we are interested in is $\text{Var}[\widehat{\text{ES}}_\alpha]$, where the 'hat' indicates an estimator for the underlying Expected Shortfall. Conditioning on the quantile estimator $\widehat{Q}_\alpha$, we have:

$$\text{Var}[\widehat{\text{ES}}_\alpha] = \text{E}[\text{Var}[\widehat{\text{ES}}_\alpha \,|\, \widehat{Q}_\alpha]] + \text{Var}[\text{E}[\widehat{\text{ES}}_\alpha \,|\, \widehat{Q}_\alpha]]. \tag{3.24}$$

The plug-in, $s_u^2/N(1-\alpha)$, estimates the first term; we need to make allowance also for the second term which considers the effect of the uncertainty in the quantile.

A way to allow for both terms in equation (3.24) is the influence function approach of Manistre and Hancock (2005). The Manistre–Hancock formula for the standard error of the Expected Shortfall estimate is

$$s_{\text{ES}_\alpha} = \sqrt{\frac{s_u^2 + \alpha(\widehat{\text{ES}}_\alpha - \widehat{Q}_\alpha)^2}{N(1-\alpha)}}. \tag{3.25}$$

Using the Table 3.1 data, with $\alpha = 0.95$, for example, we have $\widehat{Q}_{95\%} = 209.5$ using the smoothed estimator, and the 95% Expected Shortfall is estimated above as 260.68. The standard deviation of the largest 50 values in Table 3.1 is 37.74. Also, $N = 1,000$, $\alpha = 0.95$, so the standard error estimate is:

$$\sqrt{\frac{37.74^2 + 0.95(260.68 - 209.5)^2}{50}} = 8.85.$$

Another approach to the standard error is to repeat the sample simulation a large number of times and calculate the standard deviation of the estimator, exactly as we did for the quantile. This is effective, but expensive in terms of the volume of additional simulation required.

3.6.3 Uncertainty for Analytic Risk Measures

Where the VaR or Expected Shortfall is calculated analytically from a parametric distribution, there may still be some residual sampling uncertainty, if we rely on parameters estimated from data. In this case we may be able to use the delta method, described in Appendix A, to generate standard errors.

It is worth noting that all these measures of uncertainty are conditional on the correct model being used to generate the data, or estimate parameters. The uncertainty referred to in this section arises from sampling variability.

The measure of uncertainty is irrelevant if the underlying model does not adequately model the losses that we are interested in.

3.7 Other Measures of Risk

All the measures of risk listed so far are solvency measures – that is, they can be interpreted as capital requirements for uncertain future potential losses. Another class of risk measures includes measures of variability.

In Modern Portfolio Theory, the portfolio variance or standard deviation is taken as a measure of risk, where a higher variance indicates a more risky loss random variable.

Another variability risk measure is the **semi-variance**. The motivation is that only variance on the worst side is important in risk measurement. So, instead of measuring the variance σ^2 as

$$\sigma^2 = E[(X - \mu_X)^2],$$

we only look at the worst side of the mean. Since we are dealing with a loss random variable, this corresponds to higher values of X, so the semi-variance is

$$\sigma_{sv}^2 = E[(\max(0, X - \mu_X))^2] \tag{3.26}$$

which would generally be estimated by the **sample semi-variance**, for a sample size n,

$$s_{sv}^2 = \sum_{i=1}^{n} \frac{(\max(x_i - \bar{x}, 0))^2}{n - 1} \tag{3.27}$$

where $\bar{x} = \sum_{i=1}^{n} x_i / n$.

The mean may be replaced in the calculation by an arbitrary, known threshold parameter value, τ. This is sometimes called the **threshold semi-variance**, denoted $\sigma_{sv,\tau}^2$:

$$\sigma_{sv,\tau}^2 = E[(\max(0, X - \tau)^2]. \tag{3.28}$$

For a profit and loss random variable Y, where a positive value indicates a profit and a negative value a loss, the semi-variance is known as the **downside semi-variance**, so the threshold downside semi-variance, for example, is

$$\sigma_{sv,\tau}^2 = E[(\min(0, Y - \tau))^2] \tag{3.29}$$

and $\tau = 0$ would be a common threshold. This measures the variance of losses with no contribution from profits.

The **downside semi-deviation** is the square root of the downside semi-variance.

We can use the variability risk measures to construct solvency risk measures. If we let $v(X)$ denote a variability risk measure, then a solvency risk measure is $\varrho(X) = E[X] + \alpha\, v(X)$, for $\alpha \geq 0$. We have already used this format in the variance and standard deviation premium principles. However, none of the solvency risk measures of this form are coherent. The standard deviation principle $\varrho(X) = E[X] + \alpha\, \sigma$ does not satisfy the monotonicity axiom, and neither the variance principle $\varrho(X) = E[X] + \alpha\, \sigma^2$ nor the semi-variance principle $\varrho(X) = E[X] + \alpha\, \sigma_{sv}^2$ satisfy the subadditivity axiom.

3.8 Notes and Further Reading

More technical details about risk measures and their properties can be found in McNeil et al. (2015). Embrechts and Wang (2015) give seven different proofs of the subadditivity of the Expected Shortfall.

See Kim and Hardy (2007) for details of bias of order statistics, referred to in Section 3.5.2.

The term **translation equivariance** is sometimes used, in place of translation invariance, in the coherence criteria.

3.9 Exercises

Exercise 3.1 Show that the α-Expected Shortfall of a lognormal distribution with parameters μ and σ is

$$\frac{e^{\mu+\sigma^2/2}}{1-\alpha}\, \Phi\left(z_{1-\alpha} + \sigma\right). \tag{3.30}$$

Exercise 3.2 A firm is modelling its operational losses using Monte Carlo simulation. The risk analyst has generated 1,000 values for the loss random variable.

(a) The Chief Risk Officer suggests that the VaR could be calculated by approximating the loss distribution by a normal distribution with the same mean and variance.

You are given that the mean of the sample is 268 and the standard deviation is 278.

(i) Estimate the 99% VaR using the normal approximation.

(ii) Use the delta method to estimate the standard error of your VaR estimate, based on the normal distribution assumption. You are given that the covariance matrix for $\hat{\mu}$ and $\hat{\sigma}$ is

$$\Sigma = \begin{pmatrix} \sigma^2/n & 0 \\ 0 & \sigma^2/2n \end{pmatrix}.$$

(iii) Use your estimates to calculate an approximate 95% confidence interval for the 99% VaR.

(b) The table below shows the largest 20 values from the Monte Carlo sample of 1,000 loss values.

992	998	1,003	1,004	1,006	1,011	1,019	1,022	1,027	1,031
1,059	1,068	1,074	1,081	1,083	1,083	1,085	1,089	1,090	1,095

(i) Estimate the 99% VaR using the raw sample percentile method.
(ii) Estimate a 95% confidence interval for the 99% VaR.

(c) Discuss whether the confidence intervals found in (a)(iii) and (b)(ii) are reasonable.

(d) Suggest, with reasons, a better method to find a confidence interval for the 99% VaR.

Exercise 3.3

(a) Explain briefly why subadditivity is a desirable characteristic for a risk measure used for setting economic capital.

(b) The standard deviation principle is the risk measure

$$\rho(X) = \mu_X + a\,\sigma_X,$$

where a is a constant, $a > 0$, and μ_X and σ_X are the mean and standard deviation of X.

(i) Show that the standard deviation principle satisfies the translation invariance and positive homogeneity criteria.
(ii) Show that the standard deviation principle is subadditive.
(iii) Show that the standard deviation principle is not monotonic.

Exercise 3.4 Show that expected loss is a coherent risk measure.

Exercise 3.5 Let $\alpha \in (0, 1)$, and let X be an exponential random variable with mean μ.

(a) Calculate $\text{VaR}_\alpha(X)$.
(b) Calculate $\text{ES}_\alpha(X)$ using:

(i) The definition

$$\mathrm{ES}_\alpha(X) = \tfrac{1}{1-\alpha} \int\limits_\alpha^1 \mathrm{VaR}_u(X)\,du.$$

(ii) The memoryless property of the exponential distribution.

Exercise 3.6

(a) Let X and Y be independent random variables with identical cumulative distribution function $F(x) = 1 - \tfrac{1}{\sqrt{x}}, x \geq 1$.
Show that for all $\alpha \in (0, 1)$,

$$\mathrm{VaR}_\alpha(X+Y) > \mathrm{VaR}_\alpha(2X) = \mathrm{VaR}_\alpha(X) + \mathrm{VaR}_\alpha(Y).$$

(This is another example of the failure of subadditivity of VaR.)

(b) Your colleague claims that the above example shows that Expected Shortfall cannot be subadditive, despite all the mathematical proofs. After all,

$$\mathrm{ES}_\alpha(L) = \frac{1}{1-\alpha} \int\limits_\alpha^1 \mathrm{VaR}_u(L)\,du \tag{3.31}$$

and in the previous part it was shown that

$$\mathrm{VaR}_u(X+Y) > \mathrm{VaR}_u(2X) = \mathrm{VaR}_u(X) + \mathrm{VaR}_u(Y) \text{for all } u.$$

Integrating this inequality then gives that

$$\mathrm{ES}_\alpha(X+Y) > \mathrm{ES}_\alpha(X) + \mathrm{ES}_\alpha(Y).$$

What is the flaw in your colleague's reasoning?

Exercise 3.7 Show that a positive homogeneous risk measure ρ must satisfy $\rho(0) = 0$.
(Hint: Note that $\rho(0) = \rho(1 \cdot 0) = \rho(2 \cdot 0)$.)

Exercise 3.8 A risk measure is said to be convex if for all X, Y, and all constants λ such that $0 \leq \lambda \leq 1$

$$\rho\big(\lambda X + (1-\lambda)Y\big) \leq \lambda\rho(X) + (1-\lambda)\rho(Y). \tag{3.32}$$

Show that a coherent risk measure is convex.

Exercise 3.9 Calculate the semi-variance for the two example loss distributions in Section 3.3.1.

Exercise 3.10

(a) Use a software package or programming language (e.g., Excel or R) to simulate 1,000 scenarios for each of the loss distributions from Section 3.3.1.
(b) Estimate the 95% VaR for both cases.
(c) Calculate a 90% confidence interval for your VaR estimate, using the order statistics approach.
(d) Repeat (a), (b), and (c) for 50 different sets of scenarios.
(e) Comment on the confidence intervals; does the true value of the 95% VaR lie within the confidence interval in every case?
(f) Calculate a 90% confidence interval for the VaR estimates using the repeated simulation approach, based on the 50 sets of simulation generated in (d). Comment on the relationship between this interval and those calculated in (d) above.

Exercise 3.11 Rockafellar et al. (2006) defined a deviation measure $\mathcal{D}$ to be a function on random variables satisfying the following four properties:

(1) $\mathcal{D}(X + C) = \mathcal{D}(X)$ for all X and all constants C.
(2) $\mathcal{D}(0) = 0$ and $\mathcal{D}(\lambda X) = \lambda \mathcal{D}(X)$ for all X and all $\lambda > 0$.
(3) $\mathcal{D}(X + Y) \leq \mathcal{D}(X) + \mathcal{D}(Y)$ for all X, Y.
(4) $\mathcal{D}(X) \geq 0$ for all X, with $\mathcal{D}(X) > 0$ for nonconstant X.

Determine whether each of the following is a measure of deviation.

(a) standard deviation,
(b) downside semi-deviation,
(c) threshold downside semi-deviation.

Exercise 3.12

(a) Calculate the limit:

$$\lim_{\alpha \to 1} \frac{\mathrm{ES}_\alpha(L)}{\mathrm{VaR}_\alpha(L)}$$

when $L \sim \mathrm{N}(\mu, \sigma^2)$.
(b) Repeat (a) for the case where L has cumulative distribution function $F(x) = 1 - x^{-a}$, for $x \geq 1$, with $a > 1$.
(c) Comment on the implications of your results for financial risk management.

Exercise 3.13 Consider the positive homogeneity assumption of coherent risk measures,

$$\rho(\lambda X) = \lambda \rho(X) \text{ for } \lambda > 0.$$

Your colleague asserts that this assumption is unrealistic, and that doubling the size of a portfolio may *more* than double the risk.

Critique your colleague's opinion.

Exercise 3.14 Your colleague states that:

Expected Shortfall is sensitive to the assessment of potential losses far in the tail (off to infinity), and consequently is subjective and inherently subject to severe model risk. VaR (at least for short time horizons) can be estimated and validated based on available data, and as a result is therefore more objective. As a result, in spite of its theoretical/academic shortcomings, VaR is a better practical measure of risk.

Critique your colleague's opinion, and suggest how the Expected Shortfall calculation could be adapted to reduce the impact of losses far in the tail.

4

Frequency-Severity Analysis

4.1 Summary

In this chapter, we present the frequency-severity model. In this model, the total loss from a risk is treated as a random sum of random, identically distributed individual losses. If the frequency and severity random variables are independent, then the mean and variance of the aggregate loss can easily be calculated from the moments of the frequency and severity distributions. However, numerical methods are usually required for other metrics, such as VaR or Expected Shortfall. We show how to implement these numerical methods, and also discuss the limitations of this model.

4.2 Introduction

In much of the literature on enterprise risk management (ERM), event risk is quantified by multiplying the probability of the event by the loss expected if the event occurs. For example, a firm might quantify the risk from product liability by assessing the probability of a defective product line, multiplied by the expected cost if a defective product reaches the market. If there is a chance of more than one defective product, then the risk may be quantified by multiplying the expected frequency of defective products by the expected cost for each one. We call this the **frequency-severity** approach, and it comes from the classical method of analysing insurance risk. When we use statistical distributions for loss frequency and loss severity, rather than point estimates, we can develop more sophisticated and more revealing analyses by developing a picture of the full distribution of losses. This will allow us to calculate tail risk measures, such as VaR or Expected Shortfall, and will also help quantify the benefits of risk mitigation methods – for example, by comparing the potential insurance recoveries with the cost of insurance.

4.3 Modelling Loss Frequency

The number of loss events in, say, a one-year period can be modelled as a random variable, N, which can take values from $\{0, 1, 2, \ldots\}$. This is called a **counting distribution**.

Useful counting distributions include the binomial distribution, the Poisson distribution, and the negative binomial distribution. We briefly recall the probability functions, moments, and moment generating functions for these three distributions. We use $sk[X]$ to denote the third central moment of X. Also, $P_X(t) = \mathrm{E}[X^t]$ and $M_X(t) = \mathrm{E}[e^{Xt}]$ represent the probability generating function of X, and the moment generating function of X, respectively.

4.3.1 The Binomial Distribution

If N follows the binomial distribution, with parameters m and q, we say $N \sim \mathrm{Bin}(m, q)$, where m is a positive integer, and $0 \leq q \leq 1$. In this case

$$\Pr[N = k] = p_k = \binom{m}{k} q^k (1 - q)^{m-k} \qquad \text{for } k \leq m,$$

$$\mathrm{E}[N] = m\,q, \qquad \mathrm{Var}[N] = m\,q\,(1 - q), \qquad sk\,[N] = mq(1 - q)(1 - 2q),$$

$$P_N(z) = (1 + q(z - 1))^m \, ; \; M_N(z) = \left(1 + q(e^z - 1)\right)^m.$$

4.3.2 The Poisson Distribution

The Poisson distribution is known as the distribution for rare events, which is why it is particularly useful for risk assessment. The parameter, $\lambda > 0$ determines the distribution, and we write that $N \sim \mathrm{Poi}(\lambda)$. In this case we have

$$\Pr[N = k] = p_k = \frac{e^{-\lambda} \lambda^k}{k!},$$

$$\mathrm{E}[N] = \lambda, \qquad V[N] = \lambda, \qquad sk\,[N] = \lambda,$$

$$P_N(z) = e^{\lambda(z-1)}; \; M_N(z) = e^{\lambda(e^z - 1)}.$$

The Poisson distribution is very tractable and is particularly convenient for combining or dis-aggregating risks.

For combining risks, we employ the very useful result that the sum of independent Poisson random variables is also a Poisson random variable. That is, suppose we have r independent Poisson random variables, N_1, N_2, ..., N_r, where $N_j \sim \text{Poi}(\lambda_j)$ for $j = 1, 2, \ldots, r$. Then

$$\left(\sum_{j=1}^{r} N_j \right) \sim \text{Poi}(\lambda) \quad \text{where} \quad \lambda = \sum_{j=1}^{r} \lambda_j.$$

This is useful because we may want to consider several different risks together – for example, losses associated with IT risk may be associated with directed external attacks, internal security breaches, or hardware and/or software defects. Each of these risk events might be appropriately modelled as Poisson random variables with different λ parameters. Assuming independence, the total number of IT risk events can then be modelled as a Poisson random variable, with parameter equal to the sum of the three individual λ's.

For disaggregating risks we can use the reverse result. Let $N \sim \text{Poi}(\lambda)$ represent the number of risk events, and suppose events can be classified into m categories, independent of N, such that, given that an event occurs, the probability that it falls into category j is q_j, $j = 1, 2, \ldots, m$. Then the number of events in category j, N_j, say, has a Poisson distribution with parameter $\lambda_j = \lambda q_j$.

As an example, suppose the number of loss events from work-related injuries to employees for a firm has a Poisson distribution with $\lambda = 40$. Each event is categorized according to whether the underlying cause is 'human failure' ($q_1 = 0.6$), 'equipment failure' ($q_2 = 0.3$), or 'other' ($q_3 = 0.1$). Then the number of events each year arising from human failure is also Poisson distributed, with parameter $\lambda_1 = q_1 \lambda = 24$; the number arising from equipment failure is Poisson with parameters $\lambda_2 = q_2 \lambda = 12$, and the 'other' category is Poisson with parameter $\lambda_3 = q_3 \lambda = 4$.

4.3.3 The Negative Binomial Distribution

The Poisson distribution has many attractive features, but it is limited; as a single parameter distribution it is not flexible enough to provide an adequate fit to data in many situations. For a counting distribution which fits a distribution with variance greater than the mean, we may use the negative binomial. With two parameters, it offers more flexibility in fitting to frequency dates. If N has a negative binomial distribution, we write $N \sim \text{NB}(r, \beta)$, where $r, \beta > 0$, and

$$\Pr[N = k] = p_k = \frac{\Gamma(k + r)}{k! \, \Gamma(r)} \left(\frac{\beta}{1 + \beta} \right)^k \left(\frac{1}{1 + \beta} \right)^r,$$

$$E[N] = r \beta, \qquad \text{Var}[N] = r \beta (1 + \beta), \qquad sk[N] = r \beta (1 + \beta)(1 + 2\beta),$$

$$P_N(z) = \left(\frac{1}{1 - \beta(z - 1)} \right)^r ; \quad M_N(z) = \left(\frac{1}{1 - \beta(e^z - 1)} \right)^r.$$

Recall that, for integer r, $\Gamma(r) = (r-1)!$. If r is not an integer, the gamma functions for r and $k+r$ must be calculated numerically. Most quantitative software packages include built-in gamma functions. Alternatively, p_k can be calculated directly using

$$\frac{\Gamma(k + r)}{k! \, \Gamma(r)} = \frac{r \times (r+1) \times \cdots \times (r+k-1)}{k!}.$$

Note that this parametrization is slightly different from the one that is commonly used in statistics texts, where a parameter p is used, such that $p = (1 + \beta)^{-1}$.

4.3.4 Choosing the Frequency Distribution

If the binomial, Poisson, and negative binomial are being considered as potential distributions for a given sample, the first step is to calculate the sample mean and variance. The binomial variance is always smaller than the mean, the Poisson variance is equal to the mean, and the negative binomial variance is always bigger than the mean. If the sample variance is slightly larger than the mean, it is worth trying the Poisson and negative binomial distributions to see if either fits. Similarly, if the sample variance is slightly less than the mean, then the Poisson or binomial might provide an adequate fit. Assessing the goodness of fit can be achieved through standard chi-square tests.

In some cases, the distribution may be consistent with one of the three distributions, but with a distortion at zero. Typically, either there are more zero values than would be expected under any of the distributions, or the zero values are unobserved, and so only the non-zero values are available. In these cases, it may be appropriate to use a **zero-modified** distribution. A zero-modified distribution is a mixture of a degenerate distribution at $N = 0$, with a parametric distribution for $N|N \geq 1$.

For example, suppose Z is a Poisson random variable with parameter λ. Then the zero-modified Poisson random variable, N, say, can be defined as

$$N = \begin{cases} 0 & \text{with probability } q, \\ Z|Z \geq 1 & \text{with probability } 1 - q. \end{cases}$$

The probability function for $Z|Z \geq 1$ is p_k^*, say, where for $k = 1, 2, 3, \ldots$,

$$p_k^* = \frac{\Pr[Z = k]}{\Pr[Z \geq 1]} = \frac{1}{1 - e^{-\lambda}} \times \frac{\lambda^k e^{-\lambda}}{k!},$$

so the probability function for N is

$$p_0 = q,$$
$$p_k = (1 - q) \times \Pr[Z = k]$$
$$= (1 - q) p_k^* = \frac{(1 - p_0)}{1 - e^{-\lambda}} \times \frac{\lambda^k e^{-\lambda}}{k!} \quad \text{for } k = 1, 2, 3, \ldots$$

In the zero-modified distribution, q is an additional parameter. If the zero values are unobserved, then $p_0 = q = 0$; this is called the **zero-truncated distribution**.

4.3.5 The $(a, b, 0)$ class

A counting random variable, N, is in the $(a, b, 0)$ class of distributions if and only if there exist constants a and b such that

$$\frac{p_{k+1}}{p_k} = a + \frac{b}{k + 1} \quad \text{for } k = 0, 1, 2, \ldots \quad (4.1)$$

In fact, the $(a, b, 0)$ class contains only the binomial, Poisson, and negative binomial distributions.

In the binomial case, with parameters m and q, we have

$$\frac{p(k + 1)}{p(k)} = \frac{\binom{m}{k+1} q^{k+1} (1 - q)^{m-k-1}}{\binom{m}{k} q^k (1 - q)^{m-k}} \quad (4.2)$$

$$= \frac{m - k}{k + 1} \frac{q}{1 - q} \quad (4.3)$$

$$= -\frac{q}{1 - q} + \left(\frac{(m + 1)q}{1 - q} \right) \frac{1}{k + 1} \quad (4.4)$$

$$= a + \frac{b}{k + 1}, \quad \text{where } a = -\frac{q}{1 - q} \text{ and } b = \frac{(m + 1)q}{1 - q}. \quad (4.5)$$

Similarly, the Poisson distribution is $(a, b, 0)$ with $a = 0$ and $b = \lambda$ and the negative binomial distribution is $(a, b, 0)$ with $a = \frac{\beta}{1+\beta}$ and $b = (r - 1)\frac{\beta}{1+\beta}$.

The $(a, b, 0)$ property will become useful when we combine frequency and severity distributions in Section 4.5.

4.4 Loss Severity Distributions

The loss severity distribution is the distribution of the losses from a specified event, given that the event has occurred. We usually assume that the severity random variable is continuous and greater than zero, and that severities from different loss events are independent and identically distributed. Loss distributions are typically positively skewed, which means that loss events are more likely to be small than large, but may also be fat-tailed, meaning that occasionally, the loss may be very large.

The following distributions are commonly used for modelling loss severity:

4.4.1 The Exponential Distribution

$$\text{For } x > 0, \theta > 0 : \quad f(x) = \frac{e^{-x/\theta}}{\theta}; \quad F(x) = 1 - e^{-x/\theta};$$

$$E[X] = \theta; \qquad \text{Var}[X] = \theta^2;$$

$$M_X(z) = \frac{1}{1 - \theta z}.$$

The exponential distribution is very tractable. It is also positively skewed. However, with only one parameter, it is not very flexible and tends to be too thin-tailed for many loss situations. This means that it will underestimate the probability of very large losses.

It is important nevertheless as a basis for other distributions that are derived by transforming the exponential distribution.

4.4.2 The Weibull Distribution

$$\text{For } x > 0, \theta > 0, \tau > 0 : \quad f(x) = \frac{\tau \, x^{\tau-1} e^{-(x/\theta)^\tau}}{\theta^\tau}; \quad F(x) = 1 - e^{-(x/\theta)^\tau}$$

$$(4.6)$$

$$E[X] = \theta \Gamma\left(1 + \frac{1}{\tau}\right) \quad \text{Var}[X] = \theta^2 \left(\Gamma\left(1 + \frac{2}{\tau}\right) - \left(\Gamma\left(1 + \frac{1}{\tau}\right)\right)^2\right).$$

There is no closed form for the moment or probability generating functions.

The Weibull distribution is the distribution of X^τ, where X has an exponential distribution. It is fatter-tailed than the exponential if $\tau < 1$, and thinner-tailed if $\tau > 1$. The parameter θ is a scale parameter, meaning that if X has Weibull distribution with parameters θ and τ, then X/θ has a Weibull distribution with parameters 1 and τ.

4.4.3 The Gamma Distribution

For $x, a, \beta > 0$,

$$f(x) = \frac{x^{a-1} e^{-x/\beta}}{\beta^a \, \Gamma(a)}, \qquad F(x) = \Gamma(a; x/\beta),$$

$$E[X] = a\,\beta, \qquad \mathrm{Var}[X] = a\,\beta^2, \qquad sk[X] = 2a\,\beta^3,$$

$$M_X(z) = \left(\frac{1}{1 - \beta\,z} \right)^a,$$

where $\Gamma(a; y)$ is the incomplete gamma function.

The β parameter is a scale parameter; the shape of the distribution is determined by a.

For integer a, the gamma distribution can be interpreted as the sum of a independent and identically distributed exponential random variables. In this case, the distribution is called Erlang. However, the gamma distribution is well defined even for non-integer a.

The gamma distribution is positively skewed, and also quite tractable (despite having an inconvenient distribution function). It is also used as a base distribution for transforming to create other distributions.

A mixture distribution is derived from a set of distributions by applying weights to each distribution. That is, the mixture random variable is randomly drawn from a set of distributions. It has been shown that mixtures of Erlang distributions are particularly flexible for fitting loss random variables.

4.4.4 The Pareto Distribution

For $x, a, \theta > 0$,

$$f(x) = \frac{a\,\theta^a}{(x + \theta)^{a+1}}, \qquad F(x) = 1 - \left(\frac{\theta}{\theta + x} \right)^a,$$

$$E[X] = \frac{\theta}{a - 1} \quad \text{for } a > 1, \qquad E[X^2] = \frac{2\theta^2}{(a - 1)(a - 2)} \quad \text{for } a > 2,$$

$$\mathrm{Var}[X] = \left(\frac{\theta}{a - 1} \right)^2 \left(\frac{a}{a - 2} \right) \quad \text{for } a > 2.$$

The Pareto distribution can be used for very fat-tailed losses. The kth moment of the distribution exists only if $a > k$ and the moment generating function does not exist. It is also important in Extreme Value Theory, as we shall see in Chapter 5.

4.4.5 The Lognormal (LogN) Distribution

For $x, \sigma > 0$, and for real valued μ,

$$f(x) = \frac{1}{\sqrt{2\pi}\,\sigma\,x} \exp\left(-\frac{1}{2}\left(\frac{\log x - \mu}{\sigma}\right)^2\right), \qquad F(x) = \Phi\left(\frac{\log x - \mu}{\sigma}\right),$$

where Φ is the standard normal distribution function,

$$E[X] = e^{\mu + \sigma^2/2}, \qquad \text{Var}[X] = \left(e^{\mu + \sigma^2/2}\right)^2 \left(e^{\sigma^2} - 1\right),$$

$$E[X^k] = e^{k\mu + k^2\sigma^2/2}.$$

The lognormal distribution is fat-tailed and positively skewed. It does not have a moment generating function, but all of its moments exist and are finite. It is derived from the normal distribution: given $Z \sim N(\mu, \sigma^2)$, then $Y = e^Z$ has a lognormal distribution with parameters μ and σ. Equivalently, for a lognormally distributed random variable Y, the random variable $Z = \log Y$ has a normal distribution.

4.5 The Aggregate Loss Distribution

The aggregate loss random variable, S is formed by combining the loss frequency random variable N and the loss severity random variables, Y_j, say,

$$S = \begin{cases} \displaystyle\sum_{k=1}^{N} Y_j & \text{for } N = 1, 2, 3, \ldots \\ 0 & \text{for } N = 0. \end{cases} \qquad (4.7)$$

We assume, generally, that the severity is independent of the frequency random variable, that is, N and $\{Y_j\}$ are independent, and that the $\{Y_j\}$ are i.i.d. In this case we say that S has a **compound distribution**. The distribution of N is the **primary distribution**, and that of Y_j is the **secondary distribution**. More specifically, if $N \sim \text{Poi}(\lambda)$, and Y_j are independent, identically distributed, and independent of N, each with distribution function $F_Y(y)$, then we say that S has a **compound Poisson distribution**, and we write $S \sim \text{CoPoi}(\lambda, F_Y)$.

The independence assumptions mean that, for example, knowing that there is an unusually large number of loss events in a given year does not give any additional information on the distribution of losses from each individual event, and that, for example, knowing that the first few losses are larger than average does not tell us anything about subsequent losses. These are strong assumptions, and the methods for compound distributions should not be applied carelessly where there might be significant dependence between the frequency and severity variables.

The assumptions are useful because, in general, sums of random variables are difficult to work with. The independence assumptions allow us to develop simple expressions for the mean and variance of S given the distributions for N and Y_j, and even to approximate full probability distributions in some cases.

4.5.1 The Mean and Variance of S

If we have information about the loss frequency and loss severity random variables, then we can use iterated expectation for $E[S]$ and $\text{Var}[S]$, by conditioning on the number of loss events, N. Given N, S is a sum of independent and identically distributed loss severity random variables. Let μ_y and σ_y^2 denote the expected value and variance of each of the Y_j variables (they have the same moments because they are identically distributed), then

$$E[S|N] = E[Y_1 + Y_2 + \cdots + Y_N] = N\mu_y$$

$$\Rightarrow E\big[E[S|N]\big] = E[N]\mu_y$$

$$\text{and} \Rightarrow \text{Var}\big[E[S|N]\big] = \text{Var}[N\,\mu_y] = \mu_y^2\,\text{Var}[N]$$

$$\text{Var}[S|N] = \text{Var}[Y_1 + \cdots + Y_N] = N\,\sigma_y^2$$

$$\Rightarrow E\big[\text{Var}[S|N]\big] = E[N]\,\sigma_y^2 \quad \text{so}$$

$$E[S] = E\big[E[S|N]\big] = E[N]\mu_y$$

$$\text{Var}[S] = E\big[V[S|N]\big] + \text{Var}\big[E[S|N]\big] = E[N]\,\sigma_y^2 + \text{Var}[N]\,\mu_y^2.$$

In the case of the compound Poisson distribution, we have $E[N] = \lambda$ and $\text{Var}[N] = \lambda$, so the mean and variance of the aggregate distribution can be written as

$$E[S] = \lambda\,E[Y_j]; \quad \text{Var}[S] = \lambda\left(\text{Var}[Y_j] + E[Y_j]^2\right) = \lambda E\big[Y_j^2\big].$$

Example 4.1 Suppose $N \sim \text{Poi}(\lambda = 30)$ and $Y_j \sim \text{logN}(\mu = 5.0, \sigma = 1.6)$. Calculate the mean and variance of S.

Solution 4.1

$$E[N] = 30 \quad \text{Var}[N] = 30$$

$$E[Y_j] = e^{\mu + \sigma^2/2} = 533.8 \quad E[Y_j^2] = e^{2\mu + 4(\sigma^2/2)} = 1{,}919.85^2$$

$$\Rightarrow E[S] = 30 \times 533.8 = 16{,}014$$

$$\text{Var}[S] = 30 \times 1{,}919.85^2 = 10{,}515^2. \qquad \square$$

4.5.2 The Moment Generating Function and Skewness of S

We can use iterated expectation also for the moment generating function of S. We assume that N and Y_j have moment generating functions, denoted $M_N(z)$ and $M_Y(z)$ respectively. Then

$$M_S(z) = E[e^{Sz}] = E\left[E[e^{Sz}|N]\right]$$

$$= E\left[E\left[e^{z(Y_1 + Y_2 + \cdots + Y_N)}|N\right]\right] = E\left[(M_Y(z))^N\right]$$

$$= E\left[e^{N \log(M_Y(z))}\right]$$

$$= M_N(\log(M_Y(z))).$$

To derive expressions for the third central moment of S in terms of moments of N and Y, it is convenient to work with the cumulant generating function, $C_S(z) = \log M_S(z)$, that is,

$$C_S(z) = \log(M_N(\log(M_Y(z)))) = C_N(C_Y(z)).$$

The first three central moments of a distribution can be derived from its cumulant generating function by differentiating with respect to z, and evaluating at $z = 0$ (see Appendix). That is, for any cumulant generating function $C_X(z)$, we have $C_X(0) = 1$, $C_X'(0) = E[X]$, $C_X''(0) = \text{Var}[X]$, and $C_X'''(0) = sk[X]$. So,

$$C_S'(z) = C_Y'(z)\,C_N'(C_Y(z)) \Rightarrow E[S] = E[Y_j]E[N],$$

$$C_S''(z) = C_Y''(z)\,C_N'(C_Y(z)) + (C_Y'(z))^2\,C_N''(C_Y(z))$$

$$\Rightarrow \text{Var}[S] = \text{Var}[Y_j]E[N] + E[Y_j]^2\,\text{Var}[N],$$

$$C_S'''(z) = C_Y'''(z)\,C_N'(C_Y(z)) + C_Y''(z)\,C_Y'(z)\,C_N''(C_Y(z))$$

$$\quad + 2C_Y'(z)\,C_Y''(z)\,C_N''(C_Y(z)) + (C_Y'(z))^3\,C_N'''(C_Y(z))$$

$$\Rightarrow sk[S] = sk[Y_j]E[N] + 3\text{Var}[N]E[Y_j]\,\text{Var}[Y_j] + E[Y_j]^3\,sk[N].$$

So, the first three central moments of N and Y_j will give us the first three central moments of S. The variance and skewness formulas are not particularly easy to remember, but they are quite easy to derive.

In the case of a Poi(λ) frequency distribution, the first three moments simplify to

$$E[S] = \lambda\, E[Y_j], \tag{4.8}$$

$$Var[S] = \lambda\, E[Y_j^2], \tag{4.9}$$

$$sk[S] = \lambda\, E[Y_j^3]. \tag{4.10}$$

We can demonstrate this using the cumulant generating function for $S \sim \text{CoPoi}(\lambda, F_Y)$:

$$M_N(z) = \exp(\lambda(e^z - 1)),$$
$$\Rightarrow M_S(z) = M_N(\log(M_Y(z))) = \exp(\lambda(M_Y(z) - 1)),$$
$$\Rightarrow C_S(z) = \log(M_S(z)) = \lambda(M_Y(z) - 1),$$
$$\Rightarrow C_S'(z) = \lambda\, M_Y'(z),$$
$$\text{set } z = 0; \quad C_S'(0) = E[S], \quad M_Y'(0) = E[Y_j],$$
$$\Rightarrow E[S] = \lambda\, E[Y_j].$$
Similarly, $C_S''(z) = \lambda\, M_Y''(z) \quad \Rightarrow Var[S] = \lambda\, E[Y_j^2]$
and $C_S'''(z) = \lambda M_Y'''(z) \Rightarrow sk[S] = \lambda\, E[Y_j^3].$

4.5.3 Approximating the Aggregate Loss Distribution

In risk management, we are often interested in tail events. The mean and variance of the aggregate loss distribution may not be sufficient to assess the risk or determine an appropriate risk management strategy. However, deriving the full distribution for S is cumbersome, even for relatively simple combinations of primary and secondary distributions. We may be able to get quite good estimation of the distribution function of S by approximating it with another, simpler distribution. In this section, we describe two distributions used for this purpose in practice, and compare them.

The Normal Approximation

If $E[N]$ is reasonably large (at least 30, preferably more), and we are not seeking accurate values for $F_S(s)$ in the far tail of the distribution, then approximating with a normal distribution may give adequate results. It requires only the mean and variance of the aggregate loss distribution, and so may be used when more detailed information on the individual loss distributions is not available.

Applying the normal approximation is simple. We approximate S with another distribution, S^*, say, where

$$S^* \sim N\big(E[S], Var[S]\big).$$

Then,

$$Pr[S \le s] \approx Pr[S^* \le s] = \Phi\left(\frac{s - E[S]}{\sqrt{Var[S]}}\right),$$

where Φ is the standard normal distribution function.

The justification for using the normal approximation is that, under the Central Limit Theorem, the aggregate loss distribution will converge to the normal distribution as $E[N] \to \infty$, because S is a sum of independent random variables. However, aggregate loss distributions are commonly positively skewed and the normal distribution has zero skewness, which means that the normal distribution tends to underestimate the probability of large losses.

Example 4.2 Suppose $N \sim Poi(\lambda = 30)$ and $Y_j \sim logN(\mu = 5, \sigma = 1.6)$ (as in Example 4.1).

Use the normal approximation to estimate (i) $Pr[S > 35,000]$ and (ii) $Pr[S > 80,000]$.

Solution 4.2 We approximate S with $S^* \sim N(\mu = 16,014, \sigma^2 = 10,515^2)$, so

$$Pr[S > 35,000] \approx 1 - \Phi\left(\frac{35,000 - 16,014}{10,515}\right) = 0.0355,$$

$$Pr[S > 80,000] \approx 1 - \Phi\left(\frac{80,000 - 16,014}{10,515}\right) = 6 \times 10^{-10}.$$

The Translated Gamma Approximation

Because the aggregate loss distribution is typically positively skewed, when $E[N]$ is not large enough to use the normal approximation confidently we may, instead, approximate with another positively skewed distribution, and a common choice is the translated gamma distribution. This is the same as the gamma distribution described in Section 4.4.3, but with a lateral shift. That is, we approximate the distribution of S with the random variable $W + k$ where k is a constant and $W \sim Gamma(a, \beta)$. We determine a, β, and k by matching moments to the first three central moments of S.

The translated gamma approximation gives reasonable results where the coefficient of skewness of the underlying distribution is positive, but not too large – as a rule of thumb, a coefficient of skewness less than 10 would be expected to give reasonable results using this approximation.

Example 4.3 Suppose $N \sim \text{Poi}(\lambda = 30)$ and $Y_j \sim \text{logN}(\mu = 5, \sigma = 1.6)$, as in the examples above.

Use the translated gamma approximation to estimate (i) $\Pr[S > 35{,}000]$ and (ii) $\Pr[S > 80{,}000]$.

Solution 4.3 First, we find the values of the approximating distribution by matching three moments to the original compound distribution:

$$E[S] = 16{,}014 = a\,\beta + k,$$
$$\text{Var}[S] = 10{,}515^2 = a\,\beta^2,$$
$$sk[S] = 30 \times 6905^3 = 2a\,\beta^3,$$
$$\Rightarrow a = 0.0554, \quad \beta = 44{,}661, \quad k = 13{,}538.$$

Now use the incomplete gamma function for the distribution function,

$$\Pr[S > 35{,}000] \approx \Pr[W + k > 35{,}000] = \Pr[W > 21{,}462] = 0.03321,$$
$$\Pr[S > 80{,}000] \approx \Pr[W + k > 80{,}000] = \Pr[W > 66{,}462] = 0.00606. \quad \square$$

Note that this approximation is only intended to be used for right tails – that is, for estimating probabilities and metrics associated with rare, large losses. The translation factor makes the approximation very poor for left tail probabilities – that is, the probability that aggregate losses are small.

4.5.4 Calculating the Aggregate Loss Distribution Function

If we know the full distribution of the individual losses, and if the frequency distribution falls in the $(a, b, 0)$ class described in Section 4.3.5, then we can accurately compute the full distribution of aggregate losses. We introduce one element of estimation, in that we approximate the severity distribution (which is usually assumed to be continuous) with a discrete distribution. The process of approximating a continuous distribution by a discrete one is called **discretization**. If we use small steps in the discretization (meaning that we use a large number of discrete points), then the discrete approximation to the continuous distribution will be very close, and we can achieve as much accuracy in the final calculation as we could ever need.

There are two commonly used methods for computing the aggregate loss distribution using a discretized severity distribution; Panjer recursions and Fast Fourier Transforms.

Discretizing the Severity Distribution

Suppose we have a severity distribution $Y \geq 0$, with distribution function $F(y)$. We assume that our discretization maps the continuous function to the integers, $k = 0, 1, \ldots$. If we want a less granular, or more granular discretization (i.e. bigger or smaller step sizes) then we can scale the severity distribution appropriately, and re-scale at the end.

Let f_k denote the probability function of the discretized distribution. We can set $f_k = F_Y(k + 0.5) - F_Y(k - 0.5)$ for $k = 1, 2, \ldots$, and we can set $f_0 = F_Y(0.5)$.

Example 4.4 For $Y_j \sim \text{logN}(\mu = 5, \sigma = 1.6)$:

(a) Using an integer step size, calculate the first three values of the discretized probability function.
(b) Using a step size of 2.0, calculate the first three values of the discretized probability function.
(c) Using a step size of 0.5, calculate the first three values of the discretized probability function.

Solution 4.4

(a) $$f_0 = \Phi\left(\frac{\log(0.5) - 5}{1.6}\right) = 1.8669 \times 10^{-4},$$

$$f_1 = \Phi\left(\frac{\log(1.5) - 5}{1.6}\right) - \Phi\left(\frac{\log(0.5) - 5}{1.6}\right) = 1.8554 \times 10^{-3},$$

$$f_2 = \Phi\left(\frac{\log(2.5) - 5}{1.6}\right) - \Phi\left(\frac{\log(1.5) - 5}{1.6}\right) = 3.3083 \times 10^{-3}.$$

(b) We discretize a random variable $Y^* = Y/2$ in integer steps, so that for $k = 1, 2, \ldots,$

$$f_k = \Pr[k - 0.5 < Y^* \leq k + 0.5] = \Pr[2k - 1 < Y \leq 2k + 1], \text{ and}$$

$$f_0 = \Pr[Y \leq 1]$$

$$\Rightarrow f_0 = \Phi\left(\frac{\log(1) - 5}{1.6}\right) = 8.8903 \times 10^{-4},$$

$$f_1 = \Phi\left(\frac{\log(3) - 5}{1.6}\right) - \Phi\left(\frac{\log(1) - 5}{1.6}\right) = 6.4879 \times 10^{-3},$$

$$f_2 = \Phi\left(\frac{\log(5) - 5}{1.6}\right) - \Phi\left(\frac{\log(3) - 5}{1.6}\right) = 9.6641 \times 10^{-3}.$$

(c) We discretize a random variable $Y^* = 2Y$ in integer steps, so that for $k = 1, 2, \ldots,$

$$f_k = \Pr[k - 0.5 < Y^* \le k + 0.5] = \Pr\left[\tfrac{k}{2} - \tfrac{1}{4} < Y \le \tfrac{k}{2} + \tfrac{1}{4}\right], \text{and}$$

$$f_0 = \Pr[Y \le 0.25]$$

$$\Rightarrow f_0 = \Phi\left(\frac{\log(0.25) - 5}{1.6}\right) = 3.284 \times 10^{-5},$$

$$f_1 = \Phi\left(\frac{\log(0.75) - 5}{1.6}\right) - \Phi\left(\frac{\log(0.25) - 5}{1.6}\right) = 4.4238 \times 10^{-4},$$

$$f_2 = \Phi\left(\frac{\log(5) - 5}{1.6}\right) - \Phi\left(\frac{\log(3) - 5}{1.6}\right) = 9.4019 \times 10^{-4}.$$

In general, with a step size of h, we have

$$f_k = F_Y\left(h\left(k + \tfrac{1}{2}\right)\right) - F_Y\left(h\left(k - \tfrac{1}{2}\right)\right). \qquad \square$$

Panjer Recursions

If the loss frequency distribution is in the $(a, b, 0)$ class (that is, Poisson, Binomial, or Negative Binomial) then we can use the Panjer recursion formula to build the probability function for the aggregate loss.

Let p_k denote the probability function for the loss frequency. Given that this is an $(a, b, 0)$ distribution, we know that

$$\frac{p(k + 1)}{p(k)} = a + \frac{b}{k + 1} \quad \text{for } k = 0, 1, \dots \qquad (4.11)$$

We also need $P_N(z)$, the probability generating function of N.

Let f_k denote the probability function of the discretized loss severity distribution; we assume the discretization uses an integer step size, so that for the discrete severity random variable Y, $f_k = \Pr[Y = k]$.

Given that both the frequency and severity distributions are discrete and distributed on the non-negative integers, the aggregate loss distribution is also discrete and is also distributed on the non-negative integers. Let g_s denote the probability function for the discrete aggregate loss random variable S.

The Panjer algorithm calculates g_k recursively using the formulae

$$g_0 = P_N(f_0); \quad g_s = \frac{1}{1 - a f_0}\left(\sum_{j=1}^{s} f_j\, g_{s-j}\left(a + \frac{bj}{s}\right)\right). \qquad (4.12)$$

In the case of a compound Poisson distribution, we have $P_N(z) = e^{\lambda(z-1)}$, and $a = 0$, $b = \lambda$, so the recursion formula is

$$g_0 = e^{\lambda(f_0 - 1)}; \quad g_s = \frac{\lambda}{s}\left(\sum_{j=1}^{s} j\, f_j\, g_{s-j}\right). \qquad (4.13)$$

Note that if an $(a,b,0)$ distribution is zero-modified, it no longer meets the $(a,b,0)$ criterion, and it could not be used in the recursion given here. However, the recursion can be adapted to zero-modified distributions.

Example 4.5 Suppose, again, that $N \sim \text{Poi}(\lambda = 30)$ and $Y_j \sim \text{logN}(\mu = 5,$ $\sigma = 1.6)$, as in Example 4.1. Use the Panjer recursion to estimate (i) $\Pr[S > 35{,}000]$ and (ii) $\Pr[S > 80{,}000]$.

Solution 4.5 We first discretize the severity distribution. It is convenient to work in units, so we have f_0, f_1, and f_2 as in the example above, and we continue for f_k, $k = 3, 4, \ldots, 80{,}000$.

The probability generating function of the Poisson distribution is

$$P(z) = e^{\lambda(z-1)}$$

$$\Rightarrow g_0 = e^{\lambda(f_0-1)} = 9.4 \times 10^{-14},$$

$$g_1 = \lambda(f_1 \, g_0) = 5.2 \times 10^{-15},$$

$$g_2 = \frac{\lambda}{2}(2 \, f_2 \, g_0 + f_1 \, g_1) = 9.49 \times 10^{-15}.$$

Programming the recursion (e.g., in R) gives the results

$$\Pr[S > 35{,}000] = 1 - \sum_{s=0}^{35{,}000} g_s = 0.04000,$$

$$\Pr[S > 80{,}000] = 1 - \sum_{s=0}^{80{,}000} g_s = 0.00245. \qquad \square$$

Fast Fourier Transforms

The **Fast Fourier Transform** (FFT) is an algorithm for calculating and inverting Fourier transforms. It is embedded in many quantitative software resources, including Excel and R.

In the case where the original function, f_k, say, is the probability function of a discrete random variable Y, and if we assume that there is some integer M such that the probability that $Y > M$ is negligible, then the Fourier transform of Y, evaluated at the integer $k \leq M - 1$, is

$$\varphi_Y(k) = \sum_{j=0}^{M-1} f_j \, e^{j2\pi i k/M} = \text{E}\left[e^{Y(2\pi i k)/M}\right],$$

where $i = \sqrt{-1}$. This is the characteristic function for Y, and it is useful because it has a similar role to the moment generating function in compound distributions; that is, if S is the (discrete) aggregate loss, with characteristic function $\varphi_S(t)$, and P_N is the probability generating function of N then

$$\varphi_S(s) = P_N(\varphi_Y(s)).$$

So, given f_k, we can use the FFT algorithm to get $\varphi_Y(s)$ for $s = 0, 1,$ $2, \ldots, M - 1$ (the characteristic function for the loss severity distribution) and we can then use the probability generating function of N to get $\varphi_S(s)$ for $s = 0, 1, 2, \ldots, M - 1$, which is the characteristic function for the aggregate loss distribution. Finally, we can use the inverse FFT function to retrieve g_s, which is the probability function for the aggregate loss. Note that, usually, the inverse FFT functions will generate $g_s \times M$, so we divide by M to get g_s. The algorithm for the FFT is most efficient when $M = 2^n$ for some sufficiently large integer n.

Example 4.6 Suppose, as in previous examples, $N \sim \text{Poi}(\lambda = 30)$ and $Y_j \sim \log N(\mu = 5, \sigma = 1.6)$. Use Fast Fourier Transforms to estimate (i) $\Pr[S > 35{,}000]$ and (ii) $\Pr[S > 80{,}000]$.

Solution 4.6 Using the fft function in R, with $M = 2^{19}$,

$$\Pr[S > 35{,}000] = 0.04000,$$
$$\Pr[S > 80{,}000] = 0.00244.$$

Note that, even though we are only interested in g_s for $s \leq 80{,}000$, we must use the whole distribution of S, and Y, in the FFT, as we do not get an accurate value of the characteristic function if it is cut off too early.

For determining the whole distribution of S, with a long-tailed severity distribution, the FFT method is computationally more efficient than Panjer recursions (Embrechts and Frei, 2009). The difference is generally relatively minor, and in the examples above, the Panjer approach is quicker as the calculations are not required for Y or S beyond 80,000.

4.6 Risk Measures for the Aggregate Loss Distribution

If we have approximated the aggregate loss distribution with another distribution, then the estimated risk measure can be calculated as the risk measure of the approximating distribution. However, if the risk measure is far into the tail of the distribution this may not give a very accurate value.

Normal Approximation (NA)

If we approximate the aggregate loss distribution with a normal distribution, with mean $\mu = E[S]$ and $\sigma^2 = \text{Var}[S]$, then the approximations for the VaR and Expected Shortfall risk measures (from Chapter 3) are

$$\text{VaR}_\alpha(S) \approx \mu + z_\alpha \sigma,$$

$$\text{ES}_\alpha(S) \approx \mu + \frac{\sigma}{1-\alpha}\phi(z_\alpha),$$

where $\phi(x)$ is the standard normal density function.

Returning to the compound Poisson loss from Example 4.2, we have $\mu = 16{,}014$, $\sigma = 10{,}515$, so the 95% and 99% VaR and Expected Shortfall are:

$$\text{VaR}_{95\%} = \mu + 1.6448\,\sigma = 33{,}310;$$

$$\text{VaR}_{99\%} = \mu + 2.3263\,\sigma = 40{,}476;$$

$$\text{ES}_{95\%} = \mu + \frac{\sigma}{1-\alpha}\phi(1.6448) = 37{,}704;$$

$$\text{ES}_{99\%} = \mu + \frac{\sigma}{1-\alpha}\phi(2.3262) = 44{,}040.$$

Translated Gamma Approximation

We approximate the aggregate loss distribution with a translated gamma random variable, $W + k$, say, where $W \sim \text{Gamma}(a, \beta)$. Then, for example,

$$\text{VaR}_{99\%}(S) \approx F_W^{-1}(0.99) + k,$$

$$\text{ES}_{99\%}(S) \approx E S_{99\%}(W) + k.$$

The gamma distribution function and its inverse can be determined using standard software, including Excel (GAMMA.DIST and GAMMA.INV functions).

We can derive an analytic expression for the Expected Shortfall of a Gamma random variable:

$$\text{ES}_\alpha(W) = \frac{1}{1-\alpha} \int_{Q_\alpha}^{\infty} x\, f(x)dx$$

$$= \frac{1}{1-\alpha} \int_{Q_\alpha}^{\infty} \frac{x^a\, e^{-x/\beta}}{\beta^a\, \Gamma(a)}dx$$

$$= \frac{a\beta}{1-\alpha} \int_{Q_\alpha}^{\infty} \frac{x^a\, e^{-x/\beta}}{\beta^{a+1}\, \Gamma(a+1)}dx$$

$$= a\beta \left(\frac{1 - F^*(Q_\alpha)}{1-\alpha} \right) = \left(\frac{1 - F^*(Q_\alpha)}{1-\alpha} \right) E[W],$$

where $F^*(x)$ is the distribution function of a gamma random variable with parameters $a + 1$ and β.

The Expected Shortfall of a translated gamma random variable $W + k$ is $\mathrm{ES}_\alpha(W + k) = \mathrm{ES}_\alpha(W) + k$, as the Expected Shortfall is translation invariant.

Applying these formulas to the Compound Poisson example we have

$$\mathrm{VaR}_{95\%} = 27{,}145, \qquad \mathrm{VaR}_{99\%} = 65{,}185,$$

$$\mathrm{ES}_{95\%} = 51{,}222, \qquad \mathrm{ES}_{99\%} = 96{,}890.$$

Panjer Recursions and FFT

Where the aggregate distribution has been determined by the Panjer recursion or by the FFT method, we have a probability function g_s and a distribution function, G_s for the discretized aggregate claim distribution, where

$$g_s = \Pr[S = s], \qquad G_s = \Pr[S \le s].$$

The α-VaR can be calculated by finding the smallest s such that $G_s > \alpha$. Given the α-VaR, Q_α, the α-Expected Shortfall can be calculated as

$$\mathrm{ES}_\alpha = \frac{1}{1 - \alpha} \sum_{s \ge Q_\alpha} s \, g_s.$$

The results for the Poisson-lognormal example are given in Table 4.1, using $M = 2^{20}$. For comparison we have also included the risk measures using the normal and translated gamma approximations. We notice that the Panjer and FFT methods give identical results, which is not surprising as the major approximation involved comes from discretizing the severity distribution, which is the same for both cases. The accuracy of these methods will be very much greater than either the normal or translated gamma methods. In this example, the normal distribution is too thin-tailed beyond the 99th percentile, as we would expect. The translated gamma distribution does not do a very good job here either. While it can provide a reasonable approximation to tail probabilities, it does less well for tail risk measures. In this case, the translated gamma significantly overestimates the tail risk measures. It performs much better for aggregate loss distributions with coefficient of skewness between 0 and 1.

It is also worth noting that, because in this case we need the full probability function for the aggregate loss (required for the Expected Shortfall calculations), the FFT method is significantly faster than the Panjer method.

Table 4.1. *Risk Measures for the Poisson-lognormal example ($\lambda = 30$, $\mu = 5$, $\sigma = 1.6$) using normal approximation, translated gamma approximation, Panjer recursions, and fast Fourier transforms.*

Risk Measure	Panjer Recursions	Fast Fourier Transform	Normal Approximation	Translated Gamma Approximation
VaR$_{95\%}$	32,764	32,764	33,310	27,145
VaR$_{99\%}$	52,434	52,434	40,476	65,185
ES$_{95\%}$	46,528	46,528	37,704	51,222
ES$_{99\%}$	75,192	75,192	44,040	96,890

4.7 Notes and Further Reading

The frequency-severity approach is useful where we have a substantial volume of relevant data on loss frequency and severity, and where the (quite strong) independence assumptions of the compound distribution are valid. Recall that we assume that all losses are independent of each other and that the number of losses is independent of the severity of the individual losses. These assumptions would not hold in many situations. For example, suppose we were interested in losses from extreme weather events. A major storm in an urban area is likely to create many losses and they are likely to be large. So, we might find that loss severity and loss frequency are not independent. Losses arising from capital market investments will generally not be independent, as the changing state of the local or global economy will impact each loss. We can extend the analysis of this chapter to deal with dependency between losses, to some extent, but the methods are still generally applicable only where there is little dependence between units of loss.

The area that is most suited to frequency-severity analysis is operational risk. Many types of operational risk can be viewed as arising from independent loss events generating independent losses. Examples include fraud, cyber risk, product defect, workplace injury, and legal risk. Operational risk has no upside, consistent with the models of events and severity used in this chapter. However, availability of sufficient data to select and fit frequency and severity models can be a challenge.

Another limitation of the frequency-severity approach is that we are often interested in the very rare, very severe, events and these may not be well-modelled by classical statistical techniques. In Chapter 5, we consider the statistics of extreme events.

Klugman et al. (2019) is an excellent source for more information on frequency-severity models, including proofs of all the results quoted in this chapter and extension of the Panjer recursion formula to zero-modified frequency distributions.

4.8 Exercises

Exercise 4.1 An insurer is building a model of losses from wind storms in an area of significant hurricane risk. The number of wind storms each year has been shown to follow a Poisson distribution with parameter $\lambda_1 = 5$. Each wind storm generates a number of claims, say, N_j for the jth wind storm, where the N_j are independent of the total number of wind storms and are independent and identically distributed, each following a negative binomial distribution with parameters $r = 100$, $\beta = 5$.

(a) Identify the distribution of the annual number of claims.
(b) Calculate the first three central moments of the annual number of claims.
(c) Describe the assumptions required for the aggregate losses from a single wind storm to have a compound negative binomial distribution. Do you think these assumptions are reasonable?

Exercise 4.2 A manufacturer has collected the following data showing the daily number of hours of production lost over several production plants:

Number of Days Lost	Frequency
0	1,220
1	196
2	65
3	15
4	4
≥ 5	0
Total	1,500

(a) Determine the maximum likelihood estimate for λ for a Poisson model.
(b) Determine a 95% confidence interval for λ.
(c) Determine the maximum likelihood estimates for (r, β) for a Negative Binomial model. You will need to use software (e.g., Excel Solver).
(d) Do either of these models fit the data?

(e) Fit a zero modified negative binomial model to the data. You are given that the maximum likelihood estimate of p_0 is the empirical probability, i.e. $1,220/1,500$. Does this model provide a significantly better fit to the data than the unmodified distributions?

Exercise 4.3 Let N denote a loss frequency random variable, with $p_k = \Pr[N = k]$, and let Y_k denote a discrete loss severity random variable, with $f_j = \Pr[Y_k = j]$. Assume that the Y_k are i.i.d., and are independent of N. Let g_s denote the probability function for the aggregate loss random variable, S.

(a) Explain why $\Pr[S = 0] \geq \Pr[N = 0]$.
(b) Show that, in general, $g_0 = P_N(f_0)$, where $P_N(z) = \mathrm{E}[z^N]$ is the probability generating function of N.
(c) You are given that $f_0 = 0$, $f_1 = 0.4$ and $f_2 = 0.6$. Calculate g_s for $s = 0, 1, 2, 3, 4$ (i) by general reasoning and (ii) by the Panjer recursion.

Exercise 4.4 A firm models its annual losses from cyber risk as a compound Poisson random variable, with Poisson parameter $\lambda = 10$. Individual losses are independent and identically distributed Pareto random variables, with $a = 3.0$ and $\theta = 4,000$.

(a) Calculate the mean and standard deviation of the annual cyber losses.
(b) Calculate the probability that an individual loss is less than 750.
(c) By installing improved security, the firm eliminates all cyber losses that cost less than 750. What is the frequency distribution of the remaining losses?
(d) Show that, for a Pareto random variable Y, with parameters a and θ, the random variable $Y - D|Y > D$ also has a Pareto distribution, with parameters a and $\theta + D$.
    Hence calculate the mean and standard deviation of the remaining individual cyber losses after the security improvements.
(e) Calculate the mean and standard deviation of the aggregate losses from cyber risk after the security improvements.

Exercise 4.5 A manufacturer uses machines with three critical components, labelled A, B, and C. The number of critical component failures each year has a Poisson distribution with parameter $\lambda = 50$.

If a failure happens the probability that it is a component A failure is 0.2, the probability that it is a component B failure is 0.5, and the probability of a component C failure is 0.3. Component A failures cost 1,000, component B failures cost 2,000, and component C failures cost 3,000.

The number and types of failures are independent.

(a) Use the normal approximation to the compound Poisson distribution to estimate the 95% VaR for the aggregate costs.
(b) Use the translated gamma approximation to the compound Poisson distribution to estimate the 95% VaR for the aggregate costs.
(c) State, with reasons, which estimate is more accurate.
(d) You are given the following information about the probability function g_s and the distribution function G_s, for the aggregate loss random variable, where s is in 000s.

s	g_s	G_s
124	0.01164	0.89112
125	0.01078	0.90189
126	0.00995	0.91184
127	0.00915	0.92099
128	0.00839	0.92937
129	0.00767	0.93704

   (i) Use the Panjer recursion to calculate g_s and G_s for $s = 130, 131$, and 132.
   (ii) Hence, determine the 95% VaR for S.

Exercise 4.6

(a) Use R to simulate 10,000 values from a compound Poisson distribution, with Poisson parameter $\lambda = 4$ and with severity distribution $Y \sim \log N(3, 4)$.
(b) Estimate the 95% Expected Shortfall.
(c) Calculate a 98% confidence interval for your Expected Shortfall estimate using the Manistre and Hancock formula from Section 3.6.1.
(d) Repeat (a), (b), and (c) for 10 different sets of scenarios.
(e) Use the results of the 10 scenarios to calculate a 98% confidence interval, using the repeated simulation approach. Comment on the relationship between this interval and that calculated in (d) above.
(f) Using Panjer recursions or fast Fourier transforms, calculate the Expected Shortfall. Comment on the accuracy of the confidence intervals calculated in (d) and (e) above.

Exercise 4.7 A North American car manufacturer makes 3 million cars per year. The company has been offered a cheaper version of a critical component of the airbag system for the cars. The current component is made in Canada and costs $12 per car. The alternative is made in a developing country in Asia, and is offered for $5 per car.

With the original, more expensive component, the risk of a defective component failing and causing accident or injury is 10^{-7} per car per year.

Using the cheaper component, the risk of a defective component failing and causing accident or injury is 10^{-4} per car per year.

In the event that the component fails (either type), the loss severity is assumed to have expected value $50,000 and standard deviation $100,000.

(a) Calculate the mean and the standard deviation of the aggregate annual losses from component failure assuming (i) the manufacturer continues using the original component and (ii) the manufacturer switches to the cheaper component.

(b) Calculate the 99% Expected Shortfall of aggregate losses assuming the manufacturer switches to the cheaper component. Use the normal approximation to the aggregate loss distribution.

(c) The company has decided to use the new component, as it will save the company millions of dollars each year, on average.

Show that the company expects to increase profits by switching to the cheaper component. (Assume no impact on car price or sales.)

(d) Describe briefly three major risks that the company is taking by making the decision to switch components.

(e) Describe for each of the three risks whether the following risk treatments might be appropriate:

   (i) Transfer by insurance.
   (ii) Retain.
   (iii) Mitigate probability or severity (or both).

Appendix: R Code for FFT and Panjer Recursions

In this appendix, we show the R code used to calculate the 95% VaR and Expected Shortfall in Table 4.1.

The discretization here is kept quite simple. A more sophisticated discretization method would give more accuracy but the difference will be small. Note that the *actuar* package in R will do the discretization. Here we use the basic R functions only.

Fast Fourier Transform

For the fast Fourier transform we use $M = 2^{20}$, as it is a power of 2 (this makes the numerical fft algorithm more efficient) and because the probability that the aggregate loss is greater than M is negligible. To check whether the upper limit is sufficient, check the sum of the probability function for the aggregate loss. It should be very close to 1.0

The discretized severity probability function and aggregate loss probability functions below are $f[k] = f_{k-1}$, and $g[k] = g_{k-1}$, where the shift in the argument accommodates $k = 0$. Similarly for the aggregate loss distribution function, $G[k] = \Pr[S \leq k - 1]$.

Note that the inverse transform function must be re-scaled by dividing by M.

After inverting the Fourier transform, we take the real part of the probability function g. The complex part will be very close to zero, but by taking the real part we get rid of any problems from trying to combine real and complex numbers subsequently.

1. `M ←2^20`   Set the upper limit for loss at 2^{20}

2. `f←rep(0,M)`   Initialize the severity probability function (p.f.)

3. `g←rep(0,M)`   Initialize the aggregate loss p.f.

4. `G←rep(0,M)`   Initialize the aggregate loss distribution function (d.f.)

5. `lambda←30.0`   Poisson distribution parameter

6. `mu←5.0`   Lognormal distribution parameter

7. `sigma←1.6`   Lognormal distribution parameter

8. `f[1]←plnorm(0.5,mu,sigma)`   Severity distribution discretization; set $f_0 = F(0.5)$

9. `for(j in 1:(M-1))`
   `f[j+1]←plnorm(j+0.5,mu,sigma)-plnorm(j-0.5,mu,sigma)`
   $f_j = f[j+1] = F(j+0.5) - F(j-0.5)$,
   $j = 1, 2, \ldots M - 1$

10. `ff←fft(f)`   Apply the Fourier transform

11. `fg←exp(lambda*(ff-1))`   Apply the Poisson pgf to the transformed severity p.f.

12. `g←fft(fg,inverse=TRUE)/M`   Invert and scale the transformed aggregate loss p.f.

13. `g←Re(g)`   Eliminate residual complex part

14. `G[1]←g[1]`   This is $\Pr[S = 0]$.

15. `for(j in 2:M) G[j]←G[j-1]+g[j]`   Calculate the d.f. for aggregate loss

16. `Q←max(c(1:M)[G<0.95])-1`   Find the 95%-VaR

17. `C←sum(c((Q+1):(M-1))*g[(Q+2):M])/0.05`   Calculate the 95% Expected Shortfall.

Panjer Recursion

The Panjer recursion in R starts exactly as the FFT example; it is not necessary for M to be a power of 2, but we used the same M in the Chapter example, for the purposes of comparison.

Steps 1 to 9 and 14 to 17 are exactly as in the FFT case above. Steps 10 to 13 are replaced with the following code:

10. `g[1] ←exp(lambda*(f[1]-1))`   Sets the probability of zero aggregate loss, g_0.
11. `for(k in 2:M){`   The compound Poisson Panjer recursion formula.
    `s←k-1`
    `g[k]←lambda/s*sum(c(1:s)*f[2:k]*g[s:1])}`

5

Extreme Value Theory

5.1 Summary

In this chapter, we present some key results from **extreme value theory** (EVT) and illustrate how EVT can be used to supplement traditional statistical analysis. We use EVT when we are concerned about the impact of very rare, very large losses. Because they are rare, we are unlikely to have much data, but using EVT we can infer the extreme tail behaviour of most distributions.

There are two different, but related, types of models for extreme value analysis. The first considers the distribution of the maximum value in a random sample of losses. These are called the **block maxima** models. The second comes from analysing the rare, very large losses, defined as the losses exceeding some high threshold. These are the **points over threshold** models. We present the key results for both of these, and show how they are connected. We derive formulas for the Value at Risk (VaR) and Expected Shortfall risk measures using EVT that are useful when the loss distribution is fat-tailed, and the risk measure parameter α is close to 1.0. We use examples throughout to highlight the potential uses in practical applications.

We present several key theorems in this chapter without proofs, as the mathematics required is beyond the scope of this text.

5.2 Introduction

In Chapter 4, we looked at distributions for loss frequency and severity, appropriate for a wide range of quantifiable risks. We saw that, given sufficient data, we can model the loss frequency and severity separately, and, assuming independence of frequency and severity, we can construct a distribution function for aggregate losses. Generally, the estimation part of the frequency

132

and severity analysis would use conventional statistical methods, such as maximum likelihood. These methods give a good overall fit to a distribution from a reasonably sized sample of data. However, the main weight in the fitting process will, implicitly, focus on the centre of the distribution. This may create a fit that is less satisfactory in the extreme right tail of the loss distribution, where we are concerned with the very rare, but potentially disastrous extreme losses. Even if a distribution appears to fit the data satisfactorily overall, it may not adequately model the part of the distribution in the extreme tails, beyond the range of the available data. In these cases, we can use EVT to supplement the traditional analysis.

Some examples of risk management cases which are suited to EVT include the following:

- An insurer might model the claims exceeding some extreme threshold to assess the mitigation benefits of a reinsurance strategy.
- An investment bank might model the potential for extreme stock price movements as part of its risk management operations.
- A company with exposure to currency risk might use an extreme value approach to guide its purchase of currency derivatives.
- Ocean engineers model extreme weather conditions to design ocean structures that can withstand, for example, a 1-in-500-year storm event.

5.3 Distributions of Block Maxima

5.3.1 Block Maxima and the Maximum Domain of Attraction

Suppose we have an i.i.d. sample of n values, $X_1, X_2, \ldots, X_n$, with common distribution function $F(x)$. Let M_n denote the maximum of the sample, that is, $M_n = \max\{X_1, X_2, \ldots\}$. The distribution function for M_n is

$$
\begin{aligned}
F_n(m) &= \Pr[M_n \le m] \\
&= \Pr[X_1 \le m] \Pr[X_2 \le m] \Pr[X_3 \le m] \cdots \Pr[X_n \le m] \\
&= (F(m))^n.
\end{aligned}
$$

If we consider the limit of this distribution as the block size increases, there are only two possibilities:

$$
\lim_{n \to \infty} F_n(m) = 0 \qquad \text{if and only if } F(m) < 1,
$$

$$
\lim_{n \to \infty} F_n(m) = 1 \qquad \text{if and only if } F(m) = 1.
$$

This is not particularly helpful. However, the first important result of EVT tells us that if we *normalize* the block maximum – that is, if we consider the random variable

$$M_n^* = \frac{M_n - d_n}{c_n},$$

where $c_n > 0$ and d_n are deterministic functions of n (involving the parameters of underlying distribution) – then in many cases we can find a limiting distribution for M_∞^*. That is, for some M_n we can find a distribution function $H(x)$, where $H(x)$ is not degenerate – meaning that the random variable M_∞^* is not a constant – and where

$$\lim_{n \to \infty} \Pr[M_n^* \leq x] = \lim_{n \to \infty} F_n(c_n x + d_n) = H(x).$$

In this case, we say that the distribution $F(x)$ is in the **maximum domain of attraction** (MDA) of H.

5.3.2 The Generalized Extreme Value Distribution

There are three important distributions for limits of normalized block maxima: the Gumbel, Fréchet, and Weibull distributions.

The Gumbel Distribution

$$F(x) = \exp \left\{ -\exp \left(-\frac{x - \mu}{\theta} \right) \right\}, \quad \theta > 0. \tag{5.1}$$

The Fréchet Distribution

$$F(x) = \exp \left\{ - \left(\frac{x - \mu}{\theta} \right)^{-\alpha} \right\}, \quad x > \mu; \alpha > 0; \theta > 0. \tag{5.2}$$

The Weibull EV Distribution

$$F(x) = \exp \left\{ - \left(\frac{\mu - x}{\theta} \right)^{\tau} \right\}, \quad x < \mu; \tau > 0; \theta > 0. \tag{5.3}$$

Note that this version of the Weibull is different from the specification in Chapter 4, but it is related by a sign change.

We can express these three distributions as variants of a single distribution, which is called the **generalized extreme value** (GEV) **distribution** with cumulative distribution function $H_\xi(x)$, where ξ is the **shape parameter**:

$$H_\xi(x) = \begin{cases} \exp \left(-(1 + \xi x)^{-\frac{1}{\xi}} \right) & \xi \neq 0, \xi x > -1, \\ \exp \left(-e^{-x} \right) & \xi = 0. \end{cases} \tag{5.4}$$

- If $\xi = 0$ this gives the Gumbel distribution, with $\mu = 0$, $\theta = 1$.
- If $\xi > 0$ this gives the Fréchet distribution, with $\mu = -1/\xi$, $\theta = 1/\xi$, $\alpha = 1/\xi$.
- If $\xi < 0$, this gives the Weibull EV distribution, with $\mu = -1/\xi$, $\theta = -1/\xi$, $\tau = -1/\xi$.

Note that as $\xi \to 0^+$, or $\xi \to 0^-$, we find that the Gumbel distribution is the limiting case of both the Fréchet and Weibull EV distributions.

The GEV can be adjusted for scale and location, to give $H_{\xi,\mu,\theta}$ where

$$
H_{\xi,\mu,\theta}(x) = \begin{cases} \exp\left(-(1 + \xi(x - \mu)/\theta)^{-\frac{1}{\xi}}\right) & \xi \neq 0, \ (1 + \xi \, (x - \mu)/\theta) > 0, \\ \exp\left(-e^{-(x-\mu)/\theta}\right) & \xi = 0, \end{cases}
$$

(5.5)

where μ is a location parameter, and θ is a scale parameter.

The importance of the GEV distribution is apparent from the following theorem, which says that if a distribution has a non-degenerate limiting distribution for M_n^* (and most of the distributions that we use fall into this category), then the limiting distribution must be the GEV distribution (Figure 5.1).

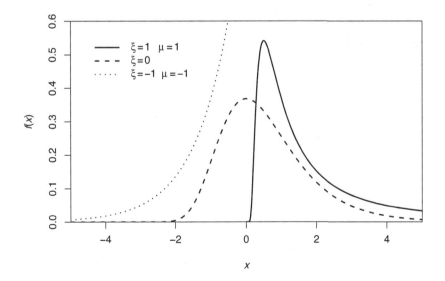

Figure 5.1 Generalized extreme value probability density functions; $\theta = 1$.

Theorem 5.1 *The Fisher–Tippett–Gnedenko Theorem*
If a distribution F lies in the MDA of a non-degenerate distribution H, then H must be the GEV distribution, H_ξ.

This classic result of EVT has some analogy to the **central limit theorem**. Consider $S_n = \sum_{j=1}^{n} X_j$ for i.i.d. X_j, with common mean $\mu > 0$ and common variance $\sigma^2 > 0$. There is, technically, no limiting distribution for S_n as n tends to infinity, as both the mean and variance of S_n will also tend to infinity. However, if we normalize the random variables, and consider

$$Z_n = \frac{S_n - n\mu}{\sigma\sqrt{n}},$$

then the central limit theorem tells us that $\lim_{n\to\infty} Z_n \sim N(0,1)$. That means that a single distribution – the standard normal distribution – is the limiting distribution of the normalized sum of any random sample of i.i.d. variables, regardless of the distribution of the individual variables, provided that they have a finite variance. In EVT, instead of considering the mean, we start by considering the maximum value in a sample, and it turns out that, like the mean, there is a limiting distribution, the GEV, that applies to the normalized sample maximum (in many cases) regardless of the distribution of the individual variables.

Example 5.1 For the exponential distribution with mean 1, you are given that $c_n = 1$ and $d_n = \log n$. Show that this distribution lies in the Gumbel MDA.

Solution 5.1 We have $F(x) = 1 - e^{-x}$. Then

$$\Pr\left[\frac{M_n - d_n}{c_n} \le x\right] = \Pr[M_n \le c_n x + d_n]$$
$$= (F(c_n x + d_n))^n = (1 - \exp(-(c_n x + d_n)))^n.$$

Now let $c_n = 1$ and $d_n = \log n$, so that

$$\Pr\left[\frac{M_n - d_n}{c_n} \le x\right] = \left(1 - e^{-x - \log n}\right)^n$$
$$= \left(1 - \frac{e^{-x}}{n}\right)^n.$$

On the right-hand side we have a term of the form $(1 + k/n)^n$ (where, in this case, $k = -e^{-x}$), and the limit of this expression as $n \to \infty$, is e^k. Hence

$$\lim_{n\to\infty} \left(1 - \frac{e^{-x}}{n}\right)^n = e^{-e^{-x}},$$

which shows that the exponential distribution is in the MDA of the H_0, or Gumbel distribution.

Example 5.2 For the exponential distribution with mean 1, calculate the probability that $M_n \leq 5$ for $n = 10$ and for $n = 100$, using the exponential distribution function directly, and using the limiting extreme value distribution.

Solution 5.2 We have $F(5) = 0.993262$, so

$$\Pr[M_{10} \leq 5] = (F(5))^{10} = 0.93463,$$
$$\Pr[M_{100} \leq 5] = (F(5))^{100} = 0.50861.$$

Using the Gumbel distribution, we have $c_n = 1, d_n = \log n$, so

$$\Pr[M_n \leq 5] = \Pr\left[\frac{M_n - d_n}{c_n} \leq \frac{5 - d_n}{c_n}\right] = \Pr[M_n - \log n \leq 5 - \log n],$$

and since the limiting distribution is Gumbel, for large n this probability is approximately

$$H_0(5 - \log n) = e^{-e^{-(5-\log n)}} = e^{-ne^{-5}},$$

which gives

$$\Pr[M_{10} \leq 5] \approx 0.93484, \qquad \Pr[M_{100} \leq 5] \approx 0.50977. \qquad \square$$

This does not appear to be all that useful at this stage, as we need to know the underlying distribution to know the normalizing functions, and if we know the underlying distribution, we can calculate the required probabilities directly. However, we shall see in Section 5.4 that we can derive some very useful information about tail risk without knowing the full distribution of the underlying random variable. The key parameter for risk management purposes will be the ξ parameter in $H_\xi(x)$.

An obvious question arising from the Fisher–Tippett–Gnedenko theorem is how we find the normalizing functions. One approach is to use the following result, which we state without proof (see Embrechts et al. (2013) for more details).

Theorem 5.2 *Consider a loss X with distribution function $F(x)$ and survival function $S(x) = 1 - F(x)$. Then $F(x)$ is in the MDA of H_ξ if and only if*

$$\lim_{n \to \infty} nS(c_n x + d_n) = -\log H_\xi(x) = \begin{cases} (1 + \xi x)^{-\frac{1}{\xi}} & \text{for } \xi \neq 0, \\ e^{-x} & \text{for } \xi = 0. \end{cases} \tag{5.6}$$

$\square$

In some cases, we can use this result to determine c_n and d_n. One example is the Pareto distribution, as we demonstrate next.

Example 5.3 Determine the limiting distribution for a maximum of Pareto(α, λ) random values, and find the normalizing sequences c_n and d_n.

Solution 5.3 The Pareto(α, λ) distribution function is

$$F(x) = 1 - \left(\frac{\lambda}{\lambda + x} \right)^\alpha,$$

so

$$nS(c_n x + d_n) = n \left(\frac{\lambda}{\lambda + d_n + c_n x} \right)^\alpha$$

$$= n \left(1 + \frac{d_n}{\lambda} + \frac{c_n}{\lambda} x \right)^{-\alpha} \tag{5.7}$$

$$= \left(n^{-1/\alpha} + \frac{n^{-1/\alpha} d_n}{\lambda} + \frac{n^{-1/\alpha} c_n}{\lambda} x \right)^{-\alpha}. \tag{5.8}$$

The form of $nS(c_n x + d_n)$ in equation (5.8) is similar to the Fréchet form of $-\log H(x)$ in equation (5.6), where $\alpha > 0$, indicating that $\xi = \frac{1}{\alpha} > 0$. To match the Fréchet form of $-\log H_\xi(x)$, we need (at least asymptotically)

$$n^{-1/\alpha} + \frac{n^{-1/\alpha} d_n}{\lambda} = 1, \quad \text{and} \quad \frac{n^{-1/\alpha} c_n}{\lambda} = \xi = \frac{1}{\alpha},$$

$$\Rightarrow d_n = (n^{1/\alpha} - 1)\lambda, \quad \text{and} \quad c_n = \frac{\lambda n^{1/\alpha}}{\alpha}.$$

In summary, the Pareto distribution is in the MDA of the Fréchet distribution with shape parameter $\xi = 1/\alpha$ and normalizing functions $c_n = \frac{\lambda n^{1/\alpha}}{\alpha}$ and $d_n = (n^{1/\alpha} - 1)\lambda$.

□

5.3.3 Notes on the Generalized Extreme Value (GEV) Distributions

The Fréchet Distribution

- The Fréchet distribution is the GEV distribution, with $\xi > 0$.
- The Fréchet distribution is bounded below, with $x > \mu - \frac{\theta}{\xi}$, for μ and θ as in equation (5.5).
- The Fréchet distribution is fat-tailed and is relatively popular for use in managing extreme risks in finance and insurance.

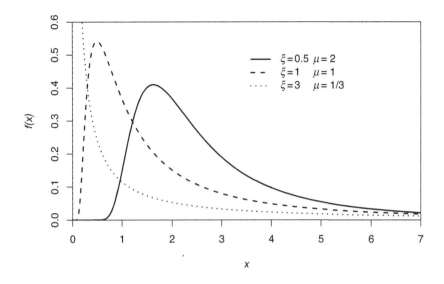

Figure 5.2 Fréchet probability density functions; $\theta = 1$.

- The distribution function is often expressed in terms of $\alpha = \frac{1}{\xi}$. This is called the **tail index** of the distribution.
- Larger values of ξ (and hence smaller values of α) indicate a fatter-tailed distribution.
- The Fréchet distribution is in the Fréchet MDA.
- For any distribution in the MDA of the Fréchet distribution, there are only a finite number of moments, up to $\alpha = 1/\xi$. That is, for a positive integer k, if $k < \frac{1}{\xi}$ we have $E[X^k] < \infty$, but for $k \geq \frac{1}{\xi}$, we have $E[X^k] = \infty$. This means that a distribution with an infinite number of moments (even if it is fat-tailed) cannot be in the MDA of the Fréchet distribution.
- Distributions in the Frechet MDA include the Pareto, Student's t, and Burr distributions.
- In Figure 5.2, we show density functions for $\xi = 0.5$, 1, and 3. The scale parameter is $\theta = 1$ and the location parameter is set at $1/\xi$ to give a distribution bounded below at 0 in each case.
- Another characterization of the Frechet MDA uses the following definition:

Definition 5.3 A positive function L is **slowly varying at** ∞ if for any $t > 0$,

$$\lim_{x \to \infty} \frac{L(tx)}{L(x)} = 1.$$

Examples of slowly varying functions include $\log(x)$ and $(k + x^{-1})^{-\alpha}$. A distribution function F is in the MDA of the Fréchet distribution with parameter ξ if and only if

$$S(x) = x^{-1/\xi} L(x), \qquad (5.9)$$

where $L(x)$ is a function which is slowly varying at ∞.

The Gumbel Distribution

- The Gumbel distribution is the GEV distribution with $\xi = 0$.
- The distribution is unbounded.
- Many distributions are in the MDA of the Gumbel distribution, ranging from quite thin-tailed distributions, such as the normal and exponential, to quite fat-tailed, such as the gamma, lognormal, and inverse Gaussian. Note that even though the Gumbel distribution is not bounded, the distributions in its MDA may be bounded (e.g., the lognormal random variable is strictly positive).
- Distributions in the Gumbel MDA have infinite number of moments – that is, $E[X^k] < \infty$ for any $k = 1, 2, 3, \ldots$
- The Gumbel distribution is in the MDA of the Gumbel distribution.
- All Gumbel distributions have the same shape, as the shape parameter, ξ, is fixed. The location and scale may vary.
- The Gumbel density function is illustrated in Figure 5.3.

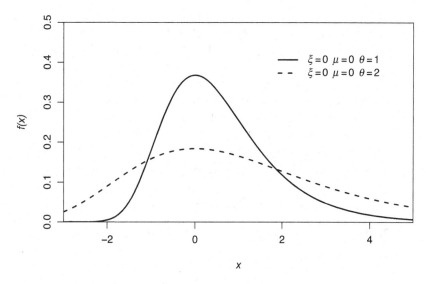

Figure 5.3 Gumbel probability density functions

The Weibull EV Distribution

- The Weibull EV distribution is the GEV distribution with $\xi < 0$.
- The Weibull EV distribution is bounded above at $\mu - 1/\xi$. It is, therefore, less useful for most large loss modelling, but can be useful for maxima of bounded losses.
- The Weibull EV distribution is related to the Weibull distribution by a sign change – that is, if Y is a Weibull EV-distributed random variable, with $\mu = 0, \theta = 1$, then $1 + \xi Y$ is a Weibull distributed random variable.
- The Weibull EV distribution, beta distribution, and uniform distribution are in the MDA of the Weibull EV distribution.
- In Figure 5.4, we show density functions for $\xi = -1, -0.5$, and -0.25. The scale parameter is $\theta = 1$, and the location parameter is set at $1/\xi$ to give a distribution bounded above at 0 in each case.

5.3.4 Estimating the GEV Parameters

For a distribution lying in the MDA of the GEV distribution, the Fisher–Tippett–Gnedenko theorem tells us that $(M_n - d_n)/c_n$ approximately follows the GEV distribution, with some parameters μ', θ', and ξ, say. In this case, the non-normalized random variable M_n also approximately follows the GEV

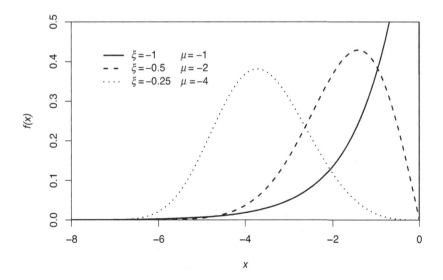

Figure 5.4 Weibull EV probability density functions; $\theta = 1$.

distribution, with adjusted location and scale parameters, μ and θ, but with the same shape parameter ξ. We can, therefore, estimate ξ, which is the key parameter for classifying the extreme value distribution, by fitting the GEV to block maxima of our data, using maximum likelihood estimation.

Assume we have a set of data, which we divide into k blocks, each with n values. This gives us k sample points of the n-block maxima. Let m_j denote the maximum of the jth block, for $j = 1, 2, \ldots, k$. The division of the data into blocks is natural for data arising as a time series, such as stock market data or flood levels. If the data has no natural ordering, then it may be randomly partitioned into blocks.

By differentiating the GEV distribution function $H_\xi(x)$, we find the GEV density function $h_\xi(x)$,

$$h_\xi(x) = (1 + \xi x)^{-(1+\frac{1}{\xi})} e^{-(1+\xi x)^{-\frac{1}{\xi}}}, \tag{5.10}$$

or, for the more general distribution, including scale and location parameters,

$$h_{\xi, \mu, \theta}(y) = \frac{1}{\theta} \left(1 + \xi \left(\frac{y - \mu}{\theta} \right) \right)^{-(1+\frac{1}{\xi})} e^{-(1+\xi(\frac{y-\mu}{\theta}))^{-\frac{1}{\xi}}}. \tag{5.11}$$

Assuming independence of the block maxima, then for the maximum likelihood estimators, we find the parameters which maximize the sum of the log densities of the sample. That is, we maximize $l(\xi, \mu, \theta)$ where

$$l(\xi, \mu, \theta) = \sum_{j=1}^{k} \log(h_{\xi, \mu, \theta}(m_j)) \tag{5.12}$$

$$= -k \log(\theta) - \left(1 + \frac{1}{\xi} \right) \sum_{j=1}^{k} \log \left(1 + \xi \left(\frac{m_j - \mu}{\theta} \right) \right)$$

$$- \sum_{j=1}^{k} \left(1 + \xi \left(\frac{m_j - \mu}{\theta} \right) \right)^{-\frac{1}{\xi}}. \tag{5.13}$$

In practice, we must balance conflicting data requirements. With a fixed sample size, we must decide how large the blocks will be. If they are very large, we can be more confident that the maxima lie in the tail of the distribution, suitable for applying the GEV distribution function, but the number of data points may be small. On the other hand, if we use smaller blocks to get a larger sample of block maxima, we may not be sufficiently near to the tail of the distribution to find accurate parameter estimates.

The result may be that even with relatively large data sets, the standard error of the parameter estimates is large. This is particularly true for the ξ parameter,

Table 5.1. *Annual maxima of monthly losses on the S&P/TSX composite index, 1956–2012, per $100 invested, in chronological order (by rows)*

5.88	10.25	0.85	5.06	4.68	2.37	8.52	3.35
0.66	6.68	7.47	5.72	4.25	11.03	10.09	6.47
3.57	11.55	10.52	5.74	7.05	5.81	5.31	10.18
19.41	14.04	10.14	5.53	3.80	6.53	4.83	25.52
2.70	6.75	8.40	3.37	4.44	3.31	6.89	1.97
3.63	4.89	22.45	6.29	8.77	14.23	7.76	3.02
3.97	5.82	3.63	6.42	18.23	6.52	3.78	9.06

which is problematic, since it is the parameter that indicates which form of the GEV distribution is appropriate.

Solving for the maximum likelihood estimates can be done very conveniently with suitable software packages.

Example 5.4 Table 5.1 shows the block maxima for monthly losses (in %) on the S&P/TSX composite index, over a period of 56 years, from 1956–2012. The block size is 12 months. Assume the values are independent and identically distributed:

(a) Find the maximum likelihood estimates of the GEV distribution parameters for this data.
(b) Find the MLE for the GEV distribution parameters using a block size of 24 months.

Solution 5.4 We used the f i t . GEV function from the R package *QRM* (Pfaff and McNeil, 2020). This generates parameter estimates and standard errors.

(a) We find, using the annual data, that the MLE parameter estimates are as follows (standard errors in parentheses):

$$\mu = 5.009(0.450), \quad \theta = 3.012(0.346), \quad \text{and } \xi = 0.1575(0.098).$$

This indicates that the Fréchet distribution is the most appropriate, although the Gumbel distribution is also possible.

(b) Using 24-month blocks, we find the following estimates and standard errors:

$$\mu = 7.144(0.60), \quad \theta = 2.655(0.53), \quad \text{and } \xi = 0.389(0.213),$$

which, again, points to the Fréchet distribution, possibly with a heavier
tail, but does not rule out the Gumbel distribution. Note that we expect the
μ and θ parameters to change, as they are functions of the block size. For
large n though, the value of ξ should be stable for different block sizes.

As we expect, the smaller sample size of block maxima (using
24-month blocks) leads to larger standard errors.   □

An interest in the tail behaviour of a random variable does not always mean
an interest in block maxima; the block maximum may not be very extreme
in some cases, and in others, a block may have several values that would be
considered extreme. In the example above, using 24-month blocks, we lose the
fifth-largest value from the 12-month blocks (14.04), because it is adjacent
to an even larger maximum. In the next section, we select extreme values
differently, by considering all the values falling beyond some threshold.

5.4 Distribution of Excess Losses Over a Threshold

In Example 5.4, we saw that much of the data is discarded and some
non-extreme data points are incorporated into the estimation. This seems,
intuitively, to be an inefficient way to model tail behaviour. We now expand
the analysis, to consider the distribution of losses which are in the tail of
the underlying distribution, where we define the tail by setting a threshold
level corresponding to a very large loss. We then consider the distribution
of exceedances, or excess losses, which are the differences between the loss
values and the threshold. That is, for an underlying loss random variable X,
and threshold $d > 0$, the **excess loss** is $Y_d = X - d | X > d$. This method is
often called the **peaks** or **points over threshold** (POT) approach.

From this definition, given that X is continuous, and that $\Pr[X > d] > 0$,
the excess loss random variable Y_d is also continuous, and $Y_d \geq 0$. We can
derive the distribution and density function for Y_d in terms of the functions for
X, as follows.

5.4.1 The Excess Loss Random Variable

The distribution function of the excess loss $Y_d = X - d | X > d$, is denoted
$F_d(y)$, and the survival function is $S_d(y) = 1 - F_d(y)$. These are related to the
underlying distribution function and survival functions, F_X and S_X, as

$$F_d(y) = \Pr[Y_d \le y] = \Pr\left[X - d \le y \mid X > d\right]$$

$$= \frac{F_X(y + d) - F_X(d)}{1 - F_X(d)}$$

$$= \frac{S_X(d) - S_X(y + d)}{S_X(d)}$$

$$= 1 - \frac{S_X(y + d)}{S_X(d)}$$

$$\Rightarrow S_d(y) = \frac{S_X(y + d)}{S_X(d)}.$$

Similarly, the probability density function for Y_d is

$$f_d(y) = \frac{f_X(y + d)}{S_X(d)}.$$

The expected value of Y, as a function of the excess threshold d, is called the **mean excess loss** (MEL) of X and is denoted $e(d)$; that is,

$$e(d) = \mathrm{E}\left[X - d \mid X > d\right]. \tag{5.14}$$

For a continuous random variable, X, we have

$$e(d) = \mathrm{E}\left[X - d \mid X > d\right] = \frac{1}{S_X(d)} \left(\int_d^\infty (y - d) f_X(y) \, dy \right) \tag{5.15}$$

$$= \frac{1}{S_X(d)} \left(\int_d^\infty y f_X(y) \, dy - d \int_d^\infty f_X(y) dy \right)$$

$$= \frac{1}{S_X(d)} \left(\int_d^\infty y f_X(y) \, dy - d \, S_X(x) \right)$$

$$= \frac{\mathrm{E}[X] - \mathrm{E}[X \wedge d]}{S_X(d)}. \tag{5.16}$$

Similarly to the GEV distribution, which provided the asymptotic distribution for block maxima, the general asymptotic distribution for excess losses is the **generalized Pareto distribution** (GPD). This distribution is closely related to the GEV distribution.

5.4.2 The Generalized Pareto Distribution (GPD)

The distribution function of the **generalized Pareto distribution** (GPD) is, for $\beta > 0$,

$$G_{\xi,\beta}(x) = \begin{cases} 1 - (1 + \xi x/\beta)^{-1/\xi} & \xi \ne 0, \\ 1 - e^{-x/\beta} & \xi = 0, \end{cases} \tag{5.17}$$

where $x \geq 0$ for $\xi \geq 0$, and $0 \leq x \leq -\beta/\xi$ for $\xi < 0$. In the GPD distribution, β is a scale parameter and ξ is the shape parameter. There is no location parameter as the distribution is fixed, with a lower bound at zero.

Notes

1. When $\xi > 0$ the GPD is a regular Pareto distribution, as in Section 4.4.4, with parameters $a = 1/\xi, \theta = \beta/\xi$.
2. For $0 < \xi < 1$, the mean of $X \sim \text{GPD}_{\xi,\beta}$ is

$$E[X] = \frac{\beta}{1 - \xi}.$$

For $\xi \geq 1$ the mean does not exist.
3. When $\xi > 0$, and for integer k, the kth moment of the GPD exists only for $k < 1/\xi$.
4. When $\xi = 0$ the GPD is the exponential distribution with mean β.
5. When $\xi < 0$, the distribution is a generalized beta distribution, which is left and right bounded. The left bound is zero, the right bound is $-\beta/\xi$.
6. $G_{\xi,\beta}(y) = 1 + \log H_\xi(y/\beta)$ where H_ξ is the GEV distribution function, from equation (5.4).

Example 5.5 Show that, if $Y \sim \text{GPD}_{\xi,\beta}$, for $\xi \geq 0$, $\beta > 0$, and $Z = Y - k | Y > k$ then

$$Z \sim \text{GPD}_{\xi,\beta^*} \text{ where } \beta^* = \beta + \xi k,$$

and hence derive the MEL function for the $\text{GPD}_{\xi,\beta}$ distribution.

Solution 5.5 Consider the survival function of Z. We assume first that $\xi > 0$, and show that the survival function for Z is GPD with ξ unchanged, and a new β^*.

$$\Pr[Z > t] = \Pr[Y - k > t | Y > k] = \Pr[Y > t + k | Y > k]$$

$$= \frac{1 - G_{\xi,\beta}(t + k)}{1 - G_{\xi,\beta}(k)}$$

$$= \frac{\left(1 + \frac{\xi}{\beta}(t + k)\right)^{-\frac{1}{\xi}}}{\left(1 + \frac{\xi}{\beta}(k)\right)^{-\frac{1}{\xi}}}$$

$$= \left(1 + \frac{\xi t}{\beta + \xi k}\right)^{-\frac{1}{\xi}}$$

$$= 1 - G_{\xi,\beta^*}(t),$$

where $\beta^* = \beta + \xi k$ as required.

If $\xi = 0$, then Y has an exponential distribution, with mean β and the survival function for Z is

$$\Pr[Z > t] = \Pr[Y > t + k | Y > k] = \frac{e^{-\frac{t+k}{\beta}}}{e^{-\frac{k}{\beta}}} = e^{-\frac{t}{\beta}},$$

which shows that the distribution of Z is also exponential with mean β (this is known as the **memoryless property** of the exponential distribution).

The mean excess loss function for the $GPD_{\xi,\beta}$ distribution is the expected value of the random variable Z (i.e. $\beta^*/(1 - \xi)$), expressed as a function of the excess point k. That is,

$$e(k) = \begin{cases} \dfrac{\beta + \xi k}{1 - \xi} & \text{for } 0 < \xi < 1, \\ \beta & \text{for } \xi = 0. \end{cases} \tag{5.18}$$

For $\xi \geq 1$, $e(k) = \infty$ since in this case the GPD distribution does not have a finite first moment. $\qquad\square$

The important point to note from this example is that for the GPD distribution, the MEL function is a straight line. If $\xi \in (0, 1)$, it has slope $\xi/(1 - \xi)$, and if $\xi = 0$, the MEL function is flat.

The relationship between the GPD and GEV distributions is captured in the following theorem.

Theorem 5.4 *The Pickands–Balkema–De Haan Theorem*
Let F denote the distribution function of a random variable X which is bounded above at $x^{sup} \leq \infty$. Then

$$F \in MDA\left(H_\xi\right) \iff \lim_{d \to x^{sup}} \sup_{0 \leq x \leq x^{sup}} \left| F_d(x) - G_{\xi,\beta}(x) \right| = 0, \tag{5.19}$$

for some function β.

What this theorem tells us is that every distribution in the MDA of H_ξ will have a distribution for excess losses that converges to the $G_{\xi,\beta}$ distribution, as the threshold tends to the maximum loss. In practice, this means that for a sufficiently high threshold d, the excess loss random variable Y_d will (approximately) follow the GPD with the same shape parameter ξ as the GEV, and with a scale parameter β. Since the left tail of Y_d is fixed at 0, there is no need for a location parameter.

In order to use the theorem, we need to identify the threshold beyond which we can assume that excess losses are close to being GPD.

One approach is to examine the empirical mean excess loss function for the data, as a function of the threshold d. Given an ordered sample,

$x_{(1)}, x_{(2)}, \ldots x_{(n)}$, we define the empirical mean excess loss function $\hat{e}(x_{(j)})$, for $j = 1, 2, \ldots, n - 1$, as

$$\hat{e}(x_{(j)}) = \sum_{k=j+1}^{n} \frac{x_{(k)}}{n - j} - x_{(j)}.$$

That is, for each ordered sample value $x_{(j)}$, we take the mean of the observations which are larger than $x_{(j)}$, and subtract $x_{(j)}$ to get an estimator of the MEL evaluated at $x_{(j)}$.

We know that the GPD mean excess loss function is a straight line, even if the mean excess loss function of the underlying distribution is not. Hence, the region where the empirical mean excess loss function becomes approximately linear indicates where the GPD becomes a good approximation to the distribution of excess losses.

Once we have chosen a suitable threshold, d^*, say, we consider the reduced sample of values of $X_{(j)} - d^*$ for all $X_{(j)} > d^*$, and fit the GPD to the reduced sample.

If the mean excess loss function has positive gradient, then we fit the tail data to the Pareto distribution. If the mean excess loss function appears flat, then we fit the tail data to the exponential distribution.

In practice, identifying an appropriate threshold can be challenging. As we get up to the largest data points, the empirical MEL tends to be very volatile. See Section 5.5 for an illustration.

5.4.3 Risk Measures for the GPD

Suppose we have a loss distribution function, F_X, and that for some threshold d, the excess loss random variable $X - d | X > d$ may be assumed to follow the GPD with parameters ξ and β.

We can estimate the VaR, assuming it lies above d, using the GPD for the excess distribution above d.

For example, for $\xi > 0$, consider first the survival function for some $x > d$. Let $S_X(x)$ denote the survival function of the original distribution, and let $S_d(y)$ denote the GPD survival function for the excess loss distribution. Then

$$\Pr[X > x] = \Pr[X > d] \Pr[X > x | X > d]$$
$$= \Pr[X > d] \Pr[X - d > x - d | X > d]$$
$$= S_X(d) S_d(x - d) \tag{5.20}$$
$$= S_X(d) \left(1 + \frac{\xi}{\beta}(x - d)\right)^{-1/\xi}. \tag{5.21}$$

So we can treat the survival function as a combination of the underlying survival function up to the threshold d, and the GPD survival function beyond d.

If we replace x with the α-VaR, $Q_\alpha(X)$, assuming $Q_\alpha(X) > d$, we have

$$\Pr[X > Q_\alpha(X)] = 1 - \alpha = \Pr[X > d]\,\Pr[X > Q_\alpha(X)|X > d]$$

$$\Rightarrow 1 - \alpha = S_X(d)\left(1 + \frac{\xi(Q_\alpha - d)}{\beta}\right)^{-\frac{1}{\xi}}$$

$$\Rightarrow Q_\alpha = d + \frac{\beta}{\xi}\left(\left(\frac{S_X(d)}{1-\alpha}\right)^{\xi} - 1\right). \tag{5.22}$$

Equation (5.22) shows that the α-VaR can be calculated using the GPD parameters β and ξ, together with $S_X(d)$, which is the survival probability at the threshold d from the original distribution. In practice, we may not know the distribution for the underlying X, which means that we must approximate $S_X(d)$. The usual (and intuitive) non-parametric estimator is the proportion of the sample which is greater than d. For example, suppose the threshold d is selected at the 950th smallest sample value from a sample size of 1,000; that is, $d = x_{(950)}$. Then there are 50 values greater than d which form the sample for estimating the GPD parameters. The empirical probability that $X > d$ is $\hat{S}(d) = 50/1,000$. So, in general, assuming that d is selected such that j sample values exceed d, out of a sample of n values,

$$S_X(d) \approx \frac{\text{Number of values of } x_i > d}{\text{Total number of values of } x_i} = \frac{j}{n}. \tag{5.23}$$

We can also use the GPD to evaluate extreme Expected Shortfall risk measures. We assume, for convenience, that losses are continuous (at least in the tail), in which case the α-Expected Shortfall of the loss is related to the α-VaR (Q_α), and the mean excess loss (MEL) function, $e_X(d)$, as follows:

$$\text{ES}_\alpha = E[X|X > Q_\alpha]$$
$$= Q_\alpha + E[X - Q_\alpha|X > Q_\alpha]$$
$$= Q_\alpha + e_X(Q_\alpha). \tag{5.24}$$

Suppose that for a continuous loss random variable X, and for a given threshold d, the distribution of $Y_d = X - d|X > d$ is GPD with parameters ξ, β. Suppose also that we are interested in the α-Expected Shortfall of X, where $Q_\alpha > d$. If $\xi \geq 1$, the Expected Shortfall does not exist (moments higher than the $(1/\xi)$th are infinite for the GPD).

If $\xi < 1$, then we consider

$$X - Q_\alpha|X > Q_\alpha = Y_d - (Q_\alpha - d)|Y_d > (Q_\alpha - d).$$

Let $k = Q_\alpha - d$, then from Example 5.5, we know that $Z = Y_d - k|Y_d > k$ follows a GPD with parameters ξ and β^* where

$$\beta^* = \beta + \xi\, k = \beta + \xi\, (Q_\alpha - d).$$

We will use $\mathrm{E}[Z]$ for the Expected Shortfall, as

$$e_X(Q_\alpha) = \mathrm{E}[Z] = \frac{\beta + \xi(Q_\alpha - d)}{1 - \xi}$$

so

$$
\begin{aligned}
\mathrm{ES}_\alpha &= Q_\alpha + e_X(Q_\alpha) \\
&= Q_\alpha + \frac{\beta + \xi(Q_\alpha - d)}{1 - \xi} \\
\Rightarrow \mathrm{ES}_\alpha &= \frac{1}{1-\xi}\left(Q_\alpha + \beta - \xi\, d\right).
\end{aligned}
\tag{5.25}
$$

Note that we have assumed that the α parameter for the risk measure is sufficiently far into the tail of the distribution that the GPD distribution is appropriate for the random variable $X - Q_\alpha | X > Q_\alpha$.

Example 5.6 An analyst is estimating risk measures for severity data for auto insurance policies. She has a sample of 200 values, and has set the GPD threshold at $d = 1.0$ (in \$ millions). The parameters of the GPD are $\xi = 0.80$ and $\beta = 0.65$.

The 24 values from the sample which exceed the threshold are given in Table 5.2, in descending order:

(a) Calculate the 95%, 99%, and 99.9% quantiles, using the GPD.
(b) Calculate the 95%, 99%, and 99.9% Expected Shortfalls, using the GPD.

Solution 5.6

(a) First, we check that the empirical 95% quantile lies above $d = 1.0$. We see from the data that $Q_{95\%} \approx X_{(191)} = 2.3 > d$ as required.

Table 5.2. *Data points exceeding threshold, $d = 1.0$, from a sample of 200, for Example 5.6*

11.33	6.17	4.67	4.41	4.20	3.31	2.97	2.65	2.58	2.29	2.12	1.76
1.35	1.34	1.28	1.27	1.25	1.15	1.13	1.10	1.09	1.07	1.02	1.01

Next, we estimate $S_X(1.0)$. From the sample, we have 24 values exceeding the threshold from a total sample of 200 data values, so $S_X(d) \approx 24/200 = 0.12$.
Then using equation (5.22) we have

$$Q_\alpha = d + \frac{\beta}{\xi}\left(\left(\frac{S_X(d)}{1-\alpha}\right)^\xi - 1\right)$$

$$\Rightarrow Q_{95\%} = 1.0 + \frac{0.65}{0.80}\left(\left(\frac{0.12}{0.05}\right)^{0.8} - 1\right) = 1.82,$$

$$Q_{99\%} = 1.0 + \frac{0.65}{0.80}\left(\left(\frac{0.12}{0.01}\right)^{0.8} - 1\right) = 6.12,$$

$$Q_{99.9\%} = 1.0 + \frac{0.65}{0.80}\left(\left(\frac{0.12}{0.001}\right)^{0.8} - 1\right) = 37.6.$$

(b) From equation (5.25) we have

$$ES_\alpha = \frac{1}{1-\xi}\left(Q_\alpha + \beta - \xi d\right)$$

$$\Rightarrow ES_{95\%} = \frac{1}{0.2}(1.82 + 0.65 - 0.8(1.0)) = 8.35,$$

$$ES_{99\%} = \frac{1}{0.2}(6.12 + 0.65 - 0.8(1.0)) = 29.85,$$

$$ES_{99.9\%} = \frac{1}{0.2}(37.6 + 0.65 - 0.8(1.0)) = 187.25. \qquad \Box$$

5.4.4 The Hill Estimator

An alternative approach to the empirical mean loss function for estimating d, β, and ξ is the **Hill estimator**, which estimates the tail index, $\alpha = 1/\xi$, for $\xi > 0$.

The Hill estimator uses the fact that for distributions in the MDA of the Fréchet distribution, the survival function can be written

$$S(x) = L(x)\, x^{-1/\xi} = L(x)\, x^{-\alpha},$$

where $L(x)$ is slowly varying at infinity. We then find that the mean excess loss function of the log of the loss data (we assume the losses are > 0) converges to $\xi = 1/\alpha$.

Suppose we have an ordered sample of loss data, $x_{(1)}, \ldots, x_{(n)}$. The Hill estimator is

$$\hat{\alpha}_j^H = \left(\sum_{k=j+1}^{n} \frac{\log(x_{(k)})}{n-j+1} - \log(x_{(j)}) \right)^{-1},$$

which is a slight variant of the empirical MEL function above, applied to the logs of the sample values.

Since different values of j will give different estimators, it is customary to plot values for a range of j, towards the higher end of the sample.

We select a threshold at the $(n - j)$th sample value, that is, at $d = x_{(n-j)}$, which means that the probability that $X > d$ is estimated to be $\hat{S}(d) = j/n$. The Hill estimator for the survival function for $x > x_{(n-j)}$ is then

$$\hat{S}^H(x) = \frac{j}{n} \left(\frac{x}{x_{(n-j)}} \right)^{-\hat{\alpha}_j^H}.$$

McNeil et al. (2015) show that this is similar to the estimate derived from equation (5.21), replacing $S_X(d)$ with the empirical estimate j/n, but without the scale parameter β.

5.5 Example: US Hurricane Losses, 1940–2012

In this section, we explore the use of extreme value distributions in the analysis of data relating to losses in the United States of America between 1940 and 2012, from 179 hurricanes and tropical storms.[1] The data is adjusted to 2017 values and losses are expressed in $millions.

The data is shown in Figure 5.5.

This analysis would be important, for example, for an insurer or reinsurer with exposure to hurricane losses. Suppose we are interested in estimating the 99% VaR or Expected Shortfall of the hurricane severity distribution. The five largest losses in the sample (in 2017 $millions) are

$L_{(175)}$	$L_{(176)}$	$L_{(177)}$	$L_{(178)}$	$L_{(179)}$
54,660	65,900	71,790	79,110	91,130

The empirical estimate of the 99% VaR from the data is approximately 81,514 (unsmoothed). The empirical estimate of the 99% Expected Shortfall is

---

[1] The data is derived from www.icatdamageestimator.com.

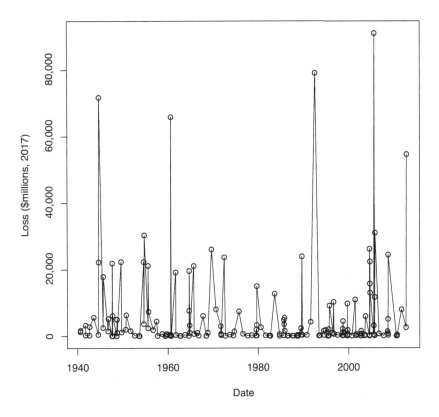

Figure 5.5 US hurricane loss data, 1940-2012, in 2017 values (millions)

the average of the values greater than 81,514, but there is only one such value, so the empirical Expected Shortfall is 91,130.

It is interesting to re-estimate the risk measures using the generalized Pareto distribution to model the tail of the severity distribution.

We first plot the empirical mean excess loss (MEL) function. The result is shown in Figure 5.6 The lower plot omits the final five values – the MEL typically fluctuates significantly in the tail. The increasing linear trend above a threshold of around 20,000 indicates that a GPD with positive ξ parameter should be the best fit.

Using the 'fit.GPD' function from the 'QRM' package in R, with a threshold of 20,000, gives maximum likelihood estimates for the GPD parameters (with associated standard errors) of

$$\hat{\xi} = 0.75(0.41), \qquad \hat{\beta} = 7,005(3,066).$$

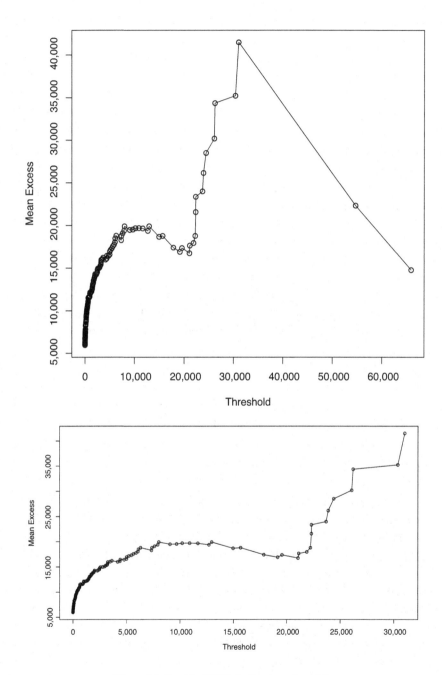

Figure 5.6 Empirical MEL for hurricane loss data

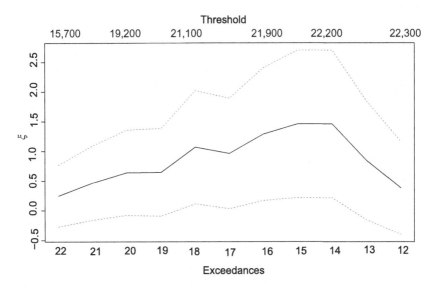

Figure 5.7 MLE estimators for ξ using different numbers of tail values, for the US hurricane loss data

Moving the threshold to 21,000 gives

$$\hat{\xi} = 1.2(0.53), \qquad \hat{\beta} = 3,850(1,960),$$

which demonstrates the difficulty of estimating the ξ parameter in practice. In Figure 5.7, we show the ξ estimates and 95% confidence intervals for the storm data, based on a range of the number of tail loss values to be included in the calculation.

In Figure 5.8, we show the estimates of ξ, with 95% confidence bands, using the Hill method. The range of thresholds is the same as in Figure 5.7, but the estimated values of ξ are quite different. The Hill estimator is less accurate than the maximum likelihood estimator used in Figure 5.7, and this sample does not generate enough tail values for the method to be suitable.

We use the fitted GPD, assuming a threshold of 20,000, to estimate the risk measures for the loss distribution. We use formula (5.22) for the estimated 99% VaR. That is

$$Q_\alpha = d + \frac{\beta}{\xi} \left(\left(\frac{1-\alpha}{S_X(d)} \right)^{-\xi} - 1 \right),$$

where $\alpha = 0.99$, $d = 20{,}000$, $\beta = 7{,}005$, $\xi = 0.75$. We estimate $S_X(d)$ using the empirical survival function at $d = 20{,}000$; that is, using the proportion of the data that is greater than 20,000. There are 179 values in the data set, and

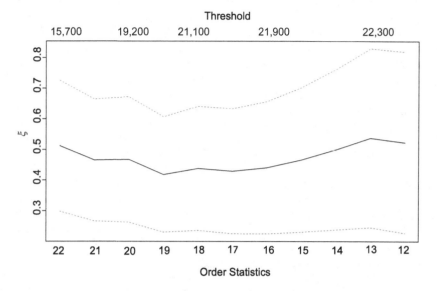

Figure 5.8 Hill estimators for ξ, using different threshold values, for the hurricane loss data, with 95% confidence interval

19 are greater than the threshold, so we use $S_X(d) = 19/179 = 0.1061$. This gives an estimate of $Q_{99\%} \approx 65{,}567$.

For the 99% Expected Shortfall we use formula (5.25),

$$ES_\alpha = \frac{1}{1-\xi}\left(Q_\alpha + \beta - \xi\, d\right),$$

with the same parameters as used for Q_α. For $\alpha = 0.99$, this gives a 99% Expected Shortfall estimate of 230,291.

We see that the VaR estimate is fairly close to the empirical estimate. The Expected Shortfall, however, is considerably larger than the maximum observed loss; we use the GPD to extrapolate beyond the data, so our estimates are not bounded by the values observed in the past. We see the influence of the extrapolation in Table 5.3, which shows the empirical estimates of the VaR and Expected Shortfall for several different values of α, using smoothed empirical estimates for the VaR. We compare them with the estimates found using the GPD. As the risk measure moves further into the tail, the Expected Shortfall is highly influenced by the GPD. In the last row, we illustrate that for risk measures using α beyond the availability in the data, the GPD extrapolation can be used to give results consistent with the upper tail of the data.

Table 5.3. *Comparison of smoothed empirical and GPD estimates of risk measures for US hurricane loss data (millions)*

α	Empirical VaR	Empirical ES	GPD VaR	GPD ES
0.90	21,140	38,783	20,424	49,716
0.95	26,070	56,273	27,081	76,345
0.99	81,514	91,130	65,567	230,291
0.999	n/a	n/a	319,429	1,245,735

5.6 Notes and Further Reading

The two perspectives on EVT discussed in this chapter, block maxima and points over threshold (POT), both have practical applications, but the POT approach is much more useful in applied risk management, as it focuses on exactly the statistic that is measured with the Expected Shortfall risk measure. Both perspectives categorize the nature of the distribution in its extreme tail using the ξ parameter; in practice, the uncertainty in the estimated value of ξ can be a significant problem. Ultimately, the nature of extreme values means that the available data is slim and, therefore, the uncertainty is high. Nevertheless, EVT offers a valuable approach for evaluating far right tail risk measures of loss.

Embrechts et al. (2013) offers a deep exploration of EVT in risk management, with a focus on insurance and finance.

5.7 Exercises

Exercise 5.1 Describe the advantages of using EVT to calculate tail risk measures of a distribution, compared with a parametric model of the full loss distribution.

Exercise 5.2 Describe the trade-off involved in selecting block sizes for the block maxima approach to estimating ξ. Explain how the selection influences (i) the bias and (ii) the variance of the estimate.

Exercise 5.3 The normal distribution is in the MDA of the Gumbel extreme value distribution.

(a) Explain in words what this means.
(b) The normal distribution is symmetric, while the Gumbel distribution is positively skewed. Explain why this is not inconsistent.

Exercise 5.4 Show that, if X follows the GEV distribution with parameters $\xi < 0$, μ, and $\theta > 0$, then $Y = 1 + \xi(x - \mu)/\theta$ follows the Weibull distribution defined in Section 4.4.2, and identify the parameters of the standard Weibull distribution.

Exercise 5.5 Consider an exponential distribution with distribution function

$$F(x) = 1 - e^{-x/\beta}.$$

(a) Show that F is in the maximum domain of attraction of the Gumbel distribution, using normalizing sequences $c_n = \beta$ and $d_n = \beta \log n$.
(b) Let M denote the maximum of 80 observations of an exponential distribution with mean 100. Calculate the probability that $M > 1,000$ using (i) the exponential distribution and (ii) the Gumbel distribution.
(c) Comment on your results.

Exercise 5.6 Describe the trade-off involved in selecting a threshold for the points over threshold approach to estimating ξ. Explain how the selection influences (i) the bias and (ii) the variance of the estimate.

Exercise 5.7 You are given the following information about three random variables that are in the MDA of the GEV distribution. State with reasons whether $\xi < 0$, $\xi = 0$, or $\xi > 0$.

(a) The first random variable, X, is greater than 0, unbounded on the right side, and has finite kth moment for all $k = 1, 2, 3, \ldots$
(b) The second random variable, Y, is equal to $-X$.
(c) The third random variable has a finite number of moments.

Exercise 5.8 A company is modelling losses from cyberattacks.
The following table shows the largest 20 values of a sample of 1,000 observations of the losses, sorted in decreasing order:

196.1	148.2	79.8	35.8	27.1	22.9	21.8	20.9	16.7	15.8
15.5	13.7	13.0	12.5	11.5	10.3	9.7	9.4	8.3	8.0

(a) Estimate the 99% VaR of X.
(b) Estimate the 99% Expected Shortfall of X.
(c) Assume that the losses are from a distribution which is GPD for $Y = X - d | X > d$, where $d = 10$, with shape parameter $\gamma = 0$, and scale parameter $\beta = 30$.

(i) Show that

$$\Pr[X > x] = S_X(d)\left(e^{-(x-d)/\beta}\right) \quad \text{for } x > d.$$

(ii) Estimate the 99% VaR and 99% Expected Shortfall using the GPD for the tail probabilities.

(iii) Comment on the differences between your estimates in (a) and (b), and your estimates using the GPD.

Exercise 5.9 Consider the one-parameter GEV distribution

$$F(x) = e^{-x^{-1/\gamma}}, \quad 0 < \gamma < 1.$$

Show that $E[X] = \Gamma(1 - \gamma)$, where $\Gamma(u) = \int_0^\infty t^{u-1} e^{-t}\, dt.$

Exercise 5.10 Consider the Pareto distribution with distribution function

$$F(x) = 1 - \left(\frac{\theta}{\theta + x}\right)^\alpha.$$

(a) Show that this distribution is in the Fréchet MDA, with distribution function $e^{-y^{-\alpha}}$, using normalizing sequences

$$c_n = \theta\, n^{1/\alpha}, \quad \text{and } d_n = -\theta.$$

(b) Hence determine the normalizing sequences c_n^* and d_n^* such that the limiting distribution for the maximum is the GEV distribution

$$H(x) = e^{-(1+\gamma x)^{-1/\gamma}}.$$

(c) Given $\theta = 200$, $\alpha = 3.0$,

(i) Compare the exact probability that $M_n \le m$ with the probability using the GEV distribution applied to normalized M_n, for $n = 25$ and $m = 500$.

(ii) Repeat (i) for $m = 500$, and $n = 50$, and $n = 100$.

(iii) Repeat (i) with $n = 25$, $m = 1{,}000$, and $m = 2{,}000$.

(iv) Comment on your results.

Exercise 5.11 You are given that the maximum of a sample of n independent variables has a Fréchet distribution, with parameters α and θ ($\mu = 0$).

Show that the maximum of a sample of $2n$ variables also has a Fréchet distribution, and determine the parameters.

Exercise 5.12 You are given that the monthly maximum for a financial series monitored daily has a Gumbel distribution, with location and scale parameters μ and θ.

Show that the annual maximum also has a Gumbel distribution, and determine the parameters.

Exercise 5.13 You are given that the Fréchet distribution with parameter α is in the MDA of the Fréchet distribution, with the same parameter α. You are also given that for this distribution the normalizing sequence $d_n = 0$. What is the c_n normalizing sequence in this case?

A distribution with the property that it lies in the MDA of the same distribution, with the same parameter is called a **max stable** distribution.

Exercise 5.14 An investment firm is interested in fitting an extreme value distribution to portfolio losses. The data set comprises 300 values for the monthly percentage loss in portfolio value.

The analyst has assumed the data is a random sample of independent identically distributed observations. She has calculated the empirical MEL function, which is shown in the figure below.

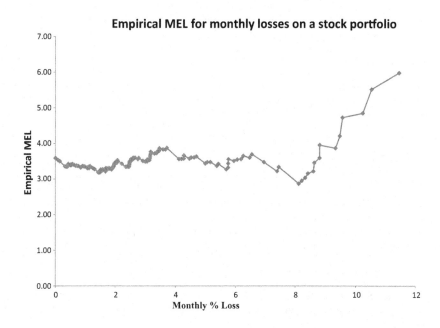

You are also given the 20 largest values from the data, sorted from high to low:

24.3	18.4	15.6	11.4	10.5	10.2	9.6	9.5	9.3	8.8
8.8	8.6	8.6	8.4	8.3	8.2	8.1	7.4	7.4	6.9

(a) (i) Estimate the 98% Expected Shortfall from the data.
   (ii) Calculate the empirical MEL function, $\hat{e}(x)$ at $x = 10.0$.
(b) The analyst decides to use the GPD with threshold $d = 8$. Explain why this choice appears reasonable.
(c) The MLE estimators for the GPD distribution, with $d = 8$, are $\hat{\xi} = 0.55$, $\hat{\beta} = 1.5$.

   (i) Calculate the 98% Expected Shortfall using the GPD distribution.
   (ii) Calculate the 99.9% Expected Shortfall using the GPD distribution.

(d) Comment on the difference between the Expected Shortfall estimates from (a)(i) and (c)(i). Which method would you recommend?

Exercise 5.15 A shipping company is reviewing its expected losses from events at sea, in order to determine how much insurance cover is needed.

The number of journeys each year, denoted N, has a Poisson distribution with expected value 100.

In 80% of journeys, there is no loss. In 19% of journeys, there is a minor loss, with severity following a lognormal distribution, with parameters $\mu = 7$, $\sigma = 1.6$. In the remaining 1% of journeys, there is a major loss, and the severity in these cases follows a Pareto distribution with parameters $a = 2.1$ and $\theta = 66,000$.

Let Y_j denote the loss from the jth voyage, and let I denote the type of loss involved, where $I \in \{$No Loss, Minor Loss, Major Loss$\}$.

You are given that Y_j are i.i.d. and are independent of N.

(a) Calculate the mean of the aggregate annual loss.
(b) The company is interested in insuring jumbo losses, defined as losses exceeding 50,000.

   (i) Calculate $\Pr[Y_j > 50,000 | I = $ Minor Loss$]$ and $\Pr[Y_j > 50,000 | I = $ Major Loss$]$, and hence determine $\Pr[Y_j > 50,000]$.
   (ii) Given that an individual loss exceeds 50,000, calculate the probability that the loss arose from a major loss event.

(c) You are given that the lognormal distribution lies in the Gumbel MDA, and the Pareto lies in the Fréchet MDA.

   A consultant claims that Y_j will be in the Gumbel MDA, because there is a higher probability that Y_j comes from the lognormal distribution than from the Pareto distribution. Critique this claim.
(d) The company insures losses from major loss events only. The remaining uninsured loss will therefore be

$$Y_j^* = \begin{cases} Y_j & I \neq \text{Major Loss}, \\ \min(Y_j, 50{,}000) & I = \text{Major Loss}. \end{cases}$$

Show that the expected value of the annual aggregate uninsured loss is 102,700 to the nearest 100.

(e) The insurer offers the cover at a cost of 47,000. As an alternative, it offers a co-insurance policy with the same expected value of insured losses for only 37,000. Under a co-insurance policy, the insurer pays a fixed proportion of all losses.

   (i) Determine the proportion of each loss retained by the shipping firm under the co-insurance.

   (ii) Comment on how the shipping company might decide between the two policies.

6

Copulas

6.1 Summary

In this chapter, we consider how individual, univariate distributions can be combined to create multivariate, joint distributions, using copula functions. This can be very valuable when a firm is looking at aggregating dependent risks from different business units. We present Sklar's seminal theorem, which states that for continuous distributions, every joint distribution can be expressed in terms of a unique copula, and every copula defines a valid joint distribution.

We present some important copulas, both explicit and implicit, and discuss their features. We show how measures of rank dependency can be more informative than traditional correlation. In keeping with our interest in tail behaviour of loss distributions, we consider how different copulas exhibit different dependency in the tails of the marginal distributions.

Finally, we discuss construction and estimation of copulas.

6.2 Introduction

In the quantitative analysis of the previous chapters, we have considered aggregate losses which are essentially independent. However, many risks that a firm faces are not independent. For example, a firm that holds corporate bonds from several different issuers must allow for the fact that the risk of default of the different bonds will not be independent – that is, if one bond defaults, it is more likely that the other bonds will also default. Different units of a firm might be exposed to different currency risk, and these risks will not be independent as global events, such as a pandemic, can impact multiple currencies. Both within business units, and when aggregating risks from different business units, it is often necessary to model dependency between risks.

There are several approaches to the statistical modelling of dependent risks. The first is to find a specific joint distribution that fits all the dependent random variables. For example, we might assume that losses from different causes have a multivariate normal distribution, or a multivariate t-distribution, or a Wishart distribution (which is a multivariate extension of the gamma distribution). In each of these cases, the marginal distribution of each individual random variable will be of the same form, but with different parameters. For example, in the multivariate normal distribution, when viewed individually, each risk is assumed to be normally distributed.

Copula functions model dependency using a bottom-up process. We start with the marginal distributions of the individual random variables. The copula function is then applied to model the dependencies between the random variables. The advantage is that copulas can be used to create multivariate distributions when the marginal distributions are not in the same family. In risk management this bottom-up capability can be very useful. It allows us to use copulas to bring together the risks from different parts of the firm, to generate a firm-wide model. For example, an insurer may offer several different lines of business; each line may develop their own loss distribution, but there are dependencies between the losses, arising from, for example, underwriting cycles or claims inflation. A copula may be used to bring together the individual loss distributions, to create a model of the joint distribution of aggregate losses from all lines of business across the enterprise. Similarly, a global conglomerate may have different business units dealing with operations in different geographical areas. Each unit may develop their own model for aggregate losses and the firm could use a copula function to create the joint probability distribution from the individual loss distributions for each unit.

Before we introduce copulas formally, we consider two specific multivariate distributions that play an important role in modelling dependency in financial risk management.

6.3 The Multivariate Normal Distribution

As it has become quite common, particularly in short-term financial applications, to assume normal distributions for stock price changes or loss variables, for example, it is natural to consider the **multivariate normal** (MVN) as a model for dependent losses.

The random vector $X = (X_1 \ X_2 \ \cdots X_d)^T$ has a multivariate normal distribution with parameters μ (a d-dimensional vector) and Σ (a $d \times d$ covariance matrix) if for any vector $w \in \mathbb{R}^d$, the random variable $w^T X$ has a univariate normal distribution with mean $w^T \mu$ and variance $w^T \Sigma w$. In the event that the matrix Σ is non-singular, the joint probability density function of X is

$$f(x) = \frac{1}{(2\pi)^{d/2} |\Sigma|^{1/2}} \exp\left\{-\frac{1}{2}\left((x-\mu)^T \Sigma^{-1}(x-\mu)\right)\right\}.$$

By definition, a covariance matrix is symmetric and positive semi-definite. The elements of the covariance matrix are $\Sigma_{ij} = \rho_{ij}\sigma_i\sigma_j$, where ρ_{ij} is the correlation between X_i and X_j, and σ_i is the standard deviation of X_i. The marginal distribution of each individual X_i is $X_i \sim N\left(\mu_i, \sigma_i^2\right)$.

6.3.1 Testing for the MVN Distribution

Suppose we have a sample of N values of a d-dimensional random variable, where the jth observed random vector from the joint distribution $X = (X_1, X_2, \ldots X_d)^T$ is $x_j = (x_{1,j} \ x_{2,j} \ldots x_{d,j})^T$. Our data can be written in matrix form as

$$\begin{pmatrix} x_{1,1} & x_{1,2} & \cdots & x_{1,N} \\ x_{2,1} & x_{2,2} & \cdots & x_{2,N} \\ \vdots & \vdots & \cdots & \vdots \\ x_{d,1} & x_{d,2} & \cdots & x_{d,N} \end{pmatrix}.$$

In this form, the columns are the repeated samples of the d-dimensional random vectors, and the rows are the marginal samples from each of the individual random variables.

We want to test whether the underlying joint distribution is MVN. We will do this in two stages.

First we test whether the marginal distributions are normally distributed, using the Jarque–Bera test for each of the marginal samples.

For the marginal distribution of X_1, the data is $x^{(1)} = (x_{11}, x_{12}, \ldots, x_{1,N})$. We calculate the empirical moments

$$\bar{x}_1 = \frac{1}{N} \sum_{j=1}^{N} x_{1,j},$$

$$s_1^2 = \frac{1}{N-1} \sum_{j=1}^{N} \left(x_{1,j} - \bar{x}_1\right)^2,$$

$$sk_1 = \frac{\left(\sum_{j=1}^{N}\left(x_{1,j} - \bar{x}_1\right)^3\right)}{N-1},$$

$$ku_1 = \frac{\left(\sum_{j=1}^{N}\left(x_{1,j} - \bar{x}_1\right)^4\right)}{N-1},$$

where sk_1 and ku_1 are the sample skewness and kurtosis, respectively. The test statistic for the Jarque–Bera test for X_1 is

$$T = \frac{N}{6}\left(\frac{sk_1}{s_1^3} + \frac{1}{4}\left(\frac{ku_1}{s_1^4} - 3\right)^2\right).$$

The normal distribution has zero skewness, and coefficient of kurtosis of 3.0, so if the data is consistent with the normal distribution, then T will be small. Under the null hypothesis that X_i has a normal distribution, T has a χ^2 distribution, with 2 degrees of freedom, so the p-value for the Jarque–Bera test is

$$p = \Pr\left[\chi_2^2 \geq T\right].$$

We repeat the test for each of the d marginal distributions.

Even if the marginal distributions are all normal, it does not follow that the joint distribution is MVN. To test for the MVN distribution we use Mardia's test, which based on the joint multivariate samples, that is, the columns of the data matrix, $\boldsymbol{x}_j = (x_{1,j} \; x_{2,j} \ldots x_{d,j})$.

The mean vector is $\bar{\boldsymbol{x}} = (\bar{x}_1 \; \bar{x}_2 \ldots \bar{x}_d)^T$, using the marginal means for each element.

Let $\mathbf{S}$ denote the sample covariance matrix.

The test statistics are based on empirical multivariate measures of skewness and kurtosis. For any two samples, say j and k, define

$$D_{jk} = (\boldsymbol{x}_j - \bar{\boldsymbol{x}})^T \mathbf{S}^{-1}(\boldsymbol{x}_k - \bar{\boldsymbol{x}}).$$

Given N samples of the d-dimensional random vector, the multivariate skewness measure is

$$b_d = \frac{1}{N^2}\sum_{j=1}^{N}\sum_{k=1}^{N} D_{jk}^3,$$

and the multivariate kurtosis measure is

$$k_d = \frac{1}{N}\sum_{j=1}^{N} D_{jj}^4.$$

Mardia's test statistics are

$$Q_1 = \frac{b_d \, N}{6} \sim \chi_\nu^2, \text{ where } \nu = \frac{d(d+1)(d+2)}{6},$$

$$Q_2 = \frac{k_d - d(d+2)}{\sqrt{8d(d+2)/N}} \sim \mathrm{N}(0,1).$$

The null hypothesis is that the joint distribution is MVN, so if the p-values are less than, say, 0.05, the null hypothesis would be rejected.

6.3.2 Simulation Algorithm for the MVN Distribution

It is often useful to be able to simulate dependent random variables from the MVN distribution, given a set of simulated independent values from the standard normal distribution.

The covariance matrix Σ, can be expressed as $\Sigma = AA^T$ where A is a lower triangular matrix; this is the Cholesky decomposition.

A simulation algorithm for the MVN distribution is as follows:

(1) Calculate A from the Cholesky decomposition of Σ.
(2) Generate $N \times d$ standard normal random variates and arrange into N d-dimensional vectors, $Z_j = (Z_{j1} \ldots, Z_{jd})^T$ for $j = 1, 2, \ldots, N$.
(3) For $j = 1, 2, \ldots, N$, set $Y_j = \mu + AZ_j$.

This algorithm generates N d-dimensional vectors, $Y_1, \ldots, Y_N$ from the MVN(μ, Σ) distribution.

6.4 The Multivariate Student's t (MVT) Distribution

The univariate Student's t distribution is symmetric, like the normal distribution, but with fatter tails. It has three parameters: μ, a location parameter, $\sigma > 0$, a scale parameter, and $\nu > 0$, a shape parameter, commonly called the **degrees of freedom** parameter. The ν parameter determines how fat-tailed the distribution is. As $\nu \to \infty$, the Student's t distribution converges to the N(μ, σ^2) distribution. The Student's t distribution has proven useful for modelling tail risks that are heavier than the normal distribution; as we noted in Chapter 5, the normal distribution is in the MDA of the Gumbel extreme value distribution ($\xi = 0$), while the Student's t distribution is in the MDA of the Fréchet distribution ($\xi > 0$). The Student's t (μ, σ, ν) distribution is also related to the normal distribution, through a transformation involving an independent χ_ν^2 random variable. Let $Z \sim N(0, \sigma^2)$ and let $V \sim \chi_\nu^2$ (that is, V has a χ^2 distribution with ν degrees of freedom), independent of Z, then

$$X = Z\sqrt{\frac{\nu}{V}} + \mu \sim \text{Student's } t(\mu, \sigma, \nu).$$

The multivariate version of the Student's t distribution models a random vector, $X = (X_1 \ X_2 \cdots X_d)^T$, say. The parameters are μ (a d-dimensional location vector), Σ (a $d \times d$ positive definite scale matrix), and $\nu > 0$ (the degrees of freedom parameter, often an integer). The marginal distribution of each individual X_i is $t(\mu_i \sigma_i, \nu)$, where $\sigma_i^2 = \Sigma_{ii}$.

The kth moments of the marginal distributions exist for $k < \nu$. If $\nu > 1$, then the mean of x is μ. If $\nu > 2$, the covariance matrix is $\nu/(\nu - 2)\Sigma$.

The relationship between the MVT and MVN distributions is similar to the univariate case. If Z is multivariate normal with mean 0 and covariance matrix Σ, and $V \sim \chi_\nu^2$ is independent of Z, then

$$X = Z\sqrt{\frac{\nu}{V}} + \mu \sim MVT(\mu, \Sigma, \nu). \tag{6.1}$$

6.4.1 Simulating a Multivariate Student's t Random Variable

Equation (6.1) indicates how we can generate a sample of N d-dimensional random vectors from the MVT distribution, with parameters μ, Σ and ν.

(1) Generate a sample of N random vectors from the d-dimensional multivariate normal distribution, with mean 0 and covariance matrix Σ, as outlined in the previous section. Let $Y_j = (Y_{j,1}, \ldots, Y_{j,d})^T$ denote the jth simulated MVN vector.
(2) Generate N random variates from the χ_ν^2 distribution, $V_1, \ldots, V_N$.
(3) Then for each j, construct the MVT random vector as

$$X_j = Y_j\sqrt{\frac{\nu}{V_j}} + \mu.$$

6.4.2 The Multivariate Non-Central t Distribution

We have that for $Z \sim N(0, \sigma^2)$ and $V \sim \chi_\nu^2$, the random variable $X = Z\sqrt{\nu/V}$ has a Student's t distribution with mean 0 and variance $\sigma^2\nu/(\nu - 2)$, provided that $\nu > 2$. If we make the same transformation to a normal random variable with non-zero mean, we have a new distribution, called the non-central t distribution. That is, for $Y \sim N(\mu, \sigma^2)$ and $V \sim \chi_\nu^2$,

$$X = Y\sqrt{\frac{v}{V}} \sim \text{non-central } t(\mu, \sigma, v).$$

If we let $Z = Y - \mu$, so that $Z \sim N(0, \sigma^2)$. We have

$$X = Y\sqrt{\frac{v}{V}} = Z\sqrt{\frac{v}{V}} + \mu\sqrt{\frac{v}{V}},$$

where the first term is a regular Student's t distributed random variable, with mean 0, and the second term is a multiple of $V^{-\frac{1}{2}}$, which is an inverse-square-root χ^2 random variable. If $v > 1$, the mean is

$$E\left[V^{-\frac{1}{2}}\right] = \frac{\sqrt{1/2}\Gamma((v-1)/2)}{\Gamma(v/2)},$$

which means that the expected value of the non-central t random variable X is

$$E[X] = \mu \frac{\sqrt{v/2}\Gamma((v-1)/2)}{\Gamma(v/2)}.$$

The effect of the second term is that the non-central t distribution is not symmetric. Similarly to the t distribution, it converges to the normal distribution as $v \to \infty$, and the asymmetry is greatest for smaller values of v.

Simulating the multivariate non-central t distribution follows exactly the same procedure as for the MVT case above, except that the normal random vectors generated in the first step have mean μ, instead of mean $\mathbf{0}$.

6.5 What Is a Copula?

The problem with relying on the multivariate normal and t distributions of the previous section is that they are very structured and very restrictive. If we have one random variable which is marginally normal, and another which is marginally gamma distributed, we already know that the multivariate normal distribution will not be suitable. The dependency structure and the marginal structure are all part of the distribution specification.

Copulas provide a methodology for creating joint distributions from *any* marginal distributions.

Suppose we have m continuous random variables, $X_1, \ldots, X_m$. Let $F_j(x_j)$ denote the marginal distribution function of X_j, so that

$$F_j(x_j) = \Pr[X_j \le x_j] \qquad \text{for } j = 1, \ldots, m.$$

A copula, C, is a function of the m probabilities, $F_1(x_1), \ldots, F_m(x_m)$ that gives the joint probability that $X_1 \leq x_1, X_2 \leq x_2, \ldots, X_m \leq x_m$. That is,

$$C\big(F_1(x_1), \ldots, F_m(x_m)\big) = \Pr[X_1 \leq x_1, X_2 \leq x_2, \ldots, X_m \leq x_m].$$

We illustrate this in the following example.

Example 6.1 Suppose we have two random variables: L^A represents annual losses from business unit A, and L^B represents annual losses from business unit B. Unit A has determined that $L^A \sim N(1,000, 300^2)$, while Unit B has determined that $L^B \sim \text{Gamma}(4, 250)$. The risk tolerance set by the Board for Unit A is 1,500 and for Unit B is 1,600. The company requires each unit to transfer losses greater than their risk tolerance threshold.

(a) What is the probability that the losses are below the threshold, for each unit?

(b) What is the probability that both losses are below the threshold, if they are independent?

(c) What is the probability that both losses are below the threshold if the copula function for the dependence is

$$C(u_1, u_2) = \min(u_1, u_2).$$

(d) What is the probability that both losses are below the threshold if the copula function for the dependence is

$$C(u_1, u_2) = \left(u_1^{-2} + u_2^{-2} - 1\right)^{-1/2}.$$

(e) What is the probability that both losses are below the threshold if the copula function for the dependence is

$$C(u_1, u_2) = \left(u_1^{-50} + u_2^{-50} - 1\right)^{-1/50}.$$

(f) You are given that all the functions in (c), (d), and (e) above are valid copulas. What is the maximum value for the probability that both losses are below the threshold?

(g) Calculate a lower bound for the probability that both losses are below the threshold.

Solution 6.1 (a) The probabilities are

$$\Pr[L^A \leq 1,500] = \Phi\left(\frac{1,500 - 1,000}{300}\right) = 0.95221,$$

$$\Pr[L^B \leq 1,600] = \Gamma(4; 1,600/250) = 0.88108,$$

where $\Gamma(\alpha; x/\beta)$ is the incomplete gamma function (e.g., evaluated using R or Excel).

(b) The probability is $0.95221 \times 0.88108 = 0.83898$.
(c) The probability is $C(0.95221, 0.88108) = 0.88108$.
(d) The probability is $C(0.95221, 0.88108) = 0.84787$.
(e) The probability is $C(0.95221, 0.88108) = 0.88075$.
(f) Let A denote the event $L^A \leq 1,500$ and let B denote the event $L^B \leq 1,600$. Then we know that

$$\Pr[A \text{ and } B] = \Pr[B] \times \Pr[A|B].$$

The maximum value for $\Pr[A|B]$ is 1.0, so

$$\Pr[A \text{ and } B] \leq \Pr[B].$$

Similarly, by symmetry, we know that $\Pr[A \text{ and } B] \leq \Pr[A]$. So the probability that both losses are less than their thresholds cannot be bigger than the probability that either loss is less than its threshold, individually, so the joint probability must be less than $\min(0.95221, 0.88108) = 0.88108$.

From (c) above, we know that the minimum function is a valid copula, so the maximum joint probability is 0.88108.

(g) Consider the probability that $L^A \leq 1,500$ or $L^B \leq 1,600$, or both. In terms of the events defined in the solution to (f), this is $\Pr[A \text{ or } B]$. This probability must, of course, be less than or equal to 1.0; it is also equal to $\Pr[A] + \Pr[B] - \Pr[A \text{ and } B]$, so

$$\Pr[A \text{ or } B] = \Pr[A] + \Pr[B] - \Pr[A \text{ and } B] \leq 1$$
$$\Rightarrow \Pr[A \text{ and } B] \geq \Pr[A] + \Pr[B] - 1.$$

This means that the probability that $L^A \leq 1,500$ and $L^B \leq 1,600$ must be at least $0.95221 + 0.88108 - 1 = 0.83329$. □

In this chapter, we will assume all loss random variables are continuous. Some of the results may not hold for discrete or mixed random variables. The interested reader can look at, for example, Genest and Nešlehová (2007) for more information on copulas for discrete (counting) random variables.

6.5.1 Copula Definition

The function $C(u_1, u_2, \ldots, u_d)$ where $0 < u_j < 1$ for $j = 1, 2, \ldots, d$, is a d-dimensional copula if and only if it is a valid joint distribution function for a d-dimensional random vector, $(U_1, U_2, \ldots, U_d)$, where the marginal distribution of each U_j is Uniform on the interval $(0, 1)$. This distribution is denoted $U(0, 1)$.

Equivalently, we require the following three conditions, for $0 \leq u_1, \ldots, u_d \leq 1$.

Increasing $C(u_1, u_2, \ldots, u_d)$ is increasing in each u_i; this ensures that the distribution function is increasing in each of the u_i.

Uniform marginals $C(1, 1, \ldots, u_i, 1, \ldots, 1) = u_i$.

Recall that, given $U_j \sim U(0, 1)$, we know that $0 \leq U_j \leq 1$ and $\Pr[U_j \leq u_j] = u_j$. Then

$$
\begin{aligned}
C(1, 1, \ldots, u_i, 1, \ldots, 1) &= \Pr[U_1 \leq 1, U_2 \leq 1, \cdots U_i \leq u_i, \cdots, U_d \leq 1] \\
&= \Pr[U_i \leq u_i] \\
&= u_i.
\end{aligned}
$$

This condition ensures that the marginal distribution for each of the U_i is uniform.

Rectangular inequality This criterion requires that for any $a_1, \ldots, a_d$ and $b_1, \ldots, b_d$, such that $b_j > a_j$, the copula function must generate a valid joint probability for a vector of $U(0, 1)$ random variables,

$$
\Pr[a_1 < U_1 < b_1, \ a_2 < U_2 < b_2, \ \ldots, \ a_d < U_d < b_d] \geq 0,
$$

which translates to the following inequality, where $u_{i,1} = a_i$ and $u_{i,2} = b_i$:

$$
\sum_{j_1=1}^{2} \sum_{j_2=1}^{2} \cdots, \sum_{j_d=1}^{2} (-1)^{j_1 + j_2 + \cdots + j_d} C(u_{1, j_1}, u_{2, j_2}, \ldots u_{d, j_d}) \geq 0.
$$

The rectangular inequality is easier to follow for $d = 2$. In this case, it requires that

$$
\big(C(b_1, b_2) - C(a_1, b_2) \big) - \big(C(b_1, a_2) - C(a_1, a_2) \big) \geq 0.
$$

Consider the first two terms of the left-hand side:

$$
\begin{aligned}
C(b_1, b_2) - C(a_1, b_2) &= \Pr[U_1 \leq b_1, U_2 \leq b_2] - \Pr[U_1 \leq a_1, U_2 \leq b_2] \\
&= \Pr[a_1 \leq U_1 \leq b_1, U_2 \leq b_2].
\end{aligned}
$$

Similarly

$$
\begin{aligned}
C(b_1, a_2) - C(a_1, a_2) &= \Pr[U_1 \leq b_1, U_2 \leq a_2] - \Pr[U_1 \leq a_1, U_2 \leq a_2] \\
&= \Pr[a_1 \leq U_1 \leq b_1, U_2 \leq a_2],
\end{aligned}
$$

and so

$$C(b_1, b_2) - C(a_1, b_2) - \big(C(b_1, a_2) - C(a_1, a_2)\big)$$
$$= \Pr[a_1 \leq U_1 \leq b_1, a_2 \leq U_2 \leq b_2],$$

and as this is a probability, it must be greater than or equal to zero.

Not all copula functions for continuous random variables are smooth, but for those that are, to verify the copula conditions it is sufficient to demonstrate (i) that the marginals are uniform, and (ii) that the implied joint probability density function for the vector $(U_1, U_2, \ldots, U_d)$ is non-negative. The joint probability density function is found by differentiating with respect to each of the u_i. That is, the copula p.d.f. is c where

$$c(u_1, u_2, \ldots, u_d) = \frac{\partial^d C(u_1, u_2, \ldots, u_d)}{\partial u_1, \partial u_2, \ldots, \partial u_d} \geq 0 \text{ for all } 0 < u_j < 1. \quad (6.2)$$

6.5.2 Sklar's Theorem

Theorem 6.1 (Sklar) *Let $F_X(x)$ denote the joint cumulative distribution function of $X = (X_1, X_2, \ldots, X_d)$ evaluated at $x = (x_1, x_2, \ldots, x_d)$, and let $F_j(x_j)$ denote the marginal c.d.f. of X_j, for each $j = 1, \ldots, d$.*

(a) Given $F_X(x)$ and $F_j(x_j)$, there exists a d-dimensional copula C such that

$$C(F_1(x_1), F_2(x_2), \ldots, F_d(x_d)) = F_X(x_1, x_2, \ldots x_d) \quad (6.3)$$

and C is unique if each X_j is continuous.
(b) Given F_j for $j = 1, 2, \ldots, d$, and given a copula function C,

$$C(F_1(x_1), F_2(x_2), \ldots, F_d(x_d)) \quad (6.4)$$

defines a joint c.d.f. for X. □

Sklar's theorem says, first, that every joint cumulative distribution function of continuous random variables can be written in the form of a unique copula, and secondly, that any valid copula function, applied to marginal distribution functions will create a valid joint distribution function.

We will not prove Sklar's theorem formally, but we can give an intuitive sketch of the reasoning.

First, we note that the random variable $F_j(X_j)$ (that is, the random variable created by applying the c.d.f. of X_j to X_j itself) is a $U(0, 1)$ random variable, as for $0 \leq q \leq 1$,

$$\Pr[F_j(X_j) \leq q] = \Pr[X_j \leq F_j^{-1}(q)] = q.$$

That is, if $U_j = F_j(X_j) \in [0, 1]$, then $\Pr[U_j \leq q] = q$, which implies that the distribution function of U_j is $U(0, 1)$.

Next, we note that, because F_j is an increasing function,

$$\Pr[X_j \leq x_j] = \Pr[F_j(X_j) \leq F_j(x_j)].$$

We can illustrate these results with an example. Suppose that X is exponentially distributed with mean 1, so that $F_X(x) = 1 - e^{-x}$. Then consider the event that $F_X(X) \leq F_X(x)$:

$$F_X(X) \leq F_X(x) \Leftrightarrow 1 - e^{-X} \leq 1 - e^{-x}$$
$$\Leftrightarrow e^{-X} \geq e^{-x}$$
$$\Leftrightarrow X \leq x$$

as required.

Now, consider the joint cumulative distribution function for X:

$$F_X(x_1, x_2, \ldots, x_d)$$
$$= \Pr[X_1 \leq x_1, \ldots, X_d \leq x_d]$$
$$= \Pr[F_1(X_1) \leq F_1(x_1), \ldots, F_d(X_d) \leq F_d(x_d)]$$
$$= \Pr[U_1 \leq u_1, \ldots, U_d \leq u_d] \quad \text{where } U_j = F_j(X_j), \, u_j = F_j(x_j)$$
$$= C(u_1, u_2, \ldots, u_d).$$

Or, in words:

(1) The cumulative distribution function of X can be written as the cumulative distribution function of the random variables $F_j(X_j)$, and these are $U(0, 1)$ distributed.
(2) Any joint distribution with $U(0, 1)$ marginals is a copula.
(3) Therefore, the joint cumulative distribution function can be written as a copula.

Part (b) of Sklar's theorem also follows:

(1) A given d-dimensional copula C applied to $U(0, 1)$ marginal random variables is a valid joint cumulative distribution function.
(2) $F_j(X_j) \sim U(0, 1)$ for $j = 1, 2, \ldots, d$.
(3) Therefore, $F(x_1, \ldots, x_d) = C(F_1(x_1), F_2(x_2), \ldots, F_d(x_d))$ defines a valid joint distribution.

The arguments of the copula are $u_j = F_j(x_j)$. It is helpful to note that x_j is the u_j-quantile of the distribution of X_j. That means that, if the copula C

models the dependence structure of the joint distribution of X and Y, then $C(u, v)$ is the probability that X lies below its u-quantile and Y lies below its v-quantile.

The fundamental equations relating the copula function C and the joint distribution function F of $X_1, \ldots, X_d$ are

$$F(x_1, \ldots, x_d) = C(F_1(x_1), \ldots, F_d(x_d)), \qquad (6.5)$$

$$C(u_1, \ldots, u_d) = F(F_1^{-1}(u_1), \ldots, F_d^{-1}(u_d)). \qquad (6.6)$$

In the remainder of this chapter we will work with bivariate copulas, for simplicity. Many of the copulas that we study can be generalized to the multivariate case.

6.5.3 Invariance of Copulas

A useful characteristic of copulas is that the copula function is unchanged when the underlying variables are transformed, provided the transformation is a strictly increasing function.

That is, if $C(u, v)$ denotes the copula describing the joint distribution of $F_X(X)$ and $F_Y(Y)$, then the same copula also describes the joint distribution of any pair of variables $X^* = g(X)$, $Y^* = h(Y)$, where g and h are strictly increasing deterministic functions.

The reason for this useful result is that the copula models how the u and v quantiles of X and Y are associated, and this association is retained when X and Y are transformed to X^* and Y^*.

6.6 Examples of Copulas

In this section, we will look at a few examples of bivariate copulas. In each case, the copula function will be denoted $C(u, v)$, where $0 < u, v < 1$. This is assumed to model the dependency between two continuous random variables, X and Y so that, $F_X(x) = u$ and $F_Y(y) = v$,

$$\Pr[X \leq x, Y \leq y] = F_{X,Y}(x, y) = C(u, v).$$

To illustrate, we apply the copulas in the context of Example 6.1. Recall from the example that for losses L^A and L^B, we have $\Pr[L^A \leq 1{,}500] = 0.95221$ and $\Pr[L^B \leq 1{,}600] = 0.88108$, so that 1,500 represents the 95.221% quantile of L^A and 1,600 represents the 88.108% quantile of L^B. Then $u = 0.95221$ and $v = 0.88108$.

6.6.1 The Independence Copula

$$C(u, v) = uv.$$

Clearly, this is the joint probability if the risks are independent. As we noted in Example 6.1, in this case $C(0.95221, 0.88108) = 0.83898$.

6.6.2 The Comonotonic Copula

$$C(u, v) = \min(u, v).$$

Two risks, X and Y, are **comonotonic** if one can be expressed as an increasing deterministic function of the other. For example, $Y = 2X$, $Y = \log X$, $Y = e^x$ are all comonotonic pairs.

The quantiles of comonotonic risks will always correspond; that is, given $Y = g(X)$, for a strictly increasing function g, we know that when X lies at its q-quantile, Y will be equal to its q-quantile. In fact, for any comonotonic risk pair (X, Y), we have that $F_X^{-1}(X) = F_Y^{-1}(Y)$.

Example 6.2 Consider the random variables $X \sim N(0, 1)$ and $Y = e^X$. Calculate $F_X(1.2816)$ and $F_Y(5.1805)$, and show that $F_{X,Y}(1.2816, 5.1805) = F_X(1.2816)$.

Solution 6.2 We have

$$F_X(1.2816) = \Phi(1.2816) = 0.90,$$

$$F_Y(5.1805) = \Pr[e^X \leq 5.1805] = \Pr[X \leq \log 5.1805]$$

$$= \Pr[X \leq 1.6449] = 0.95,$$

$$F_{X,Y}(1.2816, 5.1805) = \Pr[X \leq 1.2816 \text{ and } e^X \leq 5.1805]$$

$$= \Pr[X \leq 1.2816 \text{ and } X \leq 1.6449]$$

$$= \Pr[X \leq 1.2816] = F_X(1.2816). \qquad \square$$

Comonotonicity is the strongest form of positive dependence between risks. In the context of Example 6.1, consider the implications if L^A and L^B are comonotonic. If $L^B \leq 1,600$, then L^B lies below its 88.108% quantile, which means that, given comonotonicity, L^A must also lie below its 88.108% quantile, which (recalling that $L^A \sim N(1,000, 300^2)$) is $1,000 + z_{0.88108} \, 300 = 1,354$ (where $z_q = \Phi^{-1}(q)$).

So, when we break down the joint probability into two components as follows,

$$\Pr\left[L^A \leq 1{,}500, L^B \leq 1{,}600\right] = \Pr\left[L^B \leq 1{,}600\right]$$

$$\times \Pr\left[L^A \leq 1{,}500 \mid L^B \leq 1{,}600\right],$$

the second term on the right-hand side, the conditional probability $\Pr\left[L^A \leq 1{,}500 \mid L^B \leq 1{,}600\right]$, must be equal to 1, because we know that $L^A \leq 1{,}354$ when $L^B \leq 1{,}600$.

Hence,

$$C(u,v) = \min(u,v) = 0.88108.$$

Note that we identified this as the maximum value for the joint probability in the example.

6.6.3 The Countermonotonic Copula

$$C(u,v) = \max(u+v-1,0). \tag{6.7}$$

Two risks are **countermonotonic** if Y is a strictly decreasing function of X, which is the strongest possible negative dependence between risks. For example, $Y = -X$ and $Y = e^{-X}$ are countermonotonic pairs.

For countermonotonic pairs, the q-quantile of X corresponds to the $(1-q)$-quantile of Y. That is, $F_Y(Y) = 1 - F_X(X)$, so that when X lies at, say, its 90% quantile, Y will lie at its 10% quantile.

We will illustrate the derivation of the countermonotonic copula as follows. Assume X and Y are countermonotonic. Let $C(u,v)$ denote the copula for X and Y.

Consider first the case $C(u,v)$ where $u + v < 1$. For example, let's look at $C(0.6, 0.1)$. This is the probability that Y lies below its 10% quantile and X lies below its 60% quantile. But this is impossible – if X lies below its 60% quantile, Y must lie *above* its 40% quantile. That is,

$$C(0.6, 0.1) = \Pr[F_X(X) \leq 0.6, F_Y(Y) \leq 0.1]$$

$$= \Pr[F_X(X) \leq 0.6, F_X(X) \geq 0.9]$$

$$= 0.$$

Generalizing, we see that if $v < 1 - u$, it is impossible for Y to lie below its v-quantile when X lies below its u-quantile. Hence, $C(u,v) = 0$ when $u + v < 1$.

Now consider the case where $u + v \geq 1$, for example, $C(0.6, 0.8)$. This is the probability that X lies below its 60% quantile, and Y lies below its 80% quantile:

$$\begin{aligned}
C(0.6,\ 0.8) &= \Pr[F_X(X) \leq 0.6, F_Y(Y) \leq 0.8] \\
&= \Pr[F_X(X) \leq 0.6, F_X(X) \geq 0.2] \\
&= \Pr[0.2 \leq F_X(X) \leq 0.6] \\
&= 0.6 - 0.2 = 0.4.
\end{aligned}$$

Generalizing, we see that if $v \geq 1-u$, then $C(u,v) = u-(1-v) = u+v-1$ as required.

In terms of our example, if the losses are countermonotonic, we have

$$C(u,v) = 0.95221 + 0.88108 - 1 = 0.83329,$$

which was the lower bound identified in Example 6.1.

6.6.4 The Clayton Copula

For a parameter $\theta > 0$,

$$C(u,v) = \left(u^{-\theta} + v^{-\theta} - 1\right)^{-\frac{1}{\theta}}. \tag{6.8}$$

This was the copula used in (d) and (e) of Example 6.1. Note that as $\theta \to 0$ the Clayton copula tends to the independence copula, and as $\theta \to \infty$, it tends to the comonotonic copula.

In Figure 6.1, we show an example of a Clayton copula. The left side shows a contour plot of the joint density function. Each contour indicates a curve of equal joint density. The right side shows a scatter plot of simulated values of the copula. In both cases, the x and y axes represent the u and v variables of the copula.

6.6.5 The Gumbel Copula

For a parameter $\theta > 1$,

$$C(u,v) = \exp\left\{-\left((-\log(u))^{\theta} + (-\log(v))^{\theta}\right)^{1/\theta}\right\}. \tag{6.9}$$

When $\theta \to 1$ the Gumbel copula tends to the independence copula, and when $\theta \to \infty$ it tends to the comonotonic copula.

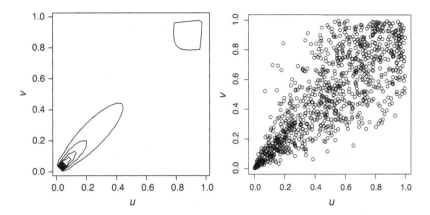

Figure 6.1 Clayton copula, density function contours and simulated values ($\theta = 3.0$).

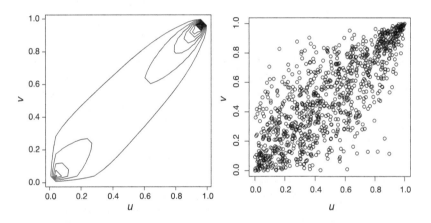

Figure 6.2 Gumbel copula, density function contours and simulated values ($\theta = 2.5$).

In Figure 6.2, we show the density function contours, and a scatterplot of simulated values, for a Gumbel copula with parameter $\theta = 2.5$.

In the context of Example 6.1, suppose first that $\theta = 1.5$, then

$$C(0.95221, 0.88108) = 0.86401,$$

and with $\theta = 50$, we have

$$C(0.95221, 0.88108) = 0.88108.$$

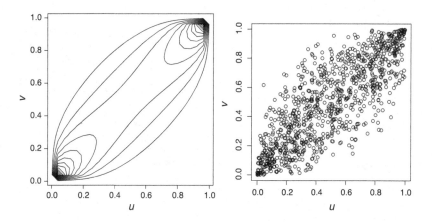

Figure 6.3 Gaussian copula, density function contours and simulated values
(the correlation parameter is $\rho = 0.81$).

6.6.6 The Gaussian Copula

For the bivariate Gaussian copula, we need a parameter ρ, representing a correlation, so $-1 \leq \rho \leq 1$. Let z_α represent the α-quantile of a standard N(0,1) distribution, i.e. $z_\alpha = \Phi^{-1}(\alpha)$, and let Φ_ρ represent the distribution function of a bivariate normal random vector, with N(0, 1) marginal distributions, and with correlation ρ. Then the bivariate Gaussian copula is

$$C(u, v) = \Phi_\rho(z_u, z_v).$$

In Figure 6.3, we show the density function contours and a scatterplot of simulated values, for a Gaussian copula with parameter $\rho = 0.81$.

The bivariate normal distribution function can be found using appropriate statistical software.

In the context of Example 6.1, setting $\rho = 0.9$, for example, we have

$$\Phi(z_u) = 0.95221 \Rightarrow z_u = 1.6667; \quad \Phi(z_v) = 0.88108 \Rightarrow z_v = 1.1804$$
$$\Rightarrow C(0.95221, 0.88108) = \Phi_{0.9}(1.6667, 1.1804) = 0.87660$$

and, if we let $\rho = -0.9$, we have

$$C(0.95221, 0.88108) = \Phi_{-0.9}(1.6667, 1.18040) = 0.83329.$$

Note that we can use the Gaussian copula even though the marginal loss distributions are not Gaussian.

6.6.7 Fundamental, Explicit, and Implicit copulas

The independent, comonotonic, and countermonotonic copulas are called **fundamental copulas**, as they are derived from fundamental relationships between the variables.

The Gaussian copula is an example of an **implicit copula**, where we impute the copula from a known multivariate distribution. We can also construct implicit copulas from the MVT distribution, called the **Student's t copula**, or from any specified multivariate distribution. For a given bivariate distribution function $F_\Theta(x)$, with associated marginal univariate distributions $F_{\theta_j}(x)$, the implicit copula is

$$C(u, v) = F_\Theta \left(F_{\theta_1}^{-1}(u), F_{\theta_2}^{-1}(v) \right).$$

For the Gaussian copula, F_Θ is the standard bivariate Gaussian distribution function, for a given correlation ρ, and F_θ is the standard normal distribution function Φ. For the t copula, F_Θ is the bivariate t distribution function, for given correlation ρ and degrees of freedom d, and F_θ is the univariate t distribution function with d degrees of freedom.

The implicit copulas are used solely for modelling the dependency between random variables. Using a Gaussian copula, for example, does not imply that the marginal distributions of the random variables are Gaussian.

The Clayton and Gumbel copulas are examples of **explicit copulas**, where the copula function has a simple closed form. There is generally no theoretical justification for using a specific explicit or implicit copula. The selection of a copula is similar to the selection of a marginal distribution for a loss. We might consider several different forms that appear consistent with the data, and use statistical inference to determine which, if any, provides the best fit to the data.

The copulas listed are all **exchangeable**, which means that $C(u, v) = C(v, u)$. Many of the commonly used bivariate copulas are exchangeable, but it is straightforward to construct examples that are not.

6.6.8 Copulas for More than Two Variables

Each of the copulas above, except the countermonotonic copula, can be quite easily extended to more than two variables. For an m-dimensional random vector $(X_1, \ldots, X_m)$, we have the following m-dimensional copulas, $C(u_1, u_2, \ldots, u_m)$:

Independence Copula

$$C(u_1, u_2, \ldots, u_m) = u_1 \times u_2 \times \cdots \times u_m.$$

Comonotonic Copula

$$C(u_1, u_2, \ldots, u_m) = \min (u_1, u_2, \ldots, u_m).$$

Clayton Copula

$$C(u_1, u_2, \ldots, u_m) = \left(u_1^{-\theta} + u_2^{-\theta} + \cdots + u_m^{-\theta} - (m - 1) \right)^{-\frac{1}{\theta}}.$$

Gumbel Copula

$$\begin{aligned} & C(u_1, u_2, \ldots, u_m) \\ & = \exp \left\{ - \left((-\log(u_1))^{\theta} + (-\log(u_2))^{\theta} + \cdots + (-\log(u_m))^{\theta} \right)^{1/\theta} \right\}. \end{aligned}$$

Gaussian Copula Let P denote a valid correlation matrix for an m-dimensional multivariate normal distribution, and let Φ_P denote the joint distribution function of a standard multivariate normal random vector, with correlation matrix P, then

$$C(u_1, u_2, \ldots, u_m) = \Phi_P \left(z_{u_1}, z_{u_2}, \ldots, z_{u_m} \right).$$

While it is possible for three or more random variables to be comonotonic, it is not possible for three or more random variables to be countermonotonic; if X and Y are countermonotonic, and Y and Z are also countermonotonic, then X and Z are comonotonic.

6.7 Survival Copulas

It is sometimes convenient to work with the joint survival function rather than the joint distribution function. In the bivariate case, the joint survival function associated with the copula $C(u, v)$ is denoted $\overline{C}(u, v)$ where, given $F_X(x) = u$ and $F_Y(y) = v$,

$$\overline{C}(u, v) = \Pr[X > x, Y > y] = \Pr[F_X(X) > u, F_Y(Y) > v].$$

Note that, in general, $\overline{C}(u, v) + C(u, v) \neq 1$. Instead, we have

$$u + v + \overline{C}(u, v) - C(u, v) = 1. \tag{6.10}$$

This is a useful formula, and it is helpful to understand why it is true. We know that

$$\Pr(A \cap B) = \Pr(A) + \Pr(B) - \Pr(A \cup B).$$

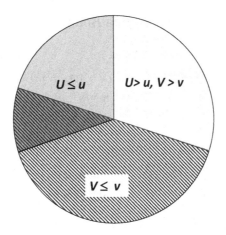

Figure 6.4 Illustration of $u + v - C(u, v) + \overline{C}(u, v) = 1$.

Let $A = \{U \le u\}$, and $B = \{V \le v\}$, so that $\Pr(A) = u$ and $\Pr(B) = v$, and

$$\Pr(A \cap B) = C(u, v),$$

$$\Pr(A \cup B) = 1 - \Pr[U > u \cap V > v] = 1 - \overline{C}(u, v)$$

$$\Rightarrow C(u, v) = u + v - \left(1 - \overline{C}(u, v)\right).$$

We illustrate this result in Figure 6.4. The figure represents a unit circle; the darker shaded part represents $\Pr[U \le u]$, which has a total area of u. The line-shaded part represents $\Pr[V \le v]$ which has a total area of v. The overlap is where $U \le u$ and $V \le v$, which has total area $C(u, v)$, and the unshaded part is where $U > u$ and $V > v$, which has total area $\overline{C}(u, v)$. The total area of the circle is 1.0, so we see that

$$1 = u + v - C(u, v) + \overline{C}(u, v).$$

The survival function $\overline{C}(u, v)$ is not a copula – it is not an increasing function of u and v, and so does not satisfy the copula requirements. However, we can utilize the **survival copula**, which is defined as

$$\widehat{C}(u, v) = \overline{C}(1 - u, 1 - v).$$

This is a true copula; it is the joint distribution function of $(1 - F_X(X))$ and $(1 - F_Y(Y))$, which is a copula because (i) it is a distribution function and (ii) $U \sim U(0, 1) \implies (1 - U) \sim U(0, 1)$, implying that $1 - F_X(X)$ and $1 - F_Y(Y)$ are both U(0,1) distributed.

6.8 Copula Bounds

For any copula $C(u_1, \ldots, u_m)$ we have

$$\max(u_1 + u_2 + \cdots + u_m - (m - 1), 0)$$
$$\leq C(u_1, \ldots, u_m) \leq \min(u_1, u_2, \ldots, u_m). \tag{6.11}$$

In the bivariate case, this simplifies to

$$\max(u + v - 1, 0) \leq C(u, v) \leq \min(u, v), \tag{6.12}$$

which shows that the lower bound for the bivariate copula is the countermono-tonic copula and the upper bound is the comonotonic copula.

We can demonstrate the bounds in the bivariate case, using the U(0,1) variables, U and V, as follows. Assume $u \leq v$:

$$C(u, v) = \Pr[U \leq u] \Pr[V \leq v | U \leq u]$$
$$\Rightarrow C(u, v) \leq Pr[U \leq u]$$
$$\Rightarrow C(u, v) \leq u,$$

which explains the upper bound.

Also, from equation (6.10) we have

$$C(u, v) = u + v + \overline{C}(u, v) - 1$$
$$\Rightarrow C(u, v) \geq u + v - 1, \quad \text{as } \overline{C}(u, v) \geq 0,$$

but since $C(u, v)$ is a probability, it must be non-negative, hence

$$C(u, v) \geq \max(u + v - 1, 0),$$

as required.

For $m \geq 3$, the upper bound is the comonotonic copula, as for the bivariate case, but the lower bound is not a copula.

6.9 Measures of Dependency

6.9.1 Pearson's ρ

We have seen that copulas can be used to add a dependency structure to random variables with different marginal distributions. Recall that the arguments of the copula function are the cumulative distribution function values of the marginal distributions. That is,

$$C(u, v) = \Pr\left[X \leq F_X^{-1}(u) \text{ and } Y \leq F_Y^{-1}(v)\right],$$

where $F_X^{-1}(u)$ is the u-quantile of X and $F_Y^{-1}(v)$ is the v-quantile of Y. It would be consistent with the copula approach to measure dependency using the association of quantiles of dependent variables. However, this is not the approach used in the classic measure of dependency, Pearson's correlation coefficient, ρ:

$$\rho(X, Y) = \frac{\text{Cov}[X, Y]}{\sqrt{\text{Var}[X]\text{Var}[Y]}} = \frac{E[XY] - E[X]E[Y]}{\sqrt{\text{Var}[X]\text{Var}[Y]}}.$$

Although ρ is widely recognized as a measure of dependency, it has some drawbacks. It measures the linear relationship between X and Y, but that can give misleading results when X and Y are highly dependent, but not necessarily linearly dependent. In particular, perfect positive correlation ($\rho = 1$) may not be attainable, even where variables are comonotonic. We demonstrate this in the following example.

Example 6.3 Suppose $X \sim \text{logN}(\mu = 0, \sigma = 1)$ and $Y = X^2$. Calculate the correlation coefficient $\rho(X, Y)$.

Solution 6.3 We know that X and Y are comonotonic, as Y is an increasing, deterministic function of $X > 0$. We also know the marginal distribution of Y, as

$$X \sim \log \text{N}(\mu, \sigma) \Rightarrow \log X \sim \text{N}(\mu, \sigma^2)$$
$$\Rightarrow \log(X^2) = 2 \log X \sim \text{N}(2\mu, (2\sigma)^2).$$

So $Y \sim \text{logN}(\mu = 0, \sigma = 2)$.

The variables X and Y are as positively dependent as possible; very large values of X will be associated with very large values of Y, and vice versa. However, when we calculate the correlation coefficient, using the fact that for a standard logN ($\mu = 0, \sigma = 1$) random variable X, $E[X^k] = e^{k^2/2}$, we have

$$E[X] = e^{0.5}, \qquad E[Y] = e^2,$$

$$E[XY] = E[X^3] = e^{4.5} \Rightarrow E[XY] - E[X]E[Y] = e^{4.5} - e^{2.5},$$

$$\text{Var}[X] = e^2 - e^1, \qquad \text{Var}[Y] = e^8 - e^4,$$

$$\Rightarrow \rho = \frac{e^{4.5} - e^{2.5}}{\sqrt{(e^2 - e^1)(e^8 - e^4)}} = 0.67.$$

We see that, despite being comonotonic, the correlation between these random variables is very much less than 1.0. Consider this from a different perspective. Given a sample of data from X and Y, if we calculated a sample correlation of $\rho = 0.67$, we would not assume a very strong dependence between the variables, but a scatter plot of the variables would show perfect, but non-linear dependency. □

Copulas model dependency in terms of the association between distribution functions of random variables, and so it is quite natural to construct measures of dependency that are based on this association. These measures are called **rank correlation measures**, as the u and v quantiles of the random variables are estimated empirically by considering the u and v rankings of a sample of bivariate data. That is, the 25%-quantile of X, say, is estimated by taking the sample value that is ranked at the 25% smallest value in the data.

We will consider two different rank correlation measures. The first is Spearman's correlation, which we denote ρ_S, to distinguish it from Pearson's correlation, which we denote ρ without subscript. The second is Kendall's rank correlation coefficient, commonly called Kendall's τ.

6.9.2 Spearman's ρ_S

Spearman's ρ_S uses the same approach as Pearson's ρ, except that instead of using the marginal random variables X and Y, Spearman's ρ_S calculates the correlation between the random variables $U = F_X(X)$ and $V = F_Y(Y)$. We know that both U and V have marginal U(0, 1) distributions, which means that

$$E[U] = E[V] = \frac{1}{2},$$

$$E[U^2] = E[V^2] = \frac{1}{3},$$

$$\text{Var}[U] = \text{Var}[V] = \frac{1}{12},$$

$$\implies \rho_S(X, Y) = \rho(U, V) = \frac{E[UV] - E[U]E[V]}{\sqrt{\text{Var}[U]\text{Var}[V]}} = \frac{E[UV] - 1/4}{1/12}$$

$$= 12E[UV] - 3.$$

The bounds for ρ_S are the same as for Pearson's ρ, that is, $-1 \leq \rho_S \leq 1$.

In the case of comonotonic risks, such as in Example 6.3, we have $U = V$ so that

$$\rho_S(X, Y) = \rho(U, U) = 12E[U^2] - 3 = 1,$$

so that comonotonic risks are always perfectly correlated using Spearman's ρ_S.

Estimating Spearman's ρ_S from data can be done by applying the usual sample correlation estimating function for Pearson's ρ to the ranking of the

Table 6.1. *Data for correlation examples*

i	x_i	y_i	i	x_i	y_i
1	21.60	44.20	11	21.15	43.20
2	22.20	44.30	12	20.50	44.50
3	21.80	45.10	13	20.30	44.10
4	21.70	55.80	14	19.80	43.80
5	22.10	45.20	15	19.10	42.90
6	21.75	43.70	16	18.40	43.10
7	21.50	44.90	17	13.50	42.30
8	21.90	45.50	18	12.10	39.70
9	22.70	45.70	19	20.20	37.60
10	37.90	45.60	20	20.00	39.00

data points, provided there are no ties (i.e. no equal values in the x or y samples). Let r_x denote the rank data for X and r_y for Y, so that (r_{x_i}, r_{y_i}) denotes the rank of observation x_i and the rank of observation y_i. Let $\bar{r}_x$ and $s_{r_x}^2$ denote the sample mean and variance of the x_i rank data, and let $\bar{r}_y$ and $s_{r_y}^2$ denote the sample mean and variance of the y_i rank data. Then, the sample Spearman correlation is

$$r = \frac{1}{n-1} \sum_{i=1}^{n} \left(\frac{r_{x_i} - \bar{r}_x}{s_{r_x}} \right) \left(\frac{r_{y_i} - \bar{r}_y}{s_{r_y}} \right),$$

but we can simplify this considerably, since

$$\bar{r}_x = \bar{r}_y = (n+1)/2 \quad \text{and} \quad s_{r_x}^2 = s_{r_y}^2 = n(n+1)/12$$

$$\Rightarrow r = \frac{12}{n(n^2-1)} \sum_{i=1}^{n} \left(r_{x_i} \times r_{y_i} \right) - \frac{3(n+1)}{n-1}. \tag{6.13}$$

If there are ties in the data we assign the average rank to the equal values. That is, if there are three observations the same, and they are all equal rank j in the sample, then assign a rank of $(j + (j + 1) + (j + 2))/3 = (j + 1)$ to each.

Example 6.4 A sample of 20 bivariate data points is presented in Table 6.1. Estimate (a) Pearson's ρ and (b) Spearman's ρ_s for these data.

Solution 6.4 (a) The sample Pearson correlation coefficient is

$$r = \frac{1}{n-1} \sum_{i=1}^{n} \left(\frac{x_i - \bar{x}}{s_x} \right) \left(\frac{y_i - \bar{y}}{s_y} \right) = 0.33.$$

This indicates a weak positive correlation.

Table 6.2. *Rank data for correlation examples*

i	rank(x_i)	rank(y_i)	i	rank(x_i)	rank(y_i)
1	9	10	11	11	14
2	3	9	12	12	8
3	6	6	13	13	11
4	8	1	14	16	12
5	4	5	15	17	16
6	7	13	16	18	15
7	10	7	17	19	17
8	5	4	18	20	18
9	2	2	19	14	20
10	1	3	20	15	19

(b) The Spearman correlation coefficient can be calculated using the same formula, but replacing the values of x_i and y_i with the rank values, and replacing the sample mean and sample standard deviations with the means and standard deviations of the rank values. For example, $x_1 = 21.6$ is the 9th largest value of the x_i, and $y_1 = 44.20$ is the 10th largest value of the y_i. The rank data set is shown in Table 6.2.

The Spearman correlation coefficient for our sample, using Table 6.2, is $r_s = 0.81$, indicating a much stronger positive relationship than suggested by the Pearson correlation. □

6.9.3 Kendall's τ_k

Let (X^*, Y^*) denote a bivariate random variable that has the same joint distribution as (X, Y), and is independent of (X, Y). Think of it as an independent draw from the same joint distribution.

Then

$$\tau_k = \Pr\left[(X - X^*)(Y - Y^*) > 0\right] - \Pr\left[(X - X^*)(Y - Y^*) < 0\right] \quad (6.14)$$

$$= \mathrm{E}\left[\mathrm{sign}\big((X - X^*)(Y - Y^*)\big)\right], \quad (6.15)$$

where

$$\mathrm{sign}(z) = \begin{cases} -1 & \text{if } z < 0, \\ 0 & \text{if } z = 0, \\ +1 & \text{if } z > 0. \end{cases}$$

The intuition here is that if larger values of X (relative to its distribution) are associated with larger relative values of Y, and smaller values of X with smaller values of Y, then $(X - X^*)(Y - Y^*)$ will tend to be positive (either both terms positive or both terms negative). In this case we say that X and Y are **concordant**. On the other hand, if larger relative values of X are associated with smaller relative values of Y, and vice versa, then $(X - X^*)(Y - Y^*)$ will tend to be negative, and we say that X and Y are **discordant**.

We can express τ_k in terms of the copula, as

$$\tau_k = 4\mathrm{E}[C(U,V)] - 1,$$

where $U = F_X(X)$ and $V = F_Y(Y)$ as usual.[1]

For comonotonic risks,

$$X < X^* \Leftrightarrow Y < Y^*$$
$$\Rightarrow \Pr\left[(X - X^*)(Y - Y^*) > 0\right] = 1 \text{ and } \Pr\left[(X - X^*)(Y - Y^*) < 0\right] = 0$$
$$\Rightarrow \tau_k = 1 - 0 = 1.$$

Alternatively, as X and Y are comonotonic, we have $V = U$ and $C(U,V) = C(U,U) = \min(U,U) = U$, so

$$4\mathrm{E}[C(U,V)] - 1 = 4\mathrm{E}[U] - 1 = 4(0.5) - 1 = 1.$$

The sample estimate of τ_k is found by considering all possible values of $\mathrm{sign}\left((x_i - x_j)(y_i - y_j)\right)$ for $i = 1, \ldots, n-1$ and where $j = i+1, \ldots, n$. We assume there are no ties in the data (the formula can be adjusted if ties exist). Then the sample estimate of τ_k is

$$t_k = \frac{2}{n(n-1)} \sum_{i=1}^{n-1} \sum_{j=i+1}^{n} \mathrm{sign}\left((x_i - x_j)(y_i - y_j)\right). \tag{6.16}$$

$$= \frac{number\ of\ concordant\ pairs - number\ of\ discordant\ pairs}{\frac{1}{2}n(n-1)} \tag{6.17}$$

where each pair is a comparison of two values from the bivariate sample, for example, comparing (x_i, y_i) with (x_j, y_j), for $i \neq j$. A concordant pair is where either $x_i > x_j$ and $y_i > y_j$, or $x_i < x_j$ and $y_i < y_j$, and a discordant pair is where either $x_i > x_j$ and $y_i < y_j$ or vice versa. The denominator, $\frac{1}{2}n(n-1)$, is the number of pairwise comparisons of the bivariate random variables, given a sample of n values. The interpretation of the formula is that t_k is the average concordance, over all the possible distinct values of i and $j > i$.

---

[1] See McNeil et al. (2015) for a proof of this result.

Table 6.3. *Calculations of concordance for* (x_1, y_1), *where* $rank(x_1) = 9$,
$rank(y_1) = 10$, *for Example 6.5*

j	$rank(x_j)$	$rank(y_j)$	$sign(x_1 - x_j)$	$sign(y_1 - y_j)$	$sign(x_1 - x_j)(y_1 - y_j)$
2	3	9	+1	+1	+1
3	6	6	+1	+1	+1
4	8	1	+1	+1	+1
5	4	5	+1	+1	+1
6	7	13	+1	-1	-1
7	10	7	-1	+1	-1
8	5	4	+1	+1	+1
9	2	2	+1	+1	+1
10	1	3	+1	+1	+1
11	11	14	-1	-1	+1
12	12	8	-1	+1	-1
13	13	11	-1	-1	+1
14	16	12	-1	-1	+1
15	17	16	-1	-1	+1
16	18	15	-1	-1	+1
17	19	17	-1	-1	+1
18	20	18	-1	-1	+1
19	14	20	-1	-1	+1
20	15	19	-1	-1	+1
			Total concordance for $i = 1$		13

We may apply equations (6.16) or (6.17) to the original data or to the ranks
of the data. The signs will be the same.

Like the other two correlation measures, both τ_k and the sample estimator
t_k are bounded by -1 and 1. If X and Y are independent, then $\tau_k = 0$, (but
$\tau_k = 0$ does not imply independence). If X and Y are countermonotonic, then
$\tau_k = -1$.

Example 6.5 Estimate τ_k for the sample data given in Table 6.1.

Solution 6.5 For each $i = 1$ to $i = 19$, we compare rank(x_i) with each
rank($x_{j>i}$) and compare rank(y_i) with each rank($y_{j>i}$).

For example, in Table 6.3 we show the 19 comparisons for $i = 1$, and
$j = 2, 3, \ldots, 20$. We have rank(x_1) = 9 and rank(y_1) = 10. If rank(x_j) < 9
then sign($x_1 - x_j$) = 1; if rank(x_j) > 9 then sign($x_1 - x_j$) = -1, and similarly
for rank(y_j).

We repeat this process for $i = 2, 3, \ldots, 19$. The results are shown in Table
6.4, which shows that we have 190 comparisons, of which 154 have positive
sign (e.g., $j = 1, i = 2$) and 36 have negative sign (e.g., $j = 2, i = 3$). This
gives a sample estimate for τ_k of $t = (154 - 36)/190 = 0.6$. ☐

Table 6.4. *Summary of concordance calculations for Example 6.5*

i	Number of comparisons	Number with positive sign	Number with negative sign	Total
1	19	16	3	13
2	18	12	6	6
3	17	16	1	15
4	16	11	5	6
5	15	14	1	13
6	14	10	4	6
7	13	13	0	13
8	12	12	0	12
9	11	10	1	9
10	10	10	0	10
11	9	6	3	3
12	8	8	0	8
13	7	7	0	7
14	6	4	2	2
15	5	2	3	−1
16	4	2	2	0
17	3	1	2	−1
18	2	0	2	−2
19	1	0	1	−1
Totals	190	154	36	118

The copulas illustrated in Figures 6.1, 6.2, and 6.3 all have a Kendall's τ correlation of $\tau_k = 0.6$, and a Spearman ρ_s correlation of around 0.8. Notice though that the single figure measures of dependency do not capture the very different dependency patterns in the simulated data. In the Clayton copula, there appears to be strong dependence for smaller values of u and v, but weak dependence in the right tail. The Gumbel copula is the other way around – dependence appears quite strong in the right tail, but is weaker in the middle and left tail. The Gaussian copula is more consistent, with fewer outliers in the middle of the distribution, but with less dense clustering in the tails. In the next section, we consider more specifically the dependence in the tails of the distribution for different copulas.

6.10 Tail Dependence

In risk management we often focus on the right tail of our loss distributions, to ensure that extreme risks are suitably managed. It is of very great interest to us to understand the tail dependency between risks. That is, if we know that Y is very large, what is the probability that X is also very large? There is a perception in financial markets that dependency is greater in extremely adverse conditions than it is in more normal conditions. So we are interested in determining whether a copula captures this perceived tendency for 'everything to go wrong together'.

We specify this question in terms of the distribution quantiles. Given, for example, that Y lies beyond its 99.9% quantile what is the probability that X is greater than its 99.9% quantile? That is, what is

$$\Pr\left[X > Q_{99.9\%}(X) \middle| Y > Q_{99.9\%}(Y)\right]?$$

In a few cases, the tail dependency is clear:

- If X and Y are independent, then knowing that $Y > Q_{99.9\%}(Y)$ tells us nothing about X, so $\Pr\left[X > Q_{99.9\%}(X) \middle| Y > Q_{99.9\%}(Y)\right] = \Pr\left[X > Q_{99.9\%}(X)\right] = 0.001$.
- If X and Y are comonotonic, then they are *always* large (or small) together, and $\Pr\left[X > Q_{99.9\%}(X) \middle| Y > Q_{99.9\%}(Y)\right] = 1.0$.
- If X and Y are countermonotonic, then they are *never* large or small together, so $\Pr\left[X > Q_{99.9\%}(X) \middle| Y > Q_{99.9\%}(Y)\right] = 0.0$.

What about other cases? If we assume, for example, that dependency can be modelled using a Gaussian copula, what does that tell us about the conditional probability in the tails?

We define the **upper tail dependence** for a pair of random losses, X and Y as

$$\lambda_U = \lim_{q \to 1} \Pr\left[X > Q_q(X) \middle| Y > Q_q(Y)\right] \tag{6.18}$$

$$= \lim_{q \to 1} \Pr\left[F_X(X) > q \middle| F_Y(Y) > q\right] \tag{6.19}$$

$$= \lim_{q \to 1} \frac{\overline{C}(q,q)}{1-q} \tag{6.20}$$

$$= \lim_{q \to 1} \frac{1 - 2q + C(q,q)}{1-q}. \tag{6.21}$$

If $\lambda_U = 0$ then X, Y are asymptotically independent in the upper tail. It is possible for dependent random variables to be asymptotically independent. If $\lambda_U > 0$ then X and Y show upper tail dependence.

Similarly, the lower tail dependence is

$$\lambda_L = \lim_{q \to 0} \Pr\left[X \le Q_q(X) \big| Y \le Q_q(Y)\right] \tag{6.22}$$

$$= \lim_{q \to 0} \Pr\left[F_X(X) \le q \big| F_Y(Y) \le q\right] \tag{6.23}$$

$$= \lim_{q \to 0} \frac{C(q, q)}{q}. \tag{6.24}$$

The Gaussian copula has no upper tail or lower tail dependence. The Clayton copula has lower tail dependence, but no upper tail dependence (this can be seen clearly in Figure 6.1), and the Gumbel copula has upper tail dependence but no lower tail dependence (see Figure 6.2).

6.11 Archimedean Copulas

Archimedean copulas are explicit copulas constructed using a generator function $\phi(u)$, with the following properties:

(1) $\phi(u)$ maps $[0, 1)$ to $[0, \infty]$.
(2) $\phi(0) = \infty$, $\phi(1) = 0$, and ϕ is continuous and strictly decreasing.
(3) For bivariate copulas, ϕ must be convex.[2]

The bivariate copula generated by the function ϕ is

$$C(u, v) = \phi^{-1}\left(\phi(u) + \phi(v)\right).$$

For bivariate Archimedean copulas, we have the following potential shortcuts for the tail dependence measures, and for Kendall's tau. Let $C(u, v)$ denote the Archimedean copula for loss variables (X, Y), with generating function $\phi(t)$. Then

$$\tau_k = 1 + 4 \int_0^1 \frac{\phi(t)}{\frac{d}{dt}\phi(t)} dt, \tag{6.25}$$

$$\lambda_U = 2 - 2 \lim_{t \to 0} \frac{\frac{d}{dt}\phi^{-1}(2t)}{\frac{d}{dt}\phi^{-1}(t)}, \tag{6.26}$$

$$\lambda_L = 2 \lim_{t \to \infty} \frac{\frac{d}{dt}\phi^{-1}(2t)}{\frac{d}{dt}\phi^{-1}(t)}. \tag{6.27}$$

---

[2] More onerous conditions apply for higher dimensional Archimedean copulas.

6.11.1 Examples of Archimedean Copulas

Clayton

$$\phi(u) = \frac{1}{\theta}\left(u^{-\theta} - 1\right) \text{ for } \theta > 0 \quad \Rightarrow \phi^{-1}(z) = (1 + \theta z)^{-\frac{1}{\theta}}.$$

The conditions for a generator function are satisfied, as

$$\phi(1) = 0, \qquad \lim_{t \to 0} \phi(t) = \infty, \qquad \frac{d}{dt}\phi(t) = -t^{-(\theta+1)} < 0,$$

$$\frac{d^2}{dt^2}\phi(t) = (\theta + 1) t^{-(\theta+2)} > 0.$$

Applying the shortcut formulas above, we find for the Clayton copula

$$\tau_k = \frac{\theta}{\theta + 2}, \qquad \lambda_U = 0, \qquad \lambda_L = 2^{-\frac{1}{\theta}}.$$

Gumbel

$$\phi(u) = (-\log(u))^{\theta} \quad \text{for } \theta \geq 1 \Rightarrow \phi^{-1}(t) = e^{-t^{1/\theta}},$$

$$\tau_k = \frac{\theta - 1}{\theta}, \qquad \lambda_U = 2 - 2^{1/\theta}, \qquad \lambda_L = 0.$$

Generalized Clayton (BB1)

$$\phi(u) = \frac{(u^{-\theta} - 1)^{\delta}}{\theta^{\delta}}.$$

6.12 Copula Estimation

6.12.1 Matching Kendall's τ_k

For smooth one-parameter copulas we can estimate the parameter θ by matching the copula τ_k to the empirical estimate t_k. This is similar to the method of moments estimation for fitting univariate distributions.

6.12.2 Maximum Likelihood

The joint density function for random variables X, Y with marginal d.f.s $F_X(x)$ and $F_Y(y)$, and with copula $C(F_X(x), F_Y(y)) = F_{X,Y}(x, y)$ is

$$f_{X,Y}(x, y) = \frac{\partial^2}{\partial x \, \partial y} F_{X,Y}(x, y) = \frac{\partial^2}{\partial x \, \partial y} C(F_X(x), F_Y(y)) \tag{6.28}$$

$$= f_X(x) \, f_Y(y) \, c(F_X(x), F_Y(y)), \tag{6.29}$$

where $f_X(x)$ and $f_Y(y)$ are the marginal p.d.f.s of X and Y, and where $c(u, v)$ is the copula density:

$$c(u, v) = \frac{\partial^2}{\partial u \, \partial v} C(u, v). \tag{6.30}$$

So, given a bivariate sample of data $(x_1, y_1), (x_2, y_2), \ldots, (x_n \, y_n)$, we can determine the log likelihood as

$$LL = \sum_{i=1}^{n} \log f_X(x_i) + \sum_{i=1}^{n} \log f_Y(y_i) + \sum_{i=1}^{n} \log c(F_X(x_i), F_Y(y_i))$$
$$= LL_m + LL_c,$$

where LL_m is the total log likelihood from the marginal distributions, and LL_c is the contribution from the copula.

If we are interested in a full parametric model fit, we will maximize the log likelihood over the full parameter space of X, Y, and $C(u, v)$. Generally, we will use some suitable software, and we need to be careful about local maxima.

If we are primarily interested in the copula parameters, then we are concerned only with LL_c. We can avoid using the full parameters of X and Y if we replace $F_X(x_i)$ with the smoothed empirical estimator,

$$\tilde{F}_X(x_i) = \frac{\text{Number of } x_j \le x_i}{n + 1} = \frac{\text{Rank of } x_i}{n + 1}.$$

We use the $n + 1$ in the denominator to avoid problems at x_n, as the copula is defined for $0 < u, v < 1$.

6.13 Monte Carlo Simulation of Bivariate Copulas

In practice, simulating joint distributions using copulas is often most easily done using software designed for the purpose. The 'copula' and 'QRM' packages in R are useful resources. In the case of implicit Gaussian and Student's t copulas, and for Archimedean bivariate copulas, the simulation algorithms are relatively straightforward, particularly for lower dimensions.

The algorithms in this section can be used to simulate from the distribution of the random pair (X, Y), with marginal distribution functions $F_X(x)$ and $F_Y(y)$ respectively, and with copula $C(u, v)$.

6.13.1 Gaussian Copula

(1) Generate N pairs of bivariate normally distributed random variables, (z_{j1}, z_{j2}), $j = 1, 2, \ldots, N$, with mean $\mathbf{0}$, and with covariance $\mathbf{\Sigma} = \left(\begin{smallmatrix} 1 & \rho \\ \rho & 1 \end{smallmatrix} \right)$, using the method from Section 6.3.

Note that the Cholesky decomposition of the correlation matrix is

$$A = \begin{pmatrix} 1 & 0 \\ \rho & \sqrt{1 - \rho^2} \end{pmatrix}.$$

(2) Convert each pair into a bivariate uniform pair, with a Gaussian copula, using the standard normal distribution function:

$$(u_j, v_j) = \big(\Phi(z_{j,1}), \ \Phi(z_{j,2}) \big).$$

(3) Convert the dependent U(0, 1) variables to marginal x_j, y_j as

$$x_j = F_X^{-1}(u_j) \qquad y_j = F_Y^{-1}(v_j).$$

6.13.2 Student's t Copula

(1) Generate N MVT pairs, $(t_{j,1}, t_{j,2})$, $j = 1, 2, \ldots, N$, using the method from Section 6.4.

(2) Convert each pair into a bivariate uniform pair with Student's t copula:

$$(u_j, v_j) = \big(t_\nu(t_{j,1}), \ t_\nu(t_{j,2}) \big),$$

where t_ν represents the (univariate) Student's t distribution function with ν degrees of freedom.

(3) Convert to marginal x_j, y_j as

$$x_j = F_X^{-1}(u_j), \qquad y_j = F_Y^{-1}(v_j).$$

Archimedean Copulas

Let $\phi(u)$ denote the generating function, and let

$$g(u) = \frac{d}{du} \phi^{-1}(u).$$

(1) Generate N i.i.d., U(0, 1) pairs, $(u_{j,1}, u_{j,2})$, $j = 1, 2, \ldots, N$.

(2) The bivariate pair (u_j, v_j) is generated from the independent values through the relationships

$$u_j = u_{j,1}, \tag{6.31}$$

$$u_{j,2} = \frac{g\left(\phi(u_j) + \phi(v_j)\right)}{g(\phi(u_j))} \tag{6.32}$$

$$\Rightarrow v_j = \phi^{-1}\left(g^{-1}\left(u_{j,2}\, g(\phi(u_j))\right) - \phi(u_j)\right). \tag{6.33}$$

(3) Convert to marginal x_j, y_j as

$$x_j = F_X^{-1}(u_j), \qquad y_j = F_Y^{-1}(v_j).$$

6.14 Notes and Further Reading

The Gaussian copula was used extensively before the 2007–8 global financial crisis, for pricing credit derivatives; analysts needed a model of dependency between the default risks of different loans. It (or its generalizations) proved to be a somewhat reasonable model for pricing but was less useful for ongoing risk management of outstanding debt, largely because of its lack of tail dependence. When markets crashed, dependencies of defaults increased, contrary to the implicit assumption in the Gaussian copula. It was even blamed in some circles for the entire financial crisis (see, e.g., Salmon (2009)), though that ignores many, many other systemic problems. One problem appeared to be that analysts were happy to have a model to insert in their pricing engines, but did not sufficiently research the characteristics of the model. The intuition that there would be increasing dependence with respect to defaults in extreme market conditions was well understood by practitioners; what may have been less well understood was that the Gaussian copula would not reflect this – and that other copulas would.

Extreme value copulas (EVC) are a class of copulas that satisfy the condition that

$$\forall t > 0, \ C(u_1^t, u_2^t, \ldots, u_d^t) = C^t(u_1, u_2, \ldots, u_d).$$

EVCs can be applied to model dependency of maxima in multivariate settings, where the marginal distributions are in the GEV family. The independence, comonotonic, and Gumbel copulas are all EV copulas. See McNeil et al. (2015) for more details and characteristics of EVCs.

6.15 Exercises

Exercise 6.1 Show that the following functions satisfy the criteria for a bivariate copula:

(a) $C(u, v) = uv$ (the independence copula).
(b) $C(u, v) = \min(u, v)$ (the comonotonic copula).
(c) $C = \max(u + v - 1, 0)$ (the countermonotonic copula).

Exercise 6.2 Outline the advantages and disadvantages of using Spearman's rank correlation to measure dependency, rather than Pearson correlation.

Exercise 6.3

(a) Show that for countermonotonic risks (X, Y), $\rho_s = -1$.
(b) Show that for countermonotonic risks (X, Y), $\tau_K = -1$.
(c) You are given that $X \sim N(0, 1)$, and $Y = 1 - e^X$:

    (i) Show that X and Y are countermonotonic.
    (ii) Calculate the correlation coefficient of (X, Y).

Exercise 6.4 Let Z be a standard normal random variable.

(a) Calculate the (Pearson) correlation between Z and $X = Z^2$.
(b) Let W be independent of Z with $\Pr[W = 1] = \Pr[W = -1] = \frac{1}{2}$. Calculate:

    (i) The (Pearson) correlation between Z and $Y = WZ$,
    (ii) $\Pr[|W| = |Z|]$.

(c) Comment on your results.

Exercise 6.5 Suppose that $C(u, v)$ and $C^*(u, v)$ are both copulas. Show that for any constant s such that $0 < s < 1$, the weighted average $sC(u, v) + (1 - s)C^*(u, v)$ is also a copula. Give a probabilistic interpretation of this copula.

Exercise 6.6 Calculate ρ_s and τ_K for the bivariate random variable (X, Y), with joint distribution function

$$F(x, y) = 0.3(C_1(F_X(x), F_Y(y))) + 0.7(C_2(F_X(x), F_Y(y))),$$

where C_1 is the countermonotonic copula and C_2 is the comonotonic copula.

Exercise 6.7 Consider the bivariate random variable (U, W) where $U \sim U(0, 1)$ and $W = (1 - U)^{0.2}$:

(a) Derive the marginal probability density function for W, and hence show that the marginal distribution of W is beta, with parameters $a = 5$, $b = 1$.
(b) Calculate the Pearson correlation coefficient, ρ, for the pair (U, W).
(c) Derive the joint distribution function, $F_{U,W}(u, w)$, and show that the copula function is the countermonotonic copula.
(d) Derive τ_K for the pair (U, W).
(e) Comment on the difference between ρ and τ_K in this case.

Exercise 6.8 Two firms, labelled Firm 1 and Firm 2, are exposed to risks X_1 and X_2, respectively, such that default for firm i will occur when $X_i \leq 1$ for $i = 1, 2$. You are given the following information:

- X_1 is modelled as an exponential random variable with $\lambda_1 = 0.03$.
- X_2 is modelled as an exponential random variable with $\lambda_2 = 0.02$.
- The dependency between X_1 and X_2 is modelled using the copula:

$$C(u, v) = \max\left(0, \left(u^{-\alpha} + v^{-\alpha} - 1\right)^{-1/\alpha}\right), \quad \text{with } \alpha = 0.8.$$

(a) Calculate the individual probabilities of default for each firm.
(b) An investor will lose 10,000 if Firm 1 fails, and 5,000 if Firm 2 fails. Identify the full probability distribution for her losses.

Exercise 6.9 Consider the copula:

$$C(u, v) = uv(1 + \theta(1 - u)(1 - v)).$$

(a) Identify the range of possible values for θ.
(b) Determine the upper and lower tail dependence for the copula.

Exercise 6.10 State with reasons which of the copulas in Figure 6.5 show the following properties (there may be more than one):

(a) Exchangeability.
(b) Positive τ_K.
(c) Negative τ_K.
(d) Lower tail dependence.

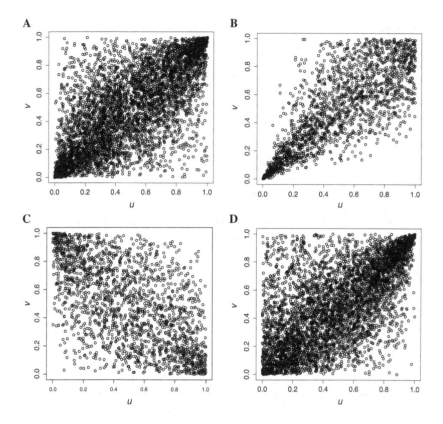

Figure 6.5 Copula examples for Exercise 6.10

Exercise 6.11 A commonly held fallacy is that the joint distribution of the random variables X_1 and X_2 is fully determined by their marginal distributions and correlation:

(a) Show that the statement is false by constructing two random pairs with the same marginal distributions and correlations, but with different joint distributions.
(b) Suppose that you know that the marginal distributions are normal, and the correlation is zero. Show (using a counterexample) that this does not imply that the random variables are independent.

Exercise 6.12 Let T_1, T_2 denote the times to failure of two independent components in a manufacturing process. Assume that T_1 and T_2 are independent, and identically distributed, with common distribution function $F(\cdot)$.

Let $X = \min(T_1, T_2)$ and $Y = \max(T_1, T_2)$.

(a) Show that X and Y are not independent.
(b) Show that

$$\Pr\left[X \le x, Y \le y\right] = 2F(\min(x,y))F(y) - (F(\min(x,y)))^2.$$

(c) Derive the marginal distribution functions for X and Y, in terms of $F(\cdot)$.
(d) Hence, derive the copula for X and Y.

Exercise 6.13 (R exercise)

(a) Using (e.g.) the 'copula' package in R (see Hofert et al., 2020), generate 1,000 random pairs, (U, V), from:

   (i) a Clayton copula, with $\theta = 0.5$;
   (ii) a Gumbel copula, with $\theta = 1.5$;
   (iii) a t copula with $\rho = -0.5$, df $= 10$.

(b) For each copula, estimate ρ_s and τ_K from the sample. Comment on the sampling error.
(c) For each copula, use the sample to generate 1,000 random pairs (X, Y), with marginal distributions

$$X \sim \log N(\mu = 3, \sigma = 1.5); \quad Y \sim \text{Pareto}(\alpha = 4.0, \theta = 195).$$

Create scatter plots of the results, and calculate the Pearson correlation coefficients.

Exercise 6.14 (R exercise) Download a data set of daily log-returns (e.g., from Yahoo.com), for the stocks of two financial firms, for a period of at least five years.

(a) Create a scatter plot of the data, (x_i, y_i), 1, 2, ..., n.
(b) Create a scatter plot of the probability-transformed pairs, (u_i, v_i), where $u_i = \frac{r_{x_i}}{n+1}$ and $v_i = \frac{r_{y_i}}{n+1}$.
(c) (i) Obtain estimates of Spearman's rho for the entire data set and also for the subsets in the upper-right and lower-left corners as the square containing the subsets gets smaller.
   (ii) Obtain estimates of $\Pr[U > u | V > u]$ as u gets close to 1. Reverse the roles of U and V. Repeat at the lower end.
   (iii) Comment on the empirical evidence of tail dependence in your data.
(d) Fit several one-parameter copulas using maximum likelihood and recommend the best model(s) based on likelihood and tests of fit.

7

Stress Testing

7.1 Summary

In this chapter, we discuss stress and scenario tests and testing frameworks. We begin with an introduction to stress testing and a discussion of where stress and scenario testing is most useful, as well as noting some limitations. This is followed by a study of methods for designing and generating stress scenarios. We then discuss regulatory stress tests and present examples of past failures and successes of real-world stress tests.

7.2 Introduction

Stress tests are tools designed to help a financial institution assess the vulnerabilities in its portfolio, the potential losses that it may suffer, and the future actions that may be taken to avoid those losses. A stress test evaluates the institution's profits and losses based a set of future stress scenarios. This evaluation may or may not include the effects of the institution's planned actions due to the impact of the scenarios (i.e. the consequences of attempts to raise new funds, either by trying to access capital markets or by selling off existing assets). Stress scenarios are descriptions of the possible future evolution of risk factors that affect the portfolio (either directly or indirectly). While stress scenarios are commonly specified in quantitative terms, they are typically not generated by models, nor are they usually assigned probabilities.

7.3 Stress and Scenario Testing

Stress testing is used to examine how risk measures and risk preparation are affected by adverse movements in one or more of the key underlying variables.

A sensitivity test might consider the impact on the results of risk modelling when small changes are made to key input variables. A stress test may be very similar to a sensitivity test, but with a focus on adverse shifts in the input variables. Or, the stress test may involve a more detailed scenario, under which many or all key inputs are adjusted in some coherent and consistent manner, to create a scenario that represents an extreme, but not impossible adverse situation for the firm. Sometimes, the term 'stress test' is used to indicate testing results against adverse changes in a single variable (or perhaps a small set of closely connected variables), while the term 'scenario test' is used when the changes are more wide ranging. In this chapter, we do not distinguish these two cases.

Example 7.1 A bank has a portfolio of mortgages covering properties in Florida and California.

If the average value of house prices falls in either state, over a 1-year period, then the bank will suffer losses. The risk manager models the losses as follows.

Let Y_F and Y_C denote the annual change in average house prices in Florida and California, respectively.

Let L denote the loss arising on the portfolio.

The risk manager calculates the 95% Expected Shortfall for this risk, assuming that Y_F and Y_C are independent, and:

$$Y_F \sim \mathrm{N}(\mu_F, \sigma_F^2), \qquad Y_C \sim \mathrm{N}(\mu_C, \sigma_C^2),$$

$$L \,|\, Y_F > 0, \, Y_C > 0 = 0,$$

$$L \,|\, Y_F \leq 0, \, Y_C > 0 = \lambda_F,$$

$$L \,|\, Y_F > 0, \, Y_C \leq 0 = \lambda_C,$$

$$L \,|\, Y_F \leq 0, \, Y_C \leq 0 = \lambda_{F\&C},$$

where

$$\mu_F = 0.050; \ \sigma_F = 0.025; \ \mu_C = 0.045; \ \sigma_C = 0.020;$$

$$\lambda_F = 20; \ \lambda_C = 15; \ \text{and } \lambda_{F\&C} = 40.$$

(a) Calculate the 95% Expected Shortfall for the aggregate loss.
(b) Determine the change in the 95% Expected Shortfall if the following inputs are stressed. In each case, keep all other variables the same as the original assumptions:

   (i) $\mu_F = 0.045$.
   (ii) $\sigma_F = 0.0275$.
   (iii) $\lambda_F = 22$.

(c) The risk manager decides to test a scenario representing a more extreme outlook, under which the probability of falling house prices is increased, the results in the two states are highly dependent, and, if house prices fall in both states, the losses in each state are more severe. The stress scenario parameters are:

- Y_F and Y_C are dependent, with copula

$$C(u, v) = \left(u^{-\theta} + v^{-\theta} - 1\right)^{-\frac{1}{\theta}}, \qquad \theta = 2.$$

- $\mu_F = 0.048$, $\sigma_F = 0.026$, $\mu_C = 0.042$, $\sigma_C = 0.022$.
- $\lambda_F = 22$, $\lambda_C = 16.5$, and $\lambda_{F\&C} = 55$.

Calculate the 95% Expected Shortfall under this stress scenario.

Solution 7.1

(a) We have

$$\Pr[Y_F \leq 0] = 0.022750; \quad \Pr[Y_C \leq 0] = 0.012224.$$

Given independence, we have

$$\Pr[Y_F \leq 0 \text{ and } Y_C \leq 0] = 0.022750 \times 0.012224 = 0.000278,$$
$$\Pr[Y_F \leq 0 \text{ and } Y_C > 0] = 0.022750 - 0.000278 = 0.022472,$$
$$\Pr[Y_F > 0 \text{ and } Y_C \leq 0] = 0.012224 - 0.000278 = 0.011946,$$
$$\Pr[Y_F > 0 \text{ and } Y_C > 0] = 0.965304,$$

which means that the distribution of the loss is

$$L = \begin{cases} 0 & \text{w.p. } 0.965304 \\ \lambda_F & \text{w.p. } 0.022472 \\ \lambda_C & \text{w.p. } 0.011946 \\ \lambda_{F\&C} & \text{w.p. } 0.000278. \end{cases}$$

The 95% quantile of L is in the probability mass at 0, (see equation (3.7)), so we have

$$\text{ES}_{0.95}$$
$$= \frac{0.022472(\lambda_F) + 0.011946(\lambda_C) + 0.000278(\lambda_{F\&C}) + 0.015304 \cdot (0)}{0.05}$$
$$= 12.795.$$

(b) (i) $\mu_F = 0.045 \Rightarrow \text{ES}_{95\%} = 18.083$.
(ii) $\sigma_F = 0.0275 \Rightarrow \text{ES}_{95\%} = 17.517$.
(iii) $\lambda_F = 22 \Rightarrow \text{ES}_{95\%} = 13.694$.

(c) Now, we have

$$\Pr[Y_F \leq 0] = 0.0.032435; \quad \Pr[Y_C \leq 0] = 0.028125,$$
$$\Pr[Y_F \leq 0 \text{ and } Y_C \leq 0] = C(0.03243, 0.02812) = 0.021254,$$
$$\Pr[Y_F \leq 0 \text{ and } Y_C > 0] = 0.032435 - 0.021254 = 0.011181,$$
$$\Pr[Y_F > 0 \text{ and } Y_C \leq 0] = 0.028125 - 0.021254 = 0.006871,$$
$$\Pr[Y_F > 0 \text{ and } Y_A > 0] = 0.960694,$$

and so the 95% Expected Shortfall under this stress scenario is

$$\frac{0.011181 * (22) + 0.006871 * (16.5) + 0.021254 * (55) + 0.01069 * (0)}{0.05}$$
$$= 30.566. \qquad \square$$

This example illustrates the difference between stress testing individual assumptions and creating a stress scenario covering multiple inputs.

It also illustrates one of the difficulties with stress testing, which is how to interpret the results. Clearly, the impact of the adverse scenario in the example is highly significant. But, does it matter? What is the probability that a scenario similar to that tested will be experienced? We usually have no objective measurement of the likelihood of the individual scenarios. If the scenario appears implausible, then the decision-makers of the firm will not be willing to invest in risk mitigation strategies to protect themselves from the implied exposure.

However, stress testing can be a useful addition to other forms of risk modelling, as we discuss in the following sections.

7.4 Purposes and Uses of Stress Testing

In previous chapters, we have discussed the statistical models and methods that can be applied to assess risk relatively objectively. Stress tests are used by most financial institutions in addition to these quantitative methods, usually in a more subjective context. In particular, stress and scenario testing can be used to focus on specific risks or scenarios that are not captured through aggregate risk modelling, or, if they are captured, are difficult to identify or interpret in the output of the aggregate model.

(a) Stress tests can be used to explore the impact of specific extreme scenarios, such as a sudden economic collapse, for example, as a result of a global pandemic similar to the 2020 COVID-19 crisis, or a systemic collapse of markets, similar to the 2007–8 financial crisis.

These scenarios might be captured in regular Monte Carlo simulations of losses, particularly if they are part of the calibrating information. In this case, one could argue that the risk is already captured in the objective quantitative analysis, and so need not be separately investigated using the more subjective scenario test. However, within a standard Monte Carlo projection, the importance of these scenarios would not be apparent; each individual projection within a Monte Carlo simulation is given equal weighting in the analysis. By using the individual historical scenario, the results can have much more impact and can give more credibility to the extreme paths in the Monte Carlo approach.

(b) Stress tests can be employed to challenge the models and assumptions used in the quantitative analysis. For example, in long periods of benign market conditions there is a danger that memories of past crises will fade, and risk will be underestimated.[1] Stress tests serve to remind risk managers and other decision-makers of potential extreme events and their consequences for the institution.

(c) In some cases, new products may arise for which there is insufficient data for statistical modelling to be adequate. The 2007–8 global financial crisis was precipitated by (among other things) losses on subprime **collaterized debt obligations** (CDOs), which were packages of home mortgages bundled together and sold through capital markets. A key variable for assessing the risk associated with these products was the dependency of mortgage defaults across the country. However, there was insufficient information available on housing market correlations, and insufficient understanding of how to model the risks. As discussed in Chapter 6, the models developed for pricing, involving Gaussian copulas, were inadequate for assessing risk because the Gaussian copula has zero tail dependency, while house prices turned out to have very significant tail dependency. Stress testing using a tail dependent scenario would not necessarily have given more information about the distribution of losses, but it would have added to the information available to risk managers.

(d) Stress tests can be used to focus on the effect of extreme scenarios on the institution's capital and liquidity. Stress scenarios can illustrate how capital may erode in a crisis; they can be used to highlight issues surrounding sources of liquidity and funding. With scenario testing, the risk manager can assess the impact of possible constraints on sources of

---

[1] *Recency bias* is a form of cognitive distortion, discussed further in Chapter 19.

funds, including the potential for some capital markets to shut down (as happened with the commercial paper market in September 2008) and the possibility that, in a crisis, assets might only be liquidated under 'fire sale conditions', that is, at severe discounts from fundamental values.

(e) Stress testing programmes should serve to facilitate communication within an institution, for example, between risk managers and other decision-makers, including the Board of Directors. In particular, applying specific historical scenarios can tell a story that may not be obvious from the quantitative reporting from large-scale Monte Carlo analysis.

(f) Stress tests can be used to establish and to communicate a firm's risk appetite. For example, specifying that the firm should maintain adequate capital to withstand a 1-in-20 year market correction.

(g) Stress tests are an integral component of deterministic microsimulation modelling. Deterministic models are often used for microsimulation of very complex processes. For example, when analysing the potential impacts of hurricanes, microsimulation models containing detailed information about the area that could be vulnerable to hurricane damage are used. The data might include individual building locations, population density, tides and currents, wind and weather patterns, and more. Deterministic scenario testing of individual hurricanes is used to estimate the likely cost of each potential path in terms of lives, property, and infrastructure damage. The results are used for planning, setting building regulations, construction of sea walls and defences, and estimating potential insurance liabilities.

(h) Stress tests are often required by regulators in assessing the capital adequacy of individual financial institutions, as well as monitoring the health of the financial system. Regulatory stress tests may be fully specified by the regulator or the firm may be required to generate its own stress scenarios; often, both external and internal stress tests are required. The advantage of externally specified stress tests is that the results should be comparable across institutions. The disadvantage is that the specified tests may not capture the risks most pertinent to the individual institution. Furthermore, if the tests are seen to constrain the activities of the firm, then there is a risk that the firm will try to work around the test, rather than use it to inform and influence their risk mitigation strategies. Some examples of regulatory stress tests are given in Section 7.6.

For stress tests to be effective and impactful on an institution, senior management must find stress testing results credible. Consequently, senior managers must be informed regarding the content of stress tests, the nature of stress scenarios, and the plans recommended by stress testing results. For a detailed discussion of this point, as well as a proposed framework to involve senior management in the specification of stress scenarios, see Rebonato (2010). Stress tests are also important vehicles for communicating the quality of an institution's capital adequacy program to its regulators.

7.5 Developing Scenarios

7.5.1 Criteria

The key to stress testing is the determination of an appropriate set of scenarios. There are many important attributes that a scenario set should have.

- The scenarios should be **comprehensive**, in that one scenario or another should stress each of the key risks facing the portfolio.
- The scenarios used for stress testing should be **extreme** in order to test the portfolio against severely adverse circumstances.
- Finally, the scenarios should be **plausible**. This means that risk managers and senior management should believe that situations such as those portrayed by the scenarios could actually occur. If stress scenarios are not considered to be plausible, decision-makers will dismiss the results of stress testing and may not be willing to take the required actions to mitigate the risks.

It is important to reflect on the conflict between the last two desirable attributes of stress scenarios mentioned above. Scenarios must simultaneously be *extreme* and *plausible*. This presents a significant challenge when designing scenario sets. Scenarios that are insufficiently extreme will tend to understate the risks faced by the portfolio, while those that are implausible (or deemed implausible by senior management) will not prompt any remedial action, even when they truly demonstrate vulnerabilities in the portfolio. The Basel Committee on Banking Supervision (2009a) identified evidence that neither criterion was met by the stress tests of banks before the financial crisis. Regarding the severity of stress scenarios, the committee stated 'scenarios tended to reflect mild shocks, assume shorter durations and underestimate the correlations between different positions, risk types and markets due to system-wide interactions and feedback effects'. However, simultaneously, "[a]t many banks, it was difficult for risk managers to obtain senior management buy-in for more severe scenarios. Scenarios that were considered extreme or innovative were often regarded as implausible by the board and senior management'.

This second quote illustrates a key problem with scenario testing. It is very common for senior management to be overconfident with respect to the firm's prospects.[2] When faced with a scenario that indicates a significant risk to the firm, they are likely to discount the scenario *because* it exposes a risk – to accept the scenario as plausible would require the individual to accept the firm's vulnerability, which would require them to challenge their own bias; much easier to dismiss the scenario.

One way to overcome the natural resistance of senior management to stress testing results is to involve them in the design and development of the stress scenarios. If they openly acknowledge that a scenario is possible before the results of that particular scenario are presented, then it will be difficult for them to subsequently deny its plausibility because the results are uncomfortable. However, there is still a risk that the 'extreme scenarios' selected are not really very extreme.

7.5.2 Top-Down vs Bottom-Up Approaches

There are two main approaches to defining stress scenarios. In the **top-down approach**, scenarios begin with a defined macro-event (e.g., Spain defaults on its debt, Greece exits the Eurozone, or a global pandemic closes down international travel). The implications of this event are then worked out for each of the risk factors that serve as inputs to the quantitative models used for portfolio valuation. A full revaluation of the portfolio (and the evolution of the portfolio value over time) can then be determined in the macro-scenario.

In the **bottom-up approach** specific weaknesses are investigated, for example, identifying sensitivities to extreme movements in particular risk factors or concentrated positions. Risk factors are then stressed along the dimensions that would lead to losses for these concentrated positions.

There are advantages and disadvantages to each approach. The bottom-up approach is simple to apply, but it has the potential to miss the underlying cause of two separate events that may stress a portfolio simultaneously; dependencies that may arise from the story surrounding a particular macro event may not be revealed through a more reductionist bottom-up approach. As Rebonato (2010) notes, this is because bottom-up stress testing can only focus on the proximate rather than the primary cause. A related observation is that bottom-up stress testing tends to be more effective over shorter, rather than longer, time horizons.

---

[2] *Overconfidence* is another cognitive bias covered in Chapter 19.

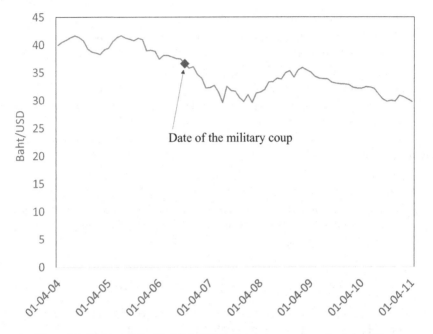

Figure 7.1 History of the Thai Baht/US Dollar exchange rate – the date of the military coup (19 September 2006) is indicated

The most significant difficulty with the top-down approach is determining how to translate scenarios that are stated in terms of macro events into specific values to be inputted into the firm's risk models. As an example, in a financial crisis will the dollar weaken because investors are worried about the US economy, or will it strengthen due to its role as a reserve currency in a flight-to-quality? Ideally, scenarios reflecting both possibilities would be considered.

The challenge of translating predictions about macro events into prescribed values of financial variables is illustrated nicely by an anecdote from the popular book *The Big Short* by Michael Lewis (2011). In it, he describes what occurred when a group of investors anticipated political events in Thailand:

> One day Ben calls me and says 'Dude, I think there's going to be a coup in Thailand' . . . He was so insistent that they went into the Thai currency market and bought what appeared to be stunningly cheap three month puts . . . on the Thai baht. One week later, the Thai military overthrew the elected prime minister. The Thai baht didn't budge. 'We predicted a coup, and we lost money', said Jamie.

Figure 7.1 shows the history of the baht–dollar exchange rate, with the date of the coup identified. The difficulty of translating a predicted macro event into the behaviour of a given (even closely connected) financial variable is apparent.

7.5.3 Historical Scenarios

Historical scenarios are top-down scenarios defined as repetitions of past periods of stress in financial markets. They are very commonly used in stress tests in modern financial institutions. Examples include a repetition of the 2007–8 global financial crisis, the Russian default in 1998, the 1997 Asian financial crisis, and the 1987 stock market crash.

Given the frequency with which financial and economic crises have occurred in the past, there is a large collection of past periods of stress which can be employed. Many such crises have been quite severe, and as a result these scenarios meet the requirement that they be extreme. Furthermore, given that the scenarios actually occurred, it is difficult to argue that they are implausible (although some will always contend that 'this time is different'). However, historical scenarios may not always be comprehensive, if they are drawn from time periods during which current financial variables or asset classes did not exist. In this case, the values of these variables must either be imputed based on available data, or postulated based on financial and economic reasoning.

Generally speaking, historical scenarios are defined in terms of relative changes that occurred in financial risk factors during the period of stress. As an example consider defining a scenario on an interest rate r. Depending on the period chosen for the historical scenario, the rates prevailing at that time may have been completely different than current market rates, so defining the scenario in terms of the level of the interest rate would not make sense. Similarly, simply considering the absolute changes of rates $\Delta r_t = r_{t+1} - r_t$ is not appropriate. A 100 basis point (1 basis point is 0.01%) change in an interest rate would represent a very different level of volatility in a high interest rate environment than it would in a low interest rate environment. Consequently, the scenario would be defined in terms of either the historically realized relative changes or log-changes – that is, either $\frac{(r_{t+1} - r_t)}{r_t}$, or $\log\left(\frac{r_{t+1}}{r_t}\right)$.

7.5.4 Synthetic Scenarios

One disadvantage of historical scenarios is that they are constrained to be no more severe than the most severe historical event. Using a synthetic scenario, we can explore events that are different from, and perhaps more extreme than historical events, whilst still remaining plausible. A particularly interesting example of a synthetic scenario is provided by Ruffle et al. (2014), who prepared a detailed description of a global pandemic scenario. It is synthetic, but aspects are drawn from historical experience, including the 1918 influenza pandemic, the SARS pandemic of 2003, and the H1N1 pandemic of 2009. The scenario develops potential impacts on GDP and the banking and insurance sectors over a period of around two years from the onset of the pandemic. As the scenario is synthetic, it can adapt the historical experience to better allow for modern circumstances, with respect to travel and communications, and global interconnectedness of business. Comparing the scenario with the experience of the COVID-19 pandemic indicates some striking areas of similarity. The pandemic stress scenario is one of a suite of synthetic stress scenarios produced by the Cambridge Centre for Risk Studies covering topics including cyber catastrophes, geopolitical conflicts, and climate change.

7.5.5 Stressing Particular Risk Factors or Risk Factor Groups

Another commonly used type of stress test focuses on a particular risk factor or collection of risk factors and applies a shock to these input variables. Such stress tests are typically constructed in a bottom-up fashion by specifying the impact on a small set of variables (e.g., 'equity market crash', 'interest rate shock') to which the portfolio is expected to be particularly sensitive. These scenarios may differ in two ways from sensitivity analysis, which applies a shock to a single risk factor and calculates the impact of that change on the portfolio value (in the manner of a partial derivative). First, the shock may be defined in terms of a set of factors, for example, shocks to the entire interest rate curve, or to a section of an implied volatility surface. Second, it may not be the case that all other variables are held constant over the stress scenario. Rather, the conditional distributions (or conditional expectations) of the other risk factors, given the specified values of the stressed factors, may be used to define a scenario set. In this way, the scenarios will respect any known or estimated codependence between the portfolio risk factors.

7.5.6 Reverse Stress Testing

In traditional stress testing, scenarios are first defined, and then the impact of those scenarios on the portfolio under consideration is evaluated. In contrast, in reverse stress testing the portfolio is given, and the risk manager seeks to identify those scenarios that are most adverse for that portfolio. The Basel Committee on Banking Supervision (2009a) recommends that '[a] stress testing programme should … determine what scenarios could challenge the viability of the bank (reverse stress tests) and thereby uncover hidden risks and interactions among risks' and provides the following description of reverse stress testing:

Reverse stress tests start from a known stress test outcome (such as breaching regulatory capital ratios, illiquidity or insolvency) and then asking what events could lead to such an outcome for the bank. As part of the overall stress testing programme, it is important to include some extreme scenarios which would cause the firm to be insolvent (i.e. stress events which threaten the viability of the whole firm). For a large complex firm, this is a challenging exercise requiring involvement of senior management and all material risk areas across the firm.

The Basel Committee identifies several important benefits of reverse stress tests, including forcing risk managers to consider events with contagion and systemic implications, informing senior management of key risk concentrations and vulnerabilities of the institution, and revealing hidden areas of vulnerability, and inconsistencies in hedging strategies. Reverse stress testing is particularly important for portfolios with significant positions in new markets and new instrument types which have yet to experience historical periods of stress.

7.5.7 Subjective Scenario Probabilities

Although scenarios are not generally developed with any objective probability associated, it is possible for those developing or mandating scenarios to assign subjective probabilities. For example, a firm might be instructed to stress test a risk at the level of a 1-in-20-year event, or a 1-in-100-year event. In some cases, one can assess this objectively, by examining the most extreme scenario in the past 100 years, for example, but in most applications, this is not realistic. In financial markets, many of the risks that are most significant today did not exist even 20 years ago. In environmental risk analysis, the effects of climate change have made so-called '1-in-100-year' events surprisingly common. For many factors, there is no historical data to even begin to assess probability objectively (e.g., cyber risk). Consequently, where probabilities are assigned to scenarios, they are usually highly subjective, based on the judgement of individual risk analysts or regulators. The problem with this is that humans – even humans who specialize in quantitative risk analysis – are notoriously bad at assessing risk and probability subjectively. In a seminal series of papers on behavioural economics, Daniel Kahneman and Amos Tversky demonstrated the almost universal tendency to underestimate low probability events – exactly the events that are supposed to be captured in scenario testing. Cumulative Prospect Theory (Tversky and Kahneman, 1992), which is described in detail in Chapter 19, was the result of factoring this cognitive bias into the theory of decision-making.

While subjective probabilities are often applied in scenario testing, even being used to weight results from individual scenarios, this is very likely to create a misplaced sense of accuracy in the analysis. It is almost always preferable to acknowledge qualitatively the uncertainty associated with scenarios than to cover it up with a spurious probabilistic facade.

7.6 Regulatory Stress Tests

Virtually all regulators of financial services firms require some stress testing. In insurance, regulators were the first to introduce formal scenario testing. For example, in the early 1990s, US insurance companies were required to report on implications of the 'New York Seven' – a list of seven scenarios for interest rates that were to be used in the emerging dynamic deterministic cash flow models of that decade.

In current regulatory systems, scenarios may be specified by the supervisory authority, just as the New York Seven were – the Dodd–Frank Act Stress Tests, European Banking Authority, and European Insurance and Occupational Pension Authority examples described below all fall into this category. In other cases, regulators outline principles for stress tests, but leave the individual firms to decide on the quantity and severity. Sometimes, a combination of externally specified tests, and internally generated tests is required. For example, Canadian insurers are required to conduct a number of specified stress tests, and then, using the results of the prescribed tests, they must test more extensively any areas where some vulnerability has been revealed.

In the remainder of this section, we briefly describe some examples and principles of stress testing that have been developed and promulgated by supervisory authorities.

Basel Stress Testing Principles

In Chapter 17, we describe the Basel Accords (Basel II, Basel III), which define a regulatory framework that is applied to banking operations across the world. Stress testing is a key component of the supervisory reporting requirement under Basel II and III. Scenarios are not described explicitly, but specific risk factors that should be stress tested (e.g., credit risk, market risk, liquidity) are identified.

As mentioned earlier, after the 2007–8 global financial crisis, a review by the Basel Committee of the stress scenarios used prior to the crisis identified serious deficiencies in the process. The scenarios tested were either insufficiently extreme or were not taken sufficiently seriously by the decision-makers (or both). Since then, the committee has worked on a series of principles for stress testing. The following principles are laid out, and discussed further, in Basel Committee on Banking Supervision (2018) and are particularly aimed at large, internationally active banks:

(a) 'Stress testing frameworks should have clearly articulated and formally adopted objectives.'

The objectives should be agreed at Board level and should be integrated within the firm's risk management structures.

(b) 'Stress testing frameworks should include an effective governance structure.'

The institution should document its stress testing framework and specify key roles and responsibilities.

(c) 'Stress testing should be used as a risk management tool and to inform business decisions.'

This means that stress testing must not simply be a compliance process, it should be integrated into decision-making.

(d) 'Stress testing frameworks should capture material and relevant risks and apply stresses that are sufficiently severe.'

The language supporting this principle does not give much more information on how 'sufficiently severe' is to be interpreted. The report does suggest that stress scenarios should be driven by a narrative, with an explanation of how the risks associated with the narrative are captured.

(e) 'Resources and organisational structures should be adequate to meet the objectives of the stress testing framework.'

(f) 'Stress tests should be supported by accurate and sufficiently granular data, and by robust IT systems.'

(g) 'Models and methodologies to assess the impacts of scenarios and sensitivities should be fit for purpose.'

(h) 'Stress testing models, results and frameworks should be subject to challenge and regular review.'

(i) 'Stress testing practices and findings should be communicated within and across jurisdictions.'

In particular, parent companies should be able to combine stress tests from individual subsidiaries, and stress tests across connected institutions should be consistent and coherent.

DFAST and CCAR

The **Dodd–Frank Act Stress Tests** (DFAST) are applied by the Federal Reserve Board to assess the capital adequacy of large bank holding companies

Table 7.1. *Excerpt from 2020 DFAST scenarios for Q1 2022*

	CPI (%)	10-yr Treasury yield (%)	BBB corporate yield (%)	Dow Jones Index	Volatility Index
Baseline	2.3	2.2	3.9	36,526	26.6
Severely adverse	1.8	1.6	4.9	22,662	32.7

in the United States, using standard scenarios for all firms. The **Comprehensive Capital Analysis and Review** (CCAR) uses scenarios that are specific to the individual firms.

Two DFAST scenarios are published each year. The first is the '*baseline scenario*', and the second is the '*severely adverse scenario*'. These define key economic variables designed to be input into deterministic projections of the bank's capital. For example, the 2020 scenarios give quarterly values for each of 28 variables (16 US, 12 international) from the first quarter of 2020 to the first quarter of 2023. The scenarios include measures of economic activity, such as GDP, unemployment rates, salary growth and inflation; financial market measures, such as equity prices, volatility and property values; interest rates by term and credit rating; and exchange rates for a range of currencies.

Excerpted values for the first quarter of 2022, from the 2020 baseline and severely adverse scenarios are given in Table 7.1 (from Federal Reserve (2020)).

European Banking Authority Stress Tests

The European Banking Authority (EBA) implements European Union (EU) wide stress tests, similar to DFAST. Rather than specify scenarios for the banks to input into their own models, the EBA constructs its own template for the calculations, which each bank must complete. Just as with DFAST, the EBA applies a baseline and adverse scenario, for deterministic projections of capital, over a three-year horizon. The scenarios are updated annually.

EIOPA Stress Tests

The European Insurance and Occupational Pensions Authority (EIOPA) runs regular (biennial) stress tests of European insurance companies. The objective (unlike the Dodd–Frank and EBA tests) is not to assess the robustness or solvency of individual companies, but to test the ability of the insurance system to withstand extreme adverse scenarios. A sample of insurers is selected to participate and the aggregate results are published. The EIOPA selects scenarios that combine financial market and insurance specific risks. For example, in 2018 three scenarios were considered. The following descriptions are taken directly from EIOPA (2018).

(a) **'Yield Curve Up'** (YCU) scenario:

> The YCU scenario assumes an abrupt and sizeable reversal of risk premiums (RP) in global financial markets leading to a tightening of financial conditions. The 10-year EUR swap rate term structure would shift upwards by 85 bps and by more than 100 bps for currencies of other major advanced economies (e.g. UK and US). The overall increase in RP would raise concerns about the debt sustainability of some EU sovereigns, widening the spreads of EU government bond yields against EU government bonds with a high credit rating. Government bond spreads increase by 36 bps on average, reaching a maximum of 134 bps. It is assumed that the economic uncertainty stemming from this abrupt change in the level of yields is not limited to the fixed income market, but also affects other financial markets.
>
> In the YCU scenario, market shocks are combined with an instantaneous shock to lapse rates and claims inflation. Lapse rates are assumed to increase by 20% for all non-mandatory life insurance products, reflecting the policyholders' reaction to the market developments. Furthermore, higher than expected inflationary pressures are assumed to induce a shortfall in liability claims reserves in the general insurance segment. This shortfall is due to 2.24% higher annual claims inflation than assumed for the existing calculation of the best estimate (BE) of non-life liabilities.

(b) **'Yield Curve Down'** (YCD) scenario:

> The YCD scenario assumes a protracted period of extremely low interest rates, with very low rates prevailing for longer maturities. The decline in interest rates reflects a slowdown in economic activity due to spillovers from outside the EU. The scenario is based on an instantaneous change of the relevant risk free interest rate term structures, including an adjustment of the ultimate forward rate (UFR), which is set at 2.04% for the euro to reflect a period of prolonged low interest rates (compared to 4.2% at the end of 2017). 10-year swap rates decline by around 80 bps in advanced economies and by around 40 bps in the emerging market economies. In the euro area, 10-year swap rates also decline by 80 bps, while 1-year swap rates fall by 11 bps. Lower economic growth is assumed to also affect other asset prices.
>
> The YCD scenario is combined with a shock to average life expectancy, which is assumed to increase significantly across the entire population. The underlying assumption is that the development of new technologies in the healthcare industry paves the way for a general revision of the mortality tables affecting BE calculations for life insurance.

(c) A **natural catastrophe** (NC) scenario:

> [T]he NC scenario assumes a set of catastrophic losses over Europe from various perils: four European windstorms, two central and eastern European

floods and two Italian earthquakes. The events were designed to hit different geographical areas in Europe and are supposed to materialise over a short period of time. Management actions were not allowed in the exercise. This means that firms were not able to reduce their exposures to scenario impacts, such as purchasing additional reinsurance, as they may have done in their usual business activities.

The scenarios are designed to be input into the calculation of standard measures of capital, as defined in the Solvency II regulatory system that applies across the EU.

7.7 Stress and Scenario Testing: Failures and Successes

In this section, we briefly examine three failures and one success of stress and scenario testing.

7.7.1 Guaranteed Annuity Options

A **guaranteed annuity option** (GAO) is a benefit provided by a life insurance company to a policyholder under which the proceeds of a maturing policy may be converted into a life annuity at a fixed rate. These guarantees began to be offered in the United Kingdom (UK) in the 1950s, and became very popular during the 1970s and 1980s. Given the nature of the contracts, there are three main sources of risk for the insurer offering GAO's. First, market prices for annuities are very sensitive to interest rates. When interest rates are low, then the market conversion rate will fall below the guaranteed rate, so that the annuity guarantee will be in-the-money. Secondly, improvements in mortality will increase the length of time over which annuity payments are made, thus making life annuities more valuable, particularly in low interest rate environments. Finally, when the guarantee is in the money, the cost is proportional to the value of the equity investment account.

The combination of very high equity returns in the late twentieth century with improvements in mortality and the low interest rate environment of the 1990s led to very large losses for insurers who had offered GAOs, most famously leading to the closure of Equitable Life Assurance Society in the UK, formerly the world's oldest mutual insurance company.

During the period when most of the UK GAOs were sold, from the mid-1970s to the mid-1980s, interest rates were quite high (see Figure 7.2). As a consequence, the GAOs were deep out-of-the money and the risks associated with the embedded options were regarded as negligible.

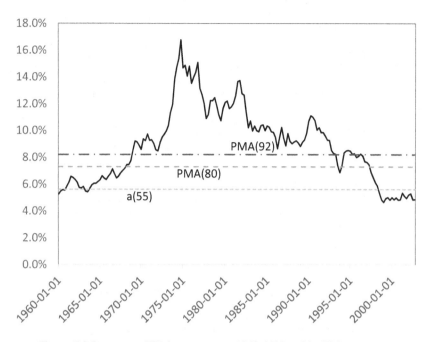

Figure 7.2 Long-term UK interest rates: 1960–2003, with GAO guarantee thresholds based on a(55), PMA(80), and PMA(92) mortality

However, this dismissal ignored the (very) long maturities of the options in question and the potential for the interest rate environment to change completely over decades. Compounding the problems, insurers did not test the sensitivity of their results to improving mortality. Insurers using the outdated mortality assumptions (the 'a(55)' tables) calculated that interest rates had to fall below 5.6% for the GAO guarantees to be in-the-money. During a prolonged period of interest rates exceeding 10%, this risk seemed negligible. If insurers in the 1980s had looked back to when GAOs were first offered, they would have seen that the double digit interest rates of the 1970s and 1980s were the anomaly – interest rates below 5.6%, over a 30-year horizon, were quite feasible, *ex ante*. Furthermore, a failure to examine the sensitivity to longevity meant that some insurers realized very late that switching from the 'a(55)' mortality to the updated tables (PMA(80), available in 1990) moved the moneyness threshold from 5.6% to 7.3%. By the time that Equitable Life closed to new business in 2000, the threshold had moved to 8.2%, based on the most recent (PMA(92)) mortality tables.

Stress testing in actuarial valuation through the GAO period involved adding or subtracting margins to the valuation assumptions, particularly interest rates, to allow for an element of conservatism in the calculations. The margins were chosen subjectively, based on the actuary's judgement. This approach failed in the case of the GAOs as the margins applied were too small to capture any of the risk. The actuaries could apply a margin of -300 basis points to interest rates through the 1970s, and still not see any liability arising from the GAO - partly because of the outdated mortality model. This example is an object lesson in the dangers of ignoring potential extreme events, and the magnitude of possible risk factor movements over long time horizons. Furthermore, note how the nature of the scenarios that could (and did) produce extreme losses in this case (high equity returns coupled with improving mortality and declining interest rates) were quite specific to the nature of the portfolio under consideration, illustrating the importance of bottom-up approaches and reverse stress testing.

7.7.2 The 2007–8 Global Financial Crisis

We have noted earlier the failures of stress testing at financial institutions before the 2007–8 global financial crisis. To reiterate, there were at least two distinct types of failures:

- At many institutions, scenarios were not extreme enough. The possibility of a widespread decline in housing prices in the US, and the extent of the potential decline should it occur, were not widely recognized. Furthermore, scenarios tended to ignore possible contagion effects arising from linkages in the financial system and made overly optimistic assumptions regarding market liquidity in a crisis.
- At institutions where risk management groups did consider extreme scenarios, those scenarios were ignored by senior management, either because the scenarios were deemed implausible or because managers did not want to face the implications of the stress testing results. There was a systemic problem within financial institutions, where risk management operations were carried out in isolation, without sufficient participation and consideration by senior management.

The global financial crisis was precipitated by a decline in housing prices in the US, leading to a spate of mortgage defaults which impacted – among other things – banks' positions in collateralized debt obligations backed by mortgages. Before the crisis, stress testing and risk management in the financial industry largely discounted the possibility of a nationwide decline in housing prices in the US. Figure 7.3 shows the annual percentage change in the

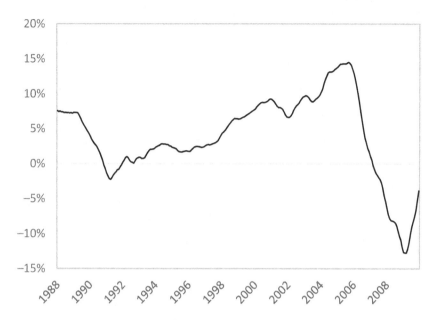

Figure 7.3 Average yearly change in US house prices, S&P Case–Shiller home-price index

S&P Case–Shiller home price index prior to, and during, the subprime crisis. The data emphasize two observations that we have made earlier. First, long periods of benign market behaviour, as occurred from the early 1990s until 2005, can breed complacency and a tendency to underestimate the probability and possible magnitude of extreme events. This is a danger that must be kept constantly in mind in risk management in general, and stress testing in particular. Secondly, much like the GAO case, if market participants had looked far enough back in time, they would have seen that the stress event they were failing to consider (a national decline in housing prices) had in fact occurred in the past.

Figure 7.4 illustrates dramatically the reduction in market liquidity during the height of the financial crisis. The TED spread is the spread between the three month US Treasury rate and the three-month LIBOR rate (the rate for interbank lending in the eurodollar market). At the time, this was a measure of the liquidity of the interbank lending market, and had historically fluctuated at around half a percent. The spread stayed consistently above 1% for almost the entire year, spiking at 2% in late March and then hitting 3% in September following the default of Lehman Brothers. In the same month, the failure of the Reserve Primary Fund to maintain a net asset value above one

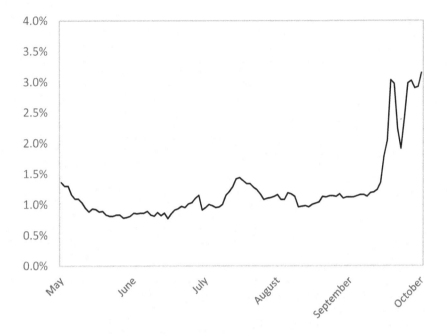

Figure 7.4 Three-month Treasury-Bill / LIBOR (TED) spread during 2008

('breaking the buck'), along with other events, led to the freezing of the commercial paper market, causing the financial crisis to have significant spillover effects on the financing needs of corporations in non-financial sectors.

7.7.3 Allied Irish Banks

Like many other financial institutions, Allied Irish Banks (AIB) suffered significant losses during 2008. The former head of the bank's retail operations later observed that 'insufficient stress testing and inadequate loan security were key reasons behind the bank's difficulties.' In February 2009, the bank received a capital injection from the Irish government and was able to continue operations. The bank participated in regulatory stress tests in July of 2010 overseen by the Committee of European Banking Supervisors (CEBS). Based on the tests, it was concluded that the bank was sufficiently capitalized and did not need to raise further capital. However, the bank suffered additional losses due to bad loans and, on 30 September 2010, required another bailout. The Irish government provided a capital injection of 3.7 billion Euros and became the majority shareholder, effectively nationalizing the bank.

Figure 7.5 shows the **credit default swap** (CDS) spread for AIB through the financial crisis. As we will discuss in Chapter 12, the CDS spread can be

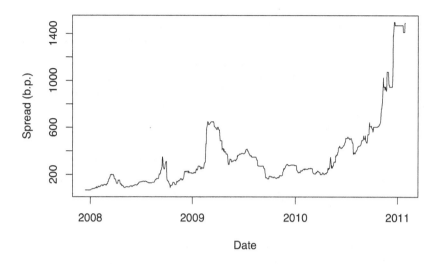

Figure 7.5 CDS Spread of AIB in basis points 2007–2010

used as a measure of the default risk of the reference entity; the higher the spread, the higher the implied default probability. We can see from Figure 7.5 that by July 2010, the AIB spread had begun to increase to roughly the same level as in early 2009, when it had required its earlier capital injection. However, this increased riskiness of the bank was not revealed in the results of the CEBS stress tests. The bank's CDS spread spiked dramatically in the months following the stress tests, reaching previously unforeseen levels in October 2010.

Each of these three cases captures several of the key challenges surrounding scenario testing. Specifically, in each case the magnitudes of the stress tests were not sufficient to capture the true risks; also in each case, the stress tests were imposed externally, without buy-in from the senior officers of the firms involved. Because the firms did not believe there was any risk involved in their strategies, they would not attach any credibility to a stress scenario that indicated otherwise.

7.7.4 H-E-B Pandemic Preparation

Contrast these examples with a successful example of scenario testing. H-E-B is the grocery chain whose preparation for the COVID-19 pandemic was described briefly in Chapter 2. In 2005, the firm became aware of the Avian Flu (H5N1) risk emerging in China and started to develop pandemic scenarios to use in developing potential procedures and plans. In early 2020, H-E-B started to implement the procedures developed and honed through its regular pandemic scenario testing. This included connecting with suppliers and other retailers as early as possible, sourcing key supplies that were most likely to experience excess demand, and tracking progress and experience from areas that were affected early in the pandemic. Thanks to its scenario testing, H-E-B was well prepared for the crisis and able to maintain much better stock levels of essential goods than its competitors. H-E-B's overall response to the emergency generated a significant amount of very positive media coverage.

Generally, success stories are less newsworthy than failures. The H-E-B case is an exception because the company's preparedness contrasted very markedly with the short-sightedness of state and federal responders. It is interesting to note, though, that this success involved a bottom-up and top-down process, initiated internally with a view not only to ensure business continuation through a crisis, but also to provide community support in the firm's areas of operations. The failures of scenario testing discussed above all involved firms making decisions that increased short-term profitability at the expense of long-term security. Perhaps H-E-B's dual focus on community and business enabled it to forego some short-term profitability in favour of long-term preparation.

7.8 Notes and Further Reading

Rebonato (2010) connects stress testing to a probabilistic model using a Bayesian framework. The Bayesian approach to probability is consistent with scenario testing, in that is interprets probability as a subjective measure of uncertainty, rather than a measure of frequency.

The Centre for Risk Studies at the University of Cambridge offers a wide variety of synthetic scenario case studies.

Guaranteed annuity options are described and analysed in Boyle and Hardy (2003). The story of how GAOs brought down Equitable Life (UK) is compellingly told in the official UK government report on the scandal, Penrose (2004); a shorter summary with a risk management focus is provided in O'Brien (2006).

7.9 Exercises

Exercise 7.1 Discuss the advantages and disadvantages of externally pre-scribed regulatory stress scenarios compared with internally developed stress scenarios.

Exercise 7.2 Explain the difference between the objectives of the EBA stress tests and the EIOPA stress tests.

Exercise 7.3 A common behavioural bias involves underestimating the chance that a low-probability event will occur. Explain the implications for the process of developing adverse scenarios for stress testing.

Exercise 7.4 A risk manager presents the stress scenarios to the senior management before inputting them into the firm's capital adequacy models. Explain why getting agreement before the results of the scenario testing are known could be valuable.

Exercise 7.5 A risk manager presents the results of 20 stress scenarios to the CEO. In 19 of the scenarios, the firm is projected to be adequately capitalized. In one scenario, the firm is projected to be insolvent. The CEO states that this represents a 95% probability that the firm will be solvent, which is within risk tolerance.

Critique this interpretation.

Exercise 7.6 An insurer issues term and whole life insurance policies. Term life policyholders who lapse receive no payment; whole life policyholders who lapse after an initial period receive a substantial sum that is pre-specified in the policy document.

Premiums are invested in a mix of equities and long duration government and corporate bonds.

The insurer decides to stress test the portfolio over a one year horizon with the following stress scenario:

- Equities fall by 10%;
- Interest rates for all bonds shift down by 50bps at all maturities;
- Policy surrenders increase by 10% at all durations.

Critique this scenario.

Exercise 7.7 An insurance portfolio has **technical provision** (TP) of 1,000 and **additional solvency capital** (ASC) of 1,200 available at the start of the year. The technical provision is the best estimate of the cost of future claims for business in force. The additional solvency capital is held to absorb adverse experience.

Assets with market value equal to the TP + ASC are invested 60% in three-year zero coupon government bonds with yield to maturity 3.5% and 40% in equities.

The aggregate claims are modelled as a lognormal distribution with mean 1,000 and standard deviation 3,000.

At the year end, the policies expire and there is no remaining technical provision required:

(a) The benchmark scenario assumes that equities increase over the year by 4%, the year end yield on two-year zero coupon bonds is 3.5%, and aggregate claims are equal to their median value. Calculate the ASC at the year end under this scenario.

(b) The adverse scenario assumes that equities fall by 25%, interest rates fall to 2.8% for all maturities, and aggregate claims are equal to the 85% quantile of the loss distribution. Calculate the ASC at the year end under this scenario.

(c) Reverse stress tests are created by stressing one assumption at a time from the benchmark scenario. Determine the stress test parameter that exhausts the ASC, if the variable assumed to change is (i) the change in equity values, (ii) the year end interest rate on two-year zero coupon bonds, and (iii) the percentile of the aggregate claims distribution at which the claims experience falls.

(d) Create a narrative explaining the adverse scenario in (b).

8

Market Risk Models

8.1 Summary

In this chapter, we review the difference between real-world and risk-neutral processes. We illustrate asset processes using two years of daily returns from the S&P 500 stock index and 30 years of monthly data from the S&P/TSX (Toronto Stock Exchange) stock index. We describe three models for modelling asset prices in discrete time: the independent lognormal model, the GARCH model, and the regime-switching lognormal model. We describe how the models are fitted to data and briefly discuss how to choose between models.

8.2 Introduction

In this chapter, we focus on three types of discrete time processes that have been found to be useful in financial risk management.

Discrete time models tend to provide a better fit to data for longer term horizons than continuous time models, and are very convenient for Monte Carlo simulation; they are also generally fairly straightforward to interpret, which is often not true of continuous time models.

8.2.1 Real-World and Risk-Neutral Processes

Real-world or $\mathbb{P}$-measure models for asset price processes are models which capture the true underlying dynamics of price movements in a simplified form.

Risk-neutral or $\mathbb{Q}$-measure models are transformed versions of the real-world models. These are not intended to give realistic probabilities or expected values; they are designed to replicate market values of assets. That is, under a

$\mathbb{Q}$-measure, the expected present value of a future payment, discounted at the risk-free rate, is the current market value of that payment. This is why the $\mathbb{Q}$ measure is called the 'risk-neutral' measure – there is no extra reward for risk under $\mathbb{Q}$-measure. In the real world, the expected return on a risky asset would be greater than the risk-free rate of interest, as there must be some reward for risk. The only purpose of a $\mathbb{Q}$-measure is to evaluate market-consistent prices of future cash flows.

There is a relationship between $\mathbb{P}$ and $\mathbb{Q}$-measure models; for a given $\mathbb{P}$-measure, a $\mathbb{Q}$-measure is a model which is both risk-neutral and **equivalent** to the $\mathbb{P}$-measure model. Equivalence means that the two measures have the same null sets, so that any event that has zero probability under the $\mathbb{P}$-measure must also have zero probability under the $\mathbb{Q}$-measure and vice versa.

For projecting cash flows with a view to assessing tail risk or analysing risk mitigation strategies, we are interested in real-world dynamics, so the main model for asset prices will be a real-world, $\mathbb{P}$-measure model. We can use standard time series methodology to calibrate the model to the historical data, and to evaluate whether the model adequately reproduces the key features of the stock price process. In some applications we are not interested in the true dynamics of the stock process, but only in market consistent values. In these cases, we use a $\mathbb{Q}$-measure calibrated to current market prices. In many cases, we need to combine $\mathbb{P}$-measure and $\mathbb{Q}$-measure processes. For example, if we are projecting the real-world value of a portfolio that includes put or call options, then we project the future stock prices under the $\mathbb{P}$-measure model, but the future option values are expectations under the $\mathbb{Q}$-measure, conditional on the stock prices projected using the $\mathbb{P}$-measure model.

Our main focus in this chapter is on real-world models, because tail risk measures such as VaR and Expected Shortfall depend on the real-world projections. We describe several of the most commonly used $\mathbb{P}$-measure models for asset prices. Where appropriate, we will comment on the potential transformation to a $\mathbb{Q}$-measure. For $\mathbb{P}$-measure models that incorporate stochastic volatility, there are typically infinitely many equivalent $\mathbb{Q}$-measures, but we will present in each case a $\mathbb{Q}$-measure that is a reasonably intuitive transformation of the given $\mathbb{P}$-measure.

8.3 Empirical Behaviour of Equity Prices

In this section, as an example of how to assess the empirical behaviour of an asset price process, we present some graphs of stock price and stock return processes for both short- and long-term horizons, and draw some general

conclusions about the qualitative behaviour of stock prices that we would like
to see reflected in our mathematical models.

The stock price at t is denoted S_t. For stock returns, we generally work
with the log-return process, $Y_{t,h} = \log(S_t/S_{t-h})$. The volatility of the process
is the standard deviation of $Y_{t,h}$, usually expressed in annual units. We will use
$Y_t = Y_{t,1}$ to denote the log-return over the unit time period from $t-1$ to t, and
σ_t to denote the volatility of the process from $t-1$ to t.

Daily Data, Short-Term Horizon

For illustrating short-term equity price movements, we use daily return data
from the S&P 500 index. This is an index tracking the price of a portfolio of the
largest 500 companies listed on US stock exchanges, weighted in proportion
to their total market capitalization.

In Figure 8.1a, we show the S&P 500 index growth over the two-year
period. We have set the index to 1.0 at 1 January 2019. The graph shows steady
price growth through 2019, with a few relatively small dips, followed by a
major disruption in 2020 associated with the onset of the COVID-19 pandemic.

We see more structure when we look at the path of the daily log-returns,
shown in Figure 8.1b, which also shows the estimated daily volatility. The
volatility is taken from the VIX index, which is a measure of the market
volatility on the S&P index based on the implied volatility underlying the
prices of options traded each day. The VIX will overestimate the true volatility
of stock returns, as the volatility used to set option prices includes margins for
profit and for uncertainty.

From Figure 8.1b, we see that, throughout 2019, returns were steady and
the volatility was reasonably stable. In 2020, prices fell and then rose again,
very dramatically, several times through March and April, with volatility rising
to about 5% per day at its peak, equivalent to over 80% per year. In Figure 8.2,
we show the annual volatility each day for the calendar years 2019 and 2020,
which demonstrates the dramatic impact of the COVID-19 crisis on volatility,
especially in the first half of 2020.

Banks are typically interested in very short-term forecasts; 1-day or 10-
day horizons are common. Often, they use models that ignore the possibility
of volatility jumps or extreme market movements, at least until the market
disruption event actually happens.

Monthly Data, Long-Term Horizon

In Figure 8.3, we show index values and log-return data for the S&P/TSX
total return index, from 1990 to 2020. The S&P/TSX is the index of the major

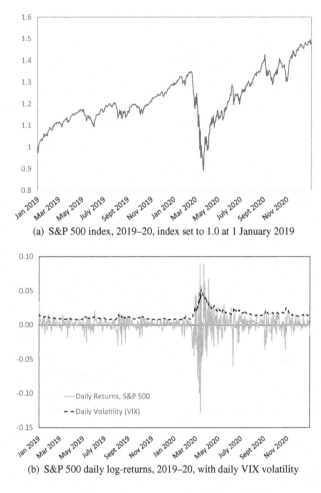

(a) S&P 500 index, 2019–20, index set to 1.0 at 1 January 2019

(b) S&P 500 daily log-returns, 2019–20, with daily VIX volatility

Figure 8.1 S&P 500 daily return data, January 2019–December 2020

companies listed on the Toronto Stock Exchange. The total return index allows for reinvestment of dividends paid on the component stocks. It is important to match the stock return model to the objective; if we fit a model to data which does not allow for the reinvestment of dividends, then we will underestimate the true returns available from holding the stocks, but we would accurately replicate the return from holding an investment in the index itself, rather than in the underlying stocks.

In Figure 8.3a, we see the big picture of market performance through this period; steady market growth through the 1990s, set back in 1998 by a crisis

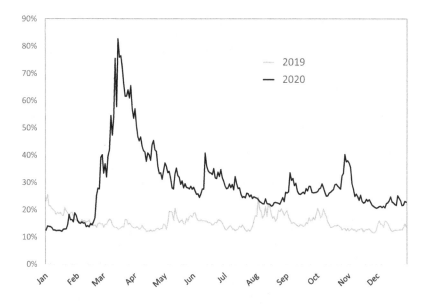

Figure 8.2 VIX (S&P volatility) 2019 and 2020, by calendar month

initiated when Russia defaulted on its sovereign debt. Around 2000, we see the 'dotcom bubble' – very fast price growth in the first stage of the bubble generated by extraordinary investment in fast growing technology companies, followed by a precipitous correction when the bubble burst. In 2007–8, we see the effect of the global financial crisis, followed by a sustained period of uncertainty.

In Figure 8.3b, we show the monthly log-returns, along with the estimated volatility. In this case, the volatility is estimated using a rolling standard deviation of the monthly log-returns, adjusted to give the annual rate. From the volatility curve, we see peaks associated with the Russian bond crisis, the dotcom bubble burst, the 2007–8 global financial crisis, and the COVID-19 crisis.

8.3.1 Stylized Facts for Stock Price Processes

From all of the figures in the previous sections, we observe four important stylized facts about the stock price movements:

(1) Volatility is stochastic, not constant. That is, the volatility appears to follow a random process.

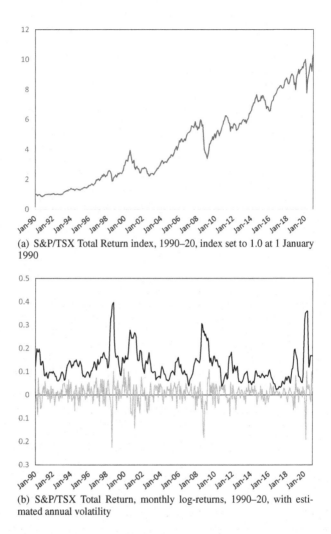

(a) S&P/TSX Total Return index, 1990–20, index set to 1.0 at 1 January 1990

(b) S&P/TSX Total Return, monthly log-returns, 1990–20, with estimated annual volatility

Figure 8.3 S&P/TSX monthly total return data, January 1990–December 2020

(2) High volatility periods are fairly rare, but tend to be clustered together. That is, if the volatility is high today, there is more chance than usual that it is also high tomorrow, and similarly for low volatility.

(3) When the absolute value of the log-return is high, the return is more likely to be negative than positive. That is, stocks are more likely to fall in value quickly, but recover more slowly, than they are to jump up in value. In both the daily and monthly graphs of log-returns, you will see more

negative spikes than positive and the negative spikes are more extreme than the positive. Furthermore, when a large positive return is recorded, it almost always follows a large negative return, so is part of a recovery from an adverse event.

(4) When volatility does move from low to high, it is far more likely to be precipitated by a sudden drop in prices (a negative return) than by a sudden increase in prices. This is referred to as the **leverage effect** and it means that high volatility is associated with crash type events and the immediate recovery period following a crash, while rising markets tend to be associated with periods of lower volatility.

As we consider some models for stock price processes, we will return to these facts to assess whether they are reflected in each case.

8.4 Geometric Brownian Motion (GBM)

Geometric Brownian Motion (GBM) is a continuous time model commonly used for asset prices, particularly for short-term applications.

Formally, GBM can be expressed as the diffusion process

$$dS_t = \mu^* S_t dt + \sigma\, S_t\, dW_t,\ \sigma > 0,$$

where μ^* and σ are parameters, and W_t is a **Wiener process**. A Wiener process is a continuous time process, under which the increment in any period of length $k > 0$ (i.e. $W_{t+k} - W_t$) is normally distributed with zero mean and variance k, and where all non-overlapping increments are independent.

One implication of the GBM $\mathbb{P}$-measure model is that the accumulation factor of the asset price over any period is lognormally distributed, specifically,

$$\frac{S_{t+k}}{S_t} \sim \text{logN}\big(k(\mu^* - \sigma^2/2),\ \sqrt{k}\sigma\big) \text{ for any } k > 0$$

$$\Rightarrow \log\left(\frac{S_{t+k}}{S_t}\right) \sim \text{N}\big(k(\mu^* - \sigma^2/2),\ k\sigma^2\big).$$

So the k-year log-return is normally distributed under the GBM model.

In Figure 8.4, we compare the S&P 2019–20 daily data with a typical path for a GBM, with parameters set to match the S&P data. We see that the GBM does not capture the extreme returns, negative and positive, of the March–May 2020 data.

One advantage of the GBM model is its tractability. Another advantage is that GBM asset prices provide the underlying assumption of the Black–Scholes

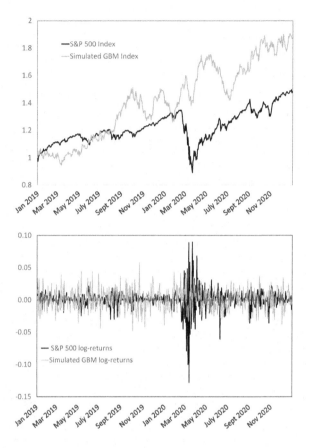

Figure 8.4 S&P Daily Returns compared with a typical GBM path

option pricing formulas. The model works as the basis for the Black–Scholes formulas because it offers an adequate fit to stock data, provided the time horizon is short, and that no significant market events occur within the time horizon. If the real world, $\mathbb{P}$-measure is GBM, with parameters μ^* and σ, then there is a unique equivalent risk-neutral, $\mathbb{Q}$-measure, which is also GBM, with parameters r (the risk-free rate) and σ.

The problem with GBM is that it fails to capture the extreme market disruptions that are often critical for risk management, as evidenced by the 2020 COVID effect that is so prominent in Figure 8.1. In fact, GBM does not comply with any of the stylized facts that we see in the data. Specifically:

(1) The volatility of the GBM is a constant, σ, and therefore there is no randomness and no clustering. In the sample GBM path in Figure 8.4,

we can see that the upward and downward movements are reasonably consistent in amplitude.

(2) Under GBM, the log-returns over each non-overlapping period (e.g., each day or month) are independent.

(3) Under GBM, the log-returns are symmetric about the mean, so jumps up are just as likely as jumps down.

(4) With constant volatility, under GBM there is no leverage effect.

There are more complex continuous time models in $\mathbb{P}$-measure and $\mathbb{Q}$-measure that address some of the shortcomings of GBM, but they are typically used for more theoretical analysis or for very specialized modelling, rather than for general risk management. In the following sections, we consider some discrete time models that have proved useful and are reasonably intuitive and easy to incorporate in quantitative risk management in practice, typically as part of a Monte Carlo simulation of losses related to financial price movements.

8.5 The Independent Lognormal Model (ILN)

If we observe the continuous time GBM process in discrete time-steps of length h years, we would see an independent Gaussian process for the log-return, $Y_{t,h}$, and an **independent lognormal** (ILN) process for S_t. That is,

$$Y_{t,h} = h\mu + \sqrt{h}\sigma \varepsilon_{t,h} \quad \text{where } \varepsilon_{t,h} \text{ are i.i.d. N}(0,1)$$

$$\Rightarrow Y_{t,h} \sim \text{N}(h\mu, h\sigma^2) \text{ and } e^{Y_{t,h}} = \frac{S_t}{S_{t-h}} \sim \text{logN}(h\mu, \sqrt{h}\sigma).$$

The process is 'independent' because the h-year log-return, $Y_{t,h}$, is independent of the previous or subsequent values, (because the ε_t are mutually independent) and so the asset price growth in any h-year period, S_{t+h}/S_t, is also independent of the previous or subsequent values.

Let $Y_t = \log S_t / S_{t-1}$, then for $t = 1, 2, \ldots$, we have

$$\frac{S_t}{S_0} = \frac{S_1}{S_0} \times \frac{S_2}{S_1} \times \cdots \times \frac{S_t}{S_{t-1}} = \exp\left(Y_1 + Y_2 + \cdots + Y_t\right).$$

Now $Y_1 + Y_2 + \cdots + Y_t \sim \text{N}(t\mu, t\sigma^2)$

(sum of independent N(μ, σ^2) variables)

$$\Rightarrow \frac{S_t}{S_0} \sim \text{logN}(t\mu, \sqrt{t}\sigma).$$

Recall that the $\mathbb{Q}$-measure equivalent of the GBM $\mathbb{P}$-measure is a GBM with shifted μ and the same σ. It should not be too surprising then that the $\mathbb{Q}$-measure equivalent to the ILN $\mathbb{P}$-measure is also ILN, with the same σ, but with μ replaced by $r - \sigma^2/2$.

All the advantages and disadvantages of the GBM model listed in the previous section also apply to the ILN model as it is essentially the same model viewed discretely.

A **scalable** time series model is one that takes the same form, with suitable adjustment of parameters, regardless of how frequently it is observed. The ILN model is scalable, because if we generate ILN returns using a daily time step, using parameters μ and σ, and then analyse the weekly returns, we would observe another ILN model with parameters (assuming a 5-day week) 5μ and $\sqrt{5}\sigma$. The weekly log-returns are just the sum of the daily log-returns, and the daily log-returns are i.i.d. random variables, each with a normal distribution. As we increase the frequency, we will converge to the underlying geometric Brownian motion. Scalability offers significant advantages in terms of tractability, but that does not compensate for the fact that the ILN model does not offer a good fit to data beyond very short time periods.

In the following sections, we consider models that allow for time varying volatility, known as heteroscedasticity.

8.6 The GARCH Model

The **generalized auto-regressive conditionally heteroscedastic** (GARCH) model is part of a family of discrete time models with time-varying volatility, developed by Bollerslev (1986) from the original ARCH model of Engle (1982). Again, it is convenient to work with the one-period log-return random process, Y_t.

The GARCH(1,1) model can be written as

$$Y_t = \mu + \sigma_t \varepsilon_t, \tag{8.1}$$

$$\sigma_t^2 = a_0 + a_1 (Y_{t-1} - \mu)^2 + b\,\sigma_{t-1}^2 \quad a_0, a_1, b > 0, \tag{8.2}$$

where $\{\varepsilon_t\}$ is an i.i.d. sequence of standard normal random variables. We see that the volatility at t, denoted σ_t, is a function of Y_{t-1} and of σ_{t-1}. If $|Y_{t-1}-\mu|$ is high, or if the previous period volatility (σ_{t-1}) is high, then the time t volatility is pushed higher. On the other hand, when Y_{t-1} is close to μ, and the previous period volatility is low, then σ_t will be at the low end of its range.

The (1,1) in GARCH(1,1) indicates that both the second and third terms in equation (8.2) use values from 1 time-step previously. A GARCH(p, q) model would use p time steps for terms in $(Y_{t-k} - \mu)^2$, and q time steps for terms in σ_{t-k}^2. These higher order GARCH processes are less often seen in practice in financial modelling, so we will consider only the GARCH(1,1) case and drop the (1,1) modifier in the rest of the chapter.

At time t, we know Y_{t-1} and σ_{t-1}, so the volatility at time t is known, but the volatility in any time period beyond time t is random, because for $k = 1, 2, 3, \ldots$, the value of σ_{t+k} depends on the unknown log-returns, Y_t, $Y_{t+1}, \ldots, Y_{t+k-1}$.

Consider a projection from a current date, which we set as $t = 0$. We assume that we know the values of $Y_0 = y_0$, μ (the mean of Y_t), and σ_0. Then we have

$$Y_1 = \mu + \sigma_1 \varepsilon_1 \text{ where } \varepsilon_1 \sim N(0,1), \text{ and}$$

$$\sigma_1^2 = a_0 + a_1 (y_0 - \mu)^2 + b\,\sigma_0^2$$

$$\Rightarrow Y_1 \sim N(\mu, \sigma_1^2).$$

So far, this looks very similar to the ILN case. Things get a little more complicated though when we proceed to Y_2:

$$Y_2 \mid Y_1 = \mu + \sigma_2 \varepsilon_2 \text{ where } \varepsilon_2 \sim N(0,1), \text{ independent of } \varepsilon_1, \text{ and}$$

$$\sigma_2^2 \mid Y_1 = a_0 + a_1 (Y_1 - \mu)^2 + b\,\sigma_1^2$$

$$= a_0 + a_1 (Y_1 - \mu)^2 + b\big(a_0 + a_1 (y_0 - \mu)^2 + b\,\sigma_0^2\big)$$

$$= a_0(1 + b) + a_1((Y_1 - \mu)^2 + b(y_0 - \mu)^2) + b^2\sigma_0^2$$

$$\Rightarrow Y_2 \mid Y_1 \sim N\big(\mu, a_0(1 + b) + a_1((Y_1 - \mu)^2 + b(y_0 - \mu)^2) + b^2\sigma_0^2\big).$$

The point of this is to show that Y_2 is *not* independent of Y_1; the variance of Y_2 is affected by the value of Y_1. Each of the future values of Y_t is conditionally normally distributed, with mean μ, and variance σ_t^2, where σ_t^2 is a function of $Y_1, \ldots, Y_{t-1}$. So,

$$Y_t \mid Y_1, Y_2, \ldots, Y_{t-1} \sim N(\mu, \sigma_t^2). \tag{8.3}$$

Recall that the accumulation factor for the asset price over t time periods from time 0 is

$$\frac{S_t}{S_0} = \exp(Y_1 + Y_2 + Y_3 + \cdots + Y_t).$$

In the ILN case, the Y_j are independent and identically distributed normal random variables, which means that the sum $Y_1 + Y_2 + \cdots + Y_t$ is also normally distributed. In the GARCH case, the Y_j are no longer independent, which means that the sum $Y_1 + Y_2 + \cdots + Y_t$ does not have a convenient closed form distribution function.

The long run, unconditional variance of the GARCH process is defined as

$$\lim_{t \to \infty} E_0[\sigma_t^2],$$

where E_t denotes the expectation given the information at time t. In terms of the GARCH process, at time $t - 1$, say, we know $Y_1, \ldots, Y_{t-1}$, and we know $\sigma_1, \ldots, \sigma_t$, as the one-step-ahead variance is known at each time point. That is,

$$E_{t-1}[\sigma_t^2] = \sigma_t^2. \tag{8.4}$$

Now we take a step backwards to time $t - 2$:

$$E_{t-2}[\sigma_t^2] = E_{t-2}\big[a_0 + a_1(Y_{t-1} - \mu)^2 + b\sigma_{t-1}^2\big].$$

Now, given all the information available at time $t - 2$, we know that Y_{t-1} is normally distributed, with variance σ_{t-1}^2, so $E_{t-2}[(Y_{t-1} - \mu)^2] = \sigma_{t-1}^2$, which gives us

$$E_{t-2}[\sigma_t^2] = a_0 + (a_1 + b)\sigma_{t-1}^2. \tag{8.5}$$

Now we take another step back, to time $t - 3$:

$$
\begin{aligned}
E_{t-3}[\sigma_t^2] &= E_{t-3}\big[a_0 + (a_1 + b)\sigma_{t-1}^2\big] \\
&= a_0 + (a_1 + b)E_{t-3}[\sigma_{t-1}^2] \\
&= a_0 + (a_1 + b)E_{t-3}\big[a_0 + a_1(Y_{t-2} - \mu)^2 + b\sigma_{t-2}^2\big] \\
&= a_0 + (a_1 + b)(a_0 + (a_1 + b)\sigma_{t-2}^2) \\
\Rightarrow E_{t-3}[\sigma_t^2] &= a_0(1 + (a_1 + b)) + (a_1 + b)^2\sigma_{t-2}^2.
\end{aligned}
$$

Similarly, $E_{t-4}[\sigma_t^2] = a_0(1 + (a_1 + b) + (a_1 + b)^2) + (a_1 + b)^3\sigma_{t-3}^2$.

Continuing down to time 0, we have

$$
\begin{aligned}
E_0[\sigma_t^2] &= a_0\Big(1 + (a_1 + b) + \cdots + (a_1 + b)^{t-2}\Big) + (a_1 + b)^{t-1}\sigma_1^2 \\
&= a_0\left(\frac{1 - (a_1 + b)^{t-1}}{1 - (a_1 + b)}\right) + (a_1 + b)^{t-1}\sigma_1^2 \quad \text{for } a_1 + b \neq 1.
\end{aligned}
$$

For the process to be covariance stationary we need $a_1 + b < 1$, otherwise the variance will increase without limit as t increases. We will assume in practice that $a_1 + b < 1$, in which case the long range, unconditional variance is

$$\lim_{t \to \infty} a_0\left(\frac{1 - (a_1 + b)^{t-1}}{1 - (a_1 + b)}\right) + (a_1 + b)^{t-1}\sigma_1^2 = \frac{a_0}{1 - (a_1 + b)}. \tag{8.6}$$

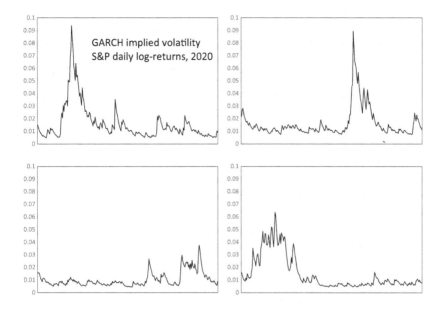

Figure 8.5 Examples of GARCH volatility, calibrated to 2020 daily S&P log-return data (the top left figure is the actual GARCH-implied volatility – the other three figures show random volatility paths from the GARCH model fitted to the S&P data)

The GARCH model incorporates stochastic volatility, through the dependence on Y_t. It also incorporates volatility clustering, through the $(Y_{t-1} - \mu)^2$ and σ_{t-1} terms. The nature of volatility clustering in GARCH tends to be a sharp or gradual increase in volatility, followed by a decline towards the long-term mean. Larger values of a_1 create higher and steeper volatility spikes; larger values of b will make the decline in volatility more gradual. In Figure 8.5, we show some examples of GARCH daily volatility paths over a 1-year period, using parameters found by calibrating the GARCH model to the 2020 daily S&P data. Note that, although we have assumed that σ_1 is known at $t = 0$, we cannot actually observe a one-period volatility, but we can estimate it given the GARCH parameters. The top left graph in Figure 8.5 shows the implied volatility for the 2020 daily S&P data after calibrating the GARCH model; it resembles the VIX volatility measure from Figure 8.2. The other three graphs show random paths from the same GARCH model. The top right path is similar to the actual implied volatility, with a single peak declining fairly slowly to a period of low volatility. The bottom right path, which is more typical of the model and parameters, shows a cluster of slightly higher volatility values towards the end of the year, but no dramatic peaks; this path is somewhat similar to the 2019 VIX path in Figure 8.2. The bottom right figure shows a path where the volatility cluster is more symmetric in its increasing and decreasing phases. We see that the GARCH volatility model, even with fixed parameters, can take a wide range of paths.

The GARCH model has no mechanism for incorporating the leverage effect, where higher volatility clusters are associated with market crashes or failures. Under the GARCH model, high volatility periods are equally likely to be instigated by a random jump up in the stock price as a random jump down. Some variations on the GARCH model address this. **Threshold GARCH** (TGARCH) models introduce an additional term in the variance equation if the previous period log-return was negative. For example,

$$\text{TGARCH variance:} \quad \sigma_t^2 = a_0 + (a_1 + \gamma \ \min(Y_{t-1},0)) \ (Y_{t-1} - \mu)^2 + b\sigma_{t-1}^2. \tag{8.7}$$

We expect $\gamma < 0$, so that there is more of a jump in volatility when Y_{t-1} is negative than when it is positive, creating the leverage effect that we identified in the data. The TGARCH model may not be very tractable, but it is easily explored numerically, and also easy to incorporate in Monte Carlo modelling of risks.

Like most models used in financial risk modelling, other than the ILN model, GARCH is *not* scalable. If we generate daily returns following a GARCH process, and observe the resulting weekly returns, we are observing the sum of dependent random variables, with no simple analytic form for the variance or the distribution. In practice, the GARCH model is pretty flexible and has been used to model returns over a wide range of frequencies, from daily to annual returns, but it is important to understand that each of these is a different model, not a scaled version of the same model.

If the $\mathbb{P}$-measure model for asset prices is a GARCH model, then a common choice for an equivalent $\mathbb{Q}$-measure retains the same variance process, but adjusts the GARCH mean. Let $\mathcal{F}_t$ denote all the information on the asset price process available at time t. We know that

$$Y_t \mid \mathcal{F}_{t-1} \sim_{\mathbb{P}} \text{N}(\mu, \sigma_t^2) \Rightarrow \text{E}_{\mathbb{P}}\big[e^{Y_t} \mid \mathcal{F}_{t-1}\big] = e^{\mu + \sigma_t^2/2}.$$

We need the equivalent $\mathbb{Q}$-measure process to be risk-neutral in the period from $t - 1$ to t, which means that

$$\text{E}_{\mathbb{Q}}\big[e^{Y_t} \mid \mathcal{F}_{t-1}\big] = e^r,$$

where r is the risk-free rate of interest. We can achieve this, retaining the original GARCH variance process, with the distribution

$$Y_t \mid \mathcal{F}_{t-1} \sim_{\mathbb{Q}} N\left(r - \tfrac{\sigma_t^2}{2}, \sigma_t^2\right)$$

$$\Rightarrow Y_t \mid \mathcal{F}_{t-1} = r - \tfrac{\sigma_t^2}{2} + \sigma_t \, \varepsilon_t, \tag{8.8}$$

$$\sigma_t^2 = a_0 + a_1 \left(Y_{t-1} - \left(r - \tfrac{\sigma_t^2}{2}\right)\right)^2 + b\sigma_{t-1}^2,$$

where a_0, a_1, and b have the same values under the $\mathbb{Q}$-measure as under the $\mathbb{P}$-measure. This $\mathbb{Q}$-measure is no longer a regular GARCH process, because of the term in σ_t^2 in equation (8.8). The process is called a **GARCH-in-Mean** (GARCH-M) process.

Example 8.1
You are given that the monthly log-returns on stock A follow a GARCH process, with $\mu = 0.004$, $a_0 = 7.5 \times 10^{-5}$, $a_1 = 0.2$, $b = 0.77$. The current price of the stock at time $t = 0$ is 90 and the price one month ago was 100.

(a) Calculate the long-run annualized volatility of the process.
(b) Assume that $\sigma_0^2 = 0.0025$.

   (i) Calculate the probability that the stock price is greater than 100 in 1 month.
   (ii) Calculate the expected value of σ_t^2 for $t = 2, 6, 12$, and 24 (in months). Comment on your calculations.

(c) Describe how your answers to (b)(ii) would change if the time 0 price of the stock is (i) 101 and (ii) 105.55. Comment.
(d) (i) Assume an investor holds 100 units of stock A. Using Monte Carlo simulation with 1,000 paths, estimate the 95% Expected Shortfall for the loss on the portfolio over two years.
   (ii) Estimate the standard error of the Expected Shortfall calculation in (d)(i).
(e) Compare the Expected Shortfall calculated in (d)(i) with the value assuming monthly log-returns are independent and identically distributed normal random variables, with $\mu = 0.004$, and variance equal to the GARCH long-run variance. Comment on the difference between the two estimates.

Solution 8.1   (a) The long-run variance, using monthly time steps, is

$$\lim_{t \to \infty} \sigma_t^2 = \frac{a_0}{1 - (a_1 + b)} = 0.0025.$$

The annualized volatility is $\sqrt{12} \times \sqrt{0.0025} = 17.3\%$.

(b)(i) We have

$$Y_0 = \log(90/100) = -0.10536, \quad \sigma_0 = 0.05,$$

which implies that $Y_1 \sim N(\mu, \sigma_1^2)$ where

$$\sigma_1^2 = a_0 + a_1(Y_0 - \mu)^2 + b\sigma_0^2 = 0.00439 = 0.066272^2,$$

$$\Pr[S_1 > 100] = \Pr\left[\frac{S_1}{S_0} > \frac{100}{90}\right] = \Pr[Y_1 > \log(100/90)]$$

$$= \Pr[Y_1 > 0.105361] = 1 - \Phi\left(\frac{0.1054 - 0.004}{0.066272}\right)$$

$$= 1 - \Phi(1.52947) = 0.06307.$$

(b)(ii)

$$E_0[\sigma_t^2] = a_0\left(\frac{1 - (a_1 + b)^{t-1}}{1 - (a_1 + b)}\right) + (a_1 + b)^{t-1}\sigma_1^2,$$

where $a_1 + b = 0.97$ and $\sigma_1^2 = 0.004392$, which gives

$$E_0[\sigma_2^2] = 0.004335, \qquad E_0[\sigma_6^2] = 0.004125,$$
$$E_0[\sigma_{12}^2] = 0.003853, \qquad E_0[\sigma_{24}^2] = 0.003439.$$

As t increases, the expected variance tends to the long-term value $\sigma^2 = 0.0025$, from the starting value, $\sigma_1^2 = 0.00439$. However, the trend is quite slow. Note that the starting value is significantly higher than the long-term value, because Y_0 is far from μ, creating a sudden spike in the volatility. This is a typical path for GARCH volatility – a sudden jump, followed by a long period trending back down to the long-term value.

(c) If the current stock price is 101, then $Y_0 = 0.00995$, and we have

$$\sigma_1^2 = 0.00201,$$
$$E_0[\sigma_2^2] = 0.00202, \qquad E_0[\sigma_6^2] = 0.00208,$$
$$E_0[\sigma_{12}^2] = 0.00215, \qquad E_0[\sigma_{24}^2] = 0.00226.$$

In this case, the $(Y_0 - \mu)^2$ term is smaller than the long-run variance, and σ_0^2 is assumed to be equal to the long-run variance, so the initial variance is expected to be smaller than the long-run value, trending slowly up to the long-run value.

If the current stock price is 105.55, then $Y_0 = 0.054$ and $(Y_0 - \mu)^2 = 0.0025 = \sigma^2$ which means that the expected variance is level at the long-run value. That is, $E_0[\sigma_t^2] = 0.0025$ for all t.

(d) The simulation can be run in R quite efficiently. The process can be summarized as follows:

A1. Enter parameters and starting values for σ_0^2 and Y_0.

A2. Generate a $1{,}000 \times 24$ matrix of independent $N(0,1)$ random variates denoted Z.

A3. For each simulation $i = 1, 2, \ldots, 1{,}000$ do the following calculations:

For each time period $t = 1, 2, \ldots, 24$ calculate

$$\sigma_t^2 = a_0 + a_1(Y_{t-1} - \mu)^2 + b\sigma_{t-1}^2 \quad \text{and} \quad Y_t = \mu + \sigma_t\, Z_{i,t}.$$

A4. Calculate the simulated loss under the ith simulation

$$L(i) = 100\big(90 - 90\, e^{Y_1 + Y_2 + \cdots Y_{24}}\big).$$

A5. The 95% Expected Shortfall estimate is the average of the worst 5% of simulated losses.

A6. The standard error uses the Manistre–Hancock formula from Section 3.5, that is,

$$s_{ES} = \sqrt{\frac{s_1^2 + \alpha(\widehat{ES}_\alpha - \widehat{Q}_\alpha)^2}{N(1 - \alpha)}},$$

where s_1^2 is the variance of the worst 5% of the simulated losses, $\alpha = 0.95$, $\widehat{ES}_\alpha$ is the estimate from step A5 above, $\widehat{Q}_\alpha$ is the estimated α-quantile, which is the 950th largest simulated loss, and $N = 1{,}000$ is the number of simulations.

The results of our simulation are

$$\widehat{ES}_{95\%} = 3{,}942.6, \qquad \widehat{Q}_\alpha = 2{,}858.5, \quad \text{and } s_{ES} = 203.$$

(e) If the Y_j are i.i.d. normally distributed, with parameters $\mu = 0.004$ and $\sigma^2 = 0.0025$, then the stock price at $t = 24$ is lognormally distributed, with parameters $\mu^* = 24\mu = 0.096$ and $\sigma^* = \sqrt{24}\sigma = 0.24495$. The Expected Shortfall for a lognormal stock price using the formula derived in Chapter 3, is

$$ES = 100\left(90\left(1 - \frac{e^{\mu^* + (\sigma^*)^2/2}}{1 - \alpha}\, \Phi\left(z_{1-\alpha} - \sigma^*\right)\right)\right)$$

$$= 2{,}999.0.$$

We see that the i.i.d. normal assumption for log-returns generates a smaller Expected Shortfall. This is reasonable, as the variances in the GARCH case tend to be larger than the long-run value, because of the large starting value of $(Y_0 - \mu)^2$. If the initial value for σ_0 is close to the long-run value σ, and the starting value of $(Y_0 - \mu)^2$ is small, then the Expected Shortfall values will be more closely aligned. $\quad\square$

8.7 Regime-Switching Models

Regime-switching models assume that the stochastic log-return process randomly switches between K different underlying processes, each with different parameters. Each process represents a different regime for the state of the economy. The model can be used for continuous or discrete time processes. In this section, we will describe the regime-switching lognormal model with two states (**RSLN-2**). We will work (as usual) with the log returns, Y_t, for $t = 1$, $2, \ldots, T$, which are assumed to follow a normal process within each regime.

Let μ_1, σ_1 denote the parameters of the first regime and μ_2, σ_2 denote the parameters of the second regime. At each time t, Y_t is in either Regime 1 or Regime 2. A separate stochastic process, $\rho_t \in \{1, 2\}$ for $t = 1, 2, \ldots$ determines which regime the process is in at time t. That means

$$Y_t | \{\rho_t = 1\} \sim N(\mu_1, \sigma_1^2), \qquad Y_t | \{\rho_t = 2\} \sim N(\mu_2, \sigma_2^2). \tag{8.9}$$

The regime process, ρ_t is assumed to be a discrete time Markov process, which means that the probability of being in, say, Regime 1 at any future date depends only on the current regime and not on any other information about the process, such as how long since the last regime change. We will use the following notation for the regime transition probabilities in each time period

$$\Pr[\rho_t = 1 \mid \rho_{t-1} = 1] = p_{11}, \quad \Pr[\rho_t = 2 \mid \rho_{t-1} = 1] = p_{12} = 1 - p_{11}, \tag{8.10}$$

$$\Pr[\rho_t = 1 \mid \rho_{t-1} = 2] = p_{21}, \quad \Pr[\rho_t = 2 \mid \rho_{t-1} = 2] = p_{22} = 1 - p_{21}. \tag{8.11}$$

The transition matrix is $P = \begin{pmatrix} p_{11} & p_{12} \\ p_{21} & p_{22} \end{pmatrix}$. The model is illustrated in Figure 8.6.

Regime-switching lognormal models with two or three regimes have proved quite robust for fitting stock prices over longer time periods, and are also relatively tractable. Generally, more frequent data requires more regimes.

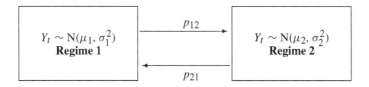

Figure 8.6 Diagram of the RSLN-2 process

For modelling monthly log-returns on stocks, typical parameters for the two regime model are given in Table 8.1. These parameters indicate a model under which the monthly volatility follows a very simple stochastic process, randomly switching between 3.5% per month (equivalent to 12.1% per year) and 7% per month (equivalent to 26.0% per year). When the process is in Regime 1, the probability of moving to Regime 2 in the next month is 5%, so the probability of staying in Regime 1 for the next month is 95%. Similarly, when the process is in Regime 2, the probability of moving to Regime 1 is 20%, so the probability of staying in Regime 2 is 80%. The result is a process that spends long periods in the low volatility regime, moving, on average, every 20 months, and rather shorter periods, averaging 5 months, in the high volatility regime.

Regime 1 represents **bull markets**, which is the term used for periods of positive returns and relative calm. Regime 2 represents **bear markets**, which are periods of falling prices and general market uncertainty.

As the parameters of the distribution depend on the regime, the parameters applying in future time periods are random variables. For example, suppose the process is in Regime 1 at time 0. At time 1 it could still be in Regime 1, with probability p_{11}, or it could have moved to Regime 2, with probability p_{12}. So, the expected value of the mean log-return at time 1, given that the process is in Regime 1 at time 0, is

$$E[Y_1 \mid \rho_0 = 1] = \mu_1 \, p_{11} + \mu_2 \, p_{12}.$$

Similarly, the expected value of the mean log-return at time 1 given that the process is in Regime 2 at time 0 is

$$E[Y_1 \mid \rho_0 = 2] = \mu_1 \, p_{21} + \mu_2 \, p_{22}.$$

We can also find the expected value of the variance of Y_1, starting from Regime 1 at time 0:

$$E\big[\mathrm{Var}[Y_1 \mid \rho_0 = 1]\big] = \sigma_1^2 \, p_{11} + \sigma_2^2 \, p_{12},$$

Table 8.1. *Typical parameters for the monthly RSLN-2 model for stock returns*

Regime 1	$\mu_1 = 0.014$	$\sigma_1 = 0.035$	$p_{12} = 0.05$
Regime 2	$\mu_2 = -0.014$	$\sigma_2 = 0.070$	$p_{21} = 0.20$

and starting from Regime 2

$$E\big[\mathrm{Var}[Y_1 \mid \rho_0 = 2]\big] = \sigma_1^2\, p_{21} + \sigma_2^2\, p_{22}.$$

The Markov regime process, ρ_t, has a stationary distribution that represents the unconditional long-term probability that the process lies in either regime. That is, if we do not know anything about the regime process or the log-return values up to time t, we can determine the unconditional probability that the process is in Regime 1 or Regime 2. Let π_1 denote the unconditional probability of being in Regime 1 and $\pi_2 = 1 - \pi_1$ denote the unconditional probability of being in Regime 2. This is called the **stationary distribution** because, given that the probabilities associated with Regime 1 and Regime 2 at time t are π_1 and π_2, respectively, then the probabilities at time $t + 1$ must be the same. That means that we can find π_1 and π_2 from the equations

$$\pi_1\, p_{11} + \pi_2\, p_{21} = \pi_1,$$

$$\pi_1\, p_{12} + \pi_2\, p_{22} = \pi_2,$$

$$\text{and } \pi_1 + \pi_2 = 1.$$

Recall that $p_{11} + p_{12} = 1$, and $p_{21} + p_{22} = 1$, giving

$$\pi_1 = \frac{p_{21}}{p_{12} + p_{21}} \quad \text{and} \quad \pi_2 = \frac{p_{12}}{p_{12} + p_{21}}. \tag{8.12}$$

Using the parameters in Table 8.1, we have $\pi_1 = 0.8$ and $\pi_2 = 0.2$, which indicates that the process is in Regime 1 approximately 80% of the time, and in Regime 2 approximately 20% of the time.

We can see that, like the GARCH model, the regime-switching model allows sudden jumps in volatility. A major difference between the models lies in the subsequent behaviour. Typically, in the GARCH model, the volatility will trend back to a lower value over some period. Under the RSLN model, the volatility switches suddenly from high to low. If we consider the estimated volatility shown in Figure 8.3b, we see that the changes from low to high and high to low volatility are both quite sudden. Although the RSLN model is less sophisticated than GARCH in some ways – in particular, the volatility can only take two values, whereas under GARCH it can take any positive value – goodness of fit tests for long-run returns have been found to favour the regime-switching framework. The swift change from low to high volatility, and from high to low volatility in the RS model is more consistent with markets, where sudden upward jumps in volatility are common, and a few market influencers switching from selling to buying can create sudden downward volatility shifts.

The RSLN model is relatively easy to use, especially in a Monte Carlo simulation, but there are some awkward features. The first is that we do not actually observe the regime, ρ_t. For example, suppose we have a RSLN-2 process with the parameters in Table 8.1 and we observe a single log-return of $y_t = -0.08$. This could be from Regime 1, but in that case, it would be an extreme observation, lying over 2.5 standard deviations away from the mean. Alternatively, it could be from Regime 2, in which case it would be less than one standard deviation away from the mean. It is more likely that the process is in Regime 2 at that time and, in fact, we can assign a probability to each regime conditional on the value of the log-return, and on the values of the previous and subsequent log-returns, if they are available. Markov models with this characteristic are called **hidden Markov models**.

When the $\mathbb{P}$-measure is RSLN, there is a $\mathbb{Q}$-measure that is also RSLN. As with the GARCH process, we find there are many equivalent $\mathbb{Q}$-measures for the RSLN $\mathbb{P}$-measure model. A simple transformation to a $\mathbb{Q}$-measure is to retain the same values for σ_1 and σ_2, and also retain the transition probabilities from the $\mathbb{P}$-measure, adjusting the μ_1 and μ_2 parameters such that the processes within each regime are risk-neutral, so that the $\mathbb{Q}$-measure mean parameter is $r - \sigma^2/2$ in Regime 1 and $r - \sigma^2/2$ in Regime 2.

Example 8.2 You are given that monthly log-returns on stock A follow a RSLN-2 process, with parameters given in Table 8.1. The current price of the stock is 90, and the price one month ago was 100. The process is assumed to be in Regime 2 at time 0.

(a) Calculate the standard deviation of the log-return at time 1 (in months).
(b) Calculate the probability that the stock price is greater than 100 in 1 month.
(c) Calculate the unconditional standard deviation of the process, per month.
(d) (i) Assume an investor holds 100 units of stock A. Using Monte Carlo simulation with 1,000 paths, estimate the 95% Expected Shortfall for the loss on the portfolio over two years.
   (ii) Estimate the standard error of your calculation in (d)(i).
   (iii) Compare your value in (d)(i) with the values in Example 8.1.

Solution 8.2

(a) We will utilize the formula for the variance of a random variable, in this
    case Y_1, which is dependent on another random variable, in this case the
    regime at time 1, ρ_1. We have

$$\text{Var}[Y_1] = E\big[\text{Var}[Y_1 \mid \rho_1]\big] + \text{Var}\big[E[Y_1 \mid \rho_1]\big]$$
$$\text{where } E[Y_1 \mid \rho_1] = \mu_{\rho_1} \text{ and } \text{Var}[Y_1 \mid \rho_1] = \sigma_{\rho_1}^2.$$

The probability that $\rho_1 = j$, $j = 1, 2$, given that we know that $\rho_0 = 2$, is

$$\Pr[\rho_1 = j \mid \rho_0 = 2] = p_{2j}.$$

Hence,

$$E[\text{Var}[Y_1 \mid \rho_1]] = p_{21} \sigma_1^2 + p_{22} \sigma_2^2 = 0.004165,$$
$$\text{Var}[E[Y_1 \mid \rho_1]] = E[E[Y_1^2 \mid \rho_1]] - E[E[Y_1 \mid \rho_1]]^2$$
$$= p_{21} \mu_1^2 + p_{22} \mu_2^2 - (p_{21} \mu_1 + p_{22} \mu_2)^2$$
$$= 0.000125$$
$$\Rightarrow V[Y_1] = 0.004290 = 0.0655^2.$$

(b)

$$\Pr[S_1 > 100] = \Pr\left[\frac{S_1}{S_0} > \frac{100}{90}\right] = \Pr[Y_1 > 0.105361]$$
$$= \Pr[Y_1 > 0.105361 \mid \rho_1 = 1] \times \Pr[\rho_1 = 1]$$
$$+ \Pr[Y_1 > 0.105361 \mid \rho_1 = 2] \times \Pr[\rho_1 = 2],$$
$$\Pr[Y_1 > 0.105361 \mid \rho_1 = 1] = 1 - \Phi\left(\frac{0.105361 - \mu_1}{\sigma_1}\right) = 0.004523,$$
$$\Pr[Y_1 > 0.105361 \mid \rho_1 = 2] = 1 - \Phi\left(\frac{0.105361 - \mu_2}{\sigma_2}\right) = 0.044083$$
$$\Rightarrow \Pr[S_1 > 100] = 0.004523 \times p_{21} + 0.044083 \times p_{22}$$
$$= 0.036171.$$

(c) This follows the solution to (a), but we use the stationary distribution
    probabilities, π_1 and π_2 in place of p_{21} and p_{22}, to calculate the
    unconditional moments for Y_t.

$$E\big[\text{Var}[Y_t \mid \rho_t]\big] = E[\sigma_{\rho_t}^2] = \pi_1 \sigma_1^2 + \pi_2 \sigma_2^2 = 0.00196,$$

$$\text{Var}\big[E[Y_t \mid \rho_t]\big] = \text{Var}[\mu_{\rho_t}] = E[\mu_{\rho_t}^2] - E[\mu_{\rho_t}]^2$$

$$= \pi_1 \mu_1^2 + \pi_2 \mu_2^2 - (\pi_1 \mu_1 + \pi_2 \mu_2)^2 = 0.000125$$

$$\Rightarrow \text{Var}[Y_t] = 0.04567^2.$$

(d) Similarly to the GARCH example, the simulation algorithm can be summarized as follows:

(i) Enter parameters and starting values for μ_1, μ_2, σ_1, σ_2, p_{21} and p_{11} and ρ_0.

(ii) Generate a $1{,}000 \times 24$ matrix of independent $N(0,1)$ random variates denoted Z.

(iii) Generate a $1{,}000 \times 24$ matrix of independent $U(0,1)$ random variates denoted U.

(iv) For each simulation $i = 1, 2, \ldots, 1{,}000$ do the following calculations:

For each time period $t = 1, 2, \ldots, 24$ determine the regime ρ_t as follows:

$$\text{if } U_{i,t} < p_{\rho_{t-1}, 1} \text{ then } \rho_t = 1, \text{ otherwise } \rho_t = 2,$$

and hence simulate a value for the log-return, using the mean and standard deviation appropriate to the simulated regime:

$$Y_t = \mu_{\rho_t} + \sigma_{\rho_t} Z_{i,t}.$$

The process then proceeds as for the GARCH example.

The results of our simulation are

$$\widehat{ES}_{95\%} = 3{,}848.9, \quad \hat{Q}_\alpha = 2{,}862.7, \quad \text{and } s_{ES} = 182.$$

The long-term standard deviation of the RSLN process is lower than the GARCH (4.567% for RSLN, compared with 5.0% for GARCH); the 1-month standard deviation of the RSLN process is higher than the GARCH (6.98% for RSLN, compared with 6.63% for GARCH). The estimated Expected Shortfall for the RSLN, of 3,848.9 is not statistically significantly different from the GARCH estimate of 3,942.6, given the standard errors are around 180–200. □

8.8 Fitting Models to Returns Data

Assume we have n observations, $x = x_1, x_2, \ldots x_n$, from a stochastic process (or time series) X_t, where t denotes the time of the observation, and for each t, assume X_t is a continuous random variable.[1] We assume that the stochastic process X_t involves unknown parameters $\theta = (\theta_1, \theta_2, \ldots, \theta_k)$. The likelihood function is the joint probability density function of the observed data, as a function of the unknown parameters,

$$L(\theta) = f_{X_1, \ldots, X_n}(x_1, x_2, \ldots, x_n; \theta).$$

We generally work with the log-likelihood, $l(\theta) = \log L(\theta)$. Maximizing the log-likelihood with respect to θ gives

Now, with time series data we cannot assume that the X_i are independent, which means that we cannot simply take the product of the individual density functions, $f(x_i)$. However, we can build up the joint density function using the conditional densities:

$$f(x_1, x_2) = f(x_1) f(x_2 \mid x_1)$$
$$f(x_1, x_2, x_3) = f(x_1) f(x_2, x_2 \mid x_1) = f(x_1) f(x_2 \mid x_1) f(x_3 \mid x_1, x_2)$$

$$\vdots \qquad \vdots$$

$$f(x_1, x_2, \ldots x_n) = f(x_1) f(x_2 \mid x_1) f(x_3 \mid x_1, x_2) \cdots f(x_n \mid x_1, x_2, \cdots, x_{n-1}).$$

So we have

$$L(\theta) = f(x_1; \theta) f(x_2 \mid x_1; \theta) f(x_3 \mid x_1, x_2; \theta) \cdots f(x_n \mid x_1, x_2, \cdots, x_{n-1}; \theta)$$

$$= \prod_{i=1}^{n} f(x_i \mid x_1, \ldots, x_{i-1}; \theta)$$

$$\Rightarrow l(\theta) = \sum_{i=1}^{n} \log f(x_i \mid x_1, \ldots, x_{i-1}; \theta). \tag{8.13}$$

We can use numerical optimization software (e.g., Solver in Excel) to determine the parameters $\theta_1, \ldots, \theta_k$ which maximize the log-likelihood function.

In the following sections we will use maximum likelihood to fit the ILN, GARCH, and RSLN-2 models to the daily S&P data shown in Figure 8.1 and the monthly S&P/TSX data shown in Figure 8.3.

---

[1] The results for discrete or mixed random variables are identical, with probability functions replacing density functions for observations from the discrete distribution.

8.8.1 The Independent Lognormal (ILN) Model

Under the **independent lognormal** (ILN) model for stock prices, the log-returns are independent and identically distributed normal random variables, with μ denoting the common mean[2] and σ^2 denoting the variance. This means that conditioning on previous values makes no difference to the density function for each successive value, so we have the following, where ϕ represents the standard normal density function:

$$f(y_i \mid y_1, y_2, \ldots, y_{i-1}; \mu, \sigma) = f(y_i; \mu, \sigma)$$

$$= \frac{1}{\sigma} \phi \left(\frac{y_i - \mu}{\sigma} \right) = \frac{1}{\sqrt{2\pi}\sigma} e^{-\frac{1}{2}\left(\frac{y_i-\mu}{\sigma}\right)^2},$$

$$l(\mu, \sigma) = -\frac{n}{2} \log 2\pi - n \log \sigma - \sum_{i=1}^{n} -\frac{1}{2} \left(\frac{y_i - \mu}{\sigma} \right)^2.$$

The maximum likelihood estimates can be derived by differentiating with respect to μ and σ, and setting the derivatives equal to zero, to get

$$\hat{\mu} = \bar{x}, \qquad \hat{\sigma} = \sqrt{\frac{\sum_{i=1}^{n} (x_i - \hat{\mu})^2}{n}}.$$

For the S&P 2019–20 daily data, we have $\hat{\mu} = 0.00079$ and $\hat{\sigma} = 0.01639$, equivalent to an annual mean log-return of 19.8% and an annual volatility of 25.9%. The log-likelihood (*ll*) value using these parameters is $ll = 1,337$.

For the S&P/TSX 1990–2020 monthly data we have $\hat{\mu} = 0.0061$ and $\hat{\sigma} = 0.0419$, equivalent to an annual mean log-return of 7.3% and an annual volatility of 14.5%. The log-likelihood value using these parameters is $ll = 653$.

8.8.2 The GARCH Model

The model parameters for the GARCH(1,1) process are μ, a_0, a_1, and b.

The conditional distribution of Y_t given σ_t is $N(\mu, \sigma_t^2)$ and σ_t is a function of Y_{t-1} and σ_{t-1}, as well as the parameters a_0, a_1, and b. We assume that σ_0 is known, so that σ_t can be written as a function of Y_1, Y_2, ..., Y_{t-1}, which allows us to build up the log-likelihood function, using (8.13), which we can maximize numerically.

---

[2] The μ parameter here corresponds to the mean of the log-returns, which is different from the drift parameter of the underlying Geometric Brownian motion.

Table 8.2. *GARCH MLE parameters for S&P daily return data (2019–20)*
and S&P/TSX monthly total return data (1990–2020) – the volatility is the
long-run unconditional value

	a_0	a_1	b	μ (annualized)	σ (annualized)
2019–20 S&P Daily data	4.8×10^{-6}	0.279	0.709	0.328	0.316
1990–2020 S&P/TSX Monthly data	1.9×10^{-4}	0.333	0.611	0.105	0.199

For the S&P 2019–20 daily data we find that if we do not constrain the parameters, the likelihood is maximized when $a_1 + b > 1$ which is not a feasible solution for a longer term model. If we constrain the parameters such that $a_1 + b < 1$ and set a maximum value for the long-run standard deviation of 0.02 per day, we find the likelihood is maximized at $ll = 1{,}607$, with parameter values given in Table 8.2.

For the S&P/TSX 1990–20 monthly data the GARCH likelihood is maximized at $ll = 682$, with the parameters given in Table 8.2. We also show in the final column the long-run annualized volatility estimate indicated by the parameters.

8.8.3 The RSLN-2 Model

The process for determining the likelihood for the RSLN model with two regimes is slightly more complex, but it does offer some insight into the model. The method uses Bayes' theorem repeatedly, exploiting the fact that the probability functions simplify significantly using appropriate conditioning.

The steps for calculating the likelihood are described below, assuming the parameters are known. This can be entered into, for example, Excel, using 'first guess' estimates for the parameters, and Excel Solver can then be applied to find the MLE parameters.

We will make use of several conditional density and probability functions. We use f to denote the probability density functions, where at least one of the variates is continuous, and p for probability functions associated with the regimes ρ_t.

Now consider the first sample value, y_1. We know that $Y_1 \mid \{\rho_1 = 1\} \sim$ N(μ_1, σ_1^2) and, similarly, $Y_1 \mid \{\rho_1 = 2\} \sim$ N(μ_2, σ_2^2). Also,

$$f(y_1) = f(y_1, \rho_1 = 1) + f(y_1, \rho_1 = 2),$$

where, for example, $f(y_1, \rho_1 = 1)$ is the joint probability density function for $Y_1 = y_1$ and $\rho_1 = 1$. Using conditional probability functions, we have

$$f(y_1) = f(y_1 \mid \rho_1 = 1) \, p(\rho_1 = 1) + f(y_1 \mid \rho_1 = 2) \, p(\rho_1 = 2).$$

Now $Y_1 \mid \{\rho_1 = j\} \sim N(\mu_j, \sigma_j^2)$, with density function

$$f(y_1 \mid \rho_1 = j) = \frac{1}{\sqrt{2\pi}\sigma_j} e^{-\frac{1}{2}\left(\frac{y_1 - \mu_j}{\sigma_j}\right)^2} = \frac{1}{\sigma_j}\phi\left(\frac{y_1 - \mu_j}{\sigma_j}\right) \quad \text{for } j = 1, 2,$$

where ϕ is the standard normal probability density function.

Assume that at time 0 the regime process is in Regime 1. Then the probability that $\rho_1 = 1$ is p_{11} and the probability that $\rho_1 = 2$ is p_{12}:

$$f(y_1) = p_{11} \times \frac{1}{\sigma_1}\phi\left(\frac{y_1 - \mu_1}{\sigma_1}\right) + p_{12} \times \frac{1}{\sigma_2}\phi\left(\frac{y_1 - \mu_2}{\sigma_2}\right).$$

Before we move on to the second value, we note that

$$p\,(\rho_1 = 1 \mid y_1) = \frac{f(y_1, \rho_1 = 1)}{f(y_1)}, \quad \text{and } p\,(\rho_1 = 2 \mid y_1) = \frac{f(y_1, \rho_1 = 2)}{f(y_1)}.$$

This gives us the probability that the hidden regime process is in each regime at time 1, based on the data point at time 1, and the parameters of the model. We will use these values for the next iteration step of the likelihood calculation.

In the second and subsequent periods we split the conditional density into four cases. For $t = 2$, we have

$$f(y_2 \mid y_1) = f(y_2, \rho_1 = 1, \rho_2 = 1 \mid y_1) + f(y_2, \rho_1 = 1, \rho_2 = 2 \mid y_1)$$
$$+ f(y_2, \rho_1 = 2, \rho_2 = 1 \mid y_1) + f(y_2, \rho_1 = 2, \rho_2 = 2 \mid y_1),$$
(8.14)

by repeated application of Bayes theorem. Consider the first of the four terms:

$$f(y_2, \rho_1 = 1, \rho_2 = 1 \mid y_1) = f(y_2 \mid y_1, \rho_1 = 1, \rho_2 = 1)$$
$$\times p\,(\rho_2 = 1 \mid y_1, \rho_1 = 1) \times p\,(\rho_1 = 1 \mid y_1).$$
(8.15)

Now $f(y_2 \mid y_1, \rho_1 = 1, \rho_2 = 1) = f(y_2 \mid \rho_2 = 1)$ because when we know ρ_2 we exactly know the distribution of y_2, and the other terms in the condition are not relevant. So this term simplifies to the normal probability density function, with the Regime 1 parameters.

Similarly, $p\,(\rho_2 = 1 \mid y_1, \rho_1 = 1)$, which is the probability that $\rho_2 = 1$, given that $\rho_1 = 1$, and given y_1, simplifies to $p(\rho_2 = 1 \mid \rho_1 = 1) = p_{11}$, because the information about y_1 makes no difference when we know ρ_1.

Table 8.3. *RSLN MLE parameters for S&P daily return data (2019–20) and S&P/TSX monthly total return data (1990–2020)*

	μ_1	μ_2	σ_1	σ_2	p_{12}	p_{21}
2019–20 S&P Daily data	0.002	−0.003	0.007	0.033	0.026	0.095
1990–2020 S&P/TSX Monthly data	0.011	−0.012	0.030	0.069	0.032	0.119

The remaining term in equation (8.15) is $p(\rho_1 = 1 \mid y_1)$ which was calculated with the $t = 1$ density calculations above.

We can similarly deconstruct the other three terms in equation (8.14); summing the four terms gives the required conditional density function $f(y_2 \mid y_1)$, and the contribution to the total log-likelihood is $\log f(y_2 \mid y_1)$.

Proceeding to $t = 3$, we have

$$f(y_3 \mid y_1, y_2) = f(y_3, \rho_2 = 1, \rho_3 = 1 \mid y_1, y_2) + f(y_3, \rho_2 = 1, \rho_3 = 2 \mid y_1, y_2)$$
$$+ f(y_3, \rho_2 = 2, \rho_3 = 1 \mid y_1, y_2) + f(y_3, \rho_2 = 2, \rho_3 = 2 \mid y_1, y_2).$$

Similarly to the $t = 2$ case, each of these terms can be broken down. For example, the first term breaks down into the three components:

$$f(y_3, \rho_2 = 1, \rho_3 = 1 \mid y_1, y_2) = f(y_3 \mid \rho_3 = 1) \times p_{11} \times p(\rho_2 = 1 \mid y_1, y_2),$$

where, as for $t = 2$, $f(y_3 \mid \rho_3 = 1)$ is just the $N(\mu_1, \sigma_1^2)$ density function and $p(\rho_2 = 1 \mid y_2)$ is taken from the likelihood calculation for y_2.

We continue, iterating through each successive data point, calculating for each one the conditional density function $f(y_t \mid y_{t-1}, y_{t-2}, \ldots, y_1)$. The total log-likelihood is the sum of the values of $\log f(y_t \mid y_{t-1}, y_{t-2}, \ldots, y_1)$ over all the data points. This is the value that is maximized to find the MLE parameters.

Note that we assumed a starting regime of $\rho_0 = 1$ above; if we do not know the starting regime, then the initial regime probabilities for the y_1 calculations can be replaced with the long-term stationary probabilities, π_1 and π_2.

The MLE parameters for the RSLN model for the daily and monthly data series are given in Table 8.3.

For the parameters fitted using the 2019–20 daily data, the long-run annualized mean log-return is 18.8% and the long-run annualized expected volatility is 26.2%. For the parameters fitted using the 1990–2020 monthly data, the long-run annualized mean log-return is 7.0% and the long-run annualized expected volatility is 14.4%. These values are very different from the mean and long-run variance results using the GARCH model.

8.9 Choosing a Model

Each of the models described in this chapter is used in practice for financial risk management. Typically, the ILN model would be used for very short-term problems with higher frequency time steps. The RSLN model needs more data for an adequate fit and would be used for longer horizons. The GARCH model is flexible and is used in a wide range of short- and long-term settings.

Another consideration is materiality. The GARCH and RSLN models have fatter tails than the ILN model and generate serial dependence in the log-returns and in the volatility. If this is not critical to the model results, then using the ILN model may be adequate. When calculating a VaR risk measure, it may not be necessary or worthwhile to ensure that a model provides a good fit in the extremes of the distribution, beyond the relevant α-quantile. On the other hand, the Expected Shortfall risk measure takes the full tail of the loss distribution into consideration, so it becomes more important to fit a fat-tailed distribution to fat-tailed data.

Statistical model selection is often based on penalized likelihood measures, such as the **Akaike information criterion** (AIC) or **Bayes information criterion** (BIC). Under the AIC we would choose the model with the largest value of $AIC = ll - k$, where ll is the maximum log-likelihood and k is the number of parameters. Under the BIC we choose the model with the largest value of $BIC = ll - (k \log(n))/2$, where n is the number of data points in the sample.[3] In Table 8.4, we summarize the results from fitting the ILN, GARCH, and RSLN models to the two data sets used throughout this chapter. We can see from this summary that the ILN fit is poor for both data sets. The GARCH model provides a better overall fit for the daily data and the RSLN model provides a slightly better fit for the monthly data.

The likelihood-based model selection criteria are straightforward, but have a couple of disadvantages. The first is that the model selection is relative – we have no information from the log-likelihood as to whether any of these models provides an adequate fit to the data. The second is that the likelihood is dominated by the fit in the centre of the distribution, where the individual values

---

[3] Note that the sample size in correlated time series data is not as clear as it would be for i.i.d. samples, but we ignore that complication here.

Table 8.4. *Log-likelihood, AIC, and BIC statistics for*
ILN, GARCH, and RSLN models, daily and monthly
data sets

	log-likelihood	k	AIC	BIC
S&P 2019–20 daily data				
ILN	1,337	2	1,335	1,331
GARCH	1,608	4	1,604	1,596
RSLN	1,581	6	1,575	1,562
S&P/TSX 1990–2020 monthly data				
ILN	652	2	650	647
GARCH	682	4	678	670
RSLN	691	6	685	673

of $f(y_t \mid y_{t-1}, \ldots, y_1)$ are highest. For risk management we are often more interested in the tails of the distribution, which may have little influence on the overall likelihood. Exploring the model residuals can indicate whether the model is providing an adequate fit to the tails of the distribution. The residuals for the three models are:

$$\text{ILN:} \qquad r_t = \frac{y_t - \mu}{\sigma},$$

$$\text{GARCH:} \qquad r_t = \frac{y_t - \mu}{\sigma_t},$$

$$\text{RSLN:} \qquad r_t \mid \rho_t = \frac{y_t - \mu_t}{\sigma_t}.$$

In the RSLN case, because the regime is not observed, we select the residual by randomly allocating ρ_t to Regime 1 or Regime 2, based on the probability $\Pr[\rho_t = j \mid y_1, \ldots, y_t]$ which was part of the likelihood calculations. For each of the models, the residuals should be approximately normally distributed. In Figure 8.7, we show the Q-Q plots for the residuals for the daily data. We note that, although the GARCH model provides a better fit than the RSLN model overall, based on likelihood statistics, the left tail fit of the GARCH model is not as good as for the RSLN model. However, all the models have tails that are less extreme than the data. This is not surprising, given the unusual market performance in 2019–20, with very high overall returns along with very high volatility.

In Figure 8.8, we show the residuals for the monthly data, which tell a similar story to the daily data. The RSLN model appears to provide a better left tail fit than the GARCH model and both are very significantly better than the ILN model.

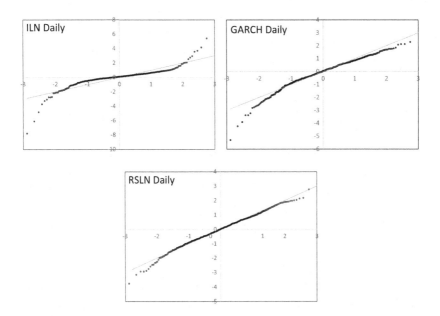

Figure 8.7 Residuals based on models calibrated to 2019–20 daily S&P log-return data

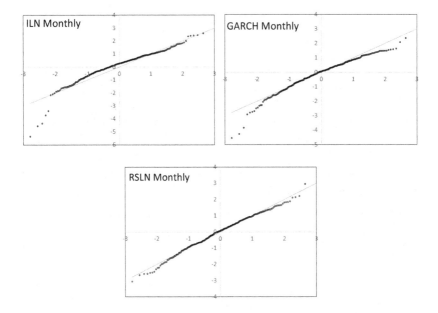

Figure 8.8 Residuals based on models calibrated to 1990–2020 monthly S&P log-return data

8.10 Notes and Further Reading

The original **ARCH model** (Engle, 1982) is similar to the GARCH process, but with a volatility process

$$\sigma_t^2 = a_0 + a_1 (Y_{t-1} - \mu)^2. \tag{8.16}$$

The introduction of the $b\sigma_{t-1}^2$ term that transforms the ARCH model into the GARCH model provides for longer clustering and less volatility in the variance process, which results in a better match to the behaviour of stock prices.

There are a number of different GARCH variants, designed to incorporate the leverage effect. We describe two of the more well-known examples below.

$$\text{EGARCH: } \log \sigma_t^2 = a_0 + a_1 \left| \frac{Y_{t-1} - \mu}{\sigma_{t-1}} \right| + \lambda \frac{Y_{t-1} - \mu}{\sigma_{t-1}} + b \log \sigma_{t-1}^2.$$
$$\tag{8.17}$$

Note that $(Y_{t-1} - \mu)/\sigma_{t-1} = \varepsilon_{t-1}$. The a_1 term uses the absolute value of ε_{t-1} in setting σ_t^2, so large movements in either direction will have the same impact. The λ term uses the absolute value, which (allowing for exponentiation) means that the model allows for different impact of positive and negative ε_{t-1}. We expect $\lambda < 0$, for consistency with the leverage effect.

$$\text{GJR-GARCH: } \sigma_t^2 = a_0 + (a_1 + \gamma I_{t-1}) (Y_{t-1} - \mu)^2 + b\sigma_{t-1}^2, \tag{8.18}$$

$$\text{where } I_t = \begin{cases} 0 & \text{if } Y_{t-1} - \mu > 0, \\ 1 & \text{if } Y_{t-1} - \mu \le 0. \end{cases} \tag{8.19}$$

The GJR-GARCH model (see Glosten et al., 1993) allows for an extra boost to the volatility at t if $Y_{t-1} - \mu < 0$, so is a form of threshold model.

Duan (1995) provides more information on option pricing with GARCH.

Regime-switching models were introduced by Hamilton (1990), where a regime-switching auto-regressive process was used to model inflation. The regime-switching framework can be combined with a wide range of within-regime processes. Gray (1996) uses a regime-switching GARCH model for interest rates, for example. The RSLN-2 model is described in more detail in Hardy (2001).

The elicitation of residuals for the RSLN model in Section 8.9 follows the method described in Hardy et al. (2006).

8.11 Exercises

Exercise 8.1 You are interested in the probability that a stock price will drop by more than 10% in the next six months. Would you use the risk-neutral or real-world measure for this calculation? Justify your answer.

Exercise 8.2

(a) Explain what is meant by 'volatility clustering'.
(b) Describe three features of the ILN model that are inconsistent with real-world stock price movements.
(c) Explain how the GARCH model captures volatility clustering. Which of the GARCH parameters has the most influence on the length of the volatility cluster?
(d) Explain how the RSLN model captures volatility clustering. Which of the RSLN parameters has the most influence on the length of the volatility cluster?

Exercise 8.3 The VIX is a measure of volatility derived from option prices, assuming that prices are determined by the Black–Scholes formulas. This is called the **implied volatility**.

You are given the following information about a European put option on one unit of a non-dividend paying stock:

(i) The current stock price is $S_0 = 100$.
(ii) The strike price is $K = 95$.
(iii) The term is $T = 0.5$ years.
(iv) The risk-free rate of interest is $r = 0.03$.
(v) The price of the put option is 5.70.

Using Excel Solver, or otherwise, determine the implied volatility.

Exercise 8.4 Assume an investor holds a portfolio of stocks. The current value is $S_0 = 100$. The daily portfolio values are assumed to follow an ILN process, with mean log-return $\mu = 0.0$ and variance of log-returns $\sigma^2 = 0.0002$ per day.

The t-day portfolio loss is defined as the difference between the value of the portfolio at time 0 and the value of the portfolio at time t.

(a) Calculate the 95% Value-at-Risk for the 1-day portfolio loss.
(b) Calculate the 95% Value-at-Risk for the 10-day portfolio loss.

Exercise 8.5 Assume Y_t follows a GARCH process with $\mu = 0$.

(a) Show that $\text{Cov}(Y_1, Y_2) = 0$.
(b) Show that $Y_1 + Y_2$ does not follow a Normal distribution.

Exercise 8.6 Assume Y_t follows a GARCH process. You are given that $\text{Cov}(Y_t, Y_s) = 0$ for all $t \neq s$.

(a) Let $\gamma = a_1 + b$, and let Var_0 denote the variance given the information available at time 0. Show that

$$\text{Var}_0\left[Y_1 + Y_2 + \cdots + Y_n\right] = \frac{a_0}{1-\gamma}\left(n - \frac{1-\gamma^n}{1-\gamma}\right) + \sigma_1^2\left(\frac{1-\gamma^n}{1-\gamma}\right).$$
(8.20)

(b) Y_t represents the daily log-return on a stock index, where t is counted in days. Given $\sigma_1 = 0.025$, $a_0 = 4 \times 10^{-6}$, $a_1 = 0.28$, and $b = 0.7$, estimate the standard deviation of the 1-year return from time 0, assuming 250 trading days in the year. Compare your answer with the annualized long-run volatility under the GARCH model.

Exercise 8.7 Assume that Y_t (t in months) follows a RSLN process, with parameters

| Regime 1 | $\mu_1 = 0.01$ | $\sigma_1 = 0.032$ | $p_{12} = 0.04$ |
| Regime 2 | $\mu_2 = -0.015$ | $\sigma_2 = 0.065$ | $p_{21} = 0.17$ |

(a) Calculate the stationary probability that the process is in Regime 1, π_1.
(b) Calculate the expected value of the number of months that the process remains in (i) Regime 1 and (ii) Regime 2, between transitions.
(c) Suppose the log-return in the first month is $Y_1 = 0.08$. State with reasons whether it is more likely that $\rho_1 = 1$ or that $\rho_1 = 2$, if you have no information about ρ_0. Does your answer change if you know that $\rho_0 = 1$?
(d) You are given that $\rho_0 = 1$.

   (i) Calculate $\Pr[Y_2 > 0.05]$.
   (ii) Calculate $E_0[Y_2]$.
   (iii) Calculate $\text{Var}_0[Y_2]$.

(e) Calculate the long-term unconditional variance of Y_t.

Exercise 8.8 You are fitting models to a series of 300 values of log-returns. The first three values in the series are $y_1 = 0.037$, $y_2 = 0.070$, and $y_3 = -0.010$.

(a) For each of the following models/parameters, calculate the values for the conditional density functions $f(y_1)$, $f(y_2|y_1)$, and $f(y_3|y_1, y_2)$.

   (A) ILN, $\mu = 0.0085$, $\sigma = 0.044$.
   (B) GARCH, $\mu = 0.0085$, $\sigma_0 = 0.044$, $a_0 = 8 \times 10^{-5}$, $a_1 = 0.10$, $b = 0.85$.

(C) RSLN-2, $\mu_1 = 0.1$, $\mu_2 = -0.005$, $\sigma_1 = 0.04$, $\sigma_2 = 0.075$, $p_{12} = 0.05$, $p_{21} = 0.25$. Assume that you have no information about p_0 (use the stationary distribution probabilities).

(b) Explain how these calculations might be used to determine maximum likelihood estimators for the model parameters.

(c) Calculate the residuals corresponding to the three values for y_t, using the ILN and GARCH models.

(d) Calculate the residuals for each regime of the RSLN model, for each of the three values of y_t. In each case, assuming the model is accurate, which is most likely to be the 'true' residual?

Exercise 8.9 You are given the following information on the maximum log-likelihoods for four models, after fitting the model using 300 data points.

Model	Maximum Log-Likelihood	Number of Parameters
ILN	595.2	2
GARCH(1,1)	611.3	4
RSLN-2	619.2	6
RSLN-3	628.5	12

(a) Recommend one of these models based only on this information.

(b) Describe any other factors you might take into consideration in deciding which model to use.

9
Short-Term Portfolio Risk

9.1 Summary

In this chapter, we describe some numerical methods used for calculating Value at Risk (VaR) and Expected Shortfall for losses related to investment portfolios, measured over short time horizons – typically 10 days or less. These are techniques commonly used for regulatory capital calculations under the Basel rules. We start with simple portfolios of investments and add derivatives. We review the covariance approach, the delta-normal approach, and the delta-gamma-normal approach to portfolio risk measures. Each of these approaches ultimately uses a normal approximation to the distribution of the portfolio value. We also consider the use of historical simulation, based on the empirical distribution of asset prices over the recent past. Finally, we discuss backtesting, which is required under the Basel regulations.

9.2 Introduction

In this chapter, we will explore some of the models and methods used by investment banks to measure short-term asset price risk. All financial services institutions must measure market risk, but the nature of the risks, and the methods used to model them, differ between the institutions with short-term horizons, including investment banks and mutual funds, and those with longer term liabilities, notably insurance companies. In this chapter our focus is on short-term changes in asset prices, specifically the 1-day and 10-day risk measures commonly tracked and managed in investment banking.

The use of VaR to measure portfolio risk became ubiquitous in banking largely because of the 1996 Market Risk Amendment to the Basel Accord, issued by the Basel Committee. The Amendment, and the subsequent Basel II

Accord, set the capital standard for loss of portfolio value as the 99% VaR over a 10-day horizon. This led to some special methods, assumptions, and conventions that we will cover in this chapter. The practice is now changing, as updated regulations (known as 'Basel III') require a 97.5% Expected Shortfall risk measure, still over 10-days, as the new standard. In most cases, the move from VaR to Expected Shortfall requires a relatively straightforward adjustment of the formulas. This is because the most common analytic methods assume that portfolio returns and portfolio losses are approximately normally distributed.

It will be useful to recall the formulas for the VaR and Expected Shortfall of normally distributed losses, derived in Chapter 3. For $L \sim N(\mu_L, \sigma_L^2)$ we have

$$\text{VaR}_\alpha(L) = \mu_L + z_\alpha \sigma_L,$$

$$\text{ES}_\alpha(L) = \mu_L + \frac{\phi(z_\alpha)}{1 - \alpha} \sigma_L,$$

where z_α is the α-quantile of the standard normal distribution (so $\Phi(z_\alpha) = \alpha$) and $\phi(z)$ is the standard normal density function,

$$\phi(z) = \frac{1}{\sqrt{2\pi}} e^{-\frac{z^2}{2}}.$$

9.3 VaR and Expected Shortfall for Portfolios

Suppose we have a portfolio of assets with value $V(t)$ at t. We are interested in the random variable measuring the loss from the portfolio between t and $t + h$, that is, $L_{t,h} = V(t) - V(t + h)$.

We may also consider the loss relative to the expected value of the portfolio at $t + h$, $L_{t,h}^{\text{mean}} = E_t[V(t + h)] - V(t + h)$, where the E_t indicates that the expectation is taken at time t.

The VaR of $L_{t,h}^{\text{mean}}$ is sometimes called the **mean-VaR** or the **VaR relative to mean**. If we are estimating 1-day or 10-day losses, it does not matter very much whether we use $L_{t,h}$ or $L_{t,h}^{\text{mean}}$ because with such a small time step it is reasonable to assume that $E_t[V(t + h)] \approx V(t)$.

We often measure risk in terms of the return on a portfolio, rather than a dollar loss. That is, we may calculate the risk measure using the return random variable

$$R_{t,h} = \frac{V(t + h)}{V(t)} - 1,$$

so we have

$$L_{t,h} = V(t) - V(t+h) = V(t) - (1 + R_{t,h})V(t) = -R_{t,h}\,V(t).$$

A consequence of working with the return random variable, $R_{t,h}$, is that the upper tail risk for the loss random variable is associated with the lower tail risk for $R_{t,h}$. So, for example, the 95% quantile for the loss distribution is generated by the 5% quantile of the return distribution – with the sign changed because the return is a measure of profit, not loss.

To illustrate, suppose the 5% quantile of the h-day return distribution is -0.08 (an 8% fall in values) and $V(t) = 100$. Then there is a 95% chance that the portfolio value at $t + h$ will be greater than 92; the 5% worst-case for the loss on the portfolio between t and $t + h$ is $100 - 92 = 8$. More specifically, if $Q_v(X)$ denotes the v quantile of the random variable X, and assuming $V(t)$ is known, we have

$$L_{t,h} = V(t) - V(t+h) = 100 - (1 + R_{t,h})100$$
$$= -R_{t,h} \times 100,$$
$$Q_{0.95}(L_{t,h}) = Q_{0.95}(-R_{t,h}) \times 100,$$
$$Q_{0.95}(-R_{t,h}) = -Q_{0.05}(R_{t,h}) = 0.08,$$
$$\implies Q_{0.95}(L_{t,h}) = Q_{0.95}(-R_{t,h}) \times 100 = -Q_{0.05}(R_{t,h}) \times 100 = 8.$$

In general, we have

$$\text{VaR}_\alpha(L_{t,h}) = Q_\alpha(L_{t,h}) = -Q_{1-\alpha}(R_{t,h})\,V(t) = Q_\alpha(-R_{t,h})\,V(t). \quad (9.1)$$

As VaR and Expected Shortfall are translation invariant and positively homogeneous, we will have consistent measures whether we work with $-V(t+h)$, $L_{t,h}$ or $-R_{t,h}$. That is, for the α-VaR, we have

$$\text{VaR}_\alpha(V(t) - V(t+h)) = \text{VaR}_\alpha(-(R_{t,h})\,V(t)) = V(t) + \text{VaR}_\alpha(-V(t+h)),$$

and similarly for the Expected Shortfall.

9.3.1 VaR and Expected Shortfall for a Single Asset

Assume a confidence level α, and a horizon h years; typically h will be 1 day or 10 days; on average there are 250 trading days in a year, so typical values will be $h = 0.004$ for a 1-day horizon or $h = 0.04$ for a 10-day horizon.

Let $S(t)$ denote the asset price at t. To keep things simple, we assume that the portfolio is comprised of a single unit of the asset, so that $S(t)$ is also the portfolio value at t. The return on the asset between t and $t + h$ is $R_{t,h} = \frac{S(t+h)-S(t)}{S(t)}$.

The common simplifying assumption is that $R_{t,h} \sim N(0, h\,\sigma_S^2)$, where σ_S is the (annual) volatility of the asset. Note that, generally, the volatility is defined as the standard deviation of the log-return on the asset,

$$\sigma_S = \sqrt{\mathrm{Var}\left[\log\left(\frac{S(t+1)}{S(t)}\right)\right]},$$

where time is measured in years. But here we are using volatility to mean the standard deviation of the annual return, not the standard deviation of the annual log-return, that is,

$$\sigma_S = \sqrt{\mathrm{Var}\left[\frac{S(t+1) - S(t)}{S(t)}\right]}.$$

For small time steps the difference will be negligible.

We have

$$L_{t,h} = S(t) - S(t + h) = -S(t)R_{t,h} \text{ and, since } R_{t,h} \sim N\big(0, h\sigma_S^2\big),$$

$$L_{t,h} \sim N\big(0, h\sigma_L^2\big) \text{ where } \sigma_L^2 = \sigma_S^2\, S(t)^2$$

$$\implies \mathrm{VaR}_\alpha(L_{t,h}) = z_\alpha \sqrt{h}\, \sigma_L = z_\alpha \sqrt{h}\, \sigma_S S(t),$$

$$\text{and } \mathrm{ES}_\alpha(L_{t,h}) = \frac{\phi(z_\alpha)}{1 - \alpha} \sqrt{h}\, \sigma_L = \frac{\phi(z_\alpha)}{1 - \alpha} \sqrt{h}\, \sigma_S\, S(t).$$

Example 9.1 Calculate the 10-day, 99% VaR and 97.5% Expected Shortfall on a stock with current price $S(0) = 100$, and with annual volatility $\sigma_S = 0.30$. Assume a normal distribution with zero mean and standard deviation $\sigma\sqrt{h}$ for the h-year stock return $R_{t,h}$. Assume 250 trading days in a year.

Solution 9.1 Ten days represents $h = 10/250 = 0.04$ years, so we assume $R_{t,h} \sim N(0, 0.04(0.30^2))$, and $L_{t,h} = -R_{t,h}\, S(t) \sim N\big(0, 0.04(100^2)(0.30^2)\big)$, that is,

$$L_{t,h} = -R_{t,h}\, S(t) \sim N(0, 6.0^2),$$

$$\mathrm{VaR}_{0.99}(L_{t,h}) = z_{0.99} \times 6.0 = 2.326 \times 6.0 = 13.96,$$

$$\mathrm{ES}_{0.975}(L_{t,h}) = \frac{\phi(z_{0.975})}{0.025} 6.0 = \frac{\phi(1.960)}{0.025} 6.0 = 14.03.$$

This means that there is a 99% probability (given all our assumptions) that the portfolio will lose less than 13.96% in value over the 10-day horizon and the average loss given that the loss falls in the worst 2.5% of the distribution is 14.03% of the stock value. ☐

We see that with losses that are normally distributed, the 97.5% Expected Shortfall is close to the 99% VaR. This will not necessarily be the case for other loss distributions. The normal distribution assumption for the asset return is not a very good model in terms of matching the historical data, but it may be close enough for very short periods and it does allow for simple calculations. It is particularly tractable when combining assets and derivatives into a portfolio, as we shall see in the following sections.

9.3.2 The Covariance Method

Suppose that, at time t, we have a portfolio of n different assets. Let $S_j(t)$ denote the price of a unit of asset j at time t, and let a_j denote the number of units of asset j in the portfolio. Let $R_{j,t,h}$ denote the return on asset j from time t to $t + h$, so

$$R_{j,t,h} = \frac{(S_j(t+h) - S_j(t))}{S_j(t)}.$$

The covariance method assumes a multivariate normal distribution for the joint distribution of the returns on the individual assets. For small h, it is common to assume that the mean return on each asset is zero, but it is easy to adapt these results for non-zero means. The annualized standard deviation of the return on asset j is σ_j. So, for each j, and for each $k \neq j$,

$$R_{j,t,h} \sim N(0, h\sigma_j^2), \text{ and } \operatorname{Cov}(R_{j,t,h}, R_{k,t,h}) = h \, \rho_{jk} \, \sigma_j \, \sigma_k,$$

where $\rho_{jk} = \rho_{kj}$ is the correlation coefficient between the annual returns on asset j and asset k, with $\rho_{jj} = 1$.

At time t, the portfolio value is $V(t)$, and the h-year loss random variable is $L_{t,h}$, where

$$V(t) = \sum_{j=1}^{n} a_j \, S_j(t), \tag{9.2}$$

$$L_{t,h} = V(t) - V(t+h) = -\sum_{j=1}^{n} a_j \left(S_j(t+h) - S_j(t)\right)$$

$$= -\sum_{j=1}^{n} a_j \, S_j(t) \frac{\left(S_j(t+h) - S_j(t)\right)}{S_j(t)}$$

$$\Rightarrow L_{t,h} = -\sum_{j=1}^{n} a_j \, S_j(t) \, R_{j,t,h}. \tag{9.3}$$

Since $L_{t,h}$ is a linear combination of the multivariate normal return random variables, it is also normally distributed. We have $L_{t,h} \sim N(0, h\sigma_L^2)$, where

$$\sigma_L^2 = \sum_{k=1}^{n}\sum_{j=1}^{n} a_j\, a_k\, S_j(t)\, S_k(t)\, \rho_{jk}\, \sigma_j\sigma_k.$$

We now proceed similarly to the single asset case:

$$\text{VaR}_\alpha(L_{t,h}) = z_\alpha\, \sqrt{h}\,\sigma_L, \tag{9.4}$$

$$\text{ES}_\alpha(L_{t,h}) = \frac{\phi(z_\alpha)}{1-\alpha}\, \sqrt{h}\,\sigma_L. \tag{9.5}$$

Example 9.2 Suppose we have a portfolio of three stocks, described in the following table. A negative value for a_j denotes a short position in stock j.

Calculate the 1-day 99.9% VaR and the 1-day 99.9% Expected Shortfall. Assume 250 trading days per year.

Stock j	$S_j(t)$	a_j	σ_j	$S_j(t)\,a_j\,\sigma_j$
1	100	5	0.25	125
2	70	10	0.20	140
3	200	−3	0.3	−180

You are also given correlations between the stock returns: $\rho_{12} = 0.8$, $\rho_{13} = 0.6$, and $\rho_{23} = 0.7$.

Solution 9.2

$$V(t) = 5 \times 100 + 10 \times 70 - 3 \times 200 = 600.$$

The annual volatility of the loss is σ_L where

$$\sigma_L^2 = \sum_{k=1}^{3}\sum_{j=1}^{3} a_j\, S_j(t)\, a_k\, S_k(t)\, \rho_{jk}\sigma_j\sigma_k$$

$$= 125^2 + 140^2 + 180^2 + 2\big((125)(140)(0.8)$$

$$- (125)(180)(0.6) - (140)(180)(0.7)\big)$$

$$= 33{,}345 = 182.61^2.$$

So, the 99.9% 1-day VaR and 1-day Expected Shortfall for the portfolio loss are

$$\text{VaR}_{99.9\%}(L_{t,h}) = z_{99.9\%}\sigma_L\sqrt{h} = 3.090 \times 182.61 \times 0.06325 = 35.69,$$

$$\text{ES}_{99.9\%}(L_{t,h}) = \frac{\phi(z_{99.9\%})}{0.001}\sigma_L\sqrt{h} = (3.3671)(182.61)(0.06325) = 38.89.$$

So, we estimate that there is a 99.9% probability that the portfolio will lose less than 35.69 (or 5.90% of its value) over the next trading day; if the 0.1% worst-case event occurs, the expected loss is 38.43 or 6.40% of its value.   □

9.4 VaR and Expected Shortfall for Portfolios of Assets and Derivatives

The linear relationship between the portfolio value and the return on the underlying assets breaks down when the portfolio contains options or other derivatives on the assets, because the change in the value of an option on an asset is not a simple multiple of the return on the underlying asset itself. However, we can adjust the calculations to make approximate allowance for derivatives using the **delta-normal** method.

9.4.1 Delta-Normal VaR and Expected Shortfall

Single Underlying Asset

Consider a non-dividend paying asset with price $S(t)$ at t. Let $V(t)$ denote the value at t of a portfolio consisting of a mix of units of the asset, together with options on the asset. The asset volatility is σ_S. The portfolio value function V is actually a function of t and of the asset price, S.

Using Taylor's expansion, we have (loosely) the following, where all derivatives are at time t:

$$V(t + h) - V(t) \approx \frac{\partial V}{\partial S}\big(S(t + h) - S(t)\big)$$

$$+ \frac{1}{2}\frac{\partial^2 V}{\partial S^2}\,(S(t + h) - S(t))^2 + \cdots + \frac{\partial V}{\partial t}h. \qquad (9.6)$$

The first derivative on the right-hand side, $\frac{\partial V}{\partial S}$, is the **delta** of the portfolio, with respect to the asset. It is the sum of the deltas of the individual options. Recall that the delta of a standard European call option on a non-dividend paying asset, maturing at T, with strike K and risk-free rate r, is $\Phi(d_1)$, where

$$d_1 = \frac{\log(S(t)/K) + (r + \sigma^2/2)(T - t)}{\sigma\sqrt{T - t}}. \qquad (9.7)$$

The delta of a put option on the same asset, with the same strike and maturity is $-\Phi(-d_1)$. For short option positions (i.e. for the option seller) the signs are reversed.

Define the function Δ as $\Delta = \frac{\partial V}{\partial S}$; $\Delta(t)$ is the function evaluated at t. Also, note that $\frac{S(t+h)-S(t)}{S(t)} = R_{t,h}$.

We ignore (for now) higher order terms in $dS(t)$, and assume that the final term, $\frac{\partial V}{\partial t} h \approx 0$. Then the loss $L_{t,h} = V(t) - V(t+h)$ is

$$L_{t,h} = V(t) - V(t+h) \approx -\frac{\partial V}{\partial S}\left(S(t+h) - S(t)\right)$$

$$\approx -\frac{\partial V}{\partial S} \frac{S(t)\left(S(t+h) - S(t)\right)}{S(t)}$$

$$\approx -\Delta(t) \, S(t) \, R_{t,h}.$$

Now we assume, as before, that $R_{t,h} \sim \mathrm{N}\!\left(0, h\sigma_S^2\right)$, so that $L_{t,h} \sim \mathrm{N}\!\left(0, h\sigma_L^2\right)$, where

$$\sigma_L^2 = \Delta(t)^2 \, S(t)^2 \, \sigma_S^2,$$

and, noting that $\Delta(t)$ may be greater or less than zero, we have

$$\sigma_L = |\Delta(t)| \, S(t) \, \sigma_S,$$

$$\mathrm{VaR}_\alpha(L_{t,h}) \approx z_\alpha \sqrt{h} \, \sigma_L = z_\alpha \sqrt{h} \, |\Delta(t)| \, S(t) \, \sigma_S,$$

$$\mathrm{ES}_\alpha(L_{t,h}) \approx \frac{\phi(z_\alpha)}{1-\alpha} \sqrt{h} \, \sigma_L = \frac{\phi(z_\alpha)}{1-\alpha} \sqrt{h} \, |\Delta(t)| \, S(t) \, \sigma_S.$$

Example 9.3 A portfolio comprises:

- 2 units of stock A (which pays no dividends), with price $S_A(0) = 100$ at $t = 0$;
- 200 European put options on stock A, with strike $K^A = 90$, maturing in 1 year.

The risk-free rate of interest is $r = 4\%$, and $\sigma_A = 0.20$.

(a) Calculate the value of the portfolio at $t = 0$.
(b) Calculate the 1-day 99% VaR using the delta-normal method.
(c) Calculate the 1-day 97.5% Expected Shortfall using the delta-normal method.

Assume 250 trading days per year.

Solution 9.3 Let p_0 denote the current value of a single put option.

$$p_0 = \left(90e^{-r}\Phi(-d_2) - 100\Phi(-d_1)\right),$$

$$\text{where } d_1 = \frac{\log(100/90) + (r + 0.2^2/2)}{0.2} = 0.82680,$$

$$d_2 = d_1 - \sigma_A = 0.62680$$

$$\implies p_0 = 2.5315,$$

$$\text{and, so} \quad V(0) = 2S_A(0) + 200p_0 = 706.3.$$

The total delta for the portfolio with respect to Stock A is the sum of the delta for the units of stock themselves ($=2$) and the delta for the options ($-200\Phi(-d_1) = -200(0.20417)$). That is,

$$\Delta(0) = \left.\frac{\partial V}{\partial S}\right|_{t=0} = 2 + 200\left.\frac{\partial p}{\partial S}\right|_{t=0} = 2 - 200\Phi(-d_1) = -38.834;$$

$$\sigma_L = S(t)\left|\Delta(0)\right|\sigma_A = 100 \times 38.834 \times 0.20 = 776.68$$

$$\implies \text{VaR}_{99\%}(L_{t,h}) \approx z_{0.99} \times \sqrt{h} \times 776.68 = 114.26,$$

$$\text{and } \text{ES}_{97.5\%}(L_{t,h}) \approx \frac{\phi(z_{0.975})}{0.025}\sqrt{h} \times 776.68 = 114.83,$$

where $h = 1/250 = 0.004$, $z_{0.99} = 2.326$, $z_{0.975} = 1.960$. $\qquad\square$

Multiple Underlying Assets

We now generalize the delta-normal method to a portfolio involving options on m different assets. Let $R_{j,t,h}$ denote the return on asset S_j between t and $t + h$. We assume that the returns on the assets in the portfolio are multivariate normal, where $R_{j,t,h} \sim N(0, h\sigma_j^2)$ and the correlation between $R_{j,t,1}$ and $R_{k,t,1}$ is ρ_{jk}.

Ignoring once again the higher order terms in dS_j and the $\partial V/\partial t$ term, the Taylor expansion gives us

$$V(t) - V(t + h) \approx -\sum_{j=1}^{m} \frac{\partial V}{\partial S_j}\left(S_j(t + h) - S_j(t)\right)$$

$$\approx -\sum_{j=1}^{m} \Delta_j(t)\, S_j(t)\, R_{j,t,h}$$

$$\text{where } \Delta_j(t) = \left.\frac{\partial V}{\partial S_j}\right|_t.$$

So the loss random variable $L_{t,h}$ is, approximately, a linear combination of the multivariate normal returns $R_{j,t,h}$, which means, again, that $L_{t,h} \sim N(0, h\, \sigma_L^2)$, where now

$$\sigma_L^2 = \text{Var}\left[\sum_{j=1}^{m} \Delta_j(t)\, S_j(t)\, R_{j,1}\right]$$

$$= \left(\sum_{j=1}^{m} \Delta_j(t)^2\, S_j(t)^2 \sigma_j^2 + 2 \sum_{k=1, k \neq j}^{m} \Delta_j(t)\, \Delta_k(t)\, S_j(t)\, S_k(t)\, \rho_{jk}\, \sigma_j \sigma_k\right).$$

We then apply the usual formulas for normally distributed losses:

$$\text{VaR}_\alpha(L_{t,h}) = z_\alpha \sqrt{h}\, \sigma_L \text{ and } \text{ES}_\alpha(L_{t,h}) = \frac{\phi(z_\alpha)}{1 - \alpha} \sqrt{h}\, \sigma_L.$$

It can be useful also to work with the relative loss random variable, $\frac{L_{t,h}}{V(t)}$, which has volatility $\sigma_V = \frac{\sigma_L}{|V(t)|}$. This is the volatility of the return on the portfolio, and can be compared with the individual asset volatilities. We then have

$$\text{VaR}_\alpha(L_{t,h}) = z_\alpha \sigma_V \sqrt{h}\, |V(t)|.$$

We use the absolute value because it is possible for the portfolio value, $V(t)$, to be negative.

Example 9.4 A portfolio comprises:

- 10 units of stock A (which pays no dividends), with price $S_A(0) = 100$ at $t = 0$,
- 5 units of stock B (which pays no dividends), with price $S_B(0) = 80$ at $t = 0$,
- 20 European put options on stock A, with strike $K^A = 90$, maturing in 1 year, and
- 15 European call options on Stock B, with strike $K^B = 85$, maturing in 3 months.

The risk-free rate of interest is $r = 4\%$. Assume volatilities for Stock A and Stock B of $\sigma_A = 0.20$ and $\sigma_B = 0.25$ respectively, and correlation between the stocks of $\rho_{AB} = 0.7$.

(a) Calculate the value of the portfolio at $t = 0$.
(b) Calculate the volatility of the portfolio return, σ_V.
(c) Calculate the 10-day 98% VaR and 95% Expected Shortfall using the Delta-Normal method.

Assume 250 trading days per year.

Solution 9.4 (a)   From Example 9.3 we know that the price of the Stock A put option is 2.5315 and the delta of the Stock A put option is −0.20417.

The price of the Stock B call option is 2.3436 and the delta of each option is 0.3660. So

$$V(0) = 10S_A(0) + 5S_B(0) + 20(2.5315) + 15(2.3436) = 1,485.78.$$

Now the total delta for the portfolio with respect to Stock A is the sum of the delta for the stocks themselves (10) and the delta for the options $(-20\Phi(-d_1))$:

$$\Delta_A(0) = 10 - 20\Phi(-d_1) = 5.9165$$

and similarly for Stock B:

$$\Delta_B(0) = 5 + 15\Phi(d_1^B) = 10.4898,$$

which gives

$$\sigma_L^2 = (\Delta_A(0)\, S_A(0)\, \sigma_A)^2 + (\Delta_B(0)\, S_B(0)\, \sigma_B)^2$$
$$+ 2\left(\Delta_A(0)\, \Delta_B(0)\, S_A(0)\, S_B(0)\, \sigma_A\, \sigma_B\, \rho_{A,B}\right)$$
$$= 304.585^2.$$

(b) $\sigma_V = \dfrac{\sigma_L}{V_0} = 20.50\%.$

(c)   The 10-day 98% delta-normal VaR is

$$z_{98\%}\sqrt{h}\,\sigma_L = 2.05375 \times \sqrt{10/250} \times 304.585 = 125.11.$$

The 10-day 95% delta-normal Expected Shortfall is

$$\frac{\phi(z_{95\%})}{0.05}\sqrt{10/250}\,\sigma_L = 2.063 \times \sqrt{10/250} \times 304.585 = 125.67. \qquad \square$$

9.4.2 Delta-Gamma-Normal VaR and Expected Shortfall

For the delta-normal method, we assumed that $\Delta_j(t)$ is constant over the period $(t, t + h)$. In fact, the Δ_j will change over time, as they are functions of t and of $S_j(t)$. We can make an adjustment to the delta-normal method that allows (somewhat roughly) for the effect of the changing Δ_j, by using an extra term of the Taylor expansion.

Single Underlying Asset

In the case where we have a single underlying asset, with price $S_j(t)$ at t, we have

$$V(t) - V(t+h) \approx -\frac{\partial V}{\partial S_j} \left(S_j(t+h) - S_j(t) \right)$$

$$-\frac{1}{2} \frac{\partial^2 V}{\partial S_j^2} \left(S_j(t+h) - S_j(t) \right)^2 - \cdots - \frac{\partial V}{\partial t} h. \qquad (9.8)$$

As before, we ignore the final term, $(\partial V / \partial t) h$.

The second derivative of V with respect to S_j is called the **gamma** of the portfolio with respect to asset j:

$$\Gamma_j(t) = \left. \frac{\partial^2 V}{\partial S_j^2} \right|_t .$$

The **Gamma** of a portfolio of options on a single asset is the sum of the gammas of the individual options. The gamma of the asset itself is zero.

The gamma of a long position (option holder) in a European call option on a non-dividend paying asset is the same as the gamma of a long position in a European put option on the asset, and both are

$$\Gamma_j(t) = \frac{\phi(d_1(t))}{S_j(t)\, \sigma \sqrt{T-t}},$$

where $\phi(x)$ is the density function of the standard normal distribution, and $d_1(t)$ is as defined in equation (9.7) above. The gamma for short option positions (i.e. for the option seller) is the negative of the gamma for the long position, which is positive for both puts and calls.

Using the return random variable $R_{j,t,h}$ over the interval $(t, t+h)$, we have $S_j(t+h) - S_j(t) = R_{j,t,h} S_j(t)$, where we assume, as before, that $R_{j,t,h} \sim N(0, h\,\sigma_j^2)$.

So

$$V(t) - V(t+h) \approx -\Delta_j(t) S_j(t) R_{j,t,h} - \frac{1}{2}\Gamma_j(t) S_j(t)^2 R_{j,t,h}^2,$$

which means that the loss random variable $L_{t,h} = V(t) - V(t+h)$ is

$$L_{t,h} \approx -\Delta_j(t) S_j(t) R_{j,t,h} - \frac{1}{2}\Gamma_j(t) S_j(t)^2 R_{j,t,h}^2. \qquad (9.9)$$

We see that if $\Gamma_j(t) > 0$ the VaR will be reduced a little, compared with the delta-normal method, and if $\Gamma_j(t) < 0$ the VaR will be a increased a little.

Now, if $R_{j,t,h}$ is normally distributed, then $L_{t,h}$ will not be normally distributed, as it is a combination of $R_{j,t,h}$ and $R_{j,t,h}^2$. Nevertheless, we will assume that $L_{t,h}$ is approximately normally distributed, with mean $h\mu_L$ and variance $h\sigma_L^2$, in order to obtain simple formulas for the risk measures. We determine μ_L and σ_L using moments of the distribution of $R_{j,t,h}$ and $R_{j,t,h}^2$.

Recall that

$$E[R_{j,t,h}] = 0, \qquad E[R_{j,t,h}^2] = \text{Var}[R_{j,t,h}] = h\sigma_j^2,$$

also, it is easy to show that $\text{Var}[R_{j,t,h}^2] = 2h^2\sigma_j^4$ using the properties of the normal distribution. So we have

$$E[L_{t,h}] = h\mu_L \approx -\Delta_j(t)\,S_j(t)\,E\big[R_{j,t,h}\big] - \frac{1}{2}\Gamma_j(t)\,S_j(t)^2\,E\big[R_{j,t,h}^2\big] \quad (9.10)$$

$$\approx -\frac{1}{2}\Gamma_j(t)\,S_j(t)^2\,\sigma_j^2\,h. \quad (9.11)$$

$$\text{Var}[L_{t,h}] = h\sigma_L^2 \approx \big(\Delta_j(t)\,S_j(t)\big)^2\,\text{Var}\big[R_{j,t,h}\big]$$

$$+ \left(\frac{1}{2}\Gamma_j(t)\,S_j(t)^2\right)^2\,\text{Var}[R_{j,t,h}^2]$$

$$+ 2\Delta_j(t)\,S_j(t)\,\frac{1}{2}\Gamma_j(t)\,S_j(t)^2\,\text{Cov}\big(R_{j,t,h}, R_{j,t,h}^2\big) \quad (9.12)$$

$$\approx \Delta_j(t)^2\,S_j(t)^2\,\sigma_j^2\,h + \frac{1}{4}\Gamma_j(t)^2\,S_j(t)^4\,2\sigma_j^4\,h^2$$

$$+ 2\,\Delta_j(t)S_j(t)\,\frac{1}{2}\Gamma_j(t)S_j(t)^2\text{Cov}\big(R_{j,t,h}, R_{j,t,h}^2\big). \quad (9.13)$$

Recall that the normal distribution has zero skewness, which means that

$$E\big[(R_j - E[R_j])^3\big] = E[R_j^3] = 0,$$

$$\text{Cov}\big(R_j, R_j^2\big) = E[R_j^3] - E[R_j]\,E[R_j^2] = 0,$$

which means that the final term in equation (9.13) is also zero, so we have

$$\text{Var}[L_{t,h}] \approx \Delta_j(t)^2\,S_j(t)^2\,\sigma_j^2\,h + \frac{1}{2}\Gamma_j(t)^2\,S_j(t)^4\,\sigma_j^4\,h^2.$$

Assuming $L_{t,h}$ is approximately normally distributed, with mean $h\mu_L$ and standard deviation $\sqrt{\text{Var}[L_{t,h}]}$, we have

$$\text{VaR}_\alpha \approx h\,\mu_L + z_\alpha\sqrt{\text{Var}[L_{t,h}]} \quad (9.14)$$

$$= -h\frac{1}{2}\Gamma_j(t)S_j(t)^2\sigma_j^2 + z_\alpha\sqrt{\Delta_j(t)^2S_j(t)^2\sigma_j^2\,h + \frac{1}{2}\Gamma_j(t)^2S_j(t)^4\sigma_j^4\,h^2} \quad (9.15)$$

and the α-Expected Shortfall is

$$\mathrm{ES}_\alpha \approx \mu_L h + \frac{\phi(z_\alpha)}{1-\alpha}\sqrt{\mathrm{Var}[L_{t,h}]}$$

$$= -h\frac{1}{2}\Gamma_j(t)S_j(t)^2\sigma_j^2$$

$$+ \frac{\phi(z_\alpha)}{1-\alpha}\sqrt{\Delta_j(t)^2 S_j(t)^2\sigma_j^2 h + \frac{1}{2}\Gamma_j(t)^2 S_j(t)^4\sigma_j^4 h^2}.$$

Example 9.5 Calculate the 99% VaR and 97.5% Expected Shortfall for Example 9.3 using the delta-gamma-normal method.

Solution 9.5 From the solution to Example 9.3 we have $\Delta_j(0) = 2 - 200 \times 0.20417 = -38.8349$.

The gamma for each option is

$$\frac{\phi(d_1)}{S_A(0)\sigma_A\sqrt{1}} = 0.014172,$$

so the gamma for the portfolio is $200(0.014172) = 2.834443$. Then

$$h\mu_L = -\frac{1}{2}\Gamma_A S_A(0)^2 \sigma_A^2 h = -2.26755,$$

$$h\sigma_L^2 = (38.8349^2)(100^2)(0.20^2)\frac{1}{250} + \frac{1}{2}(2.834443^2)(100^4)(0.2^4)\left(\frac{1}{250}\right)^2$$

$$= 49.123^2$$

$$\implies \mathrm{VaR}_{99\%} \approx -2.26755 + z_{0.99}(49.123) = 112.0,$$

$$\mathrm{ES}_{97.5\%} \approx -2.26755 + \frac{\phi(z_{0.975})}{0.025}(49.123) = 112.6.$$

These estimates are smaller than the delta-normal estimates (114.26 and 114.83), as we expect, given that gamma is less than 0. □

In this example, if the normal assumption for the distribution of $R_{j,t,h}$ is correct, we can estimate the true 99% VaR and 97.5% Expected Shortfall using Monte Carlo (MC) simulation. An accurate estimate is around 104.1 for both measures, so the gamma adjustment improves the accuracy, but not by very much. For longer horizons, such as the 10-day horizon for regulatory capital under the Basel regulations, the errors from the delta-normal and delta-gamma-normal methods are even more significant, even if the daily returns are normally distributed. The reason is that the higher order terms in the Taylor expansion have more impact, particularly in the tails. As noted above, if $R_{j,t,h}$ is normally distributed, then $L_{t,h}$ is *not* normally distributed if the portfolio includes derivatives and the deviation from the normal distribution will be most significant in the tails.

A more fundamental problem is that the normal distribution assumption for the return random variables is far from accurate, especially in the tails where most of the risk lies, as shown in Chapter 8.

Multiple Underlying Assets

We illustrate the extension of the delta-gamma-normal method to multiple underlying assets using a portfolio of assets and options on just two underlying assets, labelled A and B. The multivariate form of Taylor's theorem, using only first and second order derivatives, gives us

$$V(t+h) - V(t) = \frac{\partial V}{\partial S_A}(S_A(t+h) - S_A(t)) + \frac{\partial V}{\partial S_B}(S_B(t+h) - S_B(t))$$

$$+ \frac{1}{2}\frac{\partial^2 V}{\partial S_A^2}(S_A(t+h) - S_A(t))^2 + \frac{1}{2}\frac{\partial^2 V}{\partial S_B^2}(S_B(t+h) - S_B(t))^2$$

$$+ \frac{\partial^2 V}{\partial S_A \partial S_B}(S_A(t+h) - S_A(t))(S_B(t+h) - S_B(t)) + \cdots$$

$$+ \frac{\partial V}{\partial t}h.$$

If we assume that the options in the portfolio are written on the individual underlying assets (and not on baskets or combinations of the assets) then the second derivative cross products (i.e. the $\frac{\partial^2 V}{\partial S_A \partial S_B}$ terms) will all be zero. We also ignore the $\frac{\partial V}{\partial t}h$ term, as we did above.

What remains can be written in terms of the h-year return variables, $R_{A,t,h}$ and $R_{B,t,h}$, as

$$V(t+h) - V(t) = \Delta_A(t) S_A(t) R_{A,t,h} + \Delta_B(t) S_B(t) R_{B,t,h} \qquad (9.16)$$

$$+ \frac{1}{2}\Gamma_A(t) S_A(t)^2 R_{A,t,h}^2 + \frac{1}{2}\Gamma_B(t) S_B(t)^2 R_{B,t,h}^2$$

$$\implies L_{t,h} = -\sum_{j=A,B} \Delta_j(t) S_j(t) R_{j,t,h} - \frac{1}{2}\sum_{j=A,B} \Gamma_j(t) S_j(t)^2 R_{j,t,h}^2.$$
$$\qquad (9.17)$$

So $\mathrm{E}[L_{t,h}] = h\mu_L \approx -\frac{1}{2}\sum_{j=A,B} \Gamma_j(t) S_j(t)^2 \sigma_j^2 h, \qquad (9.18)$

$$\text{Var}[L_{t,h}] = h\sigma_L \approx \sum_{j=A,B} \Delta_j(t)^2 S_j(t)^2 \text{Var}[R_{j,t,h}]$$

$$+ \sum_{j=A,B} \frac{1}{4} \Gamma_j(t)^2 S_j(t)^4 \text{Var}[R_{j,t,h}^2]$$

$$+ 2\Delta_A(t) S_A(t) \Delta_B(t) S_B(t) \text{Cov}(R_{A,t,h}, R_{B,t,h}). \tag{9.19}$$

Note that all the remaining covariance terms involve $\text{Cov}(R_j^2, R_k)$ for some combination of $j = A, B$ and $k = A, B$, and all are zero under the multivariate normal assumption for the returns and are, therefore, omitted here. So

$$\text{Var}[L_{t,h}] = \sum_{j=A,B} \Delta_j(t)^2 S_j(t)^2 \sigma_j^2 h + \frac{1}{2} \sum_{j=A,B} \Gamma_j(t)^2 S_j(t)^4 \sigma_j^4 h^2$$

$$+ 2h \Delta_A(t) S_A(t) \Delta_B(t) S_B(t) \rho_{A,B} \sigma_A \sigma_B.$$

As in the single variable case, we proceed by assuming that $L_{t,h} \sim N(\text{E}[L_{t,h}], \text{Var}[L_{t,h}])$.

Example 9.6 Calculate the 98% VaR and 95% Expected Shortfall for Example 9.4, using the delta-gamma-normal method.

Solution 9.6 We have

Stock	$S_j(0)$	σ_j	$\Delta_j(0)$	$\Gamma_j(0)$	h
A	100	0.20	5.9165	0.283444	0.04
B	80	0.25	10.4898	0.564325	0.04

which gives $\text{E}[L_{t,h}] \approx -6.782$ and $\text{Var}[L_{t,h}] \approx 61.0^2$, so that

$$\text{VaR}_{98\%} \approx -6.782 + 2.0537(61.0) = 118.5,$$

$$\text{ES}_{95\%} \approx -6.782 + 2.0627(61.0) = 119.0,$$

compared with the delta-normal estimates of 125.1 and 125.7. The true value in each case is around 104. □

Using the delta-gamma-normal method with a large number of underlying assets is possible in theory, but estimating the correlations may be problematic, partly because the multivariate normal assumption for the joint asset returns is not consistent with the market data.

9.4.3 Delta-Gamma Monte Carlo VaR and Expected Shortfall

The delta-gamma methods from the previous two sections utilize a normal distribution assumption for the loss random variable, even though that is inconsistent with the normal distribution assumptions for the return variables. An alternative approach is to start from the delta-gamma equation (9.17), then use Monte Carlo simulation of the joint distribution of the return variables $(R_{A,t,h}, R_{B,t,h})$ to generate a pseudorandom sample for $L_{t,h}$, and use that to estimate the risk measures. This is the delta-gamma-MC method.

We illustrate the method using the portfolio from Examples 9.4 and 9.6. We have

$$L_{t,h} \approx - \sum_{j=A,B} \Delta_j(t)\, S_j(t)\, R_{j,t,h} - \frac{1}{4} \sum_{j=A,B} \Gamma_j(t)\, S_j(t)^2\, R_{j,t,h}^2 \qquad (9.20)$$

$$\approx -5.9165(100)R_{A,t,h} - 10.4898(80)R_{B,t,h}$$

$$- \frac{1}{4}0.28344(100^2)R_{A,t,h}^2 - \frac{1}{4}0.56433(80^2)R_{B,t,h}^2$$

$$\approx -591.65 R_{A,t,h} - 839.18 R_{B,t,h} - 708.6 R_{A,t,h}^2 - 902.9 R_{B,t,h}^2. \qquad (9.21)$$

Suppose we generate 100,000 pseudorandom pairs $(R_{A,t,h}, R_{B,t,h})$, from the bivariate normal distribution with mean $\mathbf{0}$ and covariance matrix $h\Sigma$,

$$\Sigma = \begin{pmatrix} \sigma_A^2 & \rho_{AB}\sigma_A\sigma_B \\ \rho_{AB}\sigma_A\sigma_B & \sigma_B^2 \end{pmatrix} = \begin{pmatrix} (0.20)^2 & (0.7)(0.20)(0.25) \\ (0.7)(0.20)(0.25) & (0.25)^2 \end{pmatrix}.$$

We substitute the simulated values of $(R_{A,t,h}, R_{B,t,h})$ into Equation (9.21) to generate 100,000 values for $L_{t,h}$. The 98% quantile of the pseudorandom sample of the $L_{t,h}$ for $h = 10/250$ is approximately 99.4 (with a standard error of around 0.4).

The true value (assuming returns are jointly normally distributed) is found by a full simulation of the portfolio value 10-days ahead and, as mentioned above, it is around 104.1, with a standard error of around 0.1. So the delta-gamma-MC method, in this case, is closer to the true value than either of the analytic approximations. This will usually be the case, as the delta-gamma-normal method requires contradictory assumptions that are not required in the delta-gamma-MC approach. The reason that the delta-gamma-MC approach is not more accurate arises from the impact of the higher order terms in the Taylor expansion that are ignored in all of the approaches except full Monte Carlo, and the impact of these higher order terms increases as the time step increases.

Table 9.1. *Different VaR approximations for the two-stock portfolio in Example 9.4, with standard errors, assuming returns on stocks are bivariate normally distributed with zero mean*

	Delta-Normal	Delta-Gamma-Normal	Delta-Gamma-MC	Full MC
1-day 98% VaR	39.6	38.9	37.7 (0.1)	37.6 (0.2)
10-day 98% VaR	125.1	119.2	99.4 (0.4)	104.1 (0.1)

The results from the delta-normal and delta-gamma-normal methods for the 10-day and 1-day 98% VaRs for Example 9.6 are shown in Table 9.1. We see that all the approximations for the 1-day VaR are within around 5% of the true value, whereas the 10-day VaR approximations are 5% to 20% different from the true value.

9.5 Empirical VaR and Expected Shortfall

The assumption of normally distributed asset price returns has been widely criticized, as records show that the empirical distribution of asset price changes is fatter tailed than the normal distribution. This means that for α close to 1.0, the delta and delta-gamma calculations will often understate the true risk measures.

One alternative method employed in practice is to use the historical record of price changes as an empirical distribution for the $R_{j,t,h}$ variables.

For example, suppose we are analysing the 1-day loss on the portfolio in Example 9.4, which depends on returns on Stock A and Stock B. We may collect, say, two years of history (i.e. 500 values) of daily price changes for the two stocks, giving a bivariate sample $(R_{A,k,h}, R_{B,k,h})$, where $h = 1/250$, and $R_{j,k,h}$ is the one-day return, on Stock j, on the kth day of the sample period, for $k = 1, 2, \ldots, 500$.

We calculate 500 values for $V(t + h)$, using the 500 values of $(R_{A,t,h}(k), R_{B,t,h}(k))$. We can then estimate the 1-day VaR and Expected Shortfall using the techniques described in Section 3.5 because the sample generated using the historical returns is analogous to a sample generated using Monte Carlo simulation. So, for example, the 95% VaR would be estimated using the 95% quantile of the sample of $L_{t,h} = V(t) - V(t+h)$. As we noted in Chapter 3, there are several ways to estimate the quantile, but the smoothed empirical approach is a good default. Using this method, we order the sample of $L_{t,h}$

from smallest to largest, say, $L_{(1)}, L_{(2)}, \ldots, L_{(500)}$, and the 95% quantile is the $0.95 \times 501 = 475.95$th value, which we find by interpolating between $L_{(475)}$ and $L_{(476)}$. The 95% Expected Shortfall is the average of the worst 5% of the values, that is, the average of $L_{(476)}, \ldots, L_{(500)}$.

Note that, by treating the historical data as a bivariate sample, we automatically capture the dependency between the daily returns on the two stocks; we always use the asset price changes for the two assets from the same day of the sample period.

We may be interested in a different horizon, for example, a 10-day horizon rather than a 1-day horizon. We could collect samples of 10-day price changes instead of 1-day, but it is difficult to collect enough data while still maintaining statistical validity – if we need 500 separate 10-day periods, we would need around 20 years of data, which may not be available (for example, if the asset is less than 20 years old) or may not be very relevant, as the company and the general market conditions of 20 years ago may be very different to the potential conditions of the next 10 days. Instead of changing the return horizon, it is common to apply a square root adjustment to the 1-day risk measures. That is, if the 1-day α-VaR estimate is $\mathrm{VaR}_\alpha^{1\text{-day}}$, then the 10-day estimate is

$$\mathrm{VaR}_\alpha^{10\text{-day}} = \sqrt{10}\, \mathrm{VaR}_\alpha^{1\text{-day}}$$

and similarly for the Expected Shortfall.

The reasoning for the square root adjustment goes back to the normal distribution, where the 1-day and 10-day horizon VaR and Expected Shortfall can be written as follows. Assume that σ_L is the annual volatility of the loss, that the mean loss is $E[L_{t,h}] = 0$, and that there are n trading days per year:

$$\mathrm{VaR}_\alpha^{1\text{-day}} = \sqrt{\frac{1}{n}}\, z_\alpha\, \sigma_L V(t),$$

$$\mathrm{VaR}_\alpha^{10\text{-day}} = \sqrt{\frac{10}{n}}\, z_\alpha\, \sigma_L V(t) = \sqrt{10}\left(\mathrm{VaR}_\alpha^{1\text{-day}}\right),$$

$$\mathrm{ES}_\alpha^{1\text{-day}} = \sqrt{\frac{1}{n}}\, \frac{\phi(z_\alpha)}{1-\alpha}\sigma_L V(t),$$

$$\mathrm{ES}_\alpha^{10\text{-day}} = \sqrt{\frac{10}{n}}\, \frac{\phi(z_\alpha)}{1-\alpha}\sigma_L V(t) = \sqrt{10}\left(\mathrm{ES}_\alpha^{1\text{-day}}\right).$$

Since the risk measures for the normal distribution (with zero mean) are proportional to the h-year standard deviation and the h-year standard deviation is proportional to $\sqrt{h}$, the risk measures can be scaled for different horizons using the square root adjustment.

Table 9.2. *Empirical 1-day price changes for Stock A and Stock B for Example 9.7*

Day	Stock A price change	Stock B price change
1	−0.256%	−1.105%
2	0.054%	−0.385%
3	−0.500%	−0.500%
4	−0.831%	−0.787%
5	0.400%	0.598%

Table 9.3. *Largest 20 values, out of a sample of 500, for the 1-day loss for Example 9.7*

31.61	33.06	33.15	33.28	33.38	34.88	36.31	37.27	37.97	39.15
39.26	40.43	40.59	49.88	51.21	51.30	52.43	53.76	61.76	62.49

However, for non-normal distributions, it will not generally be true that the risk measures are proportional to the standard deviation, and so this adjustment may create more inaccuracy. It also ignores the dependency between the daily asset price changes – there is an implicit assumption in the square root rule that each day is independent of the day before. This will underestimate the risk, because it will not adequately allow for several successive days of poor market experience, which arise because of volatility clusters and the leverage effect, as described in Chapter 8.

Example 9.7

(a) Table 9.2 shows a sample of 5 historical 1-day returns for Stock A and Stock B, taken from a larger data set of 500 values. Use this table to generate 5 values for the 1-day loss random variable.

(b) Table 9.3 shows the 20 worst 1-day losses generated using the historical dataset. Estimate the 10-day 98% VaR using the square root method.

Solution 9.7

(a) We use the values given to generate a sample of values for S_h^A and S_h^B, where h is 1-day, or 1/250 years. We then calculate the value of the portfolio of stocks and options in 1 day, assuming the given values for S^A and S^B, and allowing for the option maturities to be 1 day closer. Table 9.4 shows some intermediate calculations, together with the 1-day ahead portfolio values for each of the 5 sets of price changes.

Table 9.4. *Calculations of the 1-day loss using the empirical method,*
Example 9.7

Day	S_h^A	S_h^B	d_1^A	d_2^A	d_1^B	d_2^B	V_h	L
1	99.74	79.12	0.81441	0.61481	−0.43718	−0.56118	1474.58	11.21
2	100.05	79.69	0.82996	0.63036	−0.37868	−0.50267	1482.24	3.55
3	99.50	79.60	0.80215	0.60255	−0.38799	−0.51198	1478.05	7.73
4	99.17	79.37	0.78545	0.58585	−0.41129	−0.53529	1473.82	11.96
5	100.40	80.48	0.84726	0.64766	−0.29948	−0.42348	1492.57	−6.79

(b) We use the smoothed empirical approach to estimate the 98% 1-day VaR
from the sample of 500 values. Under this method, the α - quantile from a
sample of N values is estimated by the $\alpha(N+1)$th largest value, which in
this case is the 490.98th largest value, which from Table 9.3 is 39.26
(rounding to the 491st value, or interpolating, gives the same number
after rounding to 0.01).

We are asked for the 10-day VaR, so we apply the 'square root'
adjustment, giving the estimated 10-day VaR of

$$\text{VaR} = 39.26 \times \sqrt{10} = 124.14. \qquad \square$$

One drawback of the empirical method is that it limits the possible outcomes
to what has happened in the past. In risk management, we should always be
conscious of the possibility that things could be worse than they have ever been
before. An alternative is to use Monte Carlo simulation to generate the asset
price changes from a stochastic model, where potential future outcomes need
not be limited to past experience.

A major advantage of the Monte Carlo approach is that we no longer need
analytic formulas for the risk measures, so we can move beyond the normal
distribution to other, more complex models which provide a better fit to the
data, particularly in the tails. As we saw in Chapter 3, we can estimate risk
measures directly from the pseudosample of losses generated using the Monte
Carlo method, regardless of the underlying distributions used to generate the
sample. We can also generate asset paths, so that, if daily price changes are not
serially independent, or are not normally distributed, we can directly simulate
10-day price changes without having to use ad hoc adjustments based on the
normal distribution assumption. This is particularly useful for capturing risk
arising from prolonged periods of poor investment experience.

The major disadvantage of the Monte Carlo approach is that it may take
longer, particularly if a large number of projections is required. We also need

to select an appropriate model for the asset returns – using a more complex model needs to be empirically justified. For very short-term calculations, the approximations based on normal assumptions may be sufficient, but for longer term risk management, or where extreme tails are important, a more accurate model that captures stochastic volatility is essential.

9.6 Backtesting

The methods, models, and formulas described in this chapter are used for calculating VaR and Expected Shortfall in the context of banking and in compliance with the Basel regulations. A further requirement of the regulations is that banks should regularly backtest their VaR calculations. That means that the banks should examine the daily losses on their portfolios of the most recent past and count the number of times that the loss was greater than the 1-day VaR calculation, using whatever method is current. The period required under Basel is 250 days but the banks may also backtest over longer periods.

On each day, if the VaR$_{99\%}$ is accurate, there should be a 1% probability that the portfolio loss exceeds the VaR$_{99\%}$. Such days are called **exceptions**. Let M denote the random variable representing the number of exceptions out of, say, n days of backtesting, and let m denote the observed number of exceptions in a given period. If the VaR$_{99\%}$ is accurate, and if the days are independent, then the number of exceptions has a binomial distribution, $M \sim \text{Bin}(n, (1 - \alpha))$.

For backtesting from a regulatory or risk management perspective, we are concerned if the number of exceptions is large, so we construct a one-sided hypothesis test, where the null hypothesis is that the observed number of exceptions, m, is consistent with the binomial distribution; the alternative hypothesis is that m is significantly larger than we would expect based on the binomial distribution. To test this, we calculate the probability that $M \geq m$, given that $M \sim \text{Bin}(n, 1 - \alpha)$. That is, we set the hypothesis test p-value as

$$p = \Pr[M \geq m] = \sum_{k=m}^{n} \binom{n}{k} (1 - \alpha)^k \alpha^{n-k}$$

$$= 1 - \Pr[M \leq (m - 1)] = 1 - \sum_{k=0}^{m-1} \binom{n}{k} (1 - \alpha)^k \alpha^{n-k} = 1 - F_M(m - 1),$$

where $F_M(k)$ is the distribution function of the $\text{Bin}(n, 1 - \alpha)$ distribution.

Table 9.5. p-values for different numbers of exceptions,
99%-VaR, for 250 days of backtesting

m	p	m	p	m	p	m	p
0	1.0000	3	0.4568	6	0.0412	9	0.0011
1	0.9189	4	0.2419	7	0.0137	10	0.0004
2	0.7142	5	0.1078	8	0.0040	11	0.0001

At the usual significance level of 5%, the null hypothesis is rejected if $p < 0.05$.

Example 9.8 A bank is backtesting its 97.5% VaR calculations using 500 days of portfolio losses. It counts $m = 20$ exceptions. Determine whether the number of exceptions is consistent with the VaR confidence level of 97.5%.

Solution 9.8 Under the null hypothesis, the number of exceptions $M \sim$ Bin $(500, 0.025)$. Note that the expected number of exceptions is $500 \times 0.025 = 12.5$, so 20 is on the high side – but is it statistically significant? The p-value for the test is

$$p = 1 - F_M(19) = 0.0496,$$

so the null hypothesis is rejected at the 5% level, indicating that the probability that losses exceed the VaR is likely to be greater than the 2.5% target. □

One complication of backtesting is that the VaR calculations assume the portfolio does not change from day to day, but in fact assets are being traded all the time. Banks therefore calculate the number of exceptions on two different bases: (1) comparing the calculated VaR with the hypothetical portfolio loss, assuming no changes in the portfolio assets (known as **clean losses**); and (2) using the actual portfolio daily loss, allowing for trades, but adjusted to eliminate the impact of fees and charges arising from trading (known as **dirty losses**). Typically regulators are interested in both numbers.

For Basel compliance, banks are expected to backtest their daily 99% VaR calculations over the last 250 trading days (close to one year). The p values associated with values of m from 0 to 11 are given in Table 9.5.

A simple 'traffic light' system for backtesting was developed under which the VaR calculations were assigned a green light if the number of exceptions from 250 days of loss data was less than or equal to 4, a yellow light if the number was between 5 and 9 (even though 5 exceptions is not statistically significant at the 5% level), and a red light for 10 or more exceptions.

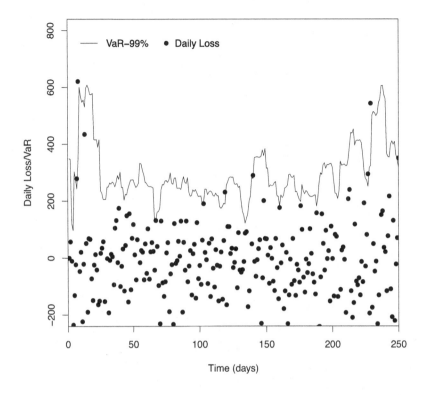

Figure 9.1 Illustration of 250-day 99%-VaR backtest

In Figure 9.1, we show an illustration of a 250-day backtest of a 99% VaR. In this example, there are 7 exceptions, on days 7, 8, 119, 140, 227, 229, and 250. In this case, the number of exceptions is high, and the model lies in the Yellow (warning) range.

The bank may also be interested in identifying whether their VaR calculations are too conservative, which would be indicated by having too few exceptions, though this would not be so interesting to the regulator. We can test simultaneously for a model that is too conservative or not conservative enough by using a two sided hypothesis test. A simple two-sided extension of the one-sided test can be constructed by choosing lower and upper limits of acceptability, m_L and m_u, where $M \sim \text{Bin}(n, 1-\alpha)$, $m_u = 2\text{E}[M] - m_L$, so the interval (m_L, m_u) is symmetric around $\text{E}[M]$, and where m_L is the largest integer satisfying the following condition:

$$\Pr[m_L \leq M \leq m_u] \geq 0.95$$

based on a 5% significance level for the hypothesis test.

Table 9.6. *Symmetric intervals*
around $E(M) = 12.5$, *with*
associated probabilities from the
Bin(300, 0.025) distribution

(m_L, m_u)	$\Pr[m_L \leq M \leq m_u]$
$\vdots$	$\vdots$
(7, 18)	0.8830
(6, 19)	0.9382
(5, 20)	0.9700

Here, the null hypothesis is that the number of exceptions is consistent with the $1-\alpha$ probability assumption for exceptions, and the alternative hypothesis is that the number of exceptions is not consistent with the $1-\alpha$ probability assumption (either too high or too low). For $n = 500$ and $1-\alpha = 0.025$, we have E[M] = 12.5, so symmetric intervals are (12, 13), (11, 14), ... ,(1, 24). We calculate the probability that M lies in each of these intervals under the assumption that $1-\alpha = 0.025$; some key results are shown in Table 9.6.

Table 9.6 shows that the largest m_L number satisfying the condition is $m_L = 5$ which gives $m_u = 20$. This means that for the two-sided test for the 97.5% VaR backtest in Example 9.8, we would accept the null hypothesis if the number of exceptions is between 5 and 20, and reject the null hypothesis (at 5% significance) if there are fewer than 5 or more than 20 exceptions from the 500 observations.[1]

A second consideration in backtesting is whether exceptions are serially independent. It is often implicitly assumed that they are, but in practice, markets do show some dependency in returns from day to day (through volatility clustering, for example). Christoffersen (1998) developed a likelihood ratio test for serial dependence of exceptions. To calculate the test statistic we need the following information from the backtesting data. An exception is a day where the portfolio loss exceeded the calculated VaR. A no-exception is a day where the portfolio loss was less than the calculated VaR:

- t^{00} denotes the number of times where a no-exception was followed by another no-exception.
- t^{01} denotes the number of times where a no-exception was followed by an exception.

---

[1] Kupiec (1995) derived a likelihood ratio statistic for a two-sided hypothesis test for the number of exceptions. It has the advantage of generating a p-value, but is based on additional assumptions not required for the binomial test in this section.

- t^{10} denotes the number of times where an exception was followed by a no-exception.
- t^{11} denotes the number of times where an exception was followed by an exception.
- $T^0 = t^{00} + t^{01}$ denotes the number of pairs of days, where the first day was a no-exception.
- $T^1 = t^{10} + t^{11}$ denotes the number of pairs of days, where the first day was an exception.
- $n - 1 = T^0 + T^1$ denotes the number of days in the backtesting period minus one, giving the total number of pairs of consecutive days.

The null hypothesis is that exceptions are not clustered, which means the probability that a day is an exception should be the same whether the previous day was an exception or not. The alternative hypothesis is that there is clustering, that is, that the probability that an exception is followed by another exception is different from the probability that an exception follows a no-exception. The test statistic is:

$$Q = -2\log\left\{\frac{\left(\frac{t^{00}+t^{10}}{n-1}\right)^{t^{00}+t^{10}}\left(\frac{t^{01}+t^{11}}{n-1}\right)^{t^{01}+t^{11}}}{\left(\frac{t^{00}}{T^0}\right)^{t^{00}}\left(\frac{t^{01}}{T^0}\right)^{t^{01}}\left(\frac{t^{10}}{T^1}\right)^{t^{10}}\left(\frac{t^{11}}{T^1}\right)^{t^{11}}}\right\}.$$

Under the null hypothesis this has a chi-squared distribution with one degree of freedom, which means that the p-value for the test is $\Pr[\chi_1^2 > Q]$. At the 5% significance level, the null hypothesis is rejected if $Q > 3.84$.

Example 9.9 Apply the clustering test to the data shown in Figure 9.1.

Solution 9.9 The times of exceptions are given as 7, 8, 119, 140, 227, 229, and 250 from a test of $n = 250$ days. So we have:

$$t^{11} = 1, \qquad t^{10} = 5, \qquad t^{01} = 6, \qquad t^{00} = (249 - 12) = 237,$$

$$T^0 = 243, \qquad T^1 = 6.$$

$$Q = -2\log\left\{\frac{\left(\frac{242}{249}\right)^{242}\left(\frac{7}{249}\right)^7}{\left(\frac{237}{243}\right)^{237}\left(\frac{6}{243}\right)^6\left(\frac{5}{6}\right)^5\left(\frac{1}{6}\right)^1}\right\} = 2.13,$$

$$p\text{-value} = \Pr[\chi_1^2 > 2.13] = 0.144.$$

As the p value is greater than 5%, the null hypothesis not rejected – that is, the results do not show significant clustering. □

Under the new Basel regulations for market risk, VaR is no longer the key risk measure. However, since backtesting VaR is relatively straightforward, and backtesting Expected Shortfall less so, it is proposed that the validation of market risk models continues to be done using VaR exceptions.

9.7 Notes and Further Reading

See Gregoriou et al. (2010) for several relevant papers on backtesting and model validation. Hull (2018) offers more information on trading processes and short-term financial risk management. Many texts cover the mathematical derivations and applications of the option greeks, including Wilmott (2013), McDonald (2009), and Hull (2022).

9.8 Exercises

Exercise 9.1

(a) Calculate the 10-day, 99% VaR and 97.5% Expected Shortfall on an asset with current price $S(0) = 100$, and with annual volatility $\sigma_S = 0.35$, assuming (i) $R_{t,h}$ follows a normal distribution with $\mu = 0$, $\sigma^2 = h\sigma_S$ and (ii) $1 + R_{t,h}$ follows a lognormal distribution with $\mu = 0$, $\sigma^2 = h\sigma_S$. Assume 250 trading days in a year.
(b) Repeat part (a), but for a 125-day period.
(c) Comment on the results, particularly with respect to (i) model risk and (ii) the square root rule.

Exercise 9.2 A portfolio comprises:

- 5 units of Stock A,
- 5 put options on Stock A, with strike price 9.75, term to expiry 3 months,
- a short holding of 10 units of Stock B,
- 5 call options on Stock B, with strike price 9.75, term to expiry 3 months.

You are given that both Stock A and Stock B have current price 10 and annual volatility $\sigma_A = \sigma_B = 0.25$. The correlation between the return on Stock A and the return on Stock B is $\rho_{A,B} = 0.7$. The risk-free rate of interest is 3% per year, continuously compounded.

(a) Calculate the current value of the portfolio.
(b) Calculate the 10-day 99% VaR using the delta-normal method. Assume 250 trading days per year.

Exercise 9.3 Repeat Exercise 9.2, but assuming that the dependency between Stock A and Stock B is a t-copula, with parameters $\nu = 7$ and $\rho = 0.75$.

- Use Monte Carlo simulation to generate 1,000 values for Stock A and Stock B at the end of the 10-day period. The 'copula' package in R (Hofert et al., 2020) has a function for random number generation from the t-copula.
- For each individual simulation, calculate the relevant put and call option prices at $t = 10/250$, using the standard Black–Scholes formulas.
- Calculate the portfolio value at $t = 10/250$ for each of the 1,000 projected pairs of stock values.
- Hence, estimate the 10-day 99% VaR and 97.5% Expected Shortfall for the portfolio.

Comment on the difference between this estimate and the values using the delta-normal approach.

Exercise 9.4

(a) Download daily return data for two years, for two stocks in the same industry sector.
(b) Use the empirical approach to calculate the 1-day 99% VaR, per unit of portfolio value, for a portfolio that is equally weighted in the two stocks.
(c) Use the square root rule to estimate the 10-day 99% VaR.
(d) Backtest the 10-day 99% VaR against your two years of empirical data.

Exercise 9.5 You are given the following information about the asset portfolio of a pension plan.

- The portfolio has a market value of 225 million and is fully allocated to equity.
- The expected return on equity is 8% p.a., and the standard deviation is 25% p.a.
- There is an imminent cash inflow of 75 million that will be fully allocated to bonds.
- The expected return on bonds is 3.5% p.a., and the standard deviation is 4% p.a.
- The correlation between the returns on the two asset classes is 0.35.

(a) (i) Calculate the 5-day 99% VaR for the equity portfolio.
    (ii) Calculate the 5-day 99% Expected Shortfall for the equity portfolio.
(b) Calculate the increase in the 5-day 99% VaR arising from the addition of the bonds, using the covariance method.

(c) Comment on the change in the VaR as a proportion of the portfolio value.

The firm wishes to reduce its equity exposure. It is considering two strategies:

(i) reallocate 20 million of the equity portfolio to cash, or
(ii) purchase a 3-month equity put option on the equity portfolio, with a strike price of 205 million.

(d) Calculate the revised 5-day 99% VaR for the portfolio, under each strategy.
(e) Comment on the advantages and disadvantages of each strategy.

Copyright 2019. The Society of Actuaries, Schaumburg, Illinois. Reproduced with permission.

10

Economic Scenario Generators

10.1 Summary

An **economic scenario generator** (ESG) is a joint model of economic indicators that is designed for use in risk measurement and risk management. Using Monte Carlo simulation, the ESG generates random paths for variables such as interest rates, inflation rates, and stock index movements, designed to reflect both suitable marginal distributions for each variable and the dependencies between variables. In this chapter, we consider first the decisions that need to be made before the model is constructed or selected. We then present two different frameworks used for ESGs: the cascade design and the vector autoregression design. We consider some of the challenges of model and parameter selection for long-term forecasting, such as structural breaks in the historical data. Finally, we illustrate the application of ESGs using an example involving an employer-sponsored pension plan.

10.2 Introduction

In Chapter 6, we considered models for dependency, based purely on statistical analysis, without considering the underlying causes of dependency. In this chapter, we consider a more structural approach to dependency, particularly where losses and expenses from different risks or risk units are all connected through some underlying economic indicators. For example, losses from different risks may depend, in different ways, on stock market movements, interest rates, exchange rates, and general economic indicators, such as GDP or the unemployment rate.

For some applications, we may use non-economic time series. For example, where losses are dependent on weather, we can work with models for projecting temperature ranges, wind speed, and precipitation, etc. However, in this chapter we focus on economic series. Typical applications involve complex dependencies which are not analytically tractable, but which can be incorporated in a Monte Carlo simulation.

10.3 Considerations for the ESG

The key preliminary considerations in ESG models include the following:

- **What Will the Model Be Used For?**
  At all stages in the design, calibration, and analysis of results of an economic model it is important to take the intended purposes of the model into consideration. A model designed specifically for pricing, where the central parts of the projected economic variables can be most critical, may not work well for risk management where we are more concerned about the extreme adverse outcomes. A model designed for producing data for quarterly statutory reporting may not perform well when applied to assess a hedging strategy with daily rebalancing (and vice versa). A model that is designed to generate future prices of financial options will need to incorporate a risk-neutral measure, as well as the overlying real-world model for projecting cash flows, and the suitability of the relationship between the real-world and risk-neutral models may be a significant source of model risk.

- **Time Step**
  Suppose that losses depend on stock price movements. We may model movements in continuous time, if it is necessary, or we may model daily, monthly, quarterly, or even annual changes. If we are considering the effectiveness of a hedging strategy that involves daily rebalancing of a stock portfolio, then we need a daily model – which will, in practice, be effectively the same as a continuous time model. On the other hand, if the main consideration is quarterly reporting, it may be sufficient to model quarterly price changes. In general, models which are designed and calibrated with very small time steps do not perform well when used for longer term applications. The micro-movements in stock markets require a different type of model than the monthly or quarterly changes. It can be very difficult to develop a model which adequately addresses both very short-term and longer term behaviour.

- **Horizon**

  In banking, a typical VaR horizon for market risk is 10 days. In short-term insurance, we might be interested in projecting economic indices for a year or two. In long-term insurance or pensions, we might be interested in a considerably longer horizon if we want to investigate the assets and liability cash flows over the lifetime of an insurance portfolio or pension plan. Typical business plans involve projections three to five years into the future.

  Similarly to the considerations in determining a suitable time step, the time horizon of the projections can have a significant impact on the form of the model. Over very short terms, we might, perhaps, ignore the possibility of very extreme, 1-in-1,000 year outcomes. But, if we are projecting 50 years ahead, then the more extreme outcomes should be represented.

- **Availability of Data to Calibrate the Model**

  If there is not sufficient data available, the model may still be constructed, but inference from the model output should be treated with caution and the model should be regularly updated to allow for additional information from new data. Some economic models are based on economic theories rather than purely on statistical grounds. Some statistical models may contradict economic theories such as no arbitrage or efficient markets.

  A rule of thumb in time series modelling is that the data used to fit the model should cover a period at least twice as long as the model horizon. However, in practice, especially for economic variables, and especially for longer projection periods, data from further back in history may not be relevant to the future. For example, changes in how governments manage inflation and interest rates could result in a structural change in the models for the future and data from before the change may not be useful for projecting future paths.

- **Dependency Modelling**

  For multivariate models, there are different ways to capture the dependence of the different series. In the two types of models described in this chapter, the dependency structure is modelled simultaneously with the individual series. This differs from the copula approach, where the univariate models can be fitted first and the dependency structure after. If the individual series and the dependency structure are fitted simultaneously, then the resulting marginal processes for each variable may have a worse fit to the data than the univariate model does. That is, if we try to fit a bivariate model of stock price returns and interest rates, we may have a worse fit to the stock price

data than if we tried a univariate model without consideration of the
dependency to interest rates.

- **Tail Behaviour and Fit**
  The tail behaviour refers to the ability of the model to reflect rare outcomes.
  How critical this aspect of a model is depends on the uses for which the
  model is designed. If the tails of the distributions are critical to the
  decisions and analysis for which the model is designed, then considerable
  care is required to ensure the extreme outcomes are appropriately
  incorporated. For example, if we intend to use an economic model to
  determine risk measures which are deep in the tail (e.g., 99% VaR), then the
  tails of the model must be given emphasis in the design and fitting stage.
  A problem with modelling tail behaviour is the scarcity of data on extreme
  outcomes. EVT can be helpful; there are time series versions of the extreme
  value distributions that were considered in Chapter 5.

- **Materiality**
  Much of the discussion above concerns materiality. If the tails of the
  distribution are not material to its purpose, then it is not worth developing
  complex extreme value processes to incorporate in the model. If day-to-day
  movements are not material, and a monthly time step is sufficient, then it is
  likely better to design a model with a monthly time step than to design a
  continuous time model and apply it to the monthly problem. However, if the
  results generated by a model impact a very significant part of a firm's
  capital management, then all aspects of the model should be subject to
  rigorous scrutiny.

- **In-House or Vendor?**
  Models may be developed in-house or may be purchased from external
  vendors. In the case of a vendor model, the firm may have to buy
  'off-the-peg', but ideally the vendor will tailor the model to the firm. In the
  discussion below, the focus is on in-house model development, but very
  similar issues arise, with some additional considerations, with vendor
  models.

- **Univariate or Multivariate?**
  Stock prices, interest rates, inflation rates, and other relevant economic
  indicators may be combined in a multivariate model that captures the
  dependencies between the series. This is valuable where a firm's assets and
  liabilities depend on several different economic variables. The disadvantage
  is that the dependencies can be difficult to ascertain, and using the data to
  try to fit the univariate time series and the dependency can lead to a worse
  fit for the individual models than using the data for a univariate model.

- **Deterministic or Stochastic?**
  We have commented that, typically, models for economic variables are incorporated in the asset and liability modelling for an enterprise using Monte Carlo simulation to generate a distribution of possible future profits and losses. This is an example of a stochastic model. It is also useful in some situations to use deterministic modelling, where a few select scenarios are used to assess the ability of the firm to withstand specific adverse future conditions. Deterministic models come under the Chapter 7 material on stress and scenario testing. In the remainder of this chapter, we assume the models under consideration are being applied in a stochastic setting.
- **Real-World Measure or Risk-Neutral?**
  For pricing and market-consistent valuation of cash flows, it is appropriate to use a risk-neutral or $\mathbb{Q}$-measure, as we discussed in Chapter 8. This is not our best estimate of the true underlying distribution, which we refer to as the real-world, or $\mathbb{P}$-measure. In general, in risk management we are interested in real-world distributions, as our objective is measuring risk, not pricing an asset. However, if the projection of assets and liabilities includes projecting prices or market-consistent valuations of derivative type cash flows, we may need to embed a risk-neutral model within the ESG, but the main, overlying structure will involve the real-world distributions.

10.4 Economic Scenario Generator Design

ESGs are multivariate models of economic series which can be used for risk management and to support strategic decision-making. ESGs are generally designed to be applied as part of a stochastic simulation exercise, projecting assets and liabilities of a financial institution.

Using an ESG allows a structural approach to dependency arising from economic factors. For example, a life insurer may have assets and liabilities in an annuity portfolio that are both dependent on long-term interest rates. It may offer embedded options to its savings products which are dependent on equity returns. In defined benefit pension plans, it is critical to manage the surplus of the plan, rather than separately manage assets and liabilities. An ESG allows the actuary to project path-dependent simulations for the surplus, using consistent, dependent models for all the major economic factors involved.

Because their main purpose is to derive a real-world picture of potential future asset and liability paths, ESGs were originally developed to generate real-world distributions, not risk-neutral. However, as the range of applications has developed, it has become common for ESGs to incorporate both real-world capabilities, for generating realistic paths of asset and liability values, and risk-neutral scenarios, for assessing how market prices may evolve over time.

There are several different ways to structure and calibrate an ESG. In this chapter, we describe two common approaches: the cascade approach and the vector autoregression approach.

10.4.1 Cascade Models

The **cascade** approach develops dependencies that feed through from one or two key series. The Wilkie models (Wilkie, 1984, 1995; Wilkie et al., 2011; Wilkie and Şahin, 2018) are a family of cascade ESGs that have significantly influenced many proprietary models in current use. In the Wilkie ESG, the consumer price inflation (CPI) model lies at the top of the cascade; the simulated value of the inflation rate feeds through to the simulated values of the other variables. The version examined in Wilkie et al. (2011) is shown diagrammatically in Figure 10.1. The rate of inflation is modelled as a straightforward autoregressive time series, of order 1 such that the continuously compounded rate of inflation at t is

$$\delta_q(t) = \mu_q + a_q(\delta_q(t-1) - \mu_q) + \sigma_q Z_q(t), \qquad (10.1)$$

where μ_q, a_q, and σ_q are parameters, and $Z_q(k) \overset{\text{i.i.d.}}{\sim} N(0,1)$, for $k = 1, 2, \ldots$. The processes below the CPI in Figure 10.1 then include $\delta_q(t)$ in their formulations. For example, the share dividend yield, $y(t)$, is modelled as

$$y(t) = \mu_y \exp(w_y \delta_q(t) + yn(t))$$
$$\text{where } yn(t) = a_y \, yn(t-1) + \sigma_y Z_y(t).$$

Again, μ_y, w_y, a_y, and σ_y are parameters, and $Z_y(k) \overset{\text{i.i.d.}}{\sim} N(0,1)$, for $k = 1, 2, \ldots$.

The long bond yield has terms in $\delta_q(t)$ and in $y(t)$, continuing through the cascade structure.

The Wilkie model is a real-world model with annual time steps. It is designed to be used for long horizon analysis – typically 20 years or more.

10.4.2 Vector Autoregression Models

An alternative to the cascade approach is to model the multivariate series as a **vector autoregressive** (VAR) process. A simple version of a VAR process

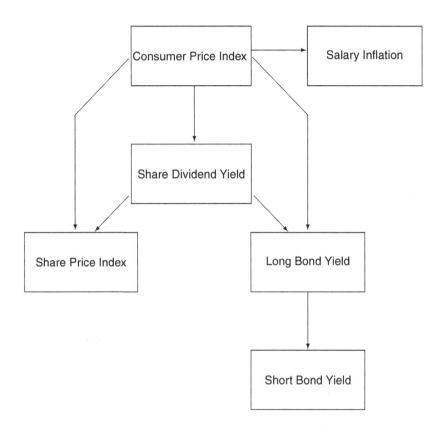

Figure 10.1 Cascade structure of the Wilkie ESG

is described here. Suppose we want to model an ESG involving three series; $x_1(t)$, representing inflation, $x_2(t)$, representing the log-return on a stock index, and $x_3(t)$, representing the long-term risk-free bond yield. We will use an autoregressive model with a lag of 1 time unit. Let $\mathbf{X}(t)$ denote the vector comprised of $x_1(t)$, $x_2(t)$, and $x_3(t)$. Then the ESG can be formulated as

$$\mathbf{X}(t) = \boldsymbol{\mu} + \mathbf{A}\left(\mathbf{X}(t-1) - \boldsymbol{\mu}\right) + \mathbf{Z}(t)$$

$$\text{where } \mathbf{X}(t) = \begin{pmatrix} x_1(t) \\ x_2(t) \\ x_3(t) \end{pmatrix}; \boldsymbol{\mu} = \begin{pmatrix} \mu_1 \\ \mu_2 \\ \mu_3 \end{pmatrix}; \mathbf{A} = \begin{pmatrix} a_{11} & a_{12} & a_{13} \\ a_{21} & a_{22} & a_{23} \\ a_{31} & a_{32} & a_{33} \end{pmatrix}$$

and $\mathbf{Z}(t) \overset{\text{i.i.d.}}{\sim} \text{MVN}(\mathbf{0}, \Sigma)$, where $\text{MVN}(\mathbf{0}, \Sigma)$ indicates a multivariate normal distribution, with mean vector $\mathbf{0}$, and covariance matrix Σ.

The μ_i parameters are the mean values for the $x_i(t)$ series. The a_{ij} parameters are the auto-covariance, and cross-covariance parameters for the model, and Σ is the covariance matrix for $X(t)$, given $X(t-1)$. Considering an individual series, say, $x_1(t)$ then, we have

$$x_1(t) = \mu_1 + (a_{11}(x_1(t-1) - \mu_1) + a_{12}(x_2(t-1) - \mu_2)$$
$$+ a_{13}(x_3(t-1) - \mu_3)) + Z_1(t).$$

We can see that the dependence between $x_1(t)$ and the other variables emerges in two ways. The first is that the $x_j(t-1) - \mu_j$ terms influence $x_1(t)$, for $j = 2, 3$. These are the cross-covariance terms. The second is that $Z_1(t)$ is correlated with the $Z_2(t)$ and $Z_3(t)$ terms through the multivariate normal distribution.

Most VAR models in current use are rather more complex than this – though it is hard to judge, as usually the model assumptions of proprietary models are not divulged. Sherris and Zhang (2009) propose a VAR ESG, with quarter-year time steps, which models 11 economic variables, including GDP, price inflation, equity yields, dividend yields, short, medium, and long-term government bond rates, average earnings growth, unemployment rates, and US bond yields. The dependencies among the variables are modelled through a regime-switching multivariate normal innovation process. Regime-switching is described in the univariate case in Chapter 8, in the context of long-term modelling of equity returns.

10.5 Model Fitting and Robustness

ESGs are generally fitted and tested using standard time series techniques, which are beyond the scope of this text. In this section, we highlight some of the challenges involved, especially for ESGs that are designed to apply over very long time horizons.

10.5.1 Stationarity and Structural Breaks

A univariate time series is weakly stationary, if the variance is finite and if the mean and autocovariance do not vary over time. That is, a time series $X(t)$ is weakly stationary iff, for any $t, s, k > 0$,

$$E[X(t)] = E[X(t+k)],$$

$$E[|X(t)|^2] < \infty,$$
$$\mathrm{Cov}(X(t), X(t+k)) = \mathrm{Cov}(X(s), X(s+k)).$$

The first condition means that the unconditional mean value is constant over time. The second means that the variance is finite. The third condition means that the covariance function between $X(t_1)$ and $X(t_2)$ only depends on the time difference, $t_2 - t_1$.

A multivariate time series is weakly stationary if the individual univariate time series are weakly stationary and, in addition, the cross-covariance functions between the different variables do not vary over time.

We usually require ESGs to be weakly stationary; there is a risk that the processes will explode over time if the mean or covariances include time trends. However, there is also a problem that the data being modelled exhibit some non-stationary traits. In a study of US data, Zhang et al. (2018) found that inflation and dividend growth exhibit non-stationarity. The main problem is structural shifts in the stochastic processes. Structural shifts mean that more distant historical data is less relevant for creating feasible scenarios. In Figure 10.2, we show the results from a statistical analysis of change points, using 1932–2014 US data, for price inflation, dividend yields, and long-term interest rates.

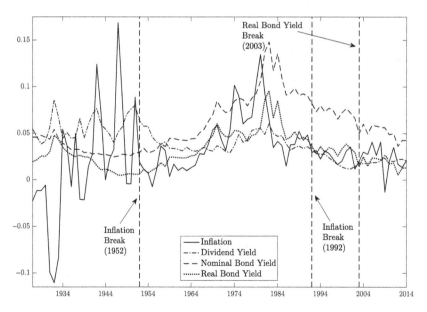

Figure 10.2 Inflation, dividend yield, and interest rates with structural breaks (from Zhang et al. (2018), © Society of Actuaries)

The 1952 inflation break point marks the end of large-scale, post-World War recessions. We see inflation subsequently sweeping upwards, to the very high rates of the 1970s, fuelled by oil crises and the unwillingness of governments to intervene. The 1992 break in inflation signifies the beginning of the modern era of more stringent government control of inflation. Since 1992, we see very modest volatility which is primarily due to energy price fluctuations. The 2009 deflation was caused by the global financial crisis, which resulted in a lower demand in energy and food, thus pushing costs down. We also see lesser momentum (no significant serial correlations), which suggests a change in the autoregressive behaviour.

Structural changes create problems in constructing and fitting long-term models. A major structural shift makes the earlier data less relevant to a model of the future behaviour of the process, but if we ignore the historical information, then we may not have sufficient data to adequately calibrate the models.

10.5.2 Parameter Uncertainty

ESGs tend to involve many parameters. The Sherris–Zhang VAR model has 11 variables, which means there are 55 different bivariate dependencies to be modelled, in addition to the mean, variance, and autoregression parameters for each individual series. The Wilkie model is fairly parsimonious, due to its reduced cascade structure, but still involves up to 30 parameters, depending on which series are included. Non-stationarity in the data, including structural shifts, as well as changes in the way that data is recorded, all increase the uncertainty in parameter estimation. The sensitivity of the parameter estimation to the period of data used to fit the model is a measure of the model robustness. In Figure 10.3, we show the estimated parameter values, with confidence intervals for the a_q and σ_q parameters for the Wilkie inflation model (see equation (10.1)). The graph shows results using a rolling 30-year window of data, starting with 1926–55, up to 1985–2014. The change points in the inflation data, at around 1952 and 1992, can be seen in these graphs. The a_q parameter models the strength of the autoregression in inflation; very high values indicate that the process will move slowly from current values towards the long-term mean values. The increase in the a_q estimate for the windows starting from 1952 through to the window starting in 1980 all reflect the inclusion of some or all of the hyperinflationary period of the 1970s. Including the 1970s data may skew the parameters away from current values, but excluding it means fitting the model to a relatively small number of data points.

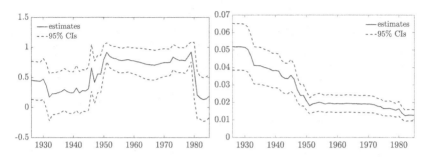

Figure 10.3 Estimation of a_q (left) and σ_q (right) for the Wilkie ESG, using a 30-year rolling window of US inflation data, by start date (from Zhang et al. (2018), © Society of Actuaries)

In practice, a significant problem arises from using different time periods to fit different variables within a multivariate model. Consultants promoting proprietary ESGs will add new modules to their models, as different investment or macroeconomic series become more prominent in the decision-making of their clients. Although the rest of their ESG is fitted to several decades of data, the new variable may have to be fitted to a much shorter period, if it is a recent innovation. But that means that there is an inconsistency created between the variables. Suppose, for example, a consultant adds a series representing returns on private equity to their existing ESG. If they use only, say, 10 years of data to calibrate the new series and then integrate that into an ESG fitted to 30 years of data, then the private equity series is fitted without being impacted (at least directly) by the experience of the 2007–8 global financial crisis. So the extreme adverse experience of that time will be reflected, within the ESG, in the forecasted returns on publicly traded stocks, but not on returns on private equities. That is likely to make the private equity returns appear misleadingly attractive. Since the ESG is often used as a tool for selecting an investment allocation strategy, it is likely to influence the client towards private investment, even if the relative advantage is not significant.

10.5.3 Forecasting with ESGs

In practice, ESGs are often provided as part of a software package, and there is a risk that they are treated as a magic black box that can predict the future for a large number of dependent market and macroeconomic series. The more variables that are included, the broader the potential applications. But including more series in the model may create less accurate forecasting for each individual series. That is, creating an ESG of, say, stock returns and long-term interest rates may give a less accurate model for each series individually than using two entirely separate models. If the ESG is being used for a risk that involves both stock returns and interest rates, then the joint model should provide a better picture of the risk than two independent models, but if the risk under analysis only involves one of the series, then it could be less accurate to use the ESG, compared with a univariate model.

A similar risk arises if the model use and the model time-step are not consistent. A model with very short time steps (e.g., continuous or daily) is likely to be best suited to shorter-term analysis; a model with longer time steps (quarterly, annual) is more suited to long-term analysis. When using a continuous time model, the calibration will focus on the moment-to-moment relationships between data points and may be unable to capture longer term trends and relationships.

10.6 A Pension Example

Even a relatively straightforward ESG, such as the Wilkie model, can be used to generate some insight into risks for financial institutions. We used the Wilkie model to examine the risk associated with a **defined benefit** (DB) pension plan. A major problem with DB plans is that liabilities are very long-term – an individual who enters employment at age 25 might be contributing to the pension for 40 years, and receiving a pension for another 40 years. In order to maintain solvency, the plan is regularly subject to actuarial review. The actuary estimates the value of the contingent liabilities, based on the accrued benefits of the current employees and retirees, and determines what level of funding the plan needs to maintain. If asset returns have been poor, or if interest rates are lower than expected, then the employer and employees will be required to increase the amount paid into the plan. Using an ESG, it is possible to gain more insight into the risks associated with the pension plan benefits and funding schedule, compared with a simple point estimate of asset and liability values. Under a dynamic financial analysis, the actuary will generate a large number of random paths for the key economic variables that impact the surplus or deficit process for the plan – specifically, interest rates, inflation rates (for projecting the value of future cost of living pension adjustments), and stock prices as pension plan assets tend to be heavily weighted to stocks.

Some results of a hypothetical pension plan asset-liability projection are shown in Figure 10.4. The figure on the left shows 30 sample paths, overlaid with the 5%, 25%, 50%, 75% and 95% quantiles, for the projected

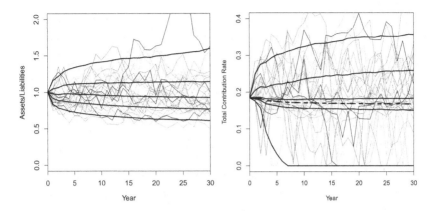

Figure 10.4 Model pension plan, Asset/Liability Ratio (left) and contribution rates (right); 5%, 25%, 50%, 75%, and 95% quantiles, with 30 sample paths

asset/liability (A/L) ratio for the plan, estimated from 10,000 scenarios. The A/L ratio is 1.0 at the start of the projection. The median A/L ratio, and the quantiles, are reasonably stable, indicating perhaps that the plan is fairly well controlled. However, the story told by the contribution rates is different. The figure on the right shows simulated paths for the total contribution rate payable each year as a percentage (%) of payroll. The contribution rate is made up of a 'normal service cost', which is the deterministic best estimate of the contribution rate plus an adjustment for surplus or deficit; when the plan is in surplus (meaning that the value of assets exceeds the value of the liabilities, then contributions are reduced. When the plan is in deficit, the employer and plan members have to pay extra contributions to restore the plan to a healthier financial position.

The normal service cost is around 19% of payroll, but the surplus/deficit adjustment is extremely volatile. From the middle of the projection, we see that there is around a 5% chance that the rate exceeds 35% of salary, very much higher than the expected rate of 19%. This sort of analysis offers important insights into the risks behind the deterministic estimation of contribution rates, which is the traditional approach to pension plan management. Many pension valuations (at least in the US and Canada) fail to consider the potential volatility of costs and funding. A justification for the deterministic approach has been the complexity of the interactions between costs and asset proceeds. By using the ESG, through Monte Carlo simulation, we can overcome this problem, with the result that we have a much more vivid understanding of the potential for adverse outcomes.

The purpose of showing the individual sample paths as well as the quantiles is that they offer a different perspective on the nature of the paths. Following the individual paths shows us that some paths stay at the 95% quantile for contribution rates for several years at a time, but also that the contribution rates can swing widely in a very short period.

10.7 Notes and Further Reading

ESGs are most prevalent in actuarial practice, as the work involves long time horizons and is often a function of several economic variables. In other areas, where the horizons are shorter, there is less need for complex multivariate models. However, in many contexts it is helpful to model equity returns and risk-free rates of interest simultaneously. However, no definitive or standard model has emerged from the research.

Figures 10.3 and 10.4 are reproduced from Zhang et al. (2018) with permission of Taylor & Francis Ltd, http://www.tandfonline.com, on behalf of the Society of Actuaries.

10.8 Exercises

Exercise 10.1 Describe the considerations relating to whether the equity model in an ESG should be based on the real-world ($\mathbb{P}$) measure or the risk-neutral ($\mathbb{Q}$) measure.

Exercise 10.2 A firm is constructing a joint model of long-term treasury bond yields and stock market returns. The CFO points out that there is data available going back 200 years. Explain why it may not be reasonable to use the full data set to calibrate the model. What steps could you take to determine how much data to use?

Exercise 10.3 A university is considering developing an ESG for the following purposes:

- Modelling pension liabilities.
- Setting investment allocation targets for the pension plan.
- Setting investment allocation targets for their endowments.
- Assessing potential impacts of wage and price inflation on their cash flows.

(a) Discuss the advantages and disadvantages of developing a single ESG to use for all the purposes described.

(b) Discuss the advantages and disadvantages of using a step-size of one-month, compared with one-year, in the ESG.

(c) The university currently does not have any foreign investments or liabilities. The CFO suggests incorporating exchange rates in the ESG, for potential future use. Discuss the advantages and disadvantages of this proposal.

Exercise 10.4 An ESG of inflation $(\delta_q(t))$ interest rates $(r(t))$, both continuously compounded, and log-returns on the market equity index $(y(t))$, is defined through the following equations:

$$\delta_q(t) = \mu_q + a_q(\delta_q(t-1) - \mu_q) + \sigma_q Z_q(t),$$

$$r(t) = \delta_q(t) + \mu_r + a_r(r(t-1) - \delta_q(t-1) - \mu_r) + \sigma_r Z_r(t),$$

$$y(t) = r(t) + \mu_y + a_y(y(t-1) - r(t-1) - \mu_y) + \sigma_y Z_y(t),$$

$$(Z_q(t), Z_r(t), Z_y(t))' \sim \text{MVN}(\mathbf{0}, \mathbf{\Sigma}); \quad \mathbf{\Sigma} = \begin{pmatrix} 1 & \rho_{qr} & \rho_{qy} \\ \rho_{qr} & 1 & \rho_{ry} \\ \rho_{qy} & \rho_{ry} & 1 \end{pmatrix}.$$

The time-step is one year.

(a) Explain why this is a cascade model and draw the cascade diagram.
(b) Interpret the variable $r(t) - \delta_q(t)$.
(c) Interpret the variable $y(t) - r(t)$.
(d) You are given the following parameters for the model:

$\mu_q = 0.025,$	$a_q = 0.8,$	$\sigma_q = 0.02,$
$\mu_r = 0.010,$	$a_r = 0.8,$	$\sigma_r = 0.01,$
$\mu_y = 0.025,$	$a_y = 0.1,$	$\sigma_y = 0.30,$
$\rho_{qr} = 0.4,$	$\rho_{qy} = 0.2,$	$\rho_{ry} = 0.0.$

In R, generate 1,000 values for the random variable $(\delta_q(t), r(t), y(t))$, for $t = 1, 2, \ldots, 10$. Plot the results, showing on a single diagram 20 sample paths, overlaid with the 5%, 50%, and 95% quantiles for the variables at each time point (similar to the graphs in Figure 10.4).

(e) Explore what happens if $a_q = 1.05$ (this makes the process non-stationary).

(f) Plot the copula scatter plots for each of the three bivariate copulas, i.e. inflation vs interest rates, inflation vs equity returns, and interest rates vs equity returns.

(g) Assume an investor deposits an amount at the start of each year for 10 years into 15-year bonds and into equities. The annual investments start at 100 in each asset class and increase with inflation. Assume a flat yield curve.

(i) Use the simulated paths to generate a sample of 1,000 values for the accumulated proceeds. Plot the density function of the accumulated proceeds, and give the mean, standard deviation, and 5%, 50%, and 95% quantiles of the results.

(ii) Repeat (i), but for real returns (net of inflation).

Exercise 10.5 The pension plan manager responsible for the plan illustrated in Figure 10.4 measures risk by considering the 95% VaR of the contribution rates. From the graph, she reports that after 10 years, the 95% VaR is over 30% each year.

Her CEO interprets that statement as meaning that, on average there will be one year between time 11 and time 30 in which contribution rates will be over 30%. Is this correct thinking? Justify your answer.

Exercise 10.6 Your colleague claims that, since the cascade model used in the Wilkie ESG has no arrows pointing back to the inflation series, and since the inflation series does not require any input from the other variables, inflation is independent of the other series. Is your colleague correct? Justify your answer.

11

Interest Rate Risk

11.1 Summary

In this chapter, we study risks associated with movements of interest rates in financial markets. We begin with a brief discussion of the term structure of interest rates. We then discuss commonly used interest rate sensitive securities. This is followed by the study of different measures of sensitivity to interest rates, including duration and convexity. We consider mitigating interest rate risk through hedging and immunization. Finally, we take a more in-depth look at the drivers of interest rate term structure dynamics.

11.2 The Term Structure of Interest Rates

In this section, we review the basic mathematics of the term structure of interest rates, including calculating present values with different compounding frequencies and different interest rates for different maturities.

11.2.1 Interest Rates and Discount Factors

Suppose that we want to calculate the present value of a cash payment to be made in 4 years at an interest rate of 6% per year, compounded half-yearly. This is equivalent to a rate of compound interest of 3% every $\frac{1}{2}$-year, so that an investment of 1 made at time 0 would accumulate to $(1.03)^8$ after 4 years, and a payment of 1 due in 4 years would have present value $\left(\frac{1}{1.03}\right)^{-8} = 0.78941$. On the other hand, if the 6% interest rate is compounded annually, then a payment of 1 due in 4 years would have present value $\left(\frac{1}{1.06}\right)^{-4} = 0.79209$. An effective rate of interest is a rate that is compounded once per time unit – that is, a rate of interest of 6% per year compounded half-yearly is the same as an effective rate of interest of 3% per $\frac{1}{2}$-year.

We let $v(t)$ denote the discount function, which gives the value at time 0 of 1 due at t. Although we have not included them as arguments, this function depends on the annual rate of interest, and the compounding frequency. Suppose we have a rate of interest of r per year, compounded every $\frac{1}{m}$ years. This is equivalent to an effective rate of interest of $\frac{r}{m}$ every $\frac{1}{m}$ years, so the discount function is

$$v(t) = \left(1 + \frac{r}{m}\right)^{-mt}.$$

If the interest rate is continuously compounded, then we have

$$v(t) = \lim_{m \to \infty} \left(1 + \frac{r}{m}\right)^{-mt} = e^{-rt}.$$

Note that the risk-free rate of interest used in financial valuation is (almost always) expressed as a continuously compounded rate. In other contexts, the more common default would be that interest rates are compounded annually.

Example 11.1 A cash flow of $C = \$150$ will be received in two years. The given interest rate for discounting the cash flow is 5% per year. What is the present value of this cash flow if this interest rate is compounded (a) annually, (b) semi-annually, (c) monthly, (d) continuously?

Solution 11.1

$$\text{(a) } PV = 150 \left(\frac{1}{1.05}\right)^2 = 136.05.$$

$$\text{(b) } PV = 150 \left(\frac{1}{1.025}\right)^4 = 135.89.$$

$$\text{(c) } PV = 150 \left(\frac{1}{1.0041667}\right)^{24} = 135.75.$$

$$\text{(d) } PV = 150 \, e^{-2(0.05)} = 135.73.$$

11.2.2 The Term Structure

In real financial markets, the interest rate that one must pay to borrow money depends on when the money will be paid back. Loans with different maturities are charged different rates.[1] At a given date, the interest rate, considered as a

---

[1] The interest rate charged may also depend on the borrower, owing to issues relating to credit risk and liquidity.

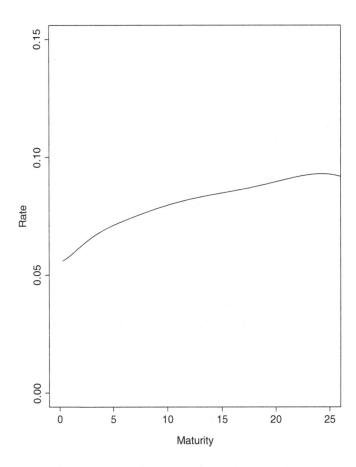

Figure 11.1 The term structure of interest rates in Canada on 25 September 1992

function of the maturity of the borrowing, is referred to as the **term structure of interest rates** or **interest rate term structure**. Figure 11.1 shows the term structure of interest rates in Canada from 25 September 1992. These are spot rates, annually compounded; a spot rate of 7% for a four-year investment means that the present value of 1 due at time 4, is $v(4) = (1.07)^{-4}$, and, conversely, an investment of 1 at time 0 will accumulate to $\frac{1}{v(4)} = (1.07)^4$ at time 4.

Note that the curve in Figure 11.1 is a snapshot of the term structure of interest rates at a single point in time. As general economic and market factors evolve, this curve will change in location and shape. If we fix the term to maturity, at one year say, we can observe the historical time series as the one-year rate changes over time.

Example 11.2 You own a bond with maturity three years, a face value of $1,000, and a 10% annual coupon rate, with coupons paid annually. The current one-year interest rate is $r_1 = 5\%$ per year effective, the current two-year interest rate is $r_2 = 6\%$ per year effective, and the current three-year interest rate is $r_3 = 7\%$ per year effective. What is the bond's current price?

Solution 11.2 The bond will pay $100 one year from now, $100 two years from now and $1,100 three years from now. Therefore, the bond's price is:

$$
\begin{aligned}
P &= \frac{100}{1+r_1} + \frac{100}{(1+r_2)^2} + \frac{1,100}{(1+r_3)^3} \\
&= \frac{100}{1.05} + \frac{100}{1.06^2} + \frac{1,100}{1.07^3} = 1,082.17. \qquad \square
\end{aligned}
$$

11.3 Interest Rate Sensitive Securities

Since pricing almost any form of financial security involves calculating the present value of the future cash flows associated with the instrument, in a certain sense it would be accurate to say that all financial securities are interest rate sensitive securities. In this section, we review securities for which the interest rate is one of the most important risk factors.

11.3.1 Bonds

A bond is a debt instrument. The issuer of the bond borrows money from the purchaser, to be repaid at a later date. There is a wide range of different types of bonds traded in the market. Bonds can vary because of the nature of the issuer (sovereign government, corporation, municipal or provincial government), the seniority of the debt in the issuer's capital structure, the nature and quality of the assets (if any) pledged to support the bond payments, and the characteristics of the promised payments. The most common examples of bonds are zero coupon bonds, bullet bonds (fixed rate bonds), and floating rate bonds.

A **zero coupon bond** makes a single promised payment of the face value at the maturity date. The bond's price will typically be less than its face value due to the time value of money. For example, consider a risk-free zero coupon bond with a face value of $1,000 and maturity date six months from now. Suppose that the one-year risk-free interest rate is $r = 0.05$, compounded continuously. The price of the bond is then $P = 1,000 \, e^{-0.5 \times 0.05} = 975.31$. Treasury Bills, or T-bills, are short-term zero-coupon bonds issued by the US government.

A **fixed rate bond**, often also called a **bullet bond**, provides a series of evenly spaced interest payments, called coupons, together with a repayment of the face value of the bond at maturity. The interest payments are all determined by applying a fixed coupon rate, which is specified in the bond contract (indenture). Typically, coupons are paid half-yearly. We have already seen an example of a fixed rate bond in Example 11.2.

A **floating rate bond** makes regular coupon payments that are based on the observed value of a given market interest rate, together with a repayment of the principal amount at maturity. There are several types of floating rate bond – a very common one is described in the next example.

Example 11.3 Let $r_h(s)$ denote the floating interest rate observed at time s for borrowing from time s to time $s + h$. Consider a bond that makes floating interest payments at times $h, 2h, 3h, \ldots, T$, together with a repayment of the face value F at time T. Show that the value of the bond at time 0 is equal to the face value, F. Ignore credit risk.

Solution 11.3 We will prove the result using a **replication argument**. That is, we show that the cash flows of the bond can be reproduced exactly by investing F dollars in the market today and then carrying out a dynamic lending strategy that requires no further investment or withdrawal of funds. In the absence of arbitrage, the cost of exactly replicating the pay-off of an asset must be equal to the cost of the asset. This is an example of arbitrage pricing using replication, a method that plays a starring role in the pricing of derivative securities.

Suppose that we invest F dollars today at the market rate $r_h(0)$. This will yield $F \times (1 + r_h(0))$ at time h. We keep $F \times r_h(0)$, which reproduces the coupon payment of the floating rate bond at time h, and reinvest the rest, which is equal to F, at the market rate prevailing at h, which is $r_h(h)$. Then, at time $2h$, we will have $F \times (1 + r_h(h))$. We again keep the coupon amount $F \times r_h(h)$ – reproducing the payment of the floating rate bond at time $2h$ – and reinvest F. Continuing in this fashion, we replicate all of the cash flows of the floating rate bond up to time $T - h$.

At time $T - h$, we reinvest F at the prevailing rate, $r_h(T - h)$, giving us $F \times (1 + r_h(T - h))$ at the maturity date T, exactly reproducing the final payment of principal, F, plus interest at the final period floating rate, $F \times r_h(T - h)$. The strategy of keeping the interest, and repeatedly reinvesting the face value at the prevailing floating rate, has exactly replicated the payments of the floating rate bond, at an initial cost of F. Consequently, the price of the floating rate bond must be F. □

Spot rates are the rates attainable for investments made immediately. Forward rates are rates that are contractually agreed at time 0, for a loan made at some future date T, say, with repayment due at time $T + \tau$. This kind of contract is called a **forward rate agreement** (FRA). We let $f(T, T + \tau)$ denote the forward rate, which is the interest rate, per year, payable over the period of the loan, from T to $T + \tau$.

We can determine the appropriate value for the forward rate by a replication argument similar to the one used above for floating rate bonds. In the discussion below, we use $v(s)$ for the discount factor, so that the present value of M due at t is $M \times v(t)$ and the accumulation at t of 1 invested at time 0 is $\frac{1}{v(t)}$.

Consider the following two strategies:

(A) Invest 1 for $T + \tau$ years for a payment of $\frac{1}{v(T+\tau)}$ at $T + \tau$.

(B) Invest 1 for T years and, simultaneously, enter into an FRA to invest the proceeds at time T for a further τ years. The payoff from the T-year investment is $\frac{1}{v(T)}$ at T, and the accumulated proceeds at time $T + \tau$ are

$$\frac{1}{v(T)} \times (1 + f(T, T + \tau))^{\tau}.$$

Both strategies have exactly the same cash flows, that is, an investment of 1 at time 0, with no further payments until the final proceeds are collected at time $T + \tau$, which, by the replication argument, means that the proceeds at $T + \tau$ must be the same. That is,

$$\frac{1}{v(T + \tau)} = \frac{(1 + f(T, T + \tau))^{\tau}}{v(T)} \Rightarrow f(T, T + \tau) = \left(\frac{v(T)}{v(T + \tau)} \right)^{\frac{1}{\tau}} - 1.$$

In terms of the current spot rates, since $v(t) = (1 + r_t)^{-t}$, we have

$$(1 + f(T, T + \tau))^{\tau} = \frac{v(T)}{v(T + \tau)} = \frac{(1 + r_{T+\tau})^{T+\tau}}{(1 + r_T)^T}.$$

Notice that the forward rate can be calculated based on today's observed term structure of interest rates, even though the borrowing is to take place in the future at time T.

A **swap** is an agreement to exchange a series of cash flows in the future according to a fixed set of rules that are determined today. Much like forward contracts and forward rate agreements, swaps are typically constructed to have zero price today. This enhances the liquidity of derivatives markets. The most common type of swap is a plain vanilla swap, in which a series of fixed payments is exchanged for a series of payments that depends on a floating interest rate. As such, it is essentially an agreement to exchange a fixed rate bond for a floating rate bond. See the exercises for information on swap pricing.

More complicated interest rate derivatives involve some degree of optionality. Examples include caps and floors, which provide protection against high (respectively low) interest rate levels, and swaptions, which are options to enter into swaps.

11.4 Duration and Convexity

In this section, we briefly examine duration and convexity. Duration is a measure of the sensitivity of a financial instrument or portfolio to changes in the interest rate. It is analogous to the delta of a derivative security, which measures the sensitivity of the derivative security to changes in the value of its underlying asset. Convexity is a second-order measure of interest rate sensitivity, analogous to the gamma of a derivative security.

When calculating and using basic duration measures, there are some important things to keep in mind.

(1) Duration-based measures often assume that the term structure of interest rates is flat, with the same rate being applied to discount cash flows at all maturities.

(2) Duration-based measures often assume that when the term structure of interest rates changes, it does so by a parallel shift, with all interest rates moving by the same amount.

(3) Duration-based measures use (mathematical) derivatives, which give approximations of changes in values of securities for small changes in the underlying interest rate.

Since duration and convexity employ mathematical derivatives of instrument values with respect to the interest rate, let us begin by calculating the first two derivatives of the discount factors given above with respect to the interest rate. For a discount factor expressed in terms of an annual effective rate of interest, r, say, we have

$$v(t) = (1 + r)^{-t} \Rightarrow \frac{\partial v(t)}{\partial r} = -t(1 + r)^{-(t+1)},$$

$$\text{and } \frac{\partial^2 v(t)}{\partial r^2} = t(t + 1)(1 + r)^{-(t+2)}.$$

If the interest rate r is continuously compounded, we have

$$v(t) = e^{-rt} \Rightarrow \frac{\partial v(t)}{\partial r} = -te^{-rt} \text{ and } \frac{\partial^2 v(t)}{\partial r^2} = t^2 e^{-rt}.$$

Observe that the first derivatives are negative (the discount factor is a decreasing function of the interest rate), and that the second derivatives are positive (the discount factor is a convex function of the interest rate).

Now, let us suppose that we have a stream of cash flows, C_k, for $k = 1, \ldots, K$; Let t_k denote the time of payment of the kth cash flow. Furthermore, we assume that the term structure of interest rates is flat (i.e. the same rate r is applied to all cash flows). Then the present value of the cash flow stream is

$$P(r) = \sum_{k=1}^{K} C_k v(t_k), \tag{11.1}$$

and by linearity, we have the derivatives

$$\frac{\partial P}{\partial r} = \sum_{k=1}^{K} C_k \frac{\partial v(t_k)}{\partial r}, \quad \frac{\partial^2 P}{\partial r^2} = \sum_{k=1}^{K} C_k \frac{\partial^2 v(t_k)}{\partial r^2}. \tag{11.2}$$

If we assume that the term structure moves in parallel (i.e. remains flat), by the (small) amount Δr, then we can approximate the change in the value of the stream of cash flows by using a first order Taylor expansion:

$$P(r + \Delta r) = P + \frac{\partial P}{\partial r} \times \Delta r + O\big((\Delta r)^2\big), \tag{11.3}$$

or using a second order Taylor expansion:

$$P(r + \Delta r) = P + \frac{\partial P}{\partial r}(r) \times \Delta r + \frac{1}{2} \frac{\partial^2 P}{\partial r^2} \times (\Delta r)^2 + O\big((\Delta r)^3\big). \tag{11.4}$$

Here, $O((\Delta r)^m)$ indicates a quantity whose absolute value is bounded by a constant multiplied by $(\Delta r)^m$.

Example 11.4 Consider a portfolio consisting of two zero-coupon bonds. The first bond has a face value of 50 and matures in 8 years, while the second bond has a face value of 1,050 and matures in 10 years. Suppose that the current term structure of interest rates is flat at 7% per year effective.

(a) Determine the current value of the portfolio, as well as its values if the interest rate were either 6% or 8%.

(b) Use a first-order Taylor expansion to approximate the value of the portfolio if the term structure of interest rates shifts in parallel to either 6% or 8%.

(c) Use a second-order Taylor expansion to approximate the value of the portfolio if the term structure of interest rates shifts in parallel to either 6% or 8%.

Solution 11.4

(a) The value of the portfolio is computed as the present value of the cash flows.

$$P(r) = \sum_{k=1}^{K} \frac{C_{t_k}}{(1+r)^{t_k}} = \frac{50}{(1+r)^8} + \frac{1,050}{(1+r)^{10}}. \qquad (11.5)$$

This gives the following prices at the given rates:

$$P(0.07) = \frac{50}{1.07^8} + \frac{1,050}{1.07^{10}} = 562.867,$$

$$P(0.06) = \frac{50}{1.06^8} + \frac{1,050}{1.06^{10}} = 617.685,$$

$$P(0.08) = \frac{50}{1.08^8} + \frac{1,050}{1.08^{10}} = 513.367.$$

(b) Using the first-order Taylor expansion:

$$P(r + \Delta r) \approx P(r) + \frac{\partial P}{\partial r} \Delta r = P(r) - \Delta r \sum_{k=1}^{K} \frac{t_k C_k}{(1+r)^{t_k+1}}$$

$$= P(0.07) - (\Delta r) \left(\frac{50 \times 8}{1.07^9} + \frac{1,050 \times 10}{1.07^{11}} \right)$$

$$= 562.867 - (\Delta r)(5{,}206.048).$$

When the rate changes to 6%, $\Delta r = -0.01$, and we get
$P(0.06) \approx 614.928$. When it changes to 8%, $\Delta r = 0.01$, and we
get $P(0.08) \approx 510.807$.

(c) Using the second-order Taylor expansion:

$$P(r + \Delta r) \approx P(r) + \frac{\partial P}{\partial r} \Delta r + \frac{1}{2} \frac{\partial^2 P}{\partial r^2} (\Delta r)^2$$

$$= P(r) - \Delta r \sum_{k=1}^{K} \frac{t_k C_k}{(1+r)^{t_k+1}} + \frac{(\Delta r)^2}{2} \sum_{k=1}^{K} \frac{t_k(t_k+1)C_k}{(1+r)^{t_k+2}}$$

$$= P(0.07) - (\Delta r) \left(\frac{50 \times 8}{1.07^9} + \frac{1,050 \times 10}{1.07^{11}} \right)$$

$$+ \frac{(\Delta r)^2}{2} \left(\frac{50 \times 8 \times 9}{1.07^{10}} + \frac{1,050 \times 10 \times 11}{1.07^{12}} \right)$$

$$= 562.867 - (\Delta r)(5{,}206.048) + \frac{(\Delta r)^2}{2}(53{,}316.78).$$

If the rate changes to 6%, $\Delta r = -0.01$, and we get $P(0.06) \approx 617.594$.
When it changes to 8%, $\Delta r = 0.01$, and we get $P(0.08) \approx 513.473$.

Example 11.5 Consider a risk-free bond that matures in one year. It will pay a coupon of 50 in 6 months, and another coupon of 50 in 1 year, together with the repayment of the face value of 1,000. Suppose that the current term structure of interest rates is flat at 7%, compounded continuously.

(a) Determine the current price of the bond, as well as the prices if the interest rate were either 6.5% or 7.5%.
(b) Use a first-order Taylor expansion to approximate the price of the bond if the term structure of interest rates shifts in parallel to cither 6.5% or 7.5%.
(c) Use a second-order Taylor expansion to approximate the price of the bond if the term structure of interest rates shifts in parallel to either 6.5% or 7.5%.

Solution 11.5

(a) The price of the bond is computed as the present value of the cash flows.

$$P(r) = \sum_{k=1}^{K} C_{t_k} \exp(-r \times t_k) = 50 \exp(-0.5r) + 1{,}050 \exp(-r). \quad (11.6)$$

This gives the following prices at the given rates:

$$P(0.07) = 50 \exp(-0.5 \times 0.07) + 1{,}050 \exp(-0.07) = 1{,}027.29,$$

$$P(0.065) = 50 \exp(-0.5 \times 0.065) + 1{,}050 \exp(-0.065) = 1{,}032.322,$$

$$P(0.075) = 50 \exp(-0.5 \times 0.075) + 1{,}050 \exp(-0.075) = 1{,}022.29.$$

(b) Using the first-order Taylor expansion:

$$P(r + \Delta r) \approx P(r) + \frac{\partial P}{\partial r} \Delta r = P(r) - \Delta r \sum_{k=1}^{K} t_k C_k \exp(-r \times t_k)$$

$$= P(0.07) - (\Delta r)(25 \exp(-0.035) + 1{,}050 \exp(-0.07))$$

$$= 1{,}027.29 - (\Delta r)(1{,}003.154).$$

When the rate changes to 6.5%, $\Delta r = -0.005$, and we get $P(0.065) \approx 1{,}032.31$. When it changes to 7.5%, $\Delta r = 0.005$, and we get $P(0.075) \approx 1{,}022.278$.

(c) Using the second-order Taylor expansion:

$$P(r + \Delta r)$$

$$\approx P(r) + \frac{\partial P}{\partial r} \Delta r + \frac{1}{2} \frac{\partial^2 P}{\partial r^2} (\Delta r)^2$$

$$= P(r) - \Delta r \sum_{k=1}^{K} t_k C_k \exp(-r \times t_k) + \frac{(\Delta r)^2}{2} \sum_{k=1}^{K} t_k^2 C_k \exp(-r t_k)$$

$$= P(0.07) - (\Delta r)(0.5 \times 50 \times \exp(-0.5 \times 0.07) + 1{,}050 \exp(-0.07))$$

$$+ \frac{(\Delta r)^2}{2} \left(0.5^2 \times 50^2 \times \exp(-0.5 \times 0.07) + 1{,}050 \exp(-0.07) \right)$$

$$= 1{,}027.29 - (\Delta r)(1{,}003.154) + \frac{(\Delta r)^2}{2} (991.0836).$$

Again, if the rate changes to 6.5%, $\Delta r = -0.005$, and we get $P(0.065) \approx$ 1,032.32. When it changes to 7.5%, $\Delta r = 0.005$, and we get $P(0.075) \approx$ 1,022.29.

We see that once again the second-order approximations are more accurate than the first-order approximations. All approximations are more accurate when the change in the interest rate Δr is smaller. Finally, the first-order approximation is more accurate – even on a percentage basis – when the cash flows are to be received sooner.

11.4.1 Duration

Consider a series of cash flows, with C_k received at time t_k, $k = 1, \ldots, K$. The **Macaulay duration** of the cash flows is defined to be:

$$M = \frac{\sum_{k=1}^{K} t_k C_k v(t_k)}{\sum_{k=1}^{K} C_k v(t_k)}. \tag{11.7}$$

The denominator is the present value of the cash flows. The numerator is the sum of the present values multiplied by the payment time, for all the cash flows. Assuming that the cash flows are all positive, if we define weights p_k:

$$p_k = \frac{C_k v(t_k)}{\sum_{j=1}^{K} C_j v(t_j)}, \tag{11.8}$$

then we see that $p_k \geq 0$ and $\sum_{k=1}^{K} p_k = 1$. The interpretation is that p_k is the proportion of the total present value contributed by the cash flow at time t_k. Furthermore, we have:

$$M = \sum_{k=1}^{K} p_k t_k, \tag{11.9}$$

which gives duration as the weighted average time that cash flows are received, where the weights are the present values of the cash flows.

Example 11.6 Consider a (default risk-free) bond that matures in one year. It will pay a coupon of 50 in 6 months, and another coupon of 50 in 1 year, together with the repayment of the face value of 1,000. Suppose that the current term structure of interest rates is flat at 7%, compounded continuously. Calculate the Macaulay duration of the bond.

Solution 11.6 This is the bond from example (11.5), for which we have already seen the price to be 1,027.29. The present value of the coupon payment received in six months is $50 \exp(-0.07 \times 0.5) = 48.28$, and the present value of the final payment of principal and interest is $1{,}050 \exp(-0.07) = 979.01$. So, the Macaulay duration of the bond is:

$$0.5 \times \frac{48.28}{1{,}027.29} + 1 \times \frac{979.01}{1{,}027.29} = 0.9765. \tag{11.10}$$

We observe that the duration is close to one, because the bulk of the cash from the bond – even in present value terms – is received at $t = 1$. However, it is not exactly one, because some of the cash from the bond is received in six months.

The **modified duration** of a stream of cash flows with value $P(r)$, where r is compounded n times per year, is defined to be

$$M_n = -\frac{P'(r)}{P(r)} = -\frac{d}{dr} \log P(r). \tag{11.11}$$

Unlike Macaulay duration, the definition of modified duration depends on the compounding frequency, n. For annual compounding,

$$P(r) = \sum_{k=1}^{K} C_k (1 + r)^{-t_k}, \tag{11.12}$$

$$P'(r) = -\sum_{k=1}^{K} C_k t_k (1 + r)^{-(t_k+1)} = -\frac{1}{1+r} \sum_{k=1}^{K} C_k t_k (1 + r)^{-t_k}, \tag{11.13}$$

so that the modified duration satisfies:

$$M_1 = \frac{1}{1+r}M, \tag{11.14}$$

where M is the Macaulay duration and the subscript 1 indicates that we are using annual compounding. For compounding n times per year, we have

$$P(r) = \sum_{k=1}^{K} C_k \left(1 + \frac{r}{n}\right)^{-nt_k}, \tag{11.15}$$

$$P'(r) = -\sum_{k=1}^{K} C_k t_k \left(1 + \frac{r}{n}\right)^{-nt_k-1} = -\frac{1}{1+\frac{r}{n}} \sum_{k=1}^{K} C_k t_k \left(1 + \frac{r}{n}\right)^{-nt_k}, \tag{11.16}$$

and we have that:

$$M_n = \frac{1}{1+\frac{r}{n}}M. \tag{11.17}$$

Letting $n \to \infty$ in the above formula, we find that for continuous compounding, we have that $M_\infty = M$. In particular,

$$P(r) = \sum_{k=1}^{K} C_k \exp(-rt_k), \tag{11.18}$$

$$P'(r) = -\sum_{k=1}^{K} t_k C_k \exp(-rt_k), \tag{11.19}$$

from which $M_\infty = M$ follows immediately.

Example 11.7 An investor is to receive a stream of cash flows consisting of 100 at time $t_1 = 1$, 200 at $t_2 = 2$, and 300 at $t_3 = 3$. The interest rate is 5%. Calculate the Macaulay duration and the modified duration if the rate is compounded (a) annually, (b) semi-annually, and (c) continuously.

Solution 11.7

(a) The Macaulay duration is:

$$M = \frac{100(1.05)^{-1} + 2 \times 200(1.05)^{-2} + 3 \times 300(1.05)^{-3}}{100(1.05)^{-1} + 200(1.05)^{-2} + 300(1.05)^{-3}} = 2.310, \tag{11.20}$$

and the modified duration is therefore $M_1 = M/(1.05) = 2.196$.

(b) With semi-annual compounding, the Macaulay duration is:

$$M = \frac{100(1.025)^{-2} + 2 \times 200(1.025)^{-4} + 3 \times 300(1.025)^{-6}}{100(1.025)^{-2} + 200(1.025)^{-4} + 300(1.025)^{-6}} = 2.306,$$

(11.21)

and the modified duration is $M_2 = M/(1.025) = 2.249$.

(c) With continuous compounding, the Macaulay duration is:

$$M = \frac{100\exp(-0.05) + 2 \times 200\exp(-0.05 \times 2) + 3 \times 300\exp(-0.05 \times 3)}{100\exp(-0.05) + 200\exp(-0.05 \times 2) + 300\exp(-0.05 \times 3)}$$

$$= 2.305,$$

(11.22)

and the modified duration is $M_\infty = M = 2.305$. □

Notice that the value for Macaulay duration changed in the solution to each of the parts above. This is because we kept the interest rate constant, but changed the compounding frequency, which altered the discount factors that appear in the definition of Macaulay duration.

Modified duration can be used as a measure of sensitivity of the price of a security to changes in the interest rate. In particular, $M_n = -P'(r)/P(r)$ gives the relative change in the price of the security per unit change in the interest rate, where the interest rate is compounded every $\frac{1}{n}$ years. This is also evident in the fact that the first-order Taylor series approximation for the new price of the security given a change Δr in the interest rate can be rewritten as:

$$P(r + \Delta r) \approx P(r) + P'(r)\Delta r = P(r) - P(r)M_n\Delta r, \qquad (11.23)$$

or, more compactly,

$$\Delta P \approx -P \times M_n \times \Delta r. \qquad (11.24)$$

Another reason that it is convenient to work with duration is the following. The duration of a portfolio is the weighted sum of the durations of the instruments contained in it, with the weights given by the fractions of the total portfolio value invested in each instrument. To see this, let $P_1(r)$ and $P_2(r)$ be the values of two instruments making up a portfolio, so that the total portfolio value is $P(r) = P_1(r) + P_2(r)$, and $w_i(r) = P_i(r)/P(r)$ is the fraction of market value invested in each instrument, for $i = 1, 2$. Then:

$$\frac{d}{dr}\log(P_1(r) + P_2(r)) = \frac{P_1'(r) + P_2'(r)}{P_1(r) + P_2(r)}$$

$$= \frac{P_1(r)}{P_1(r) + P_2(r)} \times \frac{P_1'(r)}{P_1(r)} + \frac{P_2(r)}{P_1(r) + P_2(r)} \times \frac{P_2'(r)}{P_2(r)}$$

$$= w_1(r)\frac{P_1'(r)}{P_1(r)} + w_2(r)\frac{P_2'(r)}{P_2(r)},$$

so that the portfolio duration is $w_1 M_n^{(1)} + w_2 M_n^{(2)}$ where $M_n^{(j)}$ is the modified duration of instrument j. The above calculation generalizes immediately to any portfolio consisting of N instruments.

11.4.2 Convexity

Duration is a first-order sensitivity measure of the relative change in value of a financial security due to a change in the interest rate. Convexity is the analogous measure of second-order sensitivity. Again, considering a series of cash flows, with C_k received at time t_k, $k = 1, \ldots, K$, with value $P(r)$ depending on the interest rate r (and assuming a flat term structure that only makes parallel shifts), the convexity is defined to be:

$$C = \frac{P''(r)}{P(r)}. \tag{11.25}$$

The second-order Taylor series approximation for the new value of the security given a change Δr in the interest rate can be written as:

$$P(r + \Delta r) \approx P(r) + P'(r)\Delta r + \tfrac{1}{2}P''(r)(\Delta r)^2$$
$$= P(r)\left(1 - M_n \, \Delta r + \tfrac{1}{2}C(\Delta r)^2\right), \tag{11.26}$$

or, more compactly,

$$\Delta P \approx -P \times M_n \times \Delta r + \tfrac{1}{2}P \times C \times (\Delta r)^2. \tag{11.27}$$

Similarly to modified duration, it can be shown that the portfolio convexity is the weighted sum of the convexities of the instruments in the portfolio, with the weights given by the fractions of wealth invested in each instrument.

11.5 Hedging Interest Rate Sensitive Portfolios

In this section, we discuss some strategies for hedging portfolios whose values are sensitive to the term structure of interest rates.

11.5.1 Immunization

A first approach to hedging interest rate risk is to match the duration of the assets to that of the liabilities, with the idea that this hedge should make the portfolio surplus relatively insensitive to interest rate changes. While this intuition is on the right track, it is somewhat imprecise, as demonstrated by the following examples.

Example 11.8 An insurance company has a portfolio of liabilities with a modified duration of 3.5 and current value of $V_L = 10$ million, and assets with modified duration 5 and value $V_A = 12$ million. Calculate the approximate change in the value of the surplus if the interest rate increases by 10 basis points.

Solution 11.8 The surplus is $S = V_A - V_L$, and using the duration approximation,

$$\Delta S = \Delta V_A - \Delta V_L \approx 0.001(3.5(10) - 5(12)) = -0.025, \qquad (11.28)$$

where the amounts are expressed in millions. The approximate change is a decrease in the surplus of 25,000.

Example 11.9 An insurance company has assets worth 12 million and liabilities worth 10 million, both with modified duration 22. Determine the approximate change in the value of the surplus if the interest rate decreases by one basis point.

Solution 11.9 Repeating the approach from the previous example, we have

$$\Delta S = \Delta V_A - \Delta V_L \approx -0.0001 \times 22 \times (10 - 12) = 0.0044, \qquad (11.29)$$

so that the surplus will increase by approximately 4,400. Although this is small, relative to the values assets and liabilities separately, it shows that duration matching does not provide a perfect hedge. $\square$

In general, let us denote the modified duration of the assets by M_A and the modified duration of the liabilities by M_L. The value of the surplus is $V_A - V_L$, where V_A is the value of the assets and V_L is the value of the liabilities. Using the first-order Taylor approximation as above, we have

$$\Delta S = \Delta V_A - \Delta V_L \approx \Delta r \times (M_L \times V_L - M_A \times V_A). \qquad (11.30)$$

For the surplus to be relatively insensitive to interest rate changes, we would like to have $\Delta S = 0$. From the above, the condition for this to be satisfied (at least to first order) is

$$M_L V_L = M_A V_A. \qquad (11.31)$$

This is referred to as the portfolio immunization equation, and a portfolio that satisfies it is said to be immunized. It guarantees that we have $\Delta S = 0$ to first order. However, if we use the second order approximation, we have

$$\Delta S \approx \Delta r(M_L V_L - M_A V_A) + \tfrac{(\Delta r)^2}{2}(C_A V_A - C_L V_L), \qquad (11.32)$$

where C_A and C_L are the convexity of the assets and liabilities respectively. We see that if $M_L V_L = M_A V_A$ and $V_A C_A \geq V_L C_L$, then $\Delta S \geq 0$ (to second order) regardless of the sign of Δr. This seems impressive at first glance; no matter what the direction of the change in the interest rate, the value of the surplus cannot go down. So, if a portfolio of assets and liabilities satisfies the two conditions

$$(1) \quad M_L \, V_L = M_A \, V_A,$$

$$(2) \quad V_A \, C_A \geq V_L \, C_L,$$

then a small change in the interest rate, in either direction, will lead, in principle, to a small increase in the surplus. A portfolio that satisfies these conditions is said to be **Redington immunized**. There are issues, however, with this result, which appears too good to be true. The main problem is that the positive impact on surplus relies on a parallel shift in interest rates, which is not generally how interest rate changes occur. Furthermore, since we are using Taylor expansions, our results come with an error term, which is small for small $|\Delta r|$, but which becomes significant for larger interest rate shifts.

Although our formulation of immunization has assumed constant rates of interest by term (i.e. a flat term structure), it can be applied to non-flat term structures as we show in the next section.

11.5.2 Key Rate Duration and Convexity

As we have seen, rates of interest are often far from constant across maturities, instead being represented as a continuous function of the term. In practice, the continuous structure is often replaced by a finite collection of **key rates** r_{T_j}, for times T_j, $j = 1, \ldots, m$. For example, one may consider key rates at 3 months, and 1, 2, 3, 5, 7, 10, 15, 20, 25, and 30 years. For discounting cash flows that occur between the key rate dates, from, say time t where $T_j \leq t \leq T_{j+1}$, we can interpolate. For example, using linear interpolation we have:

$$r_t \approx r_{T_j} \times \alpha_t + r_{T_{j+1}} \times (1 - \alpha_t) \text{ where } \alpha_t = \left(\frac{T_{j+1} - t}{T_{j+1} - T_j} \right). \quad (11.33)$$

In this way, we can view the value of a portfolio as a function of the key rates:

$$P = P(r_{T_1}, \ldots, r_{T_m}). \quad (11.34)$$

For simplicity, we write $r = (r_{T_1}, \ldots, r_{T_m})$. We consider the first order Taylor series approximation for changes in the value of P when the key rates move:

$$\Delta P(r) = P(r + \Delta r) - P(r) \approx \sum_{j=1}^{m} \Delta r_{T_j} \frac{\partial P}{\partial r_{T_j}}. \quad (11.35)$$

The **key-rate duration**[2] with respect to the jth key rate, r_{T_j}, is

$$M^{(j)} = -\frac{1}{P(r)}\frac{\partial P}{\partial r_{T_j}}.$$

The second order approximation is

$$\Delta P = P(r + \Delta r) - P(r) \approx \sum_{j=1}^{m} \Delta r_{T_j}\frac{\partial P}{\partial r_{T_j}} + \frac{1}{2}\sum_{k,j=1}^{m} \Delta r_{T_k}\Delta r_{T_j}\frac{\partial^2 P}{\partial r_{T_k}\partial r_{T_j}}.$$

$$(11.36)$$

As above, one could consider hedging a portfolio of liabilities with a portfolio of assets so that $\Delta S(r) = \Delta V_A(r) - \Delta V_L(r)$ is zero to first order, or non-negative to second order. With a large number of key rates, the number of terms in the above expressions (particularly the second order expansion) gets to be very large. It is possible to only consider certain terms in the expansion to approximate ΔS. For example, one may only consider the pure second partial derivatives in the second order expansion, or use a subset of the available key rates rather than the full set.

Example 11.10 Suppose that interest rates can be determined as a function of two key rates. The short rate, r_S is the rate applicable at time T_S, and the long rate r_L is the rate applicable at time T_L. For times between T_S and T_L, the rate is determined by linear interpolation, such that

$$r_t = \alpha_t \times r_S + (1 - \alpha_t) \times r_L, \text{ where } \alpha_t = \frac{T_L - t}{T_L - T_S}.$$

All rates are compounded continuously.

(a) Derive an expression for the second order approximation of ΔP for a portfolio with cash flows C_k at t_k, for $k = 1, 2, \ldots, n$, and where $T_S \leq t_k \leq T_L$ for all k.

(b) You are given that:

 (i) $r_S = 0.035$, $r_L = 0.065$, $T_S = 1$, and $T_L = 11$.
 (ii) Cash flows are 400 at time 1, 100 at times 2, 5, and 7, and 2,000 at time 10.

   Estimate the change in the portfolio value given that the short rate increases by 40 basis points, and the long rate decreases by 10 basis points.

---

[2] This is a modified duration at the key rates.

Solution 11.10

(a) $P(r) = \sum_{k=1}^{n} C_{t_k} e^{-t_k r_{t_k}} = \sum_{k=1}^{n} C_{t_k} \exp\left(-t_k\left(\alpha_{t_k} r_S + (1 - \alpha_{t_k}) r_L\right)\right),$

$\dfrac{\partial P}{\partial r_S} = \sum_{k=1}^{n} -t_k \, \alpha_{t_k} \, C_{t_k} \, e^{-t_k r_{t_k}},$

$\dfrac{\partial P}{\partial r_L} = \sum_{k=1}^{n} -t_k (1 - \alpha_{t_k}) \, C_{t_k} \, e^{-t_k r_{t_k}},$

$\dfrac{\partial^2 P}{\partial r_S^2} = \sum_{k=1}^{n} t_k^2 \, \alpha_{t_k}^2 \, C_{t_k} \, e^{-t_k r_{t_k}},$

$\dfrac{\partial^2 P}{\partial r_L^2} = \sum_{k=1}^{n} t_k^2 \, (1 - \alpha_{t_k})^2 \, C_{t_k} \, e^{-t_k r_{t_k}},$

$\dfrac{\partial^2 P}{\partial r_S \, \partial r_L} = \sum_{k=1}^{n} t_k^2 \, \alpha_{t_k} (1 - \alpha_{t_k}) \, C_{t_k} \, e^{-t_k r_{t_k}},$

$\Delta P \approx \dfrac{\partial P}{\partial r_S} \Delta r_S + \dfrac{\partial P}{\partial r_L} \Delta r_L$

$\qquad + \dfrac{1}{2} \left\{ \dfrac{\partial^2 P}{\partial r_S^2} (\Delta r_S)^2 + \dfrac{\partial^2 P}{\partial r_L^2} (\Delta r_L)^2 + 2 \dfrac{\partial^2 P}{\partial r_S \, \partial r_L} \Delta r_S \Delta r_L \right\}.$

(b) Now we have

k	t_k	α_{t_k}	r_{t_k}	$C_{t_k} e^{-r_{t_k}}$
1	1	1.0	0.035	386.24
2	2	0.9	0.038	92.68
3	5	0.6	0.047	79.06
4	7	0.4	0.053	69.00
5	10	0.1	0.062	1,075.89

which gives us

$P(r) = 1{,}702.74,$

$\dfrac{\partial P}{\partial r_S}(r) = -2{,}059.34, \qquad \dfrac{\partial P}{\partial r_L}(r) = -10{,}149.50,$

$\dfrac{\partial^2 P}{\partial r_S^2}(r) = 3{,}014.93, \qquad \dfrac{\partial^2 P}{\partial r_L^2}(r) = 88{,}684.17, \qquad \dfrac{\partial^2 P}{\partial r_S \, \partial r_L}(r) = 11{,}002.20.$

We are also given $\Delta r_S = 0.004$ and $\Delta r_L = -0.001$. Using these values in the equation for ΔP from (a), gives $\Delta P \approx 1.94$.   □

11.6 Behaviour of the Interest Rate Term Structure

The basic duration and convexity measures assume a flat term structure of interest rates, so that (i) the same interest rate is used rate to discount all cash flows and (ii) the interest rate term structure moves only in parallel. As we have seen, in real markets the term structure of interest rates is not flat. In this section, we will discuss the behaviour of the term structure in more detail. We will begin by looking at typical shapes of the term structure of interest rates.

Following this, we will look at principal component analysis, a statistical technique that can be used to explain the movements of the term structure of interest rates in terms of a small number of financially meaningful factors.

11.6.1 Common Term Structure Shapes

There are three commonly seen shapes of the term structure of interest rates: increasing, decreasing (inverted) and flat/humped. Figure 11.2 presents examples of each of these.

The **increasing term structure** is the shape that the term structure is expected to present in a normal market environment.

With an increasing term structure, shorter term loans earn a lower interest rate than longer term loans. This term structure shape is profitable for the traditional business model for a bank, in which the institution borrows for short terms (e.g., using demand deposits or short-term certificates of deposit) and then lends the proceeds of this borrowing for longer term (e.g., in mortgages). It is consistent with the view that shorter term lending is safer, and should therefore have a lower rate of return than longer term lending, which is riskier. It also leads to an obvious maturity mismatch between the bank's assets and liabilities, and significant exposure to liquidity risk. The classical manifestation of this is a run on the bank, in which depositors demand immediate return of their funds, as happened to Northern Rock in 2008 during the financial crisis.

An **inverted term structure** of interest rates is often interpreted as an indication that a recession is expected and, in particular, that expectations are that inflation will decrease. To understand this, let us consider a simplified situation in which the term structure of real interest rates is constant. We recall

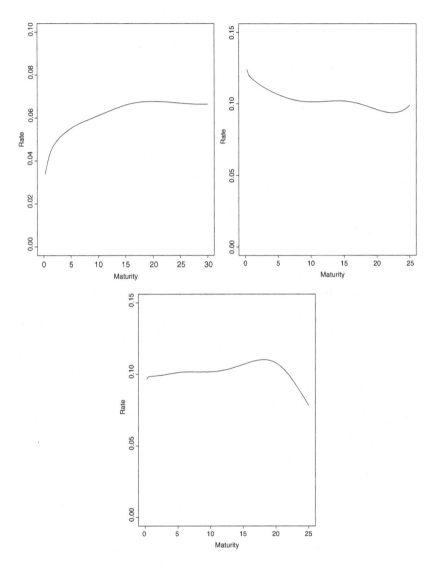

Figure 11.2 Canadian interest rates: increasing term structure (18 July 1997) (top-left), inverted term structure (23 February 1990) (top-right), and humped term structure (10 August 1988) (bottom).

the **Fisher relationship** between the inflation rate i, the real interest rate u, and the nominal interest rate r:

$$(1 + r) = (1 + u)(1 + i). \tag{11.37}$$

Let r_1 be the nominal interest rate for borrowing for one year, r_2 the interest rate for borrowing over two years, i_1 be expected inflation rate for the first year, and i_2 the expected inflation rate for the second year. From the Fisher relationship, we would expect:

$$(1 + r_1) \approx (1 + u)(1 + i_1), \tag{11.38}$$

$$(1 + r_2)^2 \approx (1 + u)^2(1 + i_1)(1 + i_2). \tag{11.39}$$

By rearranging the above equations, it is easy to see that $r_1 \gg r_2$ implies that $i_2 \ll i_1$, i.e. decreasing nominal rates of interest imply decreasing inflation expectations.

Finally, the **humped term structure** of interest rates is usually interpreted as indicating a large degree of uncertainty regarding future economic conditions in general, and inflation in particular.

11.6.2 Movements of the Interest Rate Term Structure

We have seen that the term structure of interest rates tends to take on a small number of characteristic shapes. How the term structure tends to fluctuate and move between these different shapes is the topic of this section.

As discussed above, we often analyse the term structure of interest rates by studying the rates for a fixed collection of maturities $T_k, k = 1, \ldots, K$, and the interest rates corresponding to these maturities are referred to as key rates. We denote by $r_{T_k}(t)$ the kth key rate observed at time t. Assume that we observe a time series of the key rates, with a time step of length h, for n years, that is, for $t = 0, h, 2h, \ldots, n$. Then, we can form the time series of relative changes for each of the key rates as:

$$X_{k,t} = \frac{r_{T_k}(t + h) - r_{T_k}(t)}{r_{T_k}(t)}, \quad t = 0, h, 2h, \ldots, n - h; \quad k = 1, 2, \ldots, K. \tag{11.40}$$

We emphasize that we are keeping the tenure of the rates constant, so if one of our key rates is the one-year rate and we use monthly time steps (i.e. $h = \frac{1}{12}$), then $r_{T_k}(0)$ is today's rate for borrowing for one year, and $r_{T_k}(h)$ will be the rate observed one month from now for borrowing for one-year, so that the maturity of that borrowing will be 13 months from today.

After calculating the relative changes given by equation (11.40), we have a time series of $M = n/h$ observations of the K dimensional vector of relative key rate changes. We treat these as a sample from a K dimensional random vector and try to understand the main factors driving its variation by using **principal component analysis** (PCA). PCA provides a way of understanding the variations of a random vector by decomposing it into the variations in a set of orthogonal directions. In order to carry out PCA, consider a K-dimensional random vector X, with mean vector μ, and covariance matrix V. Since V is a real, symmetric, positive semi-definite matrix, we know from linear algebra that it has K real eigenvalues, $\lambda_1 \geq \lambda_2 \geq \cdots \geq \lambda_K \geq 0$, with corresponding eigenvectors w_k, and, furthermore, the eigenvectors can be chosen to be orthonormal. That is, we have

$$V w_k = \lambda_k w_k, \quad k = 1, \ldots, K, \tag{11.41}$$

$$w_k^T w_j = \begin{cases} 0 & k \neq j, \\ 1 & k = j. \end{cases} \tag{11.42}$$

If we let W be the matrix whose kth column is w_k, then, in a more compact form, we have $V W = W \Lambda$, where Λ is the diagonal matrix with kth diagonal entry equal to λ_k. The orthonormality conditions can be written as $W W^T = W^T W = I$.

The kth principal component is $y_k = w_k^T (X - \mu)$. The covariance between the kth and jth principal components is

$$\begin{aligned} \mathrm{cov}\left(w_k^T (X - \mu), w_j^T (X - \mu) \right) &= \mathrm{cov}(w_k^T X, w_j^T X) \\ &= w_k^T V w_j \end{aligned}$$

$$\Rightarrow \mathrm{cov}\left(w_k^T (X - \mu), w_j^T (X - \mu) \right) = \begin{cases} 0 & k \neq j, \\ \lambda_k & k = j. \end{cases}$$

In particular, the principal components are uncorrelated, and the variance of the kth principal component is λ_k. If we consider the total variability of the random vector X to be the sum of the variances of its components, we have

$$\mathrm{Var}(X) = \sum_{k=1}^{K} V_{kk} = \mathrm{trace}(X) = \sum_{k=1}^{K} \lambda_k,$$

using the fact that the trace of a matrix is the sum of its eigenvectors. The fraction of the variation in the direction of the kth principal component is

$$c_k = \frac{\lambda_k}{\sum_{j=1}^{K} \lambda_j}, \tag{11.43}$$

and the fraction of the variation explained by the first k principal components is

$$C_k = \sum_{j=1}^{k} c_j = \frac{\sum_{j=1}^{k} \lambda_j}{\sum_{j=1}^{K} \lambda_j}. \tag{11.44}$$

Table 11.1. *Summary statistics for US interest rate data:*
2 January 1991 to 21 May 2021

Key Rate Tenure	Mean	Standard Deviation
1 year	1.725×10^{-4}	0.0398
2 years	2.263×10^{-4}	0.0383
3 years	1.957×10^{-4}	0.0345
5 years	0.902×10^{-4}	0.0276
7 years	0.374×10^{-4}	0.0236
10 years	0.007×10^{-4}	0.0204
15 years	-0.306×10^{-4}	0.0174
20 years	-0.483×10^{-4}	0.0156
25 years	-0.545×10^{-4}	0.0146
30 years	-0.452×10^{-4}	0.0145

Multiplying both sides of $Y = W^T(X - \mu)$ by W, we obtain:

$$WY = WW^T(X - \mu)$$
$$\Rightarrow X = WY + \mu,$$

where we have used the orthonormality condition $WW^T = I$.

PCA can be used for dimension reduction by keeping only the most important principal components, defined as those that explain a substantial proportion of the total variation of X. If we use only the first k principal components, we obtain:

$$X_i = \mu_i + \sum_{j=1}^{K} W_{ij} Y_j \approx \mu_i + \sum_{j=1}^{k} W_{ij} Y_j. \qquad (11.45)$$

It is easier to work with the smaller number of factors Y_j, $j = 1, \ldots, k$ instead of the K dimensional random vector X. Furthermore, the principal components Y_j, $j \leq k$ often have meaningful economic interpretations when applied to financial data.

To illustrate the use of principal components to analyse financial data and perform dimension reduction, we consider daily relative changes for a set of key rates on the US term structure of interest rates from 2 January 1991 to 21 May 2021. This yields a total of 7,581 observations of relative changes of our 10 key rates. Summary statistics are provided in Table 11.1 and a heat map of the correlation matrix is given in Figure 11.3. As one would expect, the

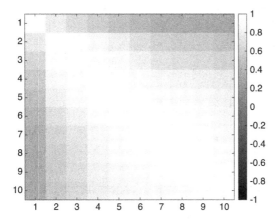

Figure 11.3 Correlation matrix for the US interest rate data described in Table 11.1

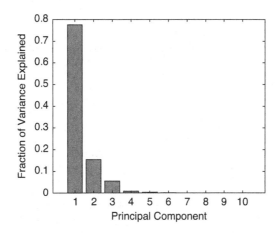

Figure 11.4 Fractions of total variation explained by each of the principal components for the US interest rate data described in Table 11.1

rate changes are all positively correlated, with particularly high correlations for rates in the same section of the curve.

To perform PCA, we calculate the spectral decomposition $\widehat{V} = W\Lambda W^T$ of the empirical covariance matrix.[3] The fractions of the total variation explained by each of the principal components are given in Figure 11.4. We see that

---

[3] PCA can also be performed using the correlation matrix. See Alexander (2008) for a discussion and financial examples.

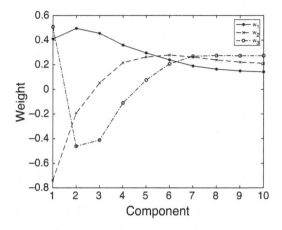

Figure 11.5 Weights of the first three eigenvectors for PCA of the US interest rate data described in Table 11.1

the first principal component explains around 77% of the total variation in the interest rate data, the second principal component just over 15%, and the third principal component around 5%. The variation explained by the remaining principal components is negligible. Depending on the application and the needs of the institution, we can explain a large proportion of the total variation of the interest rate data and work with a much more tractable model by using only a handful of principal components.

Figure 11.5 plots the eigenvectors corresponding to the first three principal components. A pattern emerges that is characteristic of the analysis of interest rate data in many markets. The first eigenvector has all weights positive and roughly the same size, and corresponds to a parallel shift of all rates in the term structure. The second eigenvector has negative weights for short maturities, and then positive weights for longer maturities; it corresponds to a change in the slope of the term structure. Finally, the third eigenvector has positive weights on the long and short ends of the term structure and negative weights in the middle; it drives changes in the convexity of the term structure of interest rates.

11.7 Notes and Further Reading

Fabozzi and Pollack (2005) gives a comprehensive coverage of fixed income markets. A good reference for the pricing of interest rate derivative securities is Brigo and Mercurio (2007).

More information on interest rate risk management can be found in Veronesi (2010) and Embrechts et al. (2013), which also contains an introduction to principal component analysis. A detailed discussion of principal component analysis and related methods is given in Jolliffe (2002).

The multi-volume work by Andersen and Piterbarg (2010) covers many aspects of interest rate modelling.

The original work on immunization was developed by Redington (1952). His immunization algorithm is still in widespread use in asset-liability management.

The term structure data used to create Figures 11.1 to 11.5 was retrieved from the Federal Reserve website.

11.8 Exercises

Exercise 11.1 (a) What is the Macaulay duration of a zero-coupon bond with maturity T?

(b) Determine the modified duration of a zero-coupon bond with maturity T under different assumptions on the compounding frequency of the interest rate r.

Exercise 11.2 Consider a bullet bond that pays regular coupons at the rate c on a principal amount F, together with the repayment of the principal at the final time.

(a) Show that the duration of the bond is a decreasing function of the coupon rate c.

(b) Give a financial interpretation of this result.

Exercise 11.3 In a plain vanilla swap, two counterparties exchange payments based on a fixed face amount F. Counterparty A will pay to counterparty B the amount $\kappa \times F \times h$, at times $h, 2h, \ldots Nh$, where the fixed rate r is set in the swap contract. Counterparty B will pay to counterparty A the amount $r_h(t - h) \times F \times h$, at the same times, where $r_h(t)$ is the rate observed in the market at time t for borrowing until time $t + h$.

(a) Determine the value of the swap contract to A. (Hint: Think of the swap as the exchange of the payments of a fixed rate bond for those of a floating rate bond. You can imagine that the two counterparties exchange equal payments of size F at the terminal time Nh.)

(b) Find a formula for the swap rate, i.e. the value of κ that makes the value of the swap to both counterparties equal to zero.

Exercise 11.4 Suppose that you have a portfolio consisting of a 3-year zero coupon bond with face value $5,000 and a 10-year zero coupon bond with face value $10,000. The term structure of interest rates is flat at the continuously compounded rate of 6%. Use first and second order Taylor approximations to determine the approximate changes in the value of your portfolio if interest rates increase or decrease by 50 basis points.

Exercise 11.5 The term structure of interest rates is flat, with all yields equal to 5% per annum effective. An insurance company faces a liability of $200,000 due in two years, and another liability of $800,000 due in seven years. The company is hedging these liabilities with $78,539.26 invested in the four-year zero-coupon bond and $671,411.70 invested in the 6-year zero coupon bond. Determine whether or not each of Redington's conditions for immunization is satisfied by the company's strategy.

Exercise 11.6 The term structure of interest rates is currently flat at 5% per year effective. Your company faces liabilities of 10,000 four years from now, 10,000 five years from now, and 20,000, seven years from now.

(a) Find the investments in the two year and eight year zero-coupon bonds necessary to immunize these liabilities, and verify that the resulting portfolio satisfies Reddington's conditions.
(b) After one year, the term structure has shifted to be flat at 6% per annum. Find the new weights for immunization (using the same bonds as those bought at time zero in (a)), and determine the amount of money that either can be withdrawn or must be added when constructing the new immunizing portfolio.

Exercise 11.7 Consider a firm that has employed portfolio immunization on its assets and liabilities. Is the firm subject to interest rate risk? Explain why or why not.

Exercise 11.8 An investor has liabilities of 500 due at times 2 and 5, and 1,000 due at times 11 and 15.

The investor assumes that the yield curve can be described using key rates at $T_1 = 2$, $T_2 = 10$, and $T_3 = 20$. Intermediate rates are determined by linear interpolation. Assume all rates are continuously compounded.

Currently, the key rates are $r_{T_1} = 0.022$, $r_{T_2} = 0.045$, and $r_{T_3} = 0.052$.

(a) Calculate the present value of the liabilities.
(b) Calculate the key rate durations of the liabilities with respect to the three key rates.

(c) Calculate the estimated change in the value of the liabilities based on the first order Taylor expansion of the present value equation, assuming that:

   (i) the key rates all fall by 50 basis points;

  (ii) the 2-year key rate falls by 70 basis points, and the other two rates fall by 40 basis points; and

 (iii) the 2-year key rate falls by 30 basis points, the 10-year key rate falls by 20 basis points, and the 20-year key rate increases by 10 basis points.

(d) Construct a portfolio of zero coupon bonds, maturing at the key-rate dates, which has the same present value as the liabilities, and the same total key rate duration. How well does this asset portfolio hedge against the interest rate movements examined in (c)?

12

Credit Risk

12.1 Summary

In this chapter, we discuss the ways that credit risk arises and how it can be modelled and mitigated. First, we consider the various types of contractual forms for loans and other obligations. We then discuss credit derivatives, which are contracts with payoffs that are contingent on credit events. We consider credit risk models based on the three fundamental components – probability of default, proportionate loss given default, and exposure at default. We consider models of default for individual firms, including the role of credit rating agencies, structural models, which are based on the underlying processes causing default, and reduced form models which are based on the empirical information, with less emphasis on an underlying story. This is followed by a description of portfolio credit risk models, where the joint credit risk of multiple entities is the modelling objective.

Credit risk is one of the oldest and most important types of financial risk. As a result, there is a huge literature on various aspects of its measurement and management, and we can only scratch the surface of this important topic. Suggestions for further reading are given at the end of the chapter.

12.2 Types of Credit Risk

In this section, we discuss the different types of credit risk that arise in financial markets. We begin by considering risk deriving from traditional lending arrangements, then proceed to consider counterparty credit risk and credit derivative securities. In each section, we discuss the mitigation techniques commonly employed when managing each type of credit risk. Finally, we discuss two different perspectives from which credit risk losses may be measured: default losses, which recognize credit losses only when the default of an obligor occurs; and mark-to-market losses, which reflect the current market value of all contracts subject to credit risk.

12.2.1 Lending

By the term 'lending', we designate any arrangement wherein one party (the lender) provides funds to another party (the borrower) to be paid back at a future date. There are many variations in the structuring of lending arrangements, including differences in repayment schedule (when the money is paid back), interest (the lender's compensation both for providing the funds, and for assuming the risk that they may not be paid back), and embedded optionality. Embedded options in common lending arrangements include a borrower's ability to either increase (through additional borrowing) or decrease (by prepayment) the size of the loan, and the lender's ability to cancel the loan and demand repayment (e.g., in a puttable bond). Once a lending agreement has been entered into, it constitutes an asset to the lender, which may be sold on to a third party, either directly in a secondary market, as with many corporate and government bonds and leveraged loans, or indirectly through a securitization procedure, as with **mortgage-backed securities** (MBS) and **collateralized debt obligations** (CDOs).

The following are examples of common traditional lending arrangements:

- **Zero coupon bond** – This is a bond in which there is a single payment P at the maturity of the contract. The initial price of the bond V is typically less than P, with the difference representing the interest on the loan. US Government Treasury Bills (T-Bills) are common examples of zero coupon bonds.
- **Coupon bonds** – A coupon bearing bond promises its holder a fixed stream of regular interest payments, together with a final repayment of a principal amount. The interest payments are typically expressed as a coupon rate multiplied by the principal. In practice, coupons are most often paid semi-annually. US Government Treasury Bonds (T-Bonds) are common examples of coupon bearing bonds.
- **Repos** – This is a short-term, collateralized lending arrangement. One party to the contract (the borrower) sells financial securities to the other (the lender), while at the same time entering into a commitment to buy the securities back at a later date. The difference between the two prices at which the securities are sold represents the interest on the loan. The loan is fully collateralized, since if the borrower fails to repay the loan (that is,

does not have the funds to repurchase the securities on schedule) then the lender simply keeps the financial securities.

- **Lines of credit** – This is a lending arrangement between a firm and a financial institution in which the firm can borrow and pay back funds (usually up to a pre-set limit) at their discretion. Interest is charged on the amount borrowed at any given time. A small fee may or may not be charged for any unused portion of the line of credit. Unlike the contracts described above, in a line of credit the amount lent may change through time as it is determined by the decisions of the borrower.
- **Mortgages** – A mortgage is a loan secured by real estate. Mortgages are often employed in order to purchase property, or in order to "access the equity" – that is, borrow against the value – of owned property. The principal on a mortgage is generally paid back gradually (amortized) over the life of the loan. The property serves as collateral for the loan and, if the borrower defaults on the loan, then the lender can seize the property (foreclose) and sell it in order to use the proceeds to cover the loan.

Credit risk in traditional lending is the risk that the borrower does not fully repay the funds owed to the lender. Aside from properly evaluating the ability and willingness to repay of the borrower, there are two main strategies for mitigating credit risk in traditional lending, which are often employed in conjunction:

- **Collateral** – Collateral consists of assets pledged by the borrower to the lender as security in case the loan is not paid back. For example, in a repo agreement, the securities serve as the collateral, and if the borrower defaults, then the lender can either keep the securities, or sell them to cover the losses due to the default of the loan. Similarly, the real estate serves as the collateral on a mortgage loan.
- **Covenants** – Lending contracts are legal agreements. Covenants are stipulations within these legal agreements which place restrictions on the borrower, including how they may use the funds. For example, mortgages typically require that the property be maintained in good order (so as not to erode the value of the collateral). Bond contracts may require that companies maintain certain financial ratios or avoid taking excessive risks with the proceeds of the loan. For example, in 2006, when it sought to spin off the donut shop chain Tim Horton's, Wendy's was sued by some of its bondholders, who alleged that the move would make the company too concentrated in a single business line, potentially contravening the terms of the covenant. The suit was unsuccessful and Wendy's was able to complete its planned divestment.

12.2.2 Counterparty Credit Risk

The term **counterparty credit risk** (CCR) refers to possible losses that may be incurred when a counterparty to an over-the-counter contract fails to honour its obligations. For example, suppose two financial institutions enter into an **over-the-counter** (OTC) derivative security; if one institution defaults when the contract has a positive value to the other institution, then a loss due to counterparty credit risk will occur.

There are two distinguishing features of counterparty credit risk, which set it apart from many traditional lending arrangements. First of all, the risk is **bilateral**, which is to say that both parties to the transaction bear some risk. This is in contrast to a traditional lending arrangement, in which the lender has assumed the risk that the borrower will fail to repay the loan. Second, the exposure associated with counterparty credit risk is often stochastic, and cannot be determined in advance.[1]

Consider a simple example where two banks enter into an OTC forward contract. Bank L (Long) agrees to purchase an asset from Bank S (Short) at future time T for the price K. K is set such that the initial value of the contract to both parties is zero. Let A_T be the value of the asset at maturity. At the time T if $A_T > K$, the contract has value $A_T - K$ to Bank L, and Bank L has an exposure to Bank S (Bank L will lose $A_T - K$ if Bank S defaults on the contract). Similarly, if $A_T < K$ then Bank S has an exposure of $K - A_T$ to Bank L. Therefore, at time T:

$$\text{Exposure of Bank L to Bank S} = (A_T - K)^+, \qquad (12.1)$$

$$\text{Exposure of Bank S to Bank L} = (K - A_T)^+. \qquad (12.2)$$

We see that counterparty risk is bilateral. When $A_T > K$, Bank L has an exposure to Bank S, while when $A_T < K$, Bank S has an exposure to Bank L. Furthermore, the exposure is stochastic, since the value of A_T is random.

Participants in OTC derivatives markets have used a number of risk mitigation techniques to attempt to reduce the impact of counterparty credit risk. The most important of these are netting, collateral, and the establishment of **central counterparties** (CCPs).

Netting

Netting is a legal arrangement whereby the positive value of one contract can be offset by the negative value of another contract. Suppose that Bank A has N contracts in force with Bank B, and that the current market value of contract

---

[1] This property is shared with some traditional lending arrangements, such as lines of credit and mortgages.

Credit Risk

j for Bank A is V_j. If there is no netting agreement in place, then in the event of its default, Bank B may seek to default only on those contracts which currently have a negative value for it (and thus a positive value for Bank A). The exposure of Bank A to Bank B in this case is

$$\text{Exposure without Netting} = \sum_{j=1}^{N} \max(V_j, 0). \tag{12.3}$$

In contrast, if negative values on some contracts are allowed to offset positive values on other contracts, then the total exposure of Bank A to Bank B is

$$\text{Exposure with Netting} = \max \left(\sum_{j=1}^{N} V_j, 0 \right). \tag{12.4}$$

The exposure with netting is always less than the exposure without netting, and the difference can be very significant in practice.

Collateral

Institutions trading in OTC credit markets will also post collateral with each other, in the event that the exposure of one institution to another becomes large. The rules for posting and returning collateral, as well as for netting, are typically set out in a master agreement between the two counterparties.

In addition to total exposure, collateral may depend on other factors such as the credit ratings of the two counterparties. Indeed, an imminent collateral call for the insurance giant AIG, due to an expected downgrade of its credit rating, provoked a major bailout of the insurance company in 2008, marking one of the key events of the 2007–8 global financial crisis. The credit downgrade itself was a response to the failure of AIG to manage the credit risk exposure it had accumulated. AIG's London subsidiary had sold credit protection on an enormous amount of debt, including tranches of subprime CDOs. When the prices of these securities plummeted during the financial crisis, AIG faced huge potential collateral payments on its contracts. It remained in business through direct government funding, provided by the US government as part of its effort to limit the systemic damage to US and global markets.

Central Counterparties

Central counterparties (CCPs) are institutions that act much like exchanges for standardized and commonly traded OTC derivatives. A central counterparty serves as an intermediary in a derivative transaction between two counterparties. In the forward contract example above, if a central counterparty C were used, then, after having agreed upon terms, rather than having a contract with each other, Bank L and Bank S would both have contracts with C. In particular, Bank L would have a long position in a contract with C, and Bank S would have a short contract with C. As a result, Bank L and Bank S would no longer be exposed to each other's default risk (although they would remained exposed to the counterparty risk with respect to C). The central counterparty C would bear no market risk, as the two positions cancel each other out. However, it would be exposed to the credit risk of both Bank L and Bank S.

CCPs have become increasingly popular since the financial crisis, both due to their role in reducing counterparty credit risk, and because centralizing a large number of trades helps to make the interconnections in the financial system less opaque. However, CCPs do create a strong concentration of risk (note that both Bank L and Bank S have exposure to C in the example) with potential systemic effects and, consequently, they must be managed and regulated carefully.

Counterparty credit risk can be a major source of risk in financial markets, even impacting the health of the overall financial system, as illustrated by the 2008 AIG bailout.

12.2.3 Credit Derivatives

Credit derivatives are derivative securities with cash flows that depend on credit events related to one or more reference entities. A simple example is a **credit default swap** (CDS), which is essentially an insurance contract written on a bond. In a credit default swap, one party (the protection buyer) makes regular premium payments to a second party (the protection seller). In return, the protection seller makes an insurance payment to the protection buyer in the event of a default of the reference entity. The size of the premium payment is typically expressed as a percentage, called the CDS spread, of a given notional amount.

The contract is illustrated in Figure 12.1. The protection buyer is purchasing insurance that will compensate them in the case that a bond issuer defaults. The protection buyer pays regular premiums to the seller. The CDS contract will specify what constitutes a default event. Criteria could include a postponement of interest or principal payments by the bond issuer or a change in coupon rates or principal amount. When a default event happens, the protection seller will reimburse the buyer for the difference between the par value and the market value of the bond. This may involve a simple payment by the seller of the difference, or the transfer of the bond from the protection buyer to the seller, in return for a payment of the par value.

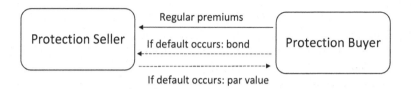

Figure 12.1 Illustration of credit default swap (CDS) cash flows

Credit default swaps can be used to mitigate credit risk. For example, if Bank A has a large position in Mexican government bonds, and is worried about its exposure to the creditworthiness of the Mexican government, it could hedge its position by entering into a CDS with Bank B as a protection buyer. In exchange for regular premium payments made by Bank A, Bank B, the protection seller, would commit to make a payment covering the losses of Bank A in the event of a Mexican government default. In this case, the government of Mexico is the reference entity. Bank A has purchased insurance against the loss from default of the Mexican government bonds. Of course, Bank A still has an exposure to the creditworthiness of Bank B.

A more complicated example of a credit derivative is a CDO, in which payments depend on the performance of a pool of underlying debts, such as bonds, loans, or mortgages. Investors in the CDO are divided into different groups, or 'tranches'. Each tranche effectively acts as if it has sold credit protection on a slice of the portfolio of underlying assets, receiving regular interest (premium) payments, and suffering losses when defaults occur. Lower rated tranches receive higher rates of interest. However, in return they suffer losses earlier when defaults hit the underlying portfolio. Higher rated tranches do not suffer losses from defaults until all lower tranches have been wiped out. In return for this safety, investors in higher rated tranches receive lower interest payments. A key concern when analysing the price and risk of CDO tranches is the probability of a very large number of defaults occurring within the underlying portfolio of assets. This is closely related to the codependence of defaults, a topic that we will return to when we discuss portfolio credit risk models below.

12.2.4 Default vs Mark-to-Market Losses

Credit risk losses can be classified into two types. Default losses are losses that result from an actual default event. Examples include the loss that a bank incurs when a homeowner defaults on a mortgage, or the losses suffered by the trading partners of Lehman Brothers when the investment bank filed for bankruptcy. In contrast, mark-to-market losses constitute decreases in the current value of a credit-sensitive portfolio owing to fluctuations in market factors. Examples include the losses to a bondholder if the issuer of the bond becomes less creditworthy, or losses incurred by a trading partner of an investment bank if current assessments of its creditworthiness (e.g., as reflected in credit default swap spreads) worsen.

While default events are more palpable, mark-to-market gains and losses contribute significantly to the volatility of the portfolios of many modern financial institutions. Indeed, in regards to credit losses during the 2007–8 global financial crisis, the Basel Committee noted that most CCR losses were mark-to-market losses, through fluctuations in the **credit valuation adjustment** (CVA), which reflects the change in market value of an OTC derivatives portfolio due to counterparty credit risk. The Basel Committee stated that: 'Mark-to-market losses due to credit valuation adjustments (CVA) were not directly capitalized. Roughly two-thirds of CCR losses were due to CVA losses and only one-third were due to actual defaults' (Basel Committee on Banking Supervision, 2009b).

Mark-to-market movements can also result in nominal gains in the value of portfolios. For example, in the first quarter of 2009, Citibank recorded a \$2.5 billion gain from the movement of a single market factor. Ironically, this was due to an *increase* in its own implied default probability, which produced a dramatically lower market value for its liabilities.

12.3 Basic Credit Model Components

In this section, we will consider the three basic components of a model of credit risk losses with respect to an individual obligor (e.g., a borrower or a counterparty to a derivative contract). These are: the **probability of default** (PD), which assesses the likelihood that the obligor will default over a given horizon; the **exposure at default** (EAD), which measures the maximum possible loss if default occurs; and the **loss given default** (LGD), which is the percentage of the exposure that is lost when a default takes place.

12.3.1 Probability of Default (PD)

In analysing potential credit losses with respect to a given obligor, the first thing we would like to have is an assessment of its probability of default, or, more generally, of the distribution of the time at which it will default.

Assuming that today is time 0, we denote by τ the time at which the obligor defaults. Then τ is a random variable, and its distribution function is

$$PD(t) = F_\tau(t) = \Pr(\tau \leqslant t) \tag{12.5}$$

for all $t \geqslant 0$. $PD(t)$ is the cumulative default probability, or the probability that the obligor will default at any time up to and including t.

Default probabilities are a fundamental component of all credit risk analysis, and are used for many different purposes. These include assessing expected losses and risk measures associated with credit sensitive portfolios, as well as pricing credit derivative securities. However, different types of default probabilities are relevant for different applications.

Real-world default probabilities are used for the estimation of portfolio risk, and for portfolio selection. They are estimated using statistical models based on historical time series of defaults and various explanatory variables, which can include firm-specific variables (such as size, accounting ratios, etc.), as well as economic covariates (such as interest rates, inflation, and unemployment). Banks commonly use non-linear regression models based on such explanatory variables to estimate PDs and develop internal rating systems, with obligors in the same rating class being of similar credit quality. Credit ratings from rating agencies such as Moody's and Standard and Poor's are also intended to reflect real-world likelihoods of default.

In contrast, risk-neutral probabilities of default are implied from observed market prices of liquid credit sensitive instruments, such as credit default swaps, and are used for the pricing of other derivative securities. For example, suppose that a zero-coupon bond with principal equal to one matures at time T, and that the continuously compounded risk-free interest rate is r. Denoting the price of the bond by B, we typically have $B < e^{-rT}$, i.e. the bond price is less than that of the corresponding risk-free bond, owing to credit risk. Suppose that if the bond does default, the total value of the principal will be lost (i.e. that loss given default is 100%, see below). Then, writing the price of the bond as the risk-neutral expectation of the present value of its payoff, we have

$$B = (1 - PD(T))e^{-rT} + PD(T) \cdot (0), \tag{12.6}$$

$$PD(T) = 1 - e^{rT}B. \tag{12.7}$$

In practice, implied risk-neutral default probabilities are derived from the observed prices of credit default swaps.

12.3.2 Exposure at Default (EAD)

The **exposure at default** (EAD) is the maximum amount that could be lost should an obligor default at a given time t. It is the amount that it would cost to replace the contract with the obligor by entering into a new contract on the same terms with another obligor in the market. Since it depends on the value of the contract at the time t, it is generally also random. Consider again the example of the forward contract between Bank L and Bank S. At time t, the value of the forward contract to bank L is $A_t - e^{-r(T-t)}K$. The exposure at default of Bank L to Bank S at time t is $EAD(t) = \max\left(A_t - e^{-r(T-t)}K, 0\right)$ (exposures are always nonnegative). In contrast, in the case of the zero coupon bond with a principal of \$1, and maturity T, the exposure at default at maturity is simply $EAD(T) = 1$.

Since exposure at default is stochastic, institutions seek to understand the distribution of their exposures to different counterparties at different future times. In general, this is a very complicated procedure. As noted above, in order to calculate the current exposure to a given counterparty, the bank must value all contracts with that counterparty. To understand the future distribution of exposures to different counterparties, the institution must model the joint distribution of all the risk factors that affect exposures to any of the counterparties. This often involves hundreds of risk factors, the joint distribution of whose values must be modelled at many future times.

Figure 12.2 plots the expected future exposure, and the 95th percentile of the distribution of exposures of Bank L to Bank S for the forward contract. We have assumed that the current asset value is $A_0 = 1$, the maturity time $T = 1$, the risk-free rate is $r = 0.05$, that the asset has no storage costs or convenience yield, so that $K = e^{rT} \approx 1.0513$, and that the value of the asset follows a geometric Brownian motion with $\mu = 0.1$, $\sigma = 0.2$.

Future exposures are used for a number of purposes, including estimating expected losses, and risk measures for credit risk. In addition, they are employed for setting risk tolerance thresholds. For example, Bank L may set a rule that the 95th percentile of its distribution of potential exposure to Bank S cannot exceed \$50 million for any time over the next two years. A new trade will not be permitted, or will require special consideration, if it violates this stated policy. Furthermore, if the value of Bank L's portfolio with Bank S changes to violate the limit, then remedial action (such as unwinding contracts or hedging some of the positions) will have to be taken.

12.3.3 Loss Given Default (LGD)

Loss given default (LGD) measures the percentage of the exposure that is lost when a default occurs. This will depend on a number of factors, including any collateral backing the exposure, the current market environment, and the nature of the debt. For example, senior corporate debt is paid before subordinated debt in the event of a corporate bankruptcy, and consequently senior debt will

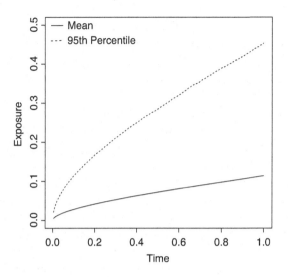

Figure 12.2 Mean and 95th percentile of potential future exposures of a forward contract

have lower loss given default. The **recovery rate** (RR) is the percentage of the exposure that the bank does receive in the event of a default, so that

$$RR = 1 - LGD.$$

Loss given default is frequently assumed to be a constant in credit risk models. In reality, it is stochastic, since it depends on market conditions.

In Chapter 4, we considered frequency-severity models for losses, and there are a lot of similarities with credit risk; in this chapter, $PD(t)$ represents the frequency of credit losses, and $LGD \times EAD$ represents the severity. However, unlike the models of Chapter 4, in credit risk the loss given default cannot be assumed to be independent of default probabilities. Consider a bank that mainly lends to firms in a single industry. When there is a downturn in the industry, more firms are likely to default on loans from the bank. Furthermore, each firm's assets, which serve as the collateral on the loans, will likely have depressed values because of the tough times. Thus, when the assets are sold in order to recover some of the value of the defaulted loan, it will be at lower values, and recovery rates will be reduced. A similar phenomenon affected mortgage lenders during the subprime crisis in the US. Housing prices declined, which simultaneously led to higher default rates on mortgages, and lower recovery rates when the homes were sold in foreclosure. The existence of a positive correlation between default frequency and losses given default is referred to as **wrong-way risk**. Wrong-way risk exacerbates the credit risk of an institution, as in a crisis it will tend to face simultaneously higher default rates and lower recoveries, leading to more severe losses. In some situations, it is also possible for a portfolio to exhibit **right-way risk** in which there is a negative correlation between default rates and losses given default.

12.4 Modelling Individual Default Behaviour

In this section, we will discuss models and measures of default behaviour for individual obligors. These could be firms that have received loans from a bank, issuers of debt securities held in a portfolio, or counterparties in OTC financial contracts. We begin by discussing credit ratings published by rating agencies, and then proceed to Markov chain models of credit rating migration. This is followed by a discussion of Merton's structural model of credit risk. Finally, we briefly discuss reduced form models of default.

12.4.1 Credit Ratings

Securities that are issued by both firms and governments are given **credit ratings** by private companies known as **rating agencies**, which specialize in the evaluation of the credit riskiness of borrowers. Credit ratings are employed by investors as indicators of the safety of investing in the securities. The three largest credit rating agencies are Standard and Poor's (S&P), Moody's, and Fitch. S&P and Fitch use the same alphabetic rating scales, while Moody's uses a similar alpha-numeric scale. The classification list is given in Table 12.1.

The highest classification, AAA or Aaa, indicates an extremely low risk of default, and is very rarely awarded. The grades from AAA to BBB⁻ (or Aaa to Baa3) are classed as **investment grade**. Lower ratings are used for firms regarded as having significant default risk, and are referred to as **high-yield, speculative**, or '**junk bonds**'. Bonds in default are rated D (S&P) or C (Moody's).

Many investors will be subject to constraints (either internally imposed or due to government regulations) that restrict their ability to invest in debt securities based on their credit ratings. For example, a municipal treasurer may be restricted to only investing excess funds in securities with a triple A credit rating. A bond fund may invest exclusively in securities with investment grade ratings, or a portfolio manager may be required to invest no more than a fixed percentage of total assets in securities of a given rating class or below.

Table 12.1. *Credit rating scales: S&P, Moody's, and Fitch*

S&P and Fitch	Moody's	Description
AAA	Aaa	Prime Grade; Extremely Strong
AA$^+$	Aa1	
AA	Aa2	High Grade; Very Strong
AA$^-$	Aa3	
A$^+$	A1	
A	A2	Upper Medium Grade; Strong
A$^-$	A3	
BBB$^+$	Baa1	
BBB	Baa2	Lower Medium Grade; Adequate
BBB$^-$	Baa3	
BB$^+$	Ba1	
BB	Ba2	Speculative
BB$^-$	Ba3	
B$^+$	B1	
B	B2	Highly Speculative
B$^-$	B3	
CCC$^+$	Caa1	
CCC	Caa2	Extremely Speculative
CCC$^-$	Caa3	
CC	Ca	Default Imminent
C	Ca	
D	C	In Default

There are certain aspects of credit ratings that should be kept in mind when using them for the evaluation of credit risk.

- Higher credit ratings correspond to lower probabilities of default. Usually, all debt from the same issuer has the same credit rating.
- The issuer of the bonds pays the rating agency to perform the rating. The motivation of the issuer in this case is to make investment in the bonds more attractive to investors. Providing more information about the riskiness of the security reduces informational asymmetry, which tends to increase liquidity (also, certain investors are restricted to only investing in higher rated securities). While the business model in which issuers pay the rating agencies for their ratings has been in place for several decades, it is subject to concerns regarding moral hazard. There is a potential for agencies to have the incentive to rate securities more favourably in order to please the

issuers (their clients). This has been the subject of considerable debate in the aftermath of the global financial crisis. Before the crisis the rating agencies made substantial revenue from rating structured credit products; and many of these securities initially received very high credit ratings, but ended up performing very poorly during 2007–8.

- Rating agencies tend to rate 'through the cycle'. In an economic downturn or recession, defaults are more likely (at least in the short-term), but credit ratings tend not to change commensurately. In other words, within any given rating class, bonds tend to show a greater historical frequency of default during recessions compared to expansions (see Kiff et al., 2013).

  Stability of credit ratings can be important to both issuers and investors, and a rating change (particularly a downgrade) can be a major event. In contrast, banks' internal rating systems tend to reflect the current economic environment, with higher default probabilities in recessionary periods and lower default probabilities in expansions. Market-based measures of default risk such as credit default swap spreads share this property.

- Credit rating transitions can exhibit a tendency to continue to move in the same direction as in the recent past; this is sometimes referred to as **momentum**. Securities can also show a tendency to persist in a given rating class if they have been in that class for a long time; this is sometimes referred to as **stickiness**.

- Ratings can sometimes reflect expected losses rather than only reflecting default probabilities. For example, the rating agency Fitch explains that its credit ratings of firms are based on default risk, but their credit ratings of specific bond issues of firms incorporate both default risk and loss severity.

12.4.2 Markov Chain Models

As changes in credit ratings have significant implications for credit risk, we may treat the future credit ratings of a firm as a random process. Rating agencies publish matrices of transition frequencies based on past historical data. A stylized example is given in Table 12.2.

According to Table 12.2, firms that began the year in rating class A have historically remained in rating class A 99% of the time, and have defaulted only 0.1% of the time. Firms that began the year in class C remained in class C 96% of the time, and migrated to class A 1.5% of the time.

A natural approach to modelling the behaviour of credit ratings is to represent them as a Markov chain, where the table of transition frequencies becomes the transition probability matrix for the Markov chain. The Markov

Table 12.2. *Sample historical transition probabilities for a simplified credit rating system*

Initial State	Year End State			
	A	B	C	D
A	0.990	0.007	0.002	0.001
B	0.030	0.950	0.015	0.005
C	0.015	0.020	0.960	0.005
D	0	0	0	1

assumption means that the only relevant information for the probability that a firm is in any specified state at some future time is which state it is in at the current time.

Example 12.1 Using the probabilities in Table 12.2, calculate the probability that a firm currently rated A will be rated C or D in two years.

Solution 12.1 Let $_k p_{ij}$ represent the probability of being in State j at time $t + k$, given that the firm is in state i at time t, for $i, j \in \{A, B, C, D\}$, and for t, $k = 0, 1, 2, \ldots$.

The probability that a firm is in State C at time $t = 2$ given that it is in State A at $t = 0$ can be calculated by considering all the possible paths for the firm to move from State A to State C over two years. This gives the following:

$$_2 p_{AC} = {}_1 p_{AA} \times {}_1 p_{AC} + {}_1 p_{AB} \times {}_1 p_{BC} + {}_1 p_{AC} \times {}_1 p_{CC} + {}_1 p_{AD} \times {}_1 p_{DC}$$
$$= 0.99 \times 0.002 + 0.007 \times 0.015 + 0.002 \times 0.96 + 0.001 \times 0 = 0.004.$$

Similarly, the probability that the firm is in State D at time $t = 2$ is

$$_2 p_{AD} = {}_1 p_{AA} \times {}_1 p_{AD} + {}_1 p_{AB} \times {}_1 p_{BD} + {}_1 p_{AC} \times {}_1 p_{CD} + {}_1 p_{AD} \times {}_1 p_{DD}$$
$$= 0.99 \times 0.001 + 0.007 \times 0.005 + 0.002 \times 0.005 + 0.001 \times 1 = 0.002.$$

So the probability that a firm moves from State A to State C or State D in 2 years is $_2 p_{AC} + {}_2 p_{AD} = 0.006$. $\square$

The Markov Chain can be summarized by its transition matrix. For example, for the four-state system in Table 12.2, we have

$$_1 P = \begin{pmatrix} {}_1 p_{AA} & {}_1 p_{AB} & {}_1 p_{AC} & {}_1 p_{AD} \\ {}_1 p_{BA} & {}_1 p_{BB} & {}_1 p_{BC} & {}_1 p_{BD} \\ {}_1 p_{CA} & {}_1 p_{CB} & {}_1 p_{CC} & {}_1 p_{CD} \\ {}_1 p_{DA} & {}_1 p_{DB} & {}_1 p_{DC} & {}_1 p_{DD} \end{pmatrix}.$$

The n-year transition probabilities are derived from the 1-year transition matrix as

$$_nP = {}_1P^n = \begin{pmatrix} _nP_{AA} & _nP_{AB} & _nP_{AC} & _nP_{AD} \\ _nP_{BA} & _nP_{BB} & _nP_{BC} & _nP_{BD} \\ _nP_{CA} & _nP_{CB} & _nP_{CC} & _nP_{CD} \\ _nP_{DA} & _nP_{DB} & _nP_{DC} & _nP_{DD} \end{pmatrix}.$$

Models that track the movement of firms through credit categories are called **credit migration** models. Although the Markov assumption is very convenient, and quite natural, it is not consistent with some features of transition probabilities in the real world. In particular, both ratings momentum and stickiness should not be present if credit ratings truly followed a Markov chain. However, the Markov model remains a useful and popular model for credit risk.

12.4.3 Structural Models

Credit risk models are often divided into structural models and reduced form models. A structural model attempts to model the underlying process that generates defaults, while a reduced form model simply tries to replicate the empirical properties of default behaviour, without any attempt to incorporate underlying causes or events.

Merton's Model

Merton's model represents the fundamental corporate securities, common shares and debt, as contingent claims on the underlying assets of a firm. In particular, it is assumed that the firm has a single liability, with a face value of $L > 0$, which is due at a future date $T > 0$. The value of the firm's assets at any time $0 \le t \le T$ is denoted by A_t. What happens on the date when the debt is due?

If the value of the assets is greater than the promised liability payment, i.e. $A_T \ge L$, then it makes sense for the shareholders of the firm to pay off the debt L, and keep the remaining assets $A_T - L$ for themselves. On the other hand, if the value of the assets is less than that of the liability payment ($A_T < L$), then the shareholders will decide to default on the debt and the bondholders will seize the assets of the firm, liquidating them in order to recover some of what they are owed. The situation is depicted in Table 12.3.

In more compact form, the payoff to the shareholders is equal to $\max(A_T - L, 0)$, and the payoff to the bondholders is $\min(A_T, L) = A_T - \max(A_T - L, 0)$. We can interpret these payoffs in the following way:

Table 12.3. *Payoffs to shareholders and bondholders at maturity of the debt in Merton's structural credit risk model*

Scenario	Shareholders' Payoff	Bondholders' Payoff
$A_T \geq L$	$A_T - L$	L
$A_T < L$	0	A_T

- Shareholders own a (European) call option on the assets of the firm, with maturity date T and strike price L.
- Bondholders own the assets of the firm, but have sold a call option on those assets, with strike price L, to the firm's shareholders.

Alternatively, the payoffs of the shareholders and the bondholders can be interpreted in terms of put options. In particular, rewriting the shareholders' payoff as $\max(A_T - L, 0) = A_T - L + \max(L - A_T, 0)$, and the bondholders' payoff as $\min(L, A_T) = L - \max(L - A_T, 0)$, we can interpret the payoffs as follows:

- The shareholders own the firm (A_T), have a debt of a risk-free bond, with face value L owed to the bondholders, and also own a (European) put option on the assets of the firm with strike price L.
- The bondholders own a risk-free bond with face value L, but have given a put option (with strike price L) on the firm's assets to the shareholders.

Merton assumed further that the firm's assets follow a geometric Brownian motion:

$$dA_t = \mu A_t dt + \sigma A_t dW_t \qquad (12.8)$$

where W is a standard Wiener Process. In Figure 12.3, we illustrate some random paths for $A(t)$, following the geometric Brownian motion assumption. At time 0, the assets have value $A_0 = 100$. The debt due at T is $L = 90$. If $A_T \geq 90$ then there is no default, and the payoff is 90 to the bondholders and $A_T - 90$ to the shareholders. If $A_T < 90$, then the payoff is A_T to the bondholders and 0 to the shareholders.

As the shareholders' equity can be written as the payoff of a call option, and as we have assumed that A_t follows a geometric Brownian motion, then we can use the Black–Scholes call option formula for the value of the shareholders' equity, E_t, for any $t < T$,

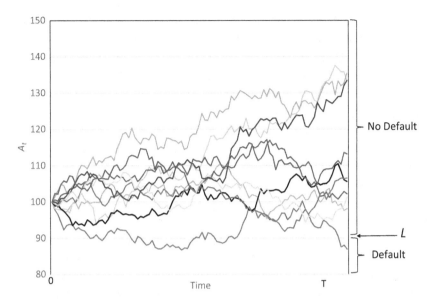

Figure 12.3 Illustration of the stochastic asset evolution and the default zone in
Merton's structural model of firm default

$$E_t = E_t^{\mathbb{Q}}\left[e^{-r(T-t)}(A_T - L)^+\right] = A_t \Phi(d_{1,t}) - e^{-r(T-t)} L \, \Phi(d_{2,t}),$$

where r is the risk-free interest rate and

$$d_{1,t} = \frac{\log\left(\frac{A_t}{L}\right) + \left(r + \frac{\sigma^2}{2}\right)(T-t)}{\sigma\sqrt{T-t}}, \quad d_{2,t} = d_{1,t} - \sigma\sqrt{T-t}. \quad (12.9)$$

We can use the Black–Scholes formula again for the value of the bondholders' payoff, D_t, but it is simpler to use the fact that at any time the value of
the firm (A_t) is equal to the value of the equity (E_t) plus the value of the debt
(D_t), so

$$D_t = A_t - E_t$$

$$= A_t \left(1 - \Phi(d_{1,t})\right) + Le^{-r(T-t)}\Phi(d_{2,t})$$

$$\Rightarrow D_t = A_t \Phi(-d_{1,t}) + Le^{-r(T-t)}\Phi(d_{2,t}).$$

We know (from Chapter 8) that if A_t follows a GBM with drift μ and
variance σ^2, then

$$\frac{A_T}{A_t} \sim \log N\big((\mu - \sigma^2/2)(T-t), \, \sigma\sqrt{T-t}\,\big).$$

Then the real-world probability of default in Merton's model, given the information available at time 0, is

$$\Pr[A_T < L] = \Pr\left[\frac{A_T}{A_0} < \frac{L}{A_0}\right] = \Phi\left(\frac{\log\frac{L}{A_0} - (\mu - \sigma^2/2)T}{\sigma\sqrt{T}}\right).$$

The risk-neutral default probability is $\Phi(-d_{2,0})$, which is

$$\Phi\left(-\left(\frac{\log\frac{A_0}{L} + (r - \sigma^2/2)T}{\sigma\sqrt{T}}\right)\right) = \Phi\left(\frac{\log\frac{L}{A_0} - (r - \sigma^2/2)T}{\sigma\sqrt{T}}\right).$$

12.4.4 Reduced Form Models

In contrast to structural models, reduced form models simply propose a mathematical object used to compute credit loss distributions. There is no 'story' that comes with the model. Nonetheless, reduced form models have been very successful in modelling credit risk, and are particularly popular in the pricing of credit derivative securities.

A simple reduced form approach models the time of default, denoted by τ, as a random variable with an exponential distribution:

$$\Pr[\tau \le t] = 1 - \exp(-\lambda t). \tag{12.10}$$

This is equivalent to modelling the default event as the first jump time of a Poisson process with intensity λ. If a random process $N(t)$ is a time homogeneous Poisson process, with intensity λ, then it is a counting process (meaning that all values are integers, $N(0) \ge 0$, and $N(t)$ is non-decreasing), and at any fixed time t, $N(t + k) - N(t) \sim \text{Poisson}(\lambda k)$, which does not depend on $N(t)$, so it is a Markov process.

A slightly more general model would be to allow the intensity to be a function of time, $\lambda(t)$. In this case, the underlying Poisson process is time inhomogeneous, which means that

$$(N(t + k) - N(t)) \sim \text{Poisson}\left(\int_t^{t+k} \lambda(s)ds\right),$$

which, again, does not depend on $N(t)$. The time to default in this model is the time of the first event of the Poisson process, which is less than t if $N(t) > 0$, so

$$\Pr[\tau \le t] = 1 - \exp\left(-\int_0^t \lambda(s)\,ds\right). \tag{12.11}$$

Even more general would be to allow the parameter λ to follow a stochastic process. For example, the Cox–Ingersoll–Ross stochastic process is

$$d\lambda_t = \alpha(\beta - \lambda_t)dt + \sigma\sqrt{\lambda_t}dW_t, \qquad (12.12)$$

where α, β, σ are positive real parameters satisfying $2\alpha\beta \geq \sigma^2$. In this case, the conditional default probability given a path for λ is given by

$$\Pr\left[\tau \leq t \mid \lambda_s; 0 \leq s \leq t\right] = 1 - \exp\left(-\int_0^t \lambda(s)\,ds\right), \qquad (12.13)$$

so that

$$\Pr[\tau \leq t] = 1 - \mathrm{E}\left[\exp\left(-\int_0^t \lambda(s)\,ds\right)\right]. \qquad (12.14)$$

Example 12.2 You are given that a firm experiences $N(t)$ significant operational losses per year, where $N(t)$ follows a Poisson process with intensity

$$\lambda(t) = \begin{cases} 0.05 & t \leq 1.25, \\ 0.07 & 1.5 < t \leq 2. \end{cases}$$

The firm will default at the first significant operational loss.

(a) Calculate (i) $\Pr[\tau < 1]$ and (ii) $\Pr[\tau < 2]$.
(b) At time 0 the firm issues a two-year zero coupon bond with nominal amount 100.

   (i) Calculate the expected loss from default on the bond, assuming that the LGD rate is 40%.
   (ii) Calculate the expected loss from default on the bond, assuming that the LGD rate is 40% if default occurs in the first year, and 55% if default occurs in the second year.

Solution 12.2

(a) (i) $\Pr[\tau \leq 1] = \Pr[N(1) \geq 1] = 1 - \Pr[N(1) = 0]$
$$= 1 - e^{-0.05} = 0.04877.$$

(ii) $\Pr[\tau \leq 2] = 1 - \Pr[N(2) = 0] = 1 - e^{-\int_0^2 \lambda(s)ds}$
$$= 1 - e^{-(1.25\times0.05+0.75\times0.07)} = 0.10863.$$

Now, let L denote the default loss, let $\mathbf{1}_A$ denote the indicator random variable, that takes the value 1 if event A occurs, and 0 otherwise. Then

(b) (i) $L = 100(0.4)\mathbf{1}_{\tau<2} \Rightarrow \mathrm{E}[L] = 100(0.4)\Pr[\tau < 2] = 4.345.$

(ii) $L = 100(0.4)\mathbf{1}_{\tau<1} + 100(0.55)\mathbf{1}_{1\le\tau<2}$

$\Rightarrow \mathrm{E}[L] = 100 \times 0.4 \times 0.04877 + 100 \times 0.55$

$\times (0.10863 - 0.04877) = 5.243.$ □

12.5 Portfolio Credit Risk Models

Modelling the default, exposure and loss given default of an individual obligor are all important topics. However, the most significant component of credit risk modelling is often specifying the *joint distribution* of the default times of several different obligors. This provides an excellent example of the importance of copulas and their role in modelling dependence in quantitative risk management.

Recall that in Merton's model, default occurs at time T if the value of the firm's assets at that time is less that the amount owed on the debt. If we strip away the structural part of the model (i.e. forget about the story), then we see that default for the firm occurs if $Z \le H$, where $Z = W_T/\sqrt{T}$ is a standard normal random variable, and H is the threshold:

$$H = \frac{\log\left(\frac{L}{A_0}\right) - \left(\mu - \frac{\sigma^2}{2}\right)T}{\sigma\sqrt{T}}. \tag{12.15}$$

Alternatively, we can define $U = \Phi(Z)$, a standard uniform random variable, and declare that the firm defaults if $U \le \Phi(H)$. Indeed, if an estimate of PD were available from another source, such as a rating agency, or the bank's internal rating system, then setting $H = \Phi^{-1}(PD)$ would yield the correct probability of default, as

$$\Pr(U \le \Phi(H)) = \Pr(U \le PD) = PD.$$

Now consider the situation in which the bank has made loans to N firms, with PD_n representing the estimated probability of default of the nth firm, $n = 1, \ldots, N$. Assume we are also given the exposure at default (EAD_n) and loss given default (LGD_n) for each firm, and that these are constants. Inspired by Merton's model, we may assign to each firm a $U(0, 1)$ random variable, U_n, and stipulate that firm n defaults if $U_n \le PD_n$. The credit loss incurred by the firm will then be

$$L = \sum_{n=1}^{N} LGD_n \times EAD_n \times \mathbf{1}_{\{U_n \le PD_n\}} = \sum_{n=1}^{N} w_n \times \mathbf{1}_{\{U_n \le PD_n\}},$$

where $w_n = EAD_n \times LGD_n$.

The expected credit loss will be

$$E[L_T] = \sum_{n=1}^{N} LGD_n \times EAD_n \times PD_n = \sum_{n=1}^{N} w_n PD_n.$$

This model inspired the copula example at the start of Chapter 6.

While the expected loss depends only on the parameters LGD_n, EAD_n, and PD_n, the distribution of losses – and, therefore measures of risk such as the standard deviation, VaR, and Expected Shortfall – will depend on the copula of the random variables $U_n, n = 1, \ldots, N$.

A strategy that has been applied frequently in practice is to use a Gaussian copula, with the credit risk of each firm driven by a combination of **systematic** and **idiosyncratic** credit factors. For the **single factor Gaussian copula model**, let Z and ε_n, $n = 1, 2, \ldots, N$ denote independent N(0,1) random variables, and let

$$Y_n = \beta_n Z + \sqrt{1 - \beta_n^2}\, \varepsilon_n, \quad n = 1, 2, \ldots, N.$$

Each Y_n is also an N(0,1) random variable, but the Y_n are now dependent, because they all depend on the same value of Z. We interpret Z as a systematic credit risk factor, reflecting the performance of the overall economy. The variable ε_n appears only in the expression for Y_n and is independent of Z and of all the variables ε_m, $m \neq n$. It is interpreted as representing the component of the risk that is unique, or idiosyncratic to firm n. This decomposition of the risk of each borrower into a systematic term and an idiosyncratic term parallels the decomposition of the returns on a stock in the capital asset pricing model (CAPM).

We assume that firm n defaults if $Y_n \leq H_n = \Phi^{-1}(PD_n)$, or, equivalently, if $\Phi(Y_n) = U_n \leq PD_n$. The random vector $\mathbf{Y} = (Y_n)_{n \leq N}$ has a multivariate normal distribution. The correlation between Y_n and Y_m $(n \neq m)$ is

$$E[Y_n Y_m] = E\left[\left(\beta_n Z + \sqrt{1 - \beta_n^2}\cdot\varepsilon_n\right)\left(\beta_m Z + \sqrt{1 - \beta_m^2}\cdot\varepsilon_m\right)\right] = \beta_n \beta_m. \quad (12.16)$$

The random variable Y_n is referred to as the **creditworthiness index** of firm n, and $\mathbf{1}_{\{Y_n \leq H_n\}}$ is its default indicator. While $\beta_n \beta_m$ is the correlation of the creditworthiness indexes of firms n and m, it is not the correlation of the default indicators. To determine this, we first begin by computing the first two moments of the default indicators:

$$E[\mathbf{1}_{\{Y_n \leq H_n\}}] = \Pr[Y_n \leq H_n] = \Phi(\Phi^{-1}(PD_n)) = PD_n, \quad (12.17)$$

$$E[\mathbf{1}_{\{Y_n \leq H_n\}}^2] = E[\mathbf{1}_{\{Y_n \leq H_n\}}] = PD_n, \quad (12.18)$$

so that $\text{Var}(\mathbf{1}_{\{Y_n \leq H_n\}}) = PD_n - PD_n^2$.

The correlation between the default indicators for firms n and m is, then,

$$
\begin{aligned}
\rho_{nm} &= \frac{\mathrm{E}\left[\mathbf{1}_{\{Y_n \leq H_n\}} \cdot \mathbf{1}_{\{Y_m \leq H_m\}}\right] - PD_n PD_m}{\sqrt{PD_n PD_m (1 - PD_n)(1 - PD_m)}} \\
&= \frac{PD_{nm} - PD_n PD_m}{\sqrt{PD_n PD_m (1 - PD_n)(1 - PD_m)}},
\end{aligned}
\tag{12.19}
$$

where PD_{nm} is the joint default probability

$$
PD_{nm} = \Pr[Y_n \leq H_n, Y_m \leq H_m] = \Phi_2(H_n, H_m, \beta_{nm}),
\tag{12.20}
$$

and where Φ_2 is the bivariate cumulative normal distribution function

$$
\Phi_2(x, y; \rho) = \frac{1}{2\pi\sqrt{1-\rho^2}} \int_{-\infty}^{x} \int_{-\infty}^{y} \exp\left(-\frac{w^2 - 2\rho wv + v^2}{2(1-\rho^2)}\right) dw\,dv.
\tag{12.21}
$$

The second moment of L can then be calculated as

$$
\mathrm{E}[L^2] = \sum_{n=1}^{N} w_n^2 PD_n + 2\sum_{n<m} w_n w_m \Phi_2(H_n, H_m, \beta_{nm}),
\tag{12.22}
$$

from which the variance of L can be derived. Unfortunately, other risk measures, such as VaR and Expected Shortfall are difficult to calculate, because L is a complicated function of $N+1$ random variables (Z and ε_n, $n = 1, \ldots, N$). A useful simplification is inspired by the CAPM. Recall that in the CAPM investors holding the market portfolio are assumed to have diversified away the idiosyncratic risk of individual stocks, and therefore only care about a stock's systematic risk, as reflected by its beta. A similar phenomenon occurs in the credit risk model we are considering, but we need the following assumptions:

- N is large.
- For each $n = 1, \ldots, N$, w_n is very small compared to $\sum_{m=1}^{N} w_m$.

The second assumption is analogous to the requirement that investors hold well-diversified portfolios in order for the conclusions of the CAPM to be applicable. In the context of credit risk, this assumption can be interpreted as saying that there are no **name concentrations** in the portfolio. In the same way that an investor who has 50% of their wealth in a given stock will care about the idiosyncratic risk of that stock, a bank which has lent out $1 million each to one hundred firms, and $1 billion to one other company, will care about the idiosyncratic risk of that company.

Under the above assumptions, we have the approximation

$$
L \approx L^s = \mathrm{E}[L|Z].
\tag{12.23}
$$

The intuition is that for large, well-diversified credit portfolios the idiosyncratic risk of obligors is diversified away and only systematic risk is relevant. Mathematically, the above approximation is very useful, because L^S is a function of only the single random variable Z, rather than the $N + 1$ random variables Z, ε_n, for $n = 1, \ldots, N$. In particular,

$$
\begin{aligned}
L^S &= \mathrm{E}[L|Z] \\
&= \sum_{n=1}^{N} w_n \mathrm{E}\left[\mathbf{1}_{\{Y_n \le H_n\}}|Z\right] \\
&= \sum_{n=1}^{N} w_n \mathrm{E}\left[\mathbf{1}\left\{\varepsilon_n \le \frac{H_n - \beta_n Z}{\sqrt{1-\beta_n^2}}\right\}\Big|Z\right] \\
&= \sum_{n=1}^{N} w_n \, \Phi\left(\frac{H_n - \beta_n Z}{\sqrt{1-\beta_n^2}}\right),
\end{aligned}
\tag{12.24}
$$

where we have used the fact that ε_n is independent of Z.

Typically, in practice, all of the β_n are non-negative. In this case, L^S is a monotone decreasing function of Z, and its Value at Risk is given by the following analytical formula where $z_\alpha = \Phi^{-1}(\alpha)$:

$$
\mathrm{VaR}_\alpha(L^S) = \sum_{n=1}^{N} w_n \Phi\left(\frac{H_n - \beta_n z_{1-\alpha}}{\sqrt{1-\beta_n^2}}\right) = \sum_{n=1}^{N} w_n \Phi\left(\frac{H_n + \beta_n z_\alpha}{\sqrt{1-\beta_n^2}}\right).
\tag{12.25}
$$

Introducing the notation $L_n = w_n \mathbf{1}_{\{Y_n \le H_n\}}$ for the loss due to the default of the nth firm, and $L_n^S = \mathrm{E}[L_n|Z]$ for its systematic component, we arrive at the important property that

$$
\mathrm{VaR}_\alpha(L^S) = \sum_{n=1}^{N} \mathrm{VaR}_\alpha(L_n^S).
\tag{12.26}
$$

So, because the systematic losses are comonotonic, the VaR of the portfolio is the sum of the VaRs of its constituents. In particular, if economic capital is calculated using VaR, then in this model, the capital charge for a position is independent of the portfolio in which it is held. This property of the above model, which is the basis for the capital charge for credit risk in the Basel Accord, is referred to as **portfolio invariance** (Gordy, 2003). While this property is very convenient for the efficient calculation of capital charges, it fails to reflect some aspects of the concentration risk that can be important in practice. For example, a loan to a company in the oil industry carries the same capital charge whether it is held by a bank that exclusively focuses on lending to oil companies, or by a bank with a large, well-diversified loan portfolio. More generally, any aspects of sector concentrations in the credit portfolio are ignored. This is a consequence of the simplistic decomposition of risk into either systematic risk (common to all obligors) or idiosyncratic risk (independent of systematic risk and idiosyncratic risk to all other obligors).

The single factor Gaussian copula model described above can be extended to a multi-factor model by defining

$$Y_n = \boldsymbol{\beta}_n^T \mathbf{Z} + c_n \varepsilon_n, \tag{12.27}$$

where now $\mathbf{Z} \in \mathbb{R}^K$ is a normal random vector with standard normal marginals, $\boldsymbol{\beta}_n \in \mathbb{R}^K$ is a vector of factor loadings, and c_n is chosen so that $Y_n \sim N(0, 1)$. The cost paid for the benefit of having a model that more accurately reflects sector concentration risk is that when the approximation $L \approx L^S = E[L|Z]$ is applied now, L^S is a function of the random vector $\mathbf{Z}$, and risk measures such as VaR are no longer analytically tractable.

Returning to the single factor Gaussian copula model, we see that while the expected loss only depends on the parameters w_n and PD_n, risk measures such as standard deviation and VaR critically depend on the parameters β_n, which describe the strength of the dependence between different obligors. To illustrate this, let us consider a homogeneous portfolio, with $w_n = \frac{1}{N}$; $PD_n \equiv PD = 0.1$, and $\beta_n \equiv \beta$, for $n = 1, \ldots, N$.

In Figure 12.4, we plot the probability density function of L^S for different values of β. We see that for small values of β the distribution is thin-tailed and close to symmetric. This makes intuitive sense; when β is close to zero, the loans are nearly independent. In particular, with $\beta = 0$ we would be adding a collection of iid random variables, and the central limit theorem would imply that L tends to a normal random variable as $N \to \infty$. On the other hand, for large β the loss distribution is skewed and thick-tailed. Again, this reflects financial intuition. When β is large, the loans are strongly correlated. Indeed, for $\beta = 1$, all of the loans are perfectly dependent, and the loss frequency is a Bernoulli random variable. Based on the shapes of the densities, we would expect that larger β would lead to larger values for tail-based risk measures. This is indeed the case, as is reflected in Figures 12.5 and 12.6, which show the VaRs and Expected Shortfalls for L^S for the homogeneous credit portfolio with $PD_n = 0.1$ for different values of β.

In Chapter 6, we noted that the tail independence property of the Gaussian copula can lead to the potential underestimation of joint extreme events. This can be particularly significant in credit risk modelling, when the joint default of two obligors corresponds exactly to the event that both $U_n \leq PD_n$ and $U_m \leq PD_m$.

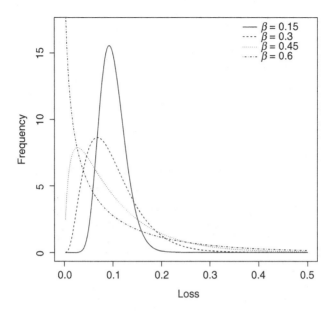

Figure 12.4 Probability density functions for the systematic credit losses L^s for a homogeneous portfolio with $PD = 0.1$ for different values of β.

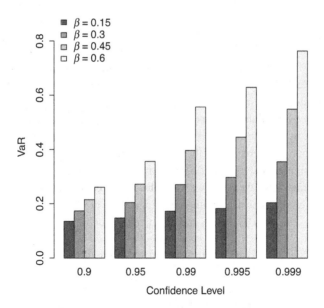

Figure 12.5 VaRs at different confidence levels (α) for the systematic credit losses L^s for a homogeneous portfolio with $PD = 0.1$, for different values of β.

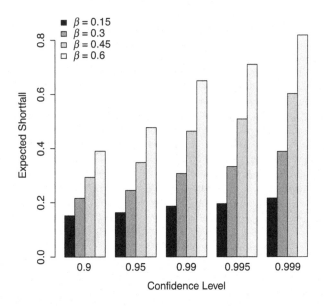

Figure 12.6 Expected shortfall at different confidence levels (α) for the systematic credit losses L^s, for a homogeneous portfolio with $PD = 0.1$, for different values of β.

Senior tranches of collateralized debt obligations are financial securities that only suffer from default losses when a significant fraction of an underlying pool of collateral loans defaults. If a model that significantly underestimates the probability of joint defaults is used to price such securities, they will be severely over-valued, because they will be viewed as far safer than they actually are by investors. This is exactly what occurred before and during the subprime mortgage crisis, and the misuse of the Gaussian copula model has received a significant amount of blame for the 2007–8 global financial crisis.

To illustrate, in Figure 12.7 we show the estimated VaRs from a simulation of the total credit losses, assuming a homogeneous portfolio with $N = 1,000$, $w_n \equiv 1/N$, $PD_n \equiv PD = 0.1$, and U_n, modelled using:

(a) A Gaussian copula with correlation matrix with all off-diagonal elements equal to $\rho = 0.16$. This is equivalent to the single-factor Gaussian copula model, with $\beta_n \equiv \beta = 0.4$.

(b) A Student's t copula with Σ the same as for the Gaussian copula, and with ν degrees of freedom, $\nu = 2, 5, 10$. The Student's t copula has upper and lower tail dependence.

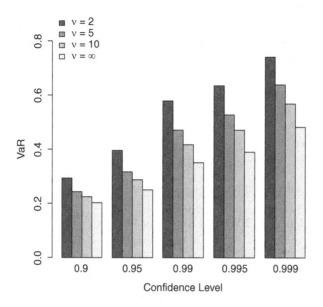

Figure 12.7 VaRs at different confidence levels (α) for the simulation of a homogeneous portfolio with $N = 1,000$, $w_n \equiv 1/N$, $PD_n \equiv 0.1$, and $\beta_n \equiv 0.4$; ν is the degrees of freedom used for the Student's t copula, with $\nu = \infty$ indicating the Gaussian copula

We observe that the risk of the credit portfolio with the Student's t copula is significantly larger than that of the Gaussian copula, particularly as we look further into the tail. This illustrates the Gaussian copula's inability to model tail dependence, and its resultant tendency to underestimate extreme risks. Imagining a (not unrealistic) world in which the true dependence structure is given by the Student's t copula with two degrees of freedom, but in which agents price credit derivative securities or manage portfolio credit risk using a Gaussian copula, we can see the potential for catastrophic consequences when using an improperly specified risk model.

12.6 Notes and Further Reading

12.6.1 The AIG Bail-Out

AIG received \$52 billion of direct government support related to AIG Financial Products between September and December 2008; \$22.4 billion of this was for collateral postings with counterparties. Among the largest recipients of collateral payments were Société Générale ($4.1 billion), Deutsche Bank ($2.6 billion), Goldman Sachs ($2.5 billion), and Merrill Lynch ($1.8 billion). This list indicates the interconnectedness of the largest financial institutions in 2008, with the consequence that the failure of one large institution threatened the entire financial system. For a popular exposition of the AIG scandal, see *Fatal Risk* by Boyd (2011).

12.6.2 Further Reading

A more in-depth introduction to credit risk modelling is contained in McNeil et al. (2015). More specialized treatments of credit risk modelling include Bluhm et al. (2010) and Bluhm and Overbeck (2007).

See Domanski et al. (2015) for more discussion of central counterparties.

For more information on the CDO market and mathematical models used to analyse credit derivatives, see Bluhm and Overbeck (2007).

For further discussion of the moral hazard risk associated with the work of credit rating agencies, and their role in the global financial crisis, see The Financial Crisis Inquiry Commission (2011) and Richardson and White (2009).

Merton's structural model is developed in Merton (1974).

For an interesting discussion of the difference between structural models and reduced form models, particularly in the context of applications to finance, see Rebonato (2007).

For a discussion of analytical aspects of credit risk models, see Lütkebohmert (2009). Estimation of the parameters of the single factor Gaussian copula model used for credit risk capital in the Basel Accord is discussed in Engelmann and Rauhmeier (2011).

For a formal mathematical justification of the approximation in equation (12.23), based on a conditional law of large numbers, see Gordy (2003).

For a somewhat sensationalized account of the role of the Gaussian copula in the global financial crisis, see Salmon (2009). For a more balanced and nuanced account, see Brigo et al. (2010).

12.7 Exercises

Exercise 12.1 Comment on the difference between the risks involved in a CDS, from the perspective of both the protection buyer and the protection seller, if the payment on default is a lump sum of par value minus market value, compared with a payout of par value in return for the physical transfer of the reference asset.

Exercise 12.2 The assumptions of the compound distributions in Chapter 4 were:

(i) that the loss severities from different loss events are independent and identically distributed, and
(ii) that loss severities are independent of loss frequency.

Explain why these assumptions may not hold when modelling the aggregate loss from credit events on a portfolio of bonds.

Exercise 12.3 Assume Merton's model, with $T = 1$, $\sigma = 0.25$, $A_0 = 100$, $L = 90$, $r = 0.03$, and $\mu = 0.04$.

(a) Calculate the real-world and risk-neutral probabilities of default.
(b) Calculate the value of the equity (E_0) and debt (D_0) at the start of the year.
(c) Calculate the expected return on equity.

Exercise 12.4

(a) Let Z be a standard normal random variable, and $b, \kappa \in \mathbb{R}$. Show that

$$\mathrm{E}[e^{bZ} \cdot \mathbf{1}\{Z \leq \kappa\}] = e^{\frac{b^2}{2}} \Phi(\kappa - b).$$

(b) Consider Merton's model. Let

$$d_1^\mu = \frac{\log\left(\frac{A_t}{L}\right) + (\mu + \frac{\sigma^2}{2})T}{\sigma\sqrt{T}}, \quad d_2^\mu = d_1^\mu - \sigma\sqrt{T}. \tag{12.28}$$

Show that the expected recovery rate given that default occurs is

$$\overline{RR} = e^{\mu T} \frac{A_0}{L} \cdot \frac{\Phi\left(-d_1^\mu\right)}{\Phi\left(-d_2^\mu\right)}. \tag{12.29}$$

Exercise 12.5 Under the risk-neutral probabilities, a company has default probability 0.1. The current risk-free interest rate is 5% per annum, compounded continuously. A one-year zero-coupon bond with face value 100 issued by the company has current price 89.42. What is the implied recovery rate of the bond?

Exercise 12.6 This exercise illustrates a model risk issue that can arise when fitting default time distributions to CDS spreads when only a few maturities are available for a given reference entity. Suppose that you are told that the default time of company A has a Weibull distribution, with CDF

$$F(x) = 1 - \exp\left(-\left(\tfrac{x}{\lambda}\right)^k\right) \tag{12.30}$$

when $x \geq 0$, and 0 otherwise. Furthermore, suppose that you are told that $F(1) = 0.04$. Calculate λ and $F(2)$ when:

(a) $k = 1$,
(b) $k = 3$,
(c) $k = 5$.

Exercise 12.7

(a) Let Z be a standard normal random variable, and let $a, b, k \in \mathbb{R}$. Show that

$$E[\Phi(a + bZ)1\{Z \leq k\}] = \Phi_2\left(\frac{a}{\sqrt{1 + b^2}}, k; -\frac{b}{\sqrt{1 + b^2}}\right). \tag{12.31}$$

(Hint: Use the fact that if Y is a standard normal random variable, independent of Z, then $\Phi(a + bZ) = E[1\{Y \leq a + bZ\}|Z]$ and the tower property of conditional expectations.)

(b) Derive a formula for the expected shortfall of L^S in the single factor Gaussian copula model.

Exercise 12.8 Consider a portfolio that has 1,000 loans. All loans have exposure 1, loss given default 1, and probability of default 0.01. To each loan n is assigned a creditworthiness indicator U_n, which has a uniform distribution on $(0, 1)$, and loan n defaults if $U_n \leq PD_n$.

(a) Simulate 100,000 loss scenarios, and report mean loss, standard deviation of losses, VaR at the 95%, 99%, 99.5%, and 99.9% confidence levels (together with non-parametric 95% confidence intervals for the VaRs), as well as Expected Shortfall at the 90% confidence level (together with a 95% confidence interval for the Expected Shortfall) when:

  (i) The U_n have a Gaussian copula, with correlation matrix equal to one on the main diagonal and 0.7 off the main diagonal.
  (ii) The U_n have a Student's t copula with correlation matrix equal to one on the main diagonal and 0.71 off the main diagonal and degrees of freedom $\nu = 4$.
  (iii) The U_n have a Gumbel copula, with $\theta = 2$.
  (iv) The U_n have a Clayton copula, with $\theta = 2.2$.

(b) Comment on your results.
(c) Compare the results of your code to the analytical results for systematic risk (e.g., for expected loss and VaR) for the Gaussian copula model. Comment on your results.

Exercise 12.9 Let (Y, Z) have a bivariate normal distribution, with standard normal marginal distributions and correlation $r \in [-1, 1]$, and let $a, b, c, d \in \mathbb{R}$. Show that

$$\mathbb{E}[\Phi(a + bY)\Phi(c + dZ)] = \Phi_2\left(\frac{a}{\sqrt{1 + b^2}}, \frac{c}{\sqrt{1 + d^2}}; \frac{bdr}{\sqrt{(1 + b^2)(1 + d^2)}}\right).$$

(Hint: Adapt the hint to Exercise 12.7.)

Exercise 12.10 Recall the definitions of the total and systematic losses for the single factor gaussian copula model

$$L = \sum_{n=1}^{N} EAD_n \cdot LGD_n \cdot \mathbf{1}_{\{Y_n \leq H_n\}},$$

$$L^S = \sum_{n=1}^{N} EAD_n \cdot LGD_n \cdot \Phi\left(\frac{H_n - \beta_n Z}{\sqrt{1 - \beta_n^2}}\right)$$

where $H_n = \Phi^{-1}(PD_n)$, and

$$Y_n = \beta_n Z + \sqrt{1 - \beta_n^2} \cdot \varepsilon_n$$

where $Z, \varepsilon_n, n = 1, \ldots, N$ are independent standard normal random variables.

(a) Find the mean and variance of L^S.
(b) Show that $\text{Var}(L) \geq \text{Var}(L^S)$ and give a simple financial reason why this must be so.
(c) Determine the probability that loan n defaults given that loan m defaults.
(d) Determine $\mathbb{E}[L|$ loan m defaults$]$.
(e) Bank A and Bank B both have portfolios of 1,000 loans of face value 1,000. Each loan has a default probability of 1%, and recovery rate of zero. The loans follow a one-factor credit risk model, as above. For bank A's portfolio, all loans have $\beta = 0$, while for bank B's portfolio all loans have $\beta = 0.4$.

   (i) Which portfolio would you expect to have the higher expected loss? Explain why.
   (ii) Which portfolio would you expect to have a higher VaR at the 99.9% confidence level? Explain why.

13

Liquidity Risk

13.1 Summary

In this chapter, we expand on the brief discussion of liquidity risk from Chapter 2. We distinguish funding liquidity from market liquidity, and idiosyncratic liquidity from systemic liquidity. We discuss the nature of highly liquid assets, and methods by which a firm might acquire liquid assets to cover short-term cash flow problems, either in normal operations, or in more extreme crises. As liquidity risk is a problem of cash flow management, we explain how cash flow scenario tests can be used to identify and mitigate risks. We describe liquidity adjusted risk measures used in banking. Finally, we describe how firms might create emergency plans for managing extreme and unexpected liquidity shocks.

13.2 Introduction

Liquidity is the ability of a firm to meet its short-term financial demands, without incurring unnecessary costs or unacceptable losses. A firm which is solvent, in that its assets are valued at more than its liabilities, may still face financial distress or even failure if the assets cannot be used to meet its short-term obligations, because they are not sufficiently liquid. Liquid assets are those that can be reliably and quickly converted into a predictable amount of cash. While short-term liquidity gaps are common and generally fairly easily managed, severe liquidity shortfall is a low probability risk, but with potentially high severity, for most firms.

Clearly, firms need to maintain a supply of cash or short-term deposits (cash-like) to pay their regular expenses, with an additional cushion of liquid assets to cover unexpected funding shortages. Examples of liquid assets (other

368

than cash) include short-term deposits, government bonds, and high quality corporate bonds, all of which can be swiftly converted into predictable amounts of cash. Examples of illiquid assets include real estate, works of art, private debt, and stocks in privately owned companies. The illiquidity of these asset types stems from possible time delays in selling the assets, and uncertainty in the amount of cash that may be raised by the sale.

Consider a firm which operates a property portfolio. Rental income is used to pay operating expenses, including maintenance, salaries, taxes, and interest on loans. Suppose that at some point the rental income is insufficient to meet those expenses – perhaps the occupancy rate dropped, or there were unexpected cost overruns. Now the firm must find cash to meet the funding shortfall. The firm may call on previously agreed credit arrangements with a financial institution to tide it over – for example, through an overdraft arrangement. However, if the liquidity gap exceeds its ability to raise funds in the short term, then it will have to monetize some of its assets. This involves either selling assets, or using its assets as collateral for a loan. Both options are problematic. Selling real estate is cumbersome and takes time. The valuation of real estate is uncertain, meaning that it may not be very attractive as collateral for short-term loans. Borrowing cash may be expensive if potential sources of credit perceive that the firm is in difficulties. Furthermore, if the whole economy is in a systemic liquidity crisis, then there may be no institutions willing to provide short-term funding, and few buyers for the real estate assets.

This example illustrates that there are different forms of liquidity, and different sources of liquidity risk. **Funding liquidity** refers to the ability to settle obligations as they fall due without recourse to uncertain markets. In the example above, funding liquidity is provided by the rental income, and is secure as long as rental income exceeds operating costs. **Market liquidity** generally refers to the ability to realize assets at full value and at short notice, if necessary, but also refers to the general availability of liquidity in the markets.

A different categorization of liquidity risk separates idiosyncratic and systemic risk. **Idiosyncratic liquidity risk** is the risk associated with an individual firm. For example, the property firm's funding risk is idiosyncratic if it arises from conditions specific to the firm – perhaps one of their larger properties requires urgent and unexpected repairs. **Systemic liquidity risk** refers to the risk from system-wide liquidity shortages. Systemic funding risk for the property firm arises when there is a system-wide slump in rental income and occupancy rates. Systemic market risk arises when markets are in crisis, leading to widespread selling, increased bid-ask spreads, and in extreme cases, an inability to raise short-term funding through normal banking procedures.

Note that we are using the term 'systemic' here where we would often use 'systematic'; in both cases, we are referring to risks that are shared by others, in contrast to idiosyncratic risks which are specific to the individual entity. The reason that we use 'systemic' here is that systematic liquidity risks generate systemic, market-wide risks, as liquidity is a crucial component of well functioning markets.

The prime modern example of systemic liquidity risk is the global financial crisis of 2007–8. During the crisis banks could not access funds; markets were in free-fall. Non-financial institutions, which are normally reasonably immune from serious liquidity crises (as long as they are solvent) found their overdrafts frozen, and their collateral insufficient. Some of the major US auto manufacturers were close to being unable to meet their wage bills, as their banks would not release funds. Some corporate bonds that were very close to maturity were sold far below intrinsic value in a desperate search for immediate cash. This was an extreme example of a systemic liquidity crisis. Government interventions to generate liquidity were rendered less effective as banks, who are relied on to provide liquidity for the economy, hoarded the cash provided by the government agencies (Cornett et al., 2011).

Firms may cover short periods of excess outgo using **wholesale funding** arrangements. This refers to liquidity provided by financial institutions, through standing loan agreements and overdraft facilities, for example.

Where wholesale funding is insufficient, the firm must select assets to monetize. One option is to sell the assets in the open market, but this is often unnecessary. It may be preferable for the firm to monetize assets without selling them – for example, by using assets as collateral for short-term borrowing, or through a **sale and repurchase agreement** or **Repo**, which is the very short-term exchange of assets for cash described in Chapter 12. A repo is very similar to a collateralized short-term loan, but it counts, technically as a sale and repurchase, as ownership of the supporting assets is transferred for the duration of the contract. The counterparty to the repo, that is, the side that provides cash in return for short-term ownership of the assets, is said to be in a **reverse repo** arrangement. **Securitization** is another more exotic way to monetize assets. Securitization involves packaging illiquid assets in a bundle, and selling them to investors, possibly through unitization. That is, investors may be willing to buy a small share in a package of illiquid assets (such as mortgages), thus allowing the issuer to avoid the problem of finding a single buyer for each of the original assets.[1]

---

[1] Securitization is described in more detail in Chapter 16.

The ability to raise liquid funds through borrowing is very dependent on the firm's credit status. A credit downgrade will significantly increase the cost of borrowing, which may then contribute further to the firm's problems. We see that liquidity and credit risk are highly interdependent.

When a firm is required to sell assets, it may not achieve the anticipated price. We use the term **fire sale** when assets are sold below their intrinsic value. This can occur when a firm is in financial distress, so that it must sell in too much volume and with too much haste to achieve full value. It can also occur when markets are generally falling, so that there is an excess of sellers over buyers, pushing prices down.

Some activities increase liquidity risk, for example:

- Derivative contracts involving margin or collateral calls. The derivative may be protecting capital, as part of a liability hedge for example, but the capital protection comes at a cost in terms of liquidity exposure, as significant price movements in the underlying assets can create unanticipated need for liquidity. If the price movements are part of a larger market event, then the risk is systemic; otherwise it is idiosyncratic.
- Credit downgrade can have a significant adverse effect on liquidity risk. It may generate calls for additional collateral posting for loans; in a stressed market, the firm may struggle to sell assets at reasonable prices. In addition, short-term funding will become more costly.
- Liquidity mismatch of assets and liabilities. For example, an institution that offers current account banking, and invests the assets into real estate through issuing home loans, may have problems from the mismatch of the on-demand liabilities (the current accounts) and the illiquid assets (home loans and foreclosures).

All firms should monitor and manage liquidity risk, but the stakes are highest for financial services firms, where providing liquidity is one of the main purposes of the organization. Idiosyncratic liquidity risk is significant for banks and insurance companies, and a liquidity crisis in a bank can lead to a systemic crisis across the economy. This means that idiosyncratic shocks can generate systemic shocks, if individual firms are sufficiently large that their distress creates a domino effect. This is the reason why, during the 2007–8 global financial crisis, some banks and insurance companies that were essentially insolvent were given cash to keep going, to mitigate the knock-on effects on the whole financial system. Subsequently, restrictions were placed on firms designated as **systemically important financial institutions** (SIFIs) to try to reduce the problems caused by firms that are 'too big to fail'.

The Basel Committee has recognized the two aspects of liquidity risk (funding and market) by setting two minimum standards. The **liquidity coverage ratio** (LCR) measures the bank's ability to manage a short-term shock to market conditions; this is a measure of market liquidity risk. The **net stable funding ratio** (NSFR) measures the bank's ability to meet funding liquidity requirements. These measures are described in more detail in Chapter 17, in the context of regulation.

13.3 Liquidity Metrics

For investment banks, measures of liquidity risk, and principles for managing liquidity, are laid out in a series of documents produced by the Basel Committee. For insurance companies, the International Association of Insurance Supervisors (IAIS) has issued some guidance on liquidity risk management. Many of the ideas and concepts from these sources can be applied to other sectors.[2]

13.3.1 Liquid Assets

The first measure of liquidity is the firm's holding of liquid assets. The Basel Committee refers to **high quality liquid assets** (HQLA), while the IAIS refers to **highly liquid assets** (HLA).

The characteristics of the most highly liquid assets are as follows:

- **Unencumbered** – Unencumbered assets are those that are free from any legal or operational restrictions on the ability of the institution to sell or transfer the asset. This excludes assets used as security for any contract, implicitly or explicitly, (e.g., as collateral, or assets transferred under repo arrangements), which are known as encumbered assets.
- **Low risk** – The Basel Committee guidance specifically references low credit risk, low legal risk, low exchange rate risk, low duration mismatch, and low inflation rate risk.
- **Ease and certainty of valuation** – The value of the asset should be transparent, and should not depend on strong assumptions. This rules out structured and exotic products.
- **Low correlation with risky assets** – In a systemic market crisis, financial institutions are the most at risk. So for liquidity purposes, stocks or bonds

---

[2] See Section 13.8: 'Notes and Further Reading' for Basel and IAIS references.

issued by financial institutions cannot be relied on to maintain value. The most liquid assets will be those that have low correlation with the value of financial sector institutions.

- **Active and sizeable market on a developed and recognized exchange** – The asset should be actively traded at high volumes, with stable, low bid-ask spreads, and low volatility. Highly liquid assets are those which are most likely to achieve intrinsic value even in a fire sale.
- **High quality** – In times of market uncertainty, investors tend to seek high quality assets, so these tend to be most liquid during times of market disruption. High quality assets are high-ranked issues from well-capitalized firms, as well as sovereign bonds issued by countries with a high credit rating.

13.3.2 Concentration Risk

Concentration risk arises from excessive exposure to a single borrower, counterparty, sector, or country. For example, a bank that does not diversify its portfolio, or a manufacturer that relies on a single supplier for a key raw material, or a firm that holds too much of its funds in a foreign currency, are all exposed to concentration risk.

Concentration risk is associated with both liquidity risk and credit risk; if a firm has too much concentration in its investments, then a small number of failures within the portfolio could trigger a credit downgrade. An insurer who relies on a single reinsurer to meet large claims may become insolvent if the reinsurer fails after a major disaster.

In the context of this chapter, we are concerned with the impact of concentration on liquidity. For example, a firm that is reliant on short-term funding arrangements with a single counterparty to manage funding liquidity gaps may be in difficulty if that counterparty withdraws from the arrangement. It would be better to negotiate with several counterparties to diversify the risk.

Concentration risk is usually monitored by assessing trends in exposures. Measures include the following:

(a) The proportion of total funding liabilities allocated to each counterparty.[3]

A counterparty is significant if it is responsible for more than some set proportion of the total. For banks, which tend to have very large numbers

---

[3] We are using the term 'counterparty' in a general sense here, meaning the party taking the other side of a financial agreement. In Chapter 12, it specifically means the other party in an OTC derivative contract.

of funding counterparties, a concentration is defined by the Basel Committee as a counterparty with more than 1% of the total.

(b) The proportion of total funding liabilities associated with each product for which the firm is responsible.

(c) The proportion of total funding liabilities by currency. Volatility in exchange rates and potential problems in inter-currency transfers could create unanticipated liquidity gaps.

(d) The proportion of total funding liabilities by term. For an extreme example, if all the firm's long-term debt expires at the same time, it may be difficult to redeem the debt and raise new capital at that time. If the debt is time-diversified, then the firm will be less vulnerable to short-term market disruptions.

Each of these measures may be used as risk limits in the risk appetite and risk tolerance statements.

The **Herfindahl index** (HI) is sometimes used as a measure of concentration. For each category (e.g., exposure to counterparty, sector, product, currency, or duration concentration) the HI is calculated as the sum of the squared proportionate exposures. So, if the exposures are $E_i, i = 1, \ldots, n$, then

$$\text{HI} = \left(\sum_{i=1}^{n} \frac{E_i}{\sum_{j=1}^{n} E_j} \right)^2 = \frac{\sum_{i=1}^{n} E_i^2}{\left(\sum_{i=1}^{n} E_i \right)^2} = \sum_{i=1}^{n} w_i^2, \qquad (13.1)$$

where

$$w_i = \frac{E_i}{\sum_{j=1}^{n} E_j}. \qquad (13.2)$$

For example, suppose a firm has total funding liabilities of 1,000, from 4 counterparties, where one counterparty is responsible for 400, and the other three for 200 each. The HI measure for funding liabilities would be

$$\text{HI} = \left(\frac{400}{1,000} \right)^2 + 3 \left(\frac{200}{1,000} \right)^2 = 0.28.$$

Suitable benchmark levels for the HI for different types of concentration could be set by the firm as part of their process for setting risk limits.

13.4 Liquidity Risk Management

A liquidity gap can create critical challenges for firms, particularly in the financial sector, and the switch from thriving to failing can be very swift.

Establishing a robust liquidity risk management strategy is a major part of the risk management function for banks and insurers.

- As with other risk categories, risk appetite and risk tolerance thresholds should be determined at the board level, communicated to the appropriate functional areas, integrated into the day-to-day operations, and subject to appropriate reporting and monitoring oversight.
- Liquidity measures and related metrics should be collected and reviewed frequently. Internal signals include concentrations, funding volatility, asset growth, currency mismatch, policyholder/customer behaviour, potential or actual credit downgrade, falling stock prices, rising funding costs. External signals include volatility indices, such as the VIX, and increasing bid-ask and credit spreads.
- The costs of maintaining sufficient liquidity should be reflected in pricing and analysing products, and in performance review. Liquidity is costly, as liquid assets have lower expected return than illiquid assets that are otherwise similar. The firm should ensure that employees are not incentivized to game the liquidity constraints, for example, by taking (and hiding) excessively leveraged positions, or under-reporting off-balance sheet funding.
- Since funding liquidity is a cash flow issue, firms should conduct regular dynamic scenario tests of projected income and outgo, using best estimate and stressed assumptions. Stressed scenarios should allow for different sources, types (institution specific or market wide) and durations of the stress situation (bearing in mind the problem with generating adequately severe but feasible stress scenarios).
- Firms should diversify sources and tenors (terms) of funding arrangements. Diversification by source means that a failure of one source does not lead to funding liquidity gaps, or credit risk for the firm. Diversification by tenor, that is, using loans that mature at a range of dates, decreases exposure to market liquidity risk because loans are not falling due or being rolled-over at the same time.
- Firms are advised to build relationships with funding counterparties, so that, in the event of an unanticipated liquidity gap, the counterparty is already familiar with the organization.
- Firms should maintain an appropriate cushion of unencumbered liquid assets.
- Firms should develop, test, and maintain a formal contingency plan that allows for a wide range of liquidity risk events.

13.5 Liquidity Stress Testing

As liquidity risk is a cash flow issue, the most common quantitative approach to risk measurement and management is projecting incoming and outgoing cash flows under a range of adverse scenarios. This links to the dynamic financial analysis analysis described in Chapter 1 as a precursor to ERM. As with all stress testing, a significant problem is determining scenarios which are sufficiently adverse, and still sufficiently realistic to be taken seriously. This is a particular problem for low frequency, high severity risks.

A liquidity stress scenario might replicate a market liquidity or a funding liquidity crisis, or a combination. Scenarios should allow for a range of counterparty behaviour, and should reflect the potential that an expected roll-over of wholesale funding may not happen during a market crisis.

Potential sources of funding that might be incorporated in the scenario include:

- Borrowing from a central bank; governments use central banks to create liquidity during market crises.
- 'Off-balance sheet' financing sources, such as:

  - **Operating leases**; under an operating lease the firm rents an asset from the owner. The rental costs appear on the firm's income statement, but there is no impact on the balance sheet.
  - Some repos – for example, where the repo asset matures at the same time as the repo contract.
  - **Financial reinsurance**: often shortened to FinRe, this is effectively a loan from a reinsurer to an insurer that does not appear as a liability on the insurer's balance sheet.

  It is worth noting that off-balance sheet financing tends to dry up during market crises.
- Lengthening liability maturities.
- Issuing new short-term and long-term debt. This may be unfeasible during a systemic market crisis.
- Intra-group transfers.
- Securitizing assets.
- Selling assets, for fire sale discounts during market crises.
- Drawing down committed facilities (such as overdrafts).
- Invoking special measure restrictions. These are terms that allow for reduction or postponement of repayments during periods of crisis, as measured, for example, by market volatility. For example, BNP Paribas

invoked a special measures clause to freeze redemptions in August 2007. In insurance, market value adjustment clauses (MVAs), are used to permit reduction or postponement of cash values during extreme market conditions.

As noted, not all of these options will be available in all scenarios; many will become unavailable, or very costly, during market crises. Even without a market crisis, some of these liquidity raising methods will take time and expense (e.g., securitization). Also, there may be reputational costs associated with some actions, for example, invoking special measures to avoid or postpone repayments.

13.5.1 Liquidity Projection Example

From the description of funding liquidity, we can see that liquidity risk can be viewed as a cash flow issue. If the cash income comfortably exceeds cash outgo, then market liquidity risk is a secondary problem. So assessing liquidity risk under various mitigation strategies requires projecting cash flows under a range of scenarios. We present a simple example here.

Example 13.1 A firm is set up with a 3-year life. The initial market value balance sheet is given below.

Assets		Liabilities	
Cash	100		
Loans Issued	695	Debt	900
Stocks	500	Equity	395

The loans issued are a two-year loan with face value 200, and a 3-year loan with face value 500, each paying annual coupons of 5% at each year end.

The debt is a two-year bond with face value 900, and with annual coupon 4.5% paid at each year end.

The stocks comprise 500 units, each priced at \$1.00 at the start; there are no dividends.

Assume all cash flows, including sale of assets or raising new capital, occur at year ends. At time 3, all assets will be converted to cash and the firm will be wound up.

Let D_t denote the MV of the debt at t; I_t denotes the interest and principal paid at t; i_t denotes the rate of interest on new debt raised at t.

Let $A_t^{(2)}$ and $A_t^{(3)}$ denote the MV at t of the 2-year and 3-year loans, respectively, after coupons and redemption at t.

Let S_t denote the MV of a unit of stock at t. At the start, the firm holds 500 units of stock.

The firm can raise cash, if required, in two ways: (1) issue new debt at a coupon rate of i_t; assume the market value of the loan is equal to the nominal value; and/or (2) sell stock at MV.

Consider the following scenarios:

Scenario 1 In this scenario, there are no defaults or market disruptions. This might be viewed as a best estimate scenario. The projected asset and debt values are:

	Time, t			
	0	1	2	3
$A_t^{(1)}$	200	200	–	–
$A_t^{(2)}$	495	495	500	–
D_t	900	900	–	–
S_t	1.0	1.06	1.12	1.19
i_t	0.045	0.045	0.045	–

Scenario 2 Scenario 2 assumes that the first borrower defaults at $t = 2$, with a 50% recovery of capital, and no coupon. There is no associated market crisis; this is assumed to represent an idiosyncratic failure of the counterparty. All other variables remain the same as in Scenario 1.

Scenario 3 Scenario 3 models a market liquidity crisis at $t = 2$, along with the partial default of the first borrower, as in Scenario 2. Interest on new debt at $t = 2$ is assumed to increase to 7% per year. The projected asset and debt values are:

	Time, t			
	0	1	2	3
$A_t^{(1)}$	200	200	–	–
$A_t^{(2)}$	495	495	400	–
D_t	900	900	–	–
S_t	1.0	1.06	0.75	0.77
i_t	0.045	0.045	0.07	–

For each scenario, project the cash flows, identify any liquidity gaps, and discuss methods of managing the liquidity gap. Assume the firm is wound up at the end of three years.

Solution 13.1

Scenario 1 At time 1, the net cash flow into the company is $0.05 \times 200 + 0.05 \times 500 - 0.045 \times 900 = -5.5$.

This is funded from cash, giving an updated MV balance sheet at $t = 1$ of

Assets		Liabilities	
Cash	94.5		
Loans Issued	695	Debt	900
Stocks	530	Equity	419.5

At time 2, the net cash flow into the company is $1.05 \times 200 + 0.05 \times 500 - 1.045 \times 900 = -705.5$.

We cover 94.5 of this from cash. We need to find an additional 611 to cover the shortfall.

Method (1): Assume that the firm issues a new 1-year bond with MV = FV = 611. The interest rate payable is $i_2 = 0.045$. The time 2 balance sheet becomes:

Assets		Liabilities	
Cash	0		
Loan Issued	500	Debt	611
Stocks	560	Equity	449

At time 3, as a result of the new debt, we have net income of $1.05 \times 500 - 1.045 \times 611 = -113.50$.

The firm is wound up at time 3, so all its shares are sold, for an amount of $500 \times 1.19 = 595$, giving a final balance sheet:

Assets		Liabilities	
Cash	481.5	Equity	481.5

Method (2): Now assume that the liquidity gap at time 2 is covered by first selling shares, and then raising additional capital through a new debt issue. The shares are sold for 560, and the new debt issue is for $611 - 560 = 51$. The revised time 2 balance sheet is:

Assets		Liabilities	
Cash	0		
Loans Issued,	500	Debt	51
Stocks	0	Equity	449

At time 3, we have:

Assets		Liabilities	
Cash	471.7	Equity	471.7

Note that the different methods of raising cash at time 2 do not effect the equity at time 2, but do make a difference at time 3 as the return on shares is different from the interest paid on debt.

Scenario 2 At time 1, the cash flow and balance sheet are exactly as in Scenario 1.

At time 2, the net cash flow into the company is -815.5.

We cover 94.5 of this from cash. We need to find an additional 721 to cover the shortfall.

Method (1): Assume the shortfall is funded by raising debt: The time 2 balance sheet becomes:

Assets		Liabilities	
Cash	0		
Loans Issued	500	Debt, D_2	721
Stocks	560	Equity	339

At time 3, as a result of the new debt, we have net income of -228.4. The firm sells all its remaining shares, giving a final balance sheet:

Assets		Liabilities	
Cash	366.6	Equity	366.6

Method (2): Again, we consider the results if we sell all the stock at $t = 2$ to meet part of the funding gap. The resulting balance sheets at time 2 is

Assets		Liabilities	
Cash	0		
Loans Issued	500	Debt	161
Stocks,	0	Equity	339

and at time 3 is

Assets		Liabilities	
Cash	356.8	Equity	356.8

Scenario 3 At time 1, the cash flow and balance sheet are exactly as in Scenario 1.

At time 2, as in Scenario 2, the net cash flow into the company is -815.5. We cover 94.5 of this from cash. We need to find an additional 721 to cover the shortfall.

Method (1): We assume first that the shortfall is raised by issuing debt. The time 2 balance sheet is:

Assets		Liabilities	
Cash	0		
Loans Issued	400	Debt	721
Stocks	375	Equity	54

In this scenario is the cost of servicing the debt has increased to 7%. Note also the change in the market value of the stock portfolio.

At time 3, as a result of the new debt, we have net cash flow into the firm of -246.5. The final balance sheet is:

Assets		Liabilities	
Cash	138.5	Equity	138.5

Method (2): Now assume that shares are sold at $t = 2$ to meet part of the funding shortfall. The resulting balance sheet at time 2 is:

Assets		Liabilities	
Cash	0		
Loans Issued, A_2	400	Debt	346
Stocks	0	Equity	54

The final time 3 balance sheet is:

Assets		Liabilities	
Cash	154.8	Equity	154.8

In this case, unlike the first two scenarios, it is advantageous to sell the shares, due to the high cost of debt, and the poor final year return on shares.   □

13.6 Liquidity-Adjusted Risk Measures

The purpose of economic capital is to provide a cushion of solvency in the event of adverse experience. Often the economic capital is assessed using risk measures, such as VaR or Expected Shortfall. These may also be used for setting risk limits, for individual business units.

One problem with the market models of VaR and Expected Shortfall is that in the extreme conditions that they are designed to provide for, the risk measures may be misleading, as they do not allow for the increasing frictions that arise when markets are in crisis mode. Liquidity adjusted VaR and Expected Shortfall are designed to allow for these frictions, to some extent.

The general principle of the liquidity adjusted risk measure is that in a crisis bid-ask spreads will be wider, and more unpredictable, than in stable markets. In Chapter 9, we modelled the h-year VaR and Expected Shortfall on a portfolio of assets using the loss random variable,

$$L = - \sum_{j=1}^{n} a_j \, S_j(t) \, R_j,$$

where a_j represents the number of units of asset j, $S_j(t)$ represents the asset price at t, R_j represents the return on asset j between t and $t + h$, and L represents the loss in portfolio value between t and $t + h$. We assumed that returns follow a multivariate normal distribution, which means that L is normally distributed. We can then calculate the VaR and Expected Shortfall of L using standard results for risk measures of normal random variables.

For a liquidity adjusted risk measure, we can replace R_j with the product $R_j \times B_j$, where B_j is a random variable representing the ratio of the market value to the bid value, for stock j, at time $t + h$. The random variables R_j and B_j are not independent; when markets are crashing, R_j will be negative, and B_j will be larger, as the bid side of the spread lengthens, exacerbating the loss. In more stable periods, B_j will likely be fairly stable, relative to R_j. The result is that the full distribution of L will be less tractable, though easy enough to analyse using Monte Carlo simulation. However, as the VaR and Expected Shortfall risk measures only involve the tail of the distribution, it is possible that ad hoc adjustments to allow for widening bid-ask spreads may be sufficient.

Example 13.2 Suppose we have the following portfolio of three stocks:

Stock j	$S_j(t)$	a_j	σ_j	ρ_{1j}	ρ_{2j}	ρ_{3j}
1	100	5	0.25	1.0	0.8	0.6
2	70	10	0.20	0.8	1.0	0.7
3	200	3	0.3	0.6	0.7	1.0

(a) Calculate the 1-day 95% VaR and the 1-day 95% Expected Shortfall without liquidity adjustment, assuming that the portfolio loss random variable is normally distributed with mean 0, and that there are 250 trading days in the year.

(b) Assume that for each stock, we have the following conditional
     distribution for B_j:

$$B_j = \begin{cases} 0.99 & \text{for } R_j > 0.0, \\ 1.02 & \text{for } -0.03 < R_j \le 0.0, \\ 1.05 & \text{for } R_j \le -0.03. \end{cases}$$

(i) Simulate 10,000 values for the return R_j for each stock, using the
     multivariate normal distribution, with mean 0 and covariance matrix
     as described above.
(ii) Use your sample to estimate the liquidity adjusted 95% 1-day VaR
     and Expected Shortfall, and compare your results with the values
     without liquidity adjustment.

Solution 13.2 (a) Let $h = 1/250$. Then the standard deviation of the 1-day
change in the portfolio value is

$$\sqrt{h}\,\sigma_L = \sqrt{\sum_{k=1}^{3}\sum_{j=1}^{3} a_j\, S_j(t)\, a_k\, S_k(t)\, \rho_{jk}\sigma_j\sigma_k\, h} = 25.13.$$

Using the method of Example 9.2, we have

$$\text{VaR}_{95\%}(L) = z_{95\%}\sigma_L\sqrt{h} = 1.645 \times 25.13 = 41.33,$$

$$\text{ES}_{99.9\%}(L) = \frac{\phi(z_{95\%})}{0.05}\sigma_L\sqrt{h} = \frac{0.1032}{0.05} \times 25.13 = 51.84.$$

(b) (i) The simulations can be done in R. We have used the MASS package
        (Ripley et al., 2020) to generate 10,000 values of the 1-day return on
        each of the stocks, using a multivariate normal distribution. Let $R_{j,k}$
        denote the kth simulated value of R_j, for $j = 1, 2, 3$ and for
        $k = 1, \ldots, 10{,}000$.
        For each $R_{j,k}$, we select a value $B_{j,k}$ using the conditional
        distribution given.
        We then calculate 10,000 values for the portfolio loss. Let L_k
        denote the kth simulated value; then

$$L_k = -\sum_{j=1}^{3} a_j \times R_{j,k} \times B_{j,k}.$$

(ii) The risk measures are estimated by sorting the simulated losses, such
     that $L_{(k)}$ is the kth smallest value. Then

$$\text{VaR}_{95\%}(L) \approx L_{(9,500)} = 43.367,$$

$$\text{ES}_{99.9\%}(L) \approx \frac{1}{500} \sum_{k=9,501}^{10,000} L_{(k)} = 54.647.$$

The standard errors for both of these estimates are around 0.5 to 0.7.

If we compare the analytic values calculated in (a), and the simulated, liquidity adjusted risk measures in (b), we see that the ratio of the VaR measures is around 1.05 and of the Expected Shortfall measures is around 1.054, but that is quite heavily influenced by sampling variation, with relatively large standard errors. A better illustration of the impact of the liquidity adjustment is to consider the relationship between simulated values of L with and without the liquidity adjustment – that is, we generate a parallel set of values for the loss random variable, for which all the B_j terms are set to 1.0. We then calculate the ratios of the liquidity adjusted and non-liquidity adjusted risk measures. We find that

$$\frac{\text{VaR}_{95\%} \text{ liquidity adjusted}}{\text{VaR}_{95\%} \text{ no adjustment}} \approx 1.030,$$

$$\frac{\text{ES}_{95\%} \text{ liquidity adjusted}}{\text{ES}_{95\%} \text{ no adjustment}} \approx 1.036.$$

These numbers make sense; the losses arise when returns are negative, so that the spread adjustment factor is either 1.02 or 1.05, depending on the severity of the price drop. The Expected Shortfall uses more extreme values, so that there will be a greater influence from the larger values of $B_{j,k}$. □

13.7 Emergency Contingency Funding Plan

Firms may wish to develop plans for raising cash in exigent circumstances. For the financial sector, which trades in liquidity, this is particularly important, but systemic liquidity crises may impact non-financial firms also. Emergency preparation should be commensurate with the level of risk involved. The emergency plan should cover the following topics:

(1) Strategies for managing liquidity gaps in emergency situations. The strategies should reflect the realistic risks to the firm. They should specify

distinct strategies for idiosyncratic funding liquidity gaps, and for systemic market liquidity scarcity.

(2) The firm should monitor liquidity quantitatively and qualitatively to assess as soon as possible whether a liquidity gap is likely, and to ensure that action to acquire the necessary liquidity can be implemented as early as possible.

(3) The firm should maintain access to a range of potential sources of liquidity, in case one source fails or is not adequate to the situation. The emergency plan might specify which sources are to be prioritized in different settings, recognizing that not all of these options will be available in all settings. For example, overdrafts and repos are likely to be difficult to secure in a systemic crisis. The firm might test its emergency financing strategy from time to time by trying to raise cash at short notice using the specified channels.

(4) Off-balance sheet financing is particularly risky; it should only be included in emergency planning if the firm is very sure that it will be available in the circumstances envisaged in the plan.

(5) The firm should monitor their ongoing access to liquidity. Terms and conditions may change as the volume of liquidity required increases. Changes in ownership or funding rules of partner financial institutions may impact emergency plans.

(6) The plan should assign key responsibilities and communication strategies for emergency situations. It should also identify individuals in partner institutions who would be notified when emergency action is triggered.

The emergency contingency funding plan may be part of a larger crisis management plan.[4]

13.8 Notes and Further Reading

Principles of liquidity risk management and detailed descriptions of liquidity ratios, as decreed by the Basel Committee, are provided in Basel Committee on Banking Supervision (2008, 2013, 2014).

The International Association of Insurance Supervisors' guidance can be found in IAIS (2020).

---

[4] Crisis management is discussed in Chapter 20.

Booth et al. (2019) provide examples of liquidity scenario testing from an insurance perspective. For a more in-depth coverage from a banking perspective, see Castagna and Fede (2013).

13.9 Exercises

Exercise 13.1 Explain why repo financing is not an option for the funding gaps in Example 13.1.

Exercise 13.2 Explain why securitization would not be a good strategy for inclusion in an emergency funding plan.

Exercise 13.3 Explain the difference between funding liquidity risk and market liquidity risk.

Exercise 13.4 Explain the advantages to a firm of issuing debt with a range of maturity dates.

Exercise 13.5 Deposit insurance refers to programs that offer full or partial protection to bank depositors, in the event that the bank cannot make the depositors funds available. Usually, deposit insurance is government run and funded. Explain how deposit insurance impacts liquidity risk, and why governments might choose to protect bank customers in this way, rather than just allow market forces to prevail.

Exercise 13.6 In some countries, including the US, individuals purchasing long-term life insurance policies have the right to terminate their policies at any time after a specified initial term. The insurer must offer a rebate, based on a schedule that is specified at the inception of the contract. This is called a **non-forfeiture clause**.

Explain the impact of the non-forfeiture clause on the liquidity risk of the insurer.

Exercise 13.7 It has been suggested that the worst number of banking counterparties for a firm is around 3 (see Elliott et al., 2014). Explain, with reference to both liquidity and credit risk, why 3 might be worse than 1, and why 10 might be better than 3.

Exercise 13.8 A bank has exposures $E_i \geq 0$, $i = 1, \ldots, n$. Calculate the Herfindahl index of the exposures if (i) $E_i = c$, $i = 1, \ldots, n$ for some constant $c > 0$ (i.e. all the exposures are equal), (ii) $E_1 = 1$, $E_i = 0$, $i \neq 1$.

It can be shown that (i) and (ii) are the two extreme cases for n exposures. The reciprocal HI^{-1} of the Herfindahl index is often reported as a measure of the **effective number of exposures**. Interpret this in light of your answers for (i) and (ii).

Exercise 13.9 A bank has the following market value balance sheet. All values are in millions.

Assets		Liabilities	
Cash	10	Deposits	670
Government Bonds – domestic	130	Long-term debt	250
Government bonds – foreign	450		
Loans	100	Equity	80
Stocks	270		
Property	40		

Assume that (i) domestic government bonds valued at 50 are encumbered as collateral against part of the long-term debt; (ii) 25% of the loans are to Bank Y; (iii) the stocks are all publicly traded at substantial volumes; (iv) Shares in Bank Y make up 10% of the stock portfolio; the remainder is well diversified, with no further investment in financial institutions; (v) the bank is required to hold unencumbered liquid asset reserves totalling 5% of the value of the deposits.

(a) Does the bank currently meet its reserve requirements?
(b) Identify the bank's highly liquid assets.
(c) Describe metrics that the bank might use to measure its liquidity risk. Which measures are likely to be the most important?
(d) Describe methods that the bank might use to manage its liquidity risk. Which methods are likely to be the most important?
(e) Describe how the bank might assess its concentration risk, and comment on possible exposure to concentration risk.
(f) The bank experiences an outflow from deposits of 100 million. Describe potential actions it might take to meet its reserve requirements, and discuss the advantages and disadvantages of each.

Exercise 13.10 A firm has the following balance sheet:

Assets		Liabilities	
Cash	0	Deposits	11,000
Govt bonds	12,000		
Property	2,000	Equity	3,000

You are given the following scenario for weekly cash flows into/out of the short-term deposits, over a 10-week period.

Week	Net Cash Flow	Week	Net Cash Flow
1	+100	6	−900
2	−200	7	−800
3	−300	8	+400
4	+100	9	−900
5	+100	10	+300

Assume:

- If there is a positive net cash flow balance, it is held in cash.
- Negative net cash flows that cannot be funded with cash are funded through weekly repo arrangements, using the government bonds. The weekly repo rate is 1%; this means that a repo which pays X at the start of the week (in return for a transfer of ownership of some of the bonds) is completed at the end of the week with a payment of $1.01X$, and a return of the bonds.
- There is no change in the market value of the individual government bonds, or of the property assets, over the 10-week period.

(a) Calculate the equity at the end of the 10-week period for this scenario.
(b) The firm has the option of taking out an overdraft of 3,000 at time 0, to be repaid at the end of 10 weeks, with a single payment of 3,150. Assume any excess funds from the overdraft are held in cash. Assess which of the overdraft and the weekly repo provides a better funding source, in terms of equity value, for this scenario.
(c) Identify advantages and disadvantages of the overdraft approach over the repo approach.

Exercise 13.11 An investor holds a portfolio with value $V(t)$ at time t. The annual growth of the market value of the portfolio is assumed to be lognormally distributed, with parameters $\mu = 0.09$ and $\sigma = 0.3$.

(a) Calculate the 98% VaR and Expected Shortfall for the portfolio, without liquidity adjustment.

(b) Now assume that if the portfolio market value falls by between 15% and 20% over the year, then the bid-ask spread will reduce the bid value of the portfolio by a factor of 0.975, compared to the market value, and if the drop is more than 20% the bid value of the portfolio will be reduced by a factor of 0.95, relative to the market value.

  (i) Calculate the liquidity-adjusted value of the 98% VaR for the 1-year portfolio loss.
  (ii) Calculate the liquidity-adjusted value of the 98% Expected Shortfall for the 1-year portfolio loss.

14

Model Risk and Governance

14.1 Summary

In this chapter, we consider qualitative and quantitative aspects of risk related to the development, implementation, and uses of quantitative models in ERM. First, we discuss the different ways that model risk arises, including defective models, inappropriate applications, and inadequate or inappropriate interpretation of the results. We consider the lifecycle of a model – from development, through regular updating and revision, to the decommissioning stage. We review quantitative approaches to measuring model and parameter uncertainty, based on a Bayesian framework. Finally, we discuss some aspects of model governance, and some potential methods for mitigating model risk.

14.2 Introduction

Increasingly, financial firms and large global enterprises employ complex models of business and economic risks as a critical part of a risk management function. The development of **own risk solvency assessment**, or ORSA, in the insurance industry has increased the importance of models and, therefore, of model governance, and similar moves are apparent in banking regulation and supervision. In 2011, the US Federal Reserve issued a bulletin titled *Supervisory Guidance of Model Risk Management* (Federal Reserve, 2011), reflecting significant concern about the lack of adequate model governance and risk management. In 2016, the Office of the Superintendent of Financial Institutions in Canada has issued similar guidelines on enterprise-wide model risk management (OSFI, 2016).

The Federal Reserve describes **model risk** as follows: 'The use of models invariably presents model risk, which is the potential for adverse consequences

391

from decisions based on incorrect or misused model outputs and reports. Model risk can lead to financial loss, poor business and strategic decision making, or damage to a bank's reputation.'

Note that this description indicates that there are two main reasons why a model is inadequate in a given situation. The first is that the model may be fundamentally flawed in construction or implementation ('incorrect'). The second is that the model is operating as originally designed, but is being used inappropriately ('misuses'). In the following section, we refer to the first category as **defective model** risk, and the second as **defective interpretation** or **defective application** risk.

The models that are generating model risk often comprise the tools that are created to measure risk across the organization, so measuring model risk can be problematic. Considered as a form of operational risk, model risk may be quantified using a frequency-severity analysis but that does not recognize the fact that the same model may be used across the company, generating a risk that is more concentrated than other operational risk.

14.3 Model Risk

14.3.1 Defective Model Risk

This category covers the risk that the model generates results which are inappropriate or misleading. Some reasons for this are listed here:

Model Errors

Model errors include **model specification errors**, by which we mean errors in the mathematical algorithms or numerical methods utilized in the model, and **model implementation errors**, which are errors associated with translating the model specification into a computer program.

Model specification errors include errors of commission, such as mistakes in the methodology or algorithms, and errors of omission, such as the failure to include adequate treatment of tail dependency. Extrapolation beyond available data is a potentially significant source of model risk.

Structural shifts in market conditions, for example in dependency or volatility can create specification errors. Old models that previously worked with sufficient accuracy can become dangerously inaccurate relatively quickly.

Model implementation errors include coding and logic errors introduced in the installation phase.

For example, Aggarwal et al. (2016) quote a case where a wrongly set logical flag completely changed the conclusions of a risk assessment of a barrage for the River Tees in Northern England, and another where a missing minus sign led to $2.6 billion of overstated capital gains in a mutual fund.

Spreadsheet errors may be particularly difficult to detect. It is not apparent if a formula has not been fully copied down, or if a range of cells used for a calculation is not suitably adjusted when new rows or columns are added. A famous spreadsheet error is the Reinhart–Rogoff controversy. In a 2010 paper entitled *Growth in a Time of Debt*, economists Carmen Reinhart and Kenneth Rogoff argued that high debt levels led to declining GDP, creating a strong case for austerity policies in the era following the 2007–8 global financial crisis. However, their spreadsheet calculations were found to have several errors, including using the wrong cell range in the calculation of averages. When the error was corrected, the association between high debt levels and negative GDP growth was eliminated.

Right Model, Wrong Parameters
The model specification may be adequate, but the results from the model could be misleading because the parameters are inappropriate. Parameters are estimated from market or historical data, or selected by subjective judgement, or determined by some combination of these. Parameter risk arises, for example, if there is insufficient data to estimate parameters accurately. In many risk management tasks, we are concerned with the tails of distributions, where data is sparse and parameter uncertainty is significant.

If there is no way to acquire additional, relevant data, then the model may have to be implemented with highly uncertain parameters. In this case, it would be appropriate to test a range of sets of parameters, or to add a margin to the parameters to bias towards safe side assumptions. In modelling economic time series, we commonly find that changes in government policy can create structural shifts, which means that data from before a change is increasingly irrelevant and even misleading in terms of estimating parameters. So, a model and parameters that initially work well, may, over time, diverge increasingly from the real-world phenomena they were designed to capture.

User-Generated Errors
This refers to errors arising after the model has been installed. It includes 'fat finger' errors, which is the colloquial term for keyboard errors, (arising from the notion that 'fat fingers' might cause a trader to buy, say, one million units of stock instead of one thousand). An example cited in Aggarwal et al. (2016) concerned a pension fund valuation program. The plan actuary left a blank in

the field for the cost of living adjustment assumption; this created a dramatic decrease in the cost of the benefits compared with the previous valuation a few years earlier. By the time the error was identified, the pension plan solvency position had been badly damaged.[1]

Software design can mitigate user-generated errors by creating checks and balances, and by ensuring that small cursor movements will not generate large changes in inputs. Where calculations are repeated at intervals, as in the pension valuation case, it is critical to reconcile the output with previous results.

Data Quality

There may not be enough data to discriminate between several models, or the data may be compromised, leading to misleading model fit and parameter estimation. Data cleaning and validation is a crucial step in model development and application, but it can be tedious and time-consuming, and therefore may not get the attention it requires.

Inconsistent Models

If different business units develop (or purchase) different models, the results may be inconsistent, leading to inefficiencies in decision-making and potential losses from inconsistent assumptions.

14.3.2 Defective Model Application Risk

Right Model, Wrong Application

A model may be adequate for some situations, but not for all. For example, it became common to use Gaussian copulas to price credit derivatives in investment banks before the 2007–8 global financial crisis. Variations on the model may have been adequate for pricing, but not for risk management where the key part of the risk is from dependence in the tails of the distributions, which is not captured by the Gaussian copula.

Poor Communication

Communication between model developers and model users is crucial. A common problem is that users do not sufficiently understand the model and, in particular, do not fully allow for the limitations or weaknesses of the model – and all models have limitations and weaknesses.

---

[1] It is likely that the results would have been more carefully examined if the change had been adverse – another example of behavioural influence on model risk.

Over-Reliance on the Model

Model users may put too much reliance on model results, overlooking the fact that models are a simplification of reality, and the fact that, especially in financial market modelling, relationships may change suddenly. An example of model over-reliance is the Long Term Capital Management (LTCM) case.

LTCM was a very high profile hedge fund, launched in 1994, famous for the involvement of Nobel Prize-winning economists (Robert Merton and Myron Scholes) alongside famous Wall Street insiders and other academics with expertise in financial modelling. The hedge fund relied on making large profits from small pricing inconsistencies in paired assets, such as sovereign bonds of European countries or stock prices of parent and subsidiary companies. The pairwise inconsistencies were thought to represent arbitrage opportunities. LTCM used sophisticated mathematical modelling to determine investment strategies to exploit the arbitrages. The fund made very high returns from these small pricing anomalies by using a lot of leverage, taking huge positions in both assets, and waiting for the prices to converge. LTCM achieved spectacular returns for the first three years, and then, in 1998, spectacular losses, sufficient to obliterate the fund. Because of their reliance on leverage, the fund owed vast sums to several major banks. Their inability to repay the loans threatened the stability of the US investment banking system.

The cause of LTCM's failure was, apparently, a succession of market crashes in Asia, leading to a sovereign default in Russia, and a widespread liquidity shortage, during which investors rushed to pick up the most liquid assets. The price discrepancies that were supposed to narrow, according to LTCM's model, actually widened, as a result of the flight to liquidity.

The LTCM model did not allow for the changing dependencies between its pairwise assets in extreme markets (recall from the study of copulas that tail behaviour may be very different from behaviour in the middle of the distribution). Had the users of the model been fully aware of these limitations, they could have applied some judgement to identify the vulnerability and protect themselves against the potential losses from extreme market conditions. The LTCM managers believed in their model too much, without adequate consideration of its limitations. This outcome is common when the users of the model do not sufficiently understand the assumptions and theories used to construct the model.

Failure to Heed the Model

On the other end of the spectrum of model misuse are cases where model results are downplayed or ignored if they do not coincide with the biases of users and decision-makers.

This is illustrated by the Deepwater Horizon case (described in Chapter 2). In the design phase, engineering models generated the number of centralizers required to safely construct the well bore. Centralizers are critical for ensuring that the cement piped into the well bore will create a smooth, clean column. If there are too few centralizers, there is a risk that gaps or crevices will be generated, creating a path for pressurized gasses to explode upwards. However, in the construction phase, the company decided to override the model, as there would be costs and delays involved in sourcing the right kind of centralizers. As a result, the construction used only 6 centralizers, instead of the 21 recommended. The results were disastrous (National Commission on the BP Deepwater Horizon Oil Spill and Offshore Drilling, 2011).

This failure is repeated, with less severe outcomes, in many business contexts, where decision-makers reject the results of their own expert modelling, because (1) following the model would generate additional costs and lower potential profits (and bonuses); and/or (2) the user is overly confident in their own judgement, and overly sceptical of model or empirically based decision-making.

We note that, in both the LTCM and the Deepwater Horizon examples, the decision-makers followed the path that seemed to promise higher profits. In the LTCM case, the decision-makers believed the model when it indicated that the proposed strategy would generate very high returns. In the Deepwater Horizon case, the decision-makers did not trust the model when it indicated that the construction should be more costly, reducing the potential for profits. Clearly, a major factor in model risk and governance is behavioural risk – that is, related to the conscious or unconscious biases of the decision-makers.[2]

Model Concentration Risk

Although it is generally considered best practice to use a single enterprise wide model for common risks such as economic market variables, this practice scales up the exposure to model risk, because if the common economic scenario generator is inadequate or flawed, then the entire business is exposed.

14.4 The Lifecycle of a Model

The stages of the lifecycle of a model are illustrated in Figure 14.1. Risk management begins at the initial proposal stage, and continues through to the decision to decommission a model.

---

[2] Behavioural risk is covered in more detail in Chapter 19.

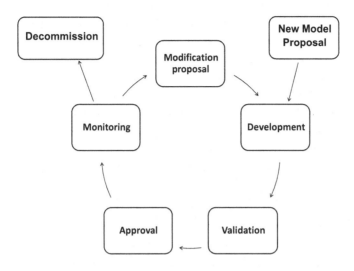

Figure 14.1 Illustration of a model lifecycle

Ultimately, model monitoring, modification, and maintenance are likely to become combined within a continuous process. Models may become out-of-date quite suddenly, due to changes in the underlying risks, improvements in the theory or practice being modelled, or availability of more or better data indicating that the model does not adequately meet its purpose.

(1) Initial Model Proposal

(a) **Identify Purpose and Risks to Be Modelled**
The risks that are easiest to incorporate are those that are well-defined, quantifiable, material, and which have sufficient relevant historical data to calibrate with some confidence. There are solid statistical methodologies that can be purposed for these risks. However, there are likely to be other material risks that require more judgement in the modelling. Ultimately, the objective is to incorporate all material risks, but where the model is particularly speculative, it is important to ensure that the users understand the limitations and that monitoring of the risk factors is maintained to allow timely updating and validation.

Many models for risk management utilize stochastic simulation. In these models, the designers must decide which factors will be modelled stochastically, and which will be modelled deterministically. Key considerations include materiality and availability of a suitable model. A particular variable or process may be material, but the random variation in the process may not be, at least relative to other factors. If the firm is concerned about the variability or uncertainty of a factor or process, it may still use deterministic scenarios, rather than stochastic, if there is no adequate model to capture the variability, as an inadequate model may do more harm than good. It is better to note that a source of risk is not captured in the model and allow for that source through, for example, stress or scenario testing, than to use an inadequate stochastic model which significantly underestimates the risk because the model or parameters are not suitable, but which may give a spurious impression that the model is capturing the full range and probability distribution of outcomes. It is also possible to use a speculative stochastic model, but highlight the weaknesses to users and apply stress testing to the model parameters.

(b) **Identify Proposed Model Users**

Where a company develops models for different parts of its business, it is important that the models are consistent across business units and are sufficiently specialized to be useful within individual business units.

In some cases a top-down, common risk model would be applied to the business as a whole, with inputs from more specialized submodels which are tailored to the needs of the individual units. The submodels should be consistent with the common risk model, in particular, with respect to external risk variables. For example, all units would use the same economic scenarios, generated by the shared model. The results from the top-down, enterprise-wide model could be used to monitor the results from the different business units, for measuring diversification benefits, for monitoring risk limits, for evaluating the potential impact of different strategic decisions, for determining economic and regulatory capital requirements, and for allocating capital to the individual business units.

The situation to be avoided is where each unit is operating different models with inconsistent parameters and assumptions. Not only is this inefficient, it can lead to mis-estimation of potential diversification benefits, or of risks from extreme adverse scenarios.

(c) **Identify and Recruit Required Expertise**

The team responsible for developing the model specification, and for determining the methodology for fitting and calibrating the model should have sufficient and appropriate expertise. The required expertise includes the science underlying the model, the business that the model will be used to analyse, and the IT supporting the model implementation and maintenance.

The model development should involve stakeholders from all the business units that will be using the model, to ensure that essential features are incorporated, but the ultimate responsibility will be allocated to a designated model owner.

If the expertise is not available in-house, the firm may choose to recruit individuals with the appropriate skills, or may outsource the model building to a third-party vendor.

(2) Model Development

The first and major requirement of a model is that it should work - that is, it should adequately model the important variables. To achieve this, the model developers should consider the following points:

(a) The time step and horizon selected should be appropriate for the range of model applications. Note that a model with long time steps cannot, in general, be used for inference about more frequent time steps.[3] A model with more frequent time steps, on the other hand, can be used for applications requiring less frequent steps.

For a simple example, suppose a firm uses a quarterly model for statutory reporting, and that as part of the model the rate of inflation at quarter year intervals is an AR(1) process. That is, if j_t is the inflation rate at time t, then, given parameters μ, a, σ, and independent N(0,1) random variates Z_t, then

$$j_t = \mu + a(j_{t-\frac{1}{4}} - \mu) + \sigma Z_t.$$

Now, the risk management function might need a more frequent model for inflation, using weekly time steps, perhaps. We cannot assume the same AR(1) structure; the quarterly model says that the inflation rate at t is related to the inflation rate at $t - \frac{1}{4}$; it says nothing about the relationship with the inflation rate at $t - \frac{1}{52}$. The more frequent model may require a higher order autoregression. However, if the firm uses the more frequent model, it can simply sample the inflation values at quarterly intervals for the accounting function, and sample at weekly intervals for the risk management function.

The natural end point of this argument could be to assume that continuous time models are the most flexible, but these can also have significant disadvantages. In particular, the long horizon goodness-of-fit

---

[3] In fact it is possible to layer a second model, such as a Brownian Bridge, to generate values between the longer time steps, but it is preferable to design the model with the most suitable time step in the first place.

of continuous time models tends to be inferior to less frequent models. The model needs to find a suitable balance between the high frequency accuracy and the long term accuracy.

(b) Data used to calibrate the model should be credible and relevant to the business use.

(c) The model should comply with sensible, objective constraints. For example, it should generate positive spot and forward rates (at least for longer terms) and should satisfy no-arbitrage principles.

(d) The fitted model should be subjected to appropriate statistical goodness of fit and validation tests.

(e) If the model uses Monte Carlo simulation, the random number generator should be validated, with consideration of the need for a large number of independent simulations.

(f) With Monte Carlo simulation, reported results should automatically include uncertainty metrics, such as standard errors.

(g) The weaknesses and limitations of the model should be documented and understood by users.

(h) The model specifications and output should be benchmarked and reconciled as far as possible against industry or academic best practice, and against any model which is being replaced.

(i) Model output should be aimed at the model users. Unnecessary technical jargon (for example, relating to the software implementation) should be avoided in documentation designed for end-users. Clarity is key. The model owners and developers share responsibility for ensuring that the end-users understand the model documentation and use the model appropriately.

(j) Reports generated by the model should be systematically integrated into the risk management decision-making. There is a danger that models are used for compliance rather than for strategic risk management. When this occurs, the results may be overlooked, especially when the news is bad, or when the results generated by the model conflict with the subjective expectations of the individual decision-makers.

(k) Model results need to be made available in a suitable time frame to influence decisions. This can be problematic when decisions are urgent but the model takes too much time to produce and disseminate results.

(3) Model Validation

(a) The model should be fully tested by an independent expert or team of experts. This involves a comprehensive review of the model specification and design, the data, the programming and user interface, and the output.

(b) The review team may reference industry or academic standard models as a benchmark for the new model.

(c) The team should also review and document model limitations, to avoid models being developed for one use, and then applied in a different, and possibly inappropriate context.

(d) The materiality of the model risk may be investigated at this stage.

(e) For organizations with extensive use of models and where model risk is material, an independent model risk unit may be designated for model validation. In other situations, a firm may use a third party vendor to validate new models – but not one that has a stake in the outcome of the validation.

(f) For vetting model modifications, the depth of analysis will reflect how major the changes are. Minor modifications would be subject to limited review, whereas major changes might be reviewed as a new model. The enterprise should have clear criteria for determining whether modifications are minor or major.

(4) Model Approval
The approval stage involves assessing the developers' documentation alongside the results of the independent review. The person responsible for final approval should be independent of the model developers, and should also be independent of any other groups with a direct stake in the model's approval and implementation.

(5) Model Monitoring
This stage involves checking that the model is still the best available for its intended purpose. Ideally, performance metrics are established to quantify how well the model is meeting its objectives. The following questions might be part of the consideration through the monitoring process:

(a) Is the model specification still valid in light of changes in the nature of the underlying business environment, changes in market conditions, or advances in the scientific foundations of a model? The model structure should be regularly reassessed as the processes being modelled may undergo short or long term changes.

(b) Are the data used sufficiently high quality? Is there a better source of data?

(c) Are the model parameters reviewed and updated as new data becomes available?

(d) Are the model uses consistent with those stated in the development phase? If a model is not being used as extensively as predicted, the users should be surveyed for an explanation. For example, are users insufficiently trained? Is the input or output format confusing or otherwise unhelpful? Do the users find the model output inconsistent with their beliefs, and if so, is it reasonable to ignore the model?

(e) Is a model being used beyond the initial use proposal?

(f) Is the model output consistent with the emerging experience?

(g) Is the model output consistent with standard industry benchmark models?

(6) Model Modification and Change Management

The result of the model monitoring will determine the extent of the modification required for the model.

If the modification required is major, the modification, vetting, and approval stages could be just as comprehensive as for a new model. For lesser changes, the process may be more streamlined, but it is always important to document changes and reconcile the output from the revised model with the original.

Decommissioned models may continue to be useful for benchmarking replacement models, and may even be brought back if the replacement model proves inadequate. Decommissioned models should be included in the firm's model inventory, along with the full model documentation.

14.5 Model and Parameter Risk

The classification in the previous section suggests that there are models that are defective, and models that are fine – but how do we know which is which? Typically, in quantitative risk management, there is no single 'true' model that we are searching for. We use models as simplified versions of reality, sufficiently complex to capture the most salient features of the risks under consideration, but not intended to reproduce reality. There may be several models that could be utilized for a given problem – in Chapter 8, we saw that both GARCH and RSLN models offered comparable fits to stock return data. There is a risk involved in selecting RSLN over GARCH or GARCH over RSLN. Statistical techniques may give some idea whether a model should not be considered at all, and may even indicate which of a set of models offers the closest fit, in some sense, to the available data, but will not indicate a single model that is 'correct'. Often, there will be a range of models with similar statistical performance, but which may generate very different outputs.

The situation is analogous to the impact of parameter risk, given a specific model. We may be able to determine a set of parameters that is consistent with the data, given the model, but there is often considerable uncertainty involved;

many different sets of parameters could be almost equally likely as the chosen set, and the results generated using different, feasible sets of parameters may vary widely.

Model and parameter risk may be explored by testing a range of plausible models and parameters to a problem. The models may be selected from a set that, broadly, offers a similar fit to the available data, and/or can be justified on structural grounds. Different sets of parameters for a given model may be constructed taking into account the estimated standard errors associated with the best-estimate parameters. The difference between the output values based on different parameters, and based on different models, is a measure of parameter and model risk. If the relevant output is not very sensitive to the different model/parameter sets, then the model risk is quite low. In this case, we would say that model risk is not material, meaning that it is small relative to other sources of variability and uncertainty. Unfortunately, this is often not the case.

It is tempting to think that if the standard error of the output statistic (say, Expected Shortfall) is small, then the model and parameter uncertainty is low. This is a common, but dangerous misconception. The standard error only measures idiosyncratic, sampling variability, for a given model and parameters; a model which is completely wrong may generate results that appear very accurate based on standard errors.

To illustrate this, consider the 99% Expected Shortfall for a loss defined as $L = 100 - S_{10}$, where S_t is the value of a stock index at t years, with $S_0 = 100$. We have simulated the loss based on two of the models described in Chapter 8; (1) the ILN model and (2) the monthly RSLN model. In both cases, we calibrated the models to the 1990–2020 monthly S&P/TSX data used in Chapter 8. In Table 14.1, we show results for the 99% Expected Shortfall, based on 1,000 simulated paths for the stock values. We also show approximate standard errors, calculated using the Manistre–Hancock formula (equation (3.25)).

Table 14.1. *Comparison of 99% Expected Shortfall values and standard errors, using the Manistre–Hancock formula; ILN and RSLN stock price models, fitted to 1990–2020 S&P/TSX monthly data*

	99% ES	99% VaR	SE of ES
ILN	39.2	31.6	2.7
RSLN	57.4	46.0	4.1

We see that the model choice makes a significant difference in the estimated Expected Shortfall, with the RSLN model generating a much larger value than the ILN model – not surprising, as the ILN model is much thinner-tailed than the RSLN. We also see that the standard error of the Expected Shortfall estimate is smaller for the ILN model. The temptation is to say 'since there's less uncertainty about the ILN estimate, that must be the better choice' – but that is a false argument; the ILN Expected Shortfall is *not* more accurate than the RSLN value. We know this because the analysis of residuals in Chapter 8 (see Figure 8.8) shows that the ILN is a much worse model than the RSLN model, in terms of its fit to the data. The low standard error simply tells us that *if* the ILN model is accurate, then the standard error in the Expected Shortfall calculation would be around 2.7. Similarly, *if* the RSLN model is accurate, the standard error would be around 4.1. We know nothing about which model is preferred from this information.

14.5.1 Parameter Uncertainty

Typically, parameters are estimated from historical data (or from market data for $\mathbb{Q}$ measures). The uncertainty involved in the estimated parameters can be quantified through their standard errors.

If the vector of estimated parameters, denoted $\hat{\theta}$, is estimated by maximum likelihood, then the asymptotic covariance of $\hat{\theta}$ (which is the Cramér–Rao lower bound) is the inverse of the expected information matrix, $I(\theta)$, where

$$I(\theta)_{i,j} = \mathrm{E}\left[-\frac{\partial^2}{\partial \theta_i\, \partial \theta_j} l(\theta)\right]. \tag{14.1}$$

When the likelihood function is not very tractable, the second derivatives required can be estimated numerically.[4]

Maximum likelihood estimates are typically asymptotically normally distributed, so for larger samples the standard error can be used to calculate an approximate confidence interval for the parameter, which can then be used in assessing the sensitivity of the model results to parameter uncertainty. Where parameter estimates are mutually dependent, the sensitivity should be assessed jointly, using the asymptotic covariances generated using the inverse information matrix. However, the asymptotic properties of maximum likelihood estimators, specifically the normal distribution and Cramér–Rao

---

[4] See Appendix A.6 for a review of maximum likelihood estimation.

lower bound covariance properties, may be quite inaccurate for small sample sizes, or where parameters are close to a boundary of the parameter space.

Bayesian Approach to Parameter Uncertainty

Maximum likelihood provides point estimates of parameters. The Bayesian approach provides full distributions associated with the parameters, capturing the range of possible values, and the probabilities associated with those values. For quantifying and incorporating parameter risk into calculations involving parameter uncertainty, the Bayesian approach offers a richer framework than the MLE approach. However, the practical application can be complex. As the distributions involved are rarely sufficiently tractable for analytical results, the most common implementation of Bayesian methods is through the computational algorithms collectively known as **Markov chain Monte Carlo** (MCMC) methods. The details of MCMC are beyond the scope of this text; references are provided at the end of the chapter. In this section, we illustrate how the results of the MCMC algorithm can be used to assess and incorporate parameter risk in modelling losses.

Under the Bayesian approach, parameters are treated as random variables.[5] Before calibrating a model to data, we assign a **prior distribution** to the parameters, representing our subjective assessment of the likely location and uncertainty for each parameter. If we have little prior information, then we use a **non-informative prior**, which has a very large variance, and will have little direct influence on the results.

We combine the information from the prior distribution with information from the data, through the likelihood function, to determine the **posterior distribution** for the parameters, which models the parameter uncertainty after taking into account information provided from the data.

More mathematically, suppose we have a model that depends on a vector of parameters, denoted $\theta = (\theta_1, \ldots, \theta_k)$. We assign a joint prior distribution, $p(\theta)$ to the parameters.

We collect a sample of data, $x = (x_1, x_2, \ldots, x_n)$. Given this data, the likelihood function is a function of the parameter vector θ, denoted here by $L_x(\theta)$.

We combine the likelihood function and the prior distribution to generate the posterior distribution for the parameters, denoted $\pi(\theta)$, as

$$\pi(\theta) = c \, L_x(\theta) \, p(\theta),$$

---

[5] See Appendix A.7 for a review of Bayesian methods and terminology.

where c is a normalizing constant, ensuring that the posterior marginal probabilities sum to 1.0.

The posterior distribution can be used to estimate parameters, typically using the mean values of each θ_i from the posterior distribution, and also to estimate the standard errors of the parameters, using the marginal standard deviations from the posterior distribution. Dependencies between parameters can be investigated through the covariance matrix, or the implied copula derived from the posterior distribution. The posterior distribution, therefore, provides the fullest information about parameter uncertainty, including dependencies between parameters.

There are two main challenges with this approach. The first is that using an inappropriate prior distribution will generate inappropriate results. The process of deriving the posterior distribution from the prior distribution is called **Bayesian updating**. If more data is subsequently collected, the posterior distribution can be repurposed as the new prior distribution, and ultimately the impact of the original prior will be mitigated, especially if it is not consistent with the data.

The second problem is that it is not possible to derive an analytic form for the posterior distribution, except in a very few special cases. However, the MCMC algorithm will generate random samples of parameter vectors from their joint posterior probability distribution. We can then use this sample to generate point estimates and standard errors for the individual parameters, based on the marginal samples for each one, and dependencies between the parameters, based on the empirical implied copula derived from the joint sample.

The Bayesian approach can be taken one step further; not only does it give us insight into the uncertainty associated with the parameters, through the posterior distribution, it also allows us to measure the effect of that uncertainty on the distribution of the original random variable, through the **predictive distribution**. Suppose that, given the parameter vector θ, the distribution function for the loss X is $F(x|\theta)$. Typically, using (for example) maximum likelihood estimation, we set $\theta = \hat{\theta}$, that is, set the parameters to their maximum likelihood values, and work with $F(x|\hat{\theta})$. But under the Bayesian framework, where θ is treated as a random variable, we can construct the unconditional distribution function for X, as

$$F(x) = \int_\theta F(x|\theta)\,\pi(\theta)\,d\theta,$$

which is the distribution function of the predictive distribution of X. The predictive distribution takes into consideration not only the variability of X

for any given set of parameter values, but also the variability in the parameter values themselves. It is a mixture of the conditional loss random variable, $X|\boldsymbol{\theta}$, and the posterior parameter distribution.

As for the posterior parameter distribution, in practice the predictive distribution will not be a tractable mathematical function. However, using MCMC allows us to simulate values from the predictive distribution, using Monte Carlo simulation, in almost exactly the same way as we would simulate from the distribution with a single point estimate for each parameter. The one difference is that each simulated loss value uses a different parameter vector, taken from the sample generated using the MCMC algorithm.

We illustrate this with a simple example. Suppose we want to generate a sample of 1,000 values of a loss random variable, X, that is assumed to be Pareto distributed with unknown parameters; we also have a sample of loss data. The traditional, frequentist, Monte Carlo approach might proceed as follows:

(1) Use MLE to estimate parameters, $\hat{a}$ and $\hat{\theta}$, say.
(2) Simulate 1,000 values from the U(0,1) (uniform) distribution, denoted U_j, $j = 1, 2, \ldots, 1{,}000$.
(3) Convert the uniform random variates to values from the Pareto($\hat{a}, \hat{\theta}$) distribution, denoted $X_1, \ldots, X_{1{,}000}$, by setting $F(X_j | a = \hat{a}, \theta = \hat{\theta}) = U_j$; that is,

$$U_j = 1 - \left(\frac{\hat{\theta}}{\hat{\theta} + X_j}\right)^{\hat{a}} \Rightarrow X_j = \hat{\theta}\left((1 - U_j)^{-\frac{1}{\hat{a}}} - 1\right).$$

Using MCMC, we can generate 1,000 values of the loss random variable based on the predictive distribution, as follows:

(1) Use MCMC to generate a sample of 1,000 pairs of values from the posterior distribution, $\pi(a, \theta)$; let (a_i, θ_i) denote the ith simulated parameter vector.
(2) Simulate 1,000 values from the U(0,1) distribution, denoted U_j, $j = 1, 2, \ldots, 1{,}000$.
(3) Convert the uniform random variates to values from the predictive distribution, denoted $X_1, \ldots, X_{1{,}000}$, by setting $F(X_j | a = a_j, \theta = \theta_j) = U_j$; that is,

$$\Rightarrow X_j = \theta_j\left((1 - U_j)^{-\frac{1}{a_j}} - 1\right).$$

Table 14.2. *GARCH parameter sets for Example 14.1*

	μ	a_0	a_1	b		μ	a_0	a_1	b
MLE	0.00880	0.00019	0.33263	0.61117					
MCMC1	0.01036	0.00024	0.30645	0.61023	MCMC6	0.00945	0.00014	0.32231	0.66125
MCMC2	0.00926	0.00013	0.26289	0.71760	MCMC7	0.01102	0.00021	0.24762	0.63905
MCMC3	0.00919	0.00016	0.32813	0.63028	MCMC8	0.00941	0.00019	0.38462	0.60490
MCMC4	0.00947	0.00028	0.41458	0.57070	MCMC9	0.00564	0.00024	0.39285	0.55245
MCMC5	0.00475	0.00016	0.41888	0.57070	MCMC10	0.00846	0.00020	0.26585	0.66347

Example 14.1 Table 14.2 shows 10 parameter sets for a monthly GARCH model, generated using MCMC, as well as the MLE parameters. You are also given that $Y_0 = 0.0109$ and $\sigma_0 = 0.0528$.

(a) Calculate $E_0\left[\sigma_{12}^2\right]$ under the GARCH distribution with the MLE parameters, and under the predictive distribution, using the MCMC parameters.

(b) Simulate 10 values for S_{12} using (i) the GARCH distribution with the MLE parameters and (ii) the predictive distribution, using the MCMC parameters. You are given that $S_0 = 100$.

Solution 14.1

(a) We saw from Chapter 8 that the expected value of σ_t^2 at time 0 can be calculated as a weighted average of σ_1^2 and the long term unconditional variance, $\sigma^2 = a_0/(1 - (a_1 + b))$, provided that $a_1 + b < 1$. The weights are $(a_1 + b)^{t-1}$ and $1 - (a_1 + b)^{t-1}$, respectively.

In Table 14.3, we show the calculated values of σ_1^2, σ^2, and $E_0[\sigma_{12}^2]$ for each parameter set. The estimate of $E_0[\sigma_{12}^2]$ using the predictive distribution is the average of the values generated using the different parameter sets, which is 0.00281.

(b) To simulate 10 paths using the GARCH model and MLE parameters, we generate ten sets of twelve standard normal random variates, $Z_{i,t}$, where $i = 1, 2, \ldots, 10$, and $t = 1, 2, \ldots, 12$. We then simulate 10 paths for σ_t, Y_t, and S_t, using the MLE parameters, where for $i = 1, 2, \ldots, 10$, we have $\sigma_{i,0} = 0.0528$, $Y_{i,0} = 0.0109$, $S_{i,0} = 100$, and

$$\sigma_{i,t} = \left(a_0 + a_1(Y_{i,t-1} - \mu)^2 + b\,\sigma_{i,t-1}^2\right)^{0.5},$$

$$Y_{i,t} = \mu + \sigma_{i,t}\,Z_{i,t},$$

$$S_{i,t} = 100e^{Y_{i,t}}.$$

Table 14.3. *Calculations for Example 14.1*

	σ_1^2	σ^2	$E_0[\sigma_{12}^2 \mid \theta]$		σ_1^2	σ^2	$E_0[\sigma_{12}^2 \mid \theta]$
MLE	0.00190	0.00338	0.00259				
MCMC1	0.00194	0.00288	0.00252	MCMC6	0.00198	0.00852	0.00307
MCMC2	0.00213	0.00666	0.00301	MCMC7	0.00199	0.00185	0.00189
MCMC3	0.00192	0.00385	0.00264	MCMC8	0.00188	0.01813	0.00366
MCMC4	0.00166	0.00313	0.00260	MCMC9	0.00179	0.00439	0.00299
MCMC5	0.00177	0.01536	0.00325	MCMC10	0.00205	0.00283	0.00248

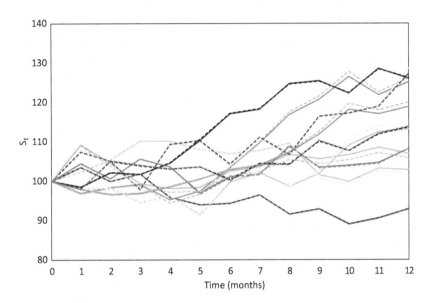

Figure 14.2 Simulated paths for stock prices under a GARCH model for Example 14.1 – unbroken lines are paths using the MLE parameters, broken lines are paths from the predictive distribution

To simulate 10 paths using the predictive model, we follow the same procedure, except that each path is generated with a different parameter set from the MCMC output.

We illustrate our results in Figure 14.2. We have used the same $Z_{i,j}$ for the GARCH and predictive distribution simulations, to isolate the impact of parameter uncertainty. The MLE paths are shown by the solid lines, and the paths simulated using the predictive distribution are shown by the broken lines. In this case, the impact of parameter uncertainty is not very significant, but that may not be the case when considering other outputs such as tail risk measures, within a much larger scale simulation exercise.   □

14.5.2 Model Uncertainty

One approach to model uncertainty in risk management is to choose the most conservative from a set of feasible models, or to choose a middling value from a larger set. This is a rather ad hoc solution, and introduces an element of subjectivity to the process that may be dangerous. It can also lead to inconsistencies, as the model that is most conservative in one context may not be the most conservative in others.

In practice, the temptation to choose the model that generates the most optimistic results appears to be strong. We have seen from the risk management failures of LTCM and Deepwater Horizon that cherry picking model results to emphasize the optimistic scenarios and ignore the pessimistic can lead to disastrous outcomes.

For a more quantitative approach, the Bayesian framework can be extended to allow for model uncertainty as well as parameter uncertainty. In this case we assign prior distributions at the model level, and, for each model, at the parameter level. We can then calculate posterior distributions for both the model and the parameters, as follows.

Assume that we have K models in the feasible set. Let $p(M_j)$ denote the prior probability function for model M_j, and let $p(\boldsymbol{\theta}_j|M_j)$ denote the prior distribution for the parameters for model M_j, $j = 1, 2, \ldots, K$. A non-informative prior would set $p(M_j) = 1/K$ for each of the K models.

The joint posterior distribution for the model and parameters is

$$\pi(M_j, \boldsymbol{\theta}_j) = p(M_j, \boldsymbol{\theta}_j|\boldsymbol{x}) = p(\boldsymbol{\theta}_j|M_j, \boldsymbol{x}) \times p(M_j|\boldsymbol{x}).$$

The first term on the right-hand side, $p(\boldsymbol{\theta}_j|M_j, \boldsymbol{x})$ is the normal posterior distribution function for the parameters of model M_j, which we denote by $\pi(\boldsymbol{\theta}_j|M_j)$. The second term is a posterior probability function for the model,

$$p(M_j|\boldsymbol{x}) \propto p(M_j) f(\boldsymbol{x}|M_j),$$
$$\text{where } f(\boldsymbol{x}|M_j) = \int L(\boldsymbol{x}; \theta, M_j) \pi(\theta|M_j) d\theta.$$

The probability function $f(\boldsymbol{x}|M_j)$ is called the **Bayes factor** for model M_j. The Bayes factors can be determined numerically (for example by Monte Carlo integration), although analytical approximations may be feasible if the x_j observations are i.i.d.

To generate a Monte Carlo sample of, say, N model and parameter sets, we can prepare, in advance, samples of parameters sets from the posterior distributions for each of the K models, using MCMC. Then, for $i = 1, 2, \ldots, N$ we first generate a model, m_i, using the probability function $p(M_j|\boldsymbol{x})$ for $j = 1, 2, \ldots, K$, and then we select at random one of the MCMC parameter sets for the given model.

It is worth noting that if the model prior distribution is non-informative, then the posterior probability functions will be determined in proportion to the Bayes factors, which are weighted average likelihoods for each model. Two models with similar maximum likelihood values may have very different Bayes factors depending on the shape of the likelihood surface; other things (specifically, number of parameters) being equal, a flatter likelihood will have a larger value for the Bayes factor than a likelihood that falls steeply away from the maximum.

14.5.3 Proxy Models

Proxy models are models of models – that is, given that a model is a simplified representation of a real-world process or risk, a proxy model is a simpler model that approximates the output of the original model.

Proxy models are used where the original model is too limited or too cumbersome for some required applications. For example, a comprehensive Monte Carlo model of the cash flows of a life insurance operation might have a very long run time for a relatively small number of simulations, particularly if there are several tiers of stochastic modelling required. Where a quicker assessment of the surplus process is required, the insurer may use a simpler proxy to replicate the full model.

Methods for proxy modelling include:

- **Representative scenarios** – Instead of running several thousand scenarios to assess its tail risk, the firm may select a small number of scenarios intended to capture the same risk.
- **Parametric curve fitting** – The enterprise may use the full set of simulations to fit a multivariate function to generate the output as a function of the key input variables.
- **Non-parametric model fitting** – The enterprise may employ a non-parametric statistical algorithm to 'learn' the outcome of a more sophisticated model and then produce an approximating function.
- The firm may replace some elements of the full model with simplified model points. For example, an insurer may replace its full portfolio of insurance

policies with a small number of representative policies, with the view that the smaller set of model points will adequately represent the full range.

- The firm may replace some less tractable parts of a model with assumptions that can obviate some of the calculations. For example, a model that has a stock price process with stochastic volatility could be approximated by a proxy with constant volatility.

In each case, the proxy may be sufficiently accurate – or it may introduce potentially catastrophic model error. The representative scenarios may fail to capture some combinations of input variables that create significant tail risk, or may only be suitable for very limited applications. An approximating function may give the appearance of sophistication, but it could be much harder to identify when the relationships start to break down, and that could happen very quickly.

The use of proxy models for material applications adds very significantly to the model risk. It is extremely important that the proxy models should be frequently benchmarked against the full model that they are simulating.

14.6 Model Governance

Model governance refers to the processes and policies established to ensure that models used by a firm are developed, reviewed, and maintained consistently with the risks involved and with the firm's risk appetite. The major functions of model risk governance include:

- Managing risk in the different life stages of a model, from initial development, through the vetting and approval processes, to monitoring and change management.
- Managing the model inventory for the enterprise.
- Assessing the materiality of the risk associated with the models being used.
- Managing the internal model audit process.
- Directing and maintaining appropriate comprehensive, accessible documentation for the models and the review of the models.

14.6.1 Model Inventory

Part of model governance includes the maintenance of a firm-wide model inventory. This is a catalogue of all the models used by the firm, whether in current use or decommissioned. The following list of information that should be included in the inventory documentation is collated from the Federal Reserve (2011) and OSFI (2016) reports:

- Model name and description of key features.
- Actual and expected uses.
- Assessment of model risk and materiality.
- Type and source of input data.
- Links to other models (for example, if the model uses output from another model as input).
- Details of all modifications.
- Vetting reports.
- Monitoring reports.
- Dates of inception and decommission, if appropriate.
- Model limitations, restrictions on use.

14.6.2 Model Materiality

Ascertaining how material a model is to the enterprise ensures that models posing the highest risk receive the highest priority in vetting, approval, and monitoring.

A model is likely to be classified as having material risk if (1) it is involved in financially significant decisions, (2) the decisions depend heavily on the results of the model, and (3) it has significant uncertainty in output, for example if the output is highly sensitive to relatively small changes in parameters, or if parameters themselves are unstable, or if the model selection is uncertain.

14.6.3 Model Ownership

The model owner is the person or team with primary responsibility for the model. Access to the model code should be managed by this team. Model risk management generally requires that access is limited to a small set of authorized individuals, with stringent documentation requirements in the event that the code is updated.

It is common practice to assign ownership to the development team, unless the model has been purchased from an external vendor. However, the model users are likely to be the first to identify problems with the model results or interpretation, and so the primary model users may be in the best position to act as the designated model owners. Secondary model users should be consulted during the monitoring and modification stages, but may not be given access to make the modifications, to ensure compliance with the model risk management process and documentation requirements, and to avoid the risk of multiple versions simultaneously in use.

For an enterprise-wide model in financial services, or other organizations which rely heavily on modelling, ownership should be assigned to a specialized model risk unit.

14.6.4 Internal Audit

A regular internal audit should address the following issues:

- Assess whether the firm's model risk management framework and policies are effective, comprehensive, and consistent with the firm's model risk appetite.
- Review of the level of compliance with the relevant policies by all parties involved in model development, vetting, monitoring, and use.
- Verify that all required documentation is complete and accurate.
- Audit the model inventory for accuracy and completeness.

14.7 Risk Treatment for Model Risk

- **Misspecification and/or Coding Errors**
  Mitigate likelihood through strong model governance, especially with respect to acquisition of highly qualified staff, together with rigorous vetting and approval requirements.
- **Misuse of Model Results**
  Mitigate likelihood and severity through:

  (1) strong training for model users;
  (2) ensuring model users are represented at the design stage;
  (3) good design of model output ensuring results are easy to interpret and to use;
  (4) creating feedback channels (possibly automated) so that mis-use of models is identified and corrected promptly; and
  (5) ensuring models cannot be deployed outside their original purpose without documented approval from a qualified model risk manager.

- **Idiosyncratic Model Errors**
  Models will never exactly reproduce reality. Idiosyncratic errors are the unavoidable differences between the model output and the real-world outcome. This is a risk that will be retained, though it can be mitigated through model design.
- **Multiple Inconsistent Models in Use**
  Remove source of risk through strong model governance and control.
- **Fat Finger Errors**
  Mitigate likelihood through design of user interface, with checks and constraints built-in.
- **Spreadsheet Errors**
  Mitigate likelihood through rigorous vetting process. Restrict access to spreadsheet formulae so that changes cannot be introduced outside the model lifecycle process.
- **Model and Parameter Uncertainty**
  Avoid behavioural risk by ensuring that any stakeholder with an interest in the model outcome is not involved in vetting or approval. For example, in investment banking, traders have an interest in minimizing constraints. Traders may be represented in the model development process, but should not be involved in vetting or approval, and should not have access to the code.
  Record standard errors of parameter estimates, and stress test results based on realistic variation in parameters. Calculate important metrics using a range of models, and select values that are at the conservative side of the range of outcomes.
  Alternatively, use a Bayesian framework to incorporate model and parameter uncertainty into the calculations through the predictive distribution.

14.8 Notes and Further Reading

For more discussion, and examples, of Bayesian model and parameter uncertainty in actuarial risk management, see Cairns (2000). For an actuarial example using MCMC to set economic capital for embedded options in life insurance, see Hardy (2002).

For more information on Bayesian methods in general, and MCMC methods in particular, see Gelman et al. (2013) and Gilks et al. (1995).

For the views of banking regulators in the US and Canada on model risk and governance, see Federal Reserve (2011) and OSFI (2016).

14.9 Exercises

Exercise 14.1 Define model risk, and describe four different ways that model risk can lead to loss events.

Exercise 14.2 The Board of Directors of a firm has proposed using the 'Three lines of defence' approach to managing model risk.

(a) Explain how the 'Three lines of defence' approach could be applied to model risk.
(b) Describe the advantages and disadvantages of using this approach in the context of model risk.

Exercise 14.3 Explain how Knightian and non-Knightian uncertainty apply to parameter and model uncertainty.

Exercise 14.4 You are working in a team responsible for the risk management of options embedded in life insurance policies.

The current model used to project cash flows assumes that returns each month are independent and lognormally distributed. You propose exploring other models. Your manager says that 'if the model is good enough for Black and Scholes, it's good enough for us'.

Outline the points you would make in response to your manager. In particular, you should identify features of the model that may not adequately capture the risks being modelled.

Exercise 14.5 You work for an international auto manufacturing company. You have been tasked with developing a model for predicting annual business interruption costs from pandemics. The model will be based on a frequency/severity approach.

(a) Discuss briefly the risks involved with the model development and application.
(b) List and briefly explain the major points that should be considered at the model development stage.
(c) Comment on the likely problems of parameter and model uncertainty.
(d) What factors would you take into consideration in deciding whether to use a Bayesian approach to (a) parameter and (b) model uncertainty?

Exercise 14.6 You are a risk analyst working for a bank. You have been asked to evaluate two economic scenario generators (ESGs). One is a cascade model, the other is a vector autoregression model. Both models are fitted to the same historical data, and both satisfy standard goodness of fit tests, although the powers of the tests are low, as there are many parameters and not that much data.

(a) Describe the features of a good ESG.
(b) Explain briefly the different structures of a cascade model and a vector autoregression model.
(c) The two ESGs generate very different economic capital values for a section of the business, even when fitted to the same historical data. The economic capital used is the 98% Expected Shortfall estimated from Monte Carlo simulation, with a 1-year time horizon. The firm also records the 98% VaR measure.

The first generates a 98% VaR of 100 million, and a 98% Expected Shortfall of 200 million. The estimated standard error of the Expected Shortfall is 30 million.

The second generates a 98% VaR of 120 million, and a 98% Expected Shortfall of 150 million. The estimated standard error of the Expected Shortfall is 20 million.

The CEO of the bank has sent the following memo:

> Since both models are shown to the fit the data, we can choose either one. The first is conservative in the Expected Shortfall, the second is conservative in VaR. Moreover, the second is more accurate, as we see from the standard error of the Expected Shortfall. I therefore propose that we adopt the second ESG.

State with reasons whether you agree with the CEO's comments. Which ESG, if either, would you recommend the bank should adopt?

Exercise 14.7 You are given the following independent samples from posterior parameter distributions for three models of daily stock log-returns. There are five parameter sets for each model:

	μ	σ
	0.00058	0.01689
ILN	0.00064	0.01669
	0.00044	0.01793
	0.00060	0.01761
	0.00054	0.01767

	μ	a_0	a_1	b
	0.00131	4.38×10^{-6}	0.33792	0.64556
GARCH	0.00087	4.36×10^{-6}	0.29301	0.69544
	0.00107	2.66×10^{-6}	0.25727	0.72890
	0.00121	2.41×10^{-6}	0.24885	0.74497
	0.00072	4.59×10^{-6}	0.31537	0.68044

	μ_1	σ_1	μ_2	σ_2	p_{12}	p_{21}
	0.00161	0.00677	0.00090	0.03698	0.01692	0.10457
RSLN	0.00155	0.00675	−0.00352	0.03657	0.02413	0.07178
	0.00157	0.00691	−0.00299	0.03543	0.02126	0.06451
	0.00120	0.00702	−0.00067	0.03398	0.01525	0.06638
	0.00155	0.00701	−0.00253	0.03828	0.02035	0.07924

(a) Simulate five values for the 20-day portfolio loss for a portfolio
    with starting value 100, using the predictive distributions for
    (i) the ILN model, (ii) the GARCH model, and (3) the RSLN-2 model.
    Comment on the results.
(b) You are given that the posterior distribution for the individual
    models is:

$$p(\text{ILN} \,|\, \boldsymbol{x}) = 0.01; \quad p(\text{GARCH} \,|\, \boldsymbol{x}) = 0.84; \quad p(\text{RSLN2} \,|\, \boldsymbol{x}) = 0.14.$$

Simulate 5 values for the 20-day portfolio loss using the Bayesian
approach to model and parameter uncertainty.
(c) One colleague says: 'The ILN parameters look pretty stable. That must be
    the most accurate model'. Is he correct? Justify your answer.
(d) Another colleague says: 'The Bayesian approach just averages the correct
    model with some incorrect models. We should identify the true model and
    discard the others'. Critique this suggestion.
(e) A third colleague says: 'We should select the most conservative model'.
    Critique this suggestion.

Exercise 14.8 Marpole Insurance Company (MIC) sells Private Mortgage
Insurance (PMI), primarily in the state of California. US lenders require that
borrowers purchase PMI for new mortgage loans when the loan is more than
80% of the property value.

MIC's PMI product has the following characteristics:

• Level premiums are paid annually by the borrower based on the initial size
  of the loan. Premium rates are a function of the borrower's credit score.
• A claim equal to the outstanding loan balance is paid to the lender in the
  event that the borrower defaults.
• The insurance can be cancelled upon request of the borrower once the
  outstanding loan balance is less than 75% of the property value.

MIC invests the supporting assets primarily in short-term US treasuries and
high quality corporate bonds.

PMI is simple to administer and is sold by general agents who receive a
modest commission based on premium.

MIC has repurposed its cash flow testing model to determine its economic
capital (EC). The model has been modified to run numerous economic
scenarios as required for the EC calculation. Attributes of the repurposed
model include:

- Economic scenarios are generated from an internal ESG, which models equity values, credit spreads, US treasuries, inflation, US home prices, and US unemployment rates.
- The claims assumption, based on previous company experience, is modeled as a function of the projected unemployment rate and loan-to-value (LTV) ratio.
- The time step in the model is one month and the projection period is the average loan maturity.

(a) Assess whether the PMI EC model is fit for its intended purpose.
(b) Describe aspects of model governance that MIC should have in place.
(c) Identify which specific aspects of the PMI EC model warrant most of the validation effort. Justify your response.
(d) Explain how you would apply each of the following model calculation validation tests to the key drivers of the PMI EC model:

    (i) Sensitivity testing parameters.
    (ii) Validation of the dynamics of the model – for example, are the outputs and modelled relationships credible?
    (iii) Backtesting.

Copyright 2016. The Society of Actuaries, Schaumburg, Illinois. Reproduced with permission.

Exercise 14.9 Your firm is developing a model for operational risk exposure, in particular considering:

- Routine operational risks

    – People.
    – Processes.
    – IT.

- Exceptional operational risks

    – External events.
    – Sales and business practices.

Two potential approaches are being proposed to develop the model. Approach A is a simplified deterministic approach, based on average frequency and average severity within individual business units, developed through a risk mapping exercise. Approach B is a more comprehensive statistical approach. Key features of the two approaches are outlined in the following table:

	Approach A (Riskmap)	Approach B (Statistical model)
Owner	Unit Manager	ERM Department
Risk Measure	Expected Loss	Value at Risk
Frequency	Point estimates of likelihood for each risk	Statistical model, not yet determined
Severity	Direct impact on the firm's financial condition	Direct and indirect impact on the firm's financial condition
Dependency	Not modelled	Historical correlation matrix
Data	Individual units' experience and managers' judgement	Company wide data

(a) Compare and contrast the two approaches, in reference to the principles for new model proposals, development, validation, and approval laid out in Section 14.4.
(b) Assess the appropriateness of Approach B to adequately model both routine and exceptional operational risk exposures.

  Justify your response by discussing the suitability of each model component.

Copyright 2018. The Society of Actuaries, Schaumburg, Illinois. Reproduced with permission.

15

Risk Mitigation Using Options and Derivatives

15.1 Summary

In this chapter, we consider how derivatives can be used as part of a risk treatment plan. First, we look at the use of options to limit asset price risk; then we consider derivatives that protect against adverse movements in interest rates, credit risk, and exchange rates. Finally, we briefly consider how commodity derivatives are used to limit the risk from changing commodity prices.

15.2 Introduction

Options and derivatives are financial contracts with payouts that are dependent on the value of an underlying asset. Examples include put options, call options, swaps, and futures contracts. Derivatives may be used for speculative investment – and can be extremely risky in that context – but they can also be used to mitigate risk, by reducing the potential severity of a loss. Several market risk factors can serve as the underlying variables for derivative securities, including stock prices, stock market indices, interest rates, and commodity and energy prices.

15.3 Market Risk

In Chapter 9 we saw that, based on the short-term risk model, the VaR and Expected Shortfall of a portfolio move with the absolute value of the delta of the portfolio. To reduce the VaR or Expected Shortfall, we can use options to reduce the absolute value of the portfolio delta. The intuition is that if an

421

investor takes a long position in Stock A, then they will lose money if Stock A falls in value; this risk can be offset, or hedged, by purchasing a put option on the stock, which will compensate the investor if the stock price falls below the strike price. Similarly, if the investor has a short position in Stock A, they are exposed to risk from rising stock prices, which can be hedged by purchasing a call option, which will compensate them if the stock price increases above the strike price.

We illustrate this in the following example. Recall that the delta of one unit of stock is 1; the delta of a call option on one unit of a non-dividend paying stock is $\Phi(d_1)$, and the delta of a put option on one unit of a non-dividend paying stock is $-\Phi(-d_1)$.

Example 15.1 An investor has \$2,000 to invest. She is interested in Stock A, which has current price $S(0) = 10$ and volatility $\sigma = 0.31$. It does not pay dividends. She is considering two possible portfolios:

(1) Invest all her funds in units of Stock A.
(2) Purchase 398 put options on Stock A, with strike $K = 9.5$, term $T = 5/12$-years. The remainder of her funds would be invested in units of Stock A.

Assume options are priced using the Black–Scholes formula, with risk-free rate $r = 0.03$.

(a) Calculate the number of units of Stock A purchased under Portfolio (2).
(b) Calculate the delta of Portfolio (2).
(c) Calculate the 1-day VaR$_{99\%}$ of each portfolio, as a percentage of the portfolio value, using the delta-normal method.

Solution 15.1

(a) The price at $t = 0$ of each put option is

$$p(0) = 9.5e^{-rT}\Phi(-d_2) - 10\Phi(-d_1) = 0.502,$$

$$\text{where } d_1 = \frac{\log(S(0)/K) + (r + \sigma^2/2)T}{\sigma\sqrt{T}}, \quad d_2 = d_1 - \sigma\sqrt{T}.$$

If the investor buys 398 of these put options, the total cost is \$200, leaving \$1,800 available to invest in the stock. So the portfolio now comprises 180 units of stock and 398 put options.

(b) At $t = 0$, the delta of Portfolio (2) is

$$180 - 398 \times \Phi(-d_1) = 180 - 398 \times 0.3377 = 45.6.$$

This compares with the delta of Portfolio (1), which is 200.

(c) Using the delta-normal method, the one-day 99% VaR for Portfolio (1) is

$$\text{VaR}_{99\%} = 200 \times 10 \times z_{99\%} \times \sqrt{1/250} \times \sigma = 91.21,$$

which is 4.56% of the portfolio value.

Portfolio (2) has a delta of 45.6 (from (b)), so the 99% VaR using the delta-normal method is

$$\text{VaR}_{99\%} = 45.6 \times 10 \times 2.326 \times \sqrt{\frac{1}{250}} \times 0.31 = 20.8,$$

which is 1.04% of the portfolio value. □

15.3.1 Delta-Neutral Hedging

We see from the previous example that reducing the portfolio delta significantly reduces the risk, as measured by the 10-day 99% VaR. Taking this to the limit, we can construct a portfolio that combines the underlying and put options on it, such that the delta on the portfolio is zero. This is called a **delta-neutral hedge**.

Suppose an investor has $V(0)$ to invest in a combination of Stock A, priced at $S(0)$, and put options on Stock A, with term T years, and strike K, priced at p_0, with delta of $-\Phi(-d_1)$. Let w_1 denote the number of units of stock purchased, and w_2 denote the number of put options. Then we can find a delta-neutral portfolio by solving the following equations for w_1 and w_2:

$$V(0) = w_1 S(0) + w_2 p_0 \qquad \text{(portfolio value)},$$
$$0 = w_1 - w_2 \Phi(-d_1) \qquad \text{(portfolio delta)}.$$

Note that there are other ways to achieve a low delta portfolio. Combinations of some or all of short call options, futures contracts or more exotic derivatives could be used. The put options used here are just one example of a delta-reducing asset.

Example 15.2 Suppose the investor in Example 15.1, with $2,000 to invest, uses the put options from that example to create a delta-neutral portfolio. Let w_1 denote the number of units of stock she will buy, at $S(0) = 10$ each, and w_2 denote the number of put options, at $p_0 = 0.50$ each. We assume that options and stock can be purchased in fractions of units.

(a) Calculate w_1 and w_2.

(b) Suppose after $t = 0.02$ years the stock price has risen by 15%. For each of Portfolios (1) and (2) from Example 15.1 and Portfolio (3) from this example, calculate (i) the value of the portfolio at t, (ii) the return on the portfolio over the interval $(0, t]$, (iii) the delta of the portfolio at t, and (iv) the 1-day VaR$_{99\%}$ relative to the portfolio value at $t = 0.02$, using the delta-normal method.

(c) Suppose after $t = 0.02$ years the stock price has fallen by 15%. For each of Portfolios (1) and (2) from Example 15.1 and Portfolio (3) from this example, calculate (i) the value of the portfolio at t, (ii) the return on the portfolio over the interval $(0, t]$, (iii) the delta of the portfolio value at t and (iv) the 1-day VaR$_{99\%}$ relative to the portfolio at $t = 0.02$, using the delta-normal method.

Solution 15.2

(a) The delta of each put option is 0.3377, and the investor has \$2,000 to invest in the portfolio, so the equations for w_1 and w_2 are

$$2{,}000 = w_1(10) + w_2(0.50)$$
$$0 = w_1 - w_2(0.338)$$
$$\implies 2{,}000 = w_2\,(10 \times 0.3377 + 0.5)$$
$$\implies w_2 = 515.6 \text{ and } w_1 = 174.1.$$

So the portfolio comprising 174.1 units of stock (valued at 1,741) together with 515.6 put options (valued at 259) has initial value 2,000 and initial delta 0.

(b), (c) At time $t < T$ we have the option price

$$p_t = Ke^{-r(T-t)}\Phi(-d_2) - S(t)\Phi(-d_1).$$

It is important to remember that d_1 and d_2 are functions of t, so the values here will be different from the values used to calculate p_0. The value of the portfolio with w_1 units of stock and w_2 put options is

$$V(t) = w_1\,S(t) + w_2\,p_t.$$

The return on the portfolio over $(0, t]$ is $\frac{V(t)}{V(0)} - 1$, and the delta of the portfolio is

$$w_1 - w_2\,\Phi(-d_1).$$

The results for the portfolio value, portfolio return, and portfolio delta at $t = 0.02$, are as follows, for the two given values for $S(t)$:

	Portfolio (1)			Portfolio (2)			Portfolio (3)		
$S(t)$	Value	Return	Delta	Value	Return	Delta	Value	Return	Delta
11.5	2,300.0	15.0%	200	2,132.2	6.6%	129.2	2,082.8	4.14%	108.4
8.5	1,700.0	−15.0%	200	2,018.4	0.9%	−82.5	2,112.7	5.63%	−166.0

We note the following:

- Adding the options to the portfolio has significantly reduced the risk of a loss, but has also reduced the profit on the portfolio if stock prices rise.
- The change in stock price (and passage of time) has a significant impact on d_1, so the deltas of the portfolios containing options have all changed significantly between time 0 and time t.
- In particular, Portfolio (3), which was delta-neutral at the start, has delta far from zero under both these scenarios by time t. In order to maintain a delta-neutral portfolio, the investor would have to sell or buy some shares or options to rebalance the portfolio. This is a form of **dynamic hedging**. In principle, maintaining a zero delta on the portfolio would require continuous rebalancing of stocks and options.

In the following table, we show the 1-day, delta-normal $VaR_{0.99}$ calculations for the three portfolios, at $t = 0$ and at $t = 0.02$:

	Portfolio (1)	Portfolio (2)	Portfolio (3)
$VaR_{99\%}$ at $t = 0$	4.56%	1.04%	0.00%
$VaR_{99\%}$ at $t = 0.02$, $S(t) = 11.5$	4.56%	3.18%	2.73%
$VaR_{99\%}$ at $t = 0.02$, $S(t) = 8.5$	4.56%	1.58%	3.04%

□

Without rebalancing, the delta-normal VaR_α values will change significantly for any portfolio containing options or derivatives. In order to protect from changes in delta, the investor may choose to hedge both delta, which measures the sensitivity of the portfolio *value* to changes in the value of the underlying asset or risk factor, and gamma, which measures the sensitivity of the portfolio *delta* to changes in the underlying asset or risk factor.

15.3.2 Delta-Gamma-Neutral Hedging

The gamma of the portfolio measures the risk arising from the change in the portfolio delta as the underlying asset or risk factor changes value. For a portfolio comprising units of stock, with no options or derivatives, the gamma is 0. If the portfolio has a long position in puts or calls, the portfolio will have a positive gamma; the gamma at time t of a long put or call option maturing at T is $\frac{\phi(d_1)}{S(t)\sigma\sqrt{T}}$.

The investor may reduce the exposure to delta risk by reducing the gamma of the portfolio, for example, by taking a short position in call or put options, as the gamma of the option seller is $-\phi(d_1)/(S(t)\sigma\sqrt{T})$. With delta-gamma hedging, the investor limits both the delta and gamma values for the portfolio, with a combination of long and short positions in the stock and in options on the stock. The following example illustrates the effect of mitigating both the delta and the gamma risk.

Example 15.3 The investor in Example 15.1 is considering including a short call position in her portfolio, to give a partial gamma hedge.

Portfolio (4) comprises 192 units of stock, 320 of the put options described in Example 15.1, together with a short position in 84 call options on the same stock, with strike price 11.0, and term 1 year.

(a) Verify that the initial value of Portfolio (4) is 2,000.
(b) Calculate the delta and gamma for Portfolio (4).
(c) Calculate the 1-day VaR$_{99\%}$ for Portfolio (4) using the delta-normal method.
(d) Compare the performance of Portfolio (2) and Portfolio (4) with respect to risk and return over the period $(0, 0.02]$, assuming (as above) (i) $S(0.02) = 11.5$ and (ii) $S(0.02) = 8.5$.

Solution 15.3

(a) The price of each call option is

$$c_0 = S(0)\Phi(d_1^c) - 11e^{-rT^c}\Phi(d_2^c) = 0.9638 \quad \text{where } d_1^c = -0.05568$$
$$\implies V(0) = 192 \times 10 + 320 \times 0.502 - 84 \times 0.9638 = 2{,}000.$$

(b) The delta for each call option is $\Phi(d_1^c) = 0.4778$, so the Portfolio (4) delta is

$$192 - 320 \cdot 0.3377 - 84 \cdot 0.4778 = 43.8.$$

Table 15.1. *Comparison of Delta, Gamma, VaR99%, and return for Portfolio (2) (stocks and long put options) and Portfolio (4) (stocks, long put options, and short call options) for Example 15.3*

	Delta	Gamma	VaR99%	Portfolio return
At $t = 0$				
Portfolio (2)	45.6	72.7	20.8	–
Portfolio (4)	43.8	47.7	20.2	–
At $t = 0.02$: $S(t) = 11.5$				
Portfolio (2)	129.2	37.1	67.7	6.6%
Portfolio (4)	96.2	11.2	50.5	5.3%
At $t = 0.02$: $S(t) = 8.5$				
Portfolio (2)	−82.5	87.9	32.0	0.9%
Portfolio (4)	−42.3	36.7	16.4	−0.4%

The gammas for each put option and call option are, respectively,

$$\frac{\phi(d_1^p)}{S(0)\,\sigma\,\sqrt{T^p}} = 0.1826, \qquad \frac{\phi(d_1^c)}{S(0)\,\sigma\,\sqrt{T^c}} = 0.1285.$$

So the portfolio gamma is

$$320 \times 0.1826 - 84 \times 0.1285 = 47.65.$$

(c) The delta-normal one-day VaR99% for Portfolio (4) is 19.98.
(d) In Table 15.1, we show the time $t = 0$ and the time $t = 0.02$ delta, gamma, and VaR99% values, as well as the portfolio returns, for $S(t) = 11.5$ and for $S(t) = 8.5$.

We see that the portfolios have similar values for delta at the start (45.6 and 43.8, respectively), which means that they have similar 1-day VaR99% values (20.8 and 20.0, respectively). However, the gamma for Portfolio (2) is significantly larger than Portfolio (4) (72.7 and 47.7, respectively), so we expect to see more change in the delta at $t = 0.02$ for Portfolio (2) than Portfolio (4), and that is supported by the values in the table, where the absolute value of delta has increased significantly more for Portfolio (2) than for Portfolio (4), giving a higher VaR99% in both scenarios for Portfolio (2). However, risk reduction comes at a price, and the return on Portfolio (4) is lower than Portfolio (2) for both scenarios. □

A delta-gamma neutral portfolio is one where both delta and gamma are set to zero. This can be achieved with a combination of the underlying asset, a long position in put options on the underlying, and a short position in call options on the underlying, similarly to the situation described in Example 15.3. We work through the construction for hedging equity risk as follows:

- Let w_1 denote the number of units of stock purchased, w_2 the number of put options purchased, and w_3 the number of call options sold. We also need to distinguish between d_1^p, say, which is the d_1 function for the put option, and d_1^c, which is the d_1 function for the call option. If the puts and calls have the same strike and term, then the two d_1 functions are the same.
- Let p_t and c_t denote the price of a single put option and call option. Respectively, at t, and let T^p and T^c denote the maturity dates for the put and call options, respectively.
- Then we have three equations for w_1, w_2, and w_3, corresponding to the equation for the portfolio value, the equation for the portfolio delta (which we set to zero), and the equation for the portfolio gamma (also set to zero). That is,

$$V(0) = w_1 S(0) + w_2 p_0 - w_3 c_0,$$

$$0 = w_1 - w_2 \Phi(-d_1^p) - w_3 \Phi(d_1^c),$$

$$0 = w_2 \left(\frac{\phi(d_1^p)}{S(0)\sigma \sqrt{T^p}} \right) - w_3 \left(\frac{\phi(d_1^c)}{S(0)\sigma \sqrt{T^c}} \right).$$

Example 15.4 Using the stock, put, and call options in Example 15.3, construct a delta-gamma neutral portfolio with initial value 2,000, and compare its performance, with respect to risk and return, to the delta-neutral Portfolio (3), under the two scenarios from the previous examples.

Solution 15.4 The three equations, for portfolio value, portfolio delta, and portfolio gamma are

$$2{,}000 = 10w_1 + 0.502w_2 - 0.964w_3,$$

$$0 = w_1 - 0.3377w_2 - 0.4778w_3,$$

$$0 = 0.1826w_2 - 0.1285w_3$$

$$\Rightarrow w_1 = 218.66, \quad w_2 = 215.06, \quad \text{and} \quad w_3 = 305.66.$$

Let Portfolio (5) denote the delta-gamma-neutral portfolio. In Table 15.2, we compare the delta neutral portfolio with the delta-gamma neutral portfolio. We see a similar, but more extreme pattern as in Table 15.1. That is, the delta-gamma neutral portfolio significantly reduces the portfolio risk, with very low

Table 15.2. *Comparison of Delta, Gamma, VaR$_{99\%}$, and return for Portfolio (3) (stocks and long put options, delta neutral) and Portfolio (5) (stocks, long put options, and short call options, delta-gamma neutral) for Example 15.4*

	Delta	Gamma	VaR$_{99\%}$	Portfolio return
At $t = 0$				
Portfolio (3)	0.0	72.7	0.0	–
Portfolio (5)	0.0	0.0	0.0	–
At $t = 0.02$: $S(t) = 11.5$				
Portfolio (3)	108.2	48.0	56.8	4.1%
Portfolio (5)	−8.5	−32.0	4.5	−0.1%
At $t = 0.02$: $S(t) = 8.5$				
Portfolio (3)	−166.0	113.9	64.3	5.6%
Portfolio (5)	−7.9	−39.7	3.1	0.2%

values for the time t 1-day VaR$_{99\%}$ in both scenarios, but at the cost of portfolio return in either scenario. □

15.3.3 Other Greeks

Delta and Gamma are two of a range of measures known as the 'greeks' of a portfolio. Each of the greeks measures the sensitivity of the portfolio value to a change in one of the underlying variables – or (as in the case of gamma) the sensitivity of another greek to a change in an underlying variable. We briefly list the most common greeks here. More detail can be found in the references listed at the end of this chapter.

- **Vega** (which is not a greek letter, but is a financial 'greek') is the sensitivity of the portfolio value to changes in the volatility of the underlying, σ.
  In this chapter, we have treated the stock volatility as a fixed constant.
  In fact, as we have seen, volatility changes all the time.
- **Theta** is used to mean the sensitivity of the portfolio value to changes in the time to maturity of options and derivatives, or the sensitivity to changes in the time of valuation, t.
- **Rho** is the sensitivity of the portfolio value to changes in the risk-free rate of interest, r.

For some options and derivatives, simple analytic formulas are available for calculating the greeks. In other cases they can be calculated using numerical differentiation.

15.4 Hedging Market Risk with Option Combinations

The delta neutral and delta-gamma neutral hedges described above are very restrictive. Ultimately, extra return is a reward for extra risk; eliminating risk means eliminating return. Sometimes, investors can use options in combination to provide a risk-return trade-off that meets their precise needs.

Suppose a pension fund has a substantial equity portfolio. It is seeking the extra returns offered by equities in the long run, but has significant shorter term risk from equity price shocks. The pension plan does not need to make windfall profits, but it does need to protect itself against severe losses from sudden falls in equity prices. That means the plan is willing to give up some upside opportunity to protect itself against downside risk, compared with an all-equity portfolio.

Example 15.5 A pension investment manager is responsible for an asset portfolio with current value 100 which is being held to support uncertain future pension payments. The assets are currently all held in an **exchange traded fund** (ETF) that tracks a market index. The current price of one unit of the ETF is $S(0) = 100$, and the return is assumed to follow an ILN process, with $\mu = 0.04$ and $\sigma = 0.25$ per year.

(a) Calculate the 1-year 95% VaR, assuming the assets are fully invested in the ETF.

(b) The pension trustees decide that the 1-year loss should be limited to a maximum of 15% of the initial fund value. The manager purchases a 1-year put option on the ETF, with strike price $K_1 = 85$, to achieve this goal. To fund the purchase of the put option, the manager sells a 1-year call option on the ETF with a strike price of K_2. The risk-free rate of return is $r = 0.04$.

　(i) Calculate the price of the put option.
　(ii) Hence, calculate K_2.
　(iii) Calculate the revised 1-year 95% VaR.
　(iv) Calculate the return on the portfolio.

Solution 15.5

(a) Consider the loss random variable 1-year ahead:

$$L = V_0 - V_1 = 100 - V_1.$$

The 95% VaR is $100 - 100\left(e^{\mu - 1.645\sigma}\right) = 31.0$ or 31% of the fund value.

(b) (i) The put option price is

$$p_0 = K_1 e^{-r} \Phi(-d_2) - S(0)\Phi(-d_1),$$

$$d_1 = \frac{\log(S(0)/K_1) + (r + \sigma^2/2)}{\sigma} = 0.9351,$$

$$d_2 = d_1 - \sigma = 0.6851$$

$$\Rightarrow p_0 = 2.656.$$

(ii) To find K_2, we need to solve the equation

$$c_0 = 2.656 = 100\Phi(d_1^*) - k_2 e^{-r} \Phi(d_2^*),$$

where d_1^* and d_2^* are as d_1 and d_2, but with K_2 replacing K_1. Solving this numerically gives $K_2 = 131.33$.

(iii) The 1-year loss on the portfolio is limited to a maximum of 15; the probability that this limit is reached is the probability that the ETF value is less than 85 at the end of the year, which is

$$\Phi\left(\frac{\log(0.85) - \mu}{\sigma}\right) = \Phi(-0.8101) = 0.2089.$$

Because this is greater than 5%, the 95% VaR is 15.

(iv) The accumulation factor for the portfolio is $Y = (V_1/V_0)$. Without the put and call options, we would have $Y \sim \text{logN}(0.04, 0.25)$. The effect of the put and call options is a floor for Y of 0.85 and a ceiling of 1.311. In between, Y follows the lognormal distribution. The expected value of Y is then

$$E[Y] = \Pr[Y = 0.85] \times 0.85$$

$$+ \Pr[Y = 1.311] \times 1.311 + \int_{0.85}^{1.311} y f(y) dy,$$

where $f(y)$ is the density function of the lognormal distribution of the ETF accumulation. We have

$$\Pr[Y = 0.85] = \Pr[S(1) \le 85] = \Phi\left(\frac{\log(0.85) - 0.04}{0.25}\right) = 0.2089,$$

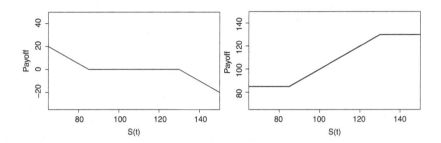

Figure 15.1 Payoff functions for a collar (left side) and a collar plus stock (right side), with strikes at $K_1 = 85$ and $K_2 = 130$.

$$\Pr[Y = 1.311] = \Pr[S(1) > 131.1]$$

$$= 1 - \Phi\left(\frac{\log(1.311) - 0.04}{0.25}\right) = 0.1780.$$

Also, we know that for the lognormal distribution,

$$\int_0^A yf(y)dy = e^{\mu + \sigma^2/2}\Phi\left(\frac{\log(A) - \mu - \sigma^2}{\sigma}\right)$$

$$\Rightarrow \int_{0.85}^{1.311} yf(y)dy = e^{\mu + \sigma^2/2}\left(\Phi\left(\frac{\log(1.311) - \mu - \sigma^2}{\sigma}\right)\right.$$

$$\left. - \Phi\left(\frac{\log(0.85) - \mu - \sigma^2}{\sigma}\right)\right)$$

$$= 0.650.$$

So the expected value of Y is

$$E[Y] = 0.2089 \times 0.85 + 0.1780 \times 1.311 + 0.65 = 1.0609,$$

and the expected return is $E[Y] - 1 = 6.09\%$.

This compares with an expected return of $e^{\mu + \sigma^2/2} - 1 = 7.38\%$ for the unprotected portfolio. □

The combination of the long put option and the short call option is called a **collar strategy**. In Figure 15.1, we show the payoff functions of the collar, and of the collar plus the stock. The diagram shows how the collar constrains both the upside and downside risk. The collar is particularly useful because, as illustrated in the example, it can be set up at zero cost. The effective price paid is the reduced return on the total investment.

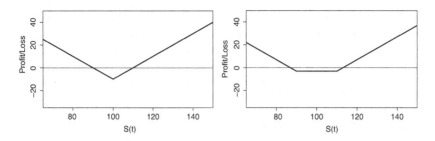

Figure 15.2 Profit/loss functions for a straddle (left side, strike = 100) and a strangle (right side, strikes at 90 and 110)

Other option combinations are frequently used in risk management. In some cases, a risk manager may be concerned about gamma risk. To offset the risk from large stock movements, the risk manager can construct a **straddle** or **strangle** option; both involve a combination of a put option and a call option. The straddle uses the same strike for both options, while the strangle uses a lower strike price for the put option and a higher strike price for the call option. These combination options provide a payoff that is large when stock prices are very low or very high. In Example 15.3, a strangle was used to reduce the portfolio gamma. Unlike the collar, these options would not be cost free. In Figure 15.2, we show profit/loss diagrams for a straddle and a strangle. The option prices assume a 3-month term, a current stock price of 100, a risk-free rate of 4%, and a volatility of 25%.

15.5 Interest Rate Derivatives

Firms may be exposed to interest rate risk in several ways. If they borrow or lend money, then they are exposed to the risk that the cost of borrowing rises, or that the interest received falls. If a firm invests funds at variable rates, but has debt that is serviced at fixed rates, then the mismatch can lead to liquidity stress or worse.

Firms may manage interest rate risk by attempting to match incoming and outgoing cash flows, or by duration matching or immunization, as described in Chapter 11. But in some cases using financial derivatives to manage interest rate risk will be a useful tool.

15.5.1 Put and Call Options On Bonds

Options on bonds work similarly to options on stocks. A put option gives the option holder the right to sell the bond at the strike price on the maturity date.

This will protect against rising interest rates, as bond prices fall when interest rates rise. Similarly, a call option protects against falling interest rates.

15.5.2 Interest Rate Forward Contract

A borrower and lender may agree on the interest rate to be paid on a future loan, with a specified start and end date, and for a specified amount. The interest rate is locked in at the date of the agreement, even though the loan is not initiated for some time.

The interest rate forward contract protects the borrower against the risk of interest rates rising between the initial agreement and the loan start date, and, similarly, protects the lender against a fall in interest rates. There is no premium or cost for this arrangement, and the appropriate rate of interest can be derived from the forward rates in force at the time of the initial agreement.

15.5.3 Interest Rate Swaps

Typical interest rate swaps involve one counterparty that agrees to pay a floating rate of interest, such as the LIBOR rate, while the other counterparty pays a fixed rate. The interest rate swap allows an organization with variable income, and fixed outgo to hedge their interest rate risk at no upfront cost.

The swap rate is the rate paid by the fixed rate counterparty (Figure 15.3). It is chosen to be consistent with the yield curve of interest rates at the issue date, based on no-arbitrage principles. That is, we know that the market value of a floating interest loan of $100, and with variable interest payable (say) yearly, is $100. So the swap rate applicable for an n year swap with annual payments, and with notional principal of $100, is c, such that the market value of a $100 bond with coupons of $100c$ per year is also equal to $100.

Suppose the yield curve discount function at the start date of the swap is $v(t)$; that is, the market value at time 0 of 1 due at t is $v(t)$. The swap rate c is then found from the equation

$$100 = 100c\,(v(1) + v(2) + \cdots + v(n)) + 100v(n)$$
$$\implies c = \frac{1 - v(n)}{\sum_{k=1}^{n} v(k)}.$$

Each swap contract specifies a notional principal, P, a payment frequency h, the floating rate (e.g., LIBOR + margin), the fixed swap rate (c), and the term (called the **tenor**). Let f_t denote the floating rate at t, then the floating

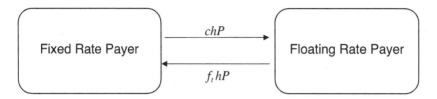

Figure 15.3 Swap transaction: P is the notional principal, h is the frequency, f_t is the floating rate at t, c is the fixed rate, and m is the margin over floating paid by the floating rate payer.

rate payer pays $(f_t - c)hP$ if $f_t > c$, and the fixed rate payer pays $(c - f_t)hP$ if $c > f_t$. In practice, the frequency is typically $h = 1/2$ or $h = 1/4$ years. Interest rate swaps are very widely used to manage interest rate risk.

15.5.4 Caps and Floors

An interest rate cap is a contract that pays at regular intervals if a reference market interest rate, such as LIBOR or a US Treasury Bill rate, exceeds a specified strike rate. The purchaser of the cap pays a premium at the start of the contract, and the cap payments are commonly set at monthly intervals. So a purchaser of a LIBOR 4% cap, with notional principal of 100, and with monthly payments, would receive a payment of $100 \max(\text{LIBOR}-0.04, 0)$ at the end of each month. For a purchaser that has a liability to pay LIBOR rates, the cap provides limit to their liability, but at a cost.

An interest rate floor is similar, but with the purchaser receiving a payment whenever the reference rate falls below the floor strike rate. So a purchaser of, say, an interest floor on one-month Treasury Bills, with notional principal of 100, strike rate 2%, and with monthly payments, would receive a payment of $100 \max(0.02-\text{Treasury Bill Rate}, 0)$ at the end of each month. For a purchaser that receives T-Bill rates, the floor provides a guarantee that at least the strike rate will be paid.

15.6 Credit Risk

As discussed in Chapter 12, a firm might be exposed to credit risk in different ways. The first and most obvious is when an individual or firm defaults on their obligations. The second arises when losses are incurred on a change in the credit quality of an institution; these are the mark-to-market losses.

For example, if a firm has its credit spread increase, the value of the outstanding bonds issued by the firm will decrease, creating losses for the bondholders.

Credit default swaps (CDS), described in Chapter 12, are the most direct way to hedge default risk using derivatives. The CDS is very similar to a traditional insurance contract, providing insurance against loss due to default or downgrade of a specified company known as the **reference entity**. The buyer pays regular premiums to the seller until a credit event occurs, or until the end of the term. The credit event may be a default, or a credit rating downgrade, of the reference entity. When a credit event occurs, the CDS issuer will pay the purchaser an amount based on the settlement mechanism, specified in the initial agreement – for example, the difference between the face value of the bond and the mid-market residual value immediately after the credit event.

A **total return swap** combines an interest swap and a credit default swap. Suppose an investor owns an asset, known as the reference asset. If the investor enters into a total return swap, then they agree to pay the counterparty all the interest paid on the asset, plus any capital gain, if positive. In return, the counterparty pays a specified rate, which may be fixed or floating (usually, whichever is not the form generated by the reference asset), plus any decrease in value of the reference asset. The total return swap then simultaneously provides interest rate protection, and protection against mark-to-market losses, for the buyer, and offers the return on the reference asset, without having to purchase it, to the counterparty, effectively creating leverage.

15.7 Exchange Rate Risk

A firm that is exposed to exchange rate risk may hedge the risk using currency derivatives.

Currency forwards allow a purchaser to lock in an exchange rate for a currency purchase made at a specified date in the future.

A **currency swap** involves a swap of payments in one currency for payments in another currency. Suppose a firm based in the US has a liability to make regular payments in euros. It can enter into a swap under which it will pay, say, 1 US dollar at the end of each year for n years, to receive x euros at the end of each year. The amount x depends on the currency forward prices and the yield curve at the start of the contract.

Let $v(t)$ again denote the yield curve discount function at the start of the contract, and let F_t denote the t-year forward price for 1 euro, at the start of the contract, meaning that an individual can contract at time 0 to purchase x euros at time t for $x F_t$ US dollars.

The value of the US dollar annuity, at the start of the contract is

$$v(1) + v(2) + \cdots + v(n).$$

The value of the x euro annuity at the start of the contract, in USD, is

$$x \left(F_1 v(1) + F_2 v(2) + \cdots + F_n v(n) \right).$$

The market value of the two payment streams is equal at the inception date, which means that

$$x = \frac{v(1) + v(2) + \cdots + v(n)}{F_1 v(1) + F_2 v(2) + \cdots + F_n v(n)}.$$

The currency swap may involve a bond swap, rather than an annuity, in which case the final payment of principal will also be included. Suppose a firm wishes to swap interest and principal payments on an n year US dollar bond, with face value 100 and annual coupons of $\$100c$, for an n year bond with the same face value, but with coupons of $100x\%$ per year, designated in Yen. The face value of the Yen bond is 100 in US dollars, which is $100/F_0$ in Yen, where F_0 is the dollar price of 1 yen at time 0. Equating the market values of the two payment streams gives

$$100c \left(v(1) + v(2) + \cdots + v(n) \right) + 100v(n)$$
$$= \frac{100x}{F_0} \left(F_1 v(1) + F_2 v(2) + \cdots + F_n v(n) \right) + \frac{100}{F_0} v(n).$$

Note that if c is the par yield of the US bond, then its market value at time 0 is 100, so we have

$$x = \frac{F_0 - v(n)}{F_1 v(1) + F_2 v(2) + \cdots + F_n v(n)}.$$

Both of these examples involve fixed payments from both swap partners. Currency swaps can also involve a fixed payment on one side and a floating payment on the other, or floating payments on both sides.

Currency options allow the purchaser to ensure a minimum or maximum exchange rate at some future date, in return for an upfront fee at the start of the contract.

15.8 Commodity Price Hedging

Commodity derivatives are forwards, futures, and options contracts, for which the underlying reference asset is a commodity. Common reference asset commodities include agricultural products, fuel and energy products, and metals. Forwards and options are over-the-counter (OTC) contracts, created for a specific buyer and seller, while futures are traded on specialized exchanges, such as the Chicago Mercantile Exchange with regulated, standardized contracts, and registered buyers and sellers, offering some protection against counterparty risk.

Commodity producers, such as farmers, oil producers, and mining companies, can use commodity derivatives to lock in a selling price for their products. Consumers, such as manufacturers, or airline companies can use commodity derivatives to lock in a price for their future purchases. For example, a car manufacturer can lock in the price it will pay for platinum, and an airline can lock in the price it will pay for aviation fuel. Unlike financial or currency derivatives, a commodity derivative often involves an actual exchange of the reference commodity at the end date.

Standardization of futures contracts means that they are issued with standard terms and conditions regarding quantity, quality, term, and location. This facilitates trading and reduces transactions costs. Many traders are not actually interested in acquiring or selling the commodity; their interest is in speculation. The commodity exchange offers a convenient forum for speculation, allowing traders to sell the contract on, before they are required to purchase or produce some quantity of the underlying commodity.

One complication of contracts on physical assets is that logistical costs relating, for example, to storage or transportation, must be taken into consideration.

15.9 Notes and Further Reading

Although LIBOR has been the standard benchmark for interest rate swaps, this is changing as a result of the LIBOR rate fixing scandal.

Many books on financial market mathematics offer more detailed coverage of the derivatives described here. Examples include Hull (2022) and McDonald (2009). For a narrative of the uses and abuses of derivatives in risk management, see Boyle and Boyle (2001).

15.10 Exercises

Exercise 15.1 An investor is considering protecting themselves from downside risk using either deep out-of-the-money put options, or a collar. Explain the advantages and disadvantages of each approach.

Exercise 15.2 A pension plan is heavily duration mismatched, with liabilities having much longer duration than assets. Explain the risk arising from the duration mismatch, and describe how the risk might be mitigated using interest rate options.

Exercise 15.3 Hilliard Co has issued a 4-year floating rate bond with face value 200 million. The interest rate, payable annually is LIBOR+40 basis points.

Hilliard's risk manager is concerned about the possibility of rising interest rates.

(a) Explain how Hilliard could mitigate the risk from rising interest rates using (i) interest rate swaps or (ii) interest rate caps. Outline the advantages and disadvantages of each approach.

(b) Avondale Bank has offered Hilliard an interest rate swap. Hilliard agrees to pay LIBOR+40 basis points; in return Avondale will pay a fixed rate of c per year. The swap payment frequency is annual, and the term is four years. The current annual spot yields are:

One-year: 2.7%, Two-year: 3.0%, Three-year: 3.2%, Four-year: 3.4%.

Calculate the swap rate, c.

Exercise 15.4 The Toronto Blue Jays baseball team pay their players in US dollars, but receive much of their revenue in Canadian dollars. Explain how currency derivatives might be used to mitigate their currency risk.

Exercise 15.5 A US university maintains a large endowment fund (UEF). Investment income is used to support student scholarships and infrastructure expenditure, both of which require a regular, predictable income stream. The fund is managed by a Trustee Board appointed by the university.

The trustees have been working closely with 'Local Investment Bank' (LIB). Currently, the UEF has entered into the following contracts with LIB to manage or mitigate financial risk:

(i) An interest rate swap, under which the university pays the short term floating rate and receives a fixed rate of 4% at each year end. The nominal principal is $100 million. The contract has three years remaining.

(ii) Credit default swaps with two years to maturity. The current Market Value (MV) is $2 million.

(iii) A European put option on the S&P 500 index with three months term to maturity. The option is far out-of-the-money. The current MV is $5 million.

(iv) A currency swap, under which the UEF pays 5% per year in euros (€) on notional principal of € 100 million and receives 4% per year in US dollars ($) on notional principal of $100 million. Payments are made at each year end. The contract has three years remaining.

(a) Each of the contracts with LIB was put in place to mitigate particular risks, based on the portfolio that the UEF has in place. Explain a potential risk that the UEF could have been intending to mitigate for each of the four contracts.

(b) The value of an interest rate swap to the party who receives an annual fixed rate of c% and pays the floating rate, with remaining term n years, is the difference in value between an n-year, c% annual coupon bond and an n-year floating rate note.

    (i) Explain why this description gives the market value of the swap.
    (ii) You are given that the current risk-free rate of interest is 3% per year, compounded continuously. Show that the current market value of the interest rate swap to the UEF is $2.7 million to the nearest $0.1 million.
    (iii) You are given that the euro payments under the currency swap are valued at a flat rate of interest of 1% per year, compounded continuously. The US dollar payments are valued at a flat rate of interest of 3% per year, compounded continuously. The current exchange rate is $1.06 to € 1.00. Show that the current market value of the currency swap is −$2.7 million, to the nearest $0.1 million.

Copyright 2016, The Society of Actuaries, Schaumburg, Illinois. Reproduced with permission.

Exercise 15.6 A trader has a constraint that her trading strategy must have a 99% VaR, based on a 7-day horizon, less than or equal to 0. Assume 250 trading days in a year.

She has constructed a portfolio of derivatives on a stock with initial value $S_0 = 100$. The value at T of S_T/S_0 follows a lognormal distribution with parameters $T\mu$ and $T\sigma^2$, where $\mu = 0.05195$ and $\sigma = 0.31$.

She has decided on the following strategy:

- purchase 1 million seven-day call options with a strike price of 87,
- sell short 1 million seven-day call options with a strike price of 88,
- finance the cost of the call options by selling short M seven-day put options with a strike price of 87.

All the options are priced using the Black–Scholes formulas, with risk-free rate $r = 0.05$, and volatility $\sigma = 0.31$ per year.

(a) Calculate the number of put options sold such that the strategy has zero initial cost.
(b) Complete the following table:

Stock Price at T	Prob. S_T at this value or lower	Loss on portfolio for this S_T (millions)
90		
89		
88		
87		
86		
85		

(c) Calculate the 99% VaR for the loss at T, and verify that it complies with the trader's constraint.
(d) Generate a Monte Carlo sample of 2,000 values for the payoff at T from the portfolio. Describe your approach, and determine a list of the largest 20 loss values in the sample.
(e) Use your sample to estimate a 95% confidence interval for the 99% VaR of the loss at T. Comment on the accuracy of the confidence interval.
(f) Use your sample to estimate the 99% Expected Shortfall for the loss at T.
(g) Estimate a 95% confidence interval for the 99% Expected Shortfall. Explain your method.
(h) Comment on the advantages and disadvantages of using the 99% VaR as a trading constraint.

16

Risk Transfer

16.1 Summary

In this chapter, we review the different methods available to a firm that wants to transfer risk. First, we consider the traditional route of insurance, or reinsurance if the firm transferring the risk is itself an insurance company. We describe the different types of insurance contracts, and analyse their advantages and disadvantages. We then consider **captive** insurance companies, which are insurance companies that are owned by the organization that is transferring risk; that is, the parent company of the insurer is also the policyholder, or the parent company of the policyholders. Next, we discuss securitization of risk, where risk is packaged into investments that are sold off in the capital markets. One of the most interesting, and better known, examples of securitized insurance risk is the **catastrophe bond** (cat bond), which has payments of interest and capital that are contingent on specified catastrophic events not occurring. If a covered event does occur, some or all of the bond principal is lost. We also look at examples of securitization of demographic risk, through pandemic bonds and through longevity derivatives, which are designed to mitigate the risk of increasing life expectancy, for example, for pension plans that have liabilities that continue through the post-retirement lifetime of the plan members.

Both securitization and captive insurance are generally categorized as **alternative risk transfer** – a term that encompasses non-traditional ways of transferring risk that would traditionally have been passed to an insurance or reinsurance company.

16.2 Introduction

The treatment of risk was classified into five broad categories in the first chapter, summarized as avoid, pursue, mitigate, transfer, or retain. In this chapter, we focus on the transfer of risk through insurance or insurance-like arrangements. Transferring risk is costly – the premium charged for insurance will usually be greater than the expected loss of the insured risk – so the firm transferring the risk must weigh carefully the impact on its overall profitability and on its risk budget. Non-traditional insurance arrangements, including securitization, can provide cheaper ways to achieve some risk transfer, but there are generally additional risks or uncertainties involved.

16.3 Risk Transfer through Traditional Insurance

Not all risks are insurable. There must be some constraints for the market between insurers and policyholders to function. Generally accepted principles for insurable risk are:

- **The Potential Loss Is Quantifiable and Well Defined.** It is important to have an objective measure of the cash value of a loss. Otherwise, there is a risk that insurers and policyholders could end up in a protracted and expensive conflict about the appropriate claim payments.
- **The Policyholder Must Have a Financial Interest No Smaller than the Potential Benefit.** This is important to avoid **moral hazard** risk. Moral hazard arises when an agent has an incentive to increase risk, because they are not exposed to the potential downsides of the risk-taking activity. So, for example, an individual who has full theft insurance for their car might not take so much care in locking it when they leave it as someone who would suffer the loss personally. Moral hazard is a well known feature of insurance, but it arises in many other situations where risk and rewards are misaligned. For example, an investment banker whose bonus is related to the return she achieves on her assets under management might take excessive risks, because she will benefit significantly from the upside, but carries none of the liability from the downside (except possibly forfeiting bonus and, worst-case, job).

  This criterion is often summarized as requiring the insured to have an **insurable interest** in the covered event.

- **The Loss Event Should Be Uncertain in Terms of Timing and Loss Severity.** Insurance is designed to indemnify against relatively rare events, not to act as a sort of bank for everyday cash flow variation.[1]
- **The Risk Is Diversifiable.** This means that by pooling risks the insurer can reduce the overall risk of extreme outcomes. This allows the insurer to charge an economic premium.

Where a firm has risks that are insurable, they must assess whether the benefits of insurance, in terms of limiting the risk, are sufficient to justify the costs.

The frequency-severity method described in Chapter 4 allows the firm to assess quantitatively the risks and benefits associated with insurance. Given an insurable risk, with potential loss S, say, the firm may choose to self-insure (that is, run the risk), to insure the risk fully, or to insure the risk partially. With full insurance, the insurer indemnifies the full loss. With partial insurance, the insurer would cover some part of the insured loss, following a predetermined formula. The two most common methods of partial insurance are **coinsurance**, also known as co-pay, where the insured and insurer share losses in predetermined proportion, and insurance deductibles, where the insured pays the first $\$D$ of loss, with the insurer covering any excess. In both cases, in practice, there will be a maximum insured loss.

From the insurer's perspective, partial insurance can have many advantages, with the most important being the reduction in moral hazard risk; the policy-holder is incentivized to mitigate risk if they continue to be at least partially responsible for losses.

16.3.1 Proportional Insurance

Suppose a firm faces an uncertain loss S. Under proportional insurance, the firm would retain a proportion of the loss, say aS where $0 < a < 1$, and the insurer would cover the remainder, $(1 - a)S$.

Example 16.1 A firm is interested in insuring losses from workers' compensation, which is the legal liability with respect to work-related injury or death of the firm's employees. Losses (in $000s) are assumed to follow a compound Poisson distribution, with Poisson parameter $\lambda = 10$, and individual severity distribution $Y_j \sim \text{Pareto}(\alpha = 11, \theta = 1,000)$.

---

[1] An exception is group health insurance policies where the insurance may be used to smooth costs, rather than as genuine insurance cover against adverse events.

The insurer charges premiums using the standard deviation premium principle, with loading ξ, so that, for a random loss S, the annual premium for insurance that would reimburse $S^I \le S$ is

$$P = \mathrm{E}[S^I] + \xi\sqrt{\mathrm{Var}[S^I]}.$$

Full insurance cover, $S^I = S$, is offered with $\xi = 0.5$.

Proportional insurance is also offered, under which the insurer covers 90% of all losses, and the firm would cover the remaining 10%, so that $S^I = 0.9S$. In this case $\xi = 0.4$.

If the firm does not fully insure the loss, the regulator requires the firm to hold capital at the 95% Expected Shortfall of any uninsured losses. This capital is treated as a loan from the shareholders, with a service charge of 10% payable annually. The expected annual cost to the firm is therefore calculated (ignoring investment returns) as:

Expected Outgo = Premium + Expected cost of uninsured losses + 10% of the 95% Expected Shortfall of uninsured losses.

For each of the three options (i) full insurance, (ii) no insurance, and (iii) partial insurance, calculate the expected annual outgo. Use the Fast Fourier Transform (FFT) for the aggregate loss distribution where required.

Solution 16.1

(i) Full insurance:

First calculate the moments of the claim severity distribution.

$$\mathrm{E}[Y_j] = \frac{\theta}{\alpha - 1} = 100, \qquad \mathrm{E}[Y_j^2] = \frac{2\theta^2}{(\alpha - 1)(\alpha - 2)} = 22{,}222.2,$$

so the mean and variance of the compound Poisson losses are

$$\mathrm{E}[S] = \lambda\,\mathrm{E}[Y_j] = 1{,}000 \qquad \mathrm{Var}[S] = \lambda\mathrm{E}[Y_j^2] = 22{,}2222 = 471.4^2.$$

The premium is

$$\mathrm{E}[S] + \xi\mathrm{SD}[S] = 1{,}000 + 0.5 \times 471.4 = 1{,}235.7,$$

and there is no uninsured loss, so the expected outgo is 1,235.7.

(ii) No insurance:

The expected cost of uninsured losses is $\mathrm{E}[S] = 1{,}000$.

The VaR and Expected Shortfall are found using the FFT approach described in Chapter 4. The 95% quantile of the loss is 1,858 and the 95% Expected Shortfall is 2,167.

Hence, the expected outgo is $\mathrm{E}[S] + 0.10\mathrm{ES}[S] = 1{,}216.7$.

(iii) Partial Insurance.

The uninsured loss is $S^U = 0.1S$. The insured loss is $S^I = 0.9S$.
The premium is

$$E[S^I] + 0.4SD[S^I] = 0.9E[S] + 0.4 \times 0.9 \times SD[S] = 1{,}069.7.$$

The expected uninsured loss is $0.1E[S] = 100$.

The Expected Shortfall of the uninsured losses is 10% of the Expected Shortfall of the full loss (as the Expected Shortfall is positive homogeneous), which is 216.7. The cost of service of the Expected Shortfall capital is therefore 21.7.

The total expected outgo is

$$1{,}069.7 + 100 + 21.7 = 1{,}191.4. \qquad \square$$

We note that in this example the expected cost of partial insurance is less than both full insurance and no insurance. The firm can assess how much insurance provides them with adequate cover, without tying up too much capital to cover uninsured losses.

16.3.2 Non-proportional Insurance

With a deductible of D, say, for each insured loss arising, the policyholder pays for losses up to D, and the insurer pays the excess above D.

Let Y_j denote the individual losses, for $j = 1, 2, \ldots, N$. The uninsured part of each loss is Y_j^U and the insured part is Y_j^I, where, for deductible D we have

$$Y_j^U = \begin{cases} Y_j & \text{for } Y_j \leq D, \\ D & \text{for } Y_j > D, \end{cases}$$

$$Y_j^I = \begin{cases} 0 & \text{for } Y_j \leq D, \\ Y_j - D & \text{for } Y_j > D. \end{cases}$$

The aggregate loss S is divided into the uninsured part S^U and the insured part S^I as

$$S^U = \sum_{j=1}^{N} Y_j^U,$$

$$S^I = \sum_{j=1}^{N} Y_j^I.$$

We note that $Y_j^U + Y_j^I = Y_j$ and $S^U + S^I = S$.

Example 16.2 Continuing Example 16.1, assume the insurer offers the firm a new option. The firm may purchase a policy with a deductible of 10, and no upper limit on each loss. The premium for this insurance would follow the standard deviation premium principle, with $\xi = 0.4$.

Calculate the firm's expected outgo, including servicing the Expected Shortfall for uninsured losses, using this insurance policy.

Solution 16.2 First, calculate the premium. As the losses are compound Poisson, the expected insured loss is $\lambda \, E[Y_j^I]$ and the standard deviation of the insured loss is $\sqrt{\lambda \, E[(Y_j^I)^2]}$. Let D denote the deductible.

Consider the random variable $Z = Y_j - D | Y_j > D$, where $D = 10$. Recall that $Y_j \sim \text{Pareto}(\alpha = 11, \theta = 1{,}000)$. The survival function of Z is

$$S_Z(z) = \frac{\Pr\left[Y_j - D > z\right]}{\Pr[Y_j > D]} = \frac{\Pr[Y_j > z + D]}{\Pr[Y_j > D]}$$

$$= \frac{\left(\dfrac{\theta}{\theta + D + z}\right)^{\alpha}}{\left(\dfrac{\theta}{\theta + D}\right)^{\alpha}}$$

$$= \left(\frac{\theta + D}{\theta + D + z}\right)^{\alpha},$$

which is the survival function of a Pareto random variable with parameters $\alpha = 11$ and $\theta + D = 1{,}010$.

Now,

$$E[Y_j^I] = E[Y_j - D \mid Y_j > D] \times \Pr[Y_j > D]$$

$$= \frac{\theta + D}{\alpha - 1} \left(\frac{\theta}{\theta + D}\right)^{\alpha} = 90.529,$$

$$E\left[(Y_j^I)^2\right] = E[(Y_j - D)^2 \mid Y_j > D] \times \Pr[Y_j > D]$$

$$= \frac{2(\theta + D)^2}{(\alpha - 1)(\alpha - 2)} \left(\frac{\theta}{\theta + D}\right)^{\alpha} = 20{,}318.60.$$

Using the compound Poisson results, we have

$$E\left[S^I\right] = 905.29, \qquad \text{Var}\left[S^I\right] = 203{,}186 = 450.76^2.$$

So the premium for the insurance is $905.29 + 0.4 \times 450.76 = 1{,}085.59$.

The expected cost of uninsured losses is $E[S^U] = E[S] - E[S^I] = 94.71$.

The 95% Expected Shortfall of the uninsured losses is 149.7, found using the FFT approach.

Hence, the expected outgo is $1,085.6 + 94.7 + 15.0 = 1,195.3$.   □

16.3.3 Comments

(1) Note that the expected cost of uninsured losses is similar for the 90% proportional insurance and the policy with deductible. However, the Expected Shortfall of the uninsured loss is greater in the proportional insurance case. Splitting each loss leaves the firm with more upside risk, as 10% of a very large loss is still a large amount, whereas under the non-proportional insurance, each individual loss is capped at 10, meaning that there are no large uninsured losses.

(2) From the insurer's perspective, offering proportional insurance cover has the advantage of limiting the moral hazard risk, more than the deductible. Under the non-proportional policy, once a loss exceeds the deductible, the policyholder's liability is capped, and there is no incentive to mitigate the severity of that loss any further. Using proportional insurance, the policyholder retains the incentive to mitigate losses for small or large events.

(3) Another motivation for the insurer to prefer partial insurance to full insurance is avoiding very small claims, which are uneconomical to manage. Proportional insurance does not achieve this, as all losses lead to claims, even small ones. The non-proportional approach is a better approach in this case, as losses below the deductible do not involve the insurer.

(4) It is possible to combine the proportional and non-proportional approaches.

(5) In practice the insurer would set a maximum claim amount for each loss event regardless of the type of coverage, leaving the insured with residual potential losses above the insurer's limit.

16.3.4 Insurance Pricing Notes

The **pure premium** or **risk premium** for an insurance cover is the expected value of the loss. The gross premium (or simply 'premium') is the premium charged, which will include a loading, on top of the risk premium, to allow for expenses, adverse experience, uncertainty in the valuation, and profit. In the examples above, the loading was determined as a multiple of the underlying standard deviation. In practice, premium loadings are more often proportional to the expected loss, although the proportional loading may vary by line of business, implicitly reflecting that some lines involve greater uncertainty than others.

Rating factors are risk characteristics used to separate policies into more homogeneous groupings, particularly for more high volume business. For example, for workers' compensation insurance, rating factors might include (i) the type of business undertaken, (ii) the nature of the hazards involved in the work, (iii) the size of the firm, by number of employees, or by total payroll, and (iv) the firm's health and safety record.

Exposure measures denote the basic unit of risk; they are quantitative measures that are expected to be linear in the potential loss. For example, for auto insurance, average losses are broadly proportional to the average annual distance driven, so mileage could be used as an exposure measure – although it usually is not, due to the fact that the insurer cannot verify the exposure. Workers' compensation will often use payroll as an exposure measure. Directors' and Officers' (D&O) insurance, which covers company directors and senior management for liability in the event of corporate malfeasance or adverse litigation, might use the market capitalization of the firm, or the D&O compensation.

Experience rating refers to any premium rating method which is based partly (and transparently) on the individual history of the risk being insured. In many countries, car insurance is priced using a **no claims bonus**, or (similar) a **Bonus-Malus** system, under which policyholders are informed of how much (proportionately) their premiums are adjusted, based on the number of claims reported over the previous years. Commercial insurance policies may also be experience rated through a return of premium arrangement, under which if claims are much lower than premiums, a proportion of the difference is returned to the insured.

For some types of insurance, the premium charged may be quite different from the actuarial assessment of the cost. For high volume business, such as auto/car insurance, market forces may have a significant influence on price. At the other end of the spectrum, more bespoke insurance policies, covering unusual risks (e.g., sporting events, terrorism risk, significant historical buildings), may be priced with very little data available to create loss distributions. For large or unusual risks, the premiums may be determined based on the opinions of the underwriter, possibly with support from experts in the broad risk area, rather than on data analysis.

A large part of the uncertainty involved in pricing insurance arises from the potential delay between a loss event and the final claim settlement. **Short tail insurance** is the collective term for business that tends to be reported and settled quickly. This includes most claims involving property damage or theft, unless they are caused by a catastrophic event, in which case the volume of claims can delay settlement, or if the claim is very large, in which case assessing the cause and agreeing the severity of the loss may take some time, especially if legal proceedings are involved. **Long tail insurance** is the term for business that involves long delays between the loss event and the final claim settlement. Often, the first delay is between the claim event and the reporting of the event, and, often, these claims involve compensation for injury or death under liability insurance. Examples include medical malpractice insurance, product liability insurance, and workers' compensation insurance.

16.3.5 Reinsurance

Reinsurance is the insurers' insurance. Reinsurance policy types are similar to policies sold by direct insurers, although some of the terminology is different, and the nature of the relationship between the direct insurer and the reinsurer is different from that of the policyholder and direct insurer. Reinsurers tend to work more closely with insurers on risk analysis and management, and can create more flexible, tailored, risk transfer solutions, compared with the more standardized arrangements common between direct insurers and policyholders. Reinsurers also buy insurance from other reinsurers – referred to as **retrocession** in the industry.

Reinsurance is typically contracted on a bulk basis (**treaty reinsurance**). The information passed to the reinsurer by the direct insurer, relating to reinsurance cover of a portfolio of contracts, will be much less detailed than the information gathered by the direct insurer for each individual contract. When the reinsurer takes some of its risk and passes it to another reinsurer through retrocession, the risk information transferred is even less detailed.

Surplus and **quota share** reinsurance are both proportional insurance contracts, under which, broadly, the insurer and reinsurer share premiums and claims in some pre-determined proportion. Quota share treaties typically cover a large number of contracts, all shared in the same proportion. Surplus insurance may use different proportions for different risks. For example, a small insurer with limited capacity might reinsure a large proportion of a larger risk, but retain all or most of a smaller risk.

Excess of loss (XL) is a non-proportional reinsurance arrangement, under which the insurer pays all losses up to the excess point (similar to a deductible) and the reinsurer pays all losses exceeding the excess point, up to a maximum. An insurer may use several XL contracts for the same risk or portfolio, each covering a different risk layer. Higher risk layers are used to cover very rare, very large losses. The lowest risk layers are called **working layers**, and these are expected to be very active – that is, there is a high probability that claims will exceed the working layer threshold. Working layers are used by small to medium sized insurers, who use reinsurance to manage capacity, optimize required capital, and smooth underwriting results. Larger insurers have less need of working layers, and are more likely to focus on the higher layers for transferring extreme losses, to cover the very large, very rare, loss events.

Excess of Loss insurance can be written on a per event basis, under which the policy may cover a limited number of events in a single policy year, or it may be based on aggregate losses from a portfolio, in which case it is also known as **stop loss** insurance. **Catastrophe excess of loss** insurance (Cat XL) covers all claims arising from specific types of catastrophic events.

16.3.6 The Underwriting Cycle

The **underwriting cycle** (also known as the **insurance cycle**) refers to cyclical patterns observed in insurance pricing and profitability. **Soft markets** refer to the portion of the cycle where premiums tend to be low, profitability is squeezed, and the market has excess capacity. Ultimately, the premiums become too low, resulting in some firms failing – often precipitated by a period of very high claims, perhaps from a natural disaster. The next stage is a contraction in capacity, and an increase in premiums, leading to a few years of **hard markets**, where premiums are high, leading to increasing profits. Gradually, market forces push premiums down, and the cycle moves back into the soft market phase. The underwriting cycle is a key feature of insurance pricing, as it can have significant impact on the cost of risk transfer.

The capacity of the reinsurance market is a key factor in the underwriting cycle – when large claim events occur, the reinsurance market capacity is diminished, as it takes time to rebuild the capital base. The resulting price increases are passed down to the direct insurers, who rely on reinsurance for much of their tail risk transfer. This is why the shift from soft to hard markets tends to follow a tail risk event such as a natural disaster.

Another contributing factor is that when market capacity is high and premiums are low, some insurers will under-state their technical provisions, to make the business appear more profitable. The technical provisions, or reserves, are funds held for insured losses that have already happened, but where the insurance claim has not yet been settled, or for losses that have not yet happened, but are covered under existing contracts. **Reserving risk** refers to the possibility that the firm underestimates these losses so significantly that the solvency of the firm is at risk. When losses emerge, the under-reserving becomes apparent, market capacity diminishes, and prices increase. From the point of view of a firm seeking insurance cover, it may not be a good idea to accept the lowest bid in a soft market, as under-reserving may lead to insurer failure just as the insurance cover is most needed.

For long tail business, investment proceeds play a significant role in pricing and profitability, as the premium income may be held for up to 10 years before the insurer is required to pay out claims. This means that general economic and business cycles will feed through to insurance pricing.

16.4 Captive Insurance

Companies that are large and diversified enough may prefer to self-insure. One way to do this is to set up an insurance company as a subsidiary of the parent. These subsidiaries are known as **captive insurance companies**. An illustration of a captive insurer structure is given in Figure 16.1.

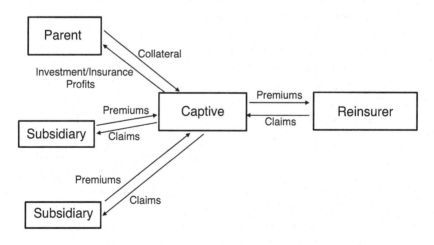

Figure 16.1 Illustration of a captive insurance arrangement

The reason for using a subsidiary company, rather than simply absorbing the risks, is largely to do with the tax treatment of insurance premiums and reserves. Suppose the firm wishes to provision for a loss with a potential cost of $1 million. If the company retains $1 million of reserve in the parent company, it is taxable. If it pays $1 million in premium to an insurance company, it is not taxable. So, corporations who wish to self-insure, and who have sufficiently diversified business to make self-insurance a reasonable risk management strategy, may be able to do so more cheaply using a captive insurer.

Typically, to maximize the tax savings, captive insurers are domiciled in low tax jurisdictions; Bermuda and the Cayman Islands are popular, although some captives of US corporations are registered in the US.

The most commonly cited benefits of captive insurance include the following:

(1) Captives can exploit tax efficiencies, as described above, compared with self-insurance. However, the captive cannot exist solely as a tax shelter. The insurance contracts written by the captive must be valid, must be appropriately priced, must cover real risk exposures, and must be appropriately risk managed, to comply with regulatory requirements in the domicile country, and possibly the jurisdiction of parent company, or of the other subsidiaries who transfer risk to the captive.

(2) Captives allow the parent to retain underwriting profits. The traditional insurance premium has loadings for risk, for advertising, for management costs, most of which are eliminated using a captive insurer.

(3) Captives can tailor insurance exactly to the needs of the corporation. Under traditional insurance, businesses are often forced to retain risks they would rather insure, because the traditional insurance market imposes contract exceptions (e.g., pandemic exception for business interruption) or is unable to offer cover at an economic price. Also, making a claim under a traditional insurance policy can become adversarial, as the insurer would prefer not to pay, if possible. This legal risk is avoided for all but the largest claims, using captive insurance.

(4) Captives facilitate access to reinsurance markets. For risks that exceed the parent company's risk tolerance, reinsurance contracts may be accessible through the captive insurer that would not generally be available through traditional insurance markets. Reinsurance contracts can be tailored to meet the needs of the corporation, focussing entirely on extreme tail risks, for example.

(5) Insurance can be made available to all subsidiaries, ensuring that insurance diversification benefits remain in-group.

(6) Captives can be used to inform and incentivize risk management across subsidiaries. Where a loss is covered by a captive insurer, particularly where there is an indication that, for example, one subsidiary is generating a disproportionate amount of claims, the parent company will be alerted, and can ensure that the subsidiary makes changes. Under traditional insurance the individual claims experience of the subsidiary is less available to the parent, and the implication of excessive claims is less immediate.

(7) Because insurers can hold reserves to smooth claims costs, the profitability of the group may be smoother using a captive compared with retaining the risk without the captive.

(8) There may be governmental grants/cost-sharing available to insurers, that can be accessed through the captive. For example, following the terrorist acts in the US on 11 September 2001, reinsurers stopped covering terrorism related losses, as the risks were too difficult to predict or quantify. This meant that direct insurers had to introduce terrorism exclusions in their contracts, and corporations lost their cover. The US government, fearing the economic implications of another large-scale attack without insurance coverage, introduced the Terrorism Risk Insurance Act of 2002, which became the Terrorism Risk Insurance Program Reauthorization Act (TRIPR) in 2007, and has since been reauthorized through to 2027. This act required insurers to include terrorism cover in business insurance, with the US government acting as reinsurer, paying for 85% of covered losses in excess of a deductible set by statute.

Disadvantages of captive insurers include the need for significant up-front capitalization, as insurance requires substantial economic capital and potentially onerous regulatory compliance. Another problem is that the need for additional capital, following some severe loss event, is likely to coincide with low availability of funds from the parent company. That is, suppose the firm selects the domicile with the lowest capital requirements for its captive. If the claims covered by the captive exceed its ability to pay, then the expectation is that the parent firm will recapitalize the captive – but it is the parent firm that has suffered the large losses that created the need for recapitalization.

Nevertheless, most large international corporations operate at least one captive subsidiary. Often, the captive has very few employees, with technical, legal, and actuarial functions outsourced to specialist consulting groups.

It is interesting to note that many insurance companies themselves have captive insurance subsidiaries. The reasons why an insurer would set up a captive subsidiary are more to do with managing capital than directly managing risk. If the insurer determines that the regulatory capital required to take on certain risks is greater than the economic capital required, then it will seek ways to circumvent the regulatory requirements. One method is to set up a captive in a favourable (low regulation) jurisdiction.

16.4.1 Captive Insurance Example – The Midtown Insurance Company

The Midtown Insurance Company is a New York domiciled captive insurance company, fully owned by the New York Times (NYT) Company, the firm that publishes the *New York Times* newspaper.

The following list of coverages was noted in a 2012 Report on Examination of the company conducted by the State of New York Insurance Department:

(a) **Terrorism coverage** under TRIPR. This provides insurance coverage up to $1.2 billion for any acts of terrorism as defined by the Act. By setting up the captive, the NYT gets to benefit directly from the reinsurance provided by the US government in the event of large losses.

(b) **Deductible liability reimbursement.** This policy provides coverage for fleet, automobile, workers' compensation, multi-media errors and omissions liability, and general liability lines. In this case, the captive is covering the deductible, with a traditional insurance policy covering losses above the deductible. Using the captive to smooth losses allows the parent company to set high deductibles for the traditional insurance contract, saving on premiums.

(c) **Excess umbrella liability indemnity**, excess property, and excess media liability. These policies can be used to cover losses that exceed the maximum sum payable under a traditional contract.

(d) **Weather policy**; this covers losses caused by unusually high rain or snow in New York – specifically, more than one standard deviation higher than the 10-year mean. This line is not connected to a traditional policy, and presumably relates to a specific risk exposure of NYT.

16.4.2 Captive Varieties

'Pure' captives are fully owned by the parent company, and only insure risks emanating from within the conglomerate headed by that parent. A corporation that is not large enough or diverse enough to justify setting up a pure captive may join with other companies to form a jointly owned **group captive**. These are often founded by groups of companies with similar risk features (e.g., from within the same industry).

Sponsored captives are not owned by the insured; they are set up by a sponsor, typically an insurer or insurance agency, who is responsible for providing the initial regulatory capital. Participating companies provide the capital to support their own insurance. Internally the assets and liabilities of each participating firm are segregated. Each of the segregated units acts as a mini-captive insurer for the participating company, so the sponsored captive operates effectively as a collective of smaller captives, with the sponsor providing the organization and regulatory requirements.

16.5 Securitization of Insurance Risk

Securitization is a form of alternative risk transfer in which tradable securities are issued whose cash flows depend on the underlying risks being managed. It has long been a tool in banking, where the cash flows associated with debt portfolios have been converted into securities marketed to investors. The long list of assets that have been pooled for debt securitization includes home and commercial mortgages, credit card receivables, automobile loans, student loans, and aircraft and equipment leases. In this section, we focus on the securitization of insurance risk, which has developed more slowly and more recently.

Securitization of insurance risk involves the creation of investments which may be purchased by public or private placement, under which the investors' principal and coupons are contingent on insurable risk events. These **insurance linked securities** (ILS) are created by a sponsoring organization – often an insurer or reinsurer – that needs to transfer some risk, typically from the extreme tail of their loss distribution. The problem with extreme tail risks, from the point of view of the insurer, is that although they may be diversifiable in principle, in practice the low frequency and high severity combination makes it difficult for insurers and reinsurers to gain adequate diversification benefits. Securitization gets around this problem by diversifying the providers of insurance, rather than diversifying the insurance portfolio.

The challenge of securitization is to package risk in a form that makes it attractive to capital market investors. In a typical arrangement, the investor purchases a bond, under which payments of coupon and principal are contingent on a specified insurance event (for example, an earthquake in California) not happening. If the insurance event does occur then some or all of the principal invested in the bonds is diverted to the sponsoring entity, usually an insurer, to offset their losses. This arrangement provides an alternative to traditional reinsurance for the sponsoring entity. From their perspective, the following list offers potential reasons for securitizing the risk, rather than (re)insuring or retaining it:

(1) Securitization spreads risk beyond the traditional reinsurance market, allowing for increased global capacity.
(2) Securitization can create efficient pricing of tail loss coverage as markets generally force prices to a fair equilibrium price, although this depends on liquid markets with full information being available to investors.
(3) The price of cover using securitization is less cyclical than through traditional channels, which are susceptible to the peaks and troughs of the underwriting cycle.
(4) Using securitization, the sponsor may relieve themselves of some regulatory capital requirements, compared with retaining the risk or reinsuring it.

To the investors, the attraction is the potential for high investment returns (achieved if the covered event does not occur), where the associated risk is at least somewhat independent of other market risks - in the CAPM language, the beta of insurance linked securities is assumed to be close to zero. An investor purchasing corporate bonds with the same risk as the insurance linked security will find that the default risks of the corporate bonds are highly correlated with falling market prices overall. On the other hand, the forfeit of principal from an insurance linked security might be triggered, for example, by a windstorm in Florida or an earthquake in Japan, and the covered event is not expected to be strongly associated with adverse returns on other investments. Typically, purchasers of insurance linked securities are large institutional investors, including pension funds and specialist hedge funds.

The earliest insurance linked securities were catastrophe bonds, commonly known as cat bonds, which are designed to provide cover for low frequency high severity losses generated by natural disasters. The introduction of cat bonds was motivated by diminished global reinsurance capacity following Hurricane Andrew in 1992. Further impetus resulted from the massive reinsurance costs associated with Hurricane Katrina in 2005 and Hurricane Sandy in 2012. More recently, the cat bond market has moved into cyber and other operational risks.

Life insurance risks have also been securitized, with two main types of instrument; one covering the risk of increased short-term mortality from pandemics, and the other covering the risk of loss from increased longevity – that

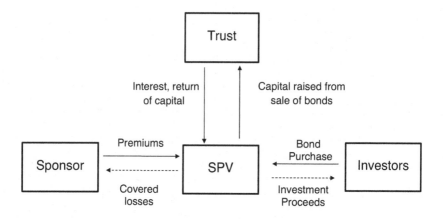

Figure 16.2 A cat bond transaction

is, the additional costs to pension plans and other life annuity providers associated with unexpected increases in population lifespans.

We discuss these three types of insurance security in the following sections.

16.6 Catastrophe Bonds

A typical cat bond transaction is illustrated in Figure 16.2. The solid arrows indicate non-contingent cash flows. The dotted lines indicate cash flows contingent on whether or not the covered event occurs. Most cat bonds are issued for terms of three to five years.

The cat bond is created by an enterprise (the sponsor or cedant) that seeks specialized loss coverage. Typically the sponsor is an insurer or reinsurer. The sponsor creates a **special purpose vehicle** (SPV), which is a separate company created for the sole purpose of issuing the cat bonds. The SPV creates the bonds and sells them to investors. The proceeds are held in a separate trust account. The investors receive regular coupon payments, as long as the covered event does not occur; the coupons are paid from the interest earned on the assets in trust, supplemented by premiums paid to the SPV by the sponsor.

If the covered event occurs, then principal is released from the trust to reimburse the sponsor. If the loss does not exhaust the principal available, the remainder is returned to the investors, and the bonds expire.

If the covered event does not occur, then the principal is returned from the SPV to the investors at the end of the specified term.

16.6.1 Cat Bond Triggers

A key element of the cat bond is the specification of the covered event – that is, defining the criteria that trigger the transfer of the investors' principal to reimburse the sponsor for losses associated with the catastrophe. There are a number of different types of triggers used in practice.

Indemnity Trigger

An indemnity trigger uses the sponsor's actual loss following the risk event.

The advantage of the indemnity trigger for the sponsor is that it relates directly to their own losses. This minimizes **basis risk**, which is the risk to the sponsor that the measure of loss used in the contract is different from the sponsor's actual losses. When basis risk is substantial, the funds reimbursed through the cat bond could be insufficient to meet the losses arising from the covered event.

The indemnity trigger is less advantageous to investors, who must rely on the sponsor to underwrite the business carefully, and to assess their losses accurately, with appropriate investigation and mitigation; there is an information asymmetry which leads to moral hazard risk from the investors' perspective.

A disadvantage of the indemnity trigger to both sides is that it can take some time to determine the full extent of the losses, which can lead to uncertainty and delays in reimbursement.

Industry Loss Index Trigger

An industry loss index trigger relies on specialist third party modelling firms to assess the total industry loss after a major catastrophe. From the sponsor's perspective, using a trigger that is not the sponsor's own losses introduces basis risk. If the cedant's losses are closely aligned with the industry as a whole, then the basis risk will be small. However, there may be substantial basis risk where the cedant's losses are significantly different from the aggregate industry losses, for example, with a different proportion of losses coming from urban and rural areas, or from commercial and private insurance.

From the investor's perspective, the industry loss index trigger reduces the moral hazard risk, as the decision as to whether the catastrophe payments are triggered is taken out of the cedant's hands. Also, typically, the modelling firms tend to produce loss estimates much more quickly than the individual firms can, reducing the period of uncertainty for both sides.

Modelled Loss Trigger

With modelled loss triggers, a third party modelling firm estimates the losses for the cedant based on the cedant's exposure data, and on the specific characteristics of the catastrophic event. This creates less basis risk for the cedant than the industry loss trigger, as the trigger is based on their own exposure, and it creates less moral hazard risk and delay risk for investors, as they are not exposed to the uncertainties of the cedant's claim management process.

Parametric Trigger

A parametric trigger uses an objective physical measure of severity to define the loss severity. Examples include windspeed thresholds at specific geographic locations for cat bonds covering hurricane events, or peak ground acceleration measures for earthquakes. In practice, the parametric trigger would use a formula incorporating a number of measures from the geographic region covered, with the objective of producing a trigger that is reasonably proportional to the cedant's potential losses.

From the cedant's perspective, the parametric approach, even where many measures are used, is likely to lead to the largest basis risk. But investors generally prefer parametric triggers, since they are objective, transparent, and do not involve any significant delay in determining whether the reimbursements to the cedant have been triggered, and how much of the investors' principal will be lost.

Hybrid Triggers can be created by combining some of the standard triggers.

The majority of cat bonds covering natural disasters use indemnity triggers (around 70% in 2020), followed by industry loss index (around 20%), and parametric (around 5%).

16.6.2 Pricing Cat Bonds

Coupons for cat bonds comprise a **benchmark rate** plus a **premium spread**. The benchmark rate is the low risk, short-term return earned on the investors' principal. Typical rates used include US treasuries or LIBOR.

The premium spread is paid by the sponsor to the SPV, who will pass it through to investors, along with the benchmark return.

The minimum premium spread that will attract investors will depend on the risk associated with the bond, and to assess this, investors are presented with the following information:

- The loss covered, the covered event, and the maximum loss payable.
- The probability that the covered event will happen, per year, called the **probability of first loss** (PFL).
- The probability that the loss will exceed the upper limit, per year, called the **probability of last loss** (PLL).
- The **expected (proportionate) loss** (EL), which is the expected value of the proportion of investors' principal forfeited, per year.

The relationship between the PFL, PLL, EL, and loss distribution are summarized below.

Let X denote the loss metric used to trigger the cat bond. The **attachment point**, denoted x_l, is the threshold triggering the payments to the cedant, so

$$\text{PFL} = \Pr[X > x_l].$$

The **exhaustion point**, x_h, is the threshold representing the maximum loss, so

$$\text{PLL} = \Pr[X > x_h].$$

Let q denote the proportion of principal lost; this is linear in X, between x_l and x_h, so that

$$q = \begin{cases} 0, & X \leq x_l, \\ \dfrac{X - x_l}{x_h - x_l}, & x_l < X \leq x_h, \\ 1, & X > x_h. \end{cases}$$

It then follows that, if f and F represent the density and distribution function of X respectively, then the EL (expected proportionate loss) is

$$\text{EL} = \text{E}[q] = \int_{x_l}^{x_h} \frac{x - x_l}{x_h - x_l} f(x)dx + (1 - F(x_h)).$$

The sponsor's loss, L, is assumed to be proportionate to X, so that $L = kX$, for some constant k. If the trigger is indemnity or modelled, then the loss will be equal to X and $k = 1$. For an industry loss index, k represents the proportion of industry losses that the sponsor carries. For parametric losses, k is the estimated ratio of the sponsor's losses to the parametric measure used.

The cat bond reimburses the sponsor for the layer of loss between kx_l and kx_h. The expected value of this loss layer is

$$k \left(\int_{x_l}^{x_h} (x - x_l) f(x)dx + (x_h - x_l)(1 - F(x_h)) \right) = k(x_h - x_l) \text{EL}.$$

Example 16.3 XYZ sponsors a one-year cat bond with a parametric trigger measure X. The attachment point is $x_l = 250$ and the exhaustion point is $x_h = 400$.

The sponsor's losses are estimated to be $0.1X$ in millions.

Suppose $X \sim \text{Pareto}(\alpha = 3.5, \lambda = 180)$, where

$$f(x) = \frac{\alpha \lambda^\alpha}{(\lambda + x)^{\alpha+1}}, \quad F(x) = 1 - \left(\frac{\lambda}{\lambda + x}\right)^\alpha,$$
$$\text{and} \quad S(x) = 1 - F(x) = \left(\frac{\lambda}{\lambda + x}\right)^\alpha.$$

(a) Calculate the PFL and PLL.
(b) Calculate the EL.
(c) Calculate the expected costs of losses to the sponsor for the loss layer covered by the cat bond.

Solution 16.3

(a) $\text{PFL} = \Pr[X > x_l] = \left(\frac{180}{180 + 250}\right)^{3.5} = 0.04746,$

$\text{PLL} = \Pr[X > x_h] = \left(\frac{180}{180 + 400}\right)^{3.5} = 0.01665.$

(b) $\text{EL} = \frac{1}{150}\left\{\int_{250}^{400}(x - 250)f(x) + 150\,S(400)\right\}$

$= \frac{1}{150}\left\{\int_{250}^{400}x\,f(x)dx - 250\int_{250}^{400}f(x)dx + 150S(400)\right\}$

$= \frac{1}{150}\left\{\int_{250}^{400}x\frac{\alpha\lambda^\alpha}{(\lambda+x)^{\alpha+1}}dx\right.$

$\left. - 250\,(S(250) - S(400)) + 150S(400)\right\}$

$= \frac{1}{150}\left\{\left[-x\left(\frac{\lambda}{\lambda+x}\right)^\alpha\right]_{250}^{400} + \int_{250}^{400}\left(\frac{\lambda}{\lambda+x}\right)^\alpha dx\right.$

$\left. - 250S(250) + 400S(400)\right\}$

$= \frac{1}{150}\left\{-\left[\frac{\lambda}{\alpha - 1}\left(\frac{\lambda}{\lambda+x}\right)^{\alpha-1}\right]_{250}^{400}\right\}$

$$= \frac{1}{150} \left\{ \frac{\lambda}{\alpha - 1} \left(\left(\frac{\lambda}{\lambda + 250} \right)^{\alpha - 1} - \left(\frac{\lambda}{\lambda + 400} \right)^{\alpha - 1} \right) \right\}$$

$$= \frac{4.300}{150} = 2.87\%.$$

(c) The sponsor's loss, in millions, for the layer covered by the cat bond, denoted L^I, is defined in terms of the full loss, L, as

$$L^I = \begin{cases} 0, & X \leq 250, \\ 0.1(X - 250), & 250 < X \leq 400, \\ 0.1(400 - 250), & X > 400, \end{cases}$$

$$= 0.1(150)q.$$

Hence, the expected layer loss is $0.1(150)\text{E}[q] = 0.42997.$ □

The cat bond is fully collateralized, which means that the capital raised, denoted C, is sufficient to pay the full layer loss in the event that the trigger measure exceeds the exhaustion point. In other words, $C = k(x_h - x_l)$.

Consider a cat bond, with a T-year term, and assume that 100% of the principal is at risk of forfeit. For simplicity, we assume settlement at the end of the contract, and that coupons are paid half-yearly for the full term.

Suppose, further, that the sponsor is choosing whether to transfer a loss layer through a reinsurance contract or through a cat bond issue, and that the reinsurance premium for the T year contract is P, paid at the start of the contract.

The coupon rate paid to the cat bond holders will be of the form $r + \rho$ per year, where r is the risk-free benchmark rate earned by the SPV on the capital received from investors, and ρ is the premium spread paid by the sponsor.

The value at issue of the sponsor's premium spread costs, assuming half-yearly coupons, and assuming that coupons are paid throughout the term of the contract, even if the catastrophe payments are triggered, is

$$\rho \, C \, (0.5) \left(e^{-0.5r} + e^{-r} + \cdots + e^{-(T-0.5)r} + e^{-Tr} \right) = \rho \, C \, a^{(2)}_{\overline{T}|},$$

where $a^{(2)}_{\overline{T}|}$ represents the present value of a T-year annuity of 1 per year, payable at the end of each half-year, that is,

$$a^{(2)}_{\overline{T}|} = \frac{1 - e^{-rT}}{2(e^{0.5r} - 1)}.$$

The cat bond has additional fixed costs compared with reinsuring the risk; let A denote the additional fixed costs associated with the cat bond, compared with the reinsurance contract. The break-even equation, where the present value of the cat bond costs equals the present value of the reinsurance policy costs, gives the maximum premium spread that the sponsor should pay; we have

$$A + \rho\, C\, a_{\overline{T}|}^{(2)} = P \Rightarrow \rho = \frac{P - A}{C\, a_{\overline{T}|}^{(2)}}.$$

If PFL is not small, we can treat T as a random variable, representing the earlier of the expiry of the bond and the triggering of the catastrophe payments. In the following example, for simplicity, we assume that the coupons continue through the term of the bond.

Example 16.4 Continuing from Example 16.3, assume that (i) the term of the cat bond is 3 years; (ii) the benchmark rate of interest is 4%, continuously compounded; (iii) the reinsurance premium to cover the risk is 1.3 million; (iv) the additional cost of issuing the cat bond is 0.5% of the face value.

Calculate the maximum premium spread the sponsor should pay for the cat bond.

Solution 16.4 The capital raised under the cat bond approach, in $millions, is $C = 15$. The extra cost of issuing the bond is $0.005 \times 15 = 0.075$. The annuity value is $a_{\overline{3}|}^{(2)} = 2.7988$. So the maximum premium spread is

$$\rho = \frac{1.3 - 0.075}{15(2.7988)} = 0.029.$$

16.6.3 Applying Extreme Value Theory to Cat Bond Analysis

Although the quantitative loss information available for cat bonds is not very extensive, we can use extreme value theory to analyse the risk distribution further.

Typically, cat bonds cover extreme tail risks for loss distributions. We recall from extreme value theory that, subject to some regularity conditions, for a random loss X, once we are far enough into the tail – that is, for $D > d$, say – the excess loss random variable, $Y = X - D \mid X > D$, will approximately follow the **generalized Pareto distribution** (GPD), with parameters β and ξ.

As the cat bond is designed for tail risks, it is likely that in most cases the attachment point x_l is sufficiently far into the tail such that, approximately,

$$Y = X - x_l | X > x_l \sim \text{GPD}(\beta, \xi).$$

The intuition here is that Y is the value of $X - x_l$ given that the covered event occurred. Recall that the survival function of the GPD distribution is

$$S_Y(y) = \left(\frac{\beta}{\beta + \xi\, y}\right)^{\frac{1}{\xi}}.$$

The **conditional probability of last loss**, denoted λ, is the probability that the trigger metric exceeds the exhaustion point, given that the trigger metric exceeds the attachment point – that is, the probability that investors lose 100% of their principal, given that they lose some of their principal.

We have

$$\lambda = \Pr[X > x_h | X > x_l] = \frac{\Pr[X > x_h]}{\Pr[X > x_l]} = \frac{\text{PLL}}{\text{PFL}},$$

and, using the GPD, we have

$$\lambda = \Pr[X > x_h | X > x_l] = \Pr[X - x_l > x_h - x_l | X > x_l]$$

$$= \Pr[Y > x_h - x_l]$$

$$= \left(\frac{\beta}{\beta + \xi\,(x_h - x_l)}\right)^{\frac{1}{\xi}}.$$

The **conditional expectation of (proportionate) loss** (CEL) is the expected proportionate loss of principal, given that the trigger metric exceeds the attachment point. So,

$$\text{CEL} = \text{E}[q|X > x_l] = \frac{\text{E}[q]}{\Pr[X > x_l]} = \frac{\text{EL}}{\text{PFL}}, \quad \text{as } q = 0 \text{ for } X < x_l.$$

In addition, using the GPD, we have

$$\text{CEL} = \text{E}[q|X > x_l] = \frac{1}{x_h - x_l}\text{E}\big[\max(Y, x_h - x_l)\big]$$

$$= \frac{1}{x_h - x_l}\left\{\int_0^{x_h - x_l} y f_Y(y)dy + (x_h - x_l)S_Y(x_h - x_l)\right\}$$

$$= \frac{1}{x_h - x_l}\left\{\int_0^{x_h - x_l} S_Y(y)dy\right\}.$$

Now, let $\beta^* = \dfrac{\beta}{\xi(x_h - x_l)}$, then $\lambda = \left(\dfrac{\beta^*}{\beta^* + 1}\right)^{\frac{1}{\xi}}$

$$\Rightarrow \lambda^\xi = \frac{\beta^*}{\beta^* + 1}, \text{ and } \beta^* = \frac{\lambda^\xi}{1 - \lambda^\xi}.$$

Then,

$$
\begin{aligned}
\text{CEL} &= \frac{1}{x_h - x_l} \left\{ \int_0^{x_h - x_l} \left(\frac{\beta}{\beta + \xi\, y} \right)^{\frac{1}{\xi}} dy \right\} \\
&= \frac{\beta}{(x_h - x_l)(1 - \xi)} \left(1 - \left(\frac{\beta}{\beta + (x_h - x_l)\xi} \right)^{\frac{1}{\xi} - 1} \right) \\
&= \frac{\beta^* \xi\, (x_h - x_l)}{(x_h - x_l)(1 - \xi)} \left(1 - \left(\frac{\beta^*}{\beta^* + 1} \right)^{\frac{1}{\xi} - 1} \right) \\
&= \frac{\xi\, \lambda^{\xi}(1 - \lambda^{1-\xi})}{(1 - \xi)(1 - \lambda^{\xi})}.
\end{aligned}
$$

Now, from the PFL and PLL information given, we can calculate λ and CEL. Then we can solve numerically for the implied ξ, which will give a strong indication of the distribution of tail losses.

Example 16.5 The International Bank for Reconstruction and Development (IBRD), a subdivision of the World Bank, issued a cat bond in March 2020, with a parametric trigger, for which the perils covered are earthquakes and named storms in Mexico. The quoted annual PFL, PLL, and EL are 1.28%, 1.01%, and 1.14% respectively.

Estimate the ξ parameter for the risk under the generalized Pareto distribution, and interpret your result.

Solution 16.5 The conditional PLL is

$$
\lambda = \frac{\text{PLL}}{\text{PFL}} = 0.789.
$$

The conditional expected loss is

$$
\text{CEL} = \frac{\text{EL}}{\text{PFL}} = 0.8906.
$$

We then have that

$$
\text{CEL} = \frac{\xi\, \lambda^{\xi}(1 - \lambda^{1-\xi})}{(1 - \xi)(1 - \lambda^{\xi})},
$$

which we can solve numerically to give $\xi = -0.06$, which indicates a short-tailed distribution. $\qquad\square$

16.6.4 Miscellaneous Notes on Cat Bonds

(1) Investors must have confidence in the PFL, PLL, and EL figures provided. If these were provided by the sponsor, there would be an incentive to understate the risk, as this would lead to a lower premium spread. Instead, these values are provided by third party modelling firms, who also provide the required information on whether industry or modelled losses exceed the trigger thresholds.

(2) The cat models used by the modelling firms generally have three main components:

- The **hazard model** is the part that determines the likelihood and severity (in terms of parametric measures) of the catastrophic events occurring in each of the sub-regions covered.
- The **vulnerability model** is the part that determines how much physical damage would be caused by the events generated by the hazard model. This may be industry-wide, for industry loss triggers, but for calculating the PFL, PLL, and EL, based on an indemnity or modelled loss trigger, the vulnerability model would be based on the insurer's specific portfolio. The vulnerability model assesses the risk exposures, often in micro-detail. It might include, for example, a list of all the buildings in the covered region, with details of the construction and occupancy type.
- The **financial (or actuarial) method** converts the information on hazard severity (from the hazard model), and exposure (from the vulnerability model) into financial losses. This would allow for deductibles and for policy claim limits. This part would be specific to the sponsor's portfolio.

There is considerable uncertainty in each step of the modelling. For the investors, the uncertainty in the vulnerability and financial modules will only be relevant if the trigger used is indemnity or modelled losses.

(3) The original cat bond design, utilized until around 2009, had the SPV pass the principal to a third party, who would arrange for a swap, receiving the benchmark rate, which was typically LIBOR. This system added a layer of counterparty risk, which became apparent when Lehman Brothers Bank collapsed in 2008, defaulting on the principal for several large cat bond issues. Subsequently, the design has tended to use collateral trusts, reducing the counterparty risk.

(4) Cat bonds are sometimes issued in tranches; if the covered event occurs, the lowest ranked tranche would be the first to be exercised.

(5) Cat bonds are often submitted to rating agencies to assess the risk to investors. Rating agencies will take into account the stated PFL, PLL, and EL, but will also consider the standing of the third party modelling firm used, and the riskiness (for investors) of the trigger used.

(6) Although most sponsors are reinsurers, or large insurance companies, other agencies also utilize the cat bond market. Individual firms may do so through captive insurers. Non-governmental agencies, such as the IBRD are also involved, as mentioned in the example above; they use cat bonds to help to provide rebuilding funds for developing countries after natural disasters.

According to Barrieu and Albertini (2009), FIFA (the international governing body for association football) issued a cat bond before the 2006 World Cup, covering event cancellation for any cause.

(7) While natural disasters still make up the majority of cat bond covered events, the market is broadening to include emerging risks, including cyber risk. The risks have also expanded to include a stop loss cat bond, covering the cedant's aggregate losses over a threshold, without requiring a specific underlying catastrophic event. The FIFA cat bond covered terrorism related risks, but otherwise terrorism has not been a popular risk for cat bond issuers, as the models for evaluating the risk are considered too uncertain.

16.7 Other Forms of Securitized P&C Insurance

There are a number of other forms of securitized property and casualty insurance. These are designed broadly for the same purpose as cat bonds – to expand global reinsurance capacity beyond the traditional reinsurance companies, into capital markets.

Industry Loss Warranties

Industry loss warranties (ILWs) are very similar to cat bonds, but with a binary payoff. The trigger for the contract is aggregate insurance industry loss arising from a covered catastrophe event. If the industry losses exceed the specified threshold (as verified by a third party cat modelling firm) then the full face value is paid to the ILW sponsor. Otherwise, it is returned to the investors.

For example, consider an ILW described as follows: '$100m limit; Japanese Earthquake, attaching at $30bn.'

Investors deposit the full $100 million through the SPV, and receive coupons of a specified base interest rate plus a specified spread in return.

If an earthquake occurs in Japan during the term of the ILW, then the third party modelling firm would track aggregate industry losses. Once the losses exceed $30 billion, then the full $100 million would be transferred to the sponsor/cedant. If the losses do not exceed the attachment point, the principal is returned to investors.

ILWs may be written as reinsurance contracts, or they may be written as financial derivatives. Even when they are written as reinsurance contracts, they are fully collateralized – that is, the full maximum payout under the policy is held as collateral. This is not the case for regular insurance or reinsurance contracts. ILWs are typically used by reinsurers for retrocession.

Reinsurance Sidecars

A sidecar is a different method for expanding reinsurance capacity through capital markets, using an SPV. The SPV is funded by an investor group. It writes quota share reinsurance for a specified subset of the insurance portfolio of the sponsoring company. All the technical actuarial work of setting premiums and reserves is done by the sponsoring company. The sidecar receives a fixed portion of the premium income and pays a fixed portion of claims. The insurance profit is generated by a combination of underwriting profit (premiums − claims) and returns on invested assets.

Collateralized Reinsurance

Collateralized reinsurance refers to any reinsurance that is fully collateralized - that is, where funds invested are sufficient to pay the maximum claim amount. The collateral is provided by investors who receive a share of the underwriting and investment profits in return.

Collateralized reinsurance is flexible, and can be tailored to specific needs. It is often used for **working layer** reinsurance – that is, for losses that are not in the tail. The investors are generally specialist institutions, including hedge funds that only invest in insurance linked securities. Liquidity is low.

16.7.1 Notes on P&C Alternative Reinsurance

The different contracts and insurance schemes described above are collectively referred to as alternative reinsurance. The demand for alternative reinsurance emanated as a result of diminishing global reinsurance capacity through the 1990s, particularly for retrocession. Between 2000 and 2020, annual P&C cat bond capital issued grew from around $800 million to $11 billion.[2] The market

---

[2] Data sourced from www.artemis.bm.

declined during and after the financial crisis, impacted particularly by the failure of Lehman Brothers, but picked up again around 2012, with a flurry of activity from 2017.

16.8 Longevity and Mortality Risk Securitization

16.8.1 Mortality/Pandemic Bonds

The early attempts to securitize mortality related risks involved pandemic bonds. These work exactly as for the natural disaster cat bonds, but the covered event is excess mortality, with severity defined in terms of excess deaths in a given reference population, over a specified period. For the original mortality bonds, issued by Swiss Re in 2003, the covered event was defined in terms of increases to population mortality by a specified minimum amount, over two consecutive calendar years, during a four-year window.

In 2017, the IBRD, issued two tranches of pandemic bonds; the Class A bonds paid coupons of US\$ six-month LIBOR + 6.5%, and the Class B bonds paid US\$ six-month LIBOR + 11.1%. In the event of a pandemic that qualifies as a covered event, the proceeds from the bonds ($16\frac{2}{3}$% of principal for Class A, 100% of principal for Class B) are distributed to developing nations impacted by the pandemic. The trigger for the World Bank pandemic bonds was less stringent than that for the original Swiss Re bonds in terms of duration and severity, but narrower in that the excess mortality must be attributable to one of a specified list of diseases. The pandemic must last longer than 12 weeks, and must meet minimum thresholds for outbreak size (at least 250 deaths), spread (at least 2 countries affected), and growth (exponentially growing case count after 12 weeks). On April 27 2020, the World Bank announced that all the trigger requirements had been met in respect of the COVID-19 coronavirus pandemic, and prepared to distribute principal to the countries involved. Despite the fact that the bonds appear to have met the objective of offsetting pandemic costs, the contracts were heavily criticized for being too slow to be triggered, resulting in critical delays in disbursement of funds. The triggers were so stringent that an earlier severe Ebola outbreak did not meet the criteria, because the deaths were concentrated in one country.

The experience of the 2020 coronavirus pandemic has challenged some beliefs about mortality bonds, most notably that activation of the bonds would be more or less independent of capital markets. The 2020 pandemic was much more severe than any of the outbreaks of the previous 30 years. Around the world, quarantine requirements led to a sudden, severe decline in economic activity, creating extensive short-term capital market losses in most countries.

16.8.2 Longevity Derivatives

Longevity Risk Exposure

Longevity securitization is a more recent phenomenon. The risk being transferred is that a group of people will, on average, live longer than expected – that is, their average longevity increases. This creates a financial risk for institutions who are liable for making life annuity payments – specifically, many pension plans and insurance companies.

Most developed nations have seen gradual improvements in longevity over the past few decades, with some sub-populations improving slightly faster or slower than others, and with occasional reverses. Broadly, mortality improvement was considered very steady and predictable through the latter decades of the 1900s. Then, around the turn of the century, actuaries and demographers started to realize that mortality improvement had suddenly become much more rapid, most notably for males in their 50s–70s. Clearly, this was a good news story, but it created significant financial pressures for annuity providers.

Life annuities are regular payments made to an individual or a couple throughout their remaining lifetime, usually as a retirement income stream. Insurance companies issue life annuities through individual policies and through group pension arrangements. Many other firms have longevity exposure through sponsored pension plans. In some industries, the most common type of pension plan is **defined benefit**, where the amount of pension earned by the employee through their working lifetime with the firm is determined by a formula, typically proportional to the number of years of service, and to salary. The firm and (usually) the employees contribute a portion of salary into the pension plan to fund the benefits during the employee's working lifetime. After retirement the pension is paid in regular instalments to the employee for their remaining lifetime; often a smaller pension is paid to the employee's widow or widower if the employee dies first. The value of the pension benefit is very sensitive to the longevity of the employees; if employees' overall longevity increases faster than anticipated, the firm will be required to to make up the resulting shortfall in the pension plan. Pension costs are also very sensitive to interest rates, as life annuities are long duration liabilities.

Q-forwards

The initial attempt to securitize longevity risk took the form of longevity bonds, designed similarly to pandemic bonds, but triggered by low mortality experience. This is not an ideal format for transferring longevity risk; a

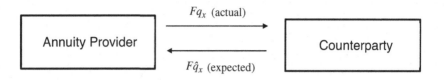

Figure 16.3 A q-forward transaction

pandemic is, usually, a short(ish) sharp shock. Longevity risk, in contrast, takes some time to emerge.

Subsequent securitization of longevity risk has been through arrangements that resemble financial swaps. A **q-forward contract** specifies a face amount, F, say, and a base table of expected mortality rates. The mortality rate at age x, denoted q_x, in actuarial notation, is the probability that a life age x will die within one year. The contract identifies a specific reference population (e.g., US males aged between 50 and 60), and identifies the expected mortality rate for this population, say $\hat{q}$, over a specified period. The actual experienced mortality rate, for the population, equal to q, say, will be published shortly after the end of the specified period. The q-forward involves two parties; one paying 'actual' and one paying 'expected'. If $q > \hat{q}$, then at maturity (say, T-years) the 'actual' counterparty pays $F(q - \hat{q})$ to the 'expected' counterparty, and vice versa if $\hat{q} > q$.

The firm or enterprise wanting to hedge its longevity risk would take the 'actual' side of the swap; when actual rates are high, they would have to make payments under the q-forward contract, but the value of their annuity liability would be lower. When actual rates are low, creating extra cost under the annuity portfolio, there would be some compensation under the q-forward contract.

For a firm with a portfolio of annuities, a hedge strategy could combine q-forward contracts with different reference populations to replicate, as far as possible, their own annuitant population. Then, in principle, q-forwards can be purchased for each age group and for each term, to match the annuity portfolio cash flows. In practice, rather than purchasing separate q-forwards for each individual age, a simpler hedge, utilizing only a few key ages, can achieve almost as good results as a fully matched portfolio. This is helpful as the available q-forwards are based on broad age groups, so a q-forward portfolio that is perfectly age matched is not actually feasible (Figure 16.3).

Base populations for q-forwards are typically in 10-year age groups, from age 40 to 90, split by male and female, for a total of 10 base population contracts. These are combined into a longevity hedge using **key q-durations**, analogous to key rate duration matching for interest rate hedging. The steps for determining the key q-forward hedge are:

(1) For each starting age cohort in the portfolio, say x, calculate the liability value, based on the expected future mortality, denoted $P_x(\hat{\boldsymbol{q}})$, where $\hat{\boldsymbol{q}}$ is the vector of expected mortality rates for all ages greater than x.
(2) We let x_j, $j = 1, \ldots, n$ denote the centre ages of the available q-forward contracts, and let $\hat{q}_{x_j}$ denote the expected mortality rate at age x_j. These are assumed to be the key ages for hedging the longevity risk.

     For each $x_j > x$, estimate, numerically, the partial derivative of P_x with respect to the mortality at x_j. This is the q-duration of the portfolio for age x_j, denoted $QD(P_x(\boldsymbol{q}), x_j)$.
(3) We hedge the portfolio by matching the q-duration of the annuity portfolio with the q-durations of the hedge portfolio, which is composed of q-forwards with varying face value for each x_j. For the q-forward with reference age x_j, and face value F_j, say, we select the term to be $T_j = x_j + 1 - x$, which means that it pays out at the end of the year that the age x cohort reaches age x_j. The value of the transaction, based on expected mortality, is

$$H_j = F_j\big(\hat{q}_{x_j} - q_{x_j}\big)e^{-rT_j}.$$

The q-duration of the forward contract for age x_j is

$$\frac{d}{dq_{x_j}}H_j = -F_j e^{-rT_j}.$$

Matching durations of the forward and the liability for each j, we have

$$-F_j e^{-rT_j} = QD(P_x(\hat{\boldsymbol{q}}), x_j) \Rightarrow F_j = -QD(P_x(\hat{\boldsymbol{q}}), x_j)\,e^{r(x_j - x + 1)},$$

which gives us the face value required for the age x_j q-forwards, to hedge the age x liability.

Example 16.6 You are given that q-forward contracts are available for reference ages 65, 75, and 85. The risk-free rate of interest, continuously compounded, is $r = 3.5\%$.

You are given the following key q-durations for a portfolio of annuities all issued to lives currently age 60.

x_j	$x_1 = 65$	$x_2 = 75$	$x_3 = 85$
q-duration	-475.7	-107.1	-27.8

(a) Explain why the q-durations are negative.

(b) Identify the term and face value of the q-forward contracts required to achieve the key q-duration match.

Solution 16.6

(a) The q-duration at age x_j is the derivative of the value of the annuity portfolio with respect to the mortality at x_j.

As mortality increases the value of the annuity decreases; a higher probability of death implies a lower probability of annuity payments. Hence, the annuity value is a decreasing function of the mortality rates, which means that the q-durations are negative.

(b) We have $x = 60$, $x_1 = 65$, $x_2 = 75$, and $x_3 = 85$, so $T_1 = 6$, $T_2 = 16$, and $T_3 = 26$.

The q-durations of the key q-forwards are $-F_1 e^{-6r}$, $-F_2 e^{-16r}$, and $-F_3 e^{-26r}$, respectively.

Matching q-durations gives $F_1 = 586.9$, $F_2 = 187.5$, and $F_3 = 69.1$. □

Basis Risk

Basis risk is a significant issue in longevity and mortality risk transfer. Hedgers are typically attempting to mitigate losses from a relatively small group – for example, the firm's retirees who are receiving pension benefits – but the reference populations for the contracts are typically whole country populations. It is likely that the age and sex specific mortality experience of the entire population will be quite different from the retiree group; mortality is strongly influenced by social factors such as income, level of education, and location. A group of retired employees of an insurance company in Iowa, and a group of retired auto workers in Michigan, are each unlikely to be well-represented by US whole-population mortality. It is possible to reduce the basis risk in a key q-duration hedge, using a joint model of mortality for the reference population and the population represented in the liability portfolio (Li and Hardy, 2011).

Other ways to avoid basis risk involve more tailored risk transfer solutions. A customized **survivor swap** can be structured to use the actual cash flows of the annuity provider, and may use the annuitants as the reference population. The annuity provider calculates a schedule of expected future cash flows. At each year end, if expected cash flows are greater than actual cash flows, meaning that the annuity cost was less than expected, the annuity provider pays the difference to the counterparty. If actual cash flows are greater than expected, then the counterparty pays the excess to the annuity provider.

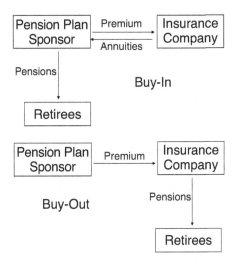

Figure 16.4 Pension buy-in and buy-out arrangements

16.8.3 Pension Buy-In and Buy-Out

Exposure to longevity risk and long-term interest rate risk is a significant challenge for many large corporations with mature defined benefit pension plans. Since the early 2000s, many companies have had to provide substantial additional funding to shore up underfunded pension plans. The underfunding was caused by (i) unexpected increases in longevity, (ii) a prolonged period of very low interest rates, and (iii) the common practice of investing heavily in equities, which lead to a dramatic collapse in pension plan asset values during the global financial crisis. Many firms with mature defined benefit pension plans found that their pension liabilities were contributing a large amount of risk and volatility to the overall operations of the firm, and that this was not a good use of their risk budget.

There are two popular methods for firms to transfer their pension-based longevity and investment risk; the **bulk annuity buy-in** (buy-in) and the **bulk annuity buy-out** (buy-out) (Figure 16.4).

Under the buy-in arrangement, the pension plan sponsor pays a premium to the insurer, who then makes regular annuity payments back to the plan sponsor, contingent on the survival of the named retirees or their spouses. The plan sponsor uses the payments from the insurer to pay the pensions to the retirees – although they do not need to do this. The annuity payments are, in principle, investment proceeds that are paid into the general funds, from which are paid the pensions. If the plan defaults, plan members with benefits covered by the

Table 16.1. *Comparison of buy-in and buy-out contracts*

Buy-in	Buy-out
The bulk annuity contract is treated as an asset of the pension plan.	The bulk annuity contract is treated as a transfer of liabilities.
Longevity and investment risk are both transferred to the insurer.	Longevity and investment risk are both transferred to the insurer.
The sponsor is liable for payment of benefits.	The insurer is liable for payment of benefits.
The sponsor is liable for administration of benefits, e.g., communicating with members, preparing tax statements.	The insurer is responsible for administration of benefits.
No special accounting implications.	A settlement cost will be reflected in the company accounts.
May transfer only part of the annuity portfolio.	Usually involves transfer of all pension liabilities.
Pension plan members are exposed to sponsor default risk.	Pension plan members are exposed to insurer default risk.
The sponsor is exposed to insurer default risk.	The sponsor retains no residual counterparty risk.
Flexible structure and coverage; may add policies to the contract or adjust payment schedules.	Inflexible contract; all terms must be negotiated up front.
Purchase of bulk annuity asset must be consistent with stated investment principles of the pension plan.	May need regulator approval. If the buy out is not related to a full wind-up, the security of benefits retained must not be diminished by the buy-out.

buy-in would have no more benefit security than plan members who were not included in the buy-in.

Buy-in contracts can be used to transfer significant longevity and investment risk for the pensions in payment, in a way that is quite flexible and customizable. The firm may include only a subset of annuities; they may bulk purchase level annuities, and then top up the pensions for example, to cover cost of living adjustments, from other funds. As insurers typically prefer not to take in inflation rate risk (and therefore charge a lot if they do), this will create a cost-effective hedge for the basic benefits, whilst allowing discretionary top up of benefits if the plan funding level is suitably healthy.

Under the buy-out arrangement, the pension plan sponsor transfers specific pension liabilities and assets to the insurer, who then takes full responsibility for paying the benefits directly to the pension plan members whose pensions were transferred. The plan sponsor takes no further role in the payment of these benefits; the buy-out contract is a full transfer of liabilities. Usually, the default risk of the insurer is very small relative to the potential default of the sponsor or the pension plan, so the benefits transferred are significantly more secure than any benefits left in the pension plan. In addition, usually the transfer of liabilities costs the pension plan more than the value of the supporting assets – the insurer will add significantly more margin than would be included in the pension valuation. If the additional assets are taken from the pension plan, then the remaining members are effectively subsidizing the members whose benefits are transferred. This is clearly undesirable; generally, if any liabilities remain within the plan, then the sponsor must make additional payments into the plan to restore the security of the benefits of remaining members. Often this is not an issue, as the buy-out is used to close out a DB pension plan.

Table 16.1 provides a brief, side-by-side comparison of buy-in and buy-out contracts.

16.9 Notes and Further Reading

For a detailed treatment of traditional securitization outside of the context of insurance, see Fabozzi and Kothari (2008).

Barrieu and Albertini (2009) is an excellent source for more in-depth coverage of insurance linked securities.

The websites run by the Artemis group (www.artemis.bm) and Lane Financial (www.lanefinancialllc.com) offer up-to-date coverage of trends in alternative risk transfer and information on recent issues of cat bonds.

For more detail on the origin and applications of q-forwards, see Li and Luo (2012) and Li and Hardy (2011).

16.10 Exercises

Exercise 16.1 Captives are often capitalized using lines of credit. Discuss advantages and disadvantages of this arrangement from the perspectives of the lender and the borrower.

Exercise 16.2 Show that the premium spread is a decreasing function of the exhaustion point. Explain this result by general reasoning.

Exercise 16.3 Put the following cat bond triggers in order of risk to (i) the investors and (ii) the sponsor. Explain your ranking.

- Industry loss.
- Indemnity.
- Modelled loss.
- Parametric.

Exercise 16.4 Explain the difference between a pension buy-in and a pension buy-out. Describe advantages and disadvantages of each approach, from the perspective of (i) the pension plan sponsor and (ii) the pension plan members and retirees.

Exercise 16.5 You are given the following information about a cat bond:

SPV	Northfarm Re
Cedant	Geneva Re
Risk modelling agents	FAIR Worldwide
Perils covered	US Earthquake
Face value	$500m
Trigger type	Industry Loss Index
Attachment Point	Index level 1,000
Exhaustion Point	Index level 1,200
Probability of First Loss (PFL)	2.44%
Expected Loss	2.1%

(a) Explain briefly the advantages and disadvantages to a reinsurer of using cat bonds to transfer risk, as compared with traditional reinsurance.
(b) Sketch a diagram of the cash transfers for the cat bond in the table. Identify the roles of Northfarm Re and Geneva Re respectively.
(c) Explain the role of the risk modelling agents.
(d) During the term of the contract an earthquake occurs, with industry loss index level 1,050. Determine the amount of principal returned to the investors.
(e) Write down formulas describing the relationship between the attachment point, the exhaustion point, and (i) the PFL and (ii) the EL.
(f) The industry loss index is modelled as a Pareto distribution, with cumulative distribution function

$$F(y) = 1 - \left(\frac{\lambda}{\lambda + y}\right)^2.$$

(i) Use the PFL to show that $\lambda = 185$ to the nearest 5.
(ii) Calculate the probability of maximum loss (PML) for the contract.

Exercise 16.6 Hamsik Insurance Company is a property insurer with most of its exposures located in the Midwest US. It currently has a reinsurance agreement with Bourbon Re on its property risks to cover weather-related losses. Bourbon provides indemnification for 75% of Hamsik's aggregate annual weather losses between $50 million and $300 million.

Recent increases in storms in the Midwest and Northwest US have deteriorated Bourbon's capitalization. Hamsik is considering terminating its reinsurance treaty and instead forming an SPV as an alternative means of transferring risk. The SPV would raise capital by issuing catastrophe bonds to investors.

(a) Outline the provisions that need to be specified and negotiated with potential investors.
(b) Explain key provisions that impact how closely the SPV's coverage matches Hamsik's existing reinsurance agreement.
(c) Explain the potential advantages and disadvantages for Hamsik if it sets up an SPV instead of continuing with its reinsurance agreement.
(d) Hamsik's primary rating agency (AM Best) is concerned with Hamsik's dependence on the existing reinsurance agreement. State whether you expect the SPV to be viewed by AM Best as a positive or negative development for Hamsik's capitalization and operating performance. Explain your answer.

Copyright 2014. The Society of Actuaries, Schaumburg, Illinois. Reproduced with permission.

Exercise 16.7 Grandview Insurance is a property and casualty insurer operating in a country prone to earthquakes. A recent series of earthquakes has strained its surplus level due to major losses from the commercial line. The commercial line insures losses from 'property damage and business interruption' (PDBI).

The CRO is considering reinsurance options to transfer some of the risk arising from earthquake claims and alleviate earnings volatility.

(a) Describe the following types of reinsurance and assess the suitability of each for PDBI risks:

(i) Quota share.
(ii) Stop loss.

The following is an excerpt from an ordered sample of 200 simulated annual losses for Grandview's PDBI line, in millions:

i	$L_{(i)}$
195	43.8
196	47.5
197	50.2
198	57.5
199	65.6
200	90.0

Grandview is considering the following three options:

(i) No reinsurance coverage.

(ii) A quota share reinsurance arrangement under which Grandview cedes 35% of the risk.

(iii) A stop loss reinsurance arrangement with a $12 million priority and $40 million capacity.

(b) Calculate the 98% Expected Shortfall of the net losses after reinsurance recoveries for each reinsurance option.

(c) (i) Estimate the standard error of the Expected Shortfall estimator in (b) for the quota share reinsurance.

(ii) Estimate the standard error of the Expected Shortfall estimator in (b) for the stop loss reinsurance.

(d) You are given the following information:

	Reinsurance Premium	Expected Recoveries
Quota Share	2.0 million	1.5 million
Stop Loss	2.5 million	1.4 million

The CFO reviews the risk measure calculations and premiums, and sends the following email:

'The expected payouts from the two reinsurance contracts are close. The Quota Share is cheaper, so we don't need any further analysis. We should go with the Quota Share.'

(i) Explain why the quota share contract is cheaper than the stop loss, per unit of expected reinsurance claim.

(ii) Critique the CFO's statement.

(e) State one advantage and one disadvantage of using securitization instead of reinsurance for Grandview's earthquake risk.

Copyright 2016. The Society of Actuaries, Schaumburg, Illinois. Reproduced with permission.

Exercise 16.8 A group of companies operating for-profit long-term care homes has formed an offshore captive insurance company, LTC Captive. The group is considering reinsurance opportunities.

(a) Outline four key risks for the companies sponsoring LTC Captive.

(b) Outline advantages to the companies in setting up LTC captive.

(c) Describe key risks that the companies might pass to LTC Captive.

(d) Explain why LTC Captive might enter quota share reinsurance contracts; give examples of risks that might be transferred using quota share.

(e) Explain why LTC Captive might enter excess of loss reinsurance contracts; give examples of risks that might be transferred using excess of loss.

(f) Outline risks remaining after quota share and excess of loss reinsurance contracts are implemented.

Copyright 2016. The Society of Actuaries, Schaumburg, Illinois. Reproduced with permission.

Exercise 16.9 A cat bond sponsored by Hannover Re, covering Florida named storms, with an indemnity trigger, has annual PFL, PLL, and EL of 4.10%, 1.64%, and 1.98% respectively.

Determine the ξ parameter of the generalized Pareto distribution, and interpret the result.

17

Regulation of Financial Institutions

17.1 Summary

In this chapter, we review some of the risk management implications of the regulation of banks and insurance companies. Banks are largely regulated through local implementation of the Basel II and Basel III Accords. Insurance regulation is more varied, but the development of the European Union (EU) directive known as Solvency II has influenced regulation more widely, and so we focus on Solvency II as an example of a modern insurance regulatory system.

17.2 Introduction

Banks and insurers are required to hold additional funds, on top of the accounting valuation of the contingent liabilities, to allow for the possibility that emerging costs exceed the amounts anticipated in the accounting valuation. The funds held in excess of the valuation of the liabilities are referred to as **capital**. Government regulations set rules for determining the minimum level of capital that a firm must hold to ensure that with high probability the assets are sufficient, even when the experience is adverse.

Firms are subject to regulation in many aspects of their operations, but in this chapter we focus on solvency regulations applying to firms working in financial services. The regulatory capital is the amount required by government regulators to protect against financial distress. A primary objective of regulation is to protect customers and creditors against firm default; individual customers are protected because capital markets are more efficient when individuals trust banks and insurance companies to act as responsible stewards of their customers' funds. In addition, regulation that reduces the risk of bank or insurer insolvency helps to avoid the possibility that the default of a single major institution sets off a chain of defaults, leading to a global systemic crisis. The 2007–8 global financial crisis followed a long period of deregulation of banking in the United States (US) and more widely.

The global regulation of banks is guided by the Basel Committee on Banking Supervision (Basel Committee) of the Bank for International Settlements. The Basel Committee currently comprises central bank governors from over 20 countries, including the US, Canada, the United Kingdom, Australia, India, and China. Since the 1970s, the Basel Committee has been developing and updating its framework for regulating banking solvency management. The Basel Accords are not binding in themselves, but have been adopted into local law by all the major countries participating in international finance. Having a single global solvency risk regulatory framework acts to reduce the impact of regulatory arbitrage, which can be a consequence of inconsistent regulation, when firms seek out the most lenient jurisdiction.

Regulation of insurance companies is more varied. The Solvency II regulations, which we describe in Section 17.4, were implemented in 2016 after a long period of development and testing. The impact of Solvency II extends beyond the European states to which it applies. The underlying framework has been used as the basis of insurance regulation in some of the fastest developing markets, such as China and India. Solvency II has not directly affected regulation in the US or Canada, but developments in insurance regulation in both countries have mirrored, to some extent, the principles of Solvency II and of the Basel Accords. In the US, insurance solvency is the responsibility of the individual states, but the National Association of Insurance Commissioners (NAIC) provides some guidance and coordination. In Canada, regulation of banks and insurers is primarily a federal responsibility and exercised through the Office of the Superintendent of Financial Institutions (OSFI).

17.3 Basel II and III

17.3.1 Three Pillars

The Basel Capital Accords (commonly known as Basel II and Basel III) provide the basis for global solvency regulations for banks. The Basel II rules were brought into force in the early 2000s. These have been updated and adjusted several times, with the major package of revisions known as Basel III due to be implemented by the mid-2020s.[1]

---

[1] The date for implementation has been delayed several times; at the time of writing, the implementation date is expected to be 1 January 2023.

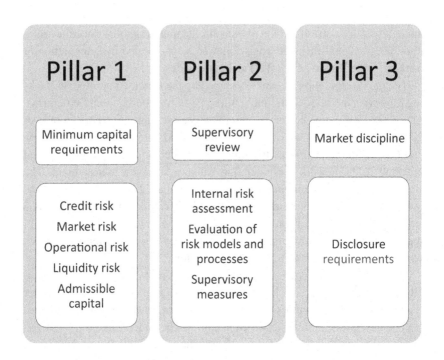

Figure 17.1 The three pillars of the Basel Accords

The framework for both Basel II and III is based on the three pillars illustrated in Figure 17.1.

The first pillar provides detailed rules and guidance for determining solvency capital requirements relating to the most quantifiable risk types, including credit risk, market risk, operational risk, and liquidity risk. It also defines what may be included as capital for the purpose of meeting the requirements.

The second pillar describes principles of supervision which are expected to be integrated into the regulatory process of banking supervision in each individual nation.

The third pillar describes how market discipline should be able to identify poorly capitalized firms, or firms with inadequate risk governance. For market participants to monitor risk management and capital adequacy of other institutions, they must be provided with sufficient information, and so the focus of the Pillar 3 requirements is disclosure.

17.3.2 Pillar 1: Minimum Capital Requirements (MCR)

The first pillar describes the calculation of the **minimum capital requirement** (MCR), which is the risk-based capital calculation determined using the particular contracts and counterparties for each individual bank.

There are four components of the MCR. The first is the determination of the capital available to the firm. The other three are the risk elements, covering (i) credit risk, (ii) market risks, and (iii) operational risks.

In the following sections, we will describe the main components and general principles of the MCR calculations, but there are many details and special cases that we omit. The objective is to give a general description of the formulas and underlying methodology. For more detailed sources, see Section 17.5.

17.3.3 Tier 1, 2, and 3 Capital

Under the Basel Accords, capital which may be used to meet minimum regulatory capital requirements is divided into three tiers, depending on the ability to absorb losses, on the permanence of the capital, and on the level of subordination to depositors and other creditors.

Under Basel III, only Tier 1 and Tier 2 capital may be used to meet the MCR.

- Tier 1 capital (also known as **core capital**) is permanent, not subordinate, and available to meet losses. Common equity is the major source of Tier 1 capital; disclosed reserves and non-redeemable, non-cumulative preferred shares[2] are also included. For some purposes the Tier 1 equity capital is separated from the other Tier 1 capital. Tier 1 capital has the highest capacity to absorb losses, and within Tier 1, the equity capital is the most flexible.
- Tier 2 capital (also known as **supplementary capital**) may include long-term subordinated debt, undisclosed reserves, which arise when a bank overstates a liability in the accounts, and revaluation reserves, where a bank understates an asset, usually because it is valued in the accounts at historical cost or book value. Some types of hybrid debt, which combine features of debt and equity, may also be used for Tier 2 capital, including

---

[2] If a company suspends dividends to survive a period of adversity, and subsequently recovers, the missed dividends on non-cumulative preferred shares are lost; on cumulative preferred shares the missed dividends must be repaid before the company can resume paying dividends on common stock.

cumulative preferred shares, perpetual debt instruments and convertible long-term bonds. Tier 2 capital is not as absorbent as Tier 1, but is sufficiently flexible to provide some protection against adverse experience.
- Tier 3 capital includes subordinated debt which is unsecured and fully paid up, and for which interest and principal payments will be waived if the bank cannot otherwise meet its MCR. Although Tier 3 capital was allowed, with restrictions, under Basel II, it has been removed from the capital calculations under Basel III.

17.3.4 Risk Weighted Assets and MCR

For each of the three risk elements, that is, credit risk, market risk, and operational risk, the Basel regulations specify the calculation of a **capital requirement factor**, CR_j, and **risk weighted assets**, RWA_j where $j = cr$ for credit risk, $j = or$ for operational risk, and $j = mr$ for market risk.

In most cases, the capital requirement is determined according to the Basel II or III specifications, and the RWA are determined as $RWA_j = 12.5 \times CR_j$.

The total RWA for the firm is the sum of the three components, $RWA = RWA_{cr} + RWA_{or} + RWA_{mr}$.

The minimum capital requirement under Basel III specifies that the following criteria must be satisfied at all times:

$$\frac{\text{Tier 1 Capital} + \text{Tier 2 Capital}}{\text{RWA}} \geq 0.08, \qquad (17.1)$$

$$\frac{\text{Tier 1 Capital}}{\text{RWA}} \geq 0.06, \qquad (17.2)$$

$$\frac{\text{Common Equity Tier 1 Capital}}{\text{RWA}} \geq 0.045. \qquad (17.3)$$

Note that the RWA is, approximately, $12.5 \times$ the total capital requirement, so that if $CR = \sum_j CR_j$, then equations (17.1) and (17.2) can be written as

$$\text{Tier 1 Capital} + \text{Tier 2 Capital} \geq CR$$

and

$$\text{Tier 1 Capital} \geq 75\% \, CR.$$

Under Basel II, only the first criterion is specified, along with a requirement that Tier 2 capital may not exceed 100% of Tier 1 capital.

Table 17.1. *Examples of risk weights for determining the credit risk (CR) required capital using the standardized approach*

Type of debt	Rating				
	$\geq$ AA−	A+ to A−	BBB+ to BBB−	BB+ to B−	<B−
Sovereign Debt	0%	20%	50%	100%	150%
Public Sector Entities	20%	50%	100%	100%	150%
Banks	20%	30%	50%	100%	150%
Corporate Bonds	20%	50%	75%	100%	150%

17.3.5 MCR: Credit Risk Component

In this section, we review the basic charge for credit risk in the Basel Accord. We consider both the basic **standardized approach** and the more sophisticated **internal models approach**. There are also regulatory capital charges in the Basel Accord related to **counterparty credit risk** (CCR) for the trading book, including a charge for potential default losses and a charge associated with the **credit valuation adjustment** (CVA), which captures mark-to-market counterparty credit risk losses. The default risk charge for CCR has a similar form to the internal models charge that we consider here, but is more complicated due to the fact that it must take into account the randomness in future counterparty exposures.

The Standardized Approach
There are two permitted methodologies for calculating the capital requirements for credit risk. The first is the **standardized approach**, which measures the RWA directly, rather than through the CR. Risk weights are applied to assets based on the nature of the issuers or counterparties, and on the credit ratings assigned to the issuers by a recognized credit rating agency, such as Standard and Poor's. Weights are also specified for loans secured on residential and commercial real estate. Some examples of weights are given in Table 17.1. The firm must calculate the risk weighted assets for the credit risk MCR (RWA_{cr}), by multiplying asset values in the different categories by the given risk weights, with some adjustment for mitigating or exacerbating factors.

The Internal Ratings-Based Approach
The alternative to the standardized approach is the **internal ratings based** (IRB) approach. Banks may apply to use the IRB approach, or may be required to do so by their regulators, depending on the jurisdiction and the size of the bank.

In the simplest cases, for exposures involving corporate bonds for example, the IRB approach involves three parameters for each borrower. The first parameter is the one-year **probability of default** (PD), which is the probability that the bond issuer will default on some or all of the funds owed within one year. The second is the **loss given default** (LGD), which is the proportion of funds lost if default occurs. The third is the **exposure at default** (EAD), which is the amount of funds owed by the obligor.[3]

The IRB method requires banks to estimate the probability of default separately for each exposure. The LGD parameter under Basel III is supposed to be a 'downturn LGD', i.e. it reflects expected losses during an economic recession. It depends on the seniority of the debt, and is adjusted in cases where there is eligible collateral supporting the loans. The EAD is the net exposure, with some adjustment for off-balance sheet items.

For the ith borrower, the capital requirement ($CR_{cr,i}$) using the IRB method is calculated as follows. Begin by determining the correlation parameter ρ_i:[4]

$$\rho_i = 0.12 \frac{1 - e^{-50PD_i}}{1 - e^{-50}} + 0.24 \left(1 - \frac{1 - e^{-50PD_i}}{1 - e^{-50}} \right). \qquad (17.4)$$

The ρ parameter is an estimate of the correlation between the ith borrower and the other borrowers in the portfolio. The minimum value for the correlation is 12%, where PD_i is close to 1, and the maximum value is 24%, where PD_i is near 0. Next we calculate three factors for each borrower:

$$MA_i = \frac{1 + (M_i - 2.5)b_i}{1 - 1.5b_i}, \qquad (17.5)$$

where

$$b_i = (0.11852 - 0.05478 \log(PD_i))^2 \qquad (17.6)$$

and

$$M_i = \min(2.5, \text{Term to maturity}). \qquad (17.7)$$

The *MA* parameter is a 'maturity adjustment' to allow for the effect on credit exposure of the term to maturity of the bond.

---

[3] In this chapter, we will use the terms 'borrower' and 'obligor' synonymously to refer to parties that owe the bank money. We reserve 'counterparty' for the counterparty to a derivative security to which the CCR capital charge would apply.

[4] This is the formula for corporate loans. It needs to be multiplied by 1.25 if the borrower is a large regulated financial institution. There are different formulas for small and medium sized enterprises, residential mortgages ($\rho_i \equiv 0.15$), qualifying revolving retail exposures ($\rho_i \equiv 0.04$), and other retail exposures.

Given these parameters, the capital requirement for the ith borrower is

$$CR_{cr,i} = \left\{ \Phi\left(\frac{z_{PD_i} + \sqrt{\rho_i}\, z_{0.999}}{\sqrt{1-\rho_i}} \right) - PD_i \right\} (LGD_i)(EAD_i)(MA_i), \quad (17.8)$$

where, as usual,

$$\Phi(z_q) = q.$$

The total capital requirement for credit risk is the sum of the capital requirements over all borrowers:

$$\mathrm{CR}_{cr} = \sum_i CR_{cr,i}.$$

It is interesting to explore the model behind this formula. Let T_i denote the time to default of the ith borrower, so that $PD_i = \Pr[T_i < 1]$. Now assume that all borrowers are connected through a **single factor Gaussian copula model**, described in Section 12.5. This models the default probability of the ith firm indirectly through a standard normal random variable Y_i, which is related to the time to default random variable T_i as

$$\Phi(Y_i) = F_{T_i}(T_i) \quad \Rightarrow \quad \Pr[T_i \le t] = \Pr[Y_i \le y] \text{ where } \Phi(y) = F_{T_i}(t).$$

The default probability for the ith firm is connected to the other firms in the portfolio through a common random variable $Z \sim N(0,1)$; for each i we have

$$Y_i = \sqrt{\rho_i} \cdot Z + \sqrt{1-\rho_i} \cdot \varepsilon_i,$$

where $\{\varepsilon_i\}$ are i.i.d. $N(0,1)$ random variables, independent of Z. All borrowers are assumed to share the same Z factor, but are otherwise independent.

Now define $y_i = \Phi^{-1}(F_{T_i}(1))$, so that the 1-year probability of default for the ith borrower is

$$PD_i = \Pr[T_i \le 1] = \Pr[Y_i \le y_i] = \Phi(y_i).$$

All the dependency among borrowers is modelled through the common factor, Z. For the capital requirement, we consider the conditional probability of default, given Z:

$$Y_i = \sqrt{\rho_i} \cdot Z + \sqrt{1-\rho_i} \cdot \varepsilon_i$$

$$\Rightarrow \Pr\left[Y_i \le y_i | Z\right] = \Pr\left[\varepsilon_i \le \frac{y_i - \sqrt{\rho_i} Z}{\sqrt{1-\rho_i}}\right] = \Phi\left(\frac{y_i - \sqrt{\rho_i} Z}{\sqrt{1-\rho_i}} \right)$$

$$= \Phi\left(\frac{z_{PD_i} - \sqrt{\rho_i}\, Z}{\sqrt{1-\rho_i}} \right).$$

The Basel risk measure for the default probability is set by assuming that the common factor, Z, lies at its 99.9% worst case value. Note that this does not give us the 99.9% VaR for the individual borrower; it is designed to capture the systematic credit risk, where adverse economic conditions lead to a large number of defaults. The idiosyncratic risk, which is the risk specific to a single borrower, is not captured, as it is assumed to be sufficiently diversified (and addressed through other measures, such as credit limits and stress testing).

Since the worst case default arises when Z is small, the 99.9% worst case for the common default risk corresponds to the 0.1% quantile of Z, and since Z is assumed to have a standard normal distribution, the 0.1% quantile is $z_{0.001} = -z_{0.999} \approx -3.090$. The result can be thought of as a stressed default probability:

$$\Pr\left[Y_i \leq y^* | Z = z_{0.001}\right] = \Phi\left(\frac{z_{PD_i} - \sqrt{\rho_i}\, z_{0.001}}{\sqrt{1 - \rho_i}}\right)$$

$$= \Phi\left(\frac{z_{PD_i} + \sqrt{\rho_i}\, z_{0.999}}{\sqrt{1 - \rho_i}}\right).$$

Recall the CR equation (17.8),

$$CR_{cr,i} = \left\{\Phi\left(\frac{z_{PD_i} + \sqrt{\rho_i}\, z_{0.999}}{\sqrt{(1 - \rho_i)}}\right) - PD_i\right\}(LGD_i)(EAD_i)(MA_i).$$

We see that the term in parentheses is the additional probability of default arising from stressing the common factor Z; it is sometimes referred to as the **worst case default rate** (WCDR). Multiplying by (LGD_i) and (EAD_i) gives the additional expected loss from default arising from the stressed default probability, compared with the expected default probability. This reflects the fact that the capital charge is meant to provide a buffer for *unexpected* losses. Expected losses are accounted for by the bank's loss reserves. The MA_i term adjusts for additional risk from long-term debt compared with shorter-term debt.

Example 17.1 Suppose a firm assesses the 1-year probability of default of a corporate bond as 1%. The loss given default is assumed to be LGD = 0.45 and the net exposure at default is EAD = 1,000,000. The term to maturity is three years. Calculate the risk weighted asset.

Solution 17.1 We have

$$\rho = 0.12(0.3935) + 0.24(0.6065) = 0.19278,$$

$$b = 0.1375, \qquad M = 2.5,$$

$$MA = \frac{1}{1 - 1.5\,(0.1375)} = 1.2598,$$

$$CR_{cr} = \left\{ \Phi\left(\frac{-2.326 + \sqrt{0.19278}\,3.0902}{\sqrt{1 - 0.19278}}\right) - 0.01 \right\}$$

$$\times\,(0.45)(1{,}000{,}000)(1.2598)$$

$$= (0.140 - 0.01)(0.45)(1{,}000{,}000)(1.2598)$$

$$= 73{,}700.$$

So the RWA$_{cr}$ for this exposure is $12.5 \times 73{,}700 = 921{,}250$.

Note that the best estimate of the 1-year probability of default is only 1%, but stressing the probability of joint default generates a default probability of 14% at the 99.9% significance level.

A second interesting point is that a bond with a 1% default probability would be rated in the B+ to BB range, which, under the standardized approach would require RWA equal to 100% of the bond nominal value, which is 1 million. In this case, given that the bond value is likely to be close to the EAD, the IRB approach generates a slightly lower capital requirement than the standardized approach.

Finally, note that in order to calculate the capital charge for the bond, we only needed to know its characteristics, and nothing about the portfolio in which it is contained. This is an illustration of the property of portfolio invariance of the capital charge in the single factor model, discussed in Chapter 12. □

To qualify for the IRB approach, a bank must demonstrate to the regulator that it is able to model its risks in a 'consistent, reliable and valid fashion'. There are a number of criteria that must be met; most critically, the bank must persuade the regulator that it is using a valid model with adequate, relevant supporting data and proven predictive capability; that the teams responsible for the models have appropriate expertise, and that the bank has effective corporate governance with respect to oversight of the estimation and modelling processes.

17.3.6 MCR: Operational Risk Component

Under Basel II, the simplest calculation of the operational risk capital requirement is the basic indicator approach, which sets the RWA at 15% of the average gross income of the bank over the previous three years. If the gross income in any year is negative it is omitted from the calculation.

As with the credit risk calculation under Basel II, banks with adequate modelling and data resources could be approved to use an internal model approach, called the **advanced measurement approach**, under which the operational risk capital is determined using the bank's own model and parameters, including allowance for risk mitigation. Under Basel III, the advanced measurement approach has been dropped, and the Basic Indicator approach has been updated to the **standardised measurement approach** (SMA), which all firms must now use. The SMA uses the **business indicator** (BI), which is a measure of income, as the operational risk exposure measure. The BI is calculated similarly to gross income, but excludes some negative contributions. It is averaged over the previous three years.

The **business indicator component** (BIC) for the firm is calculated by splitting the BI into three layers and applying different multipliers to the different layers: the first \$1 billion of BI is multiplied by 12%, the layer between \$1 billion and \$30 billion is multiplied by 15%, and the layer above \$30 billion is multiplied by 18%.

The BIC is adjusted by the **internal loss multiplier** (ILM). The ILM is 1.0 for businesses with BI < \$1 billion. For all other firms it measures whether the firm's own operational risk losses over the past 10 years are greater or less than the industry averages, relative to its BIC. The Basel committee determined that an industry average operational loss is around 1/15th of a firm's BIC, which generated the following definition of the **loss component** (LC):

$$LC = 15\big(\text{Firm's average } \textbf{operational risk losses} \text{ over the past 10 years}\big),$$

(17.9)

$$\text{ILM} = \log\left(e^1 + \left(\frac{LC}{BIC}\right)^{0.8} - 1\right).$$

(17.10)

If the firm's operational risk losses are equal to the industry average of 15% of gross income, then ILM = 1. The ILM rewards firms with relatively low internal operational risk losses, and penalizes firms with relatively high internal losses, and so introduces an increased incentive for firms to manage operational risk.

The operational risk capital requirement is

$$CR_{or} = (BIC)(ILM).$$

Example 17.2 You are given the following information for DRH Bank; all numbers are in \$ millions.

- Business indicator is equal to gross income.
- Business income in the past three years has been 4,500, 3,800, and 4,000.
- The operational risk losses over the past 10 years have averaged 42 per year.

Calculate CR_{or} and RWA_{or}.

Solution 17.2 The BI in this case is equal to the average gross income over the prior three years, which is 4,100.

Applying the layer factors gives

$$BIC = 1{,}000 \times 0.12 + 3{,}100 \times 0.15 = 585,$$

$$ILM = \log\left(e + \left(\frac{15(42)}{585}\right)^{0.8} - 1\right) = 1.022,$$

$$CR_{or} = 1.0228 \times 585 = 597.9,$$

$$RWA_{or} = 12.5 \times CR_{or} = 7{,}473.38.$$

17.3.7 MCR: Market Risk Component

Market risk covers portfolio losses from changes in market factors such as interest rates, equity prices and volatilities, foreign exchange, and commodity prices. As with credit risk, banks may choose a standardized approach or an internal model approach. The standardized approach applies prescribed correlation factors and aggregation formulas to different classes of assets. However, in most cases, banks have developed their own models which meet the regulators' standards for the internal model approach.

The original Basel II approach to internal modelling of market risk based the required capital on the 10-day 99% VaR. However, in 2019 the risk measure changed to a 10-day 97.5% Expected Shortfall. The 97.5%, 10-day Expected Shortfall must be computed daily for each trading desk, and the computed daily Expected Shortfall is further adjusted to allow for jump liquidity risk – that is, the risk of sudden changes in liquidity – with the adjustment dependent on the liquidity horizons allocated to each class of assets in the Basel standards. Although the risk measure used for regulatory compliance is the Expected Shortfall, Basel III still uses VaR for backtesting models.

17.3.8 Additional Pillar 1 Requirements

Capital Conservation Buffer (CCB)

The **capital conservation buffer** (CCB) is an additional 2.5% of RWA that must be held in common equity Tier 1 capital, meaning that, effectively, the minimum Equity Tier 1 capital ratio is 7%, rather than the 4.5% given in Section 17.3.4. The CCB is designed to allow firms to build up capital in non-stressed periods, to be available as a buffer if the bank is in difficulty. A firm that meets the 4.5% criterion, but does not have the additional CCB, may continue to operate, but will be constrained in its ability to pay dividends.

Countercyclical Capital Buffer

The goal of the **countercyclical capital buffer** (CCyB) is to protect banking systems, rather than individual banks. The CCyB is an additional capital requirement, expressed in terms of the bank's RWA, which must be met by Common Equity Tier 1 capital. The idea is that when conditions are favourable, the CCyB rate may be set to a value greater than 0%, so that firms can build up some resilience in preparation for systemic downturns. When conditions change to a more adverse state over the economy as a whole, the supervisor will cancel the CCyB requirement, allowing firms to utilize the extra capital built up in the good times. In 2018, the rate was set at 1% in the UK, and at 2% in both Sweden and Norway, with most other countries remaining at 0%. By mid-2020, the rates had been reduced to 0% almost everywhere, in recognition of the economic uncertainty associated with the COVID-19 pandemic.

Leverage Ratio (LR)

The **leverage ratio** (LR), like the CCyB, reflects the Basel Committee's recognition of some of the causes and exacerbating factors of the 2007–8 financial crisis. Excessive leverage was widely recognized as a major contributing factor to the failure or near failure of several systemically important banks. The leverage ratio is defined (loosely) as

$$LR = \frac{\text{Tier 1 Capital}}{\text{Average Total Consolidated Assets}}.$$

For most firms, the leverage ratio must exceed 3% at all times. For banks identified as **globally systemically important banks** (GSIBs) the requirements are more stringent.

Output Floor

Generally, the use of internal models will result in lower RWA and lower CR than the standardized approaches. However, the bank may not use total RWA of less than 72.5% of the total RWA calculated under the standardized approaches. This is referred to as the **output floor**.

17.3.9 Liquidity Risk

Liquidity Coverage Ratio

The **liquidity coverage ratio** (LCR) is a measure of the bank's ability to maintain sufficient short-term liquidity in the event of a stressed market. The numerator is the **high quality liquid assets** (HQLA) calculation, described loosely in Chapter 13 and reviewed with a little more detail below. The denominator is the total projected cash outflow for the next 30 days, assuming a stress market scenario similar to that experienced at the start of the 2007–8 financial crisis. It assumes, for example, loss of unsecured wholesale funding, a volatility spike, a downgrade in credit rating (leading to increased cost of borrowing and margin calls), runs on the bank, and potential costs of mitigating reputational risk. The rationale for the 30-day period is to allow for the period from the beginning of a liquidity crisis to the point where central banks intervene:

$$LCR = \frac{HQLA}{30\text{-day stressed cash outflows}}.$$

A summary of the HQLA categories is given in Table 17.2. The 'haircut' is the proportionate reduction applied to the value of assets in that category, so the total HQLA is calculated as:

HQLA = 100% of the Level 1 assets
+ 85% of the Level 2A assets
+ 75% of the qualifying residential mortgage backed securities (RMBS)
+ 50% of the Level 2B corporate debt and common shares.

Further constraints are (i) Level 2 assets are restricted to 40% of the total HQLA and (ii) Level 2B assets are restricted to 15% of the total.

Larger banks must maintain an LCR of at least 100%.

Net Stable Funding Ratio (NSFR)

The LCR measures a firm's ability to survive short-term market liquidity risk; the **net stable funding ratio** (NSFR) measures the firm's ability to manage ongoing funding liquidity. The idea is that there should be sufficient stability in the liabilities and capital to outweigh the illiquidity in the firm's assets.

The NSFR is defined as:

$$NSFR = \frac{\text{Available amount of stable funding}}{\text{Required amount of stable funding}}.$$

Table 17.2. *HQLA categories and haircuts; PSE = public sector entity; MDB = multilateral development bank; RMBS = residential mortgage backed securities; FI = financial institution or affiliate (Basel Committee on Banking Supervision, 2013)*

Item	Haircut
Level 1 Assets	0%
Coins and bank notes Marketable securities from high rated sovereigns, PSEs, and MDBs Qualifying central bank reserves	
Level 2A Assets	15%
20% credit risk weighted securities from sovereign, central bank, PSEs, and MDBs, Corporate debt rated AA− or higher (not FI)	
Level 2B Assets	
Qualifying RMBS	25%
Qualifying corporate debt rated BBB− to A+ (not FI)	50%
Qualifying equity shares (not FI)	50%

The **available amount of stable funding** (ASF) is a measure of the stability of the liabilities and capital. Broadly, longer dated debt is more stable than shorter dated debt. Liabilities and capital that contribute without haircut to the ASF include regulatory capital (excluding Tier 2 instruments with less than a year to maturity) and debt and loans with more than one year to maturity. Liabilities with a small haircut (5%–10%) include on-demand deposits of retail and small business customers. Liabilities with a 50% haircut include all debt of less than six months and debt of six months to a year, where the borrower is not a financial institution. Other liabilities and equity are not included in the ASF.

The **required amount of stable funding** (RSF) is a measure of the asset illiquidity – in a sense, it is the complement of the HQLA. Cash on hand and short-term central bank loans are considered fully liquid, and do not contribute to the RSF. Other Level 1 assets from the HQLA calculation are included in the RSF at 5% of their value, indicating a small funding liquidity risk. Short-term unencumbered loans contribute at 10%–15% of value. Unencumbered level 2B assets contribute at 50% of their value, while encumbered loans and mortgages contribute between 65% and 100% of value, depending on the term and the counterparty. The RSF also includes off-balance sheet items.

17.3.10 Approval for Internal Models

A bank may use a mixture of standardized and internal models, but once it has an approved internal model, it may not return to the standardized method, and it may not cherry pick the method that gives the lower MCR.

Approval criteria for internal models are similar for each of the three components. In each case, the bank must demonstrate to the satisfaction of the regulators that it complies with a list of quantitative and qualitative criteria. The criteria are similar to those discussed in model risk and governance, in Chapter 14. Specifically, the bank must demonstrate that it has a conceptually sound risk management system, including model risk and governance processes. Some of the major requirements are:

- The bank must have an independent risk control unit which regularly reports to the Board of Directors and Senior Management.
- The Board of Directors and Senior Management must be actively involved in the risk control process.
- The bank must have sufficient staff with appropriate expertise in the use of the models, as well as in risk control and model governance.
- The bank must apply regular (at least monthly) stress tests to identify key risks, and to assess whether the bank has sufficient equity capital to absorb potential large losses from plausible adverse scenarios.
- The bank must be able to demonstrate that its models meet requirements for the accuracy of their predicted outcomes, based on quantitative measures of historic performance.
- All relevant and material risk factors (e.g., yield curve movements, risk factors for each foreign currency included in the model, risk factors for equities by region and by sector) must be incorporated in the model.
- The valuation model should be integrated into day-to-day risk management.
- There should be an annual audit of risk management processes and practices, both at the trading level and within the risk control unit.

17.3.11 Pillar 2: Supervisory Review

Pillar 2 of the Basel Accords sets out standards and principles for the supervisory process, including internal and external monitoring.

The first principle describes the necessary requirements for internal risk management, referred to as the **internal capital adequacy assessment process** (ICAAP). It specifies, for example, that the ICAAP should be formally documented; it should be integrated into the firm's operational culture and strategic planning, it should be risk-based and fit for purpose; and it should incorporate all relevant risk factors, both internal and external; it should be forward-looking and subject to regular and rigorous review.

The second principle describes the supervisory review process. That is, how supervisors should review the ICAAP, particularly with respect to risk governance, and monitor compliance with Pillar 1 standards.

The third principle covers the capital above regulatory minimum ratios. The Pillar 1 MCR is intended to be a minimum requirement, not a target. Banking supervisors in each jurisdiction may set targets for regulatory capital, and may set thresholds above the Pillar 1 minimum which could be used to trigger intervention or closer scrutiny of the institution.

The fourth principle describes potential actions a supervisor could take to intervene in an institution's operations if there is a perceived solvency risk. The details of the supervisor's authority to intervene would be established by individual jurisdictions, and will differ from nation to nation. At the milder end of the spectrum, the supervisor might increase its monitoring of the bank, for example, requiring more detailed information or more frequent reporting. If the capital position is looking weak, the supervisor may require the bank to submit a plan to improve the position in a given time frame. If the position is more severe, intervention could take the form of restricting the bank's activities, or requiring replacement of directors or senior officers.

Implementation of these principles covers both quantitative and qualitative requirements. The requirements are quantitative in that Pillar 2 allows countries to set additional capital requirements, above those set out in Pillar 1, which then define the threshold for an institution to operate without constraint or risk of supervisor intervention. The qualitative requirements include setting standards for the ICAAP, potentially requiring institutions to increase their risk management and governance processes.

The Pillar 2 standards do set some constraints on supervisors. It is specified that regulations and supervisory requirements should be proportionate – that is, the Pillar 2 compliance should not be hugely onerous relative to the amount of risk that the institution is managing. Supervision should be flexible and forward looking, allowing well-run firms to innovate and flourish. And, ideally, supervision should be collaborative, rather than oppositional. The Pillar 2 process can be used to support firms in their development of best quality ICAAP.

17.3.12 Pillar 3: Market Discipline

Market discipline is assumed in the Basel framework to be facilitated through appropriate disclosure of firms' processes and experience. The guiding principles behind the Basel II and III disclosure requirements are as follows:

(a) Disclosures should be clear.

- Individual investors, as well as analysts, rating agencies, and other stakeholders, should be able to access and understand the information.
- Key information should be highlighted.
- Technical terms should be defined and language should be as simple as possible.

(b) Disclosures should be comprehensive.

- All major activities and risks should be included.
- Significant changes in risk exposure should be disclosed, along with a description of management responses.
- Relevant data and information supporting the explanations of risks and strategies should be included.
- The firm's risk processes and governance structure should be explained.

(c) Disclosures should be meaningful to users.

- They should include current and emerging risks and information.
- They should link to line items on statutory returns for cross validation.
- They should omit content that is not valuable or no longer relevant.

(d) Disclosures should be consistent over time, allowing readers to identify trends, and/or unexpected changes in exposure or outcomes.
(e) Disclosures should be comparable across banks. Key ratios and metrics should be consistent across institutions and jurisdictions, allowing readers to make meaningful comparisons.

17.4 Solvency II

Solvency II is a European Union (EU) directive regulating the solvency capital of all insurers and reinsurers operating in any of the member countries of the EU. The influence of Solvency II extends beyond Europe though, as several developing nations use the framework as the basis for their own insurance regulation and supervision. The International Association of Insurance Supervisors (IAIS), which is a global committee of insurance regulators, has begun work on implementing many of the key parts of Solvency II worldwide.

The structure of Solvency II is drawn from the work of the Basel Committee, but with some adaptation, reflecting the significant differences in the nature of insurance risk compared with banking risk. The three pillar structure is used, with slight differences, as shown in Figure 17.2.

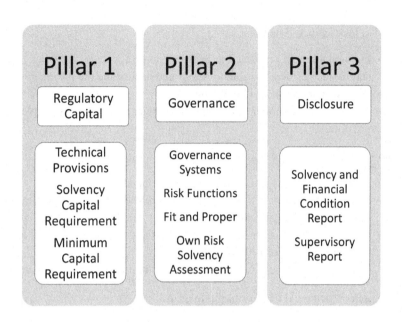

Figure 17.2 The three pillars of Solvency II

17.4.1 Pillar 1: Regulatory Capital

For insurance companies, the valuation of contingent liabilities is a more complex and critical element of the capital requirement process, as the liabilities are longer term and involve more uncertainty. Pillar 1 of Solvency II lays out the requirements for the liability valuation as well as specifying the calculation of the **solvency capital requirement** (SCR).

The Pillar 1 balance sheet is illustrated in Figure 17.3. The assets are counted at market values. Assets are designated as Tier 1, Tier 2, or Tier 3 similarly to the Basel standards.

The technical provisions are broken down into two parts for most insurance liabilities. The **best estimate liability** (BEL) is the valuation of future outgo minus income, discounted at the risk-free rate of interest. Uncertain cash flows are taken at 'best estimates', which is often interpreted as a mean value, but in practice may be closer to a median value. It specifically excludes any margins in the valuation assumptions to allow for uncertainty. Where cash flows depend on the actions of the insurer (for example in participating life insurance, where policies carry potential for discretionary bonuses or dividends) the valuation

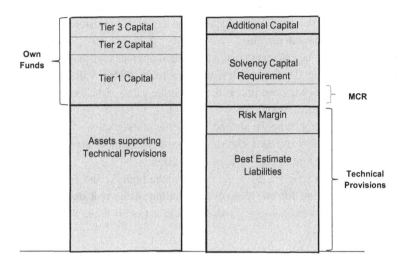

Figure 17.3 The Solvency II balance sheet

must allow for realistic management actions; where policies have options for the policyholders, realistic assessment of the policyholders' actions must be incorporated. Embedded options and guarantees are to be taken at market values. A **spread allowance** reduces the liability value if the liability cash flows are hedged with matching asset cash flows, and a **volatility adjustment** may be applied to reduce the risk of forced sales when bond spreads increase. The traditional actuarial approach to the BEL would involve a deterministic valuation based on best estimates of future cash flows, but for more complex products the valuation is more likely to involve Monte Carlo simulation of the cash flows.

The second part of the technical provision calculation is the **risk margin**. This is designed to support the additional costs to a purchaser of the cost of capital, in the event of a transfer of liabilities and supporting assets. The cost of capital is loosely interpreted as the value of the interest that an institution would have to pay investors or lenders, in return for the capital required to support the insurance portfolio. The cost of capital rate is set at 6% per year, so the risk margin is determined as the present value, at risk-free rates, of 6% of the estimated future year-end SCRs for the portfolio. So, if the projected SCR at time t is SCR_t, and the risk-free continuously compounded spot rate of interest for duration t is r_t, then the risk margin is calculated as

$$RM = \sum_{t=1}^{T} (0.06)\text{SCR}_t\, e^{-tr_t}.$$

For liabilities that are fully hedgeable, the technical provision is the market value, without any risk margin.

The SCR may be calculated using a standard approach, or may be based on internal modelling. The objective is to estimate the 99.5% VaR of the 1-year change in surplus, where surplus is defined as the value of the assets minus the value of the insurance liabilities.

To illustrate this, suppose at time $t = 0$ the market value of (admissible) assets is $A_0 = 1,200$ and the technical provision (liability value) is $L_0 = 1,000$. Then the initial surplus is $S_0 = A_0 - L_0 = 200$.

The surplus at time 1 is $S_1 = A_1 - L_1$, where both A_1 and L_1 are random variables. Allowing for one year of discounting at the risk-free rate, r, the change in surplus is $S_0 - S_1 e^{-r}$, so the SCR at time 0 is the 99.5% VaR of $S_0 - S_1 e^{-r}$, that is,

$$\text{SCR}_0 = Q_{99.5\%}\left(S_0 - S_1 e^{-r}\right) = S_0 - Q_{0.5\%}\left(S_1 e^{-r}\right),$$

where, as usual, $Q_\alpha(X)$ represents the α-quantile of a random variable X. Continuing the example above, suppose that $r = 0$, and that the 0.5% quantile of S_1 is 30, which means that there is an estimated 0.5% chance that the surplus will fall by more than 170 over the year, from 200 to less than 30. Then 170 represents the SCR at time 0.

Insurers that have internal models approved by their supervisory body will use Monte Carlo simulation to estimate the 99.5% VaR of the change in surplus. Approval of internal models is quite onerous; criteria are similar to those applied in the Basel standards, including the **use test**, which requires the models to be widely used for decision-making and risk analysis, rather than narrowly used for the capital calculations. Additionally, models must meet rigorous requirements for validation, calibration, and accuracy of out-of-sample predictive performance. The model governance must satisfy requirements around documentation and audit processes.

A key problem for the internal models is that the 99.5% VaR standard is far out in the tail; there is little relevant data on the 1-in-200 year events that are being invoked. The marginal tails of individual loss factors, and the tail dependencies between risk factors are likely to be difficult to calibrate or validate.

Insurers who do not use their own internal models must use a standard approach. This is based on stress testing individual risk factors based on the plan shown in Figure 17.4. For each of the major headings, i.e. market, life insurance, non-life (P&C) insurance, etc., there is an individual SCR calculation based on the each of the subheadings. These are combined to create

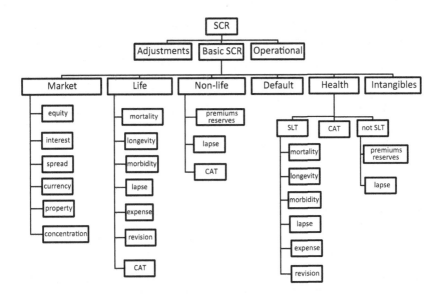

Figure 17.4 The Solvency II SCR standard formula diagram

the SCR for the category, using specified correlation matrices. The SCRs under the market and life insurance headers are largely based on stress testing the values or assumptions. Under the non-life category, the SCRs are determined by applying specified factors to the technical provisions and the earned premiums. The health insurance category is split into two parts; SLT (**similar to life techniques**) covers long-term health policies, such as long-term care or critical illness insurance, which are closer in terms of risk characteristics to life insurance, and Not-SLT which are closer to non-life insurance. The default category covers counterparty risk, and the intangible header covers risk to intangible asset values. The individual SCR values are calculated either by simple formulas or by stressing the valuation assumptions, depending on the category. The overall approach is deterministic; the application of the correlations allows for some diversification, but in a very simplistic way.

The SCR may be met by a combination of Tier 1, 2, and 3 capital, but with the constraints that at least 50% of the SCR is covered by Tier 1, and no more than 15% by Tier 3.

The MCR is smaller than the SCR, targeting an 85% VaR of the 1-year change in surplus. It is based on a relatively straightforward factor approach, with a minimum of 25% of the SCR, and a maximum of 45% of the SCR. The SCR is used to set the first level of supervisory intervention; a company whose capital dips below the SCR would experience supervisory intervention at the lighter end of the scale, such as a requirement to establish a realistic plan to return to a stronger solvency position within a set time frame. The MCR is the lower threshold, below which the insurer would lose their authorization. At this level, the supervisor would take over the operation of the firm. The MCR must be met by Tier 1 and 2 capital only, with at least 80% of the MCR being covered by Tier 1 capital.

17.4.2 Pillar 2: Governance

Pillar 2 of Solvency II sets minimum standards for the insurer's internal governance. The standards cover four main areas; these are described, briefly, in this section.

General Governance Requirements

The insurer must establish governance structures to ensure continuous, sound, and prudent management of the firm. To achieve this, the insurer must create, establish, or confirm the following:

- The Board is ultimately responsible for compliance with Solvency II and for setting the risk culture of the firm.
- Written and implemented risk governance policies.
- Written policies on the roles and responsibilities of the specific functions detailed below.
- Clearly defined and coordinated duties and responsibilities, by individual and by function.
- Clear and effective communication and cooperation across functions.
- Sufficient expertise, knowledge, and experience, both collectively and individually, at the Board and Senior Management levels.
- Remuneration processes that do not incentivize excessive risk-taking, beyond the specified risk tolerance.
- Regular internal review of all processes and systems.

Specific Functions

- The **risk management function** is responsible for implementing strategies and processes for identifying, measuring, and managing risks and risk dependencies, and for monitoring and reporting on the risks and risk management strategies. Responsibilities include: (i) underwriting and reserving standards; (ii) asset-liability management; (iii) reinsurance and risk mitigation strategies; and (iv) liquidity, investment, concentration, and operational risk management.

- The **internal control function** sets internal controls and reporting arrangements, which it uses to monitor compliance with the regulations and provisions of Solvency II, across the organization, and to assess potential internal or external events or changes that might endanger compliance.
- The **actuarial function** is responsible for the calculations of the technical provisions, the SCR and MCR, and the **own risk solvency assessment** (ORSA). It must ensure that all calculations use sound methods and models and that data quality is sufficient. It must monitor the actual emerging experience against the assumptions used in pricing and valuation, for example, with respect to claim frequency and severity, expenses, and investment return. Using this analysis, the actuarial function will provide opinions on the overall underwriting policy and on the adequacy of reinsurance provisions.
- The **internal audit function** evaluates the compliance of the various operational units with the risk management policies and processes established by the firm.
- **Outsourcing** – the firm may outsource some of its functions or activities. Outsourcing may generate additional operational risk, or may impair the ability of the internal functions to properly fulfil their responsibilities. To minimize these risks, the firm's outsourcing policy should be clearly documented and compliance monitored. Responsibility for complying fully with the Solvency II requirements remains with the firm, even where key functions are outsourced.

Own Risk and Solvency Assessment (ORSA)

The insurer is required to perform their ORSA based on the specific risk profile and risk tolerance of the individual company. The company is expected to incorporate all material risks in this analysis, including those that are not specifically covered in the SCR calculation. It would allow for the impact of new business, which is also not incorporated in the SCR calculation. This would determine the company's view of their own economic capital requirements. It would also analyse the insurer's ability to comply with the Solvency II SCR on an ongoing basis, over the next three to five years.

The ORSA must be an integral part of the firm's business decisions, for example, in strategic planning, product development, risk management strategy, and capital management.

'Fit and Proper'

The insurer must ensure that all those with responsibility for key functions in the company meet 'fit and proper' requirements. This means that all those in senior positions should have appropriate training and expertise, and can be expected to perform their duties with integrity and probity.

Similarly, the Board of Directors must include expertise in specific areas including financial markets, business strategy, actuarial analysis, insurance regulation, and finance. They must also qualify under the 'fit and proper' requirements, meaning that, in addition to having the required expertise, they must demonstrate integrity and probity in carrying out their responsibilities.

17.4.3 Pillar 3: Disclosure

The public disclosure requirements under Solvency II are in the **solvency and financial condition report**. This must be produced annually, and includes the following information:

- A **summary of the report** in clear language, accessible to policyholders.
- A description of the **business and performance** of the insurer. This would include quantitative and qualitative information on the underwriting experience and the investment experience. Any significant events or changes in the business would be included.
- A description of the **system of governance**, including:
  - The management structure and responsibilities.
  - Material changes in responsibilities or personnel or the management structure.
  - The remuneration policies and practices.
  - The policy and process for determining whether key individuals are 'fit-and-proper'.
  - The risk management function.
  - The internal control function.
  - The actuarial function.
  - The internal audit function.
  - The outsourcing policy.
  - The process for conducting the ORSA, and for integrating the ORSA results into the decision-making processes.

- Quantitative and qualitative information regarding the **risk profile** of the organization, with specific and separate coverage of underwriting risk, market risk, credit risk, liquidity risk, and operational risk.
- The results of the **solvency valuation** of the technical provisions. The insurer must describe the level of uncertainty in the calculations, and

must reconcile the solvency valuation assessment of the technical provision with the valuation included in the insurer's financial statements.

- A discussion of the insurer's **capital management** policies and processes. This section includes information on the calculation of SCR and MCR, and the eligible amounts of Tier 1, Tier 2, and Tier 3 capital. Where the firm has used internal models, the Solvency and Financial Condition Report would include a description of the models and of their broader use within the company.

There are additional supervisory reporting requirements that are not required to be publicly available. This includes in-depth results of the ORSA, as well as regular detailed quantitative reports covering assets, liabilities, risk profile, and risk management.

17.5 Notes and Further Reading

In the first part of the chapter we have described the major components of the Basel III requirements. We have omitted some additional capital charges. For example, under the market risk component, banks are required to calculate stressed Expected Shortfall values, based on historical data taken from extreme (stressed) market conditions. There is a further capital charge related to non-modellable risk factors, for which there is insufficient data to develop risk models. Also, an additional component of the market risk capital requirement is a **default risk charge** (DRC), which is evaluated using a 99.9% VaR measure of the potential loss in market value from defaults, based on a one-year horizon. The details of these calculations can be found in the Basel Committee reports. See Hull (2018) for an explanation of the stressed Expected Shortfall calculation.

The work of the Basel Committee on Banking Supervision is continuously evolving. For up to date information and in-detail specifications, visit their website at www.bis.org/bcbs/. The information in this chapter is largely taken from the following references: Basel Committee on Banking Supervision (2010, 2011, 2013, 2014, 2017). Details are given in the Bibliography.

For a comprehensive guide to Solvency II, see PwC (2020). In insurance, the implementation of Solvency II and similar legislation has driven a move towards stochastic modelling for determination of regulatory and economic capital. Most insurers prefer to use internal modelling, which relies largely on Monte Carlo simulation, rather than using the alternative – the deterministic, standardized approach. The use of internal modelling is consistent with a **principles-based** approach to regulation, while the standardized approach is closer to a **rules-based** approach. The difference is that a rules-based approach lays down the requirements in minute detail. The responsibility for determining solvency falls on the regulators who specify the rules; the sole responsibility of the insurer is to comply with the rules, even if those rules are inadequate. Under principles-based regulation, insurers are required to take appropriate actions to ensure that assets are sufficient to meet liabilities, subject to some broad principles and guidelines, and subject to stringent requirements for reporting and disclosure. Solvency II is predominantly principles-based, through the internal model approach and the ORSA requirement, but with a rules-based backstop, through the MCR.

In countries that have not adopted Solvency II style regulation, the trend has followed Solvency II in moving away from rules-based regulation towards principles-based, and in moving away from deterministic approaches towards stochastic approaches, which are more scientifically founded in statistics and data science. The strongest bastion of the rules-based approach is the US, which also still uses a book value valuation methodology for much of its life insurance business, while the rest of the world moves towards market-consistent valuations (based on IFRS-17, the fair value insurance accounting standard issued by the International Accounting Standards Board).

The problem with rules-based regulation is that it can create an adversarial situation between supervisors and insurers; insurers will try to find loopholes, potentially undermining the solvency protection targetted by the regulations. For example, insurers may design policies or reinsurance arrangements with the sole objective of avoiding capital requirements, rather than meeting a genuine need, or genuinely transferring risk. With principles-based regulation, there is no such thing as a loophole, so the 'cat and mouse' game between supervisors and insurers is more or less averted. On the other hand, the principles-based approach will fail if the insurer does not comply with the responsibility devolved to it, either through lack of expertise, or through lack of ethics.

Increasing requirements to undertake and report on ORSA are moving even the US towards a principles-based valuation system. More information on the supervision of insurance in the US can be found from the National Association of Insurance Commissioners (NAIC), who coordinate the supervisory bodies of the individual states.

17.6 Exercises

Exercise 17.1 Summarize the similarities and differences between the requirements and principles for Basel III and Solvency II. Consider each pillar separately (that is, compare Pillar 1 of Basel III with Pillar 1 of Solvency II, and so on). Explain how the similarities and differences relate to the similarities and differences between banking and insurance.

Exercise 17.2 Explain the role of disclosure in Basel III. Who are the primary stakeholders who should be able to access the information disclosed?

Exercise 17.3 For the credit risk capital requirement under the Basel rules, banks are treated as less risky than corporate bonds in the same rating category. For liquidity risk, banks and other financial institutions are treated as higher risk than non-financial institutions. Explain why banks are less risky with respect to credit, but more risky with respect to liquidity.

Exercise 17.4 A bank has the following balance sheet ($ millions):

Assets		Liabilities	
Cash	50	Retail Deposits	4,000
Sovereign Debt (A− Rated)	1,000	Equity	500
Bank Stocks	1,650	Reserves	75
Non-bank Corporate Debt (A+ Rated)	1,500	Convertible Long-Term Debt	150
Non-bank Corporate Stocks	700	Other Debt (Unsecured)	855
Fixed Assets	100		
	5,000		5,000

(a) Identify the Tier 1 and Tier 2 capital.
(b) Calculate the credit risk RWA using the standardized approach.
(c) The Business Income of the firm over the past three years has been 1,500, 3,000, and 1,260 in $millions, counting from earliest to most recent.

The annual operational losses over the past ten years average 16 per year. Calculate the CR for operational risk.

(d) Assume that the market risk CR is calculated based on the 10-day 97.5% Expected Shortfall measure on the bank's investment portfolio. The current market value is $4,850 million. The value of the portfolio is assumed to follow a geometric Brownian motion, with zero drift, and with annual volatility of 14%. Calculate the market risk CR.

(e) State whether the bank meets the regulatory capital requirements specified in equations (17.2)–(17.3).

(f) State whether the bank meets the capital conservation buffer requirement.

(g) Identify how the bank could improve its (Tier 1 + Tier 2)/RWA ratio.

Exercise 17.5 Explain the principle of the risk margin under Solvency II.

Exercise 17.6 Solvency II uses a 99.5% VaR risk measure for a 1-year loss random variable. Comment on the challenges involved in calculating this risk measure based on historical data.

Exercise 17.7 The risk measure in Solvency II assumes a transfer of the insurer's assets and liabilities at the end of one year. This has been criticized for being inconsistent with going concern accounting and strategic management. Explain how Solvency II incorporates long-term horizons and going concern assumptions.

Exercise 17.8 The disclosure requirements of Basel III generally require reports and statements to be widely available. Under Solvency II, some of the disclosure requirements (e.g., ORSA reports) only require disclosure to the regulator, not to the general public. Explain the advantages and disadvantages of full public disclosure.

Exercise 17.9 (a) The phrase 'Freedom with Publicity' was coined to summarize the UK approach to insurance regulation; insurers could select their own valuation methods and assumptions, provided that they were fully disclosed.

   (i) Explain how 'freedom with publicity' relates to the Solvency II requirements. Is it consistent with Solvency II?
   (ii) Explain how 'freedom with publicity' relates to rules-based or principles-based regulation.

(b) The phrase was later tweaked, with the advent of more stochastic valuation methods, to 'Freedom with Calibration'. Explain how this phrase is reflected in the Solvency II framework.

18

Risk-Adjusted Measures of Profit and Capital Allocation

18.1 Summary

Risk analysis and risk management is often perceived as separate from (and perhaps a drag on) the profit-generating units of a business. But exploiting the extra returns available from taking risks is a major element of business strategy, and risk management can be a proactive contributor to profit generation, not just a backstop protection against catastrophic loss.

In this chapter, we consider how traditional measures of profit, using return ratios, can be improved by considering the riskiness of the investment. The objective is to analyse which parts of the business are performing best relative to the risks involved, rather than simply comparing returns with no consideration of risk. In turn, this allows the business to decide where it should take on more risk, as the additional risk is justified by additional return, and where it should take on less.

A key part of the risk budgeting exercise is the allocation of the organization's economic capital to the individual business units. In the second part of this chapter we describe different approaches to capital allocation and assess their relative advantages and disadvantages.

18.2 Risk-Adjusted Performance Measures

Traditional accounting return ratios use the book value (BV) of the assets and the liabilities. The book value of an asset or liability is often very different from the market value (MV), as changes in market values may not be reflected in the accounts until assets are sold or liabilities are settled. The precise difference between book values and market values depends on the accounting jurisdiction

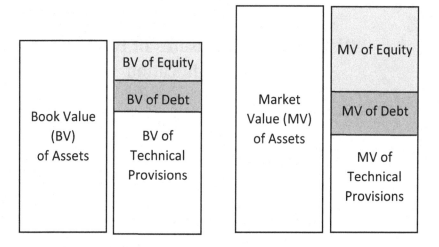

Figure 18.1 Illustration of book value and market value balance sheets

of the firm. In Figure 18.1, we illustrate a simplified balance sheet of a firm for which book values are not the same as market values. The technical provisions refers to the liabilities relating to the firm's ongoing obligations; for a bank, this would include customer deposits and other contingent liabilities. For an insurer, the technical provision would be the amount allocated to meet future claim payments on insurance policies currently in force.

Two of the more common accounting return ratios are:

$$\textbf{Return on capital} \ = \ \frac{\text{Net Income}}{\text{BV of Equity} + \text{BV of Debt}},$$

$$\textbf{Return on equity} \ = \ \frac{\text{Net Income}}{\text{BV of Equity}}.$$

Capital, here, is loosely used to mean the excess of assets over technical provisions, that is, Capital = Debt + Equity, where the debt is assumed to be long-term; short-term obligations are assumed to be included in the technical provisions. Typically, the denominator uses an average of the beginning and end year values of equity and debt.

The first problem with accounting measures is that they are based on book values, which are inconsistent between firms and within firms, due to their reliance on historical costs. Two firms holding identical assets may record different values for those assets, making it difficult to compare or interpret return ratios. There is a global trend towards fair value accounting, which, broadly, uses the market value balance sheet rather than the book value balance sheet. However, change is slow, and it is likely that book values and market values will be very different under most accounting systems for the foreseeable future.

The second problem with the traditional return ratios is that they do not take risk into consideration, either in the numerator or in the denominator. The capital provides a cushion against volatility of income, arising from the riskiness of the venture. It is not possible to interpret the traditional accounting measures in a way that informs us whether the risk-reward trade-off of the business is appropriate.

We address these two problems with **risk-adjusted measures of performance**. For risk-adjusted ratios, we always work with market values rather than book values. This ensures consistent valuation for assets and liabilities purchased or contracted at different times, and also ensures consistency between firms.

For the second problem, we can allow for risk by adjusting both the numerator and the denominator to recognize the role of risk and variability. The risk-adjusted net income is defined differently by various sources, but the most common approach uses the expected rather than the actual net income in the numerator. This smooths out the volatility arising from the riskiness of the venture, on the principle that the expected return on capital is a better measure of the risk-return trade-off than the actual return in any given year. For the denominator, we can select from two measures of capital in the market value balance sheet. The **available economic capital** (AEC) is defined as the excess of the market value of assets over the market value technical provision; this is equal to the market value of equity plus debt. The **required economic capital**, or simply **economic capital** (EC), is the firm's own assessment of how much capital (by market value) is required to conduct its business within its established risk appetite and tolerance. This might be based on a risk measure (e.g., VaR or Expected Shortfall) of the firm's net loss distribution.

The AEC must be greater than or equal to the required economic capital. If AEC < EC, then the firm must raise more capital, or curtail its risk-taking; if AEC > EC, then the firm has excess unused capital.

The most commonly cited measure of risk-adjusted performance is the **risk-adjusted return on capital** (RAROC), but the term is not well defined; it refers to a ratio of the form net income/economic capital, but whether the numerator should be the actual net income or the expected net income, and whether the denominator should be the available economic capital or the required economic capital, is not standardized. In this text, we will assume, unless otherwise noted, that the RAROC is

$$\text{RAROC} = \frac{\text{Expected Net Income}}{\text{Required Economic Capital}}.$$

However, we also note that this RAROC definition is also referred to as the **risk-adjusted return on risk-adjusted capital** (RARORAC), and that RAROC is sometimes used to mean expected net income/AEC.

Furthermore, there may be a distinction between the prospective RAROC

$$\text{Prospective RAROC} = \frac{\text{Expected Net Income}}{\text{EC}},$$

and the backwards looking

$$\text{Retrospective RAROC} = \frac{\text{Actual Net Income}}{\text{Average EC}},$$

which is based on the past year's experience.[1]

Using the RAROC gives an indication of the income expected to be generated by the risk capital available. We might compare this with the firm's weighted average cost of capital, to assess whether the risk capital is generating positive economic value.

Example 18.1 An insurer has assets with market value $10 billion. The technical provision has market value of $6.5 billion. One year ago, the MV of assets was $9.5 billion, and the technical provision was $5.8 billion. The required economic capital, which is determined using the aggregate Expected Shortfall of the liabilities, was $3.0 billion at the start of the year and $3.3 billion at the end of the year.

The net income in the past year was $0.8 billion, though that was $0.3 billion more than expected due to unusually low claims experience.

The net income in the coming year is expected to be $0.55 billion.

The book value of the assets was $8.5 billion at the start and $9.0 billion at the end of the year. The book value of the technical provision was $6.0 billion throughout.

Calculate the following ratios:

(a) The return on capital.
(b) The prospective RAROC, based on the AEC.
(c) The prospective RAROC, based on the EC.

---

[1] A further complication is that some people use the term RORAC (return on risk-adjusted capital) in place of RAROC, but others use RORAC to mean what we have called the retrospective RAROC.

(d) The retrospective RAROC, based on expected net income and the EC.

(e) The retrospective RAROC, based on actual net income and the EC.

Solution 18.1

(a) The return on capital (retrospective) is $\dfrac{0.8}{0.5(2.5+3)} = 29.1\%$.

(b) The prospective RAROC, based on the AEC, is $\dfrac{0.55}{3.5} = 15.7\%$.

(c) The prospective RAROC, based on the EC, is $\dfrac{0.55}{3.3} = 16.7\%$.

(d) The retrospective RAROC, based on expected net income and the EC, is $\frac{0.50}{0.5(3.0+3.3)} = 15.9\%$.

(e) The retrospective RAROC, based on actual net income and the EC, is $\frac{0.80}{0.5(3.0+3.3)} = 25.4\%$. □

We make the following observations:

(1) The difference between the RAROC using available economic capital, and RAROC using required economic capital indicates the potential to achieve higher returns if the entire AEC is utilized. However, it will not always be feasible to just scale the business up.

(2) The return on capital is overstated because of the significant difference between book and market values. Net income is largely a market value measure,[2] so it is more consistent to use market values than book values in the return ratios.

(3) Using actual or expected income makes a lot of difference to the calculations. In this example, we infer that the additional income, over and above the expected income, was not a reflection of superior management, but rather, a reflection of luck. So, how much should the firm rely on the results with respect to strategic risk decision-making?

(4) On the other hand, perhaps the insurer is improving its processes, in which case the expected income of $0.50 billion for the past year may be a low-side estimate. It certainly introduces some subjectivity into the calculation, compared with the actual net income.

(5) The lack of consistency surrounding the precise meaning of the RAROC is clearly problematic; in practice, any of the values in (b), (c), (d), or (e) may be quoted as the firm's RAROC.

---

[2] There are components of net income, such as depreciation and sales on credit, that do not correspond to market values or cash flows, see Ross et al. (2018) for a detailed discussion.

Risk-adjusted measures of performance give a picture of how the firm is using its economic capital as a whole, but they are also used to break down the performance of individual business units within the firm. Prospectively, the firm's RAROC can be used in risk budgeting. The firm's individual business units must operate, in aggregate, within the risk constraints imposed by the available economic capital. The RAROC, calculated at the level of individual business units, can be used to determine how much capital each unit is allocated, which determines how much risk each unit may take on.

The second purpose of the risk-adjusted profit measures is performance measurement, which is retrospective. In this context, it would be usual to replace the expected net income in the RAROC calculation with the actual net income, but this can lead to problems where there is a lot of income volatility. Nevertheless, it is common for performance-based remuneration of the managers within each business unit to be at least partially determined by the retrospective RAROC of the unit.

In order for the RAROC calculations to be performed at the level of individual business units, it is necessary for the required economic capital of the firm to be allocated to the individual business units. In the remainder of this chapter, we will discuss various approaches to allocating economic capital within the firm. We assume that the required capital has been determined using a risk measure such as VaR or Expected Shortfall. The same risk measures could be calculated for the individual business units, on a stand-alone basis, but because of diversification, the sum of the stand-alone capital calculations will (usually) be greater than the required capital of the firm as a whole (through subadditivity). We also assume hereafter that the available economic capital and the required economic capital are equal.

18.3 Economic Capital Allocation: Objectives

Allocation of capital to individual business units is used ultimately, to maximize the firm's value, within the constraints of its risk tolerance. There are several different ways that capital allocation achieves this:

- **Analysing risk-adjusted profitability by business unit** may indicate where the firm should be expanding or contracting. It can also indicate more clearly the impact of risk, through the volatility of the retrospective risk-adjusted returns. It is, therefore, a valuable tool in strategic planning.
- **Pricing** of products in different units should reflect the cost of capital for those units. For example, in insurance, there is more volatility in medical

malpractice insurance than in homeowner's insurance. We expect that the risk capital required, per unit of premium, for the medical malpractice line of business will be significantly greater than for property insurance, and the extra cost of carrying the capital should be reflected in the premium rates.

- **Risk budgeting** is the process of deciding how much risk each sub-unit of the firm should take to best achieve the overall firm objectives, within the overall risk appetite. Capital allocation is one of the key ways that the risk budget is distributed.
- **Performance-related remuneration** is used to incentivize managers to exceed their targets. The targets should be related to risk, and setting RAROC targets is a popular way to encourage appropriate risk-taking.
- **Assessing risk-taking** – Using the actual income in the RAROC calculation will give results that are volatile, reflecting the riskiness of the venture. If returns are consistently and systematically higher than the RAROC targets, then it is possible that the unit managers are taking risks that exceed their risk budget.

The principles of enterprise risk management require that the firm is treated holistically. The determination of economic capital is optimally implemented as a **top-down** process, that is, based on an enterprise-wide risk analysis. However, for allocating risk, there is some advantage in working from the **bottom up** as well, analysing the risks of the individual units as if they were independent, and collecting the results together to make up the whole. Combining top-down and bottom-up analysis allows us to identify and exploit diversification opportunities.

In principle the firm could partition its business for the purpose of allocating economic capital in many different ways; capital could be allocated across units by risk type, contract type, or by geographical exposure – and there are some advantages to this approach in assessing risk distributions. Capital could be allocated down to individual projects or contracts; this may be appropriate for major contracts. It is common in investment banking for economic capital to be allocated to each trading desk. Baer et al. (2011) suggest allocating capital to product lines or clients, in a way that minimizes internal arbitrage opportunities. In the following, we use 'business units' to mean the specific areas of the firm that are allocated risk capital.

18.3.1 Economic Capital Allocation Example

The objective of capital allocation is to allocate the total economic capital to the individual business units, in a way that is fair and consistent. Some criteria have been developed to capture the concepts of fairness and consistency more systematically, and we describe these later in this chapter. First, we present a simplified firm structure that will be used to demonstrate the various allocation methods.

Consider a firm with d business units. X_i is the random loss from the ith business unit, and $X = \sum_{i=1}^{d} X_i$ is the aggregate loss for the firm. The economic capital for the firm as a whole is EC, which is assumed to be determined using a risk measure, such that $EC = \rho(X)$.

If ρ is subadditive then the aggregate economic capital, calculated from the top down, will be less than the sum of the individual, stand-alone economic capital values, calculated from the bottom up. That is,

$$EC = \rho(X) = \rho(X_1 + X_2 + \cdots + X_d) \leq \rho(X_1) + \rho(X_2) + \cdots + \rho(X_d).$$

The individual business units are allocated risk and risk capital from the overall risk and economic capital budget. The problem is, how should the capital be allocated to the units? We illustrate with an example.

Example 18.2 Consider an insurer that writes three lines of business. Each line is considered a separate business unit. The annual losses from line i, for $i = 1, 2, 3$, are random variables, with

$$X_1 \sim N(\mu_1 = 100, \sigma_1^2 = 20^2) - 105,$$
$$X_2 \sim \text{logN}(\mu_2 = 4, \sigma_2 = 1) - 120,$$
$$X_3 \sim \text{Pareto}(\alpha = 4, \theta = 300) - 130,$$
$$L = X_1 + X_2 + X_3.$$

The losses are dependent, with Gumbel copula dependence:

$$C(u, v, w) = \exp\left\{-\left(\left(\log\frac{1}{u}\right)^{1.2} + \left(\log\frac{1}{v}\right)^{1.2} + \left(\log\frac{1}{w}\right)^{1.2}\right)^{\frac{1}{1.2}}\right\}.$$

The economic capital is determined as the 95% Expected Shortfall of the aggregate loss; using Monte Carlo simulation with 10^6 projections of the aggregate loss, L, we estimate total economic capital for the insurer as $\rho(X) = 622.0$. (The standard error is approximately 1.0.)

(a) Calculate the total **diversification benefit** – that is, the difference between the total stand-alone economic capital for the three lines, and the aggregate capital.

(b) A simple approach to allocating capital to the lines is to assign the aggregate economic capital in proportion to the stand-alone capital. Calculate the allocation of economic capital to each line using this approach.

(c) Assume that each line earns interest at 5% on their allocated economic capital and 'reserves'. The reserve is another term for the technical provision, and is 105 for Line 1, 120 for Line 2, and 130 for Line 3 (these are the amounts deducted in the X_j distributions). The aggregate **technical provision** (TP) is the sum of the technical provisions for the individual lines, i.e. TP = 355.

   (i) Calculate the RAROC for all lines combined.

  (ii) Calculate the RAROC for each unit based on their stand-alone capital.

 (iii) Calculate the RAROC for each unit based on their allocated capital, using the proportional allocation scheme.

Solution 18.2

(a)   The stand-alone capital for Line 1, using the Expected Shortfall formula for the normal distribution (see Chapter 3), is

$$\rho(X_1) = \mu_1 + \frac{\sigma_1}{0.05}\phi(z_{0.95}) - 105 = 36.3,$$

where z_q is the q-quantile of the standard normal distribution.

The stand-alone capital for Line 2, using the lognormal Expected Shortfall formula, is

$$\rho(X_2) = \frac{e^{\mu_2 + \sigma_2^2/2}}{0.05}\left(1 - \Phi(z_{0.95} - \sigma_2)\right) - 120 = 347.2.$$

For X_3, we first derive the Expected Shortfall formula for Pareto losses. Let $Q_{0.95}$ denote the 95% quantile of a Pareto-distributed loss random variable, with parameters α and θ. The density and cumulative distribution functions for the Pareto distribution are

$$f(x) = \frac{\alpha\,\theta^\alpha}{(x+\theta)^{\alpha+1}} \quad \text{and} \quad F(x) = 1 - \left(\frac{\theta}{x+\theta}\right)^\alpha,$$

$$\rho(X_3) = \mathrm{E}[X_3 \mid X_3 > Q_{0.95}] = \frac{1}{0.05}\int_{Q_{0.95}}^{\infty} x\,\frac{\alpha\theta^\alpha}{(x+\theta)^{\alpha+1}}\,dx - 130.$$

Let $y = x - Q_{0.95}$, then

$$\rho(X_3) = \frac{1}{0.05} \int_0^\infty (y + Q_{0.95}) \frac{\alpha \theta^\alpha}{(y + Q_{0.95} + \theta)^{\alpha+1}} \, dy - 130$$

$$= \frac{1}{0.05} \left(\frac{\theta}{\theta + Q_{0.95}} \right)^\alpha \int_0^\infty (y + Q_{0.95}) \frac{\alpha (\theta + Q_{0.95})^\alpha}{(y + Q_{0.95} + \theta)^{\alpha+1}} \, dy - 130.$$

Now, if we set $\theta^* = \theta + Q_{0.95}$, then the term

$$\frac{\alpha (\theta + Q_{0.95})^\alpha}{(y + Q_{0.95} + \theta)^{\alpha+1}} = \frac{\alpha (\theta^*)^\alpha}{(y + \theta^*)^{\alpha+1}}$$

is the probability density function of a Pareto distribution with parameters α and θ^*, so

$$\rho(X_3) = \frac{1}{0.05} \left(\frac{\theta}{\theta + Q_{0.95}} \right)^\alpha$$

$$\times \left\{ \int_0^\infty y \frac{\alpha (\theta^*)^\alpha}{(y + \theta^*)^{\alpha+1}} \, dy + Q_{0.95} \int_0^\infty \frac{\alpha (\theta^*)^\alpha}{(y + \theta^*)^{\alpha+1}} \, dy \right\} - 130.$$

The first term inside the curly braces is the mean of the Pareto distribution with parameters α and θ^*, which, provided $\alpha > 1$, is

$$\frac{\theta^*}{\alpha - 1} = \frac{\theta + Q_{0.95}}{\alpha - 1}.$$

The second term inside the curly braces is $Q_{0.95}$, as the Pareto probability density function must integrate to 1.0. Hence, the 95% Expected Shortfall formula for X_3 is

$$\rho(X_3) = \frac{\theta + Q_{0.95}}{\alpha - 1} + Q_{0.95} - 130 = \frac{\theta + \alpha Q_{0.95}}{\alpha - 1} - 130.$$

Finally, we have that

$$0.95 = 1 - \left(\frac{\theta}{Q_{0.95} + \theta} \right)^\alpha \implies Q_{0.95} = \theta \left((0.05)^{-\frac{1}{\alpha}} - 1 \right),$$

which gives us $\rho(X_3) = \dfrac{\theta + \alpha \theta \left((0.05)^{-\frac{1}{\alpha}} - 1 \right)}{\alpha - 1} - 130 = 415.9.$

As we expect, the sum of the three units' stand-alone economic capital, which is 799.4, is greater than the aggregate economic capital for the firm.

The total diversification benefit is $799.4 - 622.0 = 177.4$.

(b)   The capital allocation is as follows, where EC_i is the capital allocated to line i, and EC is the economic capital for the portfolio:

$$EC_1 = \frac{36.3}{799.4}(622.0) = 28.2,$$

$$EC_2 = \frac{347.2}{799.4}(622.0) = 270.2,$$

$$EC_3 = \frac{415.9}{799.4}(622.0) = 323.6.$$

(c) The expected net income for the combined portfolio is:

Expected net income, aggregate $= -E[X_1 + X_2 + X_3] + 0.05(EC + TP)$,

$E[X_1] = \mu_1 - 105 = -5.0$,

$E[X_2] = e^{4.5} - 120 = -30.0$,

$E[X_3] = \dfrac{300}{3} - 130 = -30.00$

$\implies$ Expected net income, aggregate $= 65.0 + 0.05(622.0 + 355.0) = 113.9$

$\implies$ RAROC, aggregate $= \dfrac{113.9}{622.0} = 18.3\%$.

The stand-alone RAROCs are:

RAROC, Stand-alone, Line 1 $= \dfrac{-E[X_1] + 0.05(36.3 + 105.0)}{36.3} = 33.2\%$,

RAROC, Stand-alone, Line 2 $= \dfrac{-E[X_2] + 0.05(347.2 + 120.0)}{347.2} = 15.4\%$,

RAROC, Stand-alone, Line 3 $= \dfrac{-E[X_3] + 0.05(415.9 + 130.0)}{415.9} = 13.8\%$.

The RAROCs with proportional allocation of economic capital are:

RAROC, Proportional, Line 1 $= \dfrac{-E[X_1] + 0.05(28.2 + 105.0)}{28.2} = 41.3\%$,

RAROC, Proportional, Line 2 $= \dfrac{-E[X_2] + 0.05(270.2 + 120.0)}{270.2} = 18.3\%$,

RAROC, Proportional, Line 3 $= \dfrac{-E[X_3] + 0.05(323.6 + 130.0)}{323.6} = 16.3\%$.

$\square$

There are many different ways to allocate the aggregate economic capital to the business units. Before we describe the most popular methods, we will consider some characteristics that have been proposed as desirable criteria for an allocation procedure to have. This will give us a basis for discussing the advantages and disadvantages of different methods.

18.3.2 Fair Allocation Criteria

Full Allocation

The full allocation criterion requires that the total allocated capital should be equal to the enterprise-wide allocated capital. That is,

$$EC_1 + EC_2 + \cdots + EC_d = EC = \rho(X).$$

The implication of this axiom is that the enterprise-wide economic capital should be the starting point for the allocation, which means that the approach should be top-down not bottom-up. A bottom-up approach would ignore the different diversification benefits that the units contribute to the enterprise.

No Undercut

The no undercut criterion states that the total capital allocated to each unit should be no greater than the capital that the unit would require independently.

In other words, the capital allocated to the ith business unit, EC_i, must satisfy

$$EC_i \leq \rho(X_i).$$

This also applies to subsets of business units; that is, for any $\mathcal{H} \subseteq \{1, 2, \ldots, d\}$, let $EC_{\mathcal{H}}$ denote the total economic capital allocated to the set of business units, $\mathcal{H}$. Then,

$$EC_{\mathcal{H}} \leq \rho\left(\sum_{i \in \mathcal{H}} X_i\right).$$

The reasoning here is that an individual unit should not be seen as performing worse within the firm than it would if it were independent of the firm. This criterion is analogous to the subadditivity requirement for risk measures.

Symmetry

The symmetry criterion states that if two units provide the same marginal increase in EC to all possible subsets of the firm that do not include them, then they should be allocated the same capital.

That is, let $\mathcal{H}_{\sim\{i,j\}}$ denote the set of subsets of all units of the firm that do not include unit i or unit j. Let $X_{\mathcal{K}}$ denote the sum of losses of all units in a subset $\mathcal{K}$ of the enterprise. Then the symmetry criterion requires that

$$\rho(X_{\mathcal{K}} + X_i) = \rho(X_{\mathcal{K}} + X_j) \ \forall \mathcal{K} \in \mathcal{H}_{\sim\{i,j\}} \implies EC_i = EC_j. \quad (18.1)$$

Consistency

Suppose the firm combines business units i and j, creating a new business unit $i\&j$. The consistency criterion says that the total allocation to the units should not be changed if they are considered as two units or one. That is,

$$EC_{i\&j} = EC_i + EC_j.$$

If the allocation scheme satisfies the consistency criterion, then the way that units and sub-units of the firm are combined does not affect the total capital allocated to the units and sub-units.

18.4 Capital Allocation: Methods

18.4.1 Proportional Allocation

Under proportional, or relative allocation, the firm-wide economic capital is allocated in proportion to the stand-alone capital of the individual units. That is, assuming that the firm-wide economic capital, EC, is determined using the risk measure ρ, the EC allocation to line i is determined as

$$EC_i = \left(\frac{\rho(X_i)}{\sum\limits_{j=1}^{d} \rho(X_j)} \right) EC, \quad \text{for } \sum_{j=1}^{d} \rho(X_j) > 0. \quad (18.2)$$

This is the approach used in the example of Section 18.3.1.

Proportional allocation usually satisfies three of the fair allocation criteria.

Full Allocation

Clearly, the proportional method satisfies the full allocation criterion, as

$$\sum_{i=1}^{d} EC_i = \frac{\left(\rho(X_1) + \rho(X_2) + \cdots + \rho(X_d) \right)}{\sum\limits_{j=1}^{d} \rho(X_j)} EC = EC. \quad (18.3)$$

No Undercut

If $EC = \rho(X_1 + X_2 + \cdots + X_d)$, and if ρ is a subadditive risk measure, then the proportional method satisfies the no undercut criterion, as

$$EC_i = \rho(X_i) \left(\frac{\rho(X_1 + X_2 + \cdots + X_d)}{\rho(X_1) + \rho(X_2) + \cdots + \rho(X_d)} \right).$$

If ρ is subadditive, then the numerator in the fraction is less than or equal to the denominator, so $EC_i \leq \rho(X_i)$.

Symmetry

If $\rho(X_{\mathcal{K}} + X_i) = \rho(X_{\mathcal{K}} + X_j)$ for all $\mathcal{K} \in \mathcal{H}_{\sim\{i,j\}}$, then, setting $\mathcal{K} = \emptyset$, we have that $\rho(X_i) = \rho(X_j)$. This is sufficient for $EC_i = EC_j$ under proportional allocation, as

$$EC_i = \frac{\rho(X_i)}{\displaystyle\sum_{j=1}^{d}\rho(X_j)} EC = \frac{\rho(X_j)}{\displaystyle\sum_{j=1}^{d}\rho(X_j)} EC = EC_j.$$

Consistency

In general, the proportional approach does not satisfy the consistency criterion. We will show this using a counterexample.

Consider the three-line insurance example from Section 18.3.1. If we combine Lines 1 and 2, with loss $X_{1,2} = X_1 + X_2$, the 'stand-alone' EC is $\rho(X_{1,2})$, which is 360.6 (by Monte Carlo simulation). This means that changing the structure to two units changes the proportional allocation to

$$EC_{1\&2} = \frac{\rho(X_{1,2})}{\rho(X_{1,2}) + \rho(X_3)} EC = \frac{362.0}{362.0 + 415.9}(622.0) = 289.5.$$

The proportional allocation to Lines 1 and 2 under the 3-unit structure is $28.2 + 270.2 = 298.4$, which is different from the allocation to the merged units. Hence, the proportional allocation method is not consistent.

Proportional allocation has some advantages – it is straightforward, simple to calculate, and easy to explain. However, it does not reflect the relationships between units; for example, the ability of one unit to act as a hedge against the losses of another unit does not influence the allocation. In addition, as we have shown, proportional allocation does not satisfy the consistency criterion, although it does satisfy the other three, if ρ is subadditive.

18.4.2 Discrete Marginal Allocation

A disadvantage of the proportional approach is that it does not reflect the ability of units to hedge the losses of other parts of the business. An approach which does achieve this is called the discrete marginal approach. The idea here is that we start with one unit, and then build up to the whole firm. The capital allocated to each unit is the difference between the capital required after adding that unit, and the capital required before adding that unit.

Assume, as above, that we have d units, and that the firm-wide EC is determined using the risk measure ρ. Let $X_{1,2,\dots,k}$ denote the aggregate loss from units $1, 2, 3, \dots, k$. Then, counting from unit 1 through to unit d, we have

$$EC_1 = \rho(X_1),$$
$$EC_2 = \rho(X_{1,2}) - \rho(X_1),$$
$$EC_3 = \rho(X_{1,2,3}) - \rho(X_{1,2}),$$
$$\vdots$$
$$EC_d = \rho(X) - \rho(X_{1,2,\dots,d-1}).$$

If we apply this approach to the example of Section 18.3.1, noting that $\rho(X_{1,2}) = 360.6$, we have

$$EC_1 = \rho(X_1) = 36.3, \tag{18.4}$$
$$EC_2 = \rho(X_{1,2}) - \rho(X_1) = 360.6 - 36.3 = 324.3, \tag{18.5}$$
$$EC_3 = \rho(X) - \rho(X_{1,2}) = 622.0 - 360.6 = 261.4. \tag{18.6}$$

Now, there are clearly some unsatisfactory features of this allocation. First, the order that it is applied makes a difference to the allocation – if we applied the discrete marginal approach to the same example, using the order 2,1,3, we would get

$$EC_2 = \rho(X_2) = 347.2, \tag{18.7}$$
$$EC_1 = \rho(X_{1,2}) - \rho(X_2) = 360.6 - 347.2 = 13.4, \tag{18.8}$$
$$EC_3 = \rho(X) - \rho(X_{1,2}) = 622.0 - 360.6 = 261.4. \tag{18.9}$$

The allocation to line 3 is unchanged, as it is in third place each time, but the allocations to lines 1 and 2 resulting from using the order 2,1,3 are very different from the allocations using the order 1,2,3, which does not seem satisfactory.

There is a possibility that a unit could be allocated negative risk capital, if the unit acts as a hedge against losses elsewhere in the firm, resulting in a lower capital requirement with the unit included than without.

Reviewing the discrete marginal allocation using the fair allocation axioms, we have the following results.

Full Allocation

$$EC_1 + EC_2 + \cdots + EC_d = \rho(X_1) + \big(\rho(X_{1,2}) - \rho(X_1)\big)$$
$$+ \cdots + \big(\rho(X) - \rho(X_{1,2,\ldots,d-1})\big)$$
$$= \rho(X) = EC,$$

so the full allocation criterion is satisfied.

No Undercut
If ρ is subadditive, then

$$\rho(X_{1,2,\ldots,j}) \leq \rho(X_j) + \rho(X_{1,2,\ldots,j-1})$$
$$\implies EC_j = \rho(X_{1,2,\ldots,j}) - \rho(X_{1,2,\ldots,j-1}) \leq \rho(X_j).$$

So if ρ is subadditive, the no undercut criterion is satisfied.

Symmetry
As the capital allocation depends on the order in which units are included, the discrete marginal approach is not symmetric. We can prove this with a simple counterexample.

Consider a firm with two units; the losses are i.i.d. with $X_1, X_2 \sim N(100, 10^2) - 105$. The economic capital is determined using the 95% Expected Shortfall of the loss.

The stand-alone EC for each unit is 15.6. Since the stand-alone ECs are identical, and since the firm only has two units, symmetry requires that the allocated ECs are identical.

The aggregate loss is $X = X_1 + X_2 \sim N(200, 200) - 210$, and the top-down 95% Expected Shortfall is 19.2.

So the marginal allocation to Unit 1 is $EC_1 = 15.6$ and to Unit 2 is $EC_2 = 19.2 - 15.6 = 3.6$. Hence, the discrete marginal approach does not satisfy the symmetry criterion.

Consistency
Because the method depends on the order in which units are included, it cannot be consistent. The allocation to Unit 2, say, under the unit structure 1,2,3 will be different from the allocation if line 3 is combined with line 1, if the allocation order becomes 1&3, followed by 2.

Table 18.1. *Marginal EC calculations for Shapley capital allocation, using the Section 18.3.1 example*

Order	MEC_1	MEC_2	MEC_3	Total
1,2,3	36.3	324.3	261.4	622.0
2,1,3	13.4	347.2	261.4	622.0
2,3,1	15.3	347.2	259.5	622.0
3,2,1	15.3	190.8	415.9	622.0
3,1,2	12.4	193.7	415.9	622.0
1,3,2	36.3	193.7	392.0	622.0
Mean	21.5	266.1	334.4	622.0

The discrete marginal allocation method is not proposed as a reasonable allocation method – the dependence of the allocation on the ordering of the units is clearly a major defect – but it is a useful introduction to the Shapley allocation method.

18.4.3 Shapley Allocation

The Shapley allocation method has its origins in co-operative game theory, but it can also be seen as an extension of the discrete marginal approach. Suppose we apply the discrete marginal approach to all possible orderings of the individual units. For example, with 4 units, we would have $4! = 24$ possible orderings. The average marginal capital allocation for each unit over all possible permutations is the Shapley capital allocation.

To illustrate, consider again the example from Section 18.3.1. We have three lines of business, so there are six possible permutations. We will need the 95% Expected Shortfall of all 2-unit subsets of the business; we have already used $\rho(X_{1,2}) = 360.6$; we also have $\rho(X_{1,3}) = 428.3$ and $\rho(X_{2,3}) = 606.7$, found using Monte Carlo simulation.[3] Using these values, we can calculate the discrete marginal allocations for all six permutations of the three lines. Table 18.1 gives the intermediate calculations; MEC_i is the marginal allocation to Line i, based on the specified ordering.

We see that for each unit, when they are counted first, their EC is the stand-alone Expected Shortfall. When they are counted last, their EC is independent of the ordering of the units counted before them.

---

[3] Each value was calculated using 10^6 simulations; in each case the standard error is between 1.0 and 3.0.

In order to analyse the Shapley allocation method, we first express the allocation more formally. We assume, as above, that the firm has d business units. Let $\mathcal{H}_{\sim i}^{(k)}$ denote all the k-tuple subsets of the d business units that exclude unit i. Then the Shapley allocation equation can be written as

$$EC_i = \sum_{k=0}^{d-1} \frac{k!\,(d-1-k)!}{d!} \sum_{\mathcal{K} \in \mathcal{H}_{\sim i}^{(k)}} \left(\rho(X_{\mathcal{K}} + X_i) - \rho(X_{\mathcal{K}}) \right), \qquad (18.10)$$

where $\rho(X_\emptyset) = 0$.

In cooperative game theory the Shapley value determines a fair allocation of costs and gains across players, satisfying a number of criteria that are similar, but not identical to the fair allocation principles listed above. In terms of the fair allocation principles, we have the following results for the Shapley allocation.

Full Allocation
Each individual discrete marginal allocation – that is, each row of Table 18.1 – sums to the top-down economic capital, so averaging all the rows must also generate a total which is equal to the full EC. Hence, the Shapley allocation satisfies the full allocation criterion.

No Undercut
In the previous section, we showed that each individual discrete marginal allocation satisfies the no undercut criterion, provided that ρ is subadditive. It follows that the average of the marginal allocations must also satisfy the no undercut criterion, as we are averaging over $d!$ values for MEC_i, and for each one we have that $\mathrm{MEC}_i \leq \rho(X_i)$.

Symmetry
Suppose we have two units, i and j, where, for any set $\mathcal{K}$ which does not include i or j,

$$\rho(X_{\mathcal{K}} + X_i) = \rho(X_{\mathcal{K}} + X_j). \qquad (18.11)$$

The symmetry criterion requires that $EC_i = EC_j$.

We can show that the Shapley allocation satisfies the symmetry criterion as follows.

First, we rewrite the Shapley allocation equation for Unit i, in terms of sets in $\mathcal{H}_{\sim \{i,j\}}^{(k)}$, that is, k-tuple subsets of $\{1, 2, \ldots, d\}$ that do not include i or j:

$$EC_i = \sum_{k=0}^{d-1} \frac{k!\,(d-1-k)!}{d!} \left\{ \sum_{\mathcal{K} \in \mathcal{H}^{(k)}_{\sim\{i,j\}}} \left(\rho(X_{\mathcal{K}} + X_i) - \rho(X_{\mathcal{K}}) \right) \right.$$

$$\left. + \sum_{\mathcal{K} \in \mathcal{H}^{(k-1)}_{\sim\{i,j\}}} \left(\rho(X_{\mathcal{K}} + X_j + X_i) - \rho(X_{\mathcal{K}} + X_j) \right) \right\}.$$

The first sum in the curly brackets covers all the k-tuple subsets that do not include j or i, and the second covers all the k-tuples that do include j, but do not include i.

Now, as $\mathcal{K}$ does not contain i or j, the assumption in (18.11) gives us that $\rho(X_{\mathcal{K}} + X_i) = \rho(X_{\mathcal{K}} + X_j)$. So, for each term in the first sum within the curly brackets, we have

$$\rho(X_{\mathcal{K}} + X_i) - \rho(X_{\mathcal{K}}) = \rho(X_{\mathcal{K}} + X_j) - \rho(X_{\mathcal{K}}).$$

Similarly, in the second term,

$$\rho(X_{\mathcal{K}} + X_j + X_i) - \rho(X_{\mathcal{K}} + X_j) = \rho(X_{\mathcal{K}} + X_j + X_i) - \rho(X_{\mathcal{K}} + X_i),$$

so

$$EC_i = \sum_{k=0}^{d-1} \frac{k!\,(d-1-k)!}{d!} \left\{ \sum_{\mathcal{K} \in \mathcal{H}^{(k)}_{\sim\{i,j\}}} \left(\rho(X_{\mathcal{K}} + X_i) - \rho(X_{\mathcal{K}}) \right) \right.$$

$$\left. + \sum_{\mathcal{K} \in \mathcal{H}^{(k-1)}_{\sim\{i,j\}}} \left(\rho(X_{\mathcal{K}} + X_j + X_i) - \rho(X_{\mathcal{K}} + X_j) \right) \right\}$$

$$= \sum_{k=0}^{d-1} \frac{k!\,(d-1-k)!}{d!} \left\{ \sum_{\mathcal{K} \in \mathcal{H}^{(k)}_{\sim\{i,j\}}} \left(\rho(X_{\mathcal{K}} + X_j) - \rho(X_{\mathcal{K}}) \right) \right.$$

$$\left. + \sum_{\mathcal{K} \in \mathcal{H}^{(k-1)}_{\sim\{i,j\}}} \left(\rho(X_{\mathcal{K}} + X_j + X_i) - \rho(X_{\mathcal{K}} + X_i) \right) \right\}$$

$$= EC_j.$$

Consistency
The Shapley allocation is not consistent, as can be seen from the numbers in Table 18.1, where, for example,

$$EC_{1\&2} = \frac{1}{2}\big(\rho(X_1 + X_2) + \big(\rho(X_1 + X_2 + X_3) - \rho(X_3)\big)\big) = 283.4,$$

but $EC_1 + EC_2 = 21.5 + 266.1 = 287.6$.

The Shapley allocation has some additional advantages not captured in these four criteria. When ρ is positive homogeneous, it is a linear homogeneous allocation, so that, for example, doubling X_i results in double the allocated capital to the ith business unit. However, it becomes quite cumbersome to calculate as the number of business units increases, and the failure to meet the consistency criterion is seen as a drawback.

18.4.4 Covariance Allocation

Consider a firm that uses the **standard deviation risk measure** for aggregate economic capital, that is,

$$\rho(X) = \mu_x + R\sqrt{\mathrm{Var}[X]},$$

for some $k > 0$, where μ_x is $\mathrm{E}[X]$.

The firm may use the **covariance method** to allocate capital, such that for business unit i, with $\mathrm{E}[X_i] = \mu_i$,

$$EC_i = \mu_i + k\frac{\mathrm{Cov}(X_i, X)}{\sqrt{\mathrm{Var}[X]}}. \tag{18.12}$$

We can show that the covariance method satisfies each of the fair allocation axioms. Assume the firm has d business units.

Full Allocation
For $X = X_1 + X_2 + \cdots + X_d$, we have

$$\sum_{i=1}^{d} \mathrm{Cov}(X_i, X) = \sum_{i=1}^{d} \mathrm{Var}[X_i] + \sum_{i=1}^{d}\sum_{j=1}^{d} \mathrm{Cov}(X_i, X_j) = \mathrm{Var}[X],$$

confirming that the covariance allocation method satisfies the full allocation criterion.

No Undercut

As $\dfrac{\mathrm{Cov}(X_i, X)}{\sqrt{\mathrm{Var}[X_i]}\sqrt{\mathrm{Var}[X]}}$ is the correlation coefficient between X_1 and X, we have

$$1 \geq \frac{\mathrm{Cov}(X_i, X)}{\sqrt{\mathrm{Var}[X_i]}\sqrt{\mathrm{Var}[X]}}$$

$$\Rightarrow \sqrt{\mathrm{Var}[X_i]} \geq \frac{\mathrm{Cov}(X_i, X)}{\sqrt{\mathrm{Var}[X]}}$$

$$\Rightarrow \mu_i + k\sqrt{\mathrm{Var}[X_i]} \geq \mu_i + k\frac{\mathrm{Cov}(X_i, X)}{\sqrt{\mathrm{Var}[X]}} \qquad \text{for } k > 0$$

$$\Rightarrow \rho(X_i) \geq EC_i.$$

Hence, the stand-alone EC, $\rho(X_i)$, is greater than or equal to the allocated capital, EC_i, which means that the covariance allocation method satisfies the no undercut criterion.

Symmetry

The symmetry criterion requires that if two units have the same allocation when considered within any subset of the firm, then they should have the same allocation when the firm is considered as a whole.

Suppose i and j are the two units. Then under the initial condition, that Unit i and Unit j have the same allocation when considered within any subset of the firm, we must have $\mu_i = \mu_j$, and $\sigma_i = \sigma_j$, and

$$\mu_i + k\sqrt{\mathrm{Var}[X_i]} = \mu_j + k\sqrt{\mathrm{Var}[X_j]}.$$

Now consider the subset of the firm comprising all the units except i and j; that is, let $X^* = X - X_i - X_j$. From the symmetry assumption, adding X_i to X^* will give the same risk capital as adding X_j to X^*, which means that

$$\mu_{X^*} + \mu_i + k\sqrt{\mathrm{Var}[X^* + X_i]} = \mu_{X^*} + \mu_j + k\sqrt{\mathrm{Var}[X^* + X_j]}$$
$$\implies \mathrm{Var}[X^* + X_i] = \mathrm{Var}[X^* + X_j] \qquad (18.13)$$
$$\text{Now, } \mathrm{Var}[X] = \mathrm{Var}[X^* + X_i + X_j]$$
$$= \mathrm{Var}[X^* + X_i] + \mathrm{Var}[X_j]$$
$$+ 2\mathrm{Cov}(X_i, (X^* + X_j)).$$
$$\text{Similarly, } \mathrm{Var}[X] = \mathrm{Var}[X^* + X_j] + \mathrm{Var}[X_i]$$
$$+ 2\mathrm{Cov}(X_j, (X^* + X_i))$$
$$\implies \mathrm{Cov}(X_i, (X^* + X_j)) = \mathrm{Cov}(X_j, (X^* + X_i)), \qquad (18.14)$$
$$\text{Also, } \mathrm{Cov}(X_i, X) = \mathrm{Var}[X_i] + \mathrm{Cov}(X_i, X^* + X_j) \text{ from (18.19)}$$
$$= \mathrm{Var}[X_j] + \mathrm{Cov}(X_j, X^* + X_i) \text{ from (18.13)}$$
$$= \mathrm{Cov}(X_j, X) \qquad (18.15)$$
$$\implies EC_i = EC_j, \qquad (18.16)$$

which proves that the covariance allocation method satisfies the symmetry criterion.

Consistency
We have that, for any units i, j,

$$
\begin{aligned}
EC_{i\&j} &= \mu_i + \mu_j + k\,\frac{\mathrm{Cov}(X_i + X_j, X)}{\sqrt{\mathrm{Var}[X]}} \\
&= \mu_i + \mu_j + k\,\frac{\mathrm{Cov}(X_i, X) + \mathrm{Cov}(X_j, X)}{\sqrt{\mathrm{Var}[X]}} \\
&= EC_i + EC_j,
\end{aligned}
$$

which proves that the covariance allocation method satisfies the consistency criterion.

Although the covariance allocation has attractive properties, these only apply where the aggregate economic capital is based on the standard deviation principle, and this is not a risk measure that is widely used in financial risk management.

18.4.5 Co-VaR Allocation

When the aggregate economic capital is determined using the VaR measure, we can use the co-VaR capital allocation formula,

$$
EC_i = \mathrm{E}\big[X_i \mid X = Q_\alpha(X)\big],
$$

where, as usual, $Q_\alpha(X)$ denotes the α-quantile of X.

This allocation method satisfies the full allocation, symmetry, and consistency criteria, but does not, in general, satisfy the no undercut criterion.

The co-VaR allocation formula is not very tractable analytically, but it does have a natural interpretation when the aggregate economic capital is determined through simulation. Suppose we simulate N values of $X = X_1 + X_2 + \cdots + X_d$, and sort the results such that $X_{(k)}$ represents the kth smallest simulated aggregate loss; let $X_{(k, j)}$ represent the contribution from unit j to the simulated aggregate loss, so that

$$
X_{(k)} = X_{(k, 1)} + X_{(k, 2)} + \cdots + X_{(k, d)}.
$$

Then, assuming that the α-VaR is determined using the αN order statistic, the estimated aggregate economic capital is

$$
EC = \widehat{\rho(X)} = X_{(\alpha N)},
$$

Table 18.2. *Data for Example 18.3; largest 20 simulated losses from 1,000 simulations, with component losses from three lines of business from Example 18.2*

k	$X_{(k)}$	$X_{(k,1)}$	$X_{(k,2)}$	$X_{(k,3)}$
981	540.8	33.9	254.2	252.7
982	550.0	1.5	263.4	285.1
983	553.1	−14.1	35.4	531.8
984	578.3	22.6	306.4	249.3
985	601.6	−17.6	−88.0	707.2
986	611.7	15.4	525.4	70.9
987	649.0	18.8	154.0	476.1
988	665.4	26.1	175.0	464.3
989	689.5	29.0	236.6	424.0
990	696.1	11.8	15.2	669.1
991	715.7	40.4	277.4	397.9
992	837.7	29.2	695.6	112.8
993	881.6	−1.0	−94.3	976.9
994	987.1	11.8	−10.2	985.4
995	1,031.4	16.2	195.8	819.4
996	1,092.1	53.2	475.9	563.0
997	1,191.5	39.7	52.3	1,099.4
998	1,381.4	−23.6	−54.1	1,459.2
999	2,048.5	44.1	519.1	1,485.3
1000	3,075.1	36.1	1,136.5	1,902.5

and the estimate of the co-VaR capital allocation to business unit i is

$$\widehat{EC}_i = X_{(\alpha N, i)}.$$

Example 18.3 For the insurer described in 18.3.1, we have run 1,000 simulations. The results have been sorted in ascending order of the total loss, and the 20 largest simulated values of X, along with the component values for X_1, X_2, and X_3, are given in Table 18.2.

(a) Estimate the 99% VaR using the order statistic approach, and determine the allocation of capital to each line using the co-VaR allocation method.

(b) Repeat (a), using the smoothed empirical estimator, defined in Chapter 3.

(c) For the order statistic estimator, verify that the estimated capital allocation satisfies the full allocation and consistency criteria. Does it satisfy the no undercut criterion?

Solution 18.3

(a) The order statistic method uses $X_{(\alpha N)}$ to estimate the α-VaR, so we have

$$\widehat{\text{VaR}}_\alpha(X) = X_{(990)} = 696.1,$$

$$\widehat{EC}_1 = X_{(990,1)} = 11.8,$$

$$\widehat{EC}_2 = X_{(990,2)} = 15.2,$$

$$\widehat{EC}_3 = X_{(990,3)} = 669.1.$$

(b) The smoothed empirical estimate of the α-VaR is $X_{(\alpha(N+1))} = X_{(990.99)}$. Using linear interpolation between $X_{(990)}$ and $X_{(991)}$ gives

$$\widehat{\text{VaR}}_\alpha(X) = 715.5,$$

$$\widehat{EC}_1 = 40.1,$$

$$\widehat{EC}_2 = 274.8,$$

$$\widehat{EC}_3 = 400.6.$$

(c) <u>Full allocation</u>:

$$\widehat{\text{VaR}}_\alpha(X) = 696.1, \quad EC_1 + EC_2 + EC_3 = 11.8 + 15.2 + 660.1 = 696.1.$$

<u>Consistency</u>: Clearly if we combine lines 1 and 2, say, it would make no difference to the total; we would still have

$$X_{(990)} = 696.1 = 27.0 + 669.1,$$

where

$$27.0 = EC_{1\&2} = X_{(990,1\&2)} = X_{(990,1)} + X_{(990,2)} = EC_1 + EC_2.$$

<u>No undercut</u>: The stand-alone 99% quantiles are $Q_{0.99}(X_1) = 41.5$, $Q_{0.99}(X_2) = 439.1$, and $Q_{0.99}(X_3) = 518.7$. As $\widehat{EC}_3 > \rho(3)$, in this case, empirically, the no undercut criterion is not satisfied. □

It is worth noting the very high variability of the individual line of business contributions in Table 18.2. This is not simply due to the small sample size, or large α. In a bigger experiment, with $N = 10^6$, and $\alpha = 0.99$, we found that the estimate of the aggregate VaR, using $X_{(\alpha N)}$, was relatively stable, but the allocation to the individual lines was highly variable. The results of 50 sets of 10^6 simulations are summarized in Table 18.3. This lack of stability is a serious practical constraint.[4]

---

[4] Better estimates of capital allocations can be obtained using more sophisticated simulation techniques. See, e.g., Glasserman (2005), in the context of credit risk.

Table 18.3. *Summary of 50 repetitions of Monte Carlo
simulation of 99% co-VaR allocation for the example in
Section 18.3.1; 10^6 simulations in each run*

	EC	EC_1	EC_2	EC_3
Mean	779.1	25.7	328.1	425.3
SD	3.5	16.0	239.4	239.8
Minimum	772.0	−9.1	−28.7	−109.0
Maximum	787.4	62.0	892.3	795.5

18.4.6 Co-CTE Allocation

When the aggregate economic capital is determined using the Expected Short-fall risk measure, then we can use the co-CTE allocation method (often just referred to as CTE allocation). CTE, or **Conditional Tail Expectation**, is another name for Expected Shortfall, and as it is the name associated with this allocation method, we have retained it here.

For losses which are continuous at the α-quantile,[5] the co-CTE capital allocation to Unit i is

$$EC_i = E\big[X_i \,|\, X > Q_\alpha(X)\big].$$

Similarly to the co-VaR approach, this is not particularly tractable analytically, but it has a very intuitive interpretation when estimated from Monte Carlo simulation output. Using the same notation as in the co-VaR case, we denote the kth sorted simulated loss as $X_{(k)}$, which is the sum of simulated losses for the individual business units, denoted $X_{(k,j)}$ for $j = 1, 2, \ldots, d$. Then,

$$\widehat{EC} = \widehat{\rho(X)} = \frac{1}{(1-\alpha)N} \sum_{k=\alpha N+1}^{N} X_{(k)},$$

$$\text{and } \widehat{EC_i} = \frac{1}{(1-\alpha)N} \sum_{k=\alpha N+1}^{N} X_{(k,i)}.$$

So the estimated allocated capital is the average of the simulated losses for Unit i that were components of the largest $(1 - \alpha)N$ values of X; that is, exactly

---

[5] It is straightforward to adapt the results for cases where there is a probability mass at the quantile.

the values used to calculate the aggregate EC. These are not (in general) the largest $(1 - \alpha)N$ simulated values of the individual unit losses.

The co-CTE allocation satisfies all four of the fair allocation criteria.

Full Allocation

We have

$$
\begin{aligned}
EC_1 + EC_2 + \cdots + EC_n &= \mathrm{E}[X_1 \mid X > Q_\alpha] + \mathrm{E}[X_2 \mid X > Q_\alpha] \\
&\quad + \cdots + \mathrm{E}[X_d \mid X > Q_\alpha] \\
&= \mathrm{E}[X_1 + X_2 + \cdots + X_d \mid X > Q_\alpha] \\
&= \mathrm{E}[X \mid X > Q_\alpha] \\
&= \rho(X),
\end{aligned}
$$

showing that the co-CTE allocation satisfies the full allocation criterion.

Consistency

$$
\mathrm{E}[X_i \mid X > Q_\alpha] + \mathrm{E}[X_j \mid X > Q_\alpha] = \mathrm{E}[X_i + X_j \mid X > Q_\alpha],
$$

which shows that the co-CTE allocation method also satisfies the consistency criterion.

No Undercut

Showing that the co-CTE allocation satisfies the No Undercut criterion follows a similar method to the proof that the Expected Shortfall is subadditive, from Chapter 3. In equation (3.21) we have that, for a loss random variable X,

$$
\mathrm{ES}_\alpha(X) = \lim_{n \to \infty} \frac{1}{(1 - \alpha)n} \sum_{k=n\alpha+1}^{n} X_{(k)},
$$

where the $X_{(k)}$ are order statistics from a random sample of n values from the distribution of X.

Suppose now that we have a random sample from the joint distribution of the individual business unit losses $(X_1, X_2, \ldots, X_d)$.

Let $X_{1(k)}$ denote the kth order statistic from the X_1 variables in the joint sample. That is, $X_{1(k)}$ is the kth smallest value from the Line 1 losses. Also, as above, $X_{(k,1)}$ represents the contribution of Line 1 to the kth order statistic of X; that is, it is the loss from line 1 that is a component of the kth smallest value for the aggregate loss, X. Then we have

$$
\sum_{k=\alpha N+1}^{N} X_{1(k)} \geq \sum_{k=\alpha N+1}^{N} X_{(k,1)}.
$$

This inequality follows because the sum on the left-hand side contains the largest $(1 - \alpha)N$ values of $X_{1,j}$, which must be greater than or equal to *any* sum of $(1 - \alpha)N$ values of $X_{1,j}$, including the $(1 - \alpha)N$ values on the right-hand side. Then for any n,

$$\frac{1}{n(1 - \alpha)} \sum_{k=\alpha n+1}^{n} X_{1(k)} \geq \frac{1}{n(1 - \alpha)} \sum_{k=\alpha n+1}^{n} X_{(k,1)}$$

$$\Rightarrow \lim_{n \to \infty} \frac{1}{n(1 - \alpha)} \sum_{k=\alpha n+1}^{n} X_{1(k)} \geq \lim_{n \to \infty} \frac{1}{n(1 - \alpha)} \sum_{k=\alpha n+1}^{n} X_{(k,1)}$$

$$\Rightarrow \text{ES}_\alpha(X_1) \geq EC_1,$$

which shows that the co-CTE allocation satisfies the no undercut criterion.

Symmetry

For the symmetry proof, we can again utilize the results for the co-VaR allocation. Given X_i and X_j satisfying the symmetry assumption for the co-VaR allocation, i.e. given that X_i and X_j have the same co-VaR allocation when considered within any subset of the firm, it must also be true that X_i and X_j have the same co-CTE allocation for any subset of the firm, as the co-CTE allocation is just an integral of co-VaR allocations. That is:

$$E[X_i \mid X = Q_u(X)] = E[X_j \mid X = Q_u(X)]$$

$$\Rightarrow \int_\alpha^1 E[X_i \mid X = Q_u(X)] du = \int_\alpha^1 E[X_j \mid X = Q_u(X)] du$$

$$\Rightarrow EC_i = EC_j.$$

Example 18.4 Use the data in Table 18.2 to estimate the aggregate economic capital, and the allocation to the individual lines of business, using a 98% Expected Shortfall risk measure, and the co-CTE allocation method.

Solution 18.4 The estimated 98% Expected Shortfall of the aggregate loss is the mean of the largest 2% of the 1,000 simulated values, which is the mean of the largest 20 values in the set. This gives

$$\widehat{EC} = \frac{1}{20} \sum_{k=981}^{1,000} X_{(k)} = 968.9.$$

Table 18.4. *Summary of 50 repetitions of Monte Carlo simulation of 99% CTE allocation for the example in Section 18.3.1;* 10^6 *simulations in each run*

	EC	EC_1	EC_2	EC_3
Mean	1,273.8	29.3	544.1	700.3
SD	8.9	0.2	5.0	6.7
Minimum	1,254.7	28.9	532.6	682.2
Maximum	1,294.1	29.8	555.6	713.5

The (estimated) allocation to Line 1 is the average of the $X_{(k,1)}$ values, over $k = 981, 992, \ldots, 1{,}000$ (i.e. the same rows that we used for $\widehat{EC}$), and similarly for Line 2 and Line 3, giving

$$\widehat{EC}_1 = \frac{1}{20} \sum_{k=981}^{1,000} X_{(k,1)} = 18.7,$$

$$\widehat{EC}_2 = \frac{1}{20} \sum_{k=981}^{1,000} X_{(k,2)} = 253.6,$$

$$\widehat{EC}_3 = \frac{1}{20} \sum_{k=981}^{1,000} X_{(k,3)} = 696.6. \qquad \square$$

The co-CTE allocation is much more stable than the co-VaR allocation. The same 50 repeated sets of 10^6 Monte Carlo simulations that were used to illustrate the volatility of the co-VaR allocation in Table 18.3, generate the results shown in Table 18.4 for the 99% co-CTE allocation. The standard error of the 99% Expected Shortfall for the aggregate loss is slightly larger than the VaR, but that is to be expected as it is more influenced by the extreme tail of the distribution. The standard errors of the allocations are very much smaller than those of the co-VaR allocations.

18.5 Euler Allocation Methods

The discrete marginal and Shapley methods use the increase in the aggregate economic capital required when a complete business unit is added to the firm, as the basis for allocating capital. These approaches assume that each unit is either in or out. If, instead, we use a **continuous marginal approach**, where the EC allocated to each business unit is in proportion to the rate of increase in the aggregate EC caused by an incremental increase in the weighting of that business unit, then we avoid some of the disadvantages of the discrete approach. When the risk measure used for the enterprise-wide allocation, ρ, is positive homogeneous (i.e. if $\rho(kX) = k\rho(X)$, for any constant $k > 0$), then this continuous marginal approach is called the **Euler allocation** for the risk measure ρ. The covariance, co-VaR, and co-CTE allocations are all special cases of the Euler allocation.

Euler allocation methods have attractive properties, as we have seen in the three cases discussed. For any positive homogeneous risk measure ρ, the Euler allocation will satisfy the full allocation, symmetry, and consistency criteria, and if ρ is subadditive, the Euler allocation will also satisfy the no undercut criterion.

The Euler allocation for a given risk measure ρ is derived as follows. Suppose a firm has d business units, with aggregate loss $X = X_1 + X_2 + \cdots + X_d$. Let $r(w_1, w_2, \ldots, w_d)$ denote the risk measure ρ, applied to a combination of losses where the ith business unit contributes $w_i X_i$ to the aggregate loss. That is,

$$r(w_1, w_2, \ldots, w_d) = \rho(w_1 X_1 + w_2 X_2 + \cdots + w_d X_d)$$
$$\implies r(1, 1, \ldots, 1) = \rho(X_1 + X_2 + \cdots + X_d) = \rho(X).$$

Introducing the function r allows us to model the effect on $\rho(X)$ of marginal changes in volume for each individual business unit.

If ρ is positive homogeneous, then Euler's Homogeneous Function Theorem gives us

$$r(w_1, w_2, \ldots, w_d) = w_1 \frac{\partial r}{\partial w_1} + w_2 \frac{\partial r}{\partial w_2} + \cdots + w_d \frac{\partial r}{\partial w_d} \tag{18.17}$$

$$\implies r(1, 1, \ldots, 1) = \rho(X)$$
$$= \left(\frac{\partial r}{\partial w_1} + \frac{\partial r}{\partial w_2} + \cdots + \frac{\partial r}{\partial w_d} \right) \Bigg|_{(w_1, w_2, \ldots, w_d) = (1, 1, \ldots, 1)}. \tag{18.18}$$

The Euler capital allocation for Unit i is $\frac{\partial r}{\partial w_i}$, evaluated at $(w_1, w_2, \ldots, w_d) = (1, 1, \ldots, 1)$; that is,

$$EC_i = \frac{\partial r}{\partial w_i}(1, 1, \ldots, 1),$$

and from equation (18.18) we can see that the full allocation criterion will be satisfied by the Euler allocation approach, as

$$r(1, 1, \ldots, 1) = \rho(X) = \frac{\partial r}{\partial w_1}(1, 1, \ldots, 1) + \frac{\partial r}{\partial w_2}(1, 1, \ldots, 1)$$

$$+ \cdots + \frac{\partial r}{\partial w_d}(1, 1, \ldots, 1)$$

$$\implies \rho(X) = EC_1 + EC_2 + \cdots + EC_d.$$

18.5.1 Euler – Covariance Allocation

We will show that the Euler allocation for the standard deviation risk measure, $\rho = \mu_X + k\sqrt{\text{Var}[L]}$, is the covariance allocation principle, for a firm with 3 units, and for $i = 1$. It is straightforward to generalize to d units.

We first note that, given $d = 3$,

$$\begin{aligned}
\text{Cov}(X_1, X) &= \text{Cov}(X_1, (X_1 + X_2 + X_3)) \\
&= \text{E}[X_1^2 + X_1 X_2 + X_1 X_3] - \text{E}[X_1]\text{E}[X_1 + X_2 + X_3] \\
&= \text{E}[X_1^2] + \text{E}[X_1 X_2] + \text{E}[X_1 X_3] \\
&\quad - \left(\text{E}[X_1]^2 + \text{E}[X_1]\text{E}[X_2] + \text{E}[X_1]\text{E}[X_3]\right) \\
&= \text{Var}[X_1] + \text{Cov}(X_1, X_2) + \text{Cov}(X_1, X_3). \quad (18.19)
\end{aligned}$$

We have

$$r(w_1, w_2, w_3) = \rho(w_1 X_1 + w_2 X_2 + w_3 X_3)$$

$$= w_1 \mu_1 + w_2 \mu_2 + w_3 \mu_3 + k\left(\text{Var}\left[w_1 X_1 + w_2 X_2 + w_3 X_3\right]\right)^{\frac{1}{2}}.$$

So,

$$\frac{\partial r}{\partial w_1} = \mu_1 + k\frac{\frac{\partial}{\partial w_1}\text{Var}[w_1 X_1 + w_2 X_2 + w_3 X_3]}{2\left(\text{Var}[w_1 X_1 + w_2 X_2 + w_3 X_3]\right)^{\frac{1}{2}}}.$$

Now, $\text{Var}\left[w_1 X_1 + w_2 X_2 + w_3 X_3\right] = \sum_{i=1}^{3} w_i^2 \text{Var}[X_i]$

$$+ 2\sum_{i=1}^{3}\sum_{\substack{j=1 \\ j \neq i}}^{3} w_i w_j \text{Cov}(X_i, X_j)$$

$$\implies \frac{\partial}{\partial w_1}\text{Var}\left[w_1 X_1 + w_2 X_2 + w_3 X_3\right] = 2w_1 \text{Var}[X_1] + 2w_2 \text{Cov}(X_1, X_2)$$

$$+ 2w_3 \text{Cov}(X_1, X_3)$$

$$\implies \frac{\partial r}{\partial w_1} = \mu_1 + k\frac{w_1 \text{Var}[X_1] + w_2 \text{Cov}(X_1, X_2) + w_3 \text{Cov}(X_1, X_3)}{\left(\text{Var}[w_1 X_1 + w_2 X_2 + w_3 X_3]\right)^{\frac{1}{2}}}.$$

Now set $(w_1, w_2, w_3) = (1, 1, 1)$:

$$\frac{\partial r}{\partial w_1}(1, 1, 1) = EC_1 = \mu_1 + k \frac{\text{Var}[X_1] + \text{Cov}(X_1, X_2) + \text{Cov}(X_1, X_3)}{\left(\text{Var}\big[X_1 + X_2 + X_3\big]\right)^{\frac{1}{2}}}$$

$$= \mu_1 + k \frac{\text{Cov}(X_1, X)}{\sqrt{\text{Var}[X]}} \quad \text{from (18.19)}.$$

18.5.2 Euler – Co-VaR Allocation

It is possible to show under technical assumptions that, when applied to the α-VaR risk measure, the Euler allocation principle generates the co-VaR allocation method

$$EC_i = \text{E}\big[X_i \mid X = Q_\alpha(X)\big],$$

where, as usual, $Q_\alpha(X)$ denotes the α-quantile of X.

See McNeil et al. (2015) for a proof of this result.

18.5.3 Euler – Co-CTE Allocation

When applied to the α-Expected Shortfall risk measure, the Euler allocation principle generates the co-CTE allocation. This is the best known and probably the most practical of the Euler allocation methods.

We can derive the co-CTE allocation formula, using the co-VaR result, for continuous loss distributions. Let $r_{Q_u}(w_1, w_2, \ldots, w_d)$ represent the VaR weighted risk measure, that is,

$$r_{Q_u}(w_1, w_2, \ldots, w_d) = Q_u(w_1 X_1 + w_2 X_2 + \cdots + w_d X_d).$$

From the co-VaR allocation, we have that

$$\frac{\partial r_{Q_u}}{\partial w_1}(1, 1, \ldots, 1) = \text{E}[X_1 | X = Q_u(X)].$$

For the co-CTE allocation, we have

$$r(w_1, w_2, \ldots, w_d) = \frac{1}{1 - \alpha} \int_\alpha^1 Q_u(w_1 X_1 + w_2 X_2 + \cdots + w_d X_d) du$$

$$= \frac{1}{1 - \alpha} \int_\alpha^1 r_{Q_u}(w_1, w_2, \ldots, w_d) du$$

$$\Rightarrow \frac{\partial r}{\partial w_1}(1, 1, \ldots, 1) = \frac{1}{1-\alpha} \int_{\alpha}^{1} \frac{\partial r_{Q_u}}{\partial w_1}(1, 1, \ldots, 1) du$$

$$= \frac{1}{1-\alpha} \int_{\alpha}^{1} \mathrm{E}[X_1 | X = Q_u(X)] du.$$

Now we change the variable of integration to $v = Q_u(X) = F_X^{-1}(u)$, so that, using the density function f_X of X,

$$F_X(v) = u \Rightarrow dv = dF_X(v) = f_X(v) dv$$

$$\implies \frac{\partial r}{\partial w_1}(1, 1, \ldots, 1) = \frac{1}{1-\alpha} \int_{\alpha}^{1} \mathrm{E}[X_1 | X = Q_u(X)] du$$

$$= \frac{1}{1-\alpha} \int_{Q_\alpha}^{\infty} \mathrm{E}[X_1 | X = v] f(v) dv$$

$$= \mathrm{E}[X_1 | X > Q_\alpha(X)].$$

18.6 Capital Allocation Based on Default Cost

The allocation methods described so far have broadly centred on the aggregate risk measure for the firm. Although widely used, there are some disadvantages to these methods.

- In many cases (including covariance allocation, co-VaR allocation, and co-CTE allocation), it is possible for the allocated capital to be negative. This is not helpful for calculating the RAROC, for pricing, or for performance measurement within the individual business unit. It is helpful information in terms of assessing aggregate risk, however.
- When used for pricing, the allocation may give rise to arbitrage; the fair or market value of a contingent payoff (such as an option or an insurance policy) should generally not depend on the structure of the firm that writes the contract.
- The business unit allocation does not always recognize the very different types of risk involved. For example, in the insurance example, the Euler

allocation methods may be reasonable for individual lines of business, but fail to recognize the role and risks associated with the investment management of the assets.

A different approach to the economic capital allocation problem is to consider the risk in terms of the expected default cost. The methods described below have been developed largely for application in insurance, where the cost of capital is a key factor for pricing. However, some have since been adapted to other financial services enterprises.

18.6.1 Myers–Read Allocation

The Myers and Read (2001) formula for allocating capital is based on the value of a default option. Let $L = L_1 + L_2 + \cdots + L_d$ denote the 1-year aggregate liability of a firm with d lines, and assume A is the asset value at the year end. We assume that all claims are settled at the end of one year. Because of limited liability, the insurer cannot pay more in claims than it has in assets, so the liability at time 1 is $\min(L, A) = L - (L - A)^+$. The value at the year end of the insurer's default option is $(L - A)^+$.

The value of the assets at time 0 is $V_A = \mathrm{E}^Q[Ae^{-r}]$; the value of the liabilities, ignoring default risk, is

$$V_L = \mathrm{E}^Q \left[e^{-r} \sum_{j=1}^{k} L_j \right] = \sum_{j=1}^{k} V_{L_j} \quad \text{where } V_{L_j} = \mathrm{E}^Q[e^{-r} L_j].$$

The value of the default option is

$$D = \mathrm{E}^Q \left[e^{-r} (L - A)^+ \right]$$

$$= \delta \, V_L \quad \text{where } \delta \text{ represents the default option value per unit of liability.}$$

The intuition behind the Myers–Read allocation is that the time 0 assets, V_A (including technical provisions and economic capital) should be allocated to each line according to their marginal contribution to D. For simplicity, we will assume that A is not random, and that $r = 0$, so that $V_A = A$. We also assume that we can use the $\mathbb{P}$-measure to value the liabilities (for diversifiable risks, we take $\mathbb{P} \equiv \mathbb{Q}$), so $V_{L_j} = \mathrm{E}[L_j]$. Then the default option value is

$$\delta \mathrm{E}[L] = \mathrm{E}\left[(L - A)^+ \right] = \mathrm{E}[L - A \mid L > A] \Pr[L > A]$$

$$= \mathrm{E}[L \mid L > A] \Pr[L > A] - A \Pr[L > A].$$

Let A_j denote the total asset allocation to Line j (the total asset allocation includes the technical provision as well as the economic capital allocation). Then we calculate A_j such that:

$$E[L_j - A_j | L > A] = \delta \, E[L_j] \tag{18.20}$$

$$\Rightarrow E\left[L_j \mid L > A\right] \Pr[L > A] - A_j \Pr[L > A] = \delta \, E[L_j]$$

$$\Rightarrow A_j = E[L_j \mid L > A] - \frac{\delta \, E[L_j]}{\Pr[L > A]}.$$

Notice here that the conditioning is on $L > A$, not on $L_j > A_j$. This means that we are looking at the expected value of $L_j - A_j$, conditioning on the default event, $L > A$. This is similar to the co-CTE concept, when we considered the contribution of the individual lines of business to the total loss, in the event that the total loss fell in the top $1-\alpha$ part of the distribution. Here we consider the contribution of the individual lines to the total loss, in the event that the total loss exceeds the asset value. It is straightforward to show that $\sum_{j=1}^{d} A_j = A$, meaning that the method satisfies the full allocation criterion.

To implement the Myers-Read allocation in a Monte Carlo simulation of losses, similarly to the co-VaR and co-CTE cases, let $L_{(k)} = L_{(k,1)}, + L_{(k,2)} + \cdots + L_{(k,d)}$, where, $L_{(k)}$ denotes the kth sorted simulated aggregate loss, from a set of N simulations, and $L_{(k,j)}$ represents the part of $L_{(k)}$ that comes from the jth insurance line.

Let m denote the number of simulations in which $L_k > A$.

The first step is to calculate δ given the simulated losses and the asset value A. We have

$$\delta = \frac{1}{E[L]} E[L \mid L > A] \Pr[L > A] - A \Pr[L > A],$$

where $E[L \mid L > A] \approx \dfrac{1}{m} \sum_{k=N-m+1}^{N} L_{(k)}$ and $\Pr[L > A] \approx \dfrac{m}{N}$

$$\Rightarrow E[L \mid L > A] \Pr[L > A] \approx \frac{1}{N} \sum_{k=N-m+1}^{N} L_{(k)}$$

$$\Rightarrow \delta \approx \left(\frac{\sum_{k=N-m+1}^{N} L_{(k)} - Am}{N \, E[L]} \right).$$

Next, we use this δ to set the asset allocation for each line, using the $L_{(k,j)}$ values that contributed to the simulated default losses, $L_{(k)}$:

Table 18.5. *Myers–Read asset and capital allocation for the example three-line company*

Line j	A_j	TP	EC_j
Line 1	−20.3	105.0	−125.3
Line 2	438.5	120.0	318.5
Line 3	558.8	130.0	428.8
Total	977.0	355.0	622.0

$$E[L_j - A_j | L > A] = \delta \, E[L_j] \qquad \text{from equation (18.20)}$$

$$\Rightarrow A_j = E[L_j \mid L > A] - \frac{\delta \, E[L_j]}{\Pr[L > A]},$$

$$E\left[L_j \mid L > A\right] \approx \frac{1}{m} \sum_{k=N-m+1}^{N} L_{(k,j)}$$

$$\Rightarrow A_j \approx \frac{1}{m} \left(\sum_{k=N-m+1}^{N} L_{(k,j)} - N\delta \, E[L_j] \right).$$

To illustrate the Myers–Read allocation, we have used the three line insurance example from previous sections. The liabilities are separated from the technical provision, as all the assets are collected together in A. The liability random variables for Lines 1–3 are then $L_1 \sim N(100, 20^2)$, $L_2 \sim \log N(4, 1)$, and $L_3 \sim \text{Pareto}(4, 300)$. We assume that the assets are equal to the technical provision $(105 + 120 + 130 = 355)$ plus the aggregate economic capital, 622. We ignore interest and assume asset values are fixed, so that $A = 977$. The simulated default value per unit of liability was $\delta = 0.0238$. The probability of default was estimated at 1.576%. The resulting asset allocation, and capital allocation (subtracting the technical provision for each line) are shown in Table 18.5.

Notice the negative asset and capital allocation to Line 1; this line is very thin tailed, and the diversification benefit is greater, under this measure, than its expected cost.

It is straightforward to adapt the practical implementation to allow for $r > 0$. If we allow for the asset value to be random, then we must use the $\mathbb{Q}$-measure expectation to determine δ.

The Myers–Read method is a forerunner of the co-CTE approach; basing the calculations only on the values of $L_{k,j}$ that contribute to the default cost generates an allocation method that captures some of the advantages of Euler allocation. A drawback is the lack of connection between the aggregate economic capital (which is assumed given) and the allocation method. Also, as we see from the example, the allocated capital may be negative, which indicates that it would not be helpful in providing a measure of manager performance.

18.6.2 Sherris Allocation

The Sherris (2006) allocation is similar to Myers–Read, but with the economic capital for the firm and the individual lines adjusted to allow for the value of the default option before allocation of assets.

As in the Myers–Read case, the time 0 value of the default option is

$$D = \mathrm{E}^{Q}\left[e^{-r}(L - A)^{+}\right].$$

This option value is allocated to the jth line of business as

$$D_j = \mathrm{E}^{Q}\left[e^{-r}\left(L_j - A\frac{L_j}{L}\right)^{+}\right]$$

$$= \mathrm{E}^{Q}\left[e^{-r}L_j\left(1 - \frac{A}{L}\right)\Big| L > A\right]\Pr[L > A].$$

This assumes that, for the purpose of the default option value, the assets are allocated in proportion to the liabilities; the justification for this is that all policyholders in all lines of business will be equally ranked in the event of a default, which means that the assets will be distributed in proportion to the liabilities.

Under Sherris' construction, the time 0 value of the liabilities is $V_L - D$, where V_L is the discounted expected value. Let $V_{L^*} = V_L - D$ denote the time 0 value of the liabilities net of the default option. Then the insurer's available economic capital is $EC = V_A - V_{L^*} = V_A - V_L + D$. The default-adjusted value of the liabilities for Line j is

$$V_{L_j^*} = V_{L_j} - D_j,$$

and the allocated economic capital for Line j is

$$EC_j = \alpha_j V_A - V_{L_j^*} = \alpha_j V_A - V_{L_j} + D_j, \quad \text{for some } \alpha_j \text{ with } \sum_{j=1}^{d} \alpha_j = 1.$$

Sherris offers two approaches to determine α_j. The first is to allocate capital such that the solvency ratio, $s = (\alpha_j V_A - V_{L_j})/V_{L_j}$ is the same for all lines and for the firm as a whole. That is,

$$s = \frac{V_A - V_L}{V_L} = \frac{\alpha_j V_A - V_{L_j}}{V_{L_j}} \Rightarrow \alpha_j = \frac{(1 + s)V_{L_j}}{V_A}.$$

The second method is to allocate capital such that the expected return on allocated capital is the same for all lines and for the firm as a whole, allowing for the default option. That is, the (prospective) RAROC for each line and for the whole firm is R where

$$R = \mathrm{E}^P\left[\frac{(A - L)^+}{EC}\right] = \mathrm{E}^P\left[\frac{(\alpha_j A - L_j)\,\mathbf{1}_{\{A > L\}}}{EC_j}\right]$$

$$= \mathrm{E}^P\left[\frac{(\alpha_j A - L_j)\,\mathbf{1}_{\{A > L\}}}{\alpha_j V_A - L_j + D_j}\right],$$

where $\mathbf{1}$ is the indicator function, $\mathbf{1}_{A > L} = \begin{cases} 1 & \text{if } A > L, \\ 0 & \text{if } A \le L. \end{cases}$

The key point about the Sherris allocation is that the economic capital for the firm and for the individual lines is determined taking the default option into account, explicitly, before allocating the capital.

18.6.3 Kim–Hardy Allocation

Kim and Hardy (2009) work from the same starting point as Sherris (2006), but with a different perspective; the default valuation is in the real-world measure, unlike the Sherris default, on the basis that economic capital is not a pricing measure, it is a real-world risk measure. As with the Sherris and Myers–Read methods, we consider a one-year horizon, assuming all premiums are received at the start of the year, and all claims are paid at the end of the year.

We explicitly take into consideration the premium for each line. Let L_j represent the liability for line j, and let P_j represent the premium received at the start of the year. As before, $L = L_1 + L_2 + \cdots L_d$ and the total premium income at time 0 is $P = P_1 + P_2 + \cdots P_d$ for a company with d lines. The premium is assumed to be invested in risky assets, with log-return R over the course of the year.

The aggregate economic capital at time 0 is EC, assumed determined using an appropriate risk measure, $\rho(L) - P$. The EC is assumed to be invested in risk-free assets, earning a risk-free rate of return of r.

The total asset value at the end of the year, before paying claims then due is
$A = EC\, e^r + Pe^R$.

The year end deficit is

$$(L - A)^+ = (L - EC\, e^r - Pe^R)^+ \tag{18.21}$$

with expected value $\mathrm{E}[e^{-r}(L - A)^+] = \mathrm{E}[e^{-r}(L - EC\, e^r - Pe^R)^+]$.
$$\tag{18.22}$$

We assign the expected deficit for unit j, similarly to the Sherris case, except in $\mathbb{P}$-measure. Based on the LHS of equation (18.22), we have

$$D_j = \mathrm{E}\left[e^{-r}L_j\left(1 - \frac{A}{L}\right)\,\middle|\, L > A\right]\Pr[L > A].$$

Similarly, from the RHS, we have

$$D_j = e^{-r}\Pr[L > A]\,\mathrm{E}\left[L_j - EC_j e^r - P_j e^R\right].$$

Equating the two expressions, we can solve for the economic capital allocation, EC_j as

$$EC_j = e^{-r}\mathrm{E}\left[A(L_j/L)\,|\, L > A\right] - \mathrm{E}\left[P_j e^R\,|\, L > A\right]$$

$$= e^{-r}\mathrm{E}\left[A(L_j/L) - P_j e^R\,|\, L > A\right].$$

The advantage of this allocation is that it can be decomposed into separate parts, depending on the purpose of the capital allocation exercise.

Decomposition 1

$$EC_j = (EC)\,\mathrm{E}\left[\frac{L_j}{L}\,\middle|\, L > A\right] + e^{-r}\mathrm{E}\left[e^R\left(P\frac{L_j}{L} - P_j\right)\,\middle|\, L > A\right].$$

In this expression, the first term allocates the liability risk; the total across all units is EC. The second term allocates risk of reserve inadequacy and investment. The sum over all units will be zero; some units will have negative contribution, and some positive. The advantage of this decomposition is that the liability risk has been separated from the reserve adequacy and investment risk – and further decompositions allow for the segregation of reserve and investment risk.

Decomposition 2

$$EC_j = e^{-r}\mathrm{E}\left[L_j - P_j e^R\,|\, L > A\right] - e^{-r}\mathrm{E}\left[L_j\left(1 - \frac{A}{L}\right)\,\middle|\, L > A\right],$$

$$EC_j = e^{-r}\mathrm{E}\left[L_j - P_j e^R\,|\, L > A\right] - D_j.$$

Under this decomposition, the first term provides capital to compensate for low premiums, relative to claims, or low return on premiums. The second term reduces the capital requirement in recognition of the limited liability on default.

If we add and subtract $E[L_j]$ and $P_j E[e^R]$ to the decomposition above, we have

$$EC_j = e^{-r}\left(E[L_j|L > A] - E[L_j]\right) + P_j e^{-r}\left(E[e^R] - E[e^R \mid L > A]\right)$$
$$- e^{-r}\left(P_j E[e^R] - E[L_j]\right) - D_j.$$

The first term on the RHS measures the capital required in respect of the contribution of Line j to the tail scenarios. The second term measures the capital required to protect against poor investment performance. The third term allows for a reduction in capital in recognition of the premium loading, that is, the difference between the premium and the expected cost, and the fourth term allows for a reduction in capital due to the limited liability on default.

Decomposition 3

$$EC_j = e^{-r}\left(LM_j + IM_j + RM_j - D_j\right) \quad \text{where}$$
$$LM_j = E\left[L_j \mid L_j > \rho(L_j)\right] - P_j e^r,$$
$$IM_j = P_j\left(e^r - E\left[e^R \mid e^R < -\rho(-e^R)\right]\right),$$
$$RM_j = E[L_j|L > A] - E[L_j|L_j > \rho(L_j)]$$
$$+ P_j\left(E[e^R \mid e^R < -\rho(-e^R)] - E[e^R|L > A]\right).$$

In this decomposition, we have separated the allocated capital according to the separate functions and processes that contribute to default.

The line manager for insurance line j is allocated LM_j. This is the Line j stand-alone risk measure of liabilities, minus the premiums – a bottom-up EC allocation based on excess costs over the ρ risk measure. We condition on $L_j > \rho(L_j)$, rather than $L > A$, because the team responsible for insurance Line j should be judged by how they perform on a stand-alone basis; they should not get credit for diversification arising from other lines. Similarly, we assume here that the premium earns the risk-free rate; any risk associated with the return on assets, R, belongs with the investment manager, not the line manager.

The investment manager is allocated

$$IM = \sum_{j=1}^{d} IM_j = P\left(e^r - E\left[e^R \mid e^R < -\rho\left(-e^R\right)\right]\right).$$

Each IM_j indicates the contribution to the investment manager's risk capital generated by Line j. The negative signs in $-\rho(-e^R)$ are there because for the asset return the worst case scenario is low-side not high-side. The capital allocated to the investment manager reflects the shortfall in return on invested premiums in extreme scenarios, compared with the risk-free rate.

The risk manager is allocated

$$RM = \sum_{j=1}^{d} RM_j$$

$$= \left(E[L|L > A] - \sum_{j=1}^{d} E[L_j|L_j > \rho(L_j)] \right)$$

$$+ P\left(E[e^R | e^R < -\rho(-e^R)] - E[e^R|L > A] \right).$$

This value is expected to be negative, representing the reduction in capital required due to diversification. It is possible for some values to be positive, signalling a concentration of risk. The risk manager can use the individual RM_j values to monitor the diversification benefit offered by each line, while the sum gives the total diversification benefit across all the lines.

The Kim–Hardy allocation method satisfies the full allocation, symmetry, and consistency criteria, but does not satisfy the no undercut criterion.

18.7 Using RAROC and Capital Allocation

One reason for the wide variety of capital allocation methods is that the resulting RAROC calculations are used for a number of different purposes, and an allocation that is most suitable, for example, for determining the cost of capital to be incorporated in pricing, or for risk budgeting, might be very different from the allocation that is most suitable for assessing the performance of the unit managers. Baer et al. (2011) suggest that the RAROC should be one of a package of performance indicators, and that where the allocated capital diverges significantly from the regulatory capital, the value of the RAROC diminishes.

As the RAROC reflects risk-adjusted returns, it is a useful indicator for performance based compensation. However, for salary based incentives to be effective, the measures used must be perceived by the employees to be fair, and should reward performance that is within the control of the individuals, not for factors from outside their domain. Suppose that two business units, Unit j and Unit k have identical stand-alone risks and performance, but because it offers a superior diversification benefit to the firm, the economic capital allocated to Unit j is less than the economic capital allocated to Unit k. The result is that the RAROC of Unit j is better than the RAROC of Unit k. Is it reasonable to offer a higher performance bonus to the manager of Unit j than to the manager of Unit k? Since, based on their responsibilities, their performance was identical, it does not seem appropriate. However, the higher RAROC of Unit j *would* be a reasonable consideration in determining where to expand the business. For performance pay, a bottom-up approach might be more suitable than the top-down approach. For risk budgeting, the top-down approach must be used. We should use different economic capital allocation approaches based on the different objectives of the allocation.

The Myers–Read and Sherris allocation methods are both based on the $\mathbb{Q}$-measure default cost, and were initially developed to give capital costs for pricing purposes; they are not designed for measuring manager performance. The Kim–Hardy method is designed to bridge the risk measure based allocations and the default cost allocations, and is also constructed with the view that different decompositions can be used for different purposes.

All of the capital allocation approaches assume that the distributions of the losses for sub-units of the firm are known. Where a unit appears to offer a consistently superior RAROC, it may be because the capital allocated is actually too low. The high RAROC then creates incentive to expand that line, creating a vicious circle of overstated performance and understated economic capital. The assumptions and distributions used in allocating capital need to be re-validated frequently. Consistent out-performance of prospective RAROC should be treated as a matter of concern, not necessarily as a measure of success. The other part of the RAROC calculation that requires regular review is the expected income. If the firm estimates its expected income by averaging experience over recent history, the results may be biased in periods of economic change. This can be particularly problematic when impacted by market bubbles or crashes.

18.8 Further Reading

The technical results on Euler allocation are covered more rigorously, and more comprehensively, in McNeil et al. (2015).

The symmetry and no-undercut axioms were proposed in Denault (2001), who also examines the allocation problem from a game theoretic perspective.

The simulation results in this chapter were calculated using the 'copula' package in R (Hofert et al., 2020).

18.9 Exercises

Exercise 18.1 You are given the following information for a project:

Expected revenue:	$35 million
Return on risk capital:	7%
Economic capital:	$73 million
Tax expense:	40% of net income
Operating cost:	$13 million

What is the RAROC for the project?

Exercise 18.2 You are given the following information for Example 18.2.

$$\text{Var}[X] = 221.7^2, \quad \text{Cov}(X_1, X) = 1{,}751,$$
$$\text{Cov}(X_2, X) = 20{,}401, \quad \text{Cov}(X_3, X) = 27{,}016.$$

Assume $k = 2.0$.

(a) Calculate the aggregate economic capital and the capital allocation to each line using the covariance allocation method.
(b) Calculate the diversification benefit, by line and in total.

Exercise 18.3 One criterion proposed for an economic capital allocation method is that if $\rho(X_i) > 0$, then $EC_i > 0$.

Identify which of the methods listed satisfy this criterion. Assume that the aggregate economic capital is greater than zero.

(a) Proportional
(b) Shapley
(c) Covariance
(d) Co-CTE

Exercise 18.4

(a) Prove that the co-VaR allocation method is (i) symmetric and (ii) consistent.
(b) Prove that the co-VaR allocation method does not satisfy the no undercut criterion.

Exercise 18.5 A company operates two lines of business. The capital and income information for the most recent year of operations is given in the following table. The aggregate economic capital for the business is 72.

	Line A	Line B
Undiversified capital for:		
Credit risk	5	15
Equity risk	30	6
Operational risk	19	17
Total undiversified capital	54	38
Expected net income	11.0	9.0
Actual net income	8.5	8.0

(a) Calculate the overall RAROC for the firm, using (i) the expected income and (ii) the actual income.

(b) Calculate the RAROC for each line, based on their stand-alone capital, using (i) the expected income and (ii) the actual income.

(c) Using the proportional allocation approach, calculate the RAROC for each line, using (i) the expected income and (ii) the actual income.

(d) Using the Shapley allocation, calculate the RAROC for each line, using (i) the expected income and (ii) the actual income.

(e) Discuss which of these values might be most suited to deciding on strategic allocation of risk capital.

(f) Performance pay awards for line managers require them to earn a RAROC of greater than 20%. Discuss which RAROC figure (from parts (b), (c), (d)) might be most suitable for this purpose.

(g) The firm purchases a new company which will operate as a separate line of business, Line C. You are given the following information:

	Line C
Undiversified capital for:	
Credit risk	14
Equity risk	20
Operational risk	10
Total undiversified capital	44
Expected net income	6.0
Actual net income	4.0

The impact of the new line on the aggregate economic capital is an increase to 84.

Explain why the firm might purchase Line C, despite its poor RAROC.

(h) Calculate the Shapley allocation, given that the economic capital for Lines A and C jointly is 62, and for Lines B and C jointly is 50. Comment on the impact this has made on the RAROCs of Lines A and B, compared with the Shapley allocation in (d).

Exercise 18.6 Some analysts have proposed the following two additional desirable characteristics of economic capital allocation methods, using the notation of this chapter:

- $EC_i \geq E[X_i]$.
- If X_i is constant, say, $X_i = c$, then $EC_i = c$.

(a) Explain why these are desirable characteristics.
(b) Explain whether the co-CTE method has these characteristics.
(c) Consider a firm with d business units. The economic capital allocation formula for any subset $\mathcal{K} \subseteq \{1, 2, \ldots, d\}$ of the firm is

$$EC_\mathcal{K} = \frac{E[X_\mathcal{K} X]}{E[X]}.$$

Show that this is equivalent to the covariance allocation, and state whether it satisfies the two additional criteria of this question.

Exercise 18.7 You are a risk manager in a bank. Your CEO has decided that maintaining any capital in excess of the regulatory minimum is unnecessary. Outline the points that you would make supporting or opposing this view.

Exercise 18.8 An insurer has two lines of business. All policies run for one year. Premiums are paid at time 0 and claims are paid at time 1. You are given the following information:

- The distributions of claims for the two lines are $L_1 \sim \log N(5, 2)$ and $L_2 \sim \log N(2.5, 3)$.
- The premium received for both lines is $P_1 = P_2 = 1{,}200$.
- The risk-free rate of interest is $r = 0.03$.
- Premiums are invested to earn interest at rate R, compounded continuously, where $R \sim N(0.06, 0.18^2)$.
- The dependency structure for L_1, L_2, R is modelled using a Gaussian copula $C(U, V, W)$, where

$$U = F_{L_1}(L_1), \quad V = F_{L_2}(L_2), \quad W = 1 - F_R(R),$$
$$\rho_{UV} = 0.8; \quad \rho_{UW} = \rho_{VW} = 0.2.$$

- The economic capital for the insurer is calculated using a 98% Expected Shortfall. There is no additional available capital.

  (a) Using R, simulate 100,000 values for L_1, L_2, and R. Use your simulations to estimate the economic capital for the insurer.
  (b) Calculate the allocation of capital using the Myers–Read method. Use $\mathbb{P}$-measure expectations.
  (c) Calculate the allocation of capital using the Sherris method. Use $\mathbb{P}$-measure expectations.
  (d) Calculate the allocation of capital using the Kim–Hardy method. Identify the individual components, LM_1, LM_2, IM, RM, and D, assuming the stand-alone capital $\rho(L_j)$ is the 98% Expected Shortfall measure.

19

Behavioural Risk Management

19.1 Summary

In this chapter, we discuss some of the common psychological or behavioural factors that influence risk analysis and risk management. We give examples of cases where behavioural biases created a risk management failure, and some ways in which the negative impact of biases can be mitigated. Biases are categorized, loosely, as relating to (i) self-deception, (ii) information processing (both forms of cognitive bias), and (iii) social bias, which relates to the pressures created by social norms and expectations. We provide examples of a range of common behavioural biases in risk management, and we briefly describe some strategies for overcoming the distortions created by behavioural factors in decision-making. Next, we present the foundational concepts of Cumulative Prospect Theory, which provides a mathematical framework for decision-making that reflects some universal cognitive biases.

19.2 Introduction

Economic models of human behaviour have been dominated for many years by utility theory, which assumes that individuals operate with an implicit, subconscious utility function, $u(w)$ that determines their attitude to wealth (w) and to financial risk. As all individuals are assumed to prefer more wealth to less, the utility function is assumed to be increasing, that is $u'(w) > 0$. Individuals are categorized as **risk-averse**, indicating those who prefer certainty to uncertainty, or **risk-seeking** indicating those who prefer uncertainty to certainty. We rarely concern ourselves with risk seekers (it is assumed they are off gambling somewhere, beyond the reach of neoclassical economics).

We model risk aversion through a diminishing marginal utility of wealth, that is $u''(w) < 0$. This means that the utility of an additional $\$x$ is greater for a person with little wealth than it is for a person with great wealth. If $u''(w) = 0$ then the agent is **risk-neutral**. It is generally assumed in neo-classical economics that corporations are risk-neutral, but that assumption is complicated by the fact that the decision-makers within the corporations are usually risk-averse.

Under expected utility theory, an individual, faced with a choice between strategies involving uncertain outcomes, will select the strategy that provides a higher expected utility of wealth, and will be indifferent between strategies which have the same expected utility. For risk-averse individuals, this means that a certain loss (or gain) is preferred over an uncertain loss (or gain) with the same expected value.

While expected utility is still widely applied in theoretical work, it has become clear that it does not adequately describe human behaviour. People are much more complex, contradictory, and irrational than implied by utility theory, and even the most rational person's choices will diverge from the choices implied by utility theory in some circumstances. Decisions are influenced by psychological biases, by social dynamics, and by the time available to process the background information. Everyone uses shortcuts in making decisions; it is not possible for anyone to scientifically assess all the evidence every time they make a decision. The effect of these constraints on people's ability to make strictly optimal analytic decisions is referred to as **bounded rationality**, and the shortcuts are called **heuristics**. For most decisions the heuristics that we develop are adequate and efficient, but the way that these heuristics are learned and used can lead to behavioural biases, such as oversimplifying complex situations, or failing to pay attention to key information. It is important to understand and anticipate these biases, particularly where they may impede the risk management systems of the organization.

19.3 Bias and Decision-Making

The biases that impact all the decisions we make can be classified into two categories:

Cognitive Bias refers to systematic errors in processing information. The decision-maker believes that they have made a rational decision, suitably weighing all the available information, but actually the decision is flawed. We can further divide the cognitive bias category down into biases related to self-deception, and biases relating to errors in processing information, or heuristic simplification, although the categorization is not completely clear cut.

Social bias refers to a distortion of an individual's decision processing caused by psychosocial factors.

We describe some of the biases that are relevant to risk management below. It is important to understand that these are not errors made solely by stupid people; these are biases to which we may all be susceptible, to varying degrees, regardless of our cultural background, gender, or level of education.

19.3.1 Self-Deception Biases

Overprecision Bias

It is very common that individuals have more confidence in their judgement than is justified objectively. To illustrate this, try answering the questions in the box below. You should write down your best estimate answer (even if you have no real idea), and then write down low and high bounds for each answer, such that you are 90% confident that the true answer lies within the interval.

---

(1) What is the population of Nigeria, in millions?
(2) What was the average number of planes in the air at any moment in 2016?
(3) How many islands make up the nation of Japan?
(4) What is the distance between Buenos Aires and Rio de Janeiro, by road?
(5) What was the year of birth of the mathematician, Carl Friedrich Gauss?
(6) For how many years did the Great Ming dynasty of China last?
(7) What is the length of the Beatles song 'Yesterday', in seconds?
(8) What is the height of the Empire State Building?
(9) What is the depth of the world's deepest lake?
(10) What is the ratio of the volume of the earth to the volume of the moon?

The correct answers are given in Section 19.6.1; count how many lie within your lower and upper bounds. If your bounds contained the true answer for eight or more of the questions – well done! You are an anomaly. More commonly, people tend to set adequate bounds for only around 4 to 6 questions. If people were good at assessing uncertainty, the number should average 9 out of 10, since we asked for a 90% confidence interval. Even people who know about overprecision bias are overprecise – knowing that the bias exists provides little help in overcoming the bias.

Overprecision is relevant to risk assessment. Whenever we have to manage a risk that cannot be objectively quantified, we rely on subjective judgement to assess risks or to set scenarios to assess the risk. Suppose a firm is assessing a risk by asking stakeholders to estimate the 10% worst-case outcome of the strategy under consideration. It is very unlikely that this assessment will be accurate, because of overprecision bias. This is especially true if the stakeholders have a firm belief that the strategy should be adopted, and/or if they have ownership of the project.

Overconfidence Bias

While humans have evolved to be pretty smart, many of us have also evolved to believe ourselves even smarter than we are. Overconfidence bias is sometimes called the illusion of knowledge, and it emerges in two different ways: overestimation bias and overplacement bias.

Overestimation bias applies where individuals believe their ability is better than it is, objectively. **Overplacement bias** applies where an individual believes, without foundation, that he or she is better than those around them (overestimates their placement), typically underestimating the ability of their colleagues or peer group. Most individuals consider that they are better than average drivers, that they are more ethical than others, that they have a better sense of humour. If a class of undergraduates is asked at the start of a semester what decile they expect to be in after the final exam, typically over 90% expect to be in the top 40%.

Overprecision is often included in the overconfidence category, but there is an important difference. While overprecision bias appears a very common human phenomenon, overestimation and overplacement bias are not universal. In the corporate setting, the opposite bias, where individuals underestimate themselves and overestimate their peers is also common. This is known as the **imposter syndrome**.

Extreme overconfidence bias is associated with narcissistic personality traits (Macenczak et al., 2016), and when highly narcissistic people achieve positions of power, their overconfidence increases. This is particularly risky, as overconfident decision-makers can exacerbate risks and tend to undervalue risk management. They may err in not taking adequate account of empirical evidence, believing that their subjective instinct is more reliable than objective data. They may fail to prepare adequately for meetings or negotiations. In particular, people with narcissistic personalities tend to have a fragile self-belief, which they manage by not listening to experts or advisors (having someone more knowledgeable than themselves in a conversation is too challenging), by not acknowledging any criticism or disagreement, and by not accepting responsibility for their own errors or failures.

Overconfidence bias may persuade individuals to take positions for which they are not qualified. Once in position, they tend to reinforce their sense of placement by eliminating competent advisors, and over-promoting less competent individuals, in order to maintain their sense of being the smartest person in the room. This can lead to disastrous outcomes, both in business and in politics. Overconfidence and overplacement bias is a remarkably common feature of risk management failures. McQueen (1996) tells the story of Confederation Life, which was forced into liquidation in 1994, after appointing a marketing executive as its CEO and Chair. The new CEO was not interested in hearing about actuarial analysis or asset-liability risk management. Despite warnings, he pursued an aggressive expansion plan that did not recognize the complex nature of the underlying risks. He replaced qualified and experienced employees with less qualified supporters. The CEO's determination to build the most grandiose company headquarters, the 'Taj Mahal' of Canadian architecture, is consistent with a narcissist's need for overt, grandiose symbols of success.

Studies of CEOs have identified that they are disproportionately likely to display overconfidence, and that this is exacerbated by large compensation packages, and by corporate structures that encourage deference to the CEO.

Self-Attribution Bias

While overconfidence bias relates to an illusion of knowledge, **self-attribution bias** relates to an illusion of control. It persuades individuals that their successes are explained by their innate ability, while their failures are bad luck or bad faith. When combined with overestimation bias, the individual will be resistant to risk management processes, believing that their ability will lead to success, that 'nothing bad can happen to me', so that any failures are unforeseeable or impossible. When crisis events take place, they are typically unwilling to take responsibility, and may try to shift blame or deny the situation.

Optimism Bias

Optimism bias causes individuals to underestimate the likelihood of an adverse event. It also means that low probability-high severity events are not seen as needing as much risk management as higher probability-lower severity events. A regulator may ask a firm to base their regulatory capital on a 99% VaR, but if the firm takes an over-optimistic view, for example, that the 1%

worst-case is essentially impossible, then they are more likely to try to game the system to avoid meeting the capital requirement. Optimism bias is a very common phenomenon.

Hindsight Bias

'I knew it all along' is the tag line of **hindsight bias**. It is the tendency of people to take credit, after the event, for predicting that event, even if they did not, and even if the event was essentially unpredictable. In risk management, the problems with hindsight bias are (i) hindsight bias adds to overconfidence – if the manager is persuaded that she or he predicted the adverse event, then it boosts their already exaggerated self-belief, and (ii) hindsight bias diminishes the opportunity to learn from adverse events.

Outcome Bias

Outcome bias is the tendency to judge a strategy by the outcome, rather than judge it objectively. Suppose, for example, an insurer issues a large number of policies with embedded, out-of-the-money put options, for which it charges fees, but which it does not hedge (because of optimism bias). For the first few tranches the options expire worthless, and the insurer pockets the option fees. A review of this strategy, using outcome bias, says that since it went so well, it must be a good strategy. It ignores the fact that, *ex ante*, the strategy was extremely risky.

Outcome bias can be part of a slippery slope of unethical or unlawful behaviour. A firm gets away with a small unethical act, and finds that no bad outcome ensues. The management may then become emboldened to double down on the strategy. Or, an individual who cheats on a test and does not get caught is very likely to continue to cheat on tests.

Outcome bias is different from hindsight bias; hindsight is the exaggerated assessment of the individual's ability to predict an outcome. Outcome bias is the irrational influence of the outcome on the assessment of the strategy.

19.3.2 Information Processing Biases

Confirmation Bias

Unlike some of the other biases listed, **confirmation bias** seems to be a universal human phenomenon. It is the tendency to ignore or downplay information that is contradictory to a previously held view, and to assign extra weight to information that supports the prior view.

In a famous experiment, psychologists at Stanford conducted a study in which participants were selected based on their views on capital punishment, with 50% being in favour and 50% opposed. Each participant was asked to read two studies, one of which concluded that capital punishment was a successful deterrent, and the other concluding that it was not. Both studies were fictional. Ultimately, supporters of both sides were convinced that the studies, taken as a whole, supported their prior position, finding often spurious reasons to downplay the evidence against their position.

Confirmation bias can be surprisingly persistent, with individuals holding on to wrong beliefs even when faced with evidence conclusively proving them to be false. The persistence appears to be strongest when the individual has taken a public position on an issue, creating an anchoring effect. So, for example, an individual who has stated their support for a particular politician will tend to ignore all the evidence that the politician is incompetent or worse. A person who preferred the candidate privately is more likely to be swayed by the evidence. Interestingly, when a politician is publicly disgraced, the supporter may transfer their allegiance, but is unlikely to admit to changing their mind. Instead, they persuade themselves that they were never such a big supporter in the first place.

Confirmation bias is very relevant to risk management in a number of ways. It supports the overconfident manager in their beliefs, as they discount any evidence of their lack of competence. Decision-makers may read a risk report, and only process the parts that are favourable, ignoring areas where the risk exceeds preset thresholds, or where active risk management needs to be ramped up.

A classic example of confirmation bias contributing to a crisis event is the Challenger disaster. Challenger was a NASA space shuttle which, in 1986, on its tenth flight, broke apart soon after launch, killing all seven crew. The physical cause of the disaster was the failure of an O-ring seal, which could not handle the unusually cold conditions at the launch. However, behind that explanation is a much longer story. It emerged that O-ring failures had occurred on a number of earlier flights, and engineers had become concerned about the risk of catastrophic failure, though managers remained unconvinced of the risks (outcome bias). Immediately before the scheduled launch in January 1986, the engineers recommended postponing the launch, but their information was misinterpreted by the managers, who had a strong incentive to proceed. It is reasonable to suppose that confirmation bias affected the managers' reading of the engineering report.

Framing Bias

The decisions we make are impacted by the frame in which choices are presented. In general, framing a choice in terms of a positive outcome is more likely to achieve agreement than framing it in terms of a negative outcome. Very many decisions can be framed in either a positive or negative light. For example, suppose a firm is considering buying business interruption cover, which provides funds to replace lost earnings if the company has suffered a catastrophic event. If we frame the option to buy insurance positively, we focus on the income provided if the insured event occurs. If we frame negatively, we focus on the potential bad outcomes if the insurance is not purchased. The positive frame is more likely to be persuasive than the negative.

Even the decision to adopt an enterprise risk management (ERM) process is impacted by framing. If ERM is presented by outlining the potential harms of not adopting it, it is less likely to be embraced than if it is presented in the positive light, as a strategy to make better decisions, mitigate downside risk and enhance long-term value.

Classic experiments illustrating **framing bias** were developed by Tversky and Kahneman (1981). In the first, they asked participants in an experiment to consider a situation where 600 people were expected to die from a deadly disease. Participants were then given information about two alternative programs that had been developed to combat the disease. Half the participants were presented with the alternatives which emphasized the different number of lives saved (the 'positive frame') and the other half were shown the same information, but with an emphasis on the number of deaths ('the negative frame').

Positive Frame	Negative Frame
Program A 200 people will be saved.	Program A 400 people will die.
Program B With probability 1/3, all will be saved With probability 2/3, none will be saved.	Program B With probability 2/3, all will die With probability 1/3, all will be saved.

Tversky and Kahnemann found that when the case is framed positively, 72% of participants favoured Program A, but when it is framed negatively, only 22% of participants favoured Program A. The results confirmed other experiments that indicated that individuals are risk-averse with respect to gains, preferring certainty to uncertainty, but risk seeking with respect to losses, preferring to take a chance that the outcome will be better, rather than accept a certain loss, and that these preferences apply even when the losses and gains are actually different expressions of the same outcome.

Framing bias can be exploited; to be more persuasive, emphasize the gains not the losses associated with an outcome. But, if the decision-maker is overly influenced by the initial frame, framing bias can lead to sub-optimal decisions. It can be very useful when given information to try to reframe it to see if the decision changes.

Anchoring Bias

Anchoring bias is a surprisingly widespread and powerful bias, where an individual's decision is overly influenced by an initial piece of information. The bias is persistent even when the decision-maker is aware of the potential for anchoring, and even when the initial information has little or no value. If you are negotiating a price, the initial offer will be a powerful anchor for the outcome.

The anchor does not need to be quantitative; a first impression, for example, of a person's ability, or a new strategic risk or opportunity, can anchor the subsequent decision-making. A doctor whose first impression of a patient is that they might be faking symptoms to access painkillers, is likely to misdiagnose the patient, even if they run tests indicating other more likely diagnoses (confirmation bias). A manager whose first impression of a new hire is unfavourable is likely to undervalue the employee's positive contributions and exaggerate their shortcomings.

Conservatism bias is a subcategory of anchoring bias, and also relates to confirmation bias. It refers to the reluctance of people to fully update their beliefs in the light of new information. So an investor who has researched a firm and decided that it represents a good value-investment may not update that view when negative information emerges, or may be slow to update the positive forecast.

Availability Bias

When individuals are assessing a situation, such as the chance of a plane crashing, or of a lottery win, their assessment is heavily influenced by how easily such events come to mind; we call this **availability bias**. If we see lottery winners celebrating their good fortune every week on television, we are inclined to think that maybe winning the lottery is relatively common.

Because rare events tend to create more news coverage, they are seen as being less rare than they are.

The other side of availability bias is the underestimation of the risk of events which are not well-known nor publicized. People underestimate the risk of injury from car accidents, for example, not because they are rare, but because they are so common that they are not covered in the media. We also underestimate the risk of events that have not happened, but could, or of events that have happened, but long ago.

An example from actuarial risk management is provided by the Equitable Life (UK) case described in Chapter 7. In the 1970s and 1980s, Equitable Life issued a large number of contracts that would only cost them money if interest rates fell below around 5.5%. At the time of issue long-term interest rates were well above 10%, and the actuaries did not consider any possibility that rates could fall so dramatically. But for most of the 250 years up to 1970, rates had been well below 5.5%. The availability bias led the actuaries to focus on the most recent history, of less than 10 years, even though the guarantees being written had terms exceeding 20 years. This is an example of **recency bias**, where we see decisions being made based on the individual's own life experience. A young actuary, who reached adulthood after 2008, will likely have a fairly pessimistic outlook on financial markets based on the post-financial crisis experience, which is characterized by high volatility, low average returns, and very low interest rates. An older actuary, who was around for the boom times of the 1990s might have a more optimistic view of long-term returns, as their 'normal' includes the bull market of the 1990s.

Another example of availability bias is represented by the Deepwater Horizon disaster. Because the company had not seen such a catastrophic blowout in the past, they significantly underestimated the risk that it could happen, although the conditions of the Deepwater Horizon platform were significantly more challenging than previous drilling operations. A rational analysis should have concluded that more extreme failure was a possibility. Availability bias makes it more difficult for risk managers to assess very rare risks that have not been in the news or otherwise touched their own experience.

Representativeness Bias

Representativeness bias refers to the tendency of individuals to base assessments about, say, event A by its similarity to a known event B. Perhaps event B is a stereotype, so if event A is similar to event B, representativeness bias pushes us to assume that the probability and/or impact of event A is similar to event B, even when that belief is irrational. For example, when asked which is more likely, a major electricity supply failure in Quebec, Canada, or an ice storm causing a major electricity supply failure in Quebec, many people will respond that the ice storm is more likely, as they have heard that Quebec suffers ice storms fairly regularly (and so representativeness bias is connected to availability bias). In fact, as event A (electricity supply failure) contains event B (ice storm and electricity supply failure), it cannot be less probable.

Representativeness bias can lead to the false 'law of small numbers', where small samples are expected to behave like large samples. We know from the law of large numbers that the aggregate experience of a large number of independent trials will tend to its expectation. So, over a large number of tosses of a fair coin, the proportion of heads will be close to 50%. However, if we only have a small number of trials, the proportion could be a long way from 50%. Representativeness bias makes us believe that we will still have close to 50% heads even in small scale trials, thereby underestimating the probability of other outcomes. Many people seeing a run of, say, five tails in a row will be convinced that the next toss is more than 50% likely to be a head, in order that the sequence can be more representative. This is known as the **gambler's fallacy**. Similarly, even well-informed analysts have been known to insist during periods of low investment market returns that, during a prolonged bear market, there will be increasing pressure for a 'regression to the mean', where the mean is a product of their subjective belief.

19.3.3 Social Biases

Social biases are behavioural tendencies that are thought to derive from social instincts and pressures, such as the emotional reward received from being accepted as a member of a group, or the unhappiness that results from being excluded or alienated.

Groupthink

Groupthink is the phenomenon that individuals making a decision within a group context tend to place excessive value on conformity to a collective view or attitude. If members are expected to 'go along to get along', or are discouraged from 'rocking the boat', then it is likely that groupthink is affecting the decision-making. Under groupthink, individuals are discouraged from raising concerns and the group will resist considering more than one or two options, as more options means more opportunities to disagree. The result is that decisions are based on too little information, with inadequate consideration of potential risks or of alternative courses. Decisions tend to be very rigid, with too much confidence in the collective wisdom of the group, and too much reluctance to change course even if it appears that the strategy is flawed.

It is helpful to distinguish the concepts of **group cohesion** and **group conformity**. Cohesion refers to the ability of the group to work together towards a common goal. Conformity refers to the pressure within the group to support the collective decisions without dissent. Cohesion is a positive attribute of a group; lack of cohesion means that a group is not working well together. Conformity is a negative attribute; it is healthier for groups to consider diverse views and be open to robust discussion. When we consider how conformity and cohesion combine, we have the following four broad categories:

(1) **Low Cohesion, Low Conformity** – This group will tend to split into factions; decision-making will be impaired, with multiple sub-groups making different decisions, and with a tendency for decisions to be weak or ineffectual. Individual group members or factions will often become resentful and may withdraw from the decision process entirely.

(2) **Low Cohesion, High Conformity** – This group is dominated by an authority figure or clique who will not permit disagreement. Decisions are made, but without adequate analysis. This group is very susceptible to one form of groupthink, in which individuals are afraid to disagree, or the group leader ensures that new members do not have the knowledge or experience required to contribute meaningfully. Those who try to introduce counter-arguments to the prevailing view are excluded from decision-making, and may be dismissed from the group.

(3) **High Cohesion, High Conformity** – This group is also at risk of groupthink. In this form, the group forms a single clique, where individuals do not want to disagree, because conformity engenders good feelings, like being at the cool kids' table in high school.

(4) **High Cohesion, Low Conformity** – This group will have vigorous but respectful discussions (if the discussions are not respectful, cohesion deteriorates), will be willing to consider a range of options, and will be flexible with respect to updating decisions and acknowledging errors. This type of group is likely to make the best evidence-based decisions.

It is common for groups to migrate from one category to another. In particular, a group in the High Cohesion, Low Conformity category, if kept together long enough, will tend to the High Cohesion, High Conformity category. This happens when the individual members form tighter friendship bonds, as a result of their group membership, making them increasingly less willing to present points that are in disagreement with others in the group.

An Example of Groupthink – The Oxford Union Crisis

To illustrate the potential negative consequences of groupthink, we review some decisions made during, and after, an incident at the Oxford Union in October/November 2019. The Oxford Union is a debating society established in 1823, which is technically independent of, but outwardly associated with, Oxford University. It has a long history as a place of prestige and privilege. Many of its past leaders have gone on to senior roles in politics, journalism, and public policy, including several Prime Ministers.

In October 2019, a blind Ghanaian graduate student, Ebenezer Azamati, was physically ejected from the Oxford Union debate hall for refusing to relinquish his seat, which he chose for its accessibility, there being no specific disability provisions in the chamber. The security staff who removed him were older, white, and physically imposing. Shortly after the debate, the Union's leadership team brought disciplinary charges against Azamati for 'violent misconduct', although video footage showed that he merely tried to hold onto the bench where he was sitting, whilst being grabbed, pushed, and pulled by individuals whom he could not see. A video of the incident became public, leading to widespread condemnation of the Union and its staff. After a few days, the Union withdrew the disciplinary charges, reinstated Azamati's membership, and issued a very weak apology.[1] For a week (a long time in a crisis), the Union's leadership was silent, while onlookers from inside and outside the Union grew increasingly outraged. Coverage extended to newspapers and social media around the world, to the obvious concern of Oxford University, whose reputation was being tarnished despite having virtually no control over the situation. Eventually, individual members of the Union initiated impeachment proceedings against the Union President, Brendan McGrath, that appeared highly likely to succeed. Forestalling the impeachment process, McGrath resigned and issued another weak apology. The ramifications continued with calls for the University to cut all ties with the Union, or for the Union to be disbanded entirely and replaced with a university-run debating society.

Throughout this unpleasant incident and its aftermath, the leadership team of the Union (known as the Standing Committee) seemed to make an astonishing number of bad decisions from start to finish. Why was the

---

[1] The apology was for 'the distress and any reputational damage which the publication of this charge may have caused [Azamati]'.

order given to manhandle a vulnerable black student, in plain sight of several hundred other students, with cell phones ready to record the incident? Why was that error compounded with the discipline hearing? Why did members of the leadership team not recognize the massive reputational damage that would ensue? Why, once the crisis became evident, did the leadership team double down, offering only non-apologies and unconvincing excuses for their inaction? And why did it take several weeks of increasingly heated criticism for the Standing Committee to take the situation seriously? The answers very likely lie in the impact of groupthink on the decisions of the leadership team.

Early work on groupthink was conducted by Irving Janis (1971), who proposed the following eight typical characteristics of groupthink. Each was illustrated with examples of flawed decisions taken by senior US government officials, including Presidents Kennedy and Johnson, relating to President Kennedy's decisions surrounding the Bay of Pigs invasion of Cuba and President Johnson's decision to escalate the Vietnam war. For a different type of illustration, we will use the Oxford Union incident to illustrate how groupthink might have contributed to that event.

(1) A shared illusion of **collective invulnerability**. The ability of the group to reach unchallenged decisions is seen as a sign of a superpower, rather than a danger sign (high conformity), and the decisions are seen as optimal and unchangeable, even as the ramifications indicate otherwise. In the Oxford Union case, we see the lack of timely response of the leadership team to the growing crisis as a sign that they did not believe that their position was assailable. Reports that officers of the Union were seen to be laughing about the incident are another strong indicator of groupthink; in fact, Janis specifically cites laughing at a danger signal as characteristic of the illusion of invulnerability.

(2) **Collective rationalization** refers to the ability of the group to rationalize their decision, to discount any challenges or questions, and even to discount clear evidence that a strategy is failing after it has been implemented. In the Oxford Union case, there was little effort made by the Union to explain its actions, but it appears that the initial rationale to eject Azamati arose from (i) a concern that he might not be a student (there are very few black students at Oxford University) and (ii) that he was sitting in a seat reserved for committee members. The leadership team's collective rationalization may have created the belief that these provided adequate justification for Azamati's violent removal and the humiliation of the adverse disciplinary hearing. More dispassionate

observers, not caught up in the headiness of groupthink, could see the large disconnect between the initial concerns and the subsequent actions.

In an open meeting following the initial burst of negative publicity, the leadership team criticized the press and social media posters, believing that a publicity campaign might solve the problem. Collective rationalization rendered them unable to evaluate whether the criticisms of the press, public, and fellow students might actually be valid.

(3) The group tends to believe that its cohesiveness, and its ability to make uncontested decisions, is proof of its **moral superiority**.

The Oxford Union leadership group seemed so sure that their actions were correct that they doubled down with the disciplinary case. The committee appointed to hear the case included colleagues and friends of the leadership team, and it was unsurprising that Azamati's account was dismissed.

It is notable that in his resignation letter, the Union president justified his actions by saying that in disciplining Azamati he was acting in obligation to the Union's security staff, because they were not empowered to represent themselves. Here, the president and the leadership team are signalling that they believe that they hold the moral high ground – prototypical groupthink behaviour. There remains no real indication that the leadership team ever understood why the vast majority of outside observers consider Azamati to be the victim, and the leadership team to be the perpetrators of injustice.

(4) Belief in a lack of morality of outside agents that are challenging the shared beliefs of the group. Janis refers to this as **stereotyping**. It can also be seen when groups create an 'us and them' dynamic, allowing them to discount the views of those outside the gang.

In the case of the Oxford Union, it seems likely that Azamati was stereotyped, as a black man who tried (verbally) to stand up for himself. The press was also vilified, with leadership team members claiming journalists had a vendetta against the Union. The point at which the Union slightly reversed course, withdrawing the discipline finding and reinstating membership, arose immediately after Helen Mountfield QC began to represent Azamati. As a senior academic within Oxford University, and as a renowned human rights lawyer, Professor Mountfield was harder for the leadership team to discount.

(5) Groupthink tends to result in **pressure to conform** being applied to group members who express doubts or challenge the unanimity of the group. The problem is that the benefits of groupthink are attractive. Almost everyone likes the feeling of invulnerability and moral superiority that

groupthink produces. Almost everyone is happier when they are an accepted member of a select team.

(6) Even without group pressure, individuals within the group are likely to **self-censor**. It is very difficult to be a dissenting voice amidst the collective self-certainty created by groupthink.

(7) It is common for groupthink decisions to be presented as unanimous, but **unanimity** is illusory if opposition views are suppressed through group pressure or self-censorship. If one or two group members become aware of the potential that a decision is wrong, there is a cognitive overload; what are the consequences of a wrong decision? How will the individual find the information required to make their own independent assessment of the decision? These are challenging and disturbing thoughts, so it is subconsciously tempting to just assume that since the whole group agrees on the course of action, it must be the right course of action. In some cases, including the Oxford Union example, some group members may be forced to re-evaluate the decisions, when the weight of public opinion and potential legal consequences become apparent.

(8) Sometimes members of the group are implicitly appointed as **mind-guards**, responsible for protecting the leaders from hearing dissenting views. This includes dissent from within the group. For example, the mind-guard might meet with a potential dissenter before a formal meeting, to persuade them not to raise their objections to the whole group. The mind-guard might offer an alternative opportunity to register disagreement, or suggest reasons why the dissent is inappropriate. The mind-guard also shields the group from external dissent. Perhaps letters of complaint or negative responses to group actions are not presented, or are presented in summary form with critical content removed.

The tendency to groupthink can be powerful, and the impact can be devastating. Within groups that manage to avoid the main perils, there is always a risk that a subgroup or clique emerges, sidelining the full group. Warning signs for excessive groupthink include the following:

- Dissent is discouraged or only permitted outside the plenary discussions.
- Unanimity is celebrated.
- People who do not fit in socially are ostracized or excluded from key discussions.
- The group is homogeneous with respect to age, gender, background, etc.
- Outsiders are dismissed, mocked, or demonized.
- New members are chosen based on the likelihood that they will conform, rather than for their skills and knowledge.

- Members leave meetings feeling pressed into agreeing to positions they would not support outside the pressure of the group dynamic.
- The group is dominated by one or two powerful members who have real or perceived authority over other members, and who are intolerant of dissent.

A noteworthy effect of groupthink – that was not covered in Janis' eight characteristics – is that the ultimate decisions of groups under groupthink tend to be more extreme than any of the individual positions of the group members. This happens because group members seek reasons to agree with the initial group position, while disregarding reasons to disagree. The weight of evidence in favour of the initial position becomes exaggerated. If the initial position is risk-taking, then the group will, through its overemphasis on arguments supporting the risk-taking, potentially end up taking even more risk. This effect is called **polarization**.

Shefrin (2016) gives many examples of groupthink impacting risk management decisions and, indeed, it can be observed as a factor in almost every major failure of risk or crisis management.

Endowment Effect

The **endowment effect** refers to the additional value placed on something that is owned over something that is not. This can be quantified by the difference between the amount an individual is willing to pay for an item and the amount they are willing to accept to give up the item, which is typically significantly more. In 2017, United Airlines found itself in the middle of a reputational crisis after a passenger, Dr Dao, was dragged off a plane to make space for a company employee.[2] The airline regularly 'bumped' people from flights, but typically this happens before the passenger has boarded. When United Airlines tried to take Dr Dao's seat away from him, their task was harder as, from his perspective, the seat was his until the plane landed at its destination. The gate staff, not knowing the endowment effect, did not understand that they would have to pay significantly more for an individual to give up their seat once they are in it, compared with the compensation offered before boarding.

Authority Effect

It is natural for individuals to comply or defer to authority figures. The **authority effect** is when individuals defer or obey the commands of an authority figure even when doing so contradicts the individual's beliefs or

---

[2] This incident is described in more detail in Chapter 20.

knowledge. This tendency is thought to be a product of our evolution, as it enabled humans to organize into relatively stable societies led by oracular authority figures.

The Milgram experiment vividly illustrated the power of the authority. Briefly, Milgram persuaded participants to inflict what they believed was severe pain on an innocent subject on the other side of a partition. In fact the pain was fake and the subjects were actors. Nevertheless, the participants believed they were sending electrical shocks, sometimes at life threatening levels, to the subjects. As the shocks were applied, the participants heard the subjects cry out in pain, with increasing urgency. Nevertheless, all participants in the original experiment administered shocks in the 'red zone' region of the fake electrical box (300 volts), and two-thirds of the subjects continued up to the maximum level (450 volts). Participants were visibly upset and stressed about the pain they were inflicting; most asked to stop, but were told they must continue. There was no other compulsion – the doors were not locked, and the participants were free agents. Obedience to the authority figure compelled them to remain in the room, and to continue to participate, even though doing so was very distressing.

The Milgram experiment demonstrates the strength of the tendency to obey an authority figure, and we see this also playing out in risk management situations. It contributes to groupthink effects; it can undermine risk management processes established by firms, when an authority figure gives instructions that are contradictory to the firm's risk processes. It can persuade people to ignore their instincts and responsibilities, when they conflict with the instructions of the authority figure. Bernie Madoff ran the world's largest Ponzi scheme until it collapsed in 2008. While it was still ongoing, there were rumours that all was not right, and eventually the Securities and Exchange Commission (SEC) sent some investigators to speak with him. But Madoff was a larger than life figure, who had great authority in the New York finance community. He had been the Chairman of the NASDAQ, and was on the Board of Governors of the National Association of Securities Dealers. When he spoke to the investigators, he spoke as an authority figure, persuading them not to make the simple checks that would have uncovered his deception.

The Hofling hospital experiment is another demonstration of authority bias with clear implications for risk management. In this experiment, 22 hospital nurses were contacted by a 'Dr Smith' (actually, a member of Hofling's team) and ordered to administer a large dose of a drug with which they were unfamiliar, to a specified patient. The patient was an actor, and the drug itself was fake – constructed for the experiment – and planted in the medicine cabinet of the ward. There were several reasons why the nurses should not comply: the dosage requested was twice that listed as a safe daily maximum on the label; the doctor was unknown to the nurses; paperwork required prior to administering medication had not been completed; the (fake) drug was not on the approved stock list of drugs in use in the hospital. Nevertheless, 21 out of 22 nurses were prepared to give the medication to the patient. The authority bias inherent in the doctor-nurse relationship is so strong that all of their professional training was secondary to instructions from an unknown doctor on a telephone. Interestingly, a control group of 22 nurses was given the situation as a hypothetical case study. In that context, 21 out of 22 nurses said that they would *not* comply with the order.

In highly hierarchical corporate settings, the authority effect is commonplace. Managers instruct their staff, and may punish or discourage the staff from questioning the orders. If the orders are dangerous, wrong, or just ambiguous, authority bias makes it very difficult for more junior employees to express their disagreement even if complying puts them or others in danger.

Conformity Bias

Conformity (or **herding**) **bias** is the instinct to follow the herd. The pressure to conform, similarly to the pressure to yield to authority, will often override an individual's own judgement or principles. Students who see their classmates cheating are much more likely to start cheating themselves, even if they have strong beliefs that cheating is wrong. An individual who takes a position in a discussion which is against the prevailing view is very likely to back down quickly (this is a major contributor to the groupthink problem). Psychologists have persuaded subjects in experiments to state that a clearly true fact (for example, two lines having the same length) is incorrect, by having two other people, planted for the experiment, insist that the statement is false.

Conformity bias means that it can be very difficult to change the culture of a firm that develops unethical or unsound practices. Employees tend to conform to the ethical standards around them, even if those are inconsistent with their own standards or beliefs. So when, for example, in the early 2000s, engineers working for Volkswagen (VW) started to develop software to enable their cars to cheat on US emissions tests, the fact that there were no objections, no whistle-blowers willing to report on this very obviously unlawful act, might have been because conformity bias persuaded each individual that supporting the project was more reasonable than opposing. Humans are hard-wired to conform.[3]

---

[3] The VW emissions scandal is discussed in more depth in Chapter 20.

Investment bubbles can be generated by herding behaviour, where a band-wagon effect is created around a specific sector or type of investment, leading to excessive buying, and generating prices far in excess of any inherent value. Where decisions are made sequentially, as more and more individuals join the bandwagon, ignoring any indications that would suggest not doing so, the phenomenon is called an **information cascade**.

Loss Aversion

Loss aversion refers to our tendency to feel more strongly about losses than about gains – the pleasure of a gain of 100 is not nearly as powerful as the pain of a loss of 100. Loss aversion, is related to framing bias, and both were identified and studied by Tversky and Kahneman.

The consequences of loss aversion in decision-making are considerable. Loss aversion makes it very difficult to drop an unprofitable course of action, as we must then take the certain loss of the costs to date; the tendency is to continue to invest and take increasing risks in the hope that the results will turn in our favour and the loss will be avoided. Hence, decision-makers tend to take more risks once some investment has been made than they would if the initial investment had not been made (this is the **sunk-cost fallacy**).

Loss aversion is also cited as a causal factor in corporate misbehaviour. Bernie Madoff claimed that his Ponzi scheme started in order to avoid losing reputation when his genuine investment strategy was unsuccessful. Nick Leeson was a derivatives broker who managed to bankrupt Barings bank (which was the oldest merchant bank in Britain at the time), as he took greater and greater risks to try to claw back his trading losses. In both cases, we see that the individuals were willing to take larger and larger risks, losing more and more money, in the remote hope that it would all come right and the losses would be eliminated.

The classical assumption of utility theory is that risk-averse individuals prefer certainty to uncertainty, so that, for example, a certain loss of $100 would be preferred to an outcome with a 50% chance of a loss of $0, and a 50% chance of a loss of $200. But the empirical research into loss aversion indicates that, for many individuals, the uncertain loss is preferred to the certain loss in this case. The prospect of potentially losing nothing draws people to the risky strategy, despite the chance of losing even more than the certain loss. This result, along with other related observations, has led to the development of **Prospect Theory** as an alternative to expected discounted utility. We discuss prospect theory in more detail in later sections.

Regret aversion is a form of loss aversion that inhibits decision-making through fear of future regret.

The **disposition effect** in behavioural finance is the tendency of investors to hold onto assets that have dropped in value, and to sell assets that have risen in value. It is an example of loss aversion, as investors hope to recoup the paper losses from assets that have dropped below purchase value.

Loss aversion is related to framing (negative frame emphasizes loss, engendering loss aversion) and endowment bias (loss of something already owned is more painful than loss of the potential to own something).

Ambiguity Aversion

When faced with decisions involving uncertainty, individuals tend to prefer known uncertainty to unknown uncertainty. This is different to risk aversion, which says that, all else being equal most people prefer less risk to more risk. Ambiguity aversion is about knowledge, not directly about risk.

The classic demonstration of ambiguity aversion involved an urn containing 90 balls. Thirty of the balls are red. Each of the other 60 balls is either black or yellow. There is no information on how many are black and how many are yellow. A ball will be drawn out of the urn; the decision-maker must guess what colour the ball will be. If correct, they will receive $100. Ellsberg (1961) predicted, and subsequent experiments confirmed, that subjects would bet on red rather than yellow or black. The probability of drawing a red ball is known to be $1/3$. The probability of drawing a yellow ball is unknown, but lies in the range $[0, 2/3]$. In the absence of any other information, it seems reasonable to model the uncertainty with a uniform distribution, so that the probability of drawing a yellow ball is the same as the red ball, but with more uncertainty. From this interpretation, ambiguity aversion appears to be a natural extension of risk aversion.

Status Quo Bias

Related to loss aversion is **status quo bias**, which is the tendency to prefer the current state of affairs. This makes it difficult to change direction, even where, objectively, that would be the optimal course.

Status quo bias can be seen as another expression of regret bias; a change from the status quo might be worse, and loss aversion says that the subsequent potential loss – of profits, of prestige, or of reputation, for example, is avoided. The status quo becomes a safe harbour from regret – but that can be a problem if the status quo represents a suboptimal risk management approach.

Inertia bias is a form of status quo bias. It arises where individuals are unwilling to make a decision, so the status quo is passively adopted.

Hyperbolic Discounting

Discounting in decision-making refers to the innate preference for immediate reward over delayed reward. In neoclassical economics, it is assumed that the impact of delay can be modelled using exponential discounting of utility of consumption, so that an additional delay of one day has the same impact on a decision whether the delay is from today to tomorrow, or is from one year from today to the day after that. In practice, delay, like financial reward, has diminishing impact. An immediate delay tends to be more critical in decision-making than delays applying in the future. Also, gains are discounted more than losses; we want to experience the good events as soon as possible, and to delay the negative events.

Under exponential discounting the utility of consumption of c_t in t-years would give discounted utility $\beta^t u(c_t)$ today, for some β with $0 < \beta \leq 1$. Typically, β, which is called the **subjective discount factor**, is assumed to be around 0.95 to 0.98. Under the more realistic descriptive model of hyperbolic discounting, the discounted utility would be $\frac{1}{1+\alpha t} u(c_t)$, where the discount parameter α would be in the region of 0.01 to 0.05.

Probability Distortion

We have already seen how people's perception of probability can be distorted with reference to availability bias. But there are other ways in which individuals' tendency to think deterministically can create distorted perceptions of risk and, hence, lead to poor risk management decisions.

For example, an auditor may declare, on an initial perusal of a firm's books, that fraud is very unlikely. The tendency for the auditor's team is to interpret 'unlikely' as 'impossible', so that if the team subsequently uncovers financial discrepancies, they are likely to interpret them benignly, rather than as potential indicators of fraud. The initial low probability signal becomes interpreted as a zero probability signal.

A distorted perception of risk from low probability and high severity events is noticeable in the under-insurance of extreme risks – except for those that are in the public eye through availability bias. The risk of earthquake damage in San Francisco or Los Angeles is far from negligible, but few people or firms adequately insure themselves against loss. The probability of a catastrophic event is sufficiently small that it is easy for decision-makers to ignore it entirely.

Experiments indicate that individuals tend to use a subjective distorted probability weighting to analyse risks. So, a small real-world probability may be distorted to a larger subjective probability through availability bias, or may be distorted to a zero probability through the bias towards the most likely deterministic outcome.

In Section 19.5, we return to loss aversion and probability distortion in the context of cumulative prospect theory.

19.4 Overcoming Bias

In this section we list some suggestions for overcoming bias, to attempt to de-bias risk management decision-making.

(1) Some protection against bias in corporate governance is achieved by developing the **metacognition** of the senior management. Metacognition is how individuals think about thinking; it enables us to examine our thought processes and decision-making, and in doing so to understand how we may be influenced by our cognitive biases. Metacognition can help the CEO guard against overconfidence and other biases, and it can encourage directors and senior officers to implement some of the controls described in this section, to de-bias decision-making and mitigate behavioural risks. Metacognition workshops can be very helpful, but CEOs who are very overconfident are likely to find the self-knowledge gained through metacognition training to be intolerable.

(2) The **devil's advocate system** involves appointing an individual to make as strong a case as possible against the prevailing opinion, to ensure that counter-arguments have been raised and discussed. Explicit emphasis on downside risks can protect against groupthink and overconfidence. Ensuring that risks, uncertainties, and potential bad outcomes are reviewed can help as a de-biasing technique against overconfidence and self-attribution. It is important for senior officers to understand what is, and what is not under their control. In addition, having someone whose responsibility is to dissent signals that dissent is permitted. In many firms, challenging the CEO is likely to lead to unemployment, even if the challenge is justified and necessary. Companies that have experienced significant legal crises through unethical corporate behaviour are typically companies in which dissent is not permitted, often involving dominant CEOs who would not tolerate disagreement.

(3) Encourage the Board of Directors to challenge the CEO. In particular, the Directors should take every opportunity to ask 'what could go wrong with the proposed strategy?' They are better incentivized to do this if

they are vulnerable to adverse outcomes, legally or financially. If Directors believe that they are 100% protected against legal liability by 'Directors and Officers' insurance, for example, there is a moral hazard risk that they will be less diligent in their responsibilities than they would if corporate failure or misdeeds created significant adverse personal consequences for them.

(4) Create rules for making decisions; the rules can be structured to avoid the trap of simply following the suggestion of the dominant member. Rules might include requiring some written input from each individual before and after discussions, or ensuring adequate documentation of the decision process, including alternatives considered and reasons for rejecting the alternatives.

(5) Avoid proposing solutions early in discussions, as these tend to anchor the decision-making. It is better to consider all the facts and arguments before any decisions or solutions are tabled.

(6) Change the group membership; after a time, individuals can get too comfortable within the group; as stronger friendship bonds are created, people become less willing to challenge the suggestions of others.

(7) Involve people outside the group. Subject matter experts may be consulted, or, before a decision is finalized, it could be submitted to another group or qualified individual for critical review.

(8) Encourage debate; make sure that all group members understand that they are expected to express their views, especially when they diverge from others. If someone has a compelling argument against a popular strategy, avoid blaming the individual for the outcome ('don't shoot the messenger').

(9) It can be helpful to discuss contentious issues with group members individually, outside of the setting of a formal meeting, to make it easier to present unguarded or unvarnished views. However, this can be risky if it is used to head off dissent in the group setting (as in the groupthink mind-guards).

(10) Avoid narcissists. People with narcissistic traits tend to exhibit extreme overconfidence and overplacement, resulting in grandiose, attention-seeking behaviours. They generally need those around them to admire and support them unquestioningly. They expect loyalty and deference, but will have little loyalty to others. They can be very manipulative. Narcissistic CEOs tend to take larger risks than non-narcissists, are less likely to comply with constraints imposed by Boards or regulators, and are less compliant with respect to risk management protocols. They do not respect their colleagues, and tend

not to be open to advice. They are working towards their own personal success, not the company's, and the success of those around them is perceived as threatening. The narcissist's bold actions tend to result in extreme successes and extreme failures (Chatterjee and Hambrick, 2007). Studies of long-term business successes indicate that the CEOs responsible for sustained performance tend to have opposite traits to the narcissist – they are described as 'self-effacing' and 'modest'. They ascribe success to the team rather than to themselves, but take personal responsibility for setbacks. They are less likely to be 'charismatic' (Collins, 2009).

(11) Promote diversity, in terms of education, experience, specialization, gender, nationality, and neurodiversity. A broader-based group will be more creative, and will bring a range of experience, potentially reducing both availability bias and groupthink.

(12) Emphasize individual ethics and responsibility. Encourage all employees to be aware of biases relating to herding and excessive deference to authority, and train employees in mitigation strategies. Encourage managers not to expect or reward excessive deference to authority.

(13) Have group members evaluate ideas critically, individually, in advance. We know that anchoring bias can affect the group dynamic, so that if an individual makes a proposal at the start of a decision process, that proposal will likely anchor the thinking of the group. Avoid anchoring by having each group member bring their own perspective, and use these to initiate a discussion.

(14) Ensure that the time allocated for making decisions is realistic, and sufficient to collect and examine the necessary information, avoiding the temptation to limit time allocated to dissenting opinions.

(15) Ensure that sufficient objective, quantitative analysis is available to support decision-making (but beware of **information bias**, which is a tendency to request more and more information, as a way to avoid making a decision).

(16) Reframe decisions to avoid or identify loss aversion or framing bias.

(17) Apply the **transparency test**: ask yourself, how would this decision or this course of action look if it were to appear on the front page of a newspaper tomorrow? If it would be a major embarrassment to the company (e.g., VW's decision to cheat on emissions tests), then it is probably a bad decision.

(18) Consider the **plausible worst-case outcomes** of a decision or of alternative decisions. For example, you are VW engineer, who is tempted to insert software to cheat emissions testing. The upside is that

the cars manufactured with the cheating software may be very popular. The upside is always examined extensively. Here, we focus on the plausible worst-case scenario, and decide if that is tolerable. For the VW engineer, the plausible worst-case scenario is that the deception is discovered, in which case the engineer faces severe legal consequences, including potential imprisonment. Put in those terms, it is unlikely that the cheat software would have been developed. This is a remarkably powerful thought exercise for assessing whether a decision or strategy is tolerable in a wide range of contexts. When used to select a strategy, it is a form of minimax solution – minimize the maximum loss.

19.5 Cumulative Prospect Theory

Cumulative prospect theory is an approach to decision-making under uncertainty, similar to expected utility theory, but which takes into consideration some of the cognitive biases discussed in this chapter.

Suppose a decision-maker is selecting from a number of mutually exclusive courses of action, each with uncertain payoffs. The term **prospect** is used to describe each possible course of action.

The expected utility approach to decision-making assumes that the decision-maker will select the prospect that gives them the largest expected utility of wealth. So, for example, suppose that for one prospect there are n different potential payoffs, denoted $x_1, \ldots, x_n$, with associated probabilities $p(x_1), \ldots, p(x_n)$. The expected utility for that prospect, for an individual with current wealth W, and with utility function $u(w)$, is

$$EU = \sum_j u(W + x_j)p(x_j).$$

The expected incremental utility measures the expected change to the individual's utility from the prospect, so that

$$EIU = \sum_j \big(u(W + x_j) - u(W)\big)p(x_j).$$

Using the expected utility or the expected incremental utility will generate the same decision when faced with two or more mutually exclusive prospects to choose from.

Expected utility theory was developed as a descriptive model of decision-making of rational, risk-averse agents. However, it involves some very strong, erroneous assumptions about how people make decisions in real life. In the real world, decision-makers are subject to many of the cognitive biases listed above. Prospect theory was developed by psychologists Kahneman and Tversky as a model of decision-making under uncertainty that incorporates the impact of some common cognitive biases.

19.5.1 Reference Point, Value Function, and Weighting Function

The three components of a decision under cumulative prospect theory are the **reference point**, the **value function**, and the **probability weighting function**.

The Reference Point

Under expected utility theory, we consider the impact of the payoffs on the decision-maker's total wealth. Under prospect theory, we consider the impact of the payoffs relative to some reference point. If the reference point is the decision-maker's current wealth, then this is similar to maximizing expected incremental utility.

The payoffs under each possible course of action are framed in terms of the reference point. If x_0 is defined as the reference point, then the payoffs relative to the reference point are $x_j^* = W + x_j - x_0$. If the reference point is the current wealth, then $x_j^* = x_j$ represents the incremental gain or loss under outcome j.

The reference point can be manipulated by reframing the decision, which can lead to different decisions arising from the same options, differently framed.

The Value Function

Under expected utility theory, we assume that individuals are risk-averse for all x_j, so that the same form of utility applies whether x_j is positive (a gain) or negative (a loss). But we know, empirically, that individuals are loss averse, more than they are risk-averse. Prospect theory incorporates a value function, $v(x^*)$ in place of the (incremental) utility function. Losses have negative value, and gains have positive value, so $\text{sgn}(x^*) = \text{sgn}(v(x^*))$. As we know that individuals are risk seeking for losses, and risk-averse for profits (where losses and profits are measured relative to the reference point) we generally assume a concave (risk-averse) form for the value function for $x^* > 0$ and a convex (risk-seeking) form for $x^* \leq 0$. Furthermore, as individuals dislike losses more than they like gains, the magnitude of the value function for a loss is expected to be greater than the magnitude of the value function for an equivalent gain.

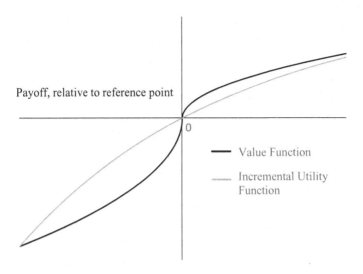

Figure 19.1 Value function and risk-averse utility function

That is, $-v(-x^*) > v(x^*)$ for $x^* > 0$. The function proposed by Kahnemann and Tversky is

$$v(x^*) = \begin{cases} (x^*)^\alpha & x^* > 0, \\ -\lambda(-(x^*)^\beta) & x^* \leq 0, \end{cases} \qquad (19.1)$$

where $0 < \alpha, \beta < 1$ and $\lambda > 0$. The values proposed by Kahnemann and Tversky are $\alpha = \beta = 0.88$ and $\lambda = 2.25$.

In Figure 19.1, we show a value function, together with a risk-averse incremental utility function. Notice that for the value function, the change from a convex curve to a concave curve at the reference point means that small differences in payoff close to the reference point may have a disproportionate effect on the value of the payoff. Compare this with the incremental utility function which is concave for all payoffs.

The Weighting Function

Under expected utility theory, individuals are assumed to know and fully take into consideration the objective probabilities, $p(x_j)$, associated with each potential payoff x_j. But individuals are not objective about probabilities. Probability distortion bias means that unlikely events are often assumed to be impossible (unless availability bias is a factor, in which case the probability of a very unlikely event may be exaggerated). Similarly, very likely events are often assumed to be certain. In between, people will generally not much distinguish between probabilities, so that, for example, if $p(x_j) = 0.5$ and $p(x_{j+1}) = 0.3$, the outcomes x_j and x_{j+1} may be treated as having, essentially, the same likelihood. The mental heuristic that people seem to employ is to divide events into three categories – 'will not happen', 'will certainly happen', and 'may happen'. If the events in the 'may happen' zone have very different probabilities, then some rough allowance may be made for the more or less likely outcomes; if not, then we tend to assign equal probability to all outcomes in the 'may happen' category. In any case, the empirical findings are that very small probabilities are re-weighted to zero; small probabilities tend to be over-weighted, and large probabilities tend to be under-weighted, except that very large probabilities tend to be rounded to 1.0. In cumulative prospect theory we allow for this cognitive probability distortion by replacing the objective probabilities with a weighting function $w(F(x))$, where $F(x)$ is the cumulative distribution function of x.

The constraints on the weighting function, $w(q), 0 \leq q \leq 1$, are

(a) $w(0) = 0$;
(b) $w(1) = 1$;
(c) $w(q)$ is non-decreasing.

In Figure 19.2, we show three weighting functions:

- The dotted line is $w(q) = q$, which is the benchmark assuming no probability distortion at all.
- The black line shows a weighting function where the weighted probability of extreme left tail loss, where $F(x) \leq 0.03$, is zero. For objective cumulative probability between 3% and 96%, the weighted distribution of loss is uniform. Above 96%, the weighted cumulative distribution jumps to 1.0, which means that outcomes in the top 4% of the distribution are also given zero weight.
- The grey line is a probability weighting function proposed by Kahneman and Tversky,

$$w(q) = \frac{q^\gamma}{(q^\gamma + (1 - q)^\gamma)^{\frac{1}{\gamma}}},$$

with $\gamma = 0.6$. This function incorporates over-weighting of the left tail probabilities and under-weighting of the right tail probabilities, but does not include rounding to zero of probabilities in the left and right tails.

If the payoff distribution is discrete, then the distorted, subjective probability associated with payoff x_j is $\pi(x_j)$ where

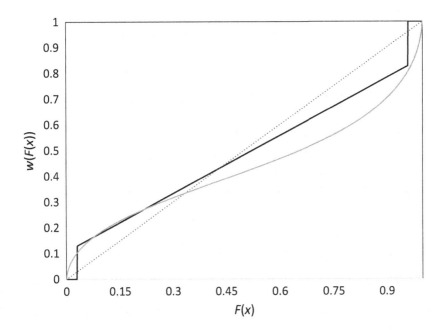

Figure 19.2 Example weighting functions for cumulative prospect theory: no distortion (broken line), Kahneman and Tversky distortion (grey line), and three-point weighting function (black line)

$$\pi(x_1) = w(F(x_1)),$$
$$\pi(x_j) = w(F(x_j)) - w(F(x_{j-1})) \quad j = 2, 3, \ldots, n.$$

If the payoff distribution is continuous, with objective pdf $f(x)$, then the distorted, subjective probability density function associated with payoff x is $f^\pi(x)$ where

$$f^\pi(x) = \frac{d}{dx} w(F(x)) = f(x) w'(F(x)).$$

19.5.2 Subjective Value under Prospect Theory

Suppose, as above, we have a prospect with discrete potential payoffs, ordered from smallest to largest, $x_1, \ldots, x_n$, with associated cumulative distribution function $F(x_j) = \sum_{k=1}^{j} p(x_j)$.

Assume that a decision-maker has subjective probability $\pi(x_j)$ associated with payoff x_j, for $j = 1, 2, \ldots, n$, and has value function $v(x)$. Then their subjective value of the prospect is

$$V = \sum_{j=1}^{n} v(x_j^*)\, \pi(x_j),$$

where x_0 is the reference point, and $x_j^* = W + x_j - x_0$.

If the payoff distribution is continuous, then the subjective value is

$$V = \int_x v(x^*)\, f^{\pi}(x)dx, \quad x^* = W + x - x_0.$$

Given a choice between several prospects, the decision-maker will select the one with the highest subjective value.

Example 19.1 A decision-maker is offered a choice between two prospects.

Under Prospect I, the potential payoffs, and associated objective probabilities are as follows:

j	x_j	$p(x_j)$
1	−4,000	0.005
2	−200	0.300
3	−5	0.200
4	100	0.300
5	600	0.190
6	12,000	0.005

Under Prospect II, the decision-maker receives $50 with probability 1.0.

(a) Assume that the decision-maker uses expected utility to decide between the two prospects. Her initial wealth is $W = \$6{,}000$. Her utility function is

$$u(w) = -\frac{10{,}000}{w}.$$

(i) Which prospect gives the higher expected incremental utility?

(ii) The certainty equivalent value of a prospect is the amount that, if paid with probability 1.0, has the same expected incremental utility as the prospect. What is the certainty equivalent of Prospect I for this decision-maker?

(b) Now assume the decision-maker uses cumulative prospect theory to make her decision. Her value function is as in equation (19.1), with $\alpha = \beta = 0.9$ and $\lambda = 2.0$. Her reference point is her current wealth.

Her subjective probabilities are:

j	x_j	$\pi(x_j)$
1	−4,000	0.00
2	−200	0.25
3	−5	0.25
4	100	0.25
5	600	0.25
6	12,000	0.00

(i) Which prospect gives the higher subjective value?

(ii) The certainty equivalent of a prospect is the certain amount that has the same subjective value as the prospect. What is the certainty equivalent of Prospect I?

(c) Now we reframe the decision. Suppose the decision-maker sets her reference point as $W + 50$ (on the grounds that this will be her wealth under the unambiguous Prospect 2). Her value function and weighting function are unchanged.

(i) Determine the prospect which gives a higher subjective value.

(ii) Determine the certainty equivalent value.

(iii) Explain why the reframing does not affect the decision under expected utility.

Solution 19.1

(a)(i) The expected incremental utility of Prospect I is

$$EU = \sum_{j=1}^{6} \left(u(W + x_j) - u(W) \right) p(x_j) = 0.008354.$$

The expected incremental utility of Prospect II is $u(W + 50) - u(W) = 0.013774$. So the decision-maker would select Prospect II, the certain payoff of 50, over the uncertain payments of Prospect I.

(a)(ii) The certainty equivalent value of Prospect I is x such that

$$u(W + x) - u(W) = 0.008354 \implies x = 31.98.$$

(b)(i) The subjective value of Prospect I is

$$V = \sum_{j=1}^{6} v(x_j)\,\pi(x_j) = 33.893.$$

The subjective value of Prospect II is

$$v(50) = 33.812.$$

So the decision-maker would choose Prospect I over Prospect II.

(b)(ii) The certainty equivalent value is x such that

$$v(x) = 33.893 \implies x^{0.9} = 33.893 \implies x = 50.133.$$

(c)(i) The payments, relative to the new reference point, are now all $50 less. So the revised subjective value of Prospect I is

$$V = \sum_{j=1}^{6} v(x_j - 50)\pi(x_j) = -8.7726.$$

The revised subjective value of Prospect II is $v(0) = 0$. Hence, the decision-maker would now choose Prospect II.

(c)(ii) The new certainty equivalent value is x, which must be negative as $V < 0$. So

$$v(x) = -8.7726 \implies -\lambda(-x^{0.9}) = -8.7726 \implies x = -5.1694.$$

(c)(iii) The expected incremental utility decision does not change with framing, even if we view the $50 change as initial income. In this case, the $50 is added to the wealth, and then subtracted from the payments, leaving the same utility for each payment. That is, the utility of x_j under the new framing is $u((W + 50) + (x_j - 50)) = u(W + x_j)$. The incremental utility changes, as we have shifted the wealth, giving incremental utility for payment x_j of $u(W + x_j) - u(W + 50)$, but the second term is the same for all x_j, and does not affect the decision. $\qquad\square$

It is clear that the payouts under the first framing in the example are exactly the same as the payouts under the second framing, but the decision is different. This is not rational, but it is realistic. Prospect theory is not intended to describe how people *should* behave, it is intended to describe how people do behave – it is descriptive, not prescriptive or normative. Expected utility theory was originally also intended to be descriptive, but is now often applied as a normative model.

Prospect theory quantifies the combined impacts of loss aversion, endowment bias and subjective probability distortion. Applications in ERM include the following:

- In executive compensation, stock options (call options on the company stock) are often used to create incentives that align the interests of senior managers and shareholders. Suppose that executives take the strike price of the options as their reference point; when the stock price is below the strike price, they tend to be risk seeking. If it is above, they tend to be risk averse. As this may not align with the shareholders' preferred risk attitude, the options can have an unexpected and unwanted impact on the firm performance.

- Traders in investment firms receive significant income from annual bonuses which are dependent on their performance. The traders tend to take the expected level of bonus as their reference point. If their performance has been below target, they are likely to become increasingly risk seeking, perhaps exceeding risk tolerance limits, in order to pull their bonus back up to the reference point. As the downside risk is constrained (providing no laws are broken, the worst-case scenario is losing the job), this is actually a rational strategy, from an individualistic perspective.

- Negotiations can be very dependent on the framing adopted by the participants. A negotiator who is in a loss frame is likely to be more aggressive and less cooperative than a negotiator in a gain frame – and, as we have seen, the same scenarios can often be described in a loss frame or a gain frame. If both negotiators are in a loss frame, then it is very hard to reach agreement; a concession received is only valued around half as much as a concession made (as $\lambda \approx 2$). This is often the case for labour negotiations.

All of these examples involve the application of prospect theory to decisions of individuals. It has also been applied (in more of a stretch of the original theory) to risk-taking of organizations. Research shows that firms tend to set an 'aspiration level' for their performance. If the performance is below the aspiration level, firms tend to be risk seeking; if above, they tend to be more risk-averse. This is consistent with prospect theory. However, the connection is less strong when the firm is well above or well below their aspiration level. Under prospect theory, decisions far away from the reference point tend to a risk-neutral valuation. Empirical research shows that, above a certain level, firms tend to become more risk seeking. If performance is very poor, firms will either throw all caution to the wind and become increasingly risk seeking, or they may become very conservative, if by doing so they can avoid bankruptcy.

In each case the behaviour can be explained by shifting reference points of the key decision-makers. If the senior management hold stock in the firm, then when the firm does very poorly they may reset their reference point to some target minimum value for their stock, and then take all risks available that maintain the possibility of achieving this target. Alternatively, the reference point could be bankruptcy, and a risk-averse approach is applied as long as the firm is at least slightly in the black.

19.6 Notes and Further Reading

Paredes (2004) offers many examples of cognitive bias in corporate governance, as well as some suggestions for de-biasing decisions. Montier (2009) describes the biases involved in investment decisions, and how to overcome or exploit them.

See Milgram (1963) for the original report on the Milgram experiment, and Hofling et al. (1966) for the original account of the Hofling experiment.

The ambiguity aversion experiment is reported in Ellsberg (1961).

The origin of the phrase 'devil's advocate' lies in the process of declaring saints in the Catholic church. The devil's advocate was an ecclesiastical lawyer who was required to make a case against sainthood for every individual under consideration.

The 'transparency test' referenced above is a loose interpretation or implementation of Rawls' *Doctrine of Public Reason* (Rawls, 1993).

For a very readable account of how biases affect almost everything we do, see *Thinking Fast and Slow*, by Daniel Kahneman, one of the architects of Cumulative Prospect Theory (Kahneman and Tversky, 1979).

19.6.1 Answers to questions from Section 19.3.1

1. The population of Nigeria is 206.63 million, according to the 2020 census.
2. The average number of planes in the air at any moment in 2016 was 9,728.
3. Japan has 6,582 islands.
4. The distance between Buenos Aires and Rio de Janeiro, by road, is 2,657 km, or 1,651 miles.
5. Carl Friedrich Gauss was born on 30 April 1777.
6. The Great Ming Dynasty lasted for 276 years.
7. 'Yesterday' is 123 seconds long.
8. The Empire State Building is 443 metres, or 1,454 feet tall.

9. The deepest lake in the world (Lake Baikal in Siberia) is 1,642 metres, or 5,387 feet, at its deepest point.

10. The ratio of the volume of the earth to the volume of the moon is

$$\frac{1.08321 \times 10^{12} \text{ km}^3}{2.1958 \times 10^{10} \text{ km}^3} \approx 49.3.$$

19.7 Exercises

Exercise 19.1 Explain the difference between risk aversion, loss aversion, and ambiguity aversion. Identify real-world examples where each can be observed.

Exercise 19.2 Explain the difference between hindsight bias and outcome bias. Give examples of each.

Exercise 19.3 Explain the biases that might be involved in the following scenarios:

(a) A fund manager has selected low performing stocks in three market sectors, but high performing stocks in the others. She claims that she was just unlucky in the low performers, and that the high performers indicate her stock picking ability.

(b) An investor holds some stock in XYZ Co. He bought the stock at $100. It is now worth $75, and has not been above $100 for a couple of years. He decides not to sell until the stock reaches $100.

(c) An investor holds some stock in MRH Co. She bought the stock at $100. It is now worth $300, but has had little growth over the past couple of years. She decides not to sell.

(d) An individual chooses to buy a printer which is very cheap, but for which the ink cartridges are very expensive, over a printer which is slightly more expensive, but for which the ink cartridges are substantially cheaper.

(e) A pension plan manager is selecting a fund manager to invest the plan assets. She chooses the manager with the best quantile results (i.e. based on rankings of managers) for the last two quarter-years.

(f) Individual investors who move to online trading tend to be more active, and less successful, than when managing their funds through intermediaries.

(g) A bank CEO disbands the risk management team, stating that the team is not profit-generating, and is interfering with his plans for the bank.

(h) A project manager reviews previous projects to identify potential savings. Noticing that the back-up equipment (held on standby in case of failure of front-line equipment) has not been utilized in the past three projects, he proposes eliminating the back-up equipment for future projects.

(i) Airlines experience a higher accident/error rate when the pilot is senior to the co-pilot than when the pilot is junior to the co-pilot.

(j) An individual is willing to pay $50 for a ticket to a football game. Luckily, he is given a ticket by a friend. When he arrives at the game, he finds he has lost the ticket; he can buy a new ticket for $50 but is unwilling to do so.

(k) Gamblers at racecourses tend to bet more on longshots, and less on favourites, towards the end of the day.

(l) Pension plan membership rates are much higher when individuals are asked to opt out of the plan than when they are asked to opt into the plan.

(m) After a major product failure, a CEO states that it could not be his company's fault, laying the blame on third party suppliers.

Exercise 19.4 For employer-sponsored defined benefit pension plans, it is common to have substantial investment of funds in risky assets, even when the plan is in surplus.

(a) Explain why this appears inconsistent with prospect theory from the point of view of the pension plan.

(b) Does the situation change if viewed from the perspective of the sponsoring employer?

(c) The decisions of the pension plan trustees are supposed to be independent of the sponsoring employer. Typically, trustees include representation from unions and management. Explain why the assumption of independence may not be reasonable.

Exercise 19.5 A firm is facing a loss with the following distribution, in 000's:

Loss	Probability
1,000	0.0001
300	0.0010
100	0.0050
50	0.0200
10	0.0200
5	0.0200
0	0.9339

Assume a value function as in equation (19.1), with $\alpha = \beta = 0.9$ and $\lambda = 2$, and a reference point of current wealth.

(a) Calculate the maximum premium the firm will pay to insure the loss fully, assuming the weighting function applied to the cumulative distribution function is

$$w(q) = \frac{q^\gamma}{(q^\gamma + (1 - q)^\gamma)^{\frac{1}{\gamma}}},$$

with $\gamma = 0.6$.

(b) Calculate the maximum premium that the firm will pay to insure the loss fully, assuming the same weighting function as in (a), but with zero weighted probability for the 1,000 loss.

(c) Explain how the value function might differ if the firm is close to bankruptcy.

20

Crisis Management

20.1 Summary

In this chapter, we discuss how to prepare for and respond to crises. Crises are inevitable, and preparing for crises is an important aspect of risk management. Effective preparation requires the firm to understand best practice in crisis response. We present some examples, good and bad, of corporate and government responses to crises. We discuss the key steps in crisis preparation, followed by the key steps in crisis response. Finally, we consider the impact of corporate structure and ethics.

20.2 Introduction

Crises are defined as events with the potential to endanger an organization's reputation, profitability, and, perhaps, its survival. Crises may arise through a failure of risk management, or through unavoidable external factors, such as the 2020 COVID-19 pandemic or the 2011 Tōhoku earthquake in Japan. **Crisis management** is the part of risk management relating to crisis preparation and response. While risk management is predominantly proactive, crisis management is more reactive, although some general preparation can mitigate the impact of the crisis when it arises.

Crises are often seen as occurring suddenly and without warning, but not all are really so unforeseeable. For example, the BP Deepwater Horizon explosion discussed in Chapter 2 was clearly a sudden and shocking event, but once the incident was fully investigated, it emerged that poor risk culture and mistaken cost-cutting had created a situation where a disaster was, in fact, quite

594

predictable. Such crises are referred to as **smouldering crises**, in contrast to **acute crises**, which are those for which there really are no prior warning signs.

Usually, crises are 'low-probability, high-severity events', necessitating swift decision-making in stressful circumstances. Examples of events with potential to create a crisis include cyberattacks, product tampering, terrorist attacks, pandemics, natural disasters, product boycotts, injury or death of customers from defective products, hostile takeovers, strikes, patent infringement, severe workplace accidents, assault of customers, assault of employees, sabotage, and theft of intellectual property.

There is some benefit in categorizing crises, as different types of triggering events will require different levels and types of preparation and response. In this chapter, we separately consider the following **crisis categories**:

(1) Crises created by natural disasters, pandemics, or random acts (e.g., terrorism) that originate from outside an organization and are not specifically targeted at the organization.
(2) Malevolent attacks from external individuals or groups, aimed specifically at the organization. Cyberattacks would fall under this category. These crises are assumed to involve illegal or unlawful activities.
(3) Confrontation crises, where individuals or groups attack the reputation of an organization, or try to disrupt a firm's activities through other means. Where the confrontation originates from outside the firm, it may be initiated by special interest groups who are opposed to some aspect of the firm's business. Such confrontation crises often involve calls to boycott the organization and its trading partners, and may also involve attempts to interrupt the firm's operations through picketing or disruption of supplies. Crises initiated internally to a firm are often associated with labour disputes. Confrontation crises do not generally involve illegal or unlawful activities, as long as any physical demonstrations or picketing remain within legal bounds.
(4) Internal errors, negligence, or bad acts of individual employees. These may, or may not, involve illegality.
(5) Crises created by management failures of omission or commission. These are the self-inflicted wounds, often involving significant failure of integrity and ethics. The crisis may involve illegal acts originating from within the organization.

Of course, not every crisis falls naturally into one of these categories, and in many cases, a crisis may fall into two or three – for example, where a crisis that is initiated by an external, non-targeted event (Type (1)) is followed by a response that involves management failures (Type (5)).

Part of crisis management involves risk avoidance, transfer, and mitigation strategies, which are covered in earlier chapters. In this chapter, we will focus on the stages beyond risk identification and mitigation.

The three stages of crisis management are:

(1) **The Planning Stage** – Identifying the team responsible for managing a crisis, specifying individual responsibilities, and ensuring that each team member, along with other senior officers, can be contacted at any time for speedy information sharing and decision-making. The firm might use simulation exercises, to test the plan and train the team members.

(2) **The Immediate Response Stage** – Acting to mitigate the crisis impact; informing key stakeholders, including customers, regulators, police, shareholders; reaching out to journalists and social media to ensure that the firm gains better control of the public messaging.

(3) **The Longer Term Response** – Reviewing how the crisis arose, assessing how to reduce future vulnerability; reviewing the effectiveness of the crisis planning and immediate response; determining appropriate reparations to affected customers; continuing communication with stakeholders and the general public to rebuild lost trust.

To illustrate the difference between crisis management and other risk management, consider the risk of cyberattack for an organization with significant personal data storage. The first task of risk management would be to prevent a successful attack, for example, by implementing sophisticated multiple level security, training employees, limiting employee access to the company's software and systems, and ensuring software is patched and updated whenever necessary. In contrast, crisis management includes planning for, and implementing responses to, a successful cyberattack.

While effective risk management can significantly mitigate the impact of a crisis on the organization, a deficient response to a crisis can exacerbate the damage. Many of the case studies discussed in this chapter involve very poor corporate crisis response, perhaps because crisis management failures are more likely to generate headlines. But, it is apparent that many highly successful corporations are very bad at preparing for and handling crises.

20.3 Examples of Crises and Responses

20.3.1 Tylenol Attacks

In 1982, an unknown assailant tampered with a number of bottles of Tylenol-brand paracetamol capsules, lacing some capsules with a deadly quantity of potassium cyanide. The contaminated pill bottles were replaced on shelves for unsuspecting customers to buy. Seven people died. The parent firm, Johnson & Johnson, immediately recalled all Tylenol products, halted production, and distributed warnings to hospitals and the public. When it started selling the product again, a few months after the recall, it was in new, tamper-proof, sealed packaging. The response of Johnson & Johnson is often cited as an example of good crisis management.

The Tylenol attacks were sudden, not smouldering, and fall under the 'external targeted attack' category (Type 2). The response was seen as swift, transparent, responsible, and decisive.

20.3.2 United Airlines and Dr Dao

In 2017, a 67-year-old physician on a United Airlines Express flight from Chicago to Kentucky was violently removed from the plane, despite having a valid ticket and boarding card. The airline wanted to accommodate some of its own employees on the plane, but Dr Dao was not willing to give up his seat, citing the necessity of returning home that day (it was the last flight of the day). The airline called airport security, whose officers assaulted Dr Dao (causing a concussion, broken nose, and loss of two teeth) and dragged him off the plane, distressed and bleeding. The attack was filmed and posted to social media, where it became a sensation. The initial response of United Airlines was to blame Dr Dao, accusing him of being the aggressor, even though millions of people had viewed the video demonstrating the untruth of this account. Their market value initially fell by around $1 billion. A few days later, the company changed tactics, took full responsibility, vowed to change its procedures, and apologized. The share price recovered quite quickly, though the company's reputation took longer to recover, especially in Asia, where the action was seen as racially motivated. Bloomberg News described the event as a public relations disaster.

The United Airlines crisis may have been smouldering rather than sudden; the airline had ignored previous social media criticisms, and so had little goodwill to start with. The practice of de-planing paying customers was long-standing, and had previously created other damaging, though less harrowing, scenes. The increasing social media scrutiny of negative customer interactions might well have been foreseen by a more active crisis preparation team. The event falls under Type (5) above. Relative to the speed with which the video of the event spread, the response from United was slow, and involved misinformation, backtracking, and a failure to take responsibility by the senior officers of the firm. However, the long-term impact of the event on the market value of United Airlines appears to be minimal; if that is all that matters, perhaps the strategy was adequate.

20.3.3 Hurricane Katrina

In August 2005, Hurricane Katrina struck the Gulf Coast of the United States (US), ultimately causing devastating damage to New Orleans and surrounding areas. Around 2,000 people died; 80% of the city of New Orleans was submerged. The federal response to the emergency fell to the Federal Emergency Management Agency (FEMA). FEMA's actions were widely criticized; not only were they ineffectual in providing aid to the victims of the hurricane, they actively hindered the work of other, more competent agencies who were trying to help. For example, FEMA turned away urgently needed supplies of water, fuel, and emergency medicines. A Select Bipartisan Committee of the US House of Representatives reported that FEMA's actions involved 'a litany of mistakes, misjudgments, lapses, and absurdities all cascading together, blinding us to what was coming and hobbling any collective effort to respond' (Davis et al., 2006).

Although a natural disaster is usually treated as an acute crisis, in this case the threat to New Orleans had been anticipated for some time before Hurricane Katrina struck, and hurricanes are a regular occurrence in that region. In fact, a simulated emergency exercise had taken place one year earlier, so this looks like a smouldering rather than a sudden crisis. It would fall under Type (1) for the initial event, and Type (5) for the mishandling of the crisis as it developed, and lack of contingency planning before the event. FEMA's response was hampered by a lack of qualified leadership and an unwillingness to cooperate with other local and federal agencies. Five of the top eight FEMA officials, including the director, were political appointees with little experience or training in large-scale disaster management.

20.3.4 Volkswagen (VW) Emissions Scandal

In 2015, the US Environmental Protection Agency found that VW had been cheating on emissions tests. The company had programmed its diesel engines to recognize when the vehicle was being put through the standard testing procedure, at which time extra controls would be activated, allowing the engine to pass the test. When not being tested, emissions were 40 times greater than the numbers recorded in the tests.

VW's immediate response was to deny the accusations of cheating. Only when presented with irrefutable evidence, did VW admit to the unlawful manipulation of emissions results. However, VW continued to insist that the cheating was the responsibility of a handful of rogue software engineers, and that senior managers had no knowledge of their actions. The financial impact on VW, from vehicle buybacks, fines, and the aggregated legal costs from criminal and civil lawsuits was very significant. The share price of VW's parent company fell swiftly by over 60%, and four years later was still 40% below its value before the scandal. VW would like to classify this as Type (4) (bad acts of rogue employees), but Type (5) seems more appropriate as more information on management involvement is revealed. VW's response has involved repeated misinformation and an unwillingness of senior officers to accept responsibility.

20.3.5 Nike Boycotts

Nike is a multinational corporation that manufactures and sells sportswear and sports equipment. Through sponsorship of popular sporting heroes, the brand has become iconic in athletic fashion. In the late 1990s, Nike expanded its production into hundreds of factories in Asia. It emerged that, in many of these factories, workers were abused, wages were below local minimum wage thresholds, and workplace conditions were unsafe. In Pakistan and Cambodia, investigators found children as young as 10 working in the factories. Meanwhile, Nike's profits rose spectacularly. Initially, Nike's response was that the subcontracted suppliers were not their responsibility, and that it was not possible to check ages of all workers in such an extensive operation. Consequently, campaigners encouraged a substantial and effective boycott of Nike products (called the 'sweatshop boycott'), which induced Nike to relent somewhat, with more extensive inspections of factories and factory records, and with a more humane list of criteria that third party manufacturers were required to comply with. Although there are some continuing concerns, the change in Nike's attitude, from denial of responsibility, to becoming champions for fair treatment of workers, has substantially repaired Nike's reputation. This was an example of a confrontation crisis (Type (3)).

In 2018, Nike signed American football quarterback Colin Kaepernick to a long-term advertising campaign. Kaepernick had been dropped from his team following his decision to kneel during the singing of the US national anthem before games, in protest against racial injustice and systematic oppression. Nike's decision was controversial, and calls to boycott the firm were widespread from right-wing commentators. Nike's share price dropped in the short term, but sales rose substantially. This was, again, a confrontation crisis, but the nature of the crisis, and Nike's strategy for managing the crisis, was completely different from the response to the sweatshop boycott.

20.3.6 Maple Leaf Foods

Maple Leaf Foods is a Canadian company that processes and distributes packaged meats. In 2008, one of their factories was identified as the source of meat which had been contaminated with the Listeria bacterium, and which had caused a number of deaths in hospitals and long-term care (LTC) homes. The company immediately issued a comprehensive recall of their products, and the Chief Executive Officer (CEO) stated publicly that the company took full responsibility. There were no outrageous failures at the factory, they followed stricter guidelines than required by law, and there seemed convincing evidence that food safety was taken very seriously. However, the firm had failed to notice that the same two assembly lines had tested positive for Listeria several times, despite extensive sanitation between each test. Each positive test was treated as a separate incident, which obscured an ongoing problem with these two lines. The company had started producing large volume packs of low sodium meats for hospitals and LTC facilities, where many patients and residents were on restricted sodium diets. Sodium provides some protection from bacteria, so the low sodium products were at more risk of contamination, but the company did not recognize this or make adjustments to their testing and sanitation processes.

The Maple Leaf Foods crisis was acute. To the extent that better monitoring of the trends in the Listeria tests might have raised the issue earlier, and that the firm failed to recognize their sanitation processes were not working, we assign this crisis as Type (5). The individual workers were doing what they were supposed to, so it would not be considered as operational negligence. Therefore, responsibility lies at the management level.

20.3.7 H-E-B Grocery Company

H-E-B Grocery Company (H-E-B) is a privately owned supermarket chain based in San Antonio, Texas, with more than 340 stores across Texas. It has a history of successfully managing environmental risks including hurricanes, floods, and disease outbreaks. At the start of the COVID-19 pandemic, the company gained recognition for its exemplary crisis management strategies and emergency preparedness. H-E-B maintained a unit dedicated to emergency preparedness, with a remit to identify potential emergencies as early as possible. The organization apparently took the COVID-19 risk very seriously even before it was addressed by local or federal agencies. H-E-B gathered information from suppliers and contacts in China and Europe, to try to prepare for the impact of the disease before it reached Texas. The firm had developed an influenza pandemic plan through simulation and scenario testing that it quickly adapted for the COVID-19 case. In order to maintain essential supplies, the company increased its inventory, opened a new warehouse, and reduced store hours to allow time to restock. Limits were placed on items such as hand sanitizer and disinfectants, to ensure, as far as possible, that stocks would not run out. In order to protect and support their employees, and to maintain service standards while limiting risk of infection, H-E-B implemented social distancing measures, extended sick leave for employees, and set up dedicated employee telephone lines.

H-E-B's response to the COVID-19 crisis was held up as a model for other companies. The organization achieved its goal of maintaining high standards of customer service, and providing a reliable resource to the local communities. It was named 'Grocer of the Year' by *Grocery Dive*, an influential industry e-journal.

The COVID-19 crisis was a Type (1) event – an acute, unavoidable, global disaster. H-E-B's commitment to crisis preparation, and their follow-through to crisis management, ensured that the negative impact on the firm was minimized, and that the reputation of the firm was ultimately enhanced.

20.3.8 The Grenfell Tower Fire

Grenfell Tower was a block of 129 apartments in West London. In June 2017, a massive fire broke out, resulting in 72 deaths and many injuries.

Grenfell Tower was owned by the local authority, the Royal Borough of Kensington and Chelsea (RBKC), and was originally designed for low-income housing. At the time of the fire, the residents were a mix of low- and middle-income families. The tower was built in 1970, and in 2015 the council arranged for the block to be renovated to improve its appearance and its energy efficiency. The original design of the tower incorporated fire-stops, so that a fire in a single apartment would, in principle, be contained within that unit. However, the refurbishment involved cladding the building using insulating materials, covered by an aluminium facade, with a ventilation gap between the insulation and the aluminium. Both the insulation and the aluminium plates failed fire safety standards, but were selected to save costs. When a fire broke out in a single apartment, the cladding materials created a chimney effect, overwhelming the built-in fire-stops, and quickly engulfing the entire building. Using fire resistant materials would have added around 3% to the refurbishment costs.

The immediate response of the leaders of the RBKC was widely criticized. The fire broke out shortly after midnight. Through the night, the firefighting and rescue operations were ongoing. Many families were evacuated with nowhere to go, and with no belongings. The Council leadership should have been on the ground, implementing crisis planning protocols, gathering information, working with the fire and police operations, organizing emergency accommodation and supplies for the survivors, helping the emergency services identify the victims, etc. None of that happened. The Council did not even meet to discuss arrangements until late the next day. A contact point for residents was set up, but the residents were not informed about it. Charity groups and local churches stepped in, while the RBKC, one of the wealthiest local authorities in the UK, failed to provide emergency assistance, failed to provide suitable emergency accommodation for survivors, failed to meet with community leaders, and failed to provide information to the press. They did not answer or return phone calls, so that offers of assistance from neighbouring local authorities and non-governmental agencies were ignored. The first council meeting following the fire was closed to the press, the survivors, and the general public. The council leader was said to appear overwhelmed and paralysed, but continued to deny any shortcomings. Within a few days, the UK government relieved the RBKC of its responsibilities with respect to Grenfell. The council leader, deputy leader, and chief executive were all forced to resign.

There were many warning signals that should have alerted the RBKC to the risks of using the cheap cladding, and to the potential failure of fire safety systems within the tower, but they were single-minded in their determination to reduce expenses at all costs. This was a Type (5) crisis for the RBKC; predictable, avoidable, and exacerbated by an incompetent response.

20.4 Crisis Preparation

It can be difficult for senior managers to allocate resources to crisis planning, especially for managers who are overconfident or over-optimistic. A person who feels that nothing bad will happen to them may have an advantage in achieving business success and recognition, but will have a significant disadvantage if called on to manage a crisis. Crises are complex and can be very emotional. The crisis may breach the individual's confidence, creating anxiety, making it difficult for them to process information quickly, or to make confident and appropriate decisions under stress. They may go into defensive mode, lashing out at journalists, regulators, or other stakeholders whom they perceive as attacking their firm and denigrating their competence. They may simply deny the crisis exists, or refuse to accept any corporate responsibility (see the above-mentioned United Airlines and VW examples). An overconfident CEO, who will not acknowledge the possibility of a catastrophic loss, will not willingly prepare for it; when a crisis does happen, if the overconfident CEO tries to manage the crisis without a competent team, and without careful planning, they are very likely to exacerbate the damage.

In a survey of firms in the US, Canada, and France, Pauchant et al. (1991) found that the managers who are most open to crisis preparation are those who have experienced poorly managed crises earlier in their careers. This has more influence than advice from professional organizations, crises experienced by other firms, or pressure from members of their Boards. Firms that are crisis-prone tend to be led by an intransigent senior management, who have reached their positions without experiencing a severe or mismanaged crisis. However, these results could also be partially explained by behavioural factors. The managers of crisis-prone firms are more likely to be overconfident or narcissistic types, who reject the idea of a crisis (even before they reach senior office) because it contravenes their illusion of control. They cannot learn from a crisis if they do not acknowledge the crisis. Those who claim to have learned from past crises are more likely to be collaborative, evidence-driven managers in the first place.

Crisis-prepared managers must question their self-confidence and their control of events; they must recognize the potentially debilitating impact of crisis-induced anxiety; they must learn to work with people who may not be their natural partners, such as journalists, regulators, and activists. Successful crisis management is more likely to be achieved by companies who are sincerely engaged in ethical business practices, particularly with respect to **environmental, social, and governance** (ESG) initiatives.

20.4.1 Educate Senior Management and Directors

Senior management must learn that crisis management is part of a successful corporate strategy, and that successful management of a crisis may not only save a company from disaster, it can enhance the firm's profits from the positive publicity generated. During a natural disaster, the firm that is well-prepared will gain business from firms that are unprepared.

The company's senior officers also need to understand the potential psychological impact of being in the eye of a media storm, or of having to publicly acknowledge corporate and individual errors of omission or commission. Training programmes can help senior managers understand and move beyond their own biases and anxiety triggers and responses. Biases that are particularly problematic during a crisis include confirmation bias, as it tends to lead people to deny the existence of a crisis; groupthink, as it can lead the firm's management to scapegoat others, (whistle-blowers, journalists, customers, or regulators) instead of taking proper responsibility for its own errors or failings (and can also create a bunker mentality amongst the leadership team), and overconfidence, which can lead the CEO to believe that they can single-handedly fix the crisis.

In a crisis, senior managers in the organization – up to, and including the CEO – may be called on to give press conferences and media interviews. Handling the media, especially live on TV, is harder than it appears. It is critical that all potential spokespersons receive prior media training specifically targeted at situations involving conflict or corporate failure.

Where senior management will not admit the possibility of a crisis, it will be very difficult for the organization to develop a working crisis management strategy. Unfortunately, many firms fall into this category, with an almost superstitious unwillingness to consider the possibility.

20.4.2 Identify Risks

Identifying vulnerability, through a **risk register** of low probability, high sever-ity potential crises, will point to risk mitigation or avoidance strategies. For example, an exercise considering the potential impact of extreme weather may identify supply chain vulnerabilities, that could be mitigated by diversification. The risk of business interruption could be mitigated by having plants operating in different regions. Risks from product tampering could be mitigated by using different packaging, or by installing more elaborate security measures. If the company's practices make it vulnerable to whistle-blowers, for example, because it uses unethical tactics such as mis-selling (UK private pensions crisis), fraudulent cross-selling (Wells Fargo), or bribery (Rolls-Royce), then mitigation might involve not doing unethical things.

The risk register will allow the firm to develop targeted contingency plans, ready to implement once a crisis event occurs.

20.4.3 Cultivate Mainstream and Social Media

Reputational risk is a key factor in many crises. A firm that has already developed good relations within the traditional media will save time in a crisis by having a network of contacts who are familiar with the firm and its culture. Furthermore, a firm that has a record of good corporate citizenship, and good faith communications with the media, will have a starting level of trust that will help it to manage its reputation through the crisis event.

Public relations crises are likely to be exposed first on social media – the United Airlines and Oxford Union crises are examples. Continuous monitoring of social media before a crisis arises is crucial for early warning, and a crisis may be averted if the organization is seen to be managing an incident appropriately through their social media responses.

20.4.4 Simulations

Crisis simulations are usually constructed by specialised crisis consultants. The objectives are to identify and correct any weaknesses in the crisis preparation and response, and to raise awareness amongst participants of the complexity and importance of crisis management.

Traditional crisis simulation involves an acute crisis scenario, where the crisis is short-term and severe. The crisis consultants create the scenario which is played out in real-time, under the consultants' directorship. Participants from the company are allocated roles according to the contingency plan, if it exists. Otherwise, the roles are determined extemporaneously. Throughout the exercise the consultants deliver information on the emerging crisis to the participants, through simulated news releases, calls from customers, emergency responders, or journalists, etc., ramping up the information received and the demand for a response. The simulation is intended to be sufficiently realistic to generate some semblance of the anxiety and stress that would be part of the real crisis, as learning about decision-making under stress is a major objective of the process. After the simulation ends, a debriefing allows participants to recognize successes and failures in their responses, and allows managers to identify ways to improve crisis preparation.

A different kind of simulation involves a smouldering crisis. Boin et al. (2004) describe longer term simulations, which they call 'institutional crises' involving, for example, obsolescence of a company's major product, failure of a key strategy, etc. The problem here is not the immediate response, but whether the firm's processes are sufficiently flexible to recognize emerging threats and adjust the direction of the corporation in time to avoid disaster.

Boin et al. (2004) report that simulations are popular with participants, but there are some risks and some drawbacks. For example, when a simulation pushes the severity of the crisis, raising the (mock) stakes, participants may withdraw from the role-playing, feeling that the simulation has 'gone too far', because they do not believe in such an extreme event. Nevertheless, simulations offer an effective, hands-on education in crisis management that (done well) will be far more effective in changing behaviours and raising awareness than PowerPoint presentations or textbooks alone.

Disaster simulations were said to have been valuable in the response and aftermath of the September 2001 terrorist attacks on New York. Several large scale disaster simulations had been run in the months before the attacks. Participants from all relevant agencies were practised in managing their responsibilities during the crisis. Well-defined command structures, communication pathways, and procedures for mass casualty events in local hospitals all helped in the emerging disaster, and also helped the community through the aftermath. Compare this with the Grenfell Tower disaster. The RBKC had run crisis simulations, but all were much smaller scale; they could not be scaled up to the level required when a real disaster occurred. The individual and organizational paralysis of the RBKC following the fire is a relatively common response to crisis-induced anxiety, when the organization has not adequately prepared for the event.

20.4.5 The Crisis Management Team

The firm should identify a high-level crisis management team (CMT). The responsibilities would usually include (i) identifying predictable risks, (ii) carrying out regular environmental scans to check for emerging risks, (iii) developing the crisis management plan, (iv) overseeing specific contingency plan creation; working with consultants on corporate training and education, and (v) maintaining emergency supplies and resources. The CMT is also responsible for the active management of the crisis response when a crisis occurs, including strategic decision-making and implementing communication strategies. Finally, the team would review successes and failures after each crisis, and help guide the firm into the rebuilding phase.

Typically, the crisis management team would involve the CEO, but they might not be an active member, depending on the size of the firm and the expertise of the CEO. If the CEO is not a member of the CMT, then one of the responsibilities of the CMT would be to ensure that the CEO is adequately informed of potential smouldering crises, and immediately informed in the event of an acute crisis. If the company has a Chief Risk Officer (CRO), they would be likely to take the lead position on the CMT, as risk and crisis management are closely connected. The Chief Financial Officer (CFO), or a senior member of the finance operations would typically be involved, as the crisis will impact the company's financial position. The Chief Operating Officer might be included, as the person with the best overall view of the firm's operations and with connections to the different business units. As crises often involve risk to employees, it would be common to involve representatives from the human resources department. Additionally, senior representatives from the firm's public relations (PR), marketing, and security teams might be involved.

The CMT will have critical responsibilities during an acute crisis, so an ability to understand and manage the effects of crisis induced anxiety and individual and organizational biases is important for all members. Ideally, the CMT members should have the following skills:

- **Ability to maintain composure under pressure** – Psychological tests can identify individuals who remain calm under stress, and who are less likely to panic, withdraw, or lose their ability to process information and make decisions in a crisis.
- **Ambiguity tolerance** – Often decision-making in a crisis must be done without full information. Some individuals are very intolerant to the ambiguity from incomplete information, and consequently are slow to make decisions, or are more likely to make bad decisions, such as 'wait-and-see' type non-decisions. The CMT members need to be able to make rational, timely decisions even where information is incomplete.
- **Communication skills** – This includes the ability to listen, to speak, and to write effectively and persuasively. Gathering information orally from different stakeholders and witnesses can be an important part of the initial assessment stage for an acute or simmering crisis. Communicating with stakeholders, including the general public through social media, is often a major element of the crisis response.
- **Critical thinking skills** – Typically, an acute crisis brings an overload of information, not all of which may be accurate, and not all of which may be pertinent. The CMT must critically evaluate the information, identify the advantages and disadvantages of the different potential strategies, and decide moment to moment on the best strategy for the immediate and longer term. In addition, it is common for the situation to progress differently than the initial predictions, so the CMT must be able to change tactics in response to new information, or to a changing environment.
- **Crisis experience** – As described above, managers who have experienced organizational crises, especially crises that were mis-managed, are more likely to be open to the education required to overcome their biases in order to better manage future crises.
- **Willingness to hear bad news** – Often, a crisis can be averted if the firm's management, represented by the CMT, is willing to listen to whistle-blowers who want to highlight risky or unethical practices of colleagues, or if the firm is open to reports of errors and 'near misses', where a crisis event was narrowly and propitiously averted. For example, in a hospital, an error

might involve administering the wrong dose of a drug. Reporting the error can lead to mitigating actions, such as proactive apology and engagement with the affected patient, and adjustments to the drug administration process to reduce the risk of the error being repeated.

In firms with a dominant CEO, crisis management is often run solely by the CEO (if the crisis is sufficiently severe), but dominant CEOs are the least likely to perform well in a crisis, as they tend to prefer individualistic leadership, when crisis response is more successful with an interdisciplinary, team-based approach.

20.4.6 The Crisis Management Plan

The crisis management plan is the high level document laying out the company's approach to crises. Specific potential crises identified by the CMT may have individual contingency plans as adjuncts to the overall plan. The plan should include information on the following issues:

(1) A list of the crisis management team members, with contact information.
(2) Individual responsibilities of each CMT member. For the separate contingency plans, additional team members may be identified, based on their technical expertise related to the specific contingency.
(3) Procedures for defining the start of a crisis and activation of the crisis response process.
(4) Plans for establishing a crisis communication centre, suitable for media briefings and other internal and external communications (for example, with employees, directors, regulators).
(5) List of phone/email information for trusted media contacts, and potential external advisors, such as legal, PR, and/or IT consultants.
(6) Statement of responsibilities and principles for social media monitoring and posting.
(7) Targets for the time taken for initial information gathering and decision-making.
(8) The designated spokesperson for the organization (may have different spokespeople for different crises).
(9) Criteria for bringing the CEO into external communications (for most severe reputational crises, for example), and ensuring that the CEO is consistent and on-message.
(10) Immediate action plan for damage limitation, including responsible persons, and target timescale for implementation.

(11) Potential corrective action project plan, including individual responsibilities, for minimizing business interruption. This may be a major part of the plan, depending on the nature of the business and the crisis.

(12) Documentation requirements.

(13) Process for debriefing after the crisis.

Crises that are exogenous to the firm, and more readily anticipated, such as natural disasters, or cyberattack, are the most likely to be identified and subject to detailed contingency planning. For example:

- Airline companies will have contingency plans for managing airplane crashes. The key components are (i) immediate action plan (e.g., facilitating rescue efforts for passengers and crew); (ii) communicating with regulators, relatives of passengers and crew, mainstream media contacts, local airport officials, etc.; (iii) setting-up a communication centre for ongoing information collection and dissemination; and (iv) corrective action plan for managing impact on operations.

- Oil companies should be prepared for spills at sea (from tankers or rigs) or on land (e.g., from pipelines). The key components might include (i) short-term damage limitation and corrective action plans (for example bringing in specialists to clean up the spill); (ii) communication with regulators and legal advisors; (iii) mainstream and social media messaging; and (iv) long-term corrective action plan for environmental repair.

- Companies that hold personal data of customers should prepare for cyberattacks leading to data theft. Key tasks would include (i) damage limitation action to stop the breach; (ii) communication with regulators; (iii) communication with customers, especially victims; and (iv) social and mainstream media messaging.

- Companies with facilities that are vulnerable to extreme weather should prepare for action, for example, in the event of a hurricane warning. Key tasks would include (i) messaging employees, to make sure they take any necessary actions to ensure their safety; (ii) damage limitation plan, such as moving vulnerable equipment, backing-up computer systems, storm-proofing buildings, and delivering generators; (iii) identifying possible actions (such as temporarily shifting production to another site) to minimize business interruption; and (iv) communicating with insurers for swift resolution of claims.

- Manufacturers should prepare for product liability crises, for example, where the firm's product has caused deaths or injuries of customers or third parties. Key tasks include (i) the damage limitation plan (product recall, production halt decisions); (ii) communicating with customers (part of damage limitation); (iii) social and mainstream media messaging; and (iv) legal liability consultation.

It is worth noting here a proposition from Pearson and Clair (1998), that: 'A modest amount of crisis preparation likely will lead executives to believe that their organization is no longer vulnerable to a crisis.'

20.5 Crisis Response

20.5.1 Strategic and Operational Responses

The strategic response is determined by the top level decision-makers, and is concerned with setting the overall strategy. The operational response falls on the workers most closely involved in the crisis, who are responsible for implementing the crisis response. Most of the crisis management literature is concerned with the strategic response, but a good strategic response can be hampered by a poor operational response.

20.5.2 Situational Assessment

It is critical for the CMT to gather as much information as possible at the initial stages of the crisis, but it is also important for them to continue gathering information, as crises often involve rapidly changing characteristics. Following the initial information gathering, the CMT would determine an initial situational assessment, identifying the likely severity of the crisis, and developing an initial response plan, both of which would be updated minute-by-minute as additional information becomes available. The CMT may at this initial stage develop several possible scenarios for the crisis, and identify possible responses suitable for each scenario.

20.5.3 Containment and Mitigation

For an acute crisis which threatens the health and safety of workers, customers or others, it is important to act quickly and decisively to contain the damage, and to put people first, even if the cost of doing so is substantial. In the case of the Tylenol attacks, the response of Johnson & Johnson to the information that contaminated Tylenol had caused several deaths was an immediate withdrawal of all of their products from all retail outlets across the United States. They might have ordered a more limited recall, based on the information that all the deaths had occurred in and around Chicago, but they chose the more conservative action. Although it cost them millions of dollars in revenue, it likely saved several lives, and was recognized and praised as socially responsible. The firm realized that the initial information involving only the Chicago area could be incomplete. The risk of more widespread contamination was not worth taking.

Even for crises that do not involve the health or safety of individuals, the advice to put people first applies, not only because it is the ethical thing to do, but also because it is the best way to minimize reputational damage. In the Dr Dao/United Airlines case, the CEO's initial response, which ignored the obvious suffering and unfair treatment of Dr Dao, created a reputational crisis that was much worse than before his communication. He could have immediately acknowledged that United Airlines had behaved badly, apologized, and offered a change of process for 'bumping' passengers, and the crisis would have been mitigated. Indeed, he did all of those things several days later, but the initial response, with its victim blaming and lack of empathy, exacerbated the problem instead of mitigating it.

The Nike sweatshop boycott was a smouldering rather than an acute crisis, but still many commentators identify the turning point in the containment of the crisis as the public statement in 2001, by Todd McKean, Nike's director of labour practices for North Asia and Europe, that the company's previous position, that 'these aren't our factories; these aren't our issues', was irresponsible and untrue.

20.5.4 Communications

Much of crisis management training and education is around communications. The communication strategy within the crisis management plan should address communicating with employees and directors, with other stakeholders, such as shareholders, clients, customers, suppliers, and regulators, and with the general public. Visibility, honesty, and empathy are seen as key components in crisis response. However, in most cases, the communication strategy should be used to highlight and support other actions taken to contain or mitigate the damage. It is rare that words alone will solve the crisis, but lack of words, or the wrong words, can make matters worse.

Communication effectiveness can substantively affect the outcome of a crisis, particularly in respect to reputational damage. A communication strategy should be developed as soon as the crisis plan is activated.

Internal communication is important as employees may be involved directly in the crisis event, for example if workplace safety is compromised, in which case they need to be given relevant information as early as possible. Even those who are not involved directly should be kept informed; otherwise, the firm risks losing their goodwill, which will make it harder to recover. Employees act as ambassadors of the firm, to customers, friends, and neighbours. Allowing employee feedback to the communications from the firm can also be helpful, both in maintaining employees' trust, and in potentially gathering new information.

External communication can make an existing crisis much worse, or it can substantively mitigate the damage, particularly with respect to the reputation of the organization.

The company should identify one or two spokespersons who are senior in the organization, have full access to all available information, and have extensive media and crisis management training. Where more technical expertise may be required the spokesperson might bring a subject matter expert to press conferences, preferably one with good communication skills and media training. The idea is, as far as possible, to be seen to be answering all possible questions as fully as possible.

Although the CEO often acts as spokesperson, particularly if the crisis is public and severe, they may not be the best choice. The televised hubris of CEOs exacerbated the reputational damage to their corporations both in the Deepwater Horizon tragedy, and in the United Airlines/Dr Dao incident. In the aftermath of the Deepwater Horizon explosion, the CEO of BP famously said that he 'wanted his life back'. The statement, made in the heat of the moment, was an explosive misstep made by a CEO who was overwhelmed, stressed, and probably sleep-deprived. It made a terrible situation even worse for BP. An apology the following day did little to assuage public anger. In the United Airlines case, the day after the Dr Dao video went viral, the CEO, Oscar Munoz, publicly blamed Dr Dao for being aggressive (this was untrue) and praised the staff responsible for ordering and carrying out the attack. Two days later, Munoz was forced to make the apology that would have been much more effective on the first day, and which was seen as forced and insincere. One reporter[1] credited Munoz' response with 'turning a public relations disaster into a crisis management shambles'.

On the other hand, when the CEO has the right message and the right tone, their impact as a spokesperson will be greater. In the Maple Leaf Foods case, the CEO, Michael McCain, appeared at a press conference immediately on hearing that the listeriosis outbreak had been sourced to one of his firm's

---

[1] www.youtube.com/watch?v=Aocjy9m1m6w

factories. He appeared grave; he explicitly took full responsibility for the deaths and illnesses, offered a full apology, and announced a widespread recall of the Maple Leaf products. In subsequent TV appearances, and press conferences, McCain was consistent in his firm and sincere message of apology and accountability. Generally, the public response was favourable to the company's message, and the reputational damage was much lower than many had anticipated. McCain[2] later explained that his approach was to be 'accepting of our accountability, very decisive in our action, and . . . transparent and open about what had happened and what we would do to correct it'.

Communication through traditional news media is often hampered by organizations treating journalists as 'the enemy'. It is the journalists' job to ask tough questions, and a company can enhance its reputation by showing that it is willing to respond to those questions, provided that the response is frank, open, and people-centred (and not predominantly shareholder centred). Many corporations develop ongoing relationships with journalists outside of crisis situations, to build up trust, and enhance the journalists' understanding of the organization and its culture.

In a press conference, the spokesperson should be candid about what is known and unknown. There may be questions that cannot be answered, because the information is not available, or because there are other considerations causing a delay in release of information, such as informing next of kin when deaths are involved. The spokesperson should explain the situation and must not be seen as evasive. Often, an early acceptance of accountability, even when all the facts are not yet known, will create the best platform for the crisis communication going forward. Sometimes revealing the truth may be very painful for the organization, but hiding it will likely lead to greater problems in the long-term (as seen in the VW emissions scandal, for example).

The corporate website will be a source for many journalists and members of the public. It is a valuable medium for communicating with customers. As the crisis develops, it is very important that the website is continuously updated.

The other source of immediate information used by the public is social media. In any public crisis, monitoring and responding to social media posts will be a major task, but it cannot be set aside or ignored. Social media can give an early signal of the direction of public sentiment, which should assist in developing the communications strategy. Also, if the firm is seen as responsive on social media, it may be able to mitigate reputational risk to some extent. Social media posts are experienced by readers as a more personal conversation, and participation makes the corporation appear more human. However, social

---

[2] www.youtube.com/watch?v=2_nZQphHq4M

media participants expect instant responses, so it can be difficult to satisfy readers if information that they seek is not yet available. Nevertheless, it is better to explain the need for time than to stay silent. It is interesting to note that United Airlines' Twitter account through the Dr Dao crisis was tone deaf to the barrage of angry tweets directed at it. The only direct reference is a tweet that says: 'Flight 3411 from Chicago to Louisville was overbooked. After our team looked for volunteers, one customer refused to leave'. This was not even true – the flight was not overbooked, the airline wanted to make space for their employees who did not have a booking. Obviously, the tweet did nothing to dissipate the anger.

20.5.5 To Apologize or Not

The crisis response team has several choices to make with respect to apologies:

- Full apology, acceptance of fault, acceptance of responsibility.
- No apology, but acceptance of responsibility.
- No apology, no acceptance of responsibility.

It is interesting to note that it was the sincere apology in the Maple Leaf Foods case that was subsequently highlighted by experts as the turning point. It was unexpected; typically, companies tend to shrink from full apologies, perhaps instead expressing regrets, or offering non-apologies, of the 'I'm sorry if you were offended' variety, both of which fall short of accepting blame or fault. The leader of the RBKC, after the Grenfell Tower fire, apologised for 'perceived failings', not for the actual failings of the council. The value of an apology lies in the perception of sincerity. In the United Airlines case, the CEO was ultimately forced to apologize, by public pressure, but because of the initial poor messaging, the apology was seen as neither sincere nor empathetic. The audience, including the public and the employees of the organization under strain, are generally looking for compassion, sincerity, and an acknowledgment of responsibility.

The apparent success of the apology strategy can create pressure to apologize early, even where the organization is not actually at fault. This can create an impression of guilt, even where it does not exist. The communications strategy, in general, should not include an apology if the organization is confident that it does not bear any blame. However, it may still acknowledge responsibility for rectifying the situation. This was the approach taken by Johnson & Johnson in the Tylenol case. It is interesting to note that some researchers (Coombs and Holladay, 2008) have found that the apology itself is less important than sympathy and a willingness to take responsibility. This gives organizations some breathing space – the expression of sympathy for victims can be part of the short-term communication, without needing to wait to find out whether any blame is attached to the organization.

The strategy attempted by United Airlines, initially, involved an aggressive defence of the organization, with an attempt to assign blame elsewhere. This can be effective in some circumstances, but will be high risk if it emerges that the organization was at fault all along.

An approach that is uniformly criticized is the 'non-apology' apology. A real apology (whether sincere or not) should convey a message acknowledging the firm or individual's error, accepting responsibility, and expressing a desire to repair harms caused by the error. The non-apology apology involves some key words, but does not include any sense of remorse or reparation. Different types of non-apology include:

(1) The **blame-shifting apology**, for example, 'We are sorry if you were offended ... '. This shifts the responsibility on to the other party, with an implication that they were just too sensitive or unreasonable.

(2) The **excuse apology**, for example: 'I am sorry we failed to keep your data safe but we were too overwhelmed with other challenges at the time ... ' implying that the actions taken were actually quite reasonable or inevitable, or were someone else's fault. The focus is on justification when it should be on reparation.

(3) The **regret non-apology**, for example: 'We regret that criminals breached our data security and stole personal information that may be used to access customers' bank accounts'. This is not an apology, it's a statement about the feelings of the speaker or their institution. Regret is inward looking, not outward (like the excuse apology). In a real-world example, in 2015, Dove soap issued a remarkably insensitive commercial where a black woman became a white woman, apparently after washing with Dove, promoting a racist meme of darker skin being less clean than lighter skin. In response to the social media storm, Dove tweeted that: 'We deeply regret the offence it caused'. No doubt they regretted the offence, since it caused a public relations hassle. But were they sorry for promoting a racist message?

(4) The **overly generic apology**, for example, after being criticized for spending over $800,000 on a trip to Las Vegas in 2010, the head of the US General Services Administration, Martha Johnston, said: 'I personally apologize to the American people for the entire situation'. The failure to

acknowledge anything more specific makes the apology seem more strategic than sincere.

(5) The **brag apology**, where the apology is subsumed in a boast about the company, for example: 'We have a long and illustrious record of exceeding our customer's expectations and are sorry that on this one occasion we did not live up to our own high standards.'

(6) **Apologizing for the wrong thing**; Equifax experienced a data breach, did not tell anyone for weeks, then when it did report it, stated: 'This is clearly a disappointing event for our company, and one that strikes at the heart of who we are and what we do. I apologize to consumers and our business customers for the concern and frustration this causes.'

20.6 Post Crisis

Post crisis evaluation of the crisis management strategy enables the organization (i) to work out the details of implementing the actions promised during the crisis, (ii) to plan the ongoing communication strategy, and (iii) to identify successes and failures in the crisis response and update the crisis management plan. The organization should be open to a change in outlook and direction if the crisis has been severe. Questions such as 'Did we miss warning signals?' 'Was our preparation as thorough and relevant as we had predicted?' 'Did the CMT work together and provide the coherent, consistent response appropriate to the crisis?' 'Are changes required to the CMT or the crisis management plan?' 'Are we currently following best practice crisis preparation?' should be considered. Documenting the successes and failures of the crisis preparation and response will support the crisis management strategy going forward.

Continuing communication through the post crisis phase can be used to help restore reputations. Where the organization has committed to an action plan, there may be benefit in reminding the public of the steps taken as the plan is implemented. For example, Maple Leaf Foods communicated its steps in leading initiatives for improving the safe processing of meat products in Canada. In addition, it may be appropriate to mark the end of the crisis with a mass communication to stakeholders, explaining the crisis response, resolution, and lessons learned.

If the crisis has interrupted the business operations, for example, after a natural disaster or a cyberattack, it is important to resume normal business activities as soon as possible. A well-prepared organization will be able to do this more quickly than the unprepared company. In the case of cyberattacks, specialist firms may help restore systems and security, and the best preparation is to establish relations with the firm before the crisis event. In the case of natural disasters, preparation might include moving goods, contacting employees, and creating makeshift premises. If employees have been displaced, then preparing systems of communication in advance will allow the organization to contact them to ensure they are aware of arrangements.

20.7 Ethics, Governance, and Crisis Management

20.7.1 Ethics

Human-induced crises occur over and over again, often in organizations that are aggressive in pursuit of profits or growth. Organizations that emphasize ethical behaviour and individual responsibility of employees are less likely to experience crises of Type (4) or (5), than those which only target profit. Apparently, the senior officers at VW did not want to know how their engineers were achieving significant performance gains whilst also meeting emissions constraints. Or, perhaps they knew but did not care as long as profits increased. But excessive diesel emissions from VW cars cause cancer and lung disease in the local populations; VW's cynical and illegal bypassing of regulations that are specifically designed to minimize risk to local communities from particulate matter, signalled that it was a corporation of low ethical values contradicting their cultivated image as friends of the environment. In the end, the focus on profits at any expense failed to provide long-term shareholder wealth maximization.

A weak ethical environment is a common factor in the most egregious risk management failures in recent history. Wells Fargo pursued an aggressive strategy of cross-selling (persuading existing customers to open additional accounts or credit cards). The senior managers created intense pressure on front-line employees to meet highly unrealistic quotas. The result was that millions of loans, credit cards, and insurance policies were created on behalf of Wells Fargo customers without their consent. The customers were charged for the unwanted contracts through direct deductions from their existing accounts. The estimated cost of fines and civil suits is around \$3 billion. The banking failures of 2008 arose from the mortgage crisis created, initially, by the cynical issuing of subprime mortgages to borrowers who were clearly going to be unable to keep up with the repayments. Ultimately, the plan failed due to a lack of understanding by the lenders of default dependency, but it is clear that the initial loan practices, whilst legal, were far from ethical.

The unethical organization is more likely to experience self-inflicted reputational crises, and is generally less able to manage the crises when they arise. The unethical CEO will generally not be able to persuade the public or regulators of their sincere apology when their pursuit of profit at all costs goes wrong. They are more likely to try to deny the event, or to try to scapegoat others for the failure.

Part of the success of Maple Leaf Foods, Johnson & Johnson, and H-E-B crisis management arose from the perception that they are ethical firms, who sincerely wanted to put things right, and to provide the best possible service to customers. On the other hand, few members of the public considered United Airlines a particularly ethical firm, and the airline's response to the Dr Dao incident hardened that view.

With increasing focus from the public, from activist shareholders, and from regulators, on corporate social responsibility, and environmental impact, the narrow focus on shareholder wealth is being displaced somewhat by a stakeholder model, where all stakeholders, including shareholders, employees, and the local community, are considered to have a role in the organization's success, and are, therefore, given consideration in the corporate strategy. The stakeholder model emphasizes business ethics, that is, the concept that business may behave morally, even where not required to do so by regulation or legislation. An ethical firm is more likely to avoid human-induced crises, and more likely to recover their reputation and business share when they do experience crises.

20.7.2 Influence of Corporate Structure

't Hart et al. (1993) suggest a distinction between **mechanistic firms** and **pragmatic firms**. Mechanistic firms are more hierarchical, rules-based, and bureaucratic. Chains of communication are formal, and decisions are expected to be made only at the top of the organization. Pragmatic firms have a flatter structure, with more devolution of decision-making to the different units.

In an acute crisis, the mechanistic organization tends to have a centralized strategy, but the operational response can be hampered by the top-down structure. For example, consider a hypothetical mechanistic firm operating a number of factories. Local managers and workers are not encouraged to make decisions; the central headquarters codifies all policies and procedures in detailed manuals. Suppose that a crisis event happens, for example, a spill of toxic chemicals into the local water supply. Suppose further that this event is not specifically covered in the manuals. The manager does not want to make any decision about the crisis (if they wanted to be decision makers, they would work for a different firm). They may not even want to inform headquarters of the incident, since rigid hierarchical structures can be brutal to bearers of bad news. Hence, there is a tendency to paralysis; the local manager takes no action, the crisis continues, until eventually the hazard is exposed, and the severity has been significantly exacerbated by the operational failure.

In a non-acute crisis, with more time for analysis and response, the mechanistic firm will have time to develop a centralized response at the senior level which is then communicated top-down for local implementation.

For the pragmatic firm, in an acute crisis the business unit that is closest to the crisis will often determine the strategy; the response is informal and decentralized. If the toxic spill event happens in a pragmatic firm, with decision making responsibility devolved to the local factories, then the local manager will be accustomed to taking responsibility, and, if the crisis is highly time-critical, the local manager is likely to make strategic decisions without waiting for approval from headquarters. During an acute winter storm in 2020, a large part of Texas was left without power or water in freezing temperatures. In a local H-E-B grocery store, when the power failed, the local manager made the decision to allow all the customers in the store to leave with their essential supplies, without paying, as the store could not operate its checkouts. The decision was highly praised for its pragmatism and empathy. However, if the local manager is not well prepared, they may withdraw from decision-making, through the crisis-induced paralysis mentioned earlier. 't Hart et al. (1993) call this **strategic evasion**. The operational response is likely to be focused on the immediate problem as perceived by the front-line workers, but there is a risk that wider issues and impacts are not taken into account.

In a non-acute crisis, the pragmatic firm might use more formal decentralization of crisis strategy, but decentralization can lead to lack of cooperation between the different units, particularly if the managers perceive themselves as being in competition with each other.

There is no prescription here for the optimal response. A centralized response may have the advantage of coherence and consistency across the organization, but the senior managers responsible may suffer from the debilitating effects of information overload and crisis-driven anxiety, particularly if the decisions fall on a single individual or small team. Furthermore, if there are technical aspects to the crisis, the senior managers may lack the expertise required to propose solutions. Centralized responses are more vulnerable to groupthink and excessive optimism biases. On the other hand, decentralized responses may be too narrowly focussed or inefficient, as different units end up separately addressing similar problems, or may just lead to strategic evasion, if the local agents become overwhelmed.

20.8 Further Reading

For a general discussion of crisis management see Lerbinger (2012) and Pearson and Clair (1998). Leadership issues are discussed in James and Wooten (2005).

't Hart et al. (1993) discusses the problems of centralized and decentralized firms' responses to crises.

Section 20.5.5 draws on Coombs and Holladay (2008).

20.9 Exercises

Exercise 20.1 Describe the advantages and disadvantages of having the CEO of the company act as spokesperson in a crisis.

Exercise 20.2 Many public organizations, such as universities, post 'emergency response plans' online. Find one of these[3] and use it to answer the following questions:

(a) How does the emergency response plan differ from a crisis management plan?
(b) Do you think the plan is sufficiently comprehensive? Has anything been left out that should have been included?
(c) Is the plan readable? Explain how it could be improved.
(d) Does the plan include debriefing and organizational learning?

Exercise 20.3 ABC is a car manufacturer. Recently, a number of ABC's vehicles have experienced power failures, which have resulted in several accidents and some deaths. Although, as a proportion of cars on the road, the number of failures is very, very small, some news outlets are beginning to pick the story up. The CMT and senior management have no warning of any problems with the car prior to reading news reports and social media posts.

(a) Describe three potential response strategies that ABC might take immediately on becoming aware of the issue.

---

[3] For example, the University of Waterloo plan is linked in https://uwaterloo.ca/emergency-planning/

(b) After a short time, ABC discovers that one contributor to the failures might be a change in materials used in a component bought from a supplier. The CEO suggests an aggressive PR strategy blaming the supplier for the accidents. Discuss the advantages and disadvantages of this approach.

(c) After some weeks, the news media have dropped the story, and it looks like ABC has avoided significant reputational damage. The CMT proposes a major recall of cars which used the faulty components. The CEO counters that this would be extremely expensive, and, in any case, the problem seems to have been resolved. Outline the points the CMT should make in response.

Exercise 20.4 Identify which of the case studies in this chapter, and in Chapter 2, have unethical, but not illegal business practices as a contributing factor. Explain how the unethical behaviour caused the crisis or made it worse. Should a firm accept some level of unethical behaviour if it is sufficiently profitable?

Exercise 20.5 Explain how internal and external crisis communication might differ. Use (a) the Maple Leaf Foods case and (b) the United Airlines/Dr Dao case as examples. More details on both cases can be found online.

Exercise 20.6 In March 2005, police officers were called to a Wendy's restaurant (Wendy's is a large franchise chain of fast food outlets) after a customer claimed to have found a human thumb in a bowl of chili. Initial reporting was sympathetic to the unnamed customer, and Wendy's sales plummeted for a week. At the start of the second week, the customer was named and sympathetically interviewed on TV. By this time, Wendy's was sure that this was an act of sabotage rather than negligence, as they verified that the thumb could not have entered the food during processing. Wendy's continued to work with police and forensic investigators, but also hired their own forensic expert, and set up a hotline with a cash reward for information identifying the source of the thumb. It turned out that the customer had put the thumb in the chili herself. She was later sentenced to nine years in prison.

(a) What type of crisis was this?

(b) As a part of Wendy's CMT, what scenarios would you have been working on in the early stages?

(c) Describe the appropriate communication strategy at the start, and then once Wendy's had established that the claim was a fraud.

(d) Do you think this crisis would have proceeded differently if it had happened in the current era of far more widespread social media?

Appendix   Probability and Statistics Review

A.1 Summary

In this appendix, we review some concepts, notation, and results from probability and statistics that are assumed as background in this book. We start with univariate random variables, their distributions, moments, and quantiles. We consider dependent random variables through conditional probabilities and joint density and distribution functions. We review the normal, lognormal, uniform, and binomial distributions. We outline the maximum likelihood (ML) estimation process and summarize key properties of ML estimators. We review Bayesian statistics, including the prior, posterior, and predictive distributions. We discuss Monte Carlo simulation, with a focus on estimation and uncertainty.

A.2 Introduction

It is assumed that much of this material is familiar to readers, as it would be covered in undergraduate courses in introductory data analysis and inference. This appendix is therefore intended as a review, rather than a comprehensive primer. Readers who have not previously covered the results that are summarily presented here are encouraged to consult an introductory text, such as Grimmett and Welsh (2014).

A.3 Random Variables

A **random variable** is a function with values determined by a random phenomenon. For example, the random variable X could be:

- The price of one unit of Apple stock in six months.

- The payoff from a six-month European at-the-money call option on one unit of Apple.
- The number of defective products manufactured in a specified plant over a one-month period.
- The time to failure of a machine component.
- Costs of patent defence litigation over a one-year period.

The **cumulative distribution function**, or just **distribution function**, of a random variable X is the function

$$F_X(x) = \Pr[X \le x].$$

The subscript X will be omitted where the associated random variable is unambiguous.

The distribution function of any random variable must satisfy the following properties, and, conversely, any function with the following properties is a distribution function:

$\lim_{x \to -\infty} F_X(x) = 0$ and $\lim_{x \to \infty} F_X(x) = 1$;
$F_X(x)$ must be a non-decreasing function of x;
$F_X(x)$ must be right-continuous.

The **survival function** or **decumulative distribution function** of a random variable X is denoted in this text by $S_X(x)$, and is defined as

$$S_X(x) = \Pr[X > x] = 1 - F_X(x).$$

The properties of $F_X(x)$ require that

$\lim_{x \to -\infty} S_X(x) = 1$ and $\lim_{x \to \infty} S_X(x) = 0$,
$S_X(x)$ must be a non-increasing function of x,
$S_X(x)$ must be right-continuous.

Random variables are classified as discrete, continuous, or mixed.

Discrete random variables take values from a range which is finite or countable. That is, the support (or range of possible values) for the random variable can be expressed as $\{x_1, x_2, \ldots, x_m\}$, where m could be infinite.[1] For discrete random variables, the distribution function is a step function which is equal to 0 for $x < x_1$ and is equal to 1 for all $x \ge x_m$; the function has jumps at each of $x_1, x_2, \ldots$, and is level between successive values. In the third example listed above, the number of defective products manufactured must be an integer, so the random variable is discrete. The distribution function is zero for $x < 0$; steps up at $x = 0, 1, 2, \ldots$, and is flat between the integer values.

---

[1] We will assume for convenience that $x_k < x_{x+1}$ in the definitions, etc.

Many of the discrete distributions we work with, like this one, are distributed on the non-negative integers.

Discrete random variables have an associated **probability function** $p(x)$, where

$$p(x) = \Pr[X = x].$$

This probability will be greater than 0 for each of the x_k in the support of X, and will be 0 for $x \neq x_k$ for any k. Properties of the probability function are

$$0 \leq p(x) \leq 1.0;$$
$$\sum_{k=1}^{m} p(x_k) = 1.0.$$

Continuous random variables take values from a continuous (uncountable) range, and have a cdf that is continuous. We generally treat future stock prices as continuous random variables,[2] even though the price is quoted in increments of 0.01. The time to failure of a component is also continuous. In both cases, $F_X(0) = 0$, and $F_X(x)$ is continuous and strictly increasing up to the maximum value for X.

For continuous random variables, the probability that the random variable is equal to any specific value is zero, so we do not use the discrete probability function. Instead, we use the **probability density function** (pdf), $f(x)$, where

$$f(x) = \frac{d}{dx} F_X(x) = -\frac{d}{dx} S_X(x).$$

A way to understand the pdf is that the probability that X lies in a very small interval, $(x, x + dx)$ is approximately $f(x)\, dx$.[3]

Properties of the probability density function are

$$f(x) \geq 0 \text{ for all } x;$$
$$\int_{-\infty}^{\infty} f(x)\, dx = 1.$$

Note that it is possible to have $f(x) > 1$ for some x.

Mixed random variables have a range which includes continuous and discrete sub-ranges. For example, the payoff of the call option may be zero, and there will be a finite probability attached to that outcome (equal to the probability that the market price of the asset at maturity lies below the strike price). If the payout is greater than zero, it can take any value on a continuous

---

[2] We ignore here the possibility of bankruptcy.
[3] As we have done above in assuming that F_X is differentiable, we will often assume that distributions and densities of continuous random variables are smooth enough to permit us to perform any mathematical manipulations that we need to, without making explicit qualifications.

range. The distribution function will have a discontinuity at $x = 0$, and will be continuous for all $x > 0$.

A mixed random variable will have discrete probability mass at each possible discrete value, and will have a density function describing the distribution over the continuous portion.

A.4 Moments and Quantiles

A.4.1 Moments

The expected value, or mean, of a discrete random variable, K say, with probability function $p(k)$, is

$$E[K] = \sum_k k\, p(k).$$

The expected value of a function of K, say $g(K)$, is

$$E[g(K)] = \sum_k g(k)\, p(k).$$

The nth **raw moment** of K is defined as $E[K^n]$, which can be calculated as

$$E[K^n] = \sum_k k^n\, p(k).$$

Similarly, the nth **central moment** of K is $E[(K - E[K])^n]$, which can be calculated as

$$E\left[(K - E[K])^n\right] = \sum_k (k - E[K])^n\, p(k).$$

For a continuous random variable X, with density function $f(x)$, we have similar results, but with the summations replaced with integrals; that is,

$$E[X] = \int_{-\infty}^{\infty} x\, f(x)\, dx,$$

$$E[g(X)] = \int_{-\infty}^{\infty} g(x)\, f(x)\, dx,$$

$$E[X^n] = \int_{-\infty}^{\infty} x^n\, f(x)\, dx,$$

$$E\left[(X - E[X])^n\right] = \int_{-\infty}^{\infty} (x - E[X])^n\, f(x)\, dx.$$

For a mixed random variable, we separate the discrete and continuous parts, and combine the appropriate sums and integrals.

If any of these sums or intervals do not converge, we say that the moment does not exist.

For a random variable X, with mean $E[X] = \mu$, we have:

(a) The **variance** of X, $\text{Var}[X]$ is the second central moment:

$$\text{Var}[X] = E\big[(X - \mu)^2\big] = E\big[X^2\big] - \mu^2.$$

The variance is commonly denoted by σ^2.

(b) The **standard deviation** of X is $\sigma = \sqrt{V[X]}$.

(c) The **skewness** of X is the third central moment:

$$sk[X] = E\big[(X - \mu)^3\big].$$

(d) The **kurtosis** of X is the fourth central moment:

$$ku[X] = E\big[(X - \mu)^4\big].$$

In this book we will use the definitions and notation above, but we note that there are some variations in usage. In particular, the term 'skewness' is often used to mean the **coefficient of skewness**, $(sk[X]/\sigma^3)$ and the term 'kurtosis' may be used to mean the **coefficient of kurtosis** $(ku[X]/\sigma^4)$ or the **excess kurtosis** $(ku[X]/\sigma^4 - 3)$.

The **limited expected value** of a random variable is the expected value up to some pre-specified maximum. Suppose X is a continuous random variable with density function $f(x)$ and distribution function $F(x)$. The limited expected value of X up to some maximum value M is denoted $E[X \wedge M]$, and is calculated as

$$E[X \wedge M] = \int_{-\infty}^{M} x \, f(x) \, dx + \int_{M}^{\infty} M \, f(x) \, dx$$

$$= \int_{-\infty}^{M} x \, f(x) \, dx + M(1 - F(M)). \qquad (A.1)$$

A.4.2 Quantiles

Quantiles of a distribution measure the value which will be greater than the random variable with a given probability. It is quite simple to express this symbolically for continuous random variables, as they have strictly increasing distribution functions. For $0 < \alpha < 1$, the α-quantile of X is Q_α such that

$$\Pr[X \leq Q_\alpha] = \alpha \quad \text{or, equivalently} \quad Q_\alpha = F_X^{-1}(\alpha).$$

For example, for the standard normal distribution, the 90% quantile is the value, $Q_{0.9}$, at which 90% of the distribution lies below $Q_{0.9}$ and 10% of the

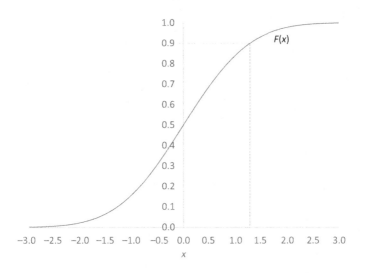

Figure A.1 Illustration of the 90% quantile of the standard normal distribution

distribution lies above $Q_{0.9}$. That is,

$$Q_{0.9} = \Phi^{-1}(0.9) \approx 1.282.$$

What this expresses is that the quantile lies at the intersection of the line $y = \alpha$ and the curve of $F(x)$. For a continuous random variable with $F(x)$ strictly increasing with values between 0 and 1, for any $\alpha \in (0, 1)$ there is a unique value $Q_\alpha = F^{-1}(\alpha)$ as above. This is illustrated in Figure A.1, where the standard normal distribution function is plotted, and the value of x corresponding to the intersection with the line $y = 0.9$ is the 90% quantile.

For a discrete random variable, taking values from the set $\{x_1, x_2, \dots, x_m\}$, we find that, using this intersection approach, the α-quantile will be unique if α lies between two values of $F(x_k)$, and will not be unique if $\alpha = F(x_k)$ for some k. For example, consider the discrete distribution with probability function:

k	x_k	$p(x_k)$	$F(x_k)$
1	1	0.3	0.3
2	5	0.3	0.6
3	7	0.3	0.9
4	8	0.1	1.0

The distribution function is illustrated in Figure A.2. Suppose we are interested in the 90% and 40% quantiles. We see that the $y = 0.9$ line intersects the curve for all x such that $7 \le x < 8$, and any number in this range may be regarded as

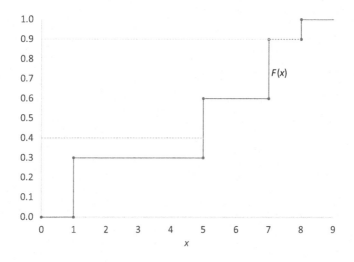

Figure A.2 Illustration of 40% and 90% quantiles of a discrete distribution

a 90% quantile. On the other hand, the $y = 0.4$ line intersects at $x = 5$, so that the 40% quantile is equal to 5 – in fact all the quantiles for α in the interval $(0.3, 0.6)$ are equal to 5.

There are different conventions for determining unique quantiles from discrete or mixed distributions. We will use the convention that sets the quantile at the smallest value where the intersection method above gives a range result. That is,

$$Q_\alpha = \min\{x : F(x) \geq \alpha\}.$$

Using this convention, the 40% quantile from the discrete distribution above would still be 5, but the 90% quantile would be equal to 7, rather than equal to all values between 7 and 8.

This convention has an intuitive interpretation. Suppose we consider the discrete distribution above as an empirical distribution from a sample of 10 values; that is, we have an underlying population of 1, 1, 1, 5, 5, 5, 7, 7, 7, 8.

The 40% quantile is the 4th (0.4×10) smallest value from the population, which is 5. The 90% quantile is the 9th smallest value from the population, which is 7.

A.4.3 Generating Functions

When summing random variables, it is often convenient to work with generating functions. The **probability generating function** (pgf) of a random variable N is

$$P_N(z) = \mathrm{E}\left[z^N\right].$$

For a counting random variable, N (that is, a random variable taking values in the non-negative integers), with $p_k = \Pr[N = k]$,

$$P_N(z) = \sum_{k=0}^{\infty} p_k\, z^k.$$

Differentiating the pgf k times, and evaluating the function at $z = 0$, gives $P_N^{(k)}(0) = k!\, p_k$.

The **moment generating function** (mgf), $M_X(t)$, say, of a random variable X, is

$$M_X(t) = \mathrm{E}\left[e^{tX}\right],$$

where the expectation exists. Differentiating the mgf k times, and evaluating the function at $t = 0$ gives the kth raw moment of the distribution, that is,

$$M'(0) = \mathrm{E}[X] \quad M''(0) = \mathrm{E}\left[X^2\right], \text{ etc.}$$

Note also that $M_X(t) = P_X\left(e^t\right)$, or, equivalently, $M_X(\log(z)) = P_X(z)$.

The mgf, where it exists, uniquely identifies the distribution of the underlying random variable X.

The **cumulant generating function** $C(z)$ is the logarithm of the moment generating function, and is useful for finding the first three central moments, as

$$C'(0) = \mathrm{E}[X], \quad C''(0) = \mathrm{Var}[X], \text{ and } C'''(0) = \mathrm{E}[(X - \mathrm{E}[X])^3].$$

This is useful because in many cases the cumulant generating function is easier to work with than the mgf, and because it directly generates the second and third central moments. However, this does not work for higher central moments.

Note that $P(0) = 0$, $M(0) = 1$, and $C(0) = 0$.

A.4.4 Tail Behaviour

We are often interested in risks arising from very rare events. One way to measure whether a distribution captures the potential financial consequences of very rate events is to assess whether the distribution is 'fat-tailed' or 'thin-tailed'. These terms are often used quite loosely, but we will use two functions to quantify whether a distribution is thin- or fat-tailed. For a continuous distribution, define the **failure rate**, $h(x)$, as the ratio of the density function to the survival function of the distribution at x, that is,

$$h(x) = \frac{f(x)}{S(x)}.$$

Both $f(x)$ and $S(x)$ converge to 0 as $x \to \infty$. If we consider a small interval $(x, x + dx)$, then $f(x)dx$ is approximately equal to the probability that X lies in the interval $(x, x + dx)$. For the same interval, we have, again somewhat loosely,

$$h(x)\, dx \approx \Pr[X \in (x, x + dx)| X > x].$$

For analysing the tail of the distribution, we consider how $h(x)$ behaves as $x \to \infty$. If $h(x)$ is an increasing function, then the further out into the tail, the higher the probability that X is close to x, given $X > x$. If $h(x)$ is a decreasing function, then far out into the tail, the probability that X is much greater than x increases. So, an increasing failure rate indicates a thin-tailed distribution, and a decreasing failure rate indicates a fat-tailed distribution.

A related function is the **mean excess loss** (MEL) function, $e(x) = \mathrm{E}[X - x | X > x]$. The MEL measures the average difference between x and the expected value of X, conditional on $X > x$. If this is an increasing function, then the further out into the tail of the distribution we go, the higher the difference between the conditional loss, $\mathrm{E}[X | X > x]$ and the tail point x, indicating a fat-tailed distribution. If $e(x)$ is a decreasing function, then the distribution is thin-tailed.

Given two continuous distributions with the same mean, we can compare tail behaviour directly by considering the ratio of their density functions as $x \to \infty$. For example, if $\lim_{x \to \infty} f(x)/g(x) = 0$, then the probability density f tends to zero faster than g, as x gets large, and a random variable with density f will have a thinner tail than a random variable with density g.

A.4.5 Conditional Random Variables

Two random variables, X and Y, say, are independent if and only if for all x and y,

$$\Pr[X \le x \text{ and } Y \le y] = \Pr[X \le x]\, \Pr[Y \le y],$$

which means that knowing everything about one of the random variables gives us no information about the other.

For dependent X, Y, we need functions which describe the probabilities jointly. We liberally utilize conditional probabilities and Bayes' theorem, which states that for two events, A and B, with the probability that A happens given that B happens, denoted by $\Pr[A|B]$ (we read 'given' for the symbol '|'), we have

$$\Pr[A|B] = \frac{\Pr[A \text{ and } B]}{\Pr[B]} = \frac{\Pr[B|A]\,\Pr[A]}{\Pr[B]}.$$

We let $F_{X,Y}(x, y)$ denote the joint distribution function, so that

$$F_{X,Y}(x, y) = \Pr[X \leq x \text{ and } Y \leq y] = \Pr[X \leq x | Y \leq y] \times \Pr[Y \leq y].$$

For continuous X, Y, with unconditional density functions $f_X(x)$ and $f_Y(y)$, we have:

- The joint density function for X, Y is

$$f_{X,Y}(x, y) = \frac{\partial^2}{\partial x \, \partial y} F_{X,Y}(x, y).$$

- The conditional density function for $X|Y$ is

$$f_{X|Y}(x|y) = \frac{f_{X,Y}(x, y)}{f_Y(y)}.$$

We interpret the conditional density function $f_{X|Y}(x|y)$ as the density for X given that $Y = y$.

The unconditional density function, $f_X(x)$, is called the **marginal density** function, and can be derived from the other functions in two ways:

$$f_X(x) = \int_{-\infty}^{\infty} f_{X,Y}(x, y)dy; \tag{A.2}$$

$$f_X(x) = \int_{-\infty}^{\infty} f_{X|Y}(x|y)f_Y(y) \, dy. \tag{A.3}$$

For discrete X, Y, we have similar probability functions.

- The joint probability function for X, Y is

$$p_{X,Y}(x, y) = \Pr[X = x \text{ and } Y = y].$$

- The conditional probability function for $X|Y$ is

$$p_{X|Y}(x|y) = \frac{p_{X,Y}(x, y)}{p_Y(y)}.$$

- The marginal probability function for X is

$$p_X(x) = \sum_y p(x, y) = \sum_y p_{X|Y}(x|y) \, p_Y(y).$$

Two very useful results follow from the relationship between the marginal and conditional probability functions. The first is the law of **iterated expectations**, also called the **tower rule**, which says that for dependent X, Y,

$$E[X] = E_Y \left[E_X \left[X|Y \right] \right]. \tag{A.4}$$

This means that we can break down the calculation of the unconditional expectation of X into two steps. In the first, we assume Y is fixed, and find $E[X|Y]$ under the conditional distribution of X. This will generally be a function of Y (unless X and Y are independent). In the second step we take expectation under the marginal distribution of Y. In this way, we can often simplify a situation that involves complex dependencies.

By using iterated expectation for $E[X^2]$, we can also derive a formula for the unconditional variance of X,

$$\text{Var}[X] = E_Y[\text{Var}_X[X|Y]] + \text{Var}_Y[E_X[X|Y]]. \tag{A.5}$$

Example A.1 Suppose X and Y are random variables such that

$$Y = \begin{cases} 1 & \text{with probability } 0.9, \\ 2 & \text{with probability } 0.1, \end{cases}$$

$$E[X|Y = 1] = 20, \quad E[X|Y = 2] = 40,$$

$$\text{Var}[X|Y = 1] = 200, \quad \text{Var}[X|Y = 2] = 1{,}000.$$

Calculate the unconditional mean and variance of X.

Solution A.1

$$E[X] = E[E[X|Y]] = 20 \times 0.9 + 40 \times 0.1 = 22,$$

$$E[\text{Var}[X|Y]] = 200 \times 0.9 + 1{,}000 \times 0.1 = 280,$$

$$\text{Var}[E[X|Y]] = 20^2 \times 0.9 + 40^2 \times 0.1 - 22^2 = 36$$

$$\Rightarrow \text{Var}[X] = 316.$$

A.5 Important Distributions

A.5.1 The Normal Distribution

The normal (or Gaussian) distribution is generally considered the most important continuous distribution in statistics. The main reason for the usefulness and ubiquity of the normal distribution is the **central limit theorem**, which says that, under some mild conditions, the (suitably normalized) sum of a large number of independent random variables will (approximately) have a normal distribution, regardless of the marginal distributions of each individual random variable.

The normal distribution has two parameters, μ and σ^2. The density function for $X \sim \mathrm{N}(\mu, \sigma^2)$ is

$$f(x) = \frac{1}{\sqrt{2\pi}\,\sigma} \exp\left(-\frac{1}{2}\left(\frac{x - \mu}{\sigma}\right)^2\right).$$

The expected value is $E[X] = \mu$, and the variance is $\mathrm{Var}[X] = \sigma^2$. The distribution function cannot be expressed in closed form, but can be calculated using using standard software.

Where the parameters of the normal distribution are $\mu = 0$ and $\sigma^2 = 1$, we have the **standard normal distribution**, denoted $\mathrm{N}(0, 1)$. The density and distribution functions of the standard normal distribution have their own notation:[4]

$$\phi(z) = \frac{1}{\sqrt{2\pi}} e^{-\frac{1}{2}z^2} \quad \text{and} \quad \Phi(z) = \int_{-\infty}^{z} \phi(y)\,dy.$$

Note that the distribution function of $X \sim \mathrm{N}(\mu, \sigma^2)$ is

$$F(x) = \Phi\left(\frac{x - \mu}{\sigma}\right).$$

The moment generating function of the $\mathrm{N}(\mu, \sigma^2)$ distribution is

$$M(t) = e^{\mu t + \frac{1}{2}\sigma^2 t^2}.$$

The normal distribution is symmetric, which means the third central moment (skewness) is always zero. The coefficient of kurtosis of the normal distribution (which is independent of μ, σ) is 3.0.

A.5.2 The Lognormal Distribution

The lognormal distribution is another continuous distribution which is particularly important in financial applications. We say that X has a lognormal distribution with parameters μ, σ, and write $X \sim \mathrm{logN}(\mu, \sigma)$, when $\log X$ has a normal distribution with parameters μ and σ^2. The density and distribution functions are derived from the standard normal distribution functions as

$$f(x) = \frac{1}{\sigma x}\phi\left(\frac{\log x - \mu}{\sigma}\right) \quad \text{and} \quad F(x) = \Phi\left(\frac{\log x - \mu}{\sigma}\right).$$

This gives us

$$E[X] = e^{\mu + \sigma^2/2} \quad \text{and} \quad \mathrm{Var}[X] = e^{2\mu + \sigma^2}\left(e^{\sigma^2} - 1\right).$$

---

[4] Note that in financial mathematics, the standard normal distribution function is often denoted $\mathrm{N}(z)$ rather than $\Phi(z)$.

A.5.3 The Uniform Distribution

The uniform distribution is particularly important in working with copula dependency models. We say that X has a uniform distribution with parameters $a, b > a$, and write $X \sim U(a, b)$, when $X \in (a, b)$, and the probability density function of X is flat between a and b, that is,

$$f(x) = \frac{1}{b - a}.$$

The $U(0, 1)$ distribution is the most common form. For the $U(0, 1)$ distribution we have

$$f(x) = 1; \ F(x) = x; \ 0 < x < 1;$$
$$E[X] = \tfrac{1}{2}; \ \text{Var}[X] = \tfrac{1}{12}.$$

A.5.4 The Binomial Distribution

The binomial is a discrete distribution on the non-negative integers. It has two parameters: m is a positive integer, and q is a real-valued parameter in $(0, 1)$. The binomial distribution arises where there are m independent 'trials' each with probability of 'success' of q; the number of successes, N, say, has a binomial distribution, denoted binomial(m, q) or $\text{Bin}(m, q)$.

We use the conventional terms 'trial' and 'success' here, but in fact the application of the binomial distribution is broad, and, especially in risk management, the 'success' that we are measuring might not be a desired outcome. For example, suppose a firm sells components in batches of 50. Each component has a probability of 0.02 of defect, and the components are independent with respect to defects. Then the number of defective components in a single batch has a binomial distribution with parameters $m = 50$, $q = 0.02$.

The probability function, mean, and variance of the $\text{Bin}(m, q)$ distribution are:

$$\Pr[N = k] = \binom{m}{k} q^k (1 - q)^{m-k}, \qquad \text{for } k \leq m,$$
$$E[N] = m\,q, \qquad \text{Var}[N] = m\,q\,(1 - q).$$

In the case where $m = 1$, the binomial distribution is called the **Bernoulli distribution**. A Bernoulli random variable is equal to 1 with probability q, or 0 with probability $1 - q$. This is particularly useful for **indicator random variables**. An indicator random variable indicates whether a random event occurs or not, and can be very useful in risk analysis. For example, an insurer might assess losses from auto insurance claims depending on whether the loss involved personal injury or not. Suppose further that the probability that a claim involves personal injury is $q = 0.1$. We could use an indicator random variable to model the event that a claim involved personal injury, that is, let

$$I = \begin{cases} 1 & \text{Personal injury involved,} \\ 0 & \text{No personal injury involved.} \end{cases}$$

Then we have

$$E[I] = 0.1 \times 1 + 0.9 \times 0 = 0.1,$$
$$\text{Var}[I] = 0.1 \times 1 - (0.1)^2 = 0.09.$$

In general, for an indicator random variable with associated probability q, we have $E[I] = q$ and $\text{Var}[I] = q(1 - q)$.

Other distributions are reviewed in Chapter 4.

A.6 Maximum Likelihood Estimation

A.6.1 The Likelihood Function

If historical loss data is available for a risk that we wish to evaluate, we can use classical statistical methods to estimate parameters for the different distributions, to analyse the goodness of fit, and to assess which distribution offers the best fit to the data.

The most common method for estimating parameters of loss distributions is **maximum likelihood estimation** (MLE).

For a given distribution, and assuming a random sample $x = (x_1, x_2, \dots x_n)$, the MLE parameter estimates are the parameter values which give the highest probability to the data set x. We find the parameters by maximizing the likelihood function, which is the multivariate probability (density) function for the data, expressed as a function of the parameters.

That is, given a sample $x = (x_1, x_2, \dots, x_n)$, taken from an underlying multivariate random variable $X = (X_1, X_2, \dots, X_n)$, and a distribution with unknown parameters $\theta = (\theta_1, \theta_2, \dots, \theta_k)$, we select values of $(\theta_1, \theta_2, \dots, \theta_k)$ to maximize the likelihood function

$$L(\theta_1, \dots, \theta_k) = f_{X_1, \dots, X_n}(x_1, x_2, \dots, x_n; \boldsymbol{\theta}).$$

The maximizing parameter vector is denoted by $\hat{\boldsymbol{\theta}}$.

In many situations, we assume the X_i are independent, which means that the joint probability function is just the product of the individual probability functions,

$$L(\theta_1, \ldots, \theta_k) = f_{X_1, \ldots, X_n}(x_1, x_2, \ldots, x_n; \boldsymbol{\theta})$$
$$= f_{X_1}(x_1; \boldsymbol{\theta}) \, f_{X_2}(x_2; \boldsymbol{\theta}), \ldots, f_{X_n}(x_n; \boldsymbol{\theta}).$$

Furthermore, if the X_i are i.i.d., then the individual probability functions are the same, so that

$$L(\theta_1, \ldots, \theta_k) = f(x_1; \boldsymbol{\theta}) \, f(x_2; \boldsymbol{\theta}), \ldots, f(x_n; \boldsymbol{\theta}).$$

The log-likelihood function $l(\boldsymbol{\theta})$ is the log of $L(\boldsymbol{\theta})$, so, in the i.i.d. case,

$$l(\boldsymbol{\theta}) = \log L(\theta) = \sum_{j=1}^{n} \log f(x_j; \boldsymbol{\theta}).$$

It is much more convenient to work with the log-likelihood than with the likelihood. For some distributions, we can determine the MLE parameter estimates analytically. In other cases, we can use numerical optimization software, such as Solver in Excel.

Note that we may use the same notation, $l(\theta)$, for the log-likelihood function applied to a data set $(x_1, \ldots, x_n)$, in which case $l(\theta)$ is a real-valued function of θ, or applied to a random sample, $(X_1, X_2, \ldots, X_n)$, in which case $l(\theta)$ is a random variable. Following most texts, we do not always distinguish these cases but allow the context to communicate which meaning is intended.

A.6.2 Properties of Maximum Likelihood Estimators

In this section, we consider the MLE parameter estimates as random variables, functions of a random sample $(X_1, \ldots, X_n)$. The useful properties of MLE estimates rely on asymptotics. That is, the results hold as the sample size $n \to \infty$, and will hold fairly well for large n, but may not be accurate for small samples.[5] Let $\hat{\boldsymbol{\theta}}$ denote the random MLE of a parameter vector $\boldsymbol{\theta}$.

Asymptotic Unbiasedness

The MLE is asymptotically unbiased, which means that

$$\lim_{n \to \infty} E\left[\hat{\theta}_j\right] = \theta_j, \quad j = 1, 2, \ldots, k.$$

In many cases $\hat{\theta}_j$ is unbiased for any sample size n.

---

[5] The properties listed below require certain regularity conditions in order to hold. For detailed statements and proofs, see, e.g., Casella and Berger (2001).

Asymptotic Minimum Variance

Suppose $\boldsymbol{\theta} = (\theta_1, \theta_2, \ldots, \theta_k)$ is a vector of unknown parameters, and $\hat{\boldsymbol{\theta}} = (\hat{\theta}_1, \hat{\theta}_2, \ldots, \hat{\theta}_k)$ is a vector of random estimators for $\boldsymbol{\theta}$.

The expected information matrix for $\boldsymbol{\theta}$, $I(\boldsymbol{\theta})$, is a $k \times k$ matrix, with i, j entry

$$I(\boldsymbol{\theta})_{i,j} = \mathrm{E}\left[-\frac{\partial^2}{\partial \theta_i \, \partial \theta_j} l(\boldsymbol{\theta})\right]. \tag{A.6}$$

The inverse of the expected information matrix, $I(\boldsymbol{\theta})^{-1}$, gives the asymptotic covariance matrix for the estimators $\hat{\theta}_1, \hat{\theta}_2, \ldots, \hat{\theta}_k$. The diagonals of $I(\boldsymbol{\theta})^{-1}$ give the asymptotic variances of the estimators $\hat{\theta}_j$, $j = 1, \ldots, k$. These variances are also the Cramér–Rao lower bounds for the estimator variance – that is, no other function of X will give an unbiased estimator with a lower variance.

This result shows that, asymptotically, the MLE is an efficient estimator. It also gives us a way to estimate the asymptotic variances and covariances of the $\hat{\theta}_j$. Although we do not know the true underlying values of θ_j, $j = 1, \ldots, k$, which may be required in equation (A.6), we can approximate them using the MLE estimators $\hat{\boldsymbol{\theta}}$ evaluated with the data set $x_1, \ldots, x_n$.

Asymptotically Normally Distributed

Asymptotically, $\hat{\boldsymbol{\theta}}$ has a multivariate normal distribution, with mean equal to the vector of true underlying values of $\boldsymbol{\theta}$, (as it is asymptotically unbiased), and with covariance matrix equal to the Cramér–Rao lower bound, which is the inverse of the expected information matrix. For large samples, we can use the normal distribution variates to determine confidence intervals for the underlying parameters.

The Delta Method

The delta method can be used to determine the MLE of a function of the parameters of a distribution, and its asymptotic variance, in terms of the MLEs for the individual parameters.

Let $\hat{\theta}$ be the MLE for a parameter θ. Then, for any differentiable function $g(z)$, we have that the MLE for $g(\theta)$ is $g(\hat{\theta})$, which is very convenient. This means, for example, that estimating σ or σ^2 will give consistent results.

Furthermore, the asymptotic variance of the estimator $g(\hat{\theta})$ is

$$\left(\frac{d}{d\theta} g(\theta)\right)^2 \mathrm{Var}[\hat{\theta}],$$

which we can estimate using the MLE based on a sample x.

In the case with more than one unknown parameter, we consider a function $g(\theta_1, \theta_2, \ldots, \theta_k)$ which is differentiable with respect to each of $\theta_1, \ldots, \theta_k$. Assume that we have MLE estimators $\hat{\theta}_j$ for $j = 1, \ldots, k$, and we have the covariance matrix Σ for the estimators θ_j. Then the MLE of $g(\theta_1, \theta_2, \ldots, \theta_k)$ is $g(\hat{\theta}_1, \hat{\theta}_2, \ldots, \hat{\theta}_k)$, and the asymptotic variance of $g(\hat{\theta}_1, \hat{\theta}_2, \ldots, \hat{\theta}_k)$ is

$$\sigma_g^2 = (\nabla g(\boldsymbol{\theta}))^T \, \Sigma \, (\nabla g(\boldsymbol{\theta})),$$

where

$$\nabla g(\boldsymbol{\theta})^T = \left(\frac{\partial}{\partial \theta_1} g(\boldsymbol{\theta}), \ \frac{\partial}{\partial \theta_2} g(\boldsymbol{\theta}), \ldots, \frac{\partial}{\partial \theta_k} g(\boldsymbol{\theta}) \right).$$

A.6.3 Limitations of Maximum Likelihood Estimation

- Unbiasedness, minimum variance, and normal distribution are only asymptotic qualities of MLEs. For smaller samples, estimators may be biased, there may be lower variance estimators available, and estimators may be very non-normal.
- If a parameter is near the boundary of its parameter space, the asymptotic results may not hold.
- MLE does not tell you how good the fit is. Even if the standard errors of parameters are small, the model may be a very bad fit to the data. However, we can use the log-likelihood as a basis for selecting the best model from a set of candidate models.
- For complex models with large numbers of parameters, the numerical methods for finding MLEs may not work well.
- MLE works well with dependent data in some cases, but not all. For time series, the asymptotic results hold for strictly stationary time series, but not for non-stationary ones.

A.7 Bayesian Statistics

Maximum likelihood estimation treats the parameters as unknown constants. Bayesian statistics addresses parameter uncertainty by modelling the parameters as random variables.

Suppose we have a random sample $\boldsymbol{x} = (x_1, x_2, \ldots, x_n)$, from a random variable X, where the probability function of X, $f(x)$, depends on an unknown parameter θ. Under the Bayesian approach, we treat θ as a random variable, with probability function $\pi(\theta)$, called the **prior distribution**. The parameters of the prior distribution are called **hyperparameters**.

Bayes' Theorem gives us

$$\pi(\theta|x) = \frac{f_X(x|\theta)\pi(\theta)}{f_X(x)} \propto f_X(x|\theta)\pi(\theta),$$

where $f_X(x|\theta) = L(x;\theta)$ is the joint probability function for the sample x, given θ, which is exactly the likelihood function from the previous section, and where $f_X(x)$ is the unconditional probability function for x, $f_X(x) = \int f_X(x|v)\,\pi(v)dv$, which does not involve θ.

The distribution $\pi^*(\theta) = \pi(\theta|x)$ is the **posterior distribution**. This is the probability function for θ updated with the information from the sample x. If we want a point estimate of the parameter θ, we can use the mean of $\pi^*(\theta)$; we can use the standard deviation as a measure of the standard error of the estimator. We can go even further, fully incorporating the range of possible values for θ in the distribution of X using the **predictive distribution**:

$$f^*(x) = \int_\theta f(x|v)\pi^*(v)dv.$$

The predictive distribution allows jointly for the uncertainty arising from the probability distribution of X, and the uncertainty associated with the parameter θ.

Typically, there are several parameters involved in the distribution of X. In this case, we replace the univariate θ with a parameter vector $\boldsymbol{\theta} = (\theta_1, \ldots, \theta_k)$, and the probability functions π and π^* are now joint probability functions for the parameter vector.

The analytic application of Bayesian statistics is limited by the complexity of the conditional and joint distributions involved. In a few cases, the functions $f(x|\theta)$ and $\pi(\theta)$ combine neatly to generate tractable, well-known distributions for $\pi^*(\theta)$ and for $f^*(x)$; examples include:

(1) The Poisson-gamma model, where $X|\theta \sim \text{Poisson}(\theta)$, and where $\theta \sim \text{Gamma}(\alpha, \beta)$. In this case, the posterior distribution is also Gamma (with updated hyperparameters) and the predictive distribution is negative binomial.

(2) The binomial-beta model, where $X|\theta \sim \text{Bin}(n, p)$, for a known n, and where $p \sim \text{Beta}(\alpha, \beta)$. In this case, the posterior distribution is also beta, with adjusted hyper-parameters, and the predictive distribution is known as the beta-binomial distribution.

(3) The normal-normal model, where $X|\theta \sim \text{N}(\theta, \sigma^2)$, for known σ, and where $\theta \sim \text{N}(\mu_\theta, \sigma_\theta^2)$. In this case, the posterior distribution for θ and the predictive distribution for X are both normal distributions.

In each of these cases, the posterior distribution of θ has the same parametric form as the prior, with parameters updated to incorporate the information provided through the likelihood. When this applies, we say that π is a **conjugate prior** to the distribution of X.

If the prior distribution of θ has a small standard deviation, that implies a low level of prior uncertainty with respect to the parameters. In this case, the prior will have more influence than the data on the posterior and predictive distributions. If the prior distribution is very dispersed, implying a high level of uncertainty, then the data will have a stronger influence on the posterior and predictive distributions, through the likelihood function. In this case, we say that π is a **non-informative prior**. Non-informative priors eliminate some of the subjectivity involved in assigning prior distributions and hyper-parameters.

For example, consider the normal-normal model, where $\sigma = 40$, and $\mu_\theta = 500$. Suppose we collect a random sample of $n = 20$ values of X, and find that the sample mean is $\bar{x} = 530$. The predictive distribution is normal, with mean

$$\mu^* = \frac{\sigma_\theta^2 \sigma^2}{n\sigma_\theta^2 + \sigma^2} \left(\frac{\mu_\theta}{\sigma_\theta^2} + \frac{n\bar{x}}{\sigma^2} \right).$$

Suppose, first, that $\sigma_\theta = 10$. The prior parameters signal a strong belief that the value of θ lies in the range $(480, 520)$, that is, within around 2 standard deviations of the prior mean. In this case, the predictive mean of X is $\mu^* = 516.7$, which is balancing the strong information from the prior, pulling the estimate towards $\mu_\theta = 500$, and the information from the data, pulling the estimate towards $\bar{x} = 530$.

Now let $\sigma_\theta = 100$, indicating that the value of θ likely lies in the range $(300, 700)$, a much weaker, non-informative prior. In this case, we find that $\mu^* = 529.8$, very close to the best estimate from the data.

In cases where the posterior and predictive distributions are not analytically tractable, we may be able to use Markov Chain Monte Carlo techniques to generate a random sample from the posterior distribution of $\boldsymbol{\theta}$.

A.8 Monte Carlo Simulation

A.8.1 Introduction

In quantitative risk management in practice, it is often the case that loss processes are too complex for analytic evaluation. A very common way to analyse risk in such cases is using **Monte Carlo simulation** (also known as **stochastic simulation**). The fundamental idea is that we use random number generators to create random scenarios, and for each scenario we can calculate the resulting cash flows. This is repeated for a large number of randomly generated scenarios. Each scenario is equally likely, and is independent of the other scenarios.[6] Thus, we can create a set of values for the cash flows that can be treated as a sample from the underlying distribution. If the sample is large enough, it can be used to estimate the loss mean, standard deviation, and quantiles. As with a real sample, the values will have some uncertainty about them, but we can quantify at least part of the uncertainty.

In this section, we describe a method for generating random variates from a distribution, using random draws from a U(0,1) distribution. We assume that the U(0,1) values are available using suitable statistical software (although in practice it is important to check the quality of the underlying random number generators).

A.8.2 The Inverse Transform Method

Consider (for simplicity of the explanation) a continuous random variable X, with distribution function $F(x)$. Let x_u denote the u-quantile of X, so that $\Pr[X \leq x_u] = F(x_u) = u$. Then consider the random variable $F(X)$. It turns out that this random variable has a standard U(0,1) distribution, regardless of the starting distribution for X. We can demonstrate this as follows:

$$\Pr[F(X) \leq u] = \Pr[X \leq F^{-1}(u)] = \Pr[X \leq x_u] = u, \qquad \text{(A.7)}$$

$$\Rightarrow F(X) \sim U(0,1). \qquad \text{(A.8)}$$

Now we can reverse the reasoning. Suppose $U \sim$ U(0,1). Then

$$F(X) \sim U \Rightarrow X \sim F^{-1}(U),$$

which means that, given a random U(0,1) variate u, we can construct a random variate from the distribution of X using $x = F^{-1}(u)$.

Note that the method works for discrete, continuous, and mixed distributions.

Example A.2 Suppose you have four draws from the U(0,1) distribution, as follows:

$$0.0289, \qquad 0.0958, \qquad 0.4905, \qquad 0.6606.$$

Generate four simulated values of a random variable with distribution function

$$F(x) = 1 - \left(\frac{\lambda}{\lambda + x} \right)^{\alpha},$$

where $\lambda = 100$ and $\alpha = 3$.

---

[6] This is not always true for more advanced methods involving variance reduction, but is true for standard Monte Carlo.

Solution A.2 Let $u = F(x)$, then

$$u = 1 - \left(\frac{\lambda}{\lambda + x}\right)^{\alpha}$$

$$\Rightarrow x = \lambda \left(\left(\frac{1}{1-u}\right)^{\frac{1}{\alpha}} - 1\right) = F^{-1}(u),$$

which gives the random variates:

$$0.9823, \qquad 3.4138, \qquad 25.2041, \qquad 43.3605.$$

Although the inverse transform method works for any distribution, it only works efficiently for large sample sizes when the distribution function is easily invertible. There are some important distributions for which this is not true, including the normal distribution. However, there are normal random number generators available in all good quantitative software, including R, Splus, Excel, etc., and there are also quite simple algorithms available for implementing your own, described fully in simulation texts such as Ross (2012).

A.8.3 A Monte Carlo Simulation Example

We use Monte Carlo simulation when the random variable that we are interested in is too complicated for analytic evaluation of its distribution function. For example, the sum of independent lognormal random variables does not have a tractable distribution function. In the following example, we use Monte Carlo simulation to estimate the tail probability for a sum of lognormal random variables.

Example A.3 Suppose $Y_1, Y_2, \ldots, Y_5$ are independent and identically distributed lognormal random variables, with parameters $\mu = 2$ and $\sigma = 2$. Generate 10,000 simulations of $S = \sum_{j=1}^{5} Y_j$, and use the sample to estimate $\Pr[S > 5{,}000]$.

Solution A.3 Assuming that we have software that can generate random variates from the standard normal distribution, the simulation would proceed as follows:

(1) Generate 10,000 sets of 5 random $N(0,1)$ values; let Z_{ij} denote the ith value in the jth simulated set, $i = 1, 2, \ldots, 5$, $j = 1, 2, \ldots, 10{,}000$.
(2) Transform the standard normal variates to the required lognormal variates as

$$Y_{ij} = e^{\mu + Z_{ij}\sigma}.$$

(3) Generate 10,000 values of the sum of each set, say, $S_j = \sum_{i=1}^{5} Y_{ij}$.

(4) Count how many of the simulated values for S_j are greater than 5,000.
(5) The estimated probability is then the number of $S_j > 5,000$ divided by the sample size, 10,000.

Since the example asks for an estimate based on a random sample, answers will be different for different trials. In our trial, (using R), we found 29 of the 10,000 simulated values for S were greater than 5,000, which gives an estimated probability of $\hat{q} = 0.0029$.

A.8.4 Estimation and Uncertainty in Monte Carlo Simulation

The Monte Carlo method is a very powerful way of exploring distributions that are not very tractable analytically, but the cost is that the simulated probabilities and moments are subject to sampling variability. As a rule, every time you use Monte Carlo simulation to estimate some statistics of a distribution, you should also determine and report a measure of the uncertainty of the estimate arising from sampling variability. This will enable users of the calculations to judge whether the accuracy is sufficient for their needs. If it is not, it can be improved by increasing the sample size, or by using more sophisticated Monte Carlo techniques.

We often quantify the sampling variability by calculating the standard error of our estimate; the standard error is the term for standard deviation of a random estimator of a parameter or other distribution metric. Sometimes we can use the standard error to construct a confidence interval, and in other cases we construct a confidence interval without calculating the standard error.

In this subsection we will consider estimators and standard errors for several commonly used statistics.

We use Monte Carlo simulation to generate a sample of N values of a random variable, L. We let L_j denote the jth simulated value, for $j = 1, 2, \ldots, N$. Assume $E[L_j] = E[L] = \mu$, say, and that $Var[L_j] = Var[L] = \sigma^2$.

Estimating a probability, q

As in the example above, suppose that we are interested in estimating $q = Pr[L > k]$ for some fixed k. Let N_k denote the number of simulations for which $L_j > k$. The estimated probability is then

$$\hat{q} = \frac{N_k}{N}. \tag{A.9}$$

The standard error of this estimate can be estimated without any additional assumptions about the underlying distribution. Consider N_k as a random variable; it is the number of values of X greater than k from N independent trials, where for each trial $\Pr[X > k] = q$, and the number of trials is fixed, so that

$$N_k \sim \text{Bin}(N, q) \Rightarrow E[N_k] = Nq, \quad \text{Var}[N_k] = N q (1 - q), \tag{A.10}$$

$$E[\hat{q}] = E\left[\frac{N_k}{N}\right] = \frac{Nq}{N} = q, \tag{A.11}$$

$$\text{Var}[\hat{q}] = \text{Var}\left[\frac{N_k}{N}\right] = \frac{1}{N^2} \text{Var}[N_k] = \frac{Nq(1-q)}{N^2} = \frac{q(1-q)}{N}. \tag{A.12}$$

This shows that the estimator is unbiased, that is, $E[\hat{q}] = q$, with standard error $\sigma_q = \sqrt{q(1-q)/N}$. For large samples the estimator is approximately normally distributed. We know this because the binomial distribution converges to a normal distribution for large N. Hence, a 95% confidence interval for q is $(\hat{q} \pm 1.96\sigma_q)$. We cannot calculate σ_q exactly, as it is a function of the unknown parameter q, but we can estimate it by using $\hat{q}$. In the example above, we have $\hat{q} = 0.0029$, $N = 10,000$, so $\sigma_q \approx 0.00054$, and the estimated 95% confidence interval for q is

$$(0.0029 - 1.96(0.00054),\, 0.0029 + 1.96(0.00054)) = (0.0018, 0.0040).$$

Estimating the mean and standard deviation

The estimate of the underlying mean is the mean of the Monte Carlo sample, that is,

$$\hat{\mu} = \frac{\sum_{j=1}^{N} L_j}{N}.$$

The estimate of the underlying variance is the variance of the Monte Carlo sample, that is,[7]

$$\hat{\sigma}^2 = \frac{\sum_{j=1}^{N} (L_j - \hat{\mu})^2}{N - 1}.$$

The expected value and variance of the mean estimator are

$$E[\hat{\mu}] = E\left[\frac{\sum_{j=1}^{N} L_j}{N}\right] = \frac{N E[L]}{N} = \frac{N\mu}{N} = \mu, \tag{A.13}$$

$$\text{Var}[\hat{\mu}] = \text{Var}\left[\frac{\sum_{j=1}^{N} L_j}{N}\right] = \frac{1}{N^2}(N\text{Var}[L]) = \frac{1}{N^2}(N\sigma^2) = \frac{\sigma^2}{N}. \tag{A.14}$$

---

[7] Here we use the sample variance, rather than the population variance, as it gives an unbiased estimator of σ^2.

From our simulation for Example A.3, we have $\hat{\mu} = 262.5$, and $\hat{\sigma} = 691.8$. The estimated standard error of $\hat{\mu}$ is $\hat{\sigma}/\sqrt{N} = 6.92$. Assuming normality of the sample mean (which is reasonable for large samples, because of the central limit theorem), gives an estimated 95% confidence interval for the mean of

$$(262.5 - 1.96(6.92), \; 262.5 + 1.96(6.92)) = (248.9, 276.1).$$

An approximate non-parametric estimator (based on the central limit theorem) of the standard error of the sample variance is

$$se(\hat{\sigma}^2) \approx \sqrt{\frac{E[(L - \mu)^4] - \sigma^4}{N}}.$$

We can estimate the fourth central moment of L, $E[(L - \mu)^4]$, using the simulated L_j values, and estimate σ^4 using the squared sample variance. In the lognormal example, the estimated fourth central moment is 8.721×10^{13}, which gives an estimated standard error of the sample variance of

$$se(\hat{\sigma}^2) \approx \sqrt{\frac{8.721 \times 10^{13} - 691.8^4}{10,000}} = 93{,}264.$$

We then have an estimated 95% confidence interval for the variance of

$$(\sigma^2 - 1.96 \times se(\hat{\sigma}^2), \sigma^2 + 1.96 \times se(\hat{\sigma}^2)),$$

and so an approximate 95% confidence interval for the standard deviation is

$$\left(\sqrt{\sigma^2 - 1.96 \times se(\hat{\sigma}^2)}, \; \sqrt{\hat{\sigma}^2 + 1.96 \times se(\hat{\sigma}^2)} \right)$$
$$= (543.9, 813.3).$$

We can compare these with the true values (which we can calculate directly for the sum of independent lognormals)

$$\mu = 5e^{2+2^2/2} = 273.0, \qquad \sigma = \sqrt{5e^8(e^4 - 1)} = 893.8.$$

We see that the 95% confidence interval for the mean captures the true value, but the 95% confidence interval for the standard deviation does not. This could just be bad luck – the confidence interval is only expected to capture the value for 95% of samples, so perhaps this sample is one of the 5%. But there are other problems here. The confidence interval is calculated assuming the variance estimator is normally distributed, which is asymptotically true, but untrue for finite samples. Even though this sample is quite large, it is also quite skewed, and the asymptotic results may not be accurate enough in this case.

Table A.1. *Results (excerpt) of 100 repeated trials of 10,000 sums of 5 lognormals*

Trial k	$\hat{q}_k$	$\hat{\mu}_k$	$\hat{\sigma}_k$
1	0.0025	268.2	680.5
2	0.0034	270.2	712.4
3	0.0030	271.5	794.0
4	0.0031	267.1	658.6
5	0.0031	275.1	1,007.9
6	0.0019	274.1	1,026.7
7	0.0036	287.7	1,788.4
8	0.0035	281.5	864.0
9	0.0031	276.0	919.7
10	0.0030	274.9	742.1
$\vdots$	$\vdots$	$\vdots$	$\vdots$
Mean	0.0031	274.6	875.9
SD	0.0006	9.3	316.7

Repeating Monte Carlo for Standard Errors

Another approach for estimating the standard error of a Monte Carlo estimator, which works for any parameter or probability estimate, is to generate a sample of estimators by repeating the Monte Carlo simulation. For example, we repeated the simulation in Example A.3 100 times, each time with 10,000 different simulated values for the sum of lognormal random variables. An excerpt from the results is shown in Table A.1.

The standard deviations indicate the uncertainty in the Monte Carlo estimators, and can be used to construct confidence intervals assuming the estimators are approximately normally distributed. So the 95% CI for $q = \Pr[S > 5,000]$ is approximately

$$(0.0031 - 1.96(0.00061), 0.0031 + 1.96(0.00061)) = (0.0019, 0.0043).$$

The 95% CI for the mean is approximately

$$(256.4, 292.8),$$

and the 95% CI for the standard deviation is approximately

$$(255.2, 1,496.6).$$

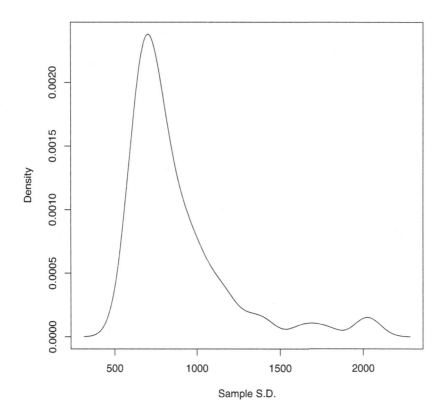

Figure A.3 Empirical probability density function of the sample standard deviations from 100 repeated trials of 10,000 sums of 5 lognormals.

We can also use the 100 values generated to construct a confidence interval, as the 95% CI for, say, σ can be estimated using the empirical 95% confidence interval from the 100 values generated – that is, the interval from the 2.5% quantile to the 97.5% quantile of the sample. This will be a more accurate approach for the uncertainty in σ, as the distribution of $\hat{\sigma}$ is not normally distributed for this sample size, as we can see from the density function of the 100 generated estimators illustrated in Figure A.3.

Using the sample quantiles gives the following 95% CIs:

For $\Pr[S > 5{,}000]$: $(0.0015, 0.0042)$;
For the mean: $(257.3, 293.3)$;
For the s.d.: $(561.0, 1{,}893.3)$.

We see that the three approaches give similar intervals for the probability q and the mean μ, but quite different intervals for the standard deviation σ. This is because the distribution of the estimators for q and μ are closer to a normal distribution, so the asymptotic approach is adequate. The uncertainty in the standard deviation is better captured using the quantiles of the resampling distribution, but the cost of this accuracy is, in computation terms, quite heavy.

A.9 Multivariate Distributions

We will review results for three-dimensional random vectors, rather then generalizing to n dimensions, as it makes the definitions and relationships easier to envisage. It will not be hard to adapt the following to other dimensions.

Suppose we have a random vector

$$X = (X_1, X_2, X_3)^T.$$

The **joint distribution function** is

$$F_X(x_1, x_2, x_3) = \Pr[X_1 \le x_1, X_2 \le x_2, X_3 \le x_3].$$

Similarly, the **joint survival function** is

$$S_X(x_1, x_2, x_3) = \Pr[X_1 > x_1, X_2 > x_2, X_3 > x_3].$$

We may write these as $F_X(x)$ and $S_X(x)$ where $x = (x_1, x_2, x_3)$.

Note that, for $n \ge 2$, in general $F_X(x) + S_X(x) \ne 1$.

We write the mean vector of X as μ where

$$\mu = \mathrm{E}[X] = (\mathrm{E}[X_1], \mathrm{E}[X_2], \mathrm{E}[X_3])^T.$$

The **covariance matrix** of X is the symmetric 3×3 matrix Σ:

$$\Sigma_{ij} = \sigma_{ij} = Cov[X_i, X_j] = \mathrm{E}[X_i X_j] - \mathrm{E}[X_i]\,\mathrm{E}[X_j] = P_{ij}\,\sigma_i\,\sigma_j$$
$$\Rightarrow \Sigma_{ii} = \sigma_i^2 = \mathrm{Var}[X_i],$$

where P_{ij} is the correlation coefficient between X_i and X_j.

The **marginal distribution** of each X_k is the distribution assuming no information about the other random variables. So, for example, the marginal distribution function of X_1 is

$$F_{X_1}(x) = F_X(x, \infty, \infty),$$

and if X_1 is a continuous random variable, its density function is

$$f_{X_1}(x) = \frac{d}{dx} F_X(x, \infty, \infty).$$

If each of the X_k is continuous, there is a joint pdf for X, which we denote $f_X(y_1, y_2, y_3)$ such that, for $x = (x_1, x_2, x_3)$,

$$F_X(x) = \int_{-\infty}^{x_1} \int_{-\infty}^{x_2} \int_{-\infty}^{x_3} f_X(y_1, y_2, y_3) dy_1 \, dy_2 \, dy_3,$$

$$f_{X_1}(x) = \int_{-\infty}^{\infty} \int_{-\infty}^{\infty} f_X(x, y_2, y_3) dy_2 \, dy_3.$$

The **conditional distribution**, for example, of $X_1 \mid X_2, X_3$ is the distribution of X_1 assuming we know the values of X_2 and X_3. Assuming all the variables are continuous, we have

$$F_{X_1 \mid X_2 \leq x_2 \, X_3 \leq x_3}(x_1) = \frac{F_X(x_1, x_2, x_3)}{F_X(\infty, x_2, x_3)}.$$

We often omit or shorten the subscripts where they can be inferred from the arguments of the functions.

The random variables X_1 and X_2 are **independent** if and only if

$$F_{X_1, X_2}(x_1, x_2) = F_{X_1}(x_1) \, F_{X_2}(x_2).$$

If X_1 and X_2 are continuous, this is equivalent to

$$f_{X_1, X_2}(x_1, x_2) = f_{X_1}(x_1) \, f_{X_2}(x_2).$$

Bibliography

Aggarwal, A., Beck, B., Cann, M., et al. (2016). Model Risk: Daring to Open Up the Black Box. *British Actuarial Journal*, **21**(2), 229–96.

Alexander, C. (2008). *Practical Financial Econometrics*. Vol. II of *Market Risk Analysis*. Hoboken, NJ: John Wiley & Sons.

Andersen, L. and Piterbarg, V. (2010). *Interest Rate Modeling*. London: Atlantic Financial Press.

Artzner, P., Delbaen, F., Eber, J. M., and Heath, D. (1999). Coherent Measures of Risk. *Mathematical Finance*, **9**(3), 203–28.

Baer, T., Mehta, A., and Samandari, H. (2011). The Use of Economic Capital in Performance Management for Banks: A Perspective. McKinsey Working Papers on Risk 24. New York: McKinsey and Company.

Barrieu, P. and Albertini, L. (2009). *The Handbook of Insurance-Linked Securities*. Chichester: John Wiley & Sons.

Basel Committee on Banking Supervision (2008). Principles for Sound Liquidity Risk Management and Supervision. Technical Report. Basel: Bank for International Settlements.

Basel Committee on Banking Supervision (2009a). Principles for Sound Stress Testing Practices and Supervision. Technical Report. Basel: Bank for International Settlements.

Basel Committee on Banking Supervision (2009b). Strengthening the Resilience of the Banking Sector. Technical Report. Basel: Bank for International Settlements.

Basel Committee on Banking Supervision (2010). Basel III: International Framework for Liquidity Risk Measurement, Standards, and Monitoring. Technical Report. Basel: Bank for International Settlements.

Basel Committee on Banking Supervision (2011). Basel III: A Global Regulatory Framework for More Resilient Banks and Banking Systems. Technical Report. Basel: Bank for International Settlements.

Basel Committee on Banking Supervision (2013). Basel III: The Liquidity Coverage Ratio and Liquidity Risk Monitoring Tools. Technical Report. Basel: Bank for International Settlements.

Basel Committee on Banking Supervision (2014). Basel III: The Net Stable Funding Ratio. Technical Report. Basel: Bank for International Settlements.

Basel Committee on Banking Supervision (2017). Basel III: Finalising Post-Crisis Reforms. Technical Report. Basel: Bank for International Settlements.

Basel Committee on Banking Supervision (2018). Stress Testing Principles. Technical Report. Basel: Bank for International Settlements.

Black, F. and Scholes, M. (1973). The Pricing of Options and Corporate Liabilities. *The Journal of Political Economy*, **81**(3), 637–54.

Bluhm, C. and Overbeck, L. (2007). *Structured Credit Portfolio Analysis, Baskets and CDOs*. Boca Raton, FL: CRC Press.

Bluhm, C., Overbeck, L., and Wagner, C. (2010). *Introduction to Credit Risk Modelling*. 2nd ed. Boca Raton, FL: CRC Press.

Boin, A., Kofman-Bos, C., and Overdijk, W. (2004). Crisis Simulations: Exploring Tomorrow's Vulnerabilities and Threats. *Simulation & Gaming*, **35**(3), 378–93.

Bollerslev, T. (1986). Generalized Autoregressive Conditional Heteroskedasticity. *Journal of Econometrics*, **31**(3), 307–27.

Booth, C., Fulcher, P., Vosvenieks, F., and Ward, R. (2019). *Liquidity Risk Management: An Area of Increased Interest for Insurers*. Technical Report. Milliman.

Boyd, R. (2011). *Fatal Risk: A Cautionary Tale of AIG's Corporate Suicide*. Chichester: John Wiley & Sons.

Boyle, P. and Hardy, M. R. (2003). Guaranteed Annuity Options. *ASTIN Bulletin: The Journal of the IAA*, **33**(2), 125–52.

Boyle, P. P. and Boyle, F. (2001). *Derivatives: The Tools That Changed Finance*. London: Risk Books.

Brigo, D. and Mercurio, F. (2007). *Interest Rate Models: Theory and Practice*. 2nd ed. Berlin: Springer.

Brigo, D., Pallavicini, A., and Torresetti, R. (2010). *Credit Models and the Crisis: A Journey into CDOs, Copulas, Correlations and Dynamic Models*. Chichester: John Wiley & Sons.

Cairns, A. J. (2000). A Discussion of Parameter and Model Uncertainty in Insurance. *Insurance: Mathematics and Economics*, **27**(3), 313–30.

Casella, G. and Berger, R. L. (2001). *Statistical Inference*. 2nd ed. Pacific Grove, CA: Duxbury Press.

Castagna, A. and Fede, F. (2013). *Measuring and Managing Liquidity Risk*. Chichester: John Wiley & Sons.

Chatterjee, A. and Hambrick, D.C. (2007). It's All about Me: Narcissistic Chief Executive Officers and Their Effects on Company Strategy and Performance. *Administrative Science Quarterly*, **52**(3), 351–86.

Christoffersen, P. F. (1998). Evaluating Interval Forecasts. *International Economic Review*, **39**(4), 841–62.

Collins, J. (2009). *Good to Great (Why Some Companies Make the Leap and Others Don't)*. New Delhi: SAGE Publications.

Committee of Sponsoring Organizations of the Treadway Commission (COSO) (2004). Enterprise Risk Management-Integrated Framework. Technical Report. New York: COSO.

Coombs, W. T. and Hollady, S. J. (2008). Comparing Apology to Equivalent Crisis Response Strategies: Clarifying Apology's Role and Value in Crisis Communication. *Public Relations Review*, **34**(3), 252–7.

Cornett, M. M., McNutt, J. J., Strahan, P. E., and Tehranian, H. (2011). Liquidity Risk Management and Credit Supply in the Financial Crisis. *Journal of Financial Economics*, **101**(2), 297–312.

Davis, T et al. (2006). A Failure of Initiative: Final Report of Select Bipartisan Committee to Investigate the Preparation for and Response to Hurricane Katrina; Technical Report.

Denault, M. (2001). Coherent Allocation of Risk Capital. *Journal of Risk*, **4**, 1–34.

Doherty, N. (2000). *Integrated Risk Management: Techniques and Strategies for Managing Corporate Risk*. New York: McGraw Hill Professional.

Domanski, D., Gambacorta, L., and Picillo, C. (2015). Central Clearing: Trends and Current Issues. *Basel Committee Quarterly Review*, **Dec.**, 59–76.

Duan, J. C. (1995). The GARCH Option Pricing Model. *Mathematical Finance*, **5**(1), 13–32.

European Insurance and Occupational Pensions Authority (EIOPA) (2018). 2018 Insurance Stress Test Report. Technical Report. Frankfurt am Main: EIOPA.

Elliott, M., Golub, B., and Jackson, M. O. (2014). Financial Networks and Contagion. *American Economic Review*, **104**(10), 3115–53.

Ellsberg, D. (1961). Risk, Ambiguity, and the Savage Axioms. *The Quarterly Journal of Economics*, **75**(4), 643–69.

Embrechts, P. and Frei, M. (2009). Panjer Recursion versus FFT for Compound Distributions. *Mathematical Methods of Operations Research*, **69**(3), 497–508.

Embrechts, P., Klüppelberg, C., and Mikosch, T. (2013). *Modelling Extremal Events for Insurance and Finance*. Vol. 33 of *Stochastic Modelling and Applied Probability*. Berlin/Heidelberg: Springer Science & Business Media.

Embrechts, P. and Wang, R. (2015). Seven Proofs of the Subadditivity of Expected Shortfall. *Dependence Modeling*, **3**(1), 126–40.

Engelmann, B. and Rauhmeier, R. (eds.) (2011). *The Basel II Risk Parameters*. 2nd ed. Berlin/Heidelberg: Springer.

Engle, R. F. (1982). Autoregressive Conditional Heteroscedasticity with Estimates of the Variance of United Kingdom Inflation. *Econometrica: Journal of the Econometric Society*, **50**(4), 987–1007.

Fabozzi, F. J. and Kothari, V. (2008). *Introduction to Securitization*. Chichester: John Wiley & Sons.

Fabozzi, F. J. and Pollack, I. M. (2005). *The Handbook of Fixed Income Securities*. Vol. 4. New York: McGraw-Hill.

Federal Reserve (2011). Supervisory Guidance on Model Risk Management. Technical Report. Washington, DC: Board of Governors of the Federal Reserve System.

Federal Reserve (2020). 2020 Supervisory Scenarios for Annual Stress Tests Required under the Dodd–Frank Act Stress Testing Rules and the Capital Plan Rule. Technical Report. Washington, DC: Board of Governors of the Federal Reserve System.

Financial Crisis Inquiry Commission (FCIC) (2011). The Financial Crisis Inquiry Report. US Government Printing Office.

Financial Stability Board (FSB) (2009). Guidance to Assess the Systemic Importance of Financial Institutions, Markets and Instruments: Initial Considerations. Report to G20 Finance Ministers and Governors. Basel: FSB.

Gelman, A., Carlin, J. B., Stern, H. S., et al. (2013). *Bayesian Data Analysis*. Boca Raton, FL: CRC Press.

Genest, C. and Nešlehová, J. (2007). A Primer on Copulas for Count Data. *ASTIN Bulletin: The Journal of the IAA*, **37**(2), 475–515.

Gilks, W. R., Richardson, S., and Spiegelhalter, D. J. (1995). *Markov Chain Monte Carlo in Practice*. Boca Raton, FL: CRC Press.

Glasserman, P. (2005). Measuring Marginal Risk Contributions in Credit Portfolios. *Journal of Computational Finance*, **9**, 1–41.

Glosten, L. R., Jagannathan, R., and Runkle, D. E. (1993). On the Relation Between the Expected Value and the Volatility of the Nominal Excess Return on Stocks. *The Journal of Finance*, **48**(5), 1779–801.

Gordy, M. B. (2003). A Risk-Factor Model Foundation for Ratings-Based Bank Capital Rules. *Journal of Financial Intermediation*, **12**(3), 199–232.

Gray, S. F. (1996). Modeling the Conditional Distribution of Interest Rates as a Regime-Switching Process. *Journal of Financial Economics*, **42**(1), 27–62.

Gregoriou, G. N., Hoppe, C., and Wehn, C. S. (2010). *The Risk Modeling Evaluation Handbook: Rethinking Financial Risk Management Methodologies in the Global Capital Markets*. New York: McGraw-Hill Finance & Investing.

Grimmett, G. and Welsh, D. (2014). *Probability: An Introduction*. Oxford: Oxford University Press.

Grossman, S. J. and Hart, O. D. (1982). Corporate Financial Structure and Managerial Incentives. In *The Economics of Information and Uncertainty*, pp. 107–40. University of Chicago Press.

Hamilton, J. D. (1990). Analysis of Time Series Subject to Changes in Regime. *Journal of Econometrics*, **45**(1–2), 39–70.

Hardy, M. R. (2001). A Regime-Switching Model of Long-Term Stock Returns. *North American Actuarial Journal*, **5**(2), 41–53.

Hardy, M. R. (2002). Bayesian Risk Management for Equity-Linked Insurance. *Scandinavian Actuarial Journal*, **2002**(3), 185–211.

Hardy, M. R., Freeland, R. K., and Till, M. C. (2006). Validation of Long-Term Equity Return Models for Equity-Linked Guarantees. *North American Actuarial Journal*, **10**(4), 28–47.

Hofert, M., Kojadinovic, I., Maechler, M., and Yan, J. (2020). *Copula: Multivariate Dependence with Copulas*. R package version 1.0-1, https://CRAN.R-project.org/package=copula.

Hofling, C. K., Brotzman, E., Dalrymple, S., Graves, N., and Pierce, C. M. (1966). An Experimental Study in Nurse-Physician Relationships. *The Journal of Nervous and Mental Disease*, **143**(2), 171–80.

Hubbard, D. W. (2020). *The Failure of Risk Management: Why It's Broken and How to Fix It*. Chichester: John Wiley & Sons.

Hull, J. (2018). *Risk Management and Financial Institutions*. 5th ed. Chichester: John Wiley & Sons.

Hull, J. (2022). *Options, Futures, and Other Derivatives*. 11th ed. Cranbury, NJ: Pearson.

Ingram, D. (2017). The Surprising Inconsistency of Risk Appetite and Risk Tolerance Statements. Technical Report. London: Willis Towers Watson Insights.

Institute of Internal Auditors (IIA) (2013). The Three Lines of Defense in Effective Risk Management and Control. Technical Report. Lake Mary, FL: IIA.

International Association of Insurance Supervisors (IAIS) (2020). Application Paper on Liquidity Risk Management. Technical Report. Basel: IAIS.

James, E. H. and Wooten, L. P. (2005). Leadership as (Un)usual: How to Display Competence in Times of Crisis. *Organizational Dynamics*, **34**(2), 141–52.

Janis, I. L. (1971). Groupthink. *Psychology Today*, **5**(6), 43–6.

Jolliffe, I. (2002). *Principal Component Analysis*. 2nd ed. New York: Springer.

Kahneman, D. and Tversky, A. (1979). Prospect Theory: An Analysis of Decision under Risk. *Econometrica*, **47**(2), 263–92.

Kiff, J., Kisser, M., and Schumacher, L. (2013). Rating through the Cycle: What does the Concept Imply for Rating Stability and Accuracy? IMF Working Paper WP/13/64.

Kim, J. H. T. and Hardy, M. R. (2007). Quantifying and Correcting the Bias in Estimated Risk Measures. *ASTIN Bulletin: The Journal of the IAA*, **37**(2), 365–86.

Kim, J. H. T. and Hardy, M. R. (2009). A Capital Allocation Based on a Solvency Exchange Option. *Insurance: Mathematics and Economics*, **44**(3), 357–66.

Klugman, S. A., Panjer, H. H., and Willmot, G. E. (2019). *Loss Models: From Data to Decisions*. 5th ed. Chichester: John Wiley & Sons.

Kupiec, P. (1995). Techniques for Verifying the Accuracy of Risk Measurement Models. *The Journal of Derivatives*, **3**(2), 73–84.

Lam, J. (2017). *Implementing Enterprise Risk Management: From Methods to Applications*. Chichester: John Wiley & Sons.

Lerbinger, O. (2012). *The Crisis Manager: Facing Disasters, Conflicts, and Failures*. 2nd ed. Abingdon: Routledge.

Lewis, M. (2011). *The Big Short: Inside the Doomsday Machine*. London: Penguin.

Li, J. S. H. and Hardy, M. R. (2011). Measuring Basis Risk in Longevity Hedges. *North American Actuarial Journal*, **15**(2), 177–200.

Li, J. S. H. and Luo., A. (2012). Key q-Duration: A Framework for Hedging Longevity Risk. *ASTIN Bulletin: The Journal of the IAA*, **42**(2), 413–52.

Lütkebohmert, E. (2009). *Concentration Risk in Credit Portfolios*. Berlin/Heidelberg: Springer.

Macenczak, L. A., Campbell, S., Henley, A. B., and Campbell, W. K. (2016). Direct and Interactive Effects of Narcissism and Power on Overconfidence. *Personality and Individual Differences*, **91**, 113–122.

Manistre, J. B. and Hancock, G. H. (2005). Variance of the CTE Estimator. *North American Actuarial Journal*, **9**(2), 129–56.

Mayers, D. and Smith, C. W. (1982). On the Corporate Demand for Insurance. In *Foundations of Insurance Economics*, pp. 190–205. New York: Springer.

McCormick, R. (2010). *Legal Risk in the Financial Markets*. Oxford: Oxford University Press.

McDonald, R. L. (2009). *Fundamentals of Derivatives Markets*. Hoboken, NJ: Pearson.

McNeil, A. J., Frey, R., and Embrechts, P. (2015). *Quantitative Risk Management: Concepts, Techniques and Tools*. Rev. ed. Princeton, NJ: Princeton University Press.

McQueen, R. (1996). *Who Killed Confederation Life?: The Inside Story*. Toronto: McClelland & Stewart.

Merton, R. C. (1973). Theory of Rational Option Pricing. *The Bell Journal of Economics and Management Science*, **4**(1), 141–83.

Merton, R. C. (1974). On the Pricing of Corporate Debt: The Risk Structure of Interest Rates. *Journal of Finance*, **29**, 449–70.

Milgram, S. (1963). Behavioral Study of Obedience. *The Journal of Abnormal and Social Psychology*, **67**(4), 371.

Montier, J. (2009). *Behavioural Investing: A Practitioner's Guide to Applying Behavioural Finance*. Chichester: John Wiley & Sons.

Myers, S. C. and Read, J. A. (2001). Capital Allocation for Insurance Companies. *Journal of Risk and Insurance*, **68**(4), 545–80.

National Commission on the BP Deepwater Horizon Oil Spill and Offshore Drilling (2011). Deep Water: Report to the President. Technical Report.

O'Brien, C. (2006). The Downfall of Equitable Life in the United Kingdom: The Mismatch of Strategy and Risk Management. *Risk Management and Insurance Review*, **9**(2), 189–204.

Office of the Superintendent of Financial Institutions (OSFI) (2016). Enterprise-Wide Model Risk Management for Deposit-Taking Institutions. Technical Report. Ottawa: OSFI.

Paredes, T. A. (2004). Too Much Pay, Too Much Deference: Behavioral Corporate Finance, CEOs, and Corporate Governance. *Florida State University Law Review*, **32**, 673.

Parliamentary Commission on Banking Standards (2013). *Changing Banking for Good*. London: The Stationery Office.

Pauchant, T. C., Mitroff, I. I., and Lagadec, P. (1991). Toward a Systemic Crisis Management Strategy: Learning from the Best Examples in the US, Canada and France. *Industrial Crisis Quarterly*, **5**(3), 209–32.

Pearson, C. M. and Clair, J. A. (1998). "Reframing Crisis Management." *Academy of Management Review*, **23**(1), 59–76.

Penrose, L. G. (2004). *Report of the Equitable Life Inquiry*. London: The Stationery Office.

Pfaff, B. and McNeil, A. (2020). *QRM: R-Language Code to Examine Quantitative Risk Management Concepts*. R package version 0.4-31, https://CRAN.R-project.org/package=QRM.

Plantin, G. and Rochet, J. C. (2016). *When Insurers Go Bust: An Economic Analysis of the Role and Design of Prudential Regulation*. Princeton, NJ: Princeton University Press.

PricewaterhouseCoopers (PwC) (2020). Solvency II: A Guide to the New Regime. Technical Report. London: PwC.

Rawls, J. (1993). *Political Liberalism*. New York: Columbia University Press.

Rebonato, R. (2007). *Plight of the Fortune Tellers*. Princeton, NJ: Princeton University Press.

Rebonato, R. (2010). *Coherent Stress Testing: A Bayesian Approach to Financial Stress*. Wiley Online Library.

Redington, F. M. (1952). Review of the Principles of Life-Office Valuations. *Journal of the Institute of Actuaries (1886–1994)*, **78**(3), 286–340.

Richardson, M. and White, L. (2009). The Rating Agencies: Is Regulation the Answer? In V. Acharya and M. Richardson (eds.), *Restoring Financial Stability: How to Repair a Failed System*, pp. 101–15. Chichester: John Wiley & Sons.

Ripley, B., Bates, D., Hornik, K., Genhardt, A., and Firth, D. (2020). *R Package 'MASS'*. http://cran.r-projectorg/web/packages/MASS/MASS.pdf.

Rockafellar, R. T., Uryasev, S., and Zabarankin, M. (2006). Optimality Conditions in Portfolio Analysis with General Deviation Measures. *Mathematical Programming*, **108**(2–3), 515–40.

Ross, S. (2012). *Simulation*. 5th ed. Amsterdam: Elsevier.

Ross, S., Westerfield, R. W., Jaffe, J., and Jordan, B. (2018). *Corporate Finance: International Edition*. New York: McGraw-Hill.

Ruffle, S., Bowman, G., Caccioli, F., et al. (2014). Stress Test Scenario: São Paulo Virus Pandemic. Cambridge Risk Framework.

Salmon, F. (2009). Recipe for Disaster: The Formula That Killed Wall Street. *Wired*, **17**(3).

Schwarcz, S. L. (2008). Systemic Risk. *Georgetown Law Journal*, **97**, 193.

Shefrin, H. (2016). *Behavioral Risk Management: Managing the Psychology That Drives Decisions and Influences Operational Risk*. New York: Springer.

Sherris, M. (2006). Solvency, Capital Allocation, and Fair Rate of Return in Insurance. *Journal of Risk and Insurance*, **73**(1), 71–96.

Sherris, M. and Zhang, B. (2009). Economic Scenario Generation with Regime Switching Models. *UNSW Australian School of Business Research Paper* (2009ACTL05).

Shin, H. S. (2009). Reflections on Northern Rock: The Bank Run that Heralded the Global Financial Crisis. *Journal of Economic Perspectives*, **23**(1), 101–19.

Stiglitz, J. E. (2010). *Freefall: America, Free Markets, and the Sinking of the World Economy*. New York: W. W. Norton.

Stulz, R. M. (2008). Risk Management Failures: What Are They and When Do They Happen? *Journal of Applied Corporate Finance*, **20**(4), 39–48.

't Hart, P., Rosenthal, U., and Kouzmin, A. (1993). Crisis Decision Making: The Centralization Thesis Revisited. *Administration & Society*, **25**(1), 12–45.

Tversky, A. and Kahneman, D. (1981). The Framing of Decisions and the Psychology of Choice. *Science*, **211**(4481), 453–8.

Tversky, A. and Kahneman, D. (1992). Advances in Prospect Theory: Cumulative Representation of Uncertainty. *Journal of Risk and Uncertainty*, **5**(4), 297–323.

Veronesi, P. (2010). *Fixed Income Securities: Valuation, Risk, and Risk Management*. Chichester: John Wiley & Sons, New Jersey.

Wilkie, A. D. (1984). A Stochastic Investment Model for Actuarial Use (with Discussion). *Transactions of the Faculty of Actuaries*, **39**, 341–403.

Wilkie, A. D. (1995). More on a Stochastic Asset Model for Actuarial Use. *British Actuarial Journal*, **1**, 777–964.

Wilkie, A. D. and Sahin, S. (2018). Yet More on a Stochastic Economic Model. Part 4: A Model for Share Earnings, Dividends, and Prices. *Annals of Actuarial Science*, **12**(1), 67–105.

Wilkie, A. D., Sahin, S., Cairns, A., and Kleinow, T. (2011). Yet More on a Stochastic Economic Model. Part 1: Updating and Refitting, 1995 to 2009. *Annals of Actuarial Science*, **5**(1), 53.

Wilmott, P. (2013). *Paul Wilmott Introduces Quantitative Finance*. Chichester: John Wiley & Sons.

Zhang, S., Hardy, M. R., and Saunders, D. (2018). Updating Wilkie's Economic Scenario Generator for US Applications. *North American Actuarial Journal*, **22**(4), 600–22.

Index

658

Printed in the United States
by Baker & Taylor Publisher Services